Get on top of this course and stay there

Student Study Guide to accompany MACROECONOMICS

Prepared by Mark Rush
University of Florida

Ask your professor and your friends and they will tell you that economics is a building block subject—so you don't want to get behind! This useful guide, which has been developed especially to increase the effectiveness of the Barro text and your learning efficiency contains:

- *Clear, straight forward overviews for each chapter,*

- *A review of the results and key points presented in each chapter.*

- *Alternative perspectives, and expansions on key theoretical issues presented in the text.*

- *True/False, multiple choice, and matching questions for reviewing chapter highlights.*

- *Numerical problems with completely worked out solutions*

Read it before class! Use it to organize your note taking! Use it to review for quizzes and exams! Expand your understanding of the finer points of the text! Save time and increase *your* learning efficiency!

Copies should be available at your College Store. If not, ask your bookstore manager to order one for you now—don't wait until the first exam!

Ask for the STUDENT STUDY GUIDE TO ACCOMPANY **MACROECONOMICS,** by Robert J. Barro, prepared by Mark Rush.

From John Wiley & Sons, Inc.

MACROECONOMICS

MACROECONOMICS

ROBERT J. BARRO
UNIVERSITY OF CHICAGO

JOHN WILEY & SONS
NEW YORK   CHICHESTER   BRISBANE   TORONTO   SINGAPORE

To Jason–
I hope this book makes him rich.

Library of Congress Cataloging in Publication Data:

Barro, Robert J.
  Macroeconomics.

  Includes index.
  1. Macroeconomics.   I. Title.
HB172.5.B36 1984   339   83-21692
ISBN 0-471-87407-8

Printed in the United States of America

10 9 8 7 6 5 4 3 2 1

ABOUT THE AUTHOR

Robert J. Barro was born in New York City, and graduated from Cal Tech in 1965. In 1969 he completed his dissertation in economics at Harvard University. Since that time, Professor Barro has held academic positions at Brown University and the University of Rochester, and is presently Professor of Economics at the University of Chicago, and a Research Associate at the National Bureau of Economic Research. A co-editor of the *Journal of Political Economy,* Professor Barro has also served in an editorial capacity for the *Journal of Monitory Economics, American Economic Review,* and *Econometrica*.

Professor Barro is the author of over 60 professional articles and books dealing with topics in macroeconomics, among them *Money, Employment and Inflation,* (with Herschel Grossman), and *Money, Expectations and Business Cycles*. His early research dealt with the interplay between money and prices during extreme inflationary conditions, and with the Keynesian approach to macroeconomics. Since 1975 his attention has been focused on the equilibrium approach to macroeconomics, the public debt, social security, government expenditures and taxes, monetary standards, and inflation.

PREFACE

Macroeconomics is in a state of flux. The Keynesian model, which was almost universally accepted as the basic paradigm until the late 1960s, has become increasingly less popular. This loss in popularity reflects embarrassments over past economic events—especially the failure of the model to deal satisfactorily with inflation and supply shocks. It also reflects the theoretical and empirical progress of an alternative "market-clearing approach," which is more closely related to the microeconomics that economists use successfully to study the behavior of individual households and businesses. Although some important problems remain, this approach provides a much more satisfactory macroeconomics than the one we had before. By more satisfactory, I mean that the approach avoids internal inconsistencies and also provides a better understanding of the real world.

While the Keynesian model has been subject to increasing skepticism by economists, it has nevertheless continued to reign supreme in the main textbooks. As a result, it has continued to organize the way the subject has been taught to students. Although aspects of the market-clearing model have been presented in textbooks, this model has not been taken seriously when it comes to studying real-world events or policy proposals. Furthermore, the explanatory power of the model has not been fully realized. This gap between textbook material and the knowledge gained in the last 15 years motivated me to write this book.

Here, I present the market-clearing approach as a general method for analyzing real-world macroeconomic problems. In addition, I discuss the material in as simple a fashion as I have found possible, so that the book will be accessible to undergraduate students. Extensive review and class-testing of the material have assured me that it is—my students tell me that the book is easier than I am. This is not, however, an attempt to provide a "balanced" treatment of alternative approaches to macroeconomics. There is no book—and probably could be none of substance—that is balanced in this respect. Although I deal in a serious manner with the Keynesian model in this book, I do not use this model for most of the analyses of economic events or policies. In any case, whatever one's ultimate judgment about the value of the Keynesian model, there is a very good reason not to start the study of macroeconomics with it. The Keynesian theory is an advanced topic that cannot be fully understood and appreciated until the market-clearing analysis has been worked out.

In writing this book I have benefited from an unusual amount of excellent advice, as well as encouragement to carry out the project. Since regular revision is a part of textbook writing, I would also appreciate any suggestions from readers. I am particularly grateful to Mark Rush, who has provided valuable and detailed comments on several versions of the text. Chitra Ramaswami, who is responsible for many of the end-of-chapter problems and the glossary, has also been a great help. I would like to thank for helpful comments my colleagues and reviewers, including James Barth, Gary Becker, Dave Denslow, William Dougan, Steve Easton, Stan Engerman, Gene Fama, Jacob Frenkel, Peter Garber, Jeremy Greenwood, Herschel Grossman, Sandy Grossman, John Haltiwanger, Bob King, Roger Kormendi, Bob Lucas, Chaipat Sahasakul, Dave Saurman, Jeremy Siegel, Dave Spencer, Dennis Starleaf, Alan Auerbach, Gene Grossman, J. Kirker Stephens, Raburn Williams, John Laitner, Michael Salemi, Tim Roth, John Eaton, Michael Wiseman, George Lamson, John Pettengill, A. Edward Day, Marc Vellrath, Michael Lovell, Stephen LeRoy, and Henry Wan, Jr.

I am also grateful to Neil Howe and Les Lenkowsky, who argued early on that this book was a good idea. Terri Fisher and Janet Mezgolits have cheerfully and efficiently typed a long succession of drafts. I would like to express my appreciation to Rich Esposito. Despite an occasional tendency to get overly excited, he is a first-rate editor and perhaps a promising economist. He in turn would like to thank Alan Stockman and Bob Lucas for first bringing us together. Finally, thanks go to my wife Judy. I am indebted to her for her patience and encouragement, as well as for direct input into many parts of the book. (She thinks that this book is better than some of my previous work.)

ROBERT J. BARRO

CONTENTS

CHAPTER 1
THE APPROACH TO MACROECONOMICS

In macroeconomics we study the overall or aggregate performance of an economy. For example, we consider the total output of goods and services as measured by the **gross national product (GNP).** Similarly, we look at the aggregates of employment and unemployment, and at the breakdown of GNP between consumer expenditures, investment (which are the purchases of new capital goods), and government purchases of goods and services.

The above terms refer to the quantities of goods or work effort. We shall also be interested in the prices that relate to these quantities. For example, we consider the dollar prices of the goods and services that the economy produces. When we look at the price of the typical or average item, we refer to the **general price level.** But we are also interested in the **wage rate,** which is the price of labor services, and the **interest rate,** which determines the cost of borrowing and the return to lending.

We shall want to know first how the private economy determines the various quantities and prices that we just mentioned. In addition, we want to know how government policies affect these variables. Specifically, we shall consider monetary policy, which involves the determination of the quantity of money and the design of monetary institutions, and fiscal policy, which pertains to the government's expenditures, taxes, and deficits.

The performance of the overall economy is, of course, a substantial concern for everyone. This performance influences our job prospects, our incomes, and the prices that we face. Thus, it is important for us—and even more important for our government policymakers—to understand how the macroeconomy works. Unfortunately, as is obvious from reading the newspapers, the theory of macroeconomics is not a settled scientific field. In fact, there is much controversy among economists about what is a useful basic approach, as well as about the detailed analysis of particular economic events and policy proposals. However, there has been a great deal of progress in recent years in designing a more satisfactory macroeconomic theory. The main objective of this book is to convey that progress to students in an accessible form.

The Behavior of Output, Unemployment, and the Price Level in the United States

In order to get an overview of the subject matter, let's look now at the historical record on some of the major macroeconomic variables for the United States. Figure 1.1 shows the total output of goods and services in the United States from 1870 to 1982. (The starting date is determined by the available data.) The measure of aggregate output is the gross national product, expressed in terms of values for a base year, which happens to be 1972. This measure, which we discuss in a later section on national-income accounting, is called **real GNP.**[1]

Two features of the graph of real GNP stand out. First, there is the general upward trend, which reflects the long-term growth or economic development of the U.S. economy. In particular, the average growth rate of real GNP from 1870 to 1982 is 3.3% per year. Thus, over 112 years, the total output increased 40-fold. If we divide through by population to determine real per capita GNP, then we find that the average growth rate is 1.7% per year. (This figure equals the 3.3% average growth rate of real GNP less the 1.6% average growth rate of population.) Hence, over 112 years, the output per person increased by a factor of 7.

The second striking feature of Figure 1.1 is the recurring ups and downs in real GNP over periods of roughly 1–5 years. These movements are called aggregate business fluctuations or the business cycle.[2] When real GNP falls toward a low point or trough, we describe the situation as a **recession** or an economic contraction. Conversely, when real GNP expands toward a high point or peak, we call it a **boom** or an economic expansion.

---

[1]The figure uses a proportionate (or logarithmic) scale on the vertical axis. Hence, each unit on this axis corresponds to an equal percentage change in real GNP.

[2]The term *business cycle* is somewhat misleading, since it suggests a much more regular pattern of ups and downs in economic activity than actually appears in the data. But the term is too entrenched in the economics literature to avoid entirely.

Figure 1.1 The Behavior of Output in the United States, 1870–1982

Sources for Figures 1.1–1.5:

For real GNP and the GNP deflator—Recent values are from the U.S. Commerce Department, *U.S. Survey of Current Business*. Figures back to 1909 are from the U.S. Commerce Department, *National Income and Product Accounts of the U.S., 1929–76*. For 1889–1908, the numbers are based on John Kendrick, *Productivity Trends in the United States,* Princeton University Press, Princeton, N.J., 1961, Tables A-I and A-III. For 1869–88, the data are unpublished estimates of Robert Gallman.

For the unemployment rate—The figures are the number unemployed divided by the total labor force, which includes military personnel. Recent data are from *Economic Report of the President,* 1983, Table B-29, and U.S. Bureau of Labor Statistics, *Handbook of Labor Statistics,* 1980, Table 1. Values before 1940 are from Stanley Lebergott, *Manpower in Economic Growth,* McGraw Hill, New York, 1964. The data from 1933–43 are adjusted to classify federal emergency workers as employed, as discussed in Michael Darby, "Three-and-a-Half Million U.S. Employees Have been Mislaid: Or, an Explanation of Unemployment, 1934–1941," *Journal of Political Economy,* February 1976.

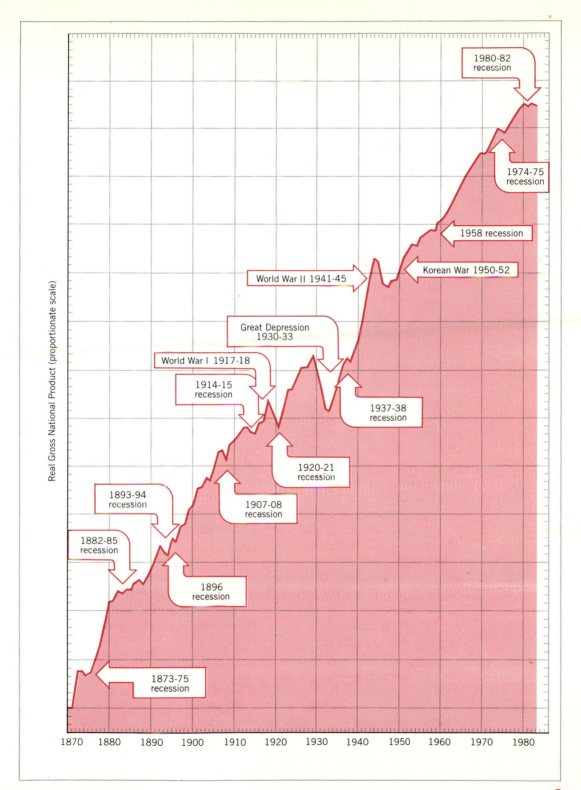

Real Gross National Product (proportionate scale)

1980-82
recession

1974-75
recession

1958 recession

Korean War 1950-52

World War II 1941-45

Great Depression
1930-33

World War I 1917-18

1914-15
recession

1937-38
recession

1920-21
recession

1893-94
recession

1907-08
recession

1882-85
recession

1896
recession

1873-75
recession

1870   1880   1890   1900   1910   1920   1930   1940   1950   1960   1970   1980

3

In Figure 1.1 we mark out the major U.S. recessions that have occurred since 1870. Note especially the **Great Depression** of 1930–33, where output fell 30% below the peak value reached in 1929. The other major economic contractions before World War II occurred in 1893–94, 1907–08, 1920–21, and 1937–38. In these cases, real GNP fell on average by 7% below its previous peak. For the post-World War II period, the three most significant recessions are those for 1958, 1974–75, and the most recent one, 1980–82. However, in these cases, real GNP declined on average by less than 1% from its previous peak. Thus, the recessions since World War II are much milder than those from before the war.

On the up side, note first the high rates of growth in output during World Wars I and II and the Korean War. Other periods of economic boom—in the sense of high growth rates of real GNP—are the 1960s (including, but not limited to the years of the Vietnam War), the recovery from the Great Depression from 1933–40 (aside from the recession of 1937–38), much of the 1920s, the period from 1896 to 1906, and the years from 1875 to 1880.

Figure 1.2 shows the growth rates of real GNP for each year from 1870 to 1982. One point that emerges clearly from this graph is the much smaller year-to-year fluctuations in real GNP since World War II than before the war. By contrast, there is little difference in the average rates of growth, which are 3.2% per year from 1870 to 1940, and 3.1% per year from 1946 to 1982.

Figure 1.3, which reports the unemployment rate for each year, gives us another way to look at recessions and booms. We measure the unemployment rate as the fraction of the total labor force that has no job. (We discuss the precise meaning of this variable in later chapters.) Over the period 1890–1982, for which data are available, the median unemployment rate is 5.4%. (The mean is 7.0%.) But during the recessions—which we already marked out in Figure 1.1—the unemployment rate rises above the median. The extreme is the Great Depression, where unemployment reached 27% of the labor force in 1932–33. But also noteworthy are the rates of 20% for 1894, 16% for 1896–97, 14% for 1938, and 13% for 1921. For the post-World War II period, the highest unemployment rates are 9.5% for 1982 and 8.3% for 1975.

Overall, when looking at Figures 1.1–1.3, we should recall the two main features that we would like to use economic analysis to understand. One is the long-term growth and the other is the short-term pattern of business fluctuations. As we develop our macroeconomic model in subsequent chapters, we shall frequently compare the theoretical propositions about these phenomena with the patterns that appear in the real-world data.

Figure 1.4 shows an index of the general level of prices in the United States from 1870 to 1982. (We shall discuss the details of the particular measure of the price level toward the end of this chapter.) One striking observation is the persistent rise in prices since World War II, as contrasted with the movements up and down from before the war. In fact, there are long periods in the earlier history—1870–92 and 1920–33—during which prices fell persistently.

Figure 1.5 looks at the year-to-year growth rate of the general price level—that is, the **inflation rate.** As already suggested, we find that almost all of the

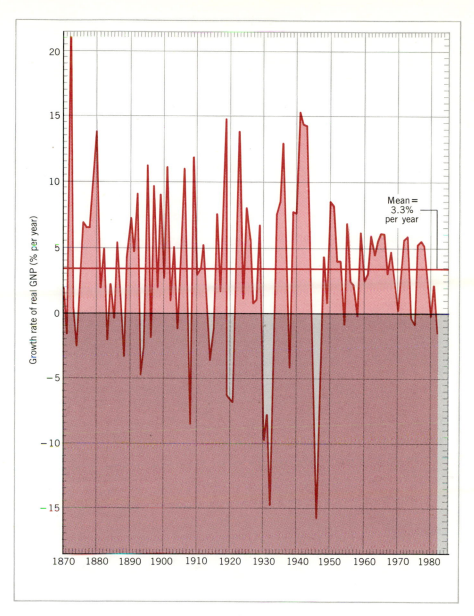

Figure 1.2 Growth Rates of Output in the United States, 1870–1982

inflation rates since World War II are positive, as contrasted with a mixture of positive and negative values from earlier periods. It is also interesting that the year-to-year fluctuations in inflation rates are smaller in recent years than they used to be. This observation parallels our earlier finding that the growth rates of output are less volatile since World War II than before the war.

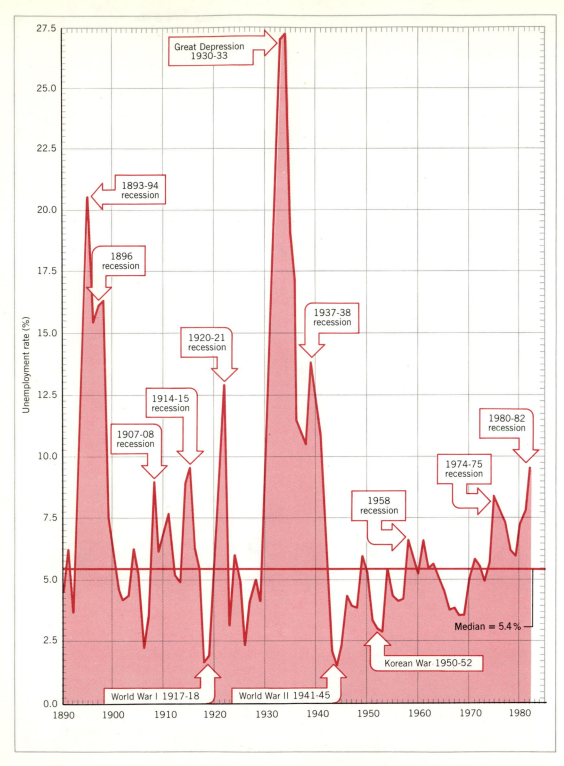

Figure 1.3 The United States Unemployment Rate, 1890–1982

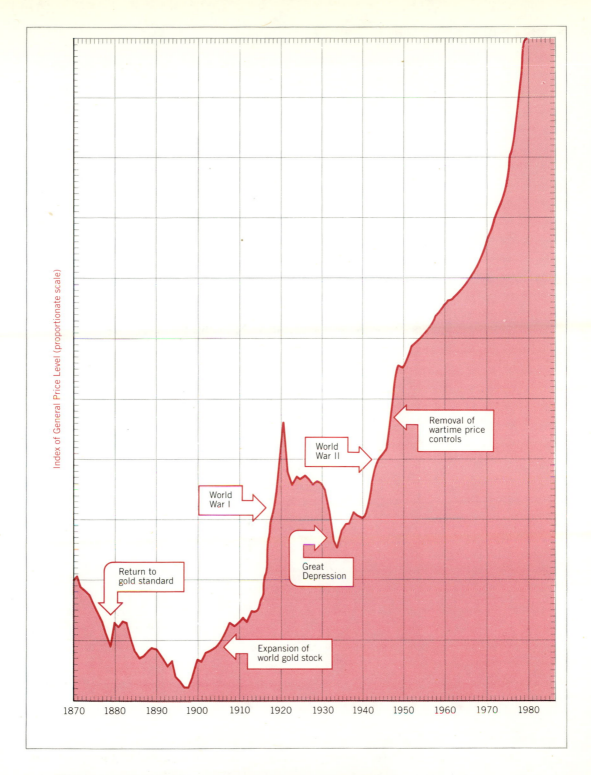

Figure 1.4 The Price Level in the United States, 1870–1982

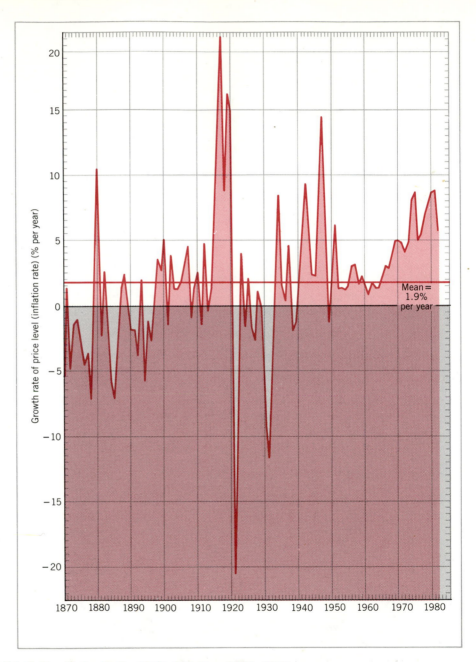

Figure 1.5 Inflation Rates in the United States, 1870–1982

In subsequent chapters we shall relate the behavior of the general price level to monetary developments, especially to changes in the quantity of money. It turns out that this analysis interacts with the nature of monetary institutions, such as whether the United States was on the gold standard (as it was from 1879 until

World War I and, to some extent, from World War I until 1933). Also important is the nature of the banking system, which has become much less vulnerable to financial crises since the 1930s. In any event, when we discuss the general price level and inflation, we shall keep in mind the behavior that shows up in Figures 1.4 and 1.5.

The Approach to Macroeconomics

We now describe the basic theoretical approach that we shall use to design a useful macroeconomic model. In setting up this model, we spend a good deal of time on economic theory. In this context we worry about whether the theory seems sensible, whether it is internally consistent, and so on. But we should always remember that the main test of the model will be its ability to explain the behavior of macroeconomic variables in the real world. Therefore, especially after we have constructed the basic theoretical framework, we shall devote considerable space to comparisons of the theory with the real world—that is, with empirical evidence.

Microeconomic Foundations of Macroeconomics

We begin by developing the basic price theory—or **microeconomic foundations**—which underlies the macroeconomic analysis of the aggregate variables in an economy. Much of this microeconomics will be familiar to students from previous courses in economics. In that sense, the macroeconomic approach in this book is a continuation of the economic reasoning that was used before to explain the behavior of individual households and businesses. Here, we apply this same economic science to understand the workings of the overall economy—that is, to study such things as real GNP, employment and unemployment, the general price level and inflation, the wage rate and the interest rate, and so on. Unfortunately, many basic courses in economics do not follow this general approach when dealing with macroeconomics. In fact, students could easily reach the conclusion that macroeconomics and microeconomics were two entirely distinct fields. A central theme of this book is that a more satisfactory macroeconomics emerges when it is linked to the underlying microeconomics. By more satisfactory, we mean first that the macroeconomic theory avoids internal inconsistencies, and second, that we obtain a better understanding of the real world.

In Chapter 2 we examine the choice problems of an isolated individual, Robinson Crusoe. Naturally, we assume that Crusoe's choices are guided by enlightened self-interest—that is, we exploit the central economic postulate of optimizing behavior. In the initial framework, the only choice problem concerns the level of work effort, which then determines the quantities of production and consumption. But by studying Crusoe's behavior, we can understand the trade-off between leisure and consumption that also applies in complicated market economies. Also, by looking at an isolated individual, we bring out the role of a resource or **budget constraint** in its simplest form. Here, when goods cannot be stored over time, Crusoe's budget constraint dictates that his consumption equals his production. As we shall see, extensions of this simple constraint are central to correct macroeconomic analyses in economies that include many consumers and producers, as well as a government.

We can use the model of Robinson Crusoe to predict his responses to changes in production opportunities—for example, to harvest failures or to discoveries of new goods or methods of production. Many of these results carry over later on to the predictions for aggregate output and employment in more realistic settings. In particular, when we consider the economy's responses to changes in production opportunities—such as the recent oil crises—we usually get the right answer by thinking of the parallel situation for Robinson Crusoe.

Chapters 3 and 4 develop the microeconomic foundations that we need to go from an analysis of Robinson Crusoe to a study of many persons who interact in various marketplaces. Once again we exploit the postulate of optimizing behavior, subject to budget constraints, in order to assess the responses of individuals to different circumstances.

In order to simplify matters, we start with only two markets. On the first market, people buy and sell goods in exchange for money. The dollar cost of goods on this market is the theoretical counterpart of the general price level. On the other market, people can borrow and lend. This credit or loan market establishes an interest rate, which borrowers must pay to lenders.

The introduction of the goods market allows people to specialize in their production activities, which adds to the economy's productivity. (Robinson Crusoe did not have this option.) The existence of the credit market means that a person's expenditure during any period can diverge from his or her income during that period. Thus, unlike Robinson Crusoe a person with a given income has choices about consuming now versus later. Similarly, people can choose between working now versus later. We discuss these choices by considering people's incentives to save—that is, to accumulate assets that pay interest income. Here, we stress the idea that a higher interest rate motivates people to save more, which means that they consume less today and plan to consume more later on. Similarly, we show that various forces can induce people to rearrange their work and production from one period to another.

Later on (in Chapter 9), we introduce a labor market on which labor services are bought and sold at an established wage rate. But in order to simplify the basic model, we do not include this market at the outset. Rather, we pretend that people work only on their own production processes—that is, each person owns his or her own business and is the only employee. For many purposes—such as studying the main determinants of aggregate output and work effort, the general price level and the interest rate—we shall find that this simplification is satisfactory. But in order to explore some other topics—such as the behavior of unemployment and the determination of wage rates—we shall have to deal explicitly with the labor market.

Throughout our analysis, we stress the role of budget constraints. Namely, over one or many periods, there must be a balance between each person's sources of funds and his or her uses of these funds. Although these budget conditions may seem tedious at times, it is extremely important to keep these matters straight. In fact, many serious errors in macroeconomic reasoning occur when economic theorists forget to impose the appropriate budget constraints in their models. We shall see that these conditions are especially important in evaluating temporary versus permanent changes in income, in studying the effects of interest rates on lenders and borrowers, and in evaluating the effects of people's money holdings. Also, when we introduce government policies in later chapters, we shall find it crucial to impose the government's budget constraint. Many errors in analyses of the government's expenditures and deficits result from a failure to impose this budget constraint.

In most of our discussion, we consider one type of economic unit, which we can think of as a combination of a household and a firm. Thus, we merge into this single unit the consumption and working activities of households with the production and hiring activities of businesses. The main reason we proceed this way is that it greatly simplifies the analysis. In any event, since some households ultimately own the private businesses in any economy, we shall find that this simplifying device does not lead us into any mistakes.

In Chapter 5 we complete our discussion of microfoundations by exploring people's incentives to hold non-interest-bearing paper money, rather than financial assets that bear interest. We assume that the **demand for money** arises out of the process of carrying out transactions, which use money as a **medium of exchange.** In particular, since people use money when they buy or sell goods or financial assets, it requires a great deal of planning and effort in order for someone to hold little or no cash. We then discuss how the quantity of money demanded depends on the price level, the interest rate, the level of income, and other variables.

Market-Clearing Conditions

When we add up the actions of all individuals, there are certain conditions that must hold. For example, the total of goods sold by suppliers must equal the total bought by demanders. Similarly, the total of funds loaned out by people on the credit market must equal the total borrowed by others. We refer to conditions such as these as **aggregate-consistency conditions.** These conditions tell us something about how aggregate quantities must behave in order for the analysis to be internally consistent. Any reasonable macromodel must satisfy these conditions.

One way to ensure that the aggregate-consistency conditions hold is to assume that the various markets—say, for goods and credit—always clear. Clearing means here that the price level and the interest rate adjust simultaneously so that the aggregate demand for goods equals the aggregate supply, and the aggregate of desired lending equals the aggregate of desired borrowing. We use this **market-clearing approach** for satisfying the aggregate-consistency conditions in the basic model.

It turns out that the idea of cleared markets is closely related to the notion that private markets function efficiently. Specifically, when markets clear, it is impossible to improve on any outcomes by matching potential borrowers and lenders or by bringing together potential buyers and sellers of goods. Cleared markets already accomplish all of these mutually advantageous trades. We can see that the idea of market clearing is closely related to the optimizing behavior of individuals, which we exploited when working out the microfoundations of the model. On the one hand, people determine their individual choices of work, consumption, and so on, in order to make themselves as well off as possible. On the other hand, market clearing reflects the idea that the people who participate in and organize markets— and who are guided by the pursuit of their own interests—do not waste resources, and thereby end up achieving efficient outcomes. Thus, market clearing is the natural macrocomplement to the microfoundations that underlie the model.

It is possible to satisfy the aggregate-consistency conditions without imposing market clearing in the sense described above. One important idea is that imperfect information makes it impossible to make the best decisions about production and work at all points in time. Later on, we explore some macroeconomic models that incorporate incomplete information (particularly in Chapter 18). But it is best to explore the workings of the economy under full information before going on to this advanced topic. Thus, we do not introduce incomplete information into the model at the outset.

Another alternative to market clearing is the **Keynesian model.** This model assumes that some prices (usually of labor services or commodities) are sticky and that some rationing of quantities bought or sold comes into play. It turns out that outcomes are generally inefficient in the Keynesian model. Notably, some mutually advantageous trades do not take place. As a reflection of this "market failure," there tends to be chronic unemployment and underproduction. These conclusions from the Keynesian model have led many economists to advocate "corrective" policy actions by the government.

The Keynesian model depends crucially on the assumption that prices are sticky. Thus, not surprisingly, the rationale for price stickiness has been a subject of substantial debate, which is still unresolved. In any event, just as in the case of models with incomplete information, the Keynesian theory is an advanced topic that cannot be appreciated without first working through the logic of a market-clearing model. Thus, we take up the Keynesian model (in Chapter 19) after the market-clearing analysis is completed.

To summarize, the basic model relies on two key elements for making predictions about the behavior of quantities and prices in the real world. First, we use the microfoundations of the model, which stem from the optimizing behavior of individuals subject to budget constraints. Second, we exploit the notion of market clearing. As mentioned, this idea reflects the efficient operation of markets—that is, the efficient matching of potential buyers and sellers of goods, credit, labor services, and so on.

Using the Market-Clearing Model

By the end of Chapter 6, we have constructed the central theoretical apparatus that we shall use throughout the remainder of the book. After this point, the discussion amounts to extensions of the basic model in order to apply the reasoning to various topics in macroeconomics. Thus, our list of applications eventually includes the following: supply shocks, business fluctuations, long-term economic growth, the role of government purchases and public services, monetary and fiscal policies, financial intermediation, incomplete information, the Keynesian model, and aspects of the international economy.

We first use the model to study various disturbances that affect opportunities for production. Specifically, we assess the effects of supply shocks on output, employment, the price level, and the interest rate.

In Chapters 7 and 8 we introduce the possibility of chronic rises in the general price level—that is, inflation. We look at inflation as primarily a monetary phenomenon. One of the major themes is that inflation and monetary growth can be largely independent of the variations in output and employment, which are examples of "real" variables. The interaction of monetary phenomena with output, employment, and other real variables is a major issue in macroeconomics, but one that is not fully resolved. In this book we deal first with simple models where the interaction between monetary forces and the real variables is unimportant. Then we extend the analysis to bring in more interesting possibilities for this interaction (in Chapters 16–19).

In Chapters 9–11 we apply the theory to aspects of business fluctuations. First, we bring in a separate labor market and thereby examine the behavior of unemployment during recessions and booms. Next, we allow for investment, which is the accumulation of capital goods. By looking at actual recessions in the United States, we find that aggregate business fluctuations involve mainly variations in investment, rather than consumption. Then we show how the theory is consistent with this important empirical observation. In order to demonstrate this consistency, we rely on two aspects of the microfoundations of the model. First, we utilize the forms of households' budget constraints, and second, we consider the incentives that people have to shift their investment and consumption from one time period to another.

In Chapter 12 we study how investment shows up over the longer term as an increase in the stock of capital and thereby in economic growth. By allowing also for growth in population and for improvements in technology, we can apply the theory to a country's long-term economic development. Accordingly, we are able to use the model to study the behavior of the major macroeconomic variables in the United States over the past century. In addition, we apply the theory to a comparison of the growth experiences of a number of industrialized countries since World War II.

Chapters 13–15 bring in government expenditures, taxes and public debt, which allow us to consider fiscal policies. First, we introduce government purchases of goods and services, which we assume are used to provide public services to consumers and producers. Then we consider how people react to income taxes and to transfer programs, such as social security. Finally, by introducing the public debt, we can evaluate the economic consequences of the government's financing its spending by deficits rather than taxes.

In order to assess changes in government activity, we again rely on the microfoundations of the model. First, we analyze individuals' incentives to react to taxes, to the provisions of various transfer programs, and to the services that they get ''free of charge'' from the government. Second, we use the budget constraints that face households and the government. It is these constraints that tell us the main difference between temporary and permanent changes in government expenditures—results that we illustrate by considering the behavior of the economy during wartime. In addition, the careful analysis of budget constraints gives us a perspective on government deficits that differs substantially from the popular view. Namely, in many circumstances, there is little economic difference between taxes and deficits.

Chapters 16–19 deal with interactions between monetary forces and real economic activity. In Chapter 16 we introduce financial intermediaries, which allows us to study the creation of deposits and the lending operations of banks and other institutions. We stress here the role of intermediaries in promoting economic efficiency. Thus, a contraction in the amount of financial intermediation—such as that during the Great Depression and in other periods of financial crisis—tends to reduce the levels of production and employment. In addition, there are important effects of changes in financial intermediation on the general price level.

Chapter 17 explores the main pieces of empirical evidence that concern the interaction between monetary variables and the real economy. Our theory can explain much of the evidence, but not all of it. Specifically, using the model that we have developed up to this point, we cannot rationalize significant effects of purely monetary shocks on real economic activity, which seem to apply at least since World War II.

In Chapter 18 we extend the market-clearing model in order to account for the observed economic effects of monetary disturbances. The new feature is that individuals have incomplete information about prices in various markets and about the overall monetary picture. However, when people do not observe something directly—such as the general price level—they are still motivated to form their expectations rationally.[3] That is, people use the available information in order to forecast the unobserved variables as well as possible. In this setting we find that monetary disturbances can affect real economic activity more or less as appears in the U.S. data on business fluctuations. However, there are some empirical puzzles that remain.

The theory in Chapter 18 also has some intriguing implications for monetary policy. Namely, there are effects on real variables only from the erratic part of monetary policy, but these effects tend to be adverse. Thus, the main message is that monetary policy should be predictable, rather than erratic.

In Chapter 19 we develop the model of business fluctuations that was stimulated by the research during the 1930s of the British economist John Maynard Keynes. This theory departs from our previous analysis by assuming that some prices do not adjust instantaneously to clear all markets. That is, the prices of goods or the wages of labor are assumed to be sticky, rather than perfectly flexible. We begin with a simple version of the Keynesian model, which brings out the idea

---

[3]Because of this feature, the approach discussed in Chapter 18 is often called ''rational-expectations macroeconomics.''

that shocks to the economy can have multiplicative effects on output. Then we work out a popular extended version of this theory, which is called the **IS/LM model.**

A basic conclusion from the Keynesian model is that recessions can result from decreases in the aggregate demand for goods, which might result from monetary contractions. Also, there is more scope for active monetary and fiscal policies in this model than there was in our market-clearing framework.

For many years, the Keynesian model was the most popular tool of macroeconomic analysis. However, the popularity of this model has diminished since the late 1960s, especially at the frontiers of macroeconomic research. There are two main reasons for this decreased popularity. First, the Keynesian model did not handle very well either inflation or supply shocks, both of which became prevalent since the late 1960s. Second, people have not found satisfactory ways to provide the Keynesian macromodel with internally consistent microfoundations. In any event, there is another good reason to postpone our consideration of the Keynesian model until late in the book. Namely, the model cannot really be fully understood—and the distinctive features of it cannot be appreciated—until the market-clearing analysis has been worked out. Thus, whatever one's ultimate judgment about the value of the Keynesian model, it is a great mistake to begin a study of macroeconomics with this model.

Finally, Chapter 20 extends the theory from the economy of one country to that of many countries, which interact on international markets. In many respects there is a parallel between a single country in the world economy and an individual in the economy of one country. Thus, we can readily apply our prior analysis to study such things as international lending and borrowing, changes in the prices of commodities such as oil, and the behavior of a country's **balance of international payments.** Then we carry out some new analysis to consider the determination of **exchange rates** among different currencies, as well as the interplay among price levels and interest rates across countries.

A Note on Mathematics and Economic Reasoning

This book does not use any advanced mathematics. Rather, it relies on graphical methods and occasional algebraic derivations. Although calculus would speed up the presentation in some places, this higher mathematics turns out to be unnecessary for the main economic arguments. Therefore, students should not find the book difficult on technical grounds.

What will be demanding from time to time is the economic reasoning. But it is this aspect of economics that really is the most difficult, as well as the most rewarding. Unfortunately, not all of this difficulty can be avoided if we wish to understand the economic events that take place in the real world. The feature that should help students to master the material is the use of a single, consistent model, which is then successively refined and applied to a variety of macroeconomic problems. Anyone who invests enough effort to understand the basic model will eventually see the simplicity of the approach, as well as the applicability to a wide variety of real-world issues.

Elements of National-Income Accounting

Up to this point, we have used terms such as *gross national product (GNP), consumer expenditure, investment,* the *general price level,* and so on without precisely defining them. Now, by looking at **national-income accounting,** we develop the meanings of these terms. There are many difficult issues that arise in the construction of the national-income accounts. Here, we consider only the basic concepts, which will be adequate for most of our subsequent analysis.

Nominal and Real GNP

We begin with the GNP. Nominal GNP measures the dollar value of all the goods and services that are produced in an economy during a specified time period. For example, in 1982 the nominal GNP in the United States was $3,059 billion. During the first quarter of 1983, the nominal GNP was $3,171 billion when expressed at an annual rate—that is, 1983's GNP would equal this amount if the dollar value of production throughout the year remained at the same rate as that for the first three months.

Let's examine the definition of nominal GNP one step at a time. The word *nominal* means that the GNP is measured in units of dollars—or, more generally, in units of some currency, such as pounds, marks, yen, and so on.

Next, for most goods and services—such as pencils, automobiles, haircuts, and so on—the dollar value is the price for which these items sell in the marketplace. However, governmental services, which include national defense, the justice system, and police services are not exchanged in markets. These items are included in nominal GNP at their dollar cost of production.

It is important to understand that the GNP includes only the goods and services that are produced during a given time period. In other words, current GNP measures only current production. For example, the construction and sale of a new house counts in GNP, but the sale of a second-hand house (which was produced earlier) does not count.

We have to be careful not to double-count **intermediate goods** when we measure GNP. An example of an intermediate good is flour used by a baker to make bread. Since the total production of goods is only the bread, we do not want to double-count the flour (once by itself and again when it is in the bread). Basically, we avoid double-counting by including in GNP only the bread, which is the final product.[4]

---

[4]Some complications arise concerning the dating of production. When the flour is produced—but before it is used to make bread—we count the extra flour in GNP as additional inventories of goods. Then when the flour is used to make bread, we add to GNP the market value of the bread, but subtract the value of the flour that is used up. Thus overall, the contribution to GNP is just the value of the bread. But when there are changes in the level of inventories, the timing of GNP from period to period can be affected substantially.

Table 1.1 The Calculation of Nominal and Real GNP

	1984			1985A			1985B		
	P_{1984}	Q_{1984}	Market Value at 1984 Prices	P_{1985A}	Q_{1985A}	Market Value at 1985A Prices	P_{1985B}	Q_{1985B}	Market Value at 1985B Prices
Butter	$2.00/lb	50 lb	$100	$2.30/lb	44 lb	$101.25	$1.80/lb	70 lb	$126
Golf balls	$1.00/ball	400 balls	$400	$1.20/ball	374 balls	$448.80	$ .80/ball	530 balls	$424
Nominal GNP			$500			$550.00			$550
	P_{1984}	Q_{1984}	Market Value at 1984 Prices	P_{1984}	Q_{1985A}	Market Value at 1984 Prices	P_{1984}	Q_{1985B}	Market Value at 1984 Prices
Butter	$2.00/lb	50 lb	$100	$2.00/lb	44 lb	$ 88	$2.00/lb	70 lb	$140
Golf balls	$1.00/ball	400 balls	$400	$1.00/ball	374 balls	$374	$1.00/ball	530 balls	$530
Real GNP (1984 base)			$500			$462			$670

If we are interested in measures of production, then the nominal GNP can be misleading. That's because this measure depends on the overall level of prices, as well as on the physical amounts of output. The top part of Table 1.1 illustrates this problem. Think about a simple economy that produces only butter and golf balls. We show the hypothetical quantities and prices of these goods for 1984 in the first columns of the table. Notice that the nominal GNP for 1984 is $500. The columns labeled 1985A and 1985B show two possibilities for prices and outputs in 1985. In both cases nominal GNP rises by 10% to $550. However, in case A the production of both goods has declined, while in case B the production of both has increased. Thus, identical figures on nominal GNP can conceal very different underlying movements in production.

We construct a measure of real GNP in order to solve the problem of changing price levels. Real GNP uses prices from only one year, which is called the base year. For example, if the base year is 1980, then we refer to real GNP as "GNP in 1980 dollar" or as "GNP in constant dollar," since we use a set of constant (1980) prices. Similarly, we refer to nominal GNP as "GNP in current dollars," since it uses the prices of the current period.

We compute real GNP by multiplying the current quantity of output of each good by the price of that good in the base year. Then we sum up over all these multiples to get the economy's aggregate real GNP. Because the prices used in this calculation do not vary from year to year, we end up with a reasonable measure for the changes over time in the overall level of production.

The bottom portion of Table 1.1 contains an example of this calculation, using 1984 as the base year. Consider the values of real GNP for the cases labeled 1985A and 1985B. These values differ substantially, even though the values of nominal GNP are the same. In the 1985A example, real GNP falls below the 1984 level by 7.6%. This figure is a weighted average of the fall in butter production by 12% and that in golf ball production by 6.5%. Thus, real GNP gives a more accurate picture of the change in output than does the 10% increase in nominal GNP. Similarly, for the 1985B case, real GNP rises by 34% (which is a remarkable achievement for 1 year!). This figure is a weighted average of the rise in butter production by 40% and that in golf ball production by 32%.

Notice that the proportional change in real GNP gives us a weighted average of the proportional changes in production for the various goods, which are butter and golf balls in the example. Generally, there would be many ways to define the weights in this calculation. It turns out that the standard method for computing real GNP—which we employed in Table 1.1—uses as weights the shares of each good (butter or golf balls) in GNP for the base year. That is, as seems reasonable, we give more weight to the goods that account for a larger share of the economy's output (in the base year). But as we move away from the base year, these shares can change significantly. For that reason, the U.S. Commerce Department changes the designation of the base year from time to time.

Although the real GNP tells us a lot about how the overall economy is performing, we cannot fully identify real GNP with an index of welfare. Some of the problems with using aggregate real GNP as a measure of overall well-being are the following:

- The measure disregards changes in the distribution of income across households.
- The calculated GNP excludes a variety of nonmarket goods. These include legal and illegal transactions in the "underground economy," as well as the services that people perform in their own homes. For example, if we mow our own lawn, then GNP does not increase—but if we hire someone to mow the lawn (and the transaction is reported to the government), then GNP increases.
- The GNP assigns no value to leisure time.

Despite these shortcomings, we typically learn a great deal about the overall performance of the economy—both in terms of short-run fluctuations and in the context of long-term development—by studying the changes in aggregate real GNP.

Components of the Gross National Product

The national accounts divide GNP into four parts, depending upon who or what buys the goods or services. The four sectors are individuals and households, business firms, all levels of government, and foreigners.

The purchase of goods and services by households for their own use is called

personal consumer expenditure. This spending for consumption accounts for the bulk of GNP—for example, for 65% of GNP in the first three months of 1983.

The national accounts distinguish between purchases of consumer goods that will be used fairly quickly, such as toothpaste and various services, and those that will last for a substantial time, such as automobiles and appliances. The first group is called **consumer nondurables and services,** while the second is called **consumer durables.** The important point is that consumer durables yield a flow of services in future periods, as well as currently.

The second major category of GNP is the purchase of goods and services by business firms. These purchases are the private **gross investment** that firms make in new capital goods, such as factories, machinery, and so on. Also, this category includes the net increase in business's inventories of goods. Note that business's capital goods are durables, which enhance production opportunities over many years. Thus, investment goods are similar to the consumer durables that we mentioned before. In fact, in the national accounts, an individual's purchase of a new home—which might be considered the ultimate consumer durable—is counted as business investment, rather than personal consumer expenditure. For many purposes, we might add the other purchases of consumer durables to the national accounts' measure of gross investment in order to get a broader concept of investment. In any case, total gross investment accounts for a relatively small, but volatile share of GNP. During the first three months of 1983, gross investment was 13% of GNP, or 21% if we include the purchases of consumer durables.

The third component of GNP is **government purchases of goods and services.** Usually, this category combines governmental consumption expenditures with public investment. However, it is possible to get separate (rough) estimates of these items. There are two points about the government sector that sometimes cause confusion. First, it includes all levels of government, whether federal, state, or local. Second, it includes purchases of goods and services, but excludes the government's **transfer payments.** (Examples of transfer payments are social security benefits and welfare payments.) The idea is that transfers do not represent payments to individuals in exchange for currently produced goods or services. Hence, they should not appear in GNP. In the first quarter of 1983, government purchases of goods and services accounted for 21% of GNP.

Finally, some of the goods and services produced in an economy are purchased by foreigners. Typically, we consider only the total of these purchases, which are the goods and services **exported** to foreign users. In addition to buying goods and services that are produced domestically, foreigners also produce goods and services that are **imported** into the domestic country. These purchases must be subtracted from the total of consumer, investment, and government purchases, since we are allocating the total production by domestic residents (GNP) among final users. So the foreign component appears in GNP as **net exports**—that is, the spending by foreigners on domestic production (exports) less the domestic spending on foreign production (imports). Notice that net exports may be either positive or negative. In the first quarter of 1983, this component was positive, but only 0.7% of GNP. (Exports were 11.5% of GNP, while imports were 10.8%.)

Net exports are often omitted in the development of a macroeconomic model for a single economy. The rationale is that first, this omission simplifies the presentation of the theory, and second, at least for the United States, exports and imports are small relative to GNP. We shall follow this tradition until Chapter 20, where we consider the role of foreign trade. When we omit the foreign sector, we get the familiar division of GNP into three parts, namely

GNP = consumer expenditure + gross investment + government purchases

One common error about national accounting arises because the spending on new physical capital is called ''investment.'' This terminology differs from the concept of investment in ordinary conversation, which refers to the allocation of savings among different financial assets, such as stocks, bonds, savings accounts, and so on. When we speak of a firm's investment, we mean the purchase of physical goods, such as a factory. Do not be confused by these two different meanings of investment.

Another point about investment concerns **depreciation.** During any period, some of the existing stock of capital tends to wear out or depreciate. Thus, a part of gross investment merely replaces the old capital that has depreciated. If we subtract depreciation from gross investment, then the remainder—called **net investment**—tells us the net change in the stock of capital goods. We shall discuss the difference between gross and net investment in Chapter 10. For now, we note that the sum of consumption expenditures, *net* investment, government purchases of goods and services, and net exports is called **net national product (NNP).** The difference between GNP and NNP reflects the difference between gross and net investment, which is the amount of depreciation. Hence, we have the condition

$$NNP = GNP - \text{depreciation}$$

Income

One of the basic relationships of national-income accounting is that between the level of production, GNP, and the income earned in this production. This income is called **national income.** In order to make clear the relation between production and income, let's think of a simple economy that has one firm producing bread as the only final product, and another firm producing flour as the only intermediate good. Suppose that the miller uses only labor to produce flour, while the baker uses labor and flour to produce bread. Sample income statements for these firms appear in Table 1.2. In this table the only sources of income are labor income and profits. We see also that total (nominal) GNP, which is the market value of the bread, is $600. This amount also equals the total revenue of the baker. The income statement shows that this revenue divides up into $350 for the cost of flour, $200 for payments to labor (or, from the workers' standpoint, $200 of labor income), and $50 of profits. For the miller, the revenue of $350 goes for $250 of labor costs (or labor income) and $100 of profits. Thus, national income equals the total labor income of $450 plus total profits of $150, which equals the $600 of GNP.

Table 1.2 Data for Calculation of Gross National Product and National Income

Baker				Miller			
Revenue		Costs and Profits		Revenue		Costs and Profits	
Total revenue from sale of bread	$600	Labor	$200	Total revenue from sale of flour	$350	Labor	$250
		Flour	$350			Profit	$100
		Profit	$ 50				

Two complications disturb the equality between GNP and national income in the real world. First, suppose that the baker uses some capital goods in the production process. Then, as the capital wears out, the baker subtracts depreciation charges from profits. Hence, we find that total income for labor and profit ends up equal to the baker's total revenue, which equals GNP, less the depreciation charges. That is, national income equals GNP less depreciation, which is NNP.

A second adjustment arises because of sales and excise taxes, which are called indirect taxes. These levies create a gap between the market price of a good—which includes the tax—and the revenue received by the producer. (The gap shows up as revenue for the government.) In our example from Table 1.2, if there had been a 5% sales tax on bread, then the consumer would have paid $630 for the bread, while the baker's total revenue would have remained at $600. As a result, national income would still be $600, while GNP would be $630. Generally, we find that national income equals GNP less depreciation and less these indirect taxes. Table 1.3 demonstrates this calculation using U.S. data for the first three months of 1983.

Recall that the definition of national income includes only the amounts earned in the production of output. Often economists also calculate the amount of income that people actually receive, which is called **personal income.** This concept differs from national income for several reasons. First, firms may retain part of their profit rather than paying it immediately to their owners. Then this income does not show up at once in the standard concept of personal income. Second, we subtract from national income the contributions paid for social insurance, since people do not receive these amounts directly as income. Next there are a series of adjustments to ensure that the amount of interest income in personal income corresponds to the amount that individuals receive. Finally we add various transfer payments, which are not included in national income, in order to calculate personal income. All of these adjustments are detailed in Table 1.3.

We can also determine the amount of income that people have left after paying taxes, which is called **disposable personal income.** Table 1.3 shows the calculation of disposable personal income from personal income.

Prices

One objective of macroeconomic theory is to explain the general level of prices and the changes in this price level over time. In order to use our theory, we need

Table 1.3 Data for Calculation of Net National Product, National Income, Personal Income, and Disposable Personal Income (Billions of Dollars)

Gross National Product (GNP)	$3,170.9
Less	
Depreciation	366.0
Equals	
Net National Product (NNP)	$2,804.9
Less	
Indirect Business Taxes and Nontax Liability	271.7
Other	9.3
Equals	
National Income	2523.9
Less	
Retained Corporate Profits	115.6
Contributions for Social Insurance	266.6
Plus	
Government Transfer Payments	381.3
Net Adjustment for Interest Income	110.7
Business Transfer Payments	14.5
Equals	
Personal Income	2,648.2
Less	
Personal Tax and Nontax Payments	401.0
Equals	
Disposable Personal Income	2,247.2

The data are for the first quarter of 1983, adjusted to an annual rate.
Source: U.S. Department of Commerce, *U.S. Survey of Current Business,* May 1983.

an empirical measure (or measures) of the general price level. Our analysis of real and nominal GNP provides one such measure. The **implicit GNP price deflator** can be calculated as

$$\text{Implicit GNP price deflator} = \left(\frac{\text{nominal } GNP}{\text{real } GNP} \right) \times 100$$

It is conventional to multiply by 100 in order to obtain an index number that takes on the value 100 for the base year (for which nominal *GNP* equals real *GNP*).

For a concrete example, consider again the data from Table 1.1. For the 1985A case, we find that the GNP deflator is (nominal *GNP*/real *GNP*) = 550/462 = 119. In other words, the price of the ''average item'' increased from 1984 to 1985 by 19%. This number is a weighted average of the percentage increase in the price of butter, which is 15%, and that of golf balls, which is 20%. It turns out that the weights used to compute the average percentage change are the shares of the two goods in the real GNP for 1985. Thus, by using the GNP deflator to measure the general level of prices, we give more weight to the items that are currently more important in the economy's market basket of produced goods.[5]

The formula for the implicit price deflator can be rearranged to see why we call it a price deflator. The rearranged equation is

$$\text{Real } GNP = \left(\frac{\text{nominal } GNP}{\text{implicit } GNP \text{ price deflator}} \right) \times 100$$

Thus, we effectively divide or deflate the nominal GNP by the price deflator in order to compute the real GNP.

The implicit GNP price deflator is called ''implicit'' because it is not directly or explicitly calculated. Real GNP and nominal GNP are computed directly and the GNP deflator is calculated by dividing the two as we have done. There are also explicit indices of the general price level. Two important examples are the **consumer price index (CPI),** and the **producer price index (PPI),** which is also called a wholesale price index. These are explicit indices since they are calculated directly.

The CPI is based on a fixed market basket of consumer goods. Every few years the government takes a statistical survey to compile the market basket and base-year prices of about 400 goods that are consumed by typical individuals. The quantities consumed serve as fixed weights until the next survey is taken. In order to calculate the CPI, we sum up the current market prices of goods, when weighted by base-year expenditures, and divide by the sum of the base-year prices, when also weighted by base-year expenditures. Typically, we also multiply the result by 100, so that the CPI for the base year is 100.

The PPI is computed in a similar manner. This index attempts to measure prices at an early stage of production, so the ''basket'' in the PPI consists of about 2,800 items sold at wholesale. These goods are primarily raw materials and semi-finished goods.[6]

We shall use primarily the implicit GNP price deflator, which appears in Figure 1.4, as our empirical measure of the general level of prices. There are several reasons for this choice. First, the PPI is too narrow a concept to reflect the general level of prices. Second, the GNP deflator reflects the importance of the various items in current market baskets of produced goods, whereas the CPI refers to base-year market baskets, which can become less relevant over time. Third, the GNP deflator contains only the prices of goods that are produced domestically, whereas the CPI includes prices of imported goods. Our attempt to understand the domestic forces that contribute to changes in the domestic price level can be confused if we use the CPI. Finally, until recently, the treatment of housing costs in the CPI was inappropriate. In particular, the index was unduly responsive to changes in mortgage interest rates.

---

[5]The GNP deflator, which weights by the importance of goods in current market baskets, is an example of a ''Paasche index of prices.'' For a discussion, see Edwin Mansfield, *Microeconomics*, 3rd edition, Norton, New York, 1979, pp. 99, ff.

[6]The CPI and PPI, which weight by the importance of goods in the base year, are examples of ''Laspeyres indices of prices.'' See Mansfield, op. cit., for a discussion.

Important Terms and Concepts

gross national product (GNP)

general price level

wage rate

interest rate

real GNP

recession

boom

Great Depression

inflation rate

microeconomic foundations

budget constraint

demand for money

medium of exchange

aggregate-consistency conditions

market-clearing approach

Keynesian model

IS/LM model

balance of international payments

exchange rate

national-income accounts

intermediate goods

personal consumer expenditures

consumer nondurables and services

consumer durables

gross investment

government purchases of goods and services

transfer payments

exports

imports

net exports

depreciation

net investment

net national product (NNP)

national income

personal income

disposable personal income

implicit GNP price deflator

consumer price index (CPI)

producer price index (PPI)

PART I

MICROECONOMIC FOUNDATIONS AND THE BASIC MARKET-CLEARING MODEL

CHAPTER 2

WORK EFFORT, PRODUCTION, AND CONSUMPTION— THE ECONOMICS OF ROBINSON CRUSOE

In this chapter we develop parts of the basic theoretical structure or **microeconomic foundations** that we shall use throughout this book. First, we describe a simple **production function,** which relates the quantity of output to the amount of work effort. We focus on the productivity of labor—that is, on how much extra output people generate by working more. Then, we discuss people's preferences for consumption and leisure. Basically, people increase their work effort and accept less leisure only if they receive a sufficient addition to consumption.

In any economic analysis, the interaction of opportunities for production with people's preferences determines the choices of work effort, production, and consumption. In order to bring out this basic interaction clearly, we begin with the simplest possible framework—namely, an economy of isolated households, each of which resembles Robinson Crusoe. Within this setting we can readily analyze the responses to changed opportunities in terms of **wealth effects** and **substitution effects.** It turns out that the primitive environment of Robinson Crusoe contains the essence of choice problems that arise in complicated market economies. So the principal findings from this chapter remain valid when we extend the analysis in later chapters to settings that look more like the present-day U.S. economy.

Production Technology

The basic theoretical model contains one type of economic unit, which we can think of as a combination of a household and a firm. Thus, we combine into this single unit the consuming and working activities of households with the production and hiring activities of businesses. For most purposes, this abstraction will be satisfactory because some households ultimately own the private businesses in any economy. Further, by merging the functions of households and businesses, we achieve some major simplifications of the analysis. From now on we refer to this composite unit as simply a household.

In our model each household uses its own labor effort as an input to production. Note that, in order to simplify matters, we do not yet consider stocks of capital as inputs to the production process. Specifically, in this chapter we concentrate on the economic incentives that make people work more or less in order to produce and consume more or fewer goods.

Formally, the quantity of a household's commodity output per period, denoted by y, is a function of the quantity of labor input, l. We write this relation as

$$y_t = f(l_t) \tag{2.1}$$

where f is the household's production function, which specifies the relation between the amount of work and the amount of output forthcoming from that work. The subscript t, which indicates the time period, is omitted when no ambiguity results.

In our abstract model there is a single physical type of commodity, so that no problems arise in measuring each household's output. The real world counterpart of this output, when added up over all producers, is the national accounts' measure of national product. Many practical problems arise in using price indices to add up goods that are physically different. Also, the standard concept of national product is limited to the flows of commodities that go through the organized market sector.[1] From an economic standpoint, we would want to make several adjustments. First, we would add the real value of the services that people produce at home; such as preparation of meals and housecleaning. Second, we might include the products from various "black markets"—including victimless crimes like prostitution and gambling, and activities such as baby-sitting and home repair work—which the official statistics exclude. Third, we might subtract from output any additions to air and water pollution, and the like. Although attempts have been made to expand the definition of national product along these lines, there are some severe problems of concept and measurement. In any case, these difficulties do not arise in our simplified theoretical framework.

We assume also in the basic model that people cannot store commodities from one period to the next, and thus, we neglect inventories of goods. We can think of the commodities in our model as perishable consumer goods. As examples, there are personal services, restaurant meals, and so on.

Work is productive in the sense that more work effort, l, means more output, y. The extra output that we get for one more unit of work is called the **marginal**

---

[1]One significant exception concerns owner-occupied housing. The U.S. Commerce Department estimates the flow of rentals that could have been obtained if these houses had been offered on rental markets. The national accounts treat this *rental equivalent* as an imputed flow of output, which appears as a component of the economy's total product.

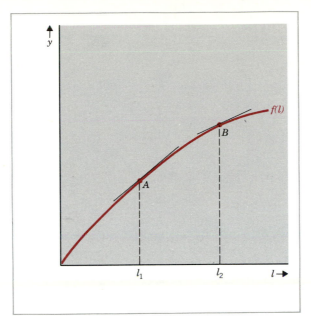

Figure 2.1 **Graph of Production Function**

The curve shows the level of output as a function of the quantity of labor input. At point A, the slope of the tangent straight line equals the marginal product of labor when $l = l_1$. Similarly, for point B where $l = l_2$.

(physical) product of labor; henceforth designated **MPL.** However, we assume **diminishing marginal productivity,** which means that each successive unit of work effort generates progressively smaller, but still positive, responses of output.

Figure 2.1, which is the graphical representation of equation (2.1), shows the relation of output to the quantity of labor input. Note that the curve goes through the origin, which means that output is zero when labor effort is nil. The positive slope of the curve (that is, of a straight line that is tangent to the curve) at any point indicates the relation between increments of output and increments in labor input, which is the marginal product of labor. For example, at the employment level l_1, the MPL equals the slope of the straight line that is tangent to the production function at point A.

The shape of the production function in Figure 2.1 implies that the slope becomes less steep as work effort increases. This property reflects the assumption of diminishing marginal productivity of labor. For example, at the employment level l_2, which exceeds l_1, the slope of the tangent straight line (at point B) is smaller than at point A. If the curve were allowed to bend over sufficiently to become almost horizontal, then close to zero extra output would be generated by an addition to labor input. That is, the marginal product of labor approaches zero as work effort tends to infinity. The full relation of the marginal product to the amount of work, as implied by the production function from Figure 2.1, appears

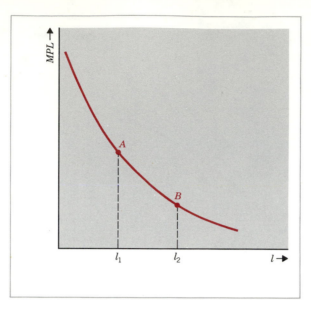

Figure 2.2 Relation of Marginal Product of Labor to Level of Work

Since $l_1 < l_2$, the marginal product of labor at point A exceeds that at point B. That is, the marginal product of labor falls as work effort rises.

in Figure 2.2. Note that the marginal product declines steadily as work effort increases.

The graph of the production function in Figure 2.3 gives us another way to look at the marginal product of labor. If we work 1 hour per day, so that $l = 1$ in the figure, then we produce the quantity Δy^1. (The symbol Δ is the Greek capital letter *delta*. The symbol denotes the increment in some quantity—in this case, the increment in output.) So in the interval up to 1 hour of work, the amount Δy^1 is a reasonable approximation to the marginal product of labor.

Now, if we work another hour, so that $l = 2$, then we produce the additional amount, Δy^2. Therefore, Δy^2 approximates the marginal product in the interval between 1 and 2 hours of work per day. Notice that the shape of the production function implies $\Delta y^1 > \Delta y^2$. Therefore, Figure 2.3 shows geometrically that the marginal product of labor declines as the amount of work effort rises. This property holds as work increases from 2 hours to 3 hours, from 3 hours to 4 hours, and so on. In Figure 2.3 the successive additions to output have the property, $\Delta y^1 > \Delta y^2 > \Delta y^3 \ldots > \Delta y^8$.

The curves in Figures 2.1–2.3 apply at some initial level of technology; that is, for a given production function, $f(l)$. We show this production function again as the solid curve in Figure 2.4. Then, the dashed curve in the figure shows the level of output for an improved technology, which we denote by $f(l)'$. The level of output is now higher at any given level of labor input.

What is the effect of an improvement in technology on the MPL? There are

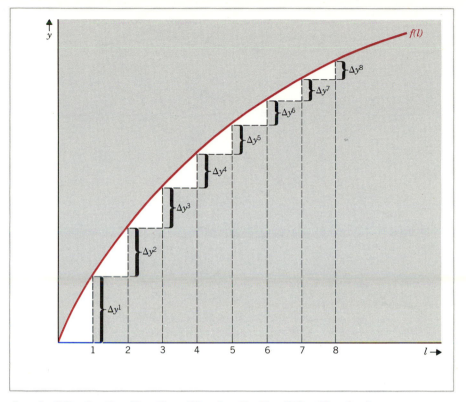

Figure 2.3 Graph of Production Function, Showing the Declining Marginal Product of Labor

The curve has the property, $\Delta y^1 > \Delta y^2 > \Delta y^3 \ldots > \Delta y^8$. That is, the marginal product of labor declines as work effort increases.

two possibilities here. In the first, the technological improvement enhances labor's productivity. For example, when hydraulic mining was applied to gold in the 19th century, each miner could process a much larger volume of ore with each hour of work. However, there are also cases where technological advances are primarily a replacement for labor services. For example, the use of robots may reduce the marginal product of workers on assembly lines.

For our purposes, we would like to capture the typical or average response of the marginal product of labor to an improvement in technology. Studies of production functions at an economy-wide level indicate that the first case is typical. That is, in the usual situation an improvement in technology raises the marginal product of labor at any given level of work effort.

The construction of the curves in Figure 2.4 reflects the assumption that the improved technology raises the productivity of labor. Namely, the curve labeled $f(l)'$—which corresponds to the improved technology—is steeper than the initial curve at any level of work effort. Recall that the slopes of the curves measure the

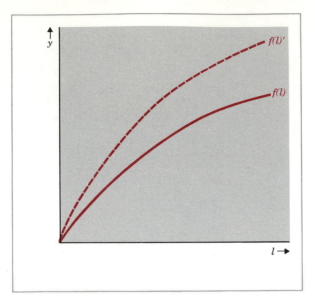

Figure 2.4 Effect of an Improvement in Technology on the Level of Production
The curve labeled $f(l)'$ corresponds to an improved technology, relative to the one labeled $f(l)$. This improvement raises the level of output for a given amount of labor input.

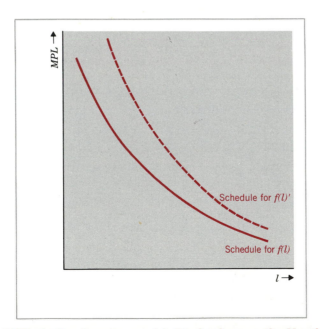

Figure 2.5 Effect of an Improvement in Technology on the Marginal Product of Labor
The dashed curve corresponds to an improved technology, $f(l)'$, relative to the initial one, $f(l)$. The technological advance shifts upward the schedule for the marginal product of labor.

marginal product of labor, MPL, at each point. In Figure 2.5 we show explicitly that, for any level of work, the MPL is higher along the new curve than it is along the initial curve. We can say that the technological advance generates an upward shift in the "schedule" for the MPL. By a schedule we mean the functional relation between the MPL and the amount of work, l. This entire relation shifts upward because of the improvement in technology.

Tastes for Consumption and Leisure

Let's pretend now that people have no opportunities to exchange commodities or anything else with other households. That is, we consider an environment of Robinson Crusoes where households are isolated from each other. In this case, each household's only option is to consume all the goods that it produces in each period. (Remember, there are no possibilities for holding commodities in storage.) Then, in the world of Robinson Crusoe we have

$$c_t = y_t = f(l_t) \qquad (2.2)$$

where c_t is the amount of consumption in physical units. The equation says that each household's consumption equals its production, which depends on its quantity of work effort.

Consumption in each period is a source of happiness or **utility** for households. (Henceforth, we use the economist's standard jargon, *utility*.) Equation (2.2) implies that people can consume more only if they raise their production. Further, for a given technology, the quantity of goods produced, y_t, depends on the level of work effort, l_t. So the amount to work in each period is the key decision that households make in our model.

In the real world, households have a lot of flexibility in their choices of work effort. For example, someone might work 4 hours per day or 8 hours. A person can pick a job that requires lots of hard work or one that does not. Someone might work only for part of the year, as is often the case for construction workers and professional sports figures. From the perspective of a family, there is a decision on how many members participate in the labor force. For example, there has been a strong increase over the last 40 years in the number of families with two full-time workers. One evidence of this trend is the growing rate of participation of women in the civilian labor force. This figure grows from 28% in 1940 to 53% in 1982 (while that for males declines from 84 to 77%).[2] In a longer time perspective, the amount of time spent at work depends also on the typical length of retirement and on the number of years that people spend in school.

---

[2]These figures refer to persons aged 16 years or more (14 years or more for 1940) who are neither full-time students nor members of the military. See *Economic Report of the President*, 1983, Table B-29.

We capture this real-world flexibility on work effort in our model by allowing people freely to choose their hours of work in each period. Thus, we neglect any institutional constraints that, for example, permit people to work on some jobs for 8 hours per day or 4 hours, but not 7½ or 2. This abstraction will be satisfactory when we think about the overall behavior of work effort for a large number of households. In this context the institutional constraints tend to average out.

In our model, households have a fixed amount of time in each period, which they can divide between work and leisure. By the term *leisure,* we mean to capture the full array of activities—other than work to produce goods—on which people spend their time. We assume that leisure time is intrinsically more enjoyable than time at work. In other words, leisure is a source of utility for households.

Let's suppose that we can define a function to measure the amount of utility that derives each period from consumption and leisure. The form of this **utility function** is

$$u_t = u(c_t, \; l_t) \tag{2.3}$$

$$(+) \; (-)$$

where u_t is the amount of utility (in units of happiness, which are sometimes called *utils*) that someone obtains for period t. We assume that the form of the utility function, u, is the same for all periods. The positive sign under the quantity of consumption, c_t, indicates that utility rises with consumption. The negative sign under work effort, l_t, signifies the negative effect on utility of more work (that is, of less leisure).

We simplify matters by assuming a type of independence for utility at different dates. Specifically, the way in which people get utility, u_t, from consumption and leisure at date t does not depend on their consumption and work during other periods. So, if someone works a lot this period, we ignore the possibility of fatigue for the next period. Similarly, if someone consumes a lot this period, we assume that the memory of this consumption binge does not make consumption any less enjoyable next period.

In the present setting the household's decisions for any period have nothing to do with choices made at other points in time. This result follows because goods are not storable and because the utility generated at one date does not depend on choices made for other dates. Therefore, we can focus on the selections of work effort and consumption for a single period. For convenience, we now drop the time subscripts and refer to period t's consumption and work as c and l, respectively.

We analyze households' decisions on working and consuming by exploiting the central economic postulate of optimizing behavior. That is, each household opts for the levels of work and consumption that are consistent with the maximization of utility in equation (2.3). Further, we observe that this maximization is subject to the constraint from equation (2.2), which says that each household's consumption in any period equals its production for the same period. We want to use these facts in order to understand the household's selection of work and consumption.

In order to make progress in our analysis of the household's choices, we must characterize further people's tastes for consumption and leisure. Accordingly, we make some additional assumptions about the form of the utility function, which appears in equation (2.3).

A basic assumption is that the utility gained from an extra unit of leisure, relative to that from an extra unit of consumption, diminishes as the ratio of leisure to consumption rises. In other words, if we have a lot of leisure, but relatively little consumption, then we are more concerned with adding to consumption, rather than to leisure. Let's think in terms of how much extra consumption we need in order to make up for the loss of a unit of leisure time—that is, how much additional consumption we require to make it worthwhile to work an extra hour. If we start with little consumption and a lot of leisure—that is, if we are working only a small amount—then it is important to add to consumption. Therefore, we are willing to work a lot more in order to get additional consumption. However, if we add more and more to consumption and are already working quite a bit, then leisure becomes more significant. We become less and less willing to work more and give up leisure in order to obtain extra consumption.

We can summarize this discussion with the curve shown in Figure 2.6. At zero work effort, $l = 0$, the curve specifies a level of consumption, c^0, on the vertical axis. This amount of consumption, together with full-time leisure (that is, $l = 0$), determines some level of utility from equation (2.3). We denote this level

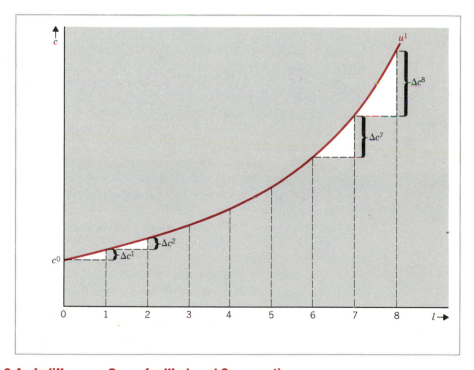

Figure 2.6 An Indifference Curve for Work and Consumption
All points, (l, c), on the curve yield the same level of utility, u^1. Hence, we are indifferent among these pairs of work effort and consumption.

of utility by u^1. Then, we construct the curve in Figure 2.6 in order to show all other possible combinations of work and consumption that provide the same level of utility, u^1, as that from the first pair, where $l = 0$ and $c = c^0$.

Suppose now that we work a positive amount, so that leisure becomes less than a full-time activity. For concreteness, assume that we work 1 hour per day, as represented by $l = 1$ in Figure 2.6. By itself, this reduction in leisure lowers utility. But we want to know how much additional consumption is needed to bring us back to the original level of utility. Suppose that we denote by Δc^1 the required amount of extra consumption. Then the new combination of work and consumption, where $l = 1$ and $c = c^0 + \Delta c^1$, yields the same utility as the initial pair, where $l = 0$ and $c = c^0$. Hence, we are indifferent between these two pairs of work and consumption. We show that these two points yield the same level of utility, u^1, by connecting them with the curve shown in Figure 2.6.

If we work another hour—that is, choose $l = 2$—then some additional consumption is again needed in order to maintain the level of utility. Figure 2.6 assumes that the required extra consumption is the amount Δc^2. Therefore, the position where $l = 2$ and $c = c^0 + \Delta c^1 + \Delta c^2$ again provides the same utility as the initial pair, where $l = 0$ and $c = c^0$.

We can continue this exercise as the amount of work rises. For example, if we raise work from 7 to 8 hours per day, then we need the extra consumption, Δc^8, in order to preserve the level of utility at the amount u^1.

All of the points, (l, c), that lie on the curve in Figure 2.6 yield the same level of utility. Therefore, we are indifferent among these hypothetical pairs of work and consumption. For this reason, the curve is usually referred to as an **indifference curve.**

Our previous discussion tells us something about the shape of an indifference curve. Namely, as we work more, each additional unit of work requires a greater amount of extra consumption in order to maintain utility. Therefore, the size of each addition to consumption, Δc, is larger the higher is the associated number of work hours. In particular, we see that $\Delta c^1 < \Delta c^2 < \ldots < \Delta c^7 < \Delta c^8$ in Figure 2.6. Eventually, if we are talking about working, say, 20 hours per day (or surely 24 hours per day), there will be no amount of extra consumption that makes an extra hour of work worthwhile. These considerations give the indifference curve the shape that it has in Figure 2.6. Specifically, the slope of this curve becomes steeper as we move to higher levels of work effort, l. In fact, at a sufficiently high level of work (somewhere less than 24 hours per day), the indifference curve must become essentially vertical.

At any point along the indifference curve, the slope of a tangent straight line tells us the increment in consumption that we require in order to make up for the loss of a unit of leisure. Each of the additions to consumption, Δc, that appear in Figure 2.6 approximate this slope in the vicinity of the corresponding level of work. For example, the amount Δc^2 is a good measure of the slope when the level of work lies between 1 and 2 hours per day.

The slope of the indifference curve in Figure 2.6 indicates the amount of consumption that we need in order to make up for the loss of a unit of leisure. Put alternatively, if we receive more than this amount of consumption, then we would be better off. So, for example, when we are already working 7 hours per day, we are willing to work an additional hour if, by doing so, we can raise consumption by at least the amount Δc^8 in Figure 2.6. If it turns out that the extra hour of work enables us to expand consumption by an amount greater than Δc^8, then economic reasoning predicts that we work that extra hour. This viewpoint allows us to determine the number of hours that people actually work.

All points on the curve in Figure 2.6 yield the same level of utility, u^1. But suppose that we look along the vertical axis and raise the consumption level above c^0; then, utility increases. So corresponding to this higher level of utility, say u^2, we can construct another indifference curve. The new curve is similar to the one shown in Figure 2.6, but it lies wholly above this curve. That is, for any level of work, l, the amount of consumption, c, is higher. That's why the new indifference curve corresponds to a higher level of utility. (We can also say that for any level of consumption, c, the amount of work effort, l, is lower along the new curve.)

Similarly, we could lower the level of consumption below c^0 along the vertical axis. In this case, we can start the construction of an indifference curve for a lower level of utility. Therefore, as a general matter, we can define a whole "family" or "map" of indifference curves, each of which corresponds to a different level of utility. Figure 2.7 shows five of these curves, labeled by their levels of utility, where $u^1 < u^2 < \ldots < u^5$. Along any curve the level of utility is constant. But

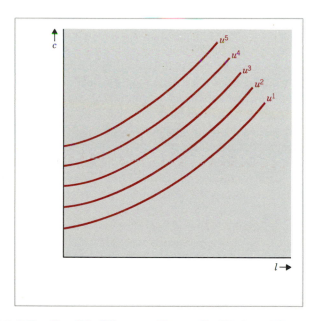

Figure 2.7 A Family of Indifference Curves for Work and Consumption
The level of utility rises as we move from the curve labeled u^1 to that labeled u^2, and so on.

as we move vertically from one curve to others—that is, raising consumption while keeping work fixed—we find that the level of utility increases. So in Figure 2.7, the level of utility rises as we move from the curve labeled u^1 to that labeled u^2, and so on. We have already mentioned the central idea that each household wants to achieve the highest possible level of utility. Therefore, we can also say that the household's objective is to reach the highest possible indifference curve among the family of curves that appear in Figure 2.7.

Deciding How Much to Work

The indifference curves in Figure 2.7 give us information about someone's willingness to give up leisure in exchange for consumption. Now suppose that we begin from a particular combination of work and consumption, (l, c). Then we can consult Figure 2.7 to find the indifference curve—that is, the level of utility—to which this point corresponds. Further, the slope of the indifference curve at this point tells us how much extra consumption, Δc, someone insists on in order to work an additional unit of time.

In order to determine how much someone actually works, we combine the indifference curves with a description of people's opportunities for raising consumption when work effort rises. In our model these opportunities come from the production function, which we introduced before and graphed in Figure 2.1. Here, the marginal product of labor (MPL), tells us the amount of extra output that derives from an extra unit of work. Further, we know from equation (2.2) that each addition to output corresponds to an equal addition to consumption.

The MPL tells us the addition to production—and therefore to consumption—that results from an extra unit of work. The slope of the indifference curve tells us the amount of extra consumption that we need in order to make up for less leisure time. Therefore, if the MPL exceeds the slope of the indifference curve, then we will be better off if we work more and use the added output to expand consumption. However, as we work more, two things happen. First, the MPL declines (because of diminishing marginal productivity). Second, the slope of the indifference curve—that is, the amount of extra consumption that we insist on—tends to rise. Therefore, as we work more and more, we tend to eliminate any initial excess of the MPL over the slope of the indifference curve. When the gap vanishes—that is, when the marginal product equals the slope of the indifference curve—it is no longer worthwhile to work more.

We depict the results in Figure 2.8. Here, we show five indifference curves, just as in Figure 2.7. The figure also shows the household's production function, $y = f(l)$.

Consider the intersection of the production function with indifference curve u^1 at point D. At this position, the slope of the production function—which is the MPL—exceeds the slope of the indifference curve. Therefore, an increase in work expands output—and thereby consumption—by more than enough to maintain the level of utility. Graphically, by raising work and moving along the production function beyond point D, we intersect higher indifference curves. Hence, we raise utility by working more.

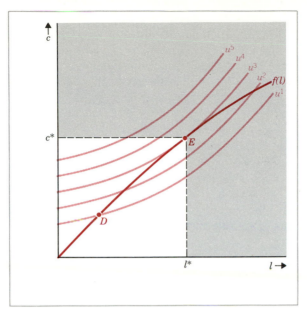

Figure 2.8 Combining the Indifference Curves with the Production Function
We move along the production function, $f(l)$, until we reach the highest possible indifference curve. This occurs at point E, where the production function is tangent to indifference curve u^3.

Assume that we raise work enough to reach point E in Figure 2.8. Here, we have moved from indifference curve u^1 to indifference curve u^3. But at point E, the slope of the production function has diminished enough to equal the slope of the indifference curve at the same point. We show this graphically by drawing the production function, $f(l)$, as tangent to indifference curve u^3 at point E. Then we designate the associated levels of work and consumption as $l*$ and $c*$. Notice that, at this point, we no longer gain utility by working more. In fact if we move along the production function beyond point E, we intersect lower indifference curves. In other words, the extra output and consumption are now insufficient to make up for the loss of utility from extra work. Therefore, utility declines if we work more than the amount $l*$.

To summarize, we choose the combination of work and consumption that maximizes utility. Therefore, we select the pair, $(l*, c*)$, at which the production function is tangent to an indifference curve.

Shifts in the Production Function

We want to understand how people change their choices of work effort and consumption when there are shifts in the opportunities for production. Here, we represent these shifts by movements up or down of the entire production function, $f(l)$, rather than by movements along a single function. Remember that we are examining the choices of work and consumption for a single period. So think here of changes in the production function that apply for that same period.

There are many examples of economic disturbances that alter production opportunities. For instance, the poor agricultural harvest in the United States for 1973 amounted to a downward shift in the production function—that is, less output materializes for a given input of labor. The oil crises of 1973–74 and 1979 led to increases in the price of oil, which meant that users of energy had to give up more resources in order to carry out their production. Hence, from the standpoint of these users, the disturbance again looks like a downward shift in the production function, $f(l)$. On the other hand, discoveries of new technology—such as practical uses of electricity, nuclear energy, and computer chips—amount to an upward shift in the production function.

In analyzing the reaction of households to economic changes, we find it useful to place the responses into two categories:

- wealth effects
- substitution effects

Briefly, a **wealth effect** (which economists also call an **income effect**) concerns the overall scale of our opportunities. If a change allows us to obtain more of the things that provide utility, then we say that our wealth increases. Note especially that we define wealth here in terms of the utility that we can attain. On the other hand, a **substitution effect** refers to the relative ease or cost with which we can obtain the different items that give us utility. For example, in the case we have been discussing, we might have a change in the possibilities for transforming more work (and, hence, less leisure) into more consumption. More generally, we could have a change in the relative costs of obtaining any two goods, such as bread and television sets.

We shall use the concepts of wealth and substitution effects extensively throughout this book. Here, we start with the details of wealth effects for the model that we have been analyzing. Throughout this discussion we assume that people have a given pattern of tastes for consumption and leisure. Specifically, people's indifference curves, which appear in Figures 2.7 and 2.8, do not move around when we shift the production function.

Wealth Effects

As a general definition we say that some change raises our wealth if it enables us to reach a higher level of utility. On the other hand, wealth declines if the change forces us to a lower level of utility.[3] Unfortunately, this definition may be difficult

---

[3]This viewpoint comes from John Hicks, as developed in his classic book, *Value and Capital*, 2nd ed., Oxford University Press, Oxford, United Kingdom, 1939, Chapter 2.

to apply in some circumstances. We want to use the notions of wealth and substitution effects to assist in analyses of various economic changes, such as a harvest failure. In some cases, we do not know at the start whether a particular change ends up raising or lowering our utility. So if we have to solve the whole problem in order to determine what happens to wealth, then there may not be much point in using the concept.

We can usually test for the sign of the change in wealth by the following method. Start with a household's initial choices of work and consumption at the position, (l^*, c^*), in Figure 2.8. Then see how the economic change alters opportunities in the vicinity of this initial point.[4] For example, we may find that the initial quantity of work effort, l^*, now allows us to consume at a higher level than before. Then, wealth surely increases (because we shall be able to attain a higher level of utility). On the other hand, we may find that the initial level of work effort, l^*, now allows only a smaller quantity of consumption than before, so wealth probably declines.

Let's be more concrete about this method for the case of a shift to the production function. An increase in wealth arises if we can produce more goods for the same amount of work effort. In the simplest case there is a parallel upward shift of the production function, at least in the vicinity of the initial level of work, l^*. Notice that a parallel upward shift means more output for a given amount of input, but no change in the slope of the production function at each level of work. That is, the marginal product of labor does not change if we maintain the level of work. We show this case in Figure 2.9. Here, the initial production function is $f(l)$, while the new one is $f(l)'$. Note that the new production function parallels the old one.

Recall that our previous cases of shifts to the production function—as shown in Figures 2.4 and 2.5—involve changes in the slope of the function. For example, a 10% rise in output at all levels of work means that the marginal product of labor is higher by 10% at each level of work. For the moment we neglect this type of change in the schedule for labor's marginal product, because it brings in substitution effects. The parallel shift shown in Figure 2.9 is easier because it involves only a wealth effect.

How do people respond to an increase in wealth? We can find the answer by combining the change to the production function that appears in Figure 2.9 with the indifference curves that appear in Figure 2.8. The results are in Figure 2.10. For clarity, we reproduce in this diagram only two indifference curves. Initially, the production function is tangent to an indifference curve at the point, (l^*, c^*). Then, as mentioned before, the upward shift to the production function enables us to reach a higher indifference curve. The new production function, $f(l)'$, is tangent to a higher indifference curve at the point, $[(l^*)', (c^*)']$. The figure indicates that

---

[4]This general approach derives from the work of the Russian economist, Eugen Slutsky. For a discussion (in the context of markets for goods), see Heinz Kohler, *Intermediate Microeconomics*, Scott, Foresman, Glenview, Illinois, 1982, p. 82.

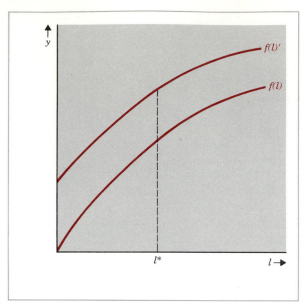

Figure 2.9 A Parallel Upward Shift of the Production Function
The new production function, $f(l)'$, lies everywhere above the old one, $f(l)$. With this type of parallel shift, the two functions have the same slope at any given level of work effort.

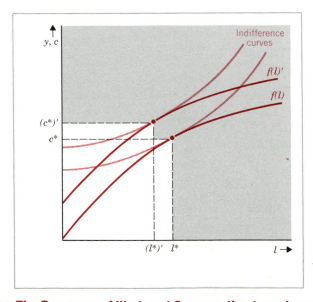

Figure 2.10 The Response of Work and Consumption to an Increase in Wealth
The parallel upward shift of the production function motivates us to consume more and work less.

consumption increases—$(c^*)' > c^*$—while work effort decreases—$(l^*)' < l^*$. In other words, we respond to the increase in wealth by raising the quantities of both things that provide utility—here, consumption and leisure. We say that consumption and leisure are **superior goods** because the quantities of both rise in response to an increase in wealth. (Sometimes economists use the term, **normal goods,** rather than superior goods.) Alternatively, we can say that the wealth effect is positive for consumption and negative for work.

Generally, when there are lots of different types of goods, we cannot be sure that the wealth effect is positive for all of them. That is, some goods may be "**inferior,**" which means that we desire less of these goods when wealth rises. (Often, economists pick on potatoes and margarine as candidates.) But when thinking of only two broad categories of things that provide utility—namely, consumption and leisure—we can be pretty sure that both goods are superior. That is, some reasonable assumptions about the nature of preferences guarantee this result. Hence, from now on, we assume that consumption and leisure are superior goods.

It is not surprising that the wealth effect on consumption is positive. Casual observation across families or countries immediately supports this proposition. Similarly, we can look over time for the United States as the economy has developed. It is no surprise that consumption per person has grown along with the rise in output per capita.

The negative effect of wealth on work effort is somewhat harder to verify. But it does show up in the long-run negative influence of economic development on average hours of work. In the United States the average hours worked per week for workers in manufacturing declines from 55 to 60 in 1890 to about 50 in 1914, 44 in 1929, and 39 in 1982.[5] Similarly, in the United Kingdom the average weekly hours of male manual workers falls from about 60 in 1850 to 55 in 1890, 54 in 1910, 48 in 1938, and 47 in 1965.[6]

If we look across countries at a point in time, we get some further indication of a negative wealth effect on work effort. For example, over the period, 1953–60, the mean over 10 industrialized countries for the average weekly hours in manufacturing is 43.9. (The 10 are the United States, Canada, Switzerland, Sweden, New Zealand, the United Kingdom, Norway, France, West Germany, and the Netherlands.) But the mean over 10 less-developed countries is 47.4. (These 10 are Yugoslavia, Colombia, the Philippines, El Salvador, Ecuador, Guatemala, Peru, Taiwan, Egypt, and Ceylon.)[7]

---

[5]The data are from U.S. Department of Commerce, *Historical Statistics of the U.S., Colonial Times to 1970,* pp. 168, 169; and *Economic Report of the President,* 1983, p. 206. For a full analysis, we should also consider changes in labor-force participation. See problem 2.10 below.

[6]The earlier data are rough averages from M. A. Bienefeld, *Working Hours in British Industry,* Weidenfeld and Nicolson, London, 1972, Chapters 4 and 5. Figures since 1938 are from B. R. Mitchell and H. G. Jones, *Second Abstract of British Historical Statistics,* Cambridge, United Kingdom, 1971, p. 148.

[7]The data are in Gordon Winston, "An International Comparison of Income and Hours of Work," *Review of Economics and Statistics,* 48, February 1966, Table 1. His study deals also with differences in labor-force participation.

On the other hand, the negative effect of economic development on average hours of work seems to weaken at high levels of development. In the United States the long-term downward trend in average hours worked per week in manufacturing apparently ends around World War II—the figure of 40.4 average hours per week for 1947 is close to that of 38.9 for 1982.[8] Similarly, for male manual workers in the United Kingdom, the value of 47.0 average hours for 1965 is nearly equal to that of 47.6 for 1946 and 47.7 for 1938.

We have to go further with our economic analysis in order to explain these observations for the recent period. As mentioned before, we want to bring in substitution effects as influences on the choices of work and consumption.

Substitution Effects for Work Versus Consumption

We started with the easy case of a parallel upward shift in the production function, as shown in Figure 2.9. This change in technology allows people to produce more goods for a given amount of work. However, there is no change in the schedule for the marginal product of labor, MPL. This last condition is artificial—that is, it does not hold for most real-world cases. In fact, we noted before that technological advances tend to raise the MPL at each level of work.

We want to understand the effects on households' choices from the type of upward shift to the production function that appears in Figure 2.11. The new production function, $f(l)'$, is proportionately higher than the initial one, $f(l)$, at each level of work. Therefore, the slope of the new curve exceeds that of the initial one at each level of work. For example, when work effort is the amount l^*, the slope of the new function at point B exceeds that of the old one at point A.

How does the proportional shift of the production function in Figure 2.11 differ from the parallel shift in Figure 2.9? At the employment level l^*, both changes indicate an increase in the level of output. We can think of the proportional shift as combining the parallel shift with a counterclockwise twist in the new function, $f(l)'$. Recall that we already understand the wealth effects from the parallel shift; therefore, we need only to study the consequences of a twist to the production function in order to assess the type of proportional shift that appears in Figure 2.11.

We graph a counterclockwise twist to the production function in Figure 2.12. Because the twist occurs at the employment level l^*, there is no change in output at this point. However, the new production function, $f(l)'$, is more steeply sloped than the old one, $f(l)$, at each level of work. For example, at the work level l^*, the dashed line labeled *new slope* in Figure 2.12 is steeper than the one labeled

---

[8]However, the available statistics refer to hours paid by employers. The actual decline in hours worked may be greater than the data indicate, because of the increasing importance of vacations and sick days. Also, more of a decline shows up when we look at the total private, nonagricultural economy. Here, average hours fall from 40.3 in 1947 to 34.8 in 1982. But these data partly reflect the changing composition of the labor force, especially toward more female workers.

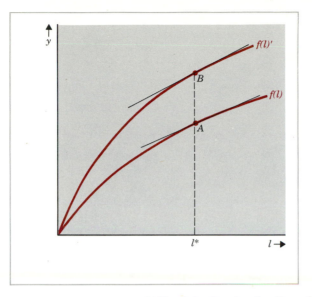

Figure 2.11 A Proportional Upward Shift of the Production Function
The new production function, $f(l)'$, is higher and more steeply sloped than the old one, $f(l)$, at each level of work.

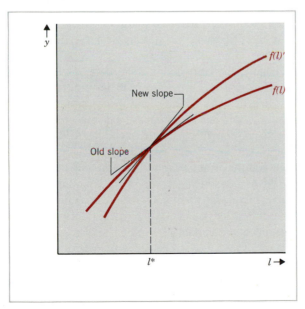

Figure 2.12 A Twist in the Production Function
At l^* the level of output is the same for the two production functions. However, the new function, $f(l)'$, is more steeply sloped than the old one, $f(l)$, at any level of work.

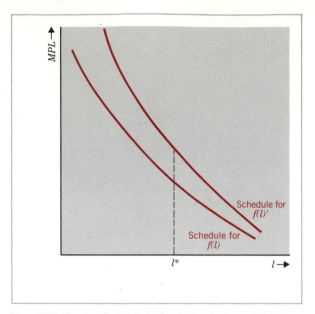

Figure 2.13 **The Shift in the Schedule for Labor's Marginal Product**
The change in the schedule for the marginal product comes from the twist in the production function, as shown in Figure 2.12. The new function, $f(l)'$, has a higher marginal product of labor than the old one, $f(l)$, at any level of work.

old slope. Hence, the twist raises the marginal product of labor at any level of work. We show the change in the schedule for the marginal product in Figure 2.13.

Figure 2.14 shows the household's response to a twist in the production function. The initial function, $f(l)$, is tangent to an indifference curve at the point, (l^*, c^*). Notice that the new function, $f(l)'$, still passes through this point. That is, it remains feasible to work the amount l^* and consume the amount c^*. Initially, we were happy to stay at this point because the MPL equals the slope of the indifference curve, but the MPL is now higher. Therefore, if we work more, we generate enough additional output (and consumption) to raise utility. That is, as we move along the new production function, $f(l)'$, in Figure 2.14, we cross higher indifference curves. Eventually, we get to one that is tangent to the new production function. This occurs at the point, $(l^{*'}, c^{*'})$, in the figure. Then, if we continue to increase work beyond this point, our utility falls.

We have shown that a rise in the schedule for the marginal product of labor induces us to work more, $(l^*)' > l^*$, and consume more, $(c^*)' > c^*$. Recall that we always have the opportunity to work one more unit of time and use the additional output to raise consumption. Further, the amount of extra output and consumption that we get equals the MPL. So in terms of the two things that provide utility—leisure and consumption—we have the option to give up 1 unit of leisure in exchange for MPL extra units of consumption. Now, when the schedule for labor's

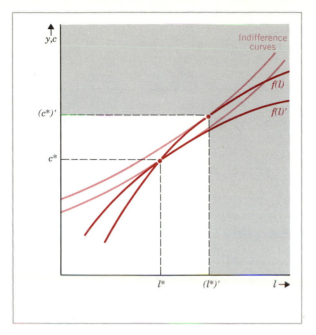

Figure 2.14 Response of Work and Consumption to a Substitution Effect
The schedule for the marginal product of labor shifts upward when we move from the old production function, $f(l)$, to the new one, $f(l)'$. The response is an increase in work—from l^* to $(l^*)'$—and a rise in consumption—from c^* to $(c^*)'$.

marginal product shifts upward, this deal becomes more favorable. That is, we can now get more consumption, MPL, when we relinquish a unit of leisure. Or, to put this another way, consumption has become less costly relative to leisure. A rational person who wants to maximize utility finds it desirable to substitute toward the things that have become less costly. Specifically, in our example, this substitution effect motivates us to opt for more consumption and less leisure (which means more work).

Combining the Wealth and Substitution Effects

We can now work out the full effects from a proportional upward shift to the production function, which appears in Figure 2.11. As mentioned before, this change amounts to a parallel upward shift in the function, combined with a counterclockwise twist in the function. That is, we have an increase in wealth, as well as a substitution effect from the rise in the schedule for the marginal product of labor.

Figure 2.15 shows the effects on the household's choices. Notice that consumption increases, $c^{*'} > c^*$. However, the effect on work effort turns out to be

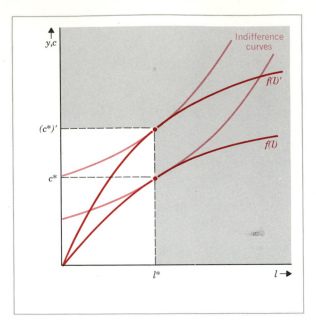

Figure 2.15 Response of Work and Consumption to Combined Wealth and Substitution Effects

When the production function shifts upward proportionately, there is an increase in consumption, but an ambiguous change in work effort.

ambiguous. Let's consider the nature of this ambiguity. First, while the positive wealth effects lead to more consumption and more leisure, which means *less* work, the substitution effect from the higher schedule for the MPL implies more consumption and less leisure. Thus, this effect means *more* work. Note that the wealth and substitution effects reinforce themselves with respect to consumption, but oppose each other with respect to work and leisure. In particular, the proportional shift of the production function leads to less work and more leisure only if the wealth effect dominates the substitution effect. We cannot say in general which force will be more important.

Let's use the perspective of wealth and substitution effects to reconsider the facts on work hours that we looked at before. Recall that over the last 40 years or so, there has been no strong trend in average hours worked per week in industry for the United States and the United Kingdom. However, there was a major decline in average hours worked at earlier stages of economic development.

Suppose that we think of economic development in the United States and the United Kingdom as represented by a series of proportional upward shifts to production functions. Figure 2.16 picks up three stages of economic development. These are a low level where the production function (for the typical producer) is $f(l)^{\mathrm{I}}$, a middle level at $f(l)^{\mathrm{II}}$, and a high level at $f(l)^{\mathrm{III}}$. We can think of the first

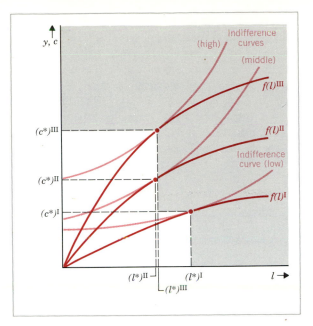

Figure 2.16 **Effect of Long-Term Economic Development on Average Work Hours**
We show three levels of the production function as the economy develops from $f(l)^I$ to $f(l)^{II}$ to $f(l)^{III}$. The indifference curves in the corresponding regions are labeled as ''low,'' ''middle,'' and ''high.'' Notice that work effort falls at early stages of economic development, but changes little at more advanced stages.

curve as applying to the United States before World War I, of the second curve as applying at the end of World War II, and of the third as applying in 1982.

In order to explain the significant decline in work hours at earlier times, we need the wealth effect from rises in the production function to dominate the substitution effect. The following property for households' tastes is consistent with the data on average work hours. Consider an economy at a low level of development—that is, a situation where the production function allows the typical person to reach only a low indifference curve. For this person, the bulk of consumption expenditure goes for items like food, clothing, and shelter, which are usually called ''necessities.'' In this circumstance people are likely to be willing to work long hours to maintain their consumption levels, even if their marginal products are low and although they are already working a lot. In other words, leisure does not become a priority until people are working 60 hours per week or more. Diagrammatically, consider the indifference curve marked *low* in Figure 2.16. We draw this curve as extremely flat until we reach a high level of work effort. The flat slope means that—at these low levels of consumption—people are willing to work a lot in order to gain a small amount of extra consumption. Notice that the first production function is tangent to the low indifference curve at the point, $[(l*)^I, (c*)^I]$. Here, people work many hours, but produce and consume relatively little because of the low level of the production function.

When production opportunities improve to the second level, $f(l)^{II}$, people respond by consuming more and working less. This production function is tangent to the indifference curve labeled *middle* at the point, $[(l^*),^{II} (c^*)^{II}]$, in Figure 2.16. Because people now consume beyond the level of necessities, we show this middle indifference curve with a slope that is generally higher and more steeply rising than that for the low indifference curve. In other words, extra leisure becomes more important relative to additional consumption. For this reason we find that a reduction in hours worked, $(l^*)^{II} < (l^*)^{I}$, accompanies the rise in consumption, $(c^*)^{II} > (c^*)^{I}$.

Finally, the move from the second production function, $f(l)^{II}$, to the third, $f(l)^{III}$, corresponds to the case that we explored before in Figure 2.15. Here, the wealth and substitution effects roughly cancel to yield little change in work hours. But consumption again increases, $(c^*)^{III} > (c^*)^{II}$.

Summary

In this chapter, we focus on the behavior of isolated households, whom we can think of as Robinson Crusoes. In particular, there are no markets on which people can trade. Thus, each household uses its own labor to produce goods via a production function. Since we treat goods as nonstorable, each household consumes what it produces.

We can express people's preferences in terms of their utility for consumption and leisure. Then we can translate these preferences into indifference curves for work and consumption. Basically, people are willing to work more only if they receive a sufficient addition to their consumption.

When we combine households' preferences with their opportunities for production, we can determine the choices of work, production, and consumption. It is convenient here to analyze these choices in terms of wealth and substitution effects. An improvement in the production function increases wealth, which motivates people to work less and consume more. That is, the wealth effect is positive for consumption and leisure. The only substitution effect in the model involves the productivity of labor. If the schedule for labor's marginal product rises, then people can obtain more consumption for an extra hour of work. Since consumption becomes cheaper relative to leisure, people work more in order to raise their consumption. That is, they substitute away from leisure and toward consumption.

Toward the end, we use the apparatus to analyze the long-term behavior of work hours. Initially, as an economy develops, we find that the increase in wealth motivates people to consume more, but to work fewer hours per week. As the economy develops further, the substitution effect from labor's higher productivity tends roughly to offset the wealth effect. Hence, there is little change in work hours, but consumption continues to rise.

Important Terms and Concepts

microeconomic foundations

production function

utility

wealth effects

substitution effects

marginal product of labor (MPL)

diminishing marginal productivity

utility function

indifference curve

superior goods (or normal goods)

inferior goods

QUESTIONS AND PROBLEMS

Mainly for Review

2.1 What is a production function? How does it represent a tradeoff that the individual *has* to make between work (and consumption) and leisure?

2.2 Distinguish between total product and marginal product. What are the implications for total product if marginal product is (a) positive and increasing, (b) positive and diminishing, and (c) negative?

2.3 What is a utility function? Show how different levels of utility can be represented by a family of indifference curves. Can these curves shift in the way that the production function can?

2.4 Show how the slope of each indifference curve indicates the tradeoff that the individual is willing to make between work (and consumption) and leisure. Explain why it may not be equal to the tradeoff represented by the slope of the production function.

2.5 Suppose that in order to remain at the same level of utility the individual would have to receive one additional unit of consumption as compensation for one less unit of leisure. Would it be utility-maximizing for the individual to work more if at that point the additional output obtained is more than one? If it is less than one? Restate your answer using the concepts of indifference curves and the production function.

2.6 Suppose there is an improvement in the production function, which is accompanied by an increase in the marginal product of labor. Will the individual work more in order to obtain more output; or work less, obtain the same or a greater amount of output, and enjoy more leisure than before? Explain your answer in terms of wealth and substitution effects. How does your answer change if either consumption or leisure is an inferior good?

Problems for Discussion

2.7 Properties of a Specific Production Function
Suppose that the production function has the form,

$$y = A \cdot \sqrt{l} + B$$

where y is output, l is labor input, A is a positive constant, and B is another constant, which may be positive, negative, or zero.

a. Graph the level of output, y, versus the quantity of labor input, l.

b. Is the marginal product of labor positive? Is it diminishing in l?

c. Describe the wealth and substitution effects from an increase in the coefficient, A.

d. Describe the wealth and substitution effects from an increase in the coefficient, B.

2.8 Effects of Shifts in the Production Function on the Choice of Work Effort

Assume again that the production function is $y = A \cdot \sqrt{l} + B$. What are the effects on a household's work effort, l, output, y, and consumption, c, from

a. an increase in the coefficient A?

b. an increase in the coefficient B?

2.9 Temporary Versus Permanent Changes in the Production Function

Suppose that we have an upward shift in the production function. Assume, as in Figure 2.9, that we have a parallel change, so that no shift occurs in the schedule for labor's marginal product. Recall that we showed in Figure 2.10 that people respond by raising consumption and reducing work.

The improvement in the production function could be permanent—as in the case of a discovery of some new technology—or it might be temporary—as in the case of good weather for this period. What difference does it make for our results whether the change is permanent or temporary? That is, do we predict different responses of consumption and work effort in the two cases?

2.10 Changes in Labor-Force Participation

In the text we mentioned some variations over time in average hours worked per week. But, we also see important changes in aggregate work effort that reflect shifts in labor-force participation. For example, people may alter their time spent at school or in retirement. Also, especially for married women in recent years, people may choose to work in the market, rather than at home. Overall, we can assess the changes in labor-force participation from the following table, which shows the ratio of the total labor force (including the military) to the adult population aged less than 65.*

Total Labor Force ÷ Population Aged 16–64 (%)	
1980	76
1960	69
1940	64
1920	63
1900	63

*The data are from U.S. Department of Commerce, *Historical Statistics of the U.S., Colonial Times to 1970*, pp. 10 and 128, and *Economic Report of the President*, 1983, pp. 195 and 196.

Notice that labor-force participation rises sharply during the post-World War II period. Further, most of this change reflects the increased activity of women, especially married women, in the market sector.

What does our analysis of wealth and substitution effects say about this behavior of labor-force participation? (Think here of effects on a family, which includes more than one potential worker.) In particular, can we reconcile the rising rate of labor-force participation with the tendency of average hours worked per worker to stay constant or fall slowly? (*Note*: this question does not have a clear-cut answer!)

2.11 Productivity

A popular measure of productivity is the ratio of output (say, real GNP) to employment (say, worker hours). In the graph of the production function below, this concept of productivity at the employment level l^1 is given by the ratio, y^1/l^1. Productivity at this point equals the slope of the dashed line that is drawn from the origin to intersect the production function at the employment level l^1.

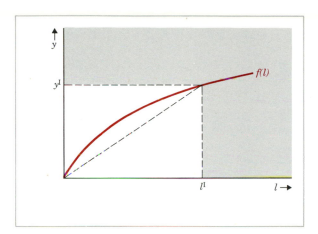

a. For the production function that is shown above and for any employment level l, show graphically that productivity, y/l, always exceeds the marginal product of labor, MPL.

b. Consider a technological change that shifts the production function upward proportionately at all levels of l (as shown in Figure 2.11). What happens to the choices of work effort, l, and output, y? What happens to productivity, y/l? (Empirically, long-run economic development is associated with a sustained rise in output per worker hour.)

c. Assume now that the form of the production function does not change. But suppose that we shift our tastes and become more willing to work. That is, at the initial levels of work and consumption, we now require a smaller addition in consumption in order to give up a unit of leisure. What happens here to the choices of work effort, l, and output, y? What happens now to productivity, y/l?

CHAPTER 3

THE BEHAVIOR OF HOUSEHOLDS WITH MARKETS FOR COMMODITIES AND CREDIT

In the previous chapter, households were Robinson Crusoe-like producers and consumers. Hence, there were no possibilities for trade between one household and another. Now we introduce two types of opportunities for exchange. First, there is a commodity market where people can sell their outputs and buy those of others. On this market, the price level tells people the amount of money that exchanges for a unit of commodities. One important aspect of this market is that it allows people to specialize in their production activities. This type of specialization is a major element in efficient economic organization.

Second, there is a credit market on which people can borrow and lend. Here, the interest rate determines the cost of borrowing and the return to lending. By using the credit market, individuals can smooth out their consumption even if their incomes vary from period to period. The effect of the interest rate on the time pattern of consumption and work is the key relation that we study in this chapter.

The Commodity Market

In the real world people consume very little of the goods that they help to produce in the marketplace. For example, an auto worker's contribution to the output of cars is much greater than that worker's expenditure on cars.[1] Typically, people

---

[1] Services produced in the home—such as cooking, child care, and so on—differ from market goods. Namely, people consume most of the goods that they produce at home. However, this production is assisted by consumer durables, which people buy on the market, and possibly by the services of maids, repair people, and so on.

work on one or a few products and receive income from the sale of these products or from the sale of their labor services, which help to create the products. Finally, they use this income to purchase a wide range of consumer goods. As Adam Smith put it, we tend to specialize with respect to occupations and production activities. This specialization aids efficiency—in fact, the national output would be many times smaller if everyone participated in the production of all types of goods. In this case, we would learn each job badly, and we would also spend most of our time shifting from task to task.

In our theoretical model we want to capture the feature that people consume little of what they produce. It is convenient to go to the extreme and assume that individuals sell their entire output on a market where people buy and sell commodities. Then, people use the proceeds from these sales to buy other goods for consumption purposes from the commodity market.

Our model will become unworkable if we try to keep track of the physical differences among many kinds of goods. In particular, we still want to pretend that there is a single physical type of good, which people produce via one type of production process.[2] Hence, as before, the production function is

$$y_t = f(l_t) \tag{3.1}$$

In our model people specialize to a single activity on the production side. The production function, $f(l_t)$, that applies here already reflects any gains in efficiency that result from this specialization. Therefore, we do not use this model in order to analyze changes in the degree of specialization for production activities.

Money

We mentioned the sales and purchases of goods on the commodity market. We have to be precise about the form of these exchanges. Let's assume, as seems reasonable, that it is inconvenient to trade one type of goods directly for another. In particular, as economists have noted for hundreds of years, this form of **barter** exchange requires us to find someone who wants exactly the goods that we have and has exactly the goods that we want. Therefore, we assume that society has settled on a **medium of exchange,** which we call money. People then sell their outputs for this stuff called money and use the money to buy other goods for consumption purposes. The use of money facilitates the exchange of one good for another.

---

[2]If all goods are identical, then we have a little problem in motivating people to sell their own products and buy those of others. The following idea (suggested by Bob Lucas of the University of Chicago) may be helpful. Think of all goods as physically identical except for color. Efficiency requires people to specialize in producing goods of one color. However, since people like to consume goods of many different colors, everyone sells most of their output on the commodity market and uses the proceeds to buy goods of different colors. We can still add up the goods in physical units to get measures of total output, consumption, and so on. However, remember that this setup is just an abstraction, which we construct in order to capture some interesting features of real-world economies in a workable model.

Table 3.1 **The U.S. Money Stock in 1982**

	Components of the Money Stock ($ billion)	Ratio to Annual GNP (%)
Currency	128	4.2
Checkable Deposits	325	10.6
*M*1 Definition of Money Stock (includes $4 billion in travelers' checks for 1982)	458	15.0

Note: All figures are annual averages of monthly data from the *Federal Reserve Bulletin*. Currency includes amounts held outside of the U.S. Treasury, Federal Reserve Banks, and the vaults of commercial banks. Checkable deposits include demand deposits at commercial banks (other than those of other domestic banks, the U.S. government, and foreign banks and official institutions), negotiable-order-of-withdrawal (NOW) accounts and automatic-transfer-service (ATS) accounts at banks and thrift institutions, credit union share draft accounts, and demand deposits at mutual savings banks.

The money in our model is analogous to a paper currency that is issued by a government. At the present time, almost all governments issue this type of currency. (Two exceptions are Panama and Liberia, which use U.S. currency. Some others that lack their own paper money are Andorra, Greenland, Guadalupe, and Liechtenstein.)

Money is denominated in an arbitrary unit, such as a ''dollar.'' We also refer to dollar amounts as **nominal** magnitudes. One important feature of money is that it maintains its value in dollar terms if we hold it. That is, unlike some assets that we introduce later, money does not bear interest.[3]

As mentioned, money takes a paper form in our model, with no allowance for backing by gold or other commodities. The monetary roles of gold and silver were important historically, but are much less significant under present-day arrangements. (Of course, the precious metals may again assume a significant monetary role at some future time.)

Table 3.1 allows us to relate our abstract concept of money to a conventional measure of the money stock for the present-day United States. Our theoretical construct corresponds closely to currency held outside of commercial banks. For 1982 the average amount of this currency was $128 billion, which amounted to 4.2% of the nominal gross national product (GNP). That is, people held a little more than 2 weeks' worth of the GNP as currency in 1982.

The term *money* typically refers to a monetary aggregate that is broader than currency. The standard definition in the United States, called **M1,** attempts to

---

[3]Historically, it is rare for currency to pay interest. Some early forms of U.S. Treasury notes, such as those issued from 1812–15, paid interest and also had some limited use as media of exchange. However, because no denomination below $100 was issued, these notes were used mostly as bank reserves. For a discussion, see Richard Timberlake, *The Origins of Central Banking in the United States*, Harvard University Press, Cambridge, Massachusetts, 1978, pp. 13–17.

classify as money the assets that serve regularly as media of exchange. Specifically, this concept also includes the checkable deposits that people hold at banks and some other financial institutions.[4] The average amount of these checkable deposits for 1982 was $325 billion, or 10.6% of annual GNP. Therefore, $M1$—the sum of currency and checkable deposits (plus about $4 billion in travelers' checks)— equaled $458 billion in 1982, or 15.0% of GNP. Put alternatively, the $M1$ definition of the money stock amounted to about eight weeks' worth of GNP in 1982.

As mentioned, we can readily identify the money in our theoretical model with currency, but our concept does not correspond precisely to a broader monetary aggregate, such as $M1$. Eventually, we expand the theoretical framework to incorporate financial institutions, such as banks—then we can also deal with checkable deposits. For now, however, we should think of money as being currency.

In our theoretical model we denote the dollar quantity of money that someone holds during period t by m_t. Then, we think of this cash as held until the start of the next period, $t + 1$. Hence, the change in someone's cash position for period t is the difference between today's money, m_t, and the amount held over from the previous period, m_{t-1}. If people add to their cash position, so that $m_t - m_{t-1} > 0$, then we say that they are positive savers in money during period t. But, if $m_t - m_{t-1} < 0$, then they dissave in money during period t.

If we add up the amount of money that people hold at any point in time, we determine the aggregate quantity of money. Here, we adopt the general convention of using a capital letter to denote an aggregate quantity. Therefore, M_t is the sum total of money held by all households during period t. For now, we do not allow the aggregate quantity of money to change over time. Therefore, $M_t - M_{t-1} = 0$ holds for all periods. This condition means that the sum total over households of saving in monetary form will be zero at all times.

The Price Level

We mentioned that goods sell for money on the commodity market. How much money do people get for each unit of goods sold? Since goods are physically the same, we expect that all can be sold for the same number of dollars. The number of dollars that people receive for each unit of goods sold is the dollar "price" of the good. We denote the price by P and measure it in units of dollars per good. Often, we refer to P as the **general price level.**

From the standpoint of a seller of commodities, the price P indicates the

---

[4]Until recently this category covered only demand deposits at commercial banks. Also, it has been illegal (since 1933) for banks to pay interest on these deposits. However, because of major changes in financial regulations, banks can now issue "negotiable orders of withdrawal" (NOW accounts), which do pay interest. The new regulations also allow savings and loan associations and other financial institutions to provide similar accounts. Therefore, the present definition of money, $M1$, includes these types of accounts, as well as demand deposits at commercial banks. The terminology, $M1$, distinguishes this asset total from broader versions, such as $M2$, which include time deposits and other forms of relatively liquid financial assets.

number of dollars obtained for each unit of goods sold. From the viewpoint of a buyer of commodities, the price is the number of dollars paid per unit of goods. Since P dollars buy 1 unit of goods, we see that $1 buys $1/P$ units of goods. Therefore, the expression, $1/P$, tells us the value of $1 in units of the commodities that it buys. Similarly, if we have $$m$, rather than $1, then we can exchange this money for $(m) \times (1/P) = m/P$ units of commodities. Whereas the quantity m defines the value of money in terms of dollars, the quantity m/P tells us the value of this money in terms of the quantity of commodities that it buys. Expressions like m/P, which are measured in commodity units, are often described as being in **real terms.** By contrast, a quantity like m is in dollar or nominal terms.

Because we have only one physical good in our model, we have only one dollar price to measure at any point in time. But in the real world there are lots of different commodities, each of which has a different price. Economists measure the general level of prices at each date by averaging over all of the individual prices for that date. Then we use this average to form a *price index,* which tells us how the average price has changed since some base year. For example, the price index that applies to personal consumption expenditures in the United States stood at 206 for 1982, relative to 100 for the base year 1972.[5] Thus, the dollar price of the typical item increased by 106% from 1972 to 1982.

Many problems arise in calculating actual price indices. By an average price we hope to measure the dollar cost of purchasing a typical market basket of goods. So, we have to know what weights to assign to different goods in constructing this market basket. In order to have a good price index, we also have to allow these weights to change over time. As an additional problem, we have to decide how to compare goods from one year with those from another. But, in what sense is a car or a computer from 1982 the same as one from 1972? Although these issues are important and interesting, we shall not spend much time on them in this book. That is because we can satisfactorily avoid these hard problems for many interesting macroeconomic questions.

One important thing to keep in mind is the distinction between the general price level and the relative prices of different goods. In our model we shall talk about the price level, which corresponds in the real world to a general index of prices. By a relative price we mean the dollar cost of one good expressed as a ratio to the dollar cost of another good. So we can say that the price of oil rose in 1973 relative to the price of hamburger or relative to the general level of prices. With only one physical good in the model, we cannot talk about changes in relative

---

[5]This index is the deflator for the component of gross national product that covers personal consumption expenditures. By the term, deflator, we refer to the price index that we use to convert (or deflate) a nominal variable—here, the dollar amount of personal consumption expenditures—to a magnitude expressed in real terms. (By real terms, we mean here the value of today's commodities, when evaluated with the prices from the base year, 1972.) For a number of reasons, the deflator for personal consumption expenditures is superior to the more widely known consumer price index or CPI. In particular, the weights attached to the various commodities in the CPI do not accurately reflect the weights of the commodities in consumers' current market baskets of goods.

prices. But occasionally, we shall stretch our imaginations by referring to real-world examples where some relative prices do change.

In the present chapter, we assume that people perceive the price level to be constant over time. However, we drop this unrealistic assumption in Chapter 7, which begins our study of inflation. In any case, we assume throughout the analysis that each household views itself as sufficiently small that it can buy or sell any amount of goods in the commodity market without influencing the established price. Economists call this **perfect competition.**

The Credit Market

In the Robinson Crusoe model of Chapter 2, people had no way to shift resources over time. For example, these isolated individuals could not borrow funds from others and repay these loans at another time. Also, people were unable to store produced goods from one period to the next.

We retain the assumption here that goods cannot be stored over time. However, we introduce possibilities for borrowing and lending on a credit market. This market will enable individuals to shift resources from one period to another. For example, borrowing now and repaying later allows people to consume now rather than later. On the other hand, lending now and collecting later permits people to consume later instead of now.

Someone who lends funds receives a piece of paper that indicates the terms of the contract. In our model we call this piece of paper a **bond.** The holder of a bond has a claim to a specified payment stream from the borrower. The borrower is the issuer of the bond.

Recall that we are dealing with households that proxy for the array of firms and households in the real world. Therefore, the bonds in our model might correspond to securities issued by corporations, loans made by banks, residential mortgages (by far the most important form of private, nonbusiness borrowing), or personal loans through credit cards or other means.

As a general background for our theoretical concept of loans, we can refer to Table 3.2. This table gives a breakdown for 1981 of the outstanding debt of private, domestic, nonfinancial borrowers.[6] Hence, the table excludes the obligations of governments, foreigners, and financial institutions, such as banks and insurance companies. From the standpoint of the identity of the borrower, the total debt breaks down into 50% for households,[7] 38% for corporations, and 12% for noncorporate businesses including farms. Expressed in terms of the type of debt, there is 37% in mortgages, 13% in consumer credit (which includes installment loans on automobiles and other purchases, personal loans, and charge accounts), 13% in

---

[6]The table includes corporate bonds, but not corporate stock.

[7]Indirectly, the households own the various corporations and noncorporate businesses. Therefore, the households ultimately also owe these other components of the debt.

Table 3.2 Breakdown of Debt for Private, Domestic, Nonfinancial Borrowers in the U.S. at the End of 1981

Borrowing Sector	Amount of Debt ($ Billion)	% of Total	Type of Debt	Amount of Debt ($ Billion)	% of Total
Households	1,550	50	Residential Mortgages	1,155	37
Corporate Business	1,180	38	Consumer Credit	411	13
Noncorporate,			Corporate Bonds	395	13
Nonfarm Business	202	$6\frac{1}{2}$	Commercial Mortgages	278	9
Farms	173	$5\frac{1}{2}$	Farm Mortgages	102	3
			Bank Loans (other than those included above)	423	14
			Other	339	11
Total	3,103	100	Total	3,103	100

Source: Board of Governers of the Federal Reserve System, *Annual Statistical Digest*, 1981, flow-of-funds accounts, p. 120.

corporate bonds, 12% in commercial and farm mortgages, 14% in bank loans (other than those included in previous categories), and 11% in other forms.

In our theory, business loans become more interesting in later chapters when we introduce possibilities for financing additions to the stock of capital. At present, we can think of the bonds in our model as consumer loans that people arrange on a credit market. In particular, people use this market in order to achieve a desired pattern of consumption over time. For example, an individual can adjust his or her borrowing and lending in order to smooth the time pattern of consumption, even if the amount of income varies greatly from period to period.

Bonds in our model come in units of dollars. When we buy 1 unit of these bonds with $1 of money, we lend $1 on the credit market. On the other hand, if we issue 1 unit of bonds in exchange for $1 of money, then we borrow $1.

For convenience, we assume that all bonds have a maturity of one period. That is, each dollar unit of these bonds commits the borrower to pay the lender the **principal**, $1, plus **interest**, R, in the next period. The variable R is the **interest rate**—that is, the ratio of the interest payments, R, to the amount borrowed, which is $1. For the buyer of a bond, the interest rate represents the return per period to lending, while for the issuer of the bond, the interest rate dictates the cost per period of borrowing.

We assume that the credit market treats all bonds the same, regardless of the issuer. That is, in order to keep things manageable, we do not differentiate among persons with respect to their credit-worthiness, the type of collateral that they put up for a loan, and so on. Accordingly, the interest rate, R, must be the same for all bonds. Further, any household is small enough to be able to buy or sell any amount of bonds without affecting the interest rate. Again, this is an assumption of perfect competition. Later on, we can modify this framework in order to bring in various real-world complications, such as limitations on individuals' access to borrowing. Also, we can readily consider loans with different payment streams, such as mortgages or securities with long maturities.

Suppose now that we look at the borrowing or lending status of various households at any point in time. Some people have a history of borrowing on the credit market—for example, students who are financing their college education may have taken out a large amount of loans. Similarly, people who have recently purchased homes or automobiles are likely to have incurred substantial debts. On the other side of the credit market, there are people who have positive holdings of bonds. For example, people who are nearing retirement or have already retired are likely to have accumulated financial assets. Also, persons who are near their peak earning years—such as business executives, middle-aged college professors, and unionized workers with seniority—are likely to have amassed substantial assets. Some of these people plan to use their assets to leave a bequest for their children.

Let b_t represent the number of bonds in dollar units that a household holds during period t. Recall that the amount of bonds may be either positive or negative for an individual household. Notice, however, that for any dollar borrowed by one person, there must be a corresponding dollar lent by someone else. Hence, the sum total of positive bond holdings for lenders must exactly match the aggregate of negative bond holdings for borrowers. In our model we allow only one type of economic unit, namely, households, to borrow and lend. In particular, we do not yet deal with governments, foreigners, financial institutions, or corporations as participants in the credit market. (We shall see later that the essential ideas do not change when we make these additions.) Therefore, in our model the sum total of bonds held by all households must always be zero.

Recall that a capital letter designates the aggregate value of a variable. Accordingly, B_t represents the total of bond holdings by all households during period t. We have just shown that $B_t = 0$ holds at all points in time in our model.

As noted before, b_{t-1} measures the dollar amount of bonds that someone holds during period $t - 1$. Then in period t these bonds pay the interest, Rb_{t-1}, and principal, b_{t-1}. Thus, the receipts from bonds are positive for lenders—for whom b_{t-1} is positive—and negative for borrowers. Recall that the aggregate stock of bonds for period $t - 1$, B_{t-1}, is zero. Therefore, it follows that the aggregates of interest and principal payments for period t must also be zero. In other words, the total of interest receipts always balances the total of interest expenses.

We measure saving in the form of bonds as the net change in someone's asset position, $b_t - b_{t-1}$. For example, retirees are likely to have built up a positive amount of financial assets, $b_{t-1} > 0$, but tend to run down these assets during their retirement. Hence, these people undertake negative saving in bonds, $b_t - b_{t-1} < 0$, although their bond holdings, b_{t-1} and b_t, are still positive. Other people— especially those in prime working years—have positive bond holdings, and also carry out additional saving in bonds, so that $b_t - b_{t-1} > 0$.

The same considerations apply to borrowers, who have a negative position in bonds, $b_{t-1} < 0$. If these people maintain the level of indebtedness, so that $b_t = b_{t-1} < 0$, then they carry out zero saving in bonds. But if they pay off part of their debts, so that $b_t - b_{t-1} > 0$ (that is, if b_t is less negative than b_{t-1}), then they are positive savers in bonds. Alternatively, if they add to the principal of their outstanding debts, so that $b_t - b_{t-1} < 0$, then they are negative savers in bonds.

When we sum up across households, we know that $B_t = B_{t-1} = 0$ applies. Therefore, the aggregate of saving in bonds, $B_t - B_{t-1}$, must also be zero in each period. In the aggregate the additions to loans balance the additions to debts.

In our model an individual's total of financial assets equals the sum of money and bonds, $m_t + b_t$. Recall that money holdings are nonnegative for all persons, $m_t \geq 0$—that is, only the government can issue money in our model. However, bond holdings can be either positive or negative. In the aggregate, since $B_t = 0$, the stock of financial assets in our model equals the total money stock, M_t.

The change in an individual's financial assets, $(m_t + b_t) - (m_{t-1} + b_{t-1})$, determines that individual's total saving for period t. This saving is partly in money, $m_t - m_{t-1}$, and partly in bonds, $b_t - b_{t-1}$. When summing up across all households, we know that $M_t - M_{t-1} = 0$ (because the total stock of money is constant), and $B_t - B_{t-1} = 0$. Therefore, the aggregate of total saving is zero at all points in time in the present model. (Later on, when we introduce investment in Chapter 10, this result will change.)

Budget Constraints

Budget Constraints for One Period

Each household receives income from sales of output, y_t, to the commodity market. As before, the quantity of this output depends on the amount of labor input, l_t, through the production function, $y_t = f(l_t)$. Since the price of goods is P, the dollar income from selling output is Py_t. Recall that interest income from the bond market, Rb_{t-1}, is positive for lenders and negative for borrowers. Also, remember that people receive no interest income on their holdings of money.

Each household purchases the quantity of consumable goods, c_t, from the commodity market. Since the price of goods is P, the amount of consumption expenditure in dollars is Pc_t.

If someone's total income exceeds his or her consumption expenditures, then the person is a positive saver and experiences an increase over time in the dollar value of total financial assets, money plus bonds. Note that this statement is satisfactory even for people who are initially borrowers—that is, for households whose initial holdings of bonds are negative. For example, if the quantity of money held does not change, then the positive saving corresponds here to a reduction in the amount owed. Similarly, households whose total income is below their consumption expenditures are dissavers. If the quantity of money held does not change, then the dissaving shows up either as a reduction in bond holdings (for people whose initial stocks of bonds are positive) or as an increase in borrowings.

At the start of any period, each household has a given total of financial assets. Then, given this total, the household can choose the breakdown between money and bonds. In particular, people use the credit market in order to exchange money for bonds, or vice versa, and thereby achieve the desired composition of their financial assets. Recall that the amount held as bonds, b_t, determines the interest income (positive or negative) for period $t + 1$. Now the motivation for holding a portion of financial assets as money derives from money's convenience in carrying out market exchanges. That is, people save on transaction costs by holding money. However, for expositional purposes, we do not deal explicitly with these transaction costs until Chapter 5. So, for now, we just assume that people hold some money.

We can express the equality between a household's total sources and uses of funds in the form of a **budget constraint.** The condition for period t is

$$Py_t + b_{t-1}(1 + R) + m_{t-1} = Pc_t + b_t + m_t \tag{3.2}$$

The left side of equation (3.2) measures current sources of funds, which include current income from the commodity market, Py_t, the principal received on last period's bonds, b_{t-1}, the interest receipts from these bonds, Rb_{t-1}, and the stock of money held over from the previous period, m_{t-1}. The right side of the equation expresses uses of funds, which consist of consumption expenditures, Pc_t, holdings of bonds, b_t, and holdings of money, m_t. Since we treat the price level and interest rate as constants, these variables appear without time subscripts in the equation.

If we rearrange terms in equation (3.2), then we obtain an expression for a household's dollar value of total saving, which equals the change over time in the dollar value of financial assets,

$$\text{Nominal Saving} = (b_t + m_t) - (b_{t-1} + m_{t-1}) = Py_t + Rb_{t-1} - Pc_t \tag{3.3}$$

Notice that nominal saving equals the income from the commodity market plus interest receipts less consumption expenditures.

As an illustration, suppose that we start with $b_0 = \$10,000$ in bonds and $m_0 = \$100$ in money. Then, if $R = 10\%$ per year, we receive $\$1,000$ in interest and $\$10,000$ in principal during the next year. Suppose that our annual income from the commodity market is $Py_1 = \$20,000$, and that we consume the amount, $Pc_1 = \$19,000$. Finally, assume that we hold a constant amount of money, so that $m_1 = \$100$. Given these assumptions, equation (3.2) tells us the amount of bonds, b_1, held at the end of the next year. That is,

$$\underset{(Py_1)}{20,000} + \underset{(b_0)}{10,000} + \underset{(Rb_0)}{1,000} + \underset{(m_0)}{100} = \underset{(Pc_1)}{19,000} + b_1 + \underset{(m_1)}{100}$$

Hence we find that next period's holdings of bonds, b_1, is $\$12,000$.

Alternatively, equation (3.3) says that total saving is the difference between total income and consumption expenditures. Therefore, total saving equals $\$20,000$ $(Py_1) + \$1,000 (Rb_0) - \$19,000 (Pc_1) = \$2,000$. Since the holdings of money do not change, all of this saving goes into bonds; therefore, the holdings of bonds rise over the year from $b_0 = \$10,000$ to $b_1 = \$12,000$.

One thing to notice is the connection between consumption and saving. The more we spend on current consumption, Pc_1, the smaller is the amount of saving. For example, if we increase current consumption expenditure by $\$1,000$ to $Pc_1 = \$20,000$, then saving falls from $\$2,000$ to $\$1,000$. Correspondingly, the bonds that we hold the next period, b_1, fall from $\$12,000$ to $\$11,000$. More consumption today means that we have less assets available for the future.

Households can also leave saving intact while making simultaneous changes in today's income and consumption. For example, suppose that we work more and raise current income, Py_1, by \$1,000. Then, if we also raise current consumption spending, Pc_1, by \$1,000, current saving does not change. Therefore, the budget constraint allows people to work more and raise consumption during any period, without altering the amounts of assets that they carry over to the following period. This choice between consumption and leisure in a single period was the only one available to Robinson Crusoe in the model from Chapter 2. The expanded model retains this option but introduces new possibilities that exploit the credit market. Specifically, individuals can vary current saving, which is the difference between today's income and today's expenditure. Thereby, people alter the amount of assets that they carry over to the future.

Recall that equation (3.3) specifies the saving for an individual household. As mentioned before, the sum total of this saving across households is zero in our model. In other words, when we add up the right side of equation (3.3) over all the households, we find that aggregate income equals aggregate spending, $PY_t = PC_t$. (Note that the aggregate stock of bonds, B_{t-1}, is zero.) For Robinson Crusoe, the equality between production and consumption holds individually at every point in time. Now, because of the credit market, some people can consume more than their income (dissave), while others consume less (save). But it is still true for the economy as a whole that total output cannot depart from total consumption. Consumption is the only use for commodities in the present model.

Budget Constraints for Two Periods

The previous discussion brings out the effects of current consumption and work on the assets that someone carries over to the future. We can bring out this interplay more clearly by studying a household's choices over more than one period. We can go a long way by considering just two periods.

The budget constraint from equation (3.2) holds for any period. For example, for period 1, the condition is

$$Py_1 + b_0(1 + R) + m_0 = Pc_1 + b_1 + m_1 \qquad (3.4)$$

Now we shall find it convenient to assume that each household's cash holdings are constant over time—that is, $m_1 = m_0$. Anyone who maintains a constant quantity of money carries out any saving or dissaving in the form of bonds. By making this assumption, we avoid a clutter of minor terms in the household's budget constraint over more than one period. But we shall return later (in Chapter 5) to reconsider the case where someone's holdings of money change over time.

Using the condition, $m_1 = m_0$, the budget constraint from equation (3.4) simplifies to

$$Py_1 + b_0(1 + R) = Pc_1 + b_1 \qquad (3.5)$$

Now, we can solve out this equation to find the amount of bonds, b_1, that someone carries forward to period 2. This amount is given by

$$b_1 = b_0(1 + R) + Py_1 - Pc_1 \qquad (3.6)$$

Notice that the quantity of bonds, b_1, is higher the greater is the initial stock of bonds, b_0, the higher is period 1's income from the commodity market, Py_1, and the lower is period 1's consumption spending, Pc_1.

Equation (3.6) applies also for the next period. Therefore, the amount of bonds carried over from period 2 to period 3 is given by

$$b_2 = b_1(1 + R) + Py_2 - Pc_2 \tag{3.7}$$

(We again assume constancy of money balances over time—that is, $m_2 = m_1$.) As before, the amount of bonds carried over to the next period depends positively on the starting stock of bonds, which is now b_1. However, equation (3.6) implies that this starting stock depends on some previous decisions. We can make this connection explicit by using equation (3.6) to substitute out for b_1 in equation (3.7). Then, after rearranging some terms, we get

$$b_2 = b_0(1 + R)^2 + Py_1(1 + R) + Py_2 - Pc_1(1 + R) - Pc_2 \tag{3.8}$$

We see from equation (3.8) that the amount of bonds carried over to period 3, b_2, depends positively on the initial bond stock, b_0. It also depends positively on incomes from the commodity market for periods 1 and 2, Py_1 and Py_2, but negatively on consumption expenditures for the two periods, Pc_1 and Pc_2.

Now, let's rearrange equation (3.8), so that the total sources of funds appear on the left side of the equation, while the total uses of funds appear on the right. Also, although it is not essential for our analysis, we divide through the entire equation by the term, $(1 + R)$. This adjustment places all of the terms on what is called a **present-value** basis—a concept that we shall explore in a moment. So, after rearrangement of equation (3.8) and division by the term $(1 + R)$, we can derive the following form of the household's budget constraint for two periods.

$$\underset{\text{SOURCES OF FUNDS}}{\underbrace{Py_1 + Py_2/(1 + R) + b_0(1 + R)}} = \underset{\text{USES OF FUNDS}}{\underbrace{Pc_1 + Pc_2/(1 + R) + b_2/(1 + R)}} \tag{3.9}$$

The left side of equation (3.9) involves the income from the commodity market for periods one and two, Py_1 and Py_2, and the initial stock of bonds, b_0. All of the items on the left side represent sources of funds for the household. On the right side, we have terms that involve consumption expenditures over the two periods, Pc_1 and Pc_2, and the stock of bonds held at the end of the second period, b_2. All of the items on the right side represent uses of the household's available funds. Recall that we already substituted out for the interim bond stock, b_1, which does not appear in equation (3.9).

Observe the manner in which the incomes, Py_1 and Py_2, appear in equation (3.9). We divide next period's amount, Py_2, by the term, $(1 + R)$, before adding it to this period's, Py_1. It is important for us to understand why incomes from the two periods, Py_1 and Py_2, are not just added together in the household's two-period budget constraint. Similarly, on the right side of equation (3.9), we divide next period's expenditure, Pc_2, by the term, $(1 + R)$, before adding it to this period's

Pc_1. Again, we want to understand why we combine expenditures from different dates in this manner.

Present Values

If the interest rate is positive—that is, $R > 0$—then a given dollar amount of today's bonds translates into a larger number of dollars next period. Accordingly, individuals who can buy or sell bonds on the economy-wide credit market (that is, people who can lend or borrow) regard a dollar's worth of income or expenses differently depending on when it arises. Specifically, a dollar received or spent earlier is equivalent to more than one dollar later. Or, viewed in reverse, dollars received or spent in the future must be discounted in order to express them in terms that are comparable to dollar values in the present.

Suppose, for example, that $R = 10\%$ per year. Assume that we have $100 of income today, but plan to spend these funds in the future. Then, we can buy $100 of bonds now and have $110 available next year. Hence, $100 today is worth just as much as $110 next year. Equivalently, we discount the $110 by asking how much income would we need today in order to generate $110 next year? We find the answer by solving the equation,

$$\text{(income needed today)} \times (1 + 10\%) = \$110$$

So, the required amount of current income is $\$110/(1.1) = \$100$.

More generally, if we substitute any value of the interest rate, R, for 10%, then we divide the income for next period, Py_2, by the term, $(1 + R)$, in order to find the equivalent amount for this period. The result, $Py_2/(1 + R)$, is the **present value** of this income. Also, economists call the term, $(1 + R)$, the **discount factor.** When we discount by this factor—that is, when we divide by the term, $1 + R$—we determine the present value of next period's income.

Equation (3.9) shows that we express the second period's income as a present value, $Py_2/(1 + R)$, before combining it with the first period's income Py_1. Thus, the sum, $Py_1 + Py_2/(1 + R)$, is the total present value of income from the commodity market over periods 1 and 2.

So far, the discussion refers to present values of incomes. But the same reasoning applies to expenditures. For example, assume that we are currently borrowing at an interest rate of 10% per year in order to buy some good that costs $100. But suppose that we were able to defer buying the good until next year. Then we can avoid borrowing $100 now, which means that we can eliminate $110 in loan payments for next year. Therefore, if the price of the good next year were $110, we would be in exactly the same position as before. In other words, an expenditure of $110 next year is equivalent to an outlay of $100 this year. Again, for any value of R, we divide next period's expenses, Pc_2, by the discount factor, $(1 + R)$, in order to find the present value of these expenses.

Equation (3.9) shows that we express next period's expenditures as the present value, $Pc_2/(1 + R)$, before adding them to this period's spending, Pc_1. Hence, the sum, $Pc_1 + Pc_2/(1 + R)$, is the total present value of consumption expenditures over periods 1 and 2.

The Household's Budget Line

We now begin our analysis of how individuals choose their levels of consumption and work over two periods. In doing so, we assume that people face a given price level, P, and interest rate, R. In particular, an individual can save either a positive or negative amount in each period. However, remember that saving must add to zero in each period when we sum up across all of the households. Later on (in Chapter 6), we see how to ensure that aggregate saving is always zero. But for the moment, we ignore this aggregate condition and consider only the behavior of individuals.

The two-period budget constraint in equation (3.9) brings out the choices that a credit market allows to a household. Notice that the stock of bonds carried over to the third period, b_2, falls if we raise consumption expenditures, Pc_1 and Pc_2, during either of the two periods. Similarly, this stock of bonds declines if we receive less income, Py_1 or Py_2, over either of the two periods. Also, we maintain this stock of bonds, b_2, if we change consumption expenditures and income by equal amounts in either period 1 or period 2.

The new element from equation (3.9) is the choice between consuming now or later—that is, Pc_1 versus Pc_2—and earning income (by working now or later— that is, Py_1 versus Py_2. Assume, for example, that we raise today's spending, Pc_1, by $1,000. This change reduces our assets at the end of the first period, b_1, by $1,000 (see equation [3.6]). Then, for the second period, we lose $1,000 in receipts of principal from bonds and $100 in receipts of interest (assuming that $R = 10\%$). Therefore, we have $1,100 less during the second period. Now we can decrease next period's spending, Pc_2, by this amount in order to keep the final asset position, b_2, intact. Therefore, the increase in today's spending by $1,000 balances against a decrease in next period's spending by $1,100.

Put alternatively, in order to offset the increase by $1,000 in period 1's spending, we must lower the present value of period 2's spending, $Pc_2/(1 + R)$, by $1,000. But, with an interest rate of 10%, this requires a decrease in next period's spending, Pc_2, by $1,100. Generally, the required decrease in spending for the next period equals the increase in this period's spending, Pc_1, multiplied by the discount factor, $(1 + R)$.

Let's focus now on the choices of consumption over two periods, c_1 and c_2. For this purpose, it is convenient to divide through equation (3.9) by the price level, P. Then, if we rearrange terms to place those involving consumption on the left side, we get

$$c_1 + c_2/(1 + R) = y_1 + y_2/(1 + R) + b_0(1 + R)/P - b_2/P(1 + R) \qquad (3.10)$$

Each term in equation (3.10) now appears in units of commodities, rather than as dollar values. For example, y_1 is period 1's real income from the commodity market, in the sense of indicating the number of commodity units that we can buy during period 1 with the dollar income of Py_1. Similarly, y_2 is the real income for period 2. Also, the quantities, c_1 and c_2, are the real expenditures for consumption during periods 1 and 2.

The dollar amount of the initial principal and interest receipts from bonds is $b_0(1 + R)$. When we divide this amount by the price level, P, in equation (3.10), we determine the real value of these principal and interest payments. That is,

$$\frac{b_0(1 + R)(\$)}{P(\$ \text{ per good})} = \frac{b_0(1 + R)}{P} \text{ (in units of goods)}$$

Similarly, we divide the dollar value of the final stock of bonds, b_2, by the price level in equation (3.10). (Notice that the division by the discount factor, $(1 + R)$, converts this amount into a present value.)

Suppose now that we fix the total of the items on the right side of equation (3.10) at some amount, which we can call x. So, we can think of fixing the starting real value of bonds, $b_0(1 + R)/P$, the real present value of bonds carried over to period 3, $b_2/P(1 + R)$, and the total present value of real income from the commodity market, $y_1 + y_2/(1 + R)$. Then we can rewrite equation (3.10) as

$$c_1 + c_2/(1 + R) = x \tag{3.11}$$

where $x = b_0(1 + R)/P - b_2/P(1 + R) + y_1 + y_2/(1 + R)$. Equation (3.11) makes clear that for a given quantity x, we can change today's consumption, c_1, if we make the appropriate adjustment in next period's consumption, c_2.

The straight line in Figure 3.1 shows the possibilities. Notice that if we consume nothing in the second period, so that $c_2 = 0$ (which would probably cause us to starve and therefore be undesirable), then equation (3.11) says that today's consumption, c_1, equals x. Hence, the line in the figure intersects the horizontal axis at this point. Alternatively, if we consume nothing today, so that $c_1 = 0$, then the real present value of next period's consumption, $c_2/(1 + R)$, equals x. In other words, next period's consumption is given by $c_2 = x \cdot (1 + R)$. Therefore, the line in the figure intersects the vertical axis at this point.

The straight line in Figure 3.1 connects the value x on the horizontal axis to the value $x(1 + R)$ on the vertical. Therefore, this **budget line** shows all the combinations of consumptions, c_1 and c_2, which satisfy the household's budget condition from equation (3.11). The important point is that the budget line shows the attainable pairs of consumption, c_1 and c_2, for a given value of x—that is, for a given real present value of spending over the two periods.

Notice that the budget line in Figure 3.1 has a slope of $-(1 + R)$. (The magnitude of the slope is the ratio of the vertical intercept, $x[1 + R]$, to the horizontal, x.) Therefore, along this line, an increase by 1 unit in today's real spending, c_1, is matched by a decrease of $(1 + R)$ units in next period's real spending, c_2. These offsetting changes just maintain the real present value of spending over the two periods at the amount x, as equation (3.11) requires.

So far, our analysis describes a household's opportunities for consuming in one period versus another. But we have not yet studied people's preferences for

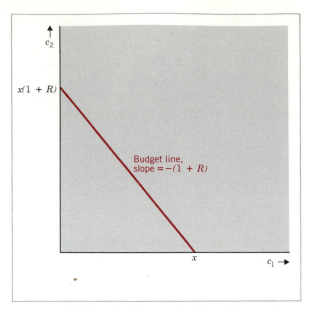

Figure 3.1 The Possibilities for Consuming Now Versus Consuming One Period Later
The budget line with slope $-(1 + R)$ shows the attainable combinations of consumption levels, c_1 and c_2. Along this line, the total real present value of expenditures over the two periods equals the fixed amount, x.

consumption at different dates. When we combine the opportunities with the preferences, we shall determine the actual choices of consumption over time. Thus, we now turn our attention to these preferences.

Preferences for Consuming Now Versus Later

We mentioned in Chapter 2 that people receive utility from consumption and leisure in each period. In particular, a family's utility for period 1 is given by $u_1 = u(c_1, l_1)$, while that for period 2 is $u_2 = u(c_2, l_2)$. But how do people weigh the units of utility or utils obtained today, u_1, versus those received next period, u_2? Usually, economists assume that people prefer to get their utils earlier rather than later. Here, we model this preference by discounting the units of future utility in a simple manner. Specifically, we assume that each household cares about total utility, U, over the two periods, as measured by

$$U = u(c_1, l_1) + \frac{1}{(1 + \rho)} u(c_2, l_2) \tag{3.12}$$

Note that we do not look beyond period 2. Implicitly, we assume in the following that people's choices from date 3 onward are givens.

Notice in expression (3.12) that we divide the utility received during period 2 by a type of discount factor, $(1 + \rho)$, where the parameter ρ is a positive constant (ρ is the Greek letter *rho*). In effect, we calculate the present value of utility, but we use the number ρ, rather than the market interest rate, R, to calculate the present value. We shall call the number ρ the **utility rate of time preference.** The higher is this utility rate of time preference, the greater is the discount applied to future utility. Put another way, for each unit of utility that we give up today, we need $(1 + \rho)$ extra units next period in order to maintain total utility, U. So a higher value of ρ signifies a greater preference for current utils relative to future ones. We assume here that each household has the same value for the utility rate of time preference, ρ.

Suppose for the moment that we have already decided on our levels of work effort, l_1 and l_2. To keep things simple, assume for now that we work the same amount in each period, so that $l_1 = l_2$. Then, we want to model our attitude toward different combinations of consumption for the two periods, c_1 and c_2. In the language of Chapter 2, we want to draw indifference curves for consumption now versus consumption next period. These curves will reveal the different combinations of consumptions, c_1 and c_2, that yield the same level of total utility, U, as defined in expression (3.12).

Figure 3.2 shows an indifference curve for consumption today versus consumption next period. Here, the total level of utility is the amount U^1. For very

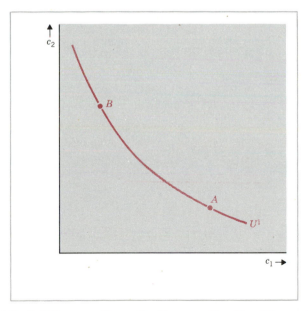

Figure 3.2 An Indifference Curve for Consumption Now Versus Consumption Next Period
We are equally happy with any combination of consumptions, c_1 and c_2, that lie along the curve. Today's consumption is high relative to next period's at point A, and low relative to next period's at point B. Hence, the curve is steeper at point B than at point A.

high levels of today's consumption, relative to next period's—for example, at point A in the figure—we are much more interested in adding to next period's consumption rather than this period's. Hence, a small increase in c_2 makes up for the loss of a unit of c_1. Thus, in the figure the curve has a relatively flat slope at point A. Similarly, the indifference curve has a steep slope when today's consumption, c_1, is relatively low, as at point B in the figure. Here, we need a large addition to next period's consumption, c_2, in order to make up for the loss of a unit of this period's consumption, c_1.

The slope of the indifference curve at any point reveals the amount of next period's consumption that we need to make up for the loss of a unit of current consumption. Generally, this slope depends on two factors. First, as shown in Figure 3.2, the slope steepens as current consumption, c_1, falls relative to future consumption, c_2. Second, the slope depends on the utility rate of time preference, ρ, which appears in expression (3.12). For any given combination of consumptions, c_1 and c_2, a rise in the parameter ρ means that we value future consumption less relative to current consumption. So for any combination of consumptions, c_1 and c_2, a rise in this parameter raises the number of units of future consumption that we need to make up the loss of a unit of current consumption. Hence, the indifference curve shown in Figure 3.2 becomes steeper throughout if the utility rate of time preference, ρ, rises.

Now, let's define the slope of the indifference curve at any point to be the quantity, $-(1 + \lambda)$ (λ is the Greek letter *lambda*). The number λ indicates the bonus in next period's consumption that we need to make up for the loss of a unit of today's consumption. For example, if $\lambda = 0.1$, then we require 1.1 extra units of next period's consumption in order to compensate for the loss of 1 unit of this period's consumption. We shall call the variable λ the **consumption rate of time preference.** Notice that unlike the utility rate of time preference ρ, the consumption rate of time preference, λ, is surely not constant. Specifically, if today's consumption is relatively low (as at point B in Figure 3.2), then the consumption rate of time preference is high. But the opposite applies when today's consumption is relatively high (as at point A in the figure).

Figure 3.3 shows the positive relation between the consumption rate of time preference, λ, and the ratio of next period's consumption to today's, c_2/c_1. But what happens when the levels of consumption, c_1 and c_2, are equal? Then we see from expression (3.12) that the only difference between consuming today versus next period derives from the discounting of future utility by the factor, $(1 + \rho)$.[8] In particular, at this point one small extra unit of today's consumption, c_1, contributes just as much to total utility as do $(1 + \rho)$ extra units of next period's consumption, c_2. But this means that the consumption rate of time preference, λ, equals the utility rate of time preference, ρ, at the point of equal consumptions,

---

[8]Recall that we also assume equal levels of work, $l_1 = l_2$. Otherwise, some other differences might arise between consuming now and consuming later. But, for now, we bring out the main effects by neglecting this possibility.

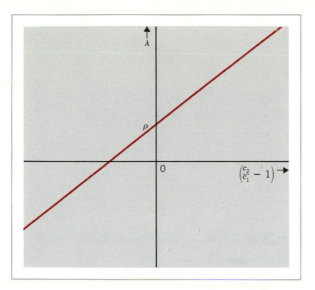

Figure 3.3 **Rates of Time Preference**
The consumption rate of time preference, λ, is the bonus in next period's consumption that we need to compensate for the loss of a unit of today's consumption. The figure shows that the number λ rises as we increase the ratio, c_2/c_1. Also, the consumption rate of time preference, λ, equals the utility rate of time preference, ρ, when $c_2 = c_1$.

$c_1 = c_2$. Hence, we draw the line in Figure 3.3 so that $\lambda = \rho$ applies when $c_2/c_1 = 1$.

As in Chapter 2, we can define a family of indifference curves, each one applying to a different level of utility. Figure 3.4 shows three of these curves, labeled by their levels of total utility, where $U^1 < U^2 < U^3$.

Choosing Consumption Over Two Periods

The budget line in Figure 3.1 describes the opportunities for shifting between consumption now and consumption next period. These opportunities come from the credit market, which designates the value of the interest rate, R. Then the family of indifference curves shown in Figure 3.4 describes people's willingness to exchange consumption now for consumption next period. Therefore, if we combine the market opportunities from Figure 3.1 with the indifference map from Figure 3.4, we can determine the choices of consumption over the two periods.[9]

---

[9]This method comes from Irving Fisher, *The Theory of Interest,* Macmillan, New York, 1930, especially Chapter 10. (Interestingly, Fisher, who did his main work at Yale University, is one of the few macroeconomists who is popular today at both Yale and Chicago.)

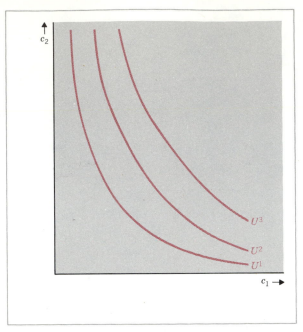

Figure 3.4 A Family of Indifference Curves for Consumption Now Versus Consumption Next Period

Along each curve the level of utility is constant. Utility increases as we move from the curve labeled U^1 to that labeled U^2, and so on.

Figure 3.5 shows how the credit-market opportunities interact with the indifference curves. Note that we move along the budget line until we reach the highest possible indifference curve, which occurs at the point of tangency shown in the figure. Here, we label the levels of consumption for the two periods as c_1^* and c_2^*. Recall that the slope of the budget line is $-(1 + R)$, while that of an indifference curve is $-(1 + \lambda)$, where λ is the consumption rate of time preference. Notice also that the slope of the budget line equals the slope of the tangent indifference curve at the chosen point, (c_1^*, c_2^*). Hence, people choose their amounts of consumption so as to equate their consumption rate of time preference, λ, to the market interest rate, R.

Recall that the number λ measures the bonus in next period's consumption that we need to compensate for giving up a unit of this period's consumption. On the other hand, the interest rate, R, tells us the premium that we get if we lend on the credit market (or that we must pay if we borrow). Therefore, if $R > \lambda$, we can raise utility by saving more—that is, by reducing consumption today, c_1, and raising consumption next period, c_2. Note that utility rises because the bonus that we receive in next period's consumption, which equals the interest rate, exceeds the amount, λ, that we need to maintain our total utility. However, as we raise the ratio of consumption next period to consumption this period, we also increase the

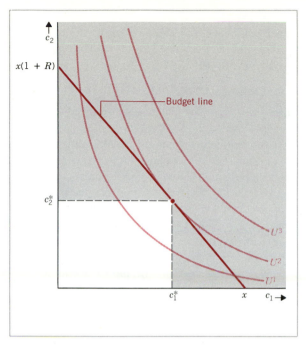

Figure 3.5 Choosing Consumption Today and Next Period
The choice of consumption levels, c_1^* and c_2^*, occurs where the budget line is tangent to an indifference curve.

consumption rate of time preference (see Figure 3.3). Then, we eventually get to a point—namely, at the tangency shown in Figure 3.5—where the consumption rate of time preference equals the interest rate. Then we no longer gain from an increase in saving.

To sum up, we combined people's opportunities (the budget line) with their preferences (the indifference curves) in order to determine the choices of consumption over two periods. Thus, we can use this analysis to see how the time pattern of consumption changes when there are shifts in the interest rate or other variables. The effects of changes in the interest rate turn out to be especially important for our subsequent macroeconomic analysis.

Wealth and Substitution Effects

As in Chapter 2, we want to use the notions of wealth and substitution effects to analyze people's choices. In the present setting wealth effects relate to the quantity previously denoted as x, which is the total present value of real consumption expenditures for periods 1 and 2. The important substitution variable for consuming now versus later turns out to be the interest rate, R.

Wealth Effects on Consumption

Before, we found that changes in the position of the production function imply wealth effects. Here, these effects show up as shifts in the total real present value of expenditures, x, which is given by

$$x = c_1 + c_2/(1 + R) = y_1 + y_2/(1 + R) + b_0(1 + R)/P - b_2/P(1 + R) \qquad (3.13)$$

Also, recall that the amounts of real income from the commodity market come from the production function as $y_1 = f(l_1)$ and $y_2 = f(l_2)$.

Assume that the production function shifts upward for periods 1 and 2. (For simplicity, we can think here of a parallel shift that does not change the schedule for labor's marginal product.) Then assuming for the moment that we do not change the levels of work, l_1 and l_2, there are increases in the amounts of real income, y_1 and y_2. Now suppose that we hold constant the initial and final stocks of bonds, b_0 and b_2. In particular, by holding fixed the final stock, b_2, we do not change our provision of assets for the future. Then the increases in real incomes, y_1 and y_2, raise the total real present value of spending, x, from equation (3.13). Now we have to decide how to allocate this increase in total spending between consumption today and next period, c_1 and c_2.

Figure 3.6 shows how an increase in the total real present value of spending affects the choices of consumption, c_1 and c_2. Notice that the increase in total

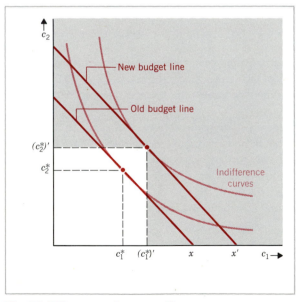

Figure 3.6 Wealth Effects on Consumption

The total real present value of consumption expenditures for periods 1 and 2 rises from x to x'. Consumption increases from c_1^* to $(c_1^*)'$ in period 1, and from c_2^* to $(c_2^*)'$ in period 2.

spending appears as a parallel outward shift of the budget line. (The slope stays the same because the interest rate does not change.) In particular, the horizontal intercept rises from the initial value, x, to the higher value, x'.

The new budget line allows us to reach a higher indifference curve than before. Note especially that the new point of tangency between the budget line and an indifference curve occurs at higher levels of consumption for the two periods. Hence, the wealth effect is positive for consumption in both periods. Equivalently, we can say that both period's consumptions, c_1 and c_2, are superior goods.

The Interest Rate and Intertemporal Substitution

If the interest rate is R, then each household faces the budget line that we label as "old" in Figure 3.7. Given the total real present value of spending for periods 1 and 2, which equals x, the household selects the consumption pair, (c_1^*, c_2^*). But suppose that the interest rate rises to R'; then the new budget line is steeper than the old one. However, there are many places that we could draw this new line in

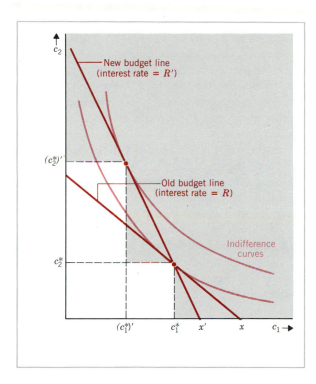

Figure 3.7 Effect on the Time Path of Consumption From an Increase in the Interest Rate
When the interest rate is R on the old budget line, the household chooses the consumption pair, (c_1^*, c_2^*). But if the interest rate rises to R' on the new budget line, the household opts for the pair $[(c_1^*)', (c_2^*)']$. Notice that the increase in the interest rate motivates people to choose a higher ratio of consumption next period to consumption this period.

Figure 3.7—it all depends on what happens to the total real present value of spending, x. For example, if we hold fixed this present value, then the new budget line starts from the value x on the horizontal axis, but otherwise lies everywhere to the right of the old budget line. But then the new budget line allows us to consume the same amount today, c_1^*, and more next period. Hence, as in our previous example, there is an increase in wealth.

Here we want to isolate the substitution effect from a change in the interest rate. As an approximation, we can do this by rotating the budget line around the point where we initially chose the levels of consumption.[10] Therefore, as shown in Figure 3.7, the new budget line intersects the old one at the point, (c_1^*, c_2^*). Then we can just manage to buy this initial pair of consumptions if we still want to. But we cannot increase either quantity unless we give up some of the other. (Notice that this construction implies a decrease in the total real present value of spending—that is, $x' < x$ on the horizontal axis.)

Although the new budget line passes through the point, (c_1^*, c_2^*), in Figure 3.7, this new line is not tangent to an indifference curve at this point. Specifically, this budget line is steeper than the slope of the indifference curve—that is, the interest rate, R', exceeds the consumption rate of time preference, λ. Accordingly, each household raises saving, which means that current consumption, c_1, falls and future consumption, c_2, rises. The new choices, labeled as $[(c_1^*)', (c_2^*)']$ in Figure 3.7, occur where the new budget line is tangent to an indifference curve.[11] But the important point is that the increase in the interest rate motivates people to raise future consumption, c_2, relative to current consumption, c_1. Equivalently, the rise in the interest rate means that an individual wants to save a larger fraction of his or her total current income.

Let's look at the results from another perspective. Recall that the total real present value of spending over periods 1 and 2 is $c_1 + c_2/(1 + R)$. Note again that we divide the next period's consumption, c_2, by the discount factor, $(1 + R)$, before adding it to current consumption, c_1. Therefore, a rise in the interest rate effectively lowers the cost of next period's consumption relative to that of current consumption. Specifically, we can obtain more units of consumption next period for each unit of current consumption that we forego. It is this change in relative costs that motivates us to substitute future goods, c_2, for the relatively more expensive current ones, c_1. Economists often refer to this result as an **intertemporal-substitution effect.** Namely, the rise in the interest rate induces us to postpone spending from the present to the future. Equivalently, the higher interest rate makes

---

[10]This method for isolating a substitution effect is the one developed by Eugen Slutsky. We used this method before in Chapter 2 when studying a shift in labor's marginal product.

[11]Note that we reach a higher indifference curve. Hence, wealth increases, even though we rotated the budget line through the point where we initially chose consumption, (c_1^*, c_2^*). But it turns out that the wealth effect becomes negligible, relative to the substitution effect, when we look at smaller and smaller changes in the interest rate. So, at least when we consider small changes, we can neglect the wealth effect as a satisfactory approximation.

it worthwhile for us to save more of our current income in order to consume more goods later.

Choosing Work Effort at Different Dates

In Chapter 2 we studied the choice of work and consumption for a single period. There we stressed substitution effects from changes in the schedule for labor's marginal product. Also, we explored wealth effects from shifts in the position of the production function.

In the present chapter we examined an individual's choices of consumption over time. But so far we have held fixed the behavior of work effort. However, if we combine the previous analysis of work and consumption with the present analysis of consumption over time, then we shall also understand how people choose work effort over time.

Wealth Effects on Work Effort

We can write the household's budget constraint over two periods as

$$f(l_1) + f(l_2)/(1 + R) + b_0(1 + R)/P = c_1 + c_2/(1 + R) + b_2/P(1 + R) \qquad (3.14)$$

Here, we make the substitutions, $y_1 = f(l_1)$ and $y_2 = f(l_2)$, in the expression for the real sources of funds on the left side.

Suppose that the production function shifts up in a parallel fashion for periods 1 and 2. Then, if we hold fixed the amounts of work, l_1 and l_2, we increase the real sources of funds on the left side of equation (3.14). As we saw before, we respond to this increase in wealth by raising the levels of consumption in each period, c_1 and c_2.

However, recall from Chapter 2, that people also react to more wealth by taking more leisure. Hence, the levels of work, l_1 and l_2, tend to decline, rather than staying fixed.

Often, macroeconomists stress the positive wealth effect on consumption, but neglect the effect on leisure. However, the evidence on hours of work, which we reviewed in Chapter 2, indicates that this effect on leisure is important. For example, at least at the early stages of economic development, the wealth effect is strong enough so that average hours worked tend to diminish as the economy develops.

The Interest Rate and Choices of Work Effort

Figure 3.7 shows that an increase in the interest rate motivates us to reduce current consumption, c_1, and raise next period's consumption, c_2. So far, we held fixed the amounts of work, l_1 and l_2. Let's see now whether this is correct.

Notice from the right side of equation (3.14) that an increase in the interest rate, R, makes next period's consumption, c_2, cheaper relative to this period's, c_1.

That is why we substitute toward next period's consumption and away from this period's when the interest rate rises. But the same argument holds for leisure in the two periods. Namely, if we take leisure in period 2 then we discount the loss in output, $f(l_2)$, by the factor, $(1 + R)$. Therefore, when the interest rate rises, the leisure from period 2 becomes cheaper relative to that in period 1. That is, the future output that we lose by working less in period 2 has a smaller present value than before. Our conclusion is that the increase in the interest rate motivates us to substitute toward next period's leisure and away from this period's. Or, equivalently, we raise this period's work, l_1, relative to next period's, l_2.

Overall, an increase in the interest rate has two types of intertemporal-substitution effects. First, we reduce today's consumption, c_1, relative to next period's, c_2. Then second, we raise today's work, l_1, relative to next period's, l_2. Notice that both effects—the reduction in current spending and the increase in current income—show up as an increase in current saving. Thus, both responses reflect the positive response of an individual's desired saving to the return from saving, which is the interest rate.

Summary

We introduced a commodity market on which people buy and sell goods at the price P. The existence of this market allows producers to specialize, which aids efficiency.

We also introduced a credit market on which people borrow and lend at the interest rate, R. By using this market, individuals can choose a time pattern for consumption that differs from that for income. In particular, a higher interest rate motivates people to reduce current consumption in favor of consumption next period. Similarly, people decrease current leisure relative to leisure next period, which means that they increase today's work relative to tomorrow's. Overall, these intertemporal-substitution effects from a higher interest rate show up as an increase in today's saving.

Finally, the choices of consumption and work react also to wealth effects. Specifically, an increase in wealth tends to raise consumption and reduce work in the various periods.

Important Terms and Concepts

barter	real terms
medium of exchange	price index
nominal terms	deflator for GNP
currency	CPI
$M1$ concept of money	perfect competition
general price level	bond

interest rate	discount factor
principal of bond	budget line
budget constraint	utility rate of time preference
saving	consumption rate of time preference
present value	intertemporal-substitution effect

QUESTIONS AND PROBLEMS

Mainly for Review

3.1 Why would individuals be interested only in the real value of consumption expenditures, income, and assets such as money and bonds? Would a fall in the dollar amount of consumption spending leave the individual worse off when it is accompanied by an equi-proportionate fall in the price level?

3.2 Distinguish clearly between an individual's initial asset position and the change in that position. Which is affected by current consumption and saving decisions? Is an individual who is undertaking negative saving necessarily a borrower in the sense of having a negative position in bonds?

3.3 Write down an individual's budget constraint for one period, and show how it limits the consumption possible in that period. What amounts of consumption would be possible if the individual could not borrow or lend on the credit market?

3.4 Derive the two-period budget constraint, and draw a graph of it. Why are there no terms involving money holdings on the side of sources of funds?

3.5 Show how taking a present value involves giving different weights to dollar values in different periods. Why is income in the present more "valuable" than income in the future? Why is consumption in the future "cheaper" than consumption in the present?

3.6 Define the utility rate of time preference. Would it be higher for an individual who is more "impatient"?

3.7 Review the factors that determine the individual's choice of c_1 and c_2, and show this choice graphically. What tradeoff would the individual make at a point where the interest rate exceeds the consumption rate of time preference?

Problems for Discussion

3.8 Discount Bonds

The one-period bonds in our model pay a single interest payment or "coupon" of R and a principal of $1. Alternatively, we could consider a one-period discount bond like a U.S. Treasury Bill. This type of asset has no coupons, but pays a

principal of $1 (or, more realistically, $10,000) next period. Let P^B be the dollar price for each unit of discount bonds, where each unit is a claim to $1 next period.
  a. Is P^B greater or less than $1?
  b. What is the one-period rate of interest that we get from holding discount bonds?
  c. How does the price, P^B, relate to this one-period rate of interest?
  d. Suppose that, instead of coming due next period, the discount bond comes due (matures) two periods from now. Then, what is the interest rate *per period* that we get from holding this bond? How do the results generalize if the bond matures n periods from now?

3.9 Financial Intermediaries

Consider a financial intermediary, such as a bank or savings and loan association, that enters the credit market. This intermediary borrows from some people and lends the proceeds to others. (The loan to a bank from its customers often takes the form of a ''deposit.'')
  a. How does the existence of intermediaries affect our result that the aggregate amount of loans is zero?
  b. What interest rate would the intermediary charge to its borrowers and pay to its lenders? Why must there be some spread between these two rates?
  c. Can you give some reasons to explain why intermediaries might be useful?

3.10 Changes in the Schedule for Labor's Marginal Product

Suppose that labor's marginal product rises at each level of work. Discuss the effects on today's work and consumption, assuming that
  a. the change in the marginal product applies for periods 1 and 2, and
  b. the change applies only for the current period.
In what ways does the existence of the credit market change people's reactions to a change in labor's marginal product?

CHAPTER 4

MORE ON THE BEHAVIOR OF HOUSEHOLDS

So far, we have examined the behavior of households over two periods. But in order to carry out this analysis, we had to hold fixed the amount of bonds that someone carries over to later periods. In fact, this amount is not a given, since it depends on people's plans for consuming and earning income later on. Now, we make this connection explicit by dealing with households' plans over many periods. Essentially, we think here of a lifetime plan, or even of a plan that considers descendants and, therefore, extends beyond people's own lifetimes.

The extensions in this chapter are important for distinguishing between temporary and permanent changes in variables. For example, we may have changes in income—possibly resulting from shifts in the production function—that last for either one or many periods. Then, we shall see that today's responses are very different in the two cases. Similarly, we shall distinguish changes in the interest rate or in labor's marginal product, depending on whether they are transitory or long lasting.

Budget Constraints

Budget Constraints for Three Periods

In order to proceed with the analysis, we have to examine people's behavior for more than two periods. We start by extending a household's budget constraint from two periods to three. Then we can readily expand to any number of periods.

Start with the two-period budget constraint, which we used extensively in the previous chapter,

$$Py_1 + Py_2/(1 + R) + b_0(1 + R) = Pc_1 + Pc_2/(1 + R) + b_2/(1 + R) \qquad (4.1)$$

Now, the final stock of bonds from the second period, b_2, determines the initial stock for period 3. Specifically, for period 3 the budget constraint is

$$Py_3 + b_2(1 + R) = Pc_3 + b_3 \qquad (4.2)$$

(Note that we still assume constancy of money balances, so that $m_2 = m_3$.)

We can solve out for the stock of bonds, b_2, from equation (4.1) and substitute the result into equation (4.2). Then we determine a budget constraint for three periods. The results from this substitution can be written as

$$Py_1 + Py_2/(1 + R) + Py_3/(1 + R)^2 + b_0(1 + R)$$

$$= Pc_1 + Pc_2/(1 + R) + Pc_3/(1 + R)^2 + b_3/(1 + R)^2$$

(4.3)

There are two main differences between the three-period budget constraint from equation (4.3) and the two-period constraint from equation (4.1). First, the right side of the three-period constraint involves the amount of bonds, b_3, held at the end of the third period, rather than the second. Second, the three-period constraint shows how to include the incomes and expenses from period 3. Notice that we divide these amounts, Py_3 and Pc_3, by the factor, $(1 + R)^2$, before adding them to the present values of incomes and expenses, respectively, for the first two periods. In other words, we calculate the present values of income and expenditure for period 3 by dividing by the factor $(1 + R)^2$.

Numerical Illustration

Let's use a numerical example to verify that equation (4.3) treats correctly the income and expenditure for period 3. Suppose that $R = 10\%$ per year. If we hold $100 of bonds this year, we receive $110 of funds next year. Then, if we place the $110 into new bonds next year, we obtain $110(1 + 10\%) = \$121$ during the following year. Hence, in comparing the $121 with the $100 of bonds bought two years earlier, we get

$$\$121 = \$100(1 + 10\%)(1 + 10\%) = \$100(1 + 10\%)^2$$

The term, $(1 + 10\%)^2$, represents the accumulation of earnings on funds that we hold as bonds for two years. Therefore, $121 in income (or expense) accruing two years from now is equivalent to $100 in income (or expense) right now. In this example, we calculate present values for incomes and expenses from two years ahead from division by the term, $(1 + 10\%)^2$. More generally, we derive this present value by dividing by the factor $(1 + R)^2$.

Budget Constraints for Any Number of Periods

By now we see how to construct a budget constraint that applies for any number of periods. For example, the budget constraint for n periods is

$$Py_1 + Py_2/(1 + R) + Py_3/(1 + R)^2 + \cdots + Py_n/(1 + R)^{n-1} + b_0(1 + R) =$$

$$Pc_1 + Pc_2/(1 + R) + Pc_3/(1 + R)^2 + \cdots + Pc_n/(1 + R)^{n-1}$$

(4.4)

$$+ b_n/(1 + R)^{n-1}$$

(We again assume constancy of money balances, so that $m_0 = m_1 = m_2 = \ldots = m_n$.) Note that our previous examples of budget constraints are special cases of equation [4.4]. For example, if we set $n = 2$, then we get the two-period budget constraint in equation [4.1]. Similarly, if $n = 3$, then we get the three-period constraint in equation [4.3].)

Notice two things about the budget constraint for n periods in equation (4.4). First, the right side involves the stock of bonds, b_n, held at the end of period n. Second, we calculate the present value of income or expense for any period t by dividing by the factor $(1 + R)^{t-1}$. This factor represents the accumulation of interest between period 1 and period t—that is, over $(t - 1)$ periods.

The Household's Planning Horizon

Suppose that someone is choosing today's consumption and work effort, c_1 and l_1. Typically, people make these choices in the context of a long-term plan that considers future levels of consumption and income. In particular, these future values relate to the current choices through the n-period budget constraint in equation (4.4). Here, we can refer to the number, n, as someone's **planning horizon.**

How long a horizon should someone consider in making current decisions? Because we are dealing with people who have access to a credit market, a long planning horizon generally applies. That is, people can borrow or lend in order effectively to use future income to finance current spending, or current income to pay for future spending. When expressed appropriately as a present value, prospective incomes and expenses from the distant future are just as pertinent for current decisions as are today's incomes and expenses.

Economists often assume that the planning horizon is long, but finite. For example, in a class of theories that are called **life-cycle models,**[1] the horizon, n, represents an individual's expected remaining lifetime. If people do not care about things that occur after their death, then they have no reason to carry assets beyond period n. Therefore, they set to zero the final asset stock, b_n, which appears on the right side of the budget constraint in equation (4.4). (Here, we also have to rule out the possibility of dying in debt, which corresponds to $b_n < 0$.)

Usually, researchers who use life-cycle models also assume that the working span, which is the interval where $l_t > 0$, is shorter than the length of life. In this case, people have retirement periods during which consumption must be financed either from the savings that have been accumulated during working years or from transfer payments. These transfers could come from the government (**social security**) or from one's children.

It is reasonably straightforward to define the anticipated lifetime—and thereby a finite planning horizon—for an isolated individual who has no concern for any descendants. However, the appropriate horizon is not obvious for a family in which

---

[1]See especially Franco Modigliani and Richard Brumberg, "Utility Analysis and the Consumption Function: An Interpretation of Cross-Section Data," in K. Kurihara, ed., *Post-Keynesian Economics,* Rutgers University Press, New Brunswick, New Jersey, 1954; and Albert Ando and Franco Modigliani, "The 'Life Cycle' Hypothesis of Saving: Aggregate Implications and Tests," *American Economic Review,* March 1963.

the parents care about their children. (The children may also care about their parents!) In this context, the applicable horizon extends beyond someone's expected lifetime. In particular, people give some weight to the expected future incomes and expenses of their children. Further, since children care about the welfare of their children—should they have any—and so on for each subsequent generation, there is no clear point at which to terminate the planning period. Of course, this argument does not imply that anticipated incomes and expenses for the distant future count as much as those from a few years off. But by using present values, the budget constraint from equation (4.4) already places a large discount on future incomes and expenses. Specifically, we divide the amounts for t periods ahead (that is, for period $t + 1$) by the factor, $(1 + R)^t$, which produces a large discount for the distant future. For example, if $R = 5\%$ per year, then we divide the amounts for 20 years ahead by 2.7, and those for 50 years ahead by 11.5.[2] It may be that these large discounts for determining present values are sufficient. That is, we may not want also to introduce a finite planning horizon, which would mean that the incomes and expenses (for us or our descendants) from after this date get exactly zero weight in our calculations.

Instead of imposing a finite horizon, we can allow the household's plan to extend into the indefinite future. That is, we can treat the length of the planning interval, n, as though it were infinite. There are two good reasons for proceeding in this way:

- First, if we think of the typical person as part of a family that has concerns about the members of future generations—such as children, grandchildren, etc.—into the indefinite future, then this setup is the correct one. In particular, it would be inappropriate to identify the horizon with the typical person's expected lifetime.

- Second, although it is not obvious at this point, an infinite planning horizon is the easiest thing to work with.

Budget Constraints for an Infinite Horizon

When the planning horizon is infinite, the budget constraint includes the present values of incomes and expenses for the indefinite future. Then, using equation (4.4), we have

$$Py_1 + Py_2/(1 + R) + Py_3/(1 + R)^2 + \cdots + b_0(1 + R) \qquad (4.5)$$
$$= Pc_1 + Pc_2/(1 + R) + Pc_3/(1 + R)^2 + \cdots$$

Here, we no longer terminate the sums for incomes and expenses at some finite date, n, as we did in equation (4.4). Notice also that the final stock of bonds, b_n, no longer appears in the budget constraint. In effect, there is no "final" period to consider here.

---

[2]Because $(1 + 0.05)^{20} = 2.7$ and $(1 + 0.05)^{50} = 11.5$.

For most purposes, we prefer to deal with the budget constraint when expressed in real terms. If we divide through equation (4.5) by the price level, P, we get

$$y_1 + y_2/(1 + R) + y_3(1 + R)^2 + \cdots + b_0(1 + R)/P \qquad (4.6)$$

$$= c_1 + c_2/(1 + R) + c_3/(1 + R)^2 + \cdots$$

Equation (4.6) says that the present value of real income from sales to the commodity market over an infinite horizon, plus the real value of the receipts from the initial stock of bonds, equals the present value of real consumption expenditure over an infinite horizon. We shall use this form of the budget constraint when studying the choices of consumption and work over time.

Preferences Over an Infinite Horizon

Here, we extend our earlier ideas about time preference from two periods to an infinite horizon. Specifically, each household cares about total utility, U, as defined by the sum,

$$U = u(c_1, l_1) + u(c_2, l_2)/(1 + \rho) + u(c_3, l_3)/(1 + \rho)^2 + \cdots \quad (4.7)$$

Again, we calculate an expression that looks like the present value of utility, but we use the utility rate of time preference ρ, rather than the interest rate, to calculate the present value.

The use of an infinite horizon also gives us an interesting way to interpret the utility rate of time preference. Namely, this rate may not be positive just because an individual prefers to get his or her utils earlier rather than later. Rather, particularly for the distant future, we can think of people as preferring their own utils to those of their children, grandchildren, and so on. Therefore, they discount the utils of these later generations. In other words, we care about our descendents, but not quite as much as we do about ourselves!

Choosing Consumption over Many Periods

Before, we discussed the choices of consumption over two periods, c_1 and c_2. Now, we consider the entire time path of consumption, $c_1, c_2, c_3, \ldots$ As before, let's start by holding fixed the time path of work. In particular, suppose that work is the same in each period, $l_1 = l_2 = l_3 = \ldots$

In some of our previous discussion, we thought about a given total present value of real spending over two periods, $x = c_1 + c_2/(1 + R)$. Here, we proceed analogously by looking at the total present value of real spending over an infinite horizon. That is, we consider the expression,

$$x = c_1 + c_2/(1 + R) + c_3/(1 + R)^2 + \cdots \qquad (4.8)$$

Notice from equation (4.6) that the quantity x equals the total real present value of income from the commodity market plus the real value of the receipts from the initial stock of bonds.

The Interest Rate and Consumption over Time

Given the total present value of real spending over an infinite horizon, x, we can still substitute between the amounts of consumption, c_1 and c_2. In particular, for each unit of consumption for period 1 that we forego, we can obtain $(1 + R)$ additional units of consumption for period 2. But there is nothing special about the substitution between periods 1 and 2. In fact, we can substitute in a similar manner between the consumptions of any two adjacent periods, such as c_2 and c_3, c_3 and c_4, and so on. In general, if we give up 1 unit of consumption for period t, then the credit market allows us to raise the next period's consumption by $(1 + R)$ units.

Consider an increase in the interest rate, R. As before, we want to abstract from wealth effects in order to isolate the substitution effect from this change. Recall, when we considered only two periods, that we rotated the budget line around the point where we initially chose consumptions, (c_1^*, c_2^*). Then we could just manage to buy the initial quantities of goods if we still wanted to. In order to do this we had to think of reducing the total present value of real spending over the two periods. Here, we do something similar, but over an infinite horizon. That is, assume that we change the total present value of real spending, x, so that—after the increase in the interest rate—we can just manage to buy the initial array of consumptions, $c_1^*, c_2^*, c_3^* \ldots$, if we still desire. Most importantly, we cannot increase consumption for any period unless we give up something for at least one other period. (However, for subsequent purposes it is unnecessary for us to compute the exact amount by which the total present value, x, changes.)

We know already that an increase in the interest rate motivates people to reduce current consumption, c_1, relative to the next period's consumption, c_2. That's because the higher interest rate makes today's consumption more expensive relative to the next period's. But the same reasoning applies to any pair of consumptions, c_t and c_{t+1}. Therefore, an increase in the interest rate lowers each period's consumption, c_t, relative to the next period's, c_{t+1}. In other words, since c_{t+1}/c_t rises, the higher interest rate motivates people to plan for a more steeply rising time path of consumption.

We show these results in Figure 4.1. In the figure we assume that the initial plan, shown by the solid line, dictates constant levels of consumption, $c_1 = c_2 = c_3 = \ldots$. Then, an increase in the interest rate causes the time path of consumption to tilt upward, as shown by the dotted line in the figure. Notice that, in comparison with the initial plan, the new one involves a higher ratio, c_{t+1}/c_t, at any date.

Observe from Figure 4.1 that the quantity consumed falls during the early periods and rises during the later ones. (Recall that, with no increase or decrease in wealth, the amounts consumed cannot all increase or decrease.) Further, the decrease in consumption is greatest for the current period, c_1, while the increase in consumption becomes larger the further out we look. Thus, in general, the intertemporal-substitution effect from a higher interest rate motivates us to shift consumption away from the near term and toward the future. Finally, let's note that the decrease in current consumption, c_1, shows up as an increase in current saving.

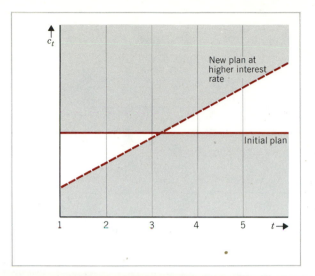

Figure 4.1 **Effect of a Higher Interest Rate on the Time Path of Consumption**

An increase in the interest rate motivates us to defer consumption. Therefore, the new time path of consumption is more steeply sloped than the old one.

The Effects of a Temporary Change in the Interest Rate

In this section, we examine what difference it makes if the increase in the interest rate is temporary, rather than permanent. Suppose that the interest rate, R_1, rises during the current period. However, people anticipate that future interest rates, R_2, R_3, . . . , will remain at the initial value, R. (Again, we assume that the present value of real spending, x, changes in such a way that there is no wealth effect.)

Consider again the incentive to substitute between consumptions for adjacent periods. As before, we reduce current consumption, c_1, relative to that for the next period, c_2. But since the interest rate during period 2 does not change, we do not shift the second period's consumption, c_2, relative to the third's, c_3. Similarly, we make no changes in any later quantity of consumption, c_t, relative to that for the following period, c_{t+1}. Therefore, the new plan for consumption looks like the dotted line shown in Figure 4.2. Notice that the new plan is more steeply sloped than the old one for the first period, but otherwise parallels the old plan.[3]

There is one other important result, which follows from a comparison of Figures 4.1 and 4.2. Suppose that the current increase in the interest rate is the same for the two cases. Then the relation of this period's consumption, c_1, to the next

---

[3]Again, we reduce the total real present value of real spending, x, so that people can just manage to buy the initial array of consumptions if they still desire. Therefore, the new quantity of consumption is lower for period 1, but higher for all subsequent periods.

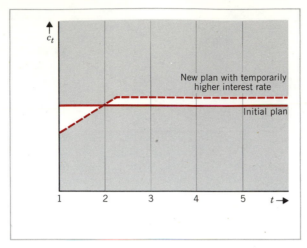

Figure 4.2 Effect of a Temporarily Higher Interest Rate on the Time Path of Consumption
The interest rate rises during the first period, but then returns to its initial value. Therefore, the new time path of consumption is more steeply sloped than the old one for the first period. But after that, it has the same slope as before.

period's, c_2, will also be the same. (That is, the two dotted lines have the same slopes between dates 1 and 2.) But if the increase in the interest rate is permanent, as in Figure 4.1, then the second period's consumption also falls relative to the third period's, which falls relative to the fourth period's, and so on. By contrast, when the change in the interest rate is temporary, as in Figure 4.2, these later changes do not occur. Overall, this means that the reduction in current consumption, c_1, is substantially larger when the rise in the interest rate is permanent, rather than temporary. Hence, the positive effect of the higher interest rate on current saving is also much greater if people think that this higher rate will persist into the future.

Wealth Effects on Consumption

As before, wealth effects on consumption involve changes in the total present value of real spending, x. Recall from the household's budget constraint (equation [4.6]) that this total equals the present value of real income from the commodity market plus the real value of the receipts from the initial stock of bonds, that is,

$$x = y_1 + y_2/(1 + R) + \cdots + b_0(1 + R)/P \qquad (4.9)$$

Remember that the aggregate value of the initial stock of bonds, B_0, is zero. Therefore, if we think about the typical or average household, for whom $b_0 = 0$, then wealth effects will arise only from changes in the present value of real income from the commodity market. But for a given amount of work effort in each period, these changes must involve shifts in the production function.

Permanent Shifts in the Production Function

Consider first the case where the production function, $f(l_t)$, shifts upward for all periods. As examples, we can think of discoveries of new technology or natural resources—that is, changes that create permanent improvements in productive capacity. If we hold constant the amounts of work, l_t, then we raise the level of output, y_t, in each period. Hence, the total real present value of spending, x, increases in equation (4.9).

Typically, an increase in the present value of real spending, x, shows up as an increase in consumption, c_t, for each period. That is, consumption in any period is a superior good, which means that the wealth effect is positive. In the previous chapter we illustrated this finding for two periods with an indifference-curve diagram. But nothing basically different arises when we consider more periods.

The Propensity to Consume

Suppose, as an example, that real income, y_t, rises by 1 unit in each period. Then, as one possibility, a person can also raise consumption, c_t, by 1 unit in each period. In particular, this response satisfies the budget constraint, which is again

$$y_1 + y_2/(1 + R) + \cdots + b_0(1 + R)/P = c_1 + c_2/(1 + R) + \cdots$$

If someone does respond this way, then we say that their current **propensity to consume** is one—that is, current consumption, c_1, rises by the same amount as current real income, y_1. Since consumption and income change by equal amounts, there is no change in saving. That is, the **propensity to save** is zero.

If someone increases current consumption, c_1, by less than 1 unit, then the current propensity to consume is less than one and the current propensity to save is positive. However, people must use this extra current saving to expand some future level of consumption. Then there must be at least one period later on during which consumption, c_t, rises by even more than one unit.

Suppose that we were planning initially for a roughly constant time path of consumption, such as the solid lines shown in Figures 4.1 and 4.2. Then the increase in period t's consumption, c_t, by more than 1 unit means that this consumption increases relative to today's, c_1. That is, we shift consumption away from the present and toward the future. Now we know that this type of shift is appropriate if the interest rate increases. But since the interest rate does not change here, we would want to maintain the relative amounts of consumption at different dates. For the case at hand, this happens only if we increase consumption in every period by 1 unit. Hence, if the improvement in the production function is permanent, then the propensity to consume is one. Correspondingly, the propensity to save is zero.

We have to modify our conclusions if the initial path of consumption is either rising or falling over time. Then with a given interest rate, we would make proportionately equal changes in consumption for each period. (Consequently, we do not change any of the ratios, c_t/c_{t+1}.) But since the initial levels of consumption differ, we no longer increase each quantity of consumption by precisely 1 unit.

Typically, we can still say as an approximation that the propensity to save will be small if the improvement in the production function is permanent. However, the true propensity may be either slightly positive or slightly negative. Correspondingly, the propensity to consume will now be either slightly below or slightly above one.

Permanent Income

Our findings correspond to Milton Friedman's concept of **permanent income**.[4] Suppose that someone has the initial stock of bonds, b_0, and the time path of real income, y_1, y_2, ... Then, in order to analyze consumption, we can look just at the total real present value of these sources of funds,[5] which is again,

$$x = y_1 + y_2/(1 + R) + \cdots + b_0(1 + R)/P$$

It is convenient to construct a hypothetical, constant level of real income—call it permanent income, $\bar{y}$—which also has a present value of the amount x. That is, we define permanent income implicitly by the condition,

$$x = \bar{y} + \bar{y}/(1 + R) + \bar{y}/(1 + R)^2 + \cdots$$

$$= \bar{y}[1 + 1/(1 + R) + 1/(1 + R)^2 + \cdots] = \bar{y}(1 + R)/R$$

We get the last term on the right from the formula for a geometric progression, which we describe in the box below. Therefore, substituting for the variable x from above, the amount of permanent income is

$$\bar{y} = x \cdot R/(1 + R) = [R/(1 + R)] \cdot [y_1 + y_2/(1 + R) + \cdots] + Rb_0/P \qquad (4.10)$$

Geometric Progression

Consider the geometric progression, $1 + z + z^2 + \cdots$ If $-1 < z < 1$, this sum equals $1/(1 - z)$. We can verify this answer by multiplying the expression, $(1 + z + z^2 + \cdots)$, by the term, $(1 - z)$. Then we get $1 - z + z - z^2 + z^2 - \cdots = 1$. (If the magnitude of z is one or greater, then the sum is unbounded.) In the present case, $z = 1/(1 + R)$, which is between 0 and 1. Therefore, $1 + 1/(1 + R) + 1/(1 + R)^2 + \cdots = 1/[1 - 1/(1 + R)] = (1 + R)/R$.

The term on the extreme right of equation (4.10) is the real income received as interest on the initial stock of bonds, b_0. We can think of the other term on the

---

[4]He develops the idea in his well-known book, *A Theory of the Consumption Function*, Princeton University Press, Princeton, New Jersey, 1957, especially Chapters 2 and 3.

[5]Actually, this statement is correct only if the amounts worked, l_1, l_2, . . . , are all equal, as we are assuming so far.

right side in a parallel fashion. Suppose that we take the entire present value of real income from the commodity market, $y_1 + y_2/(1 + R) + \cdots$, and use it to buy bonds today. Then the first term on the right side of equation (4.10) is the real income that we would receive as interest on these bonds. (Note that we divide by the discount factor $[(1 + R)]$, because the interest does not arrive until the second period.) Therefore, permanent income is the real interest receipts from this hypothetical stock of bonds plus that on the initial stock, b_0.

We can think of permanent income in two ways. First, it is the constant level of real income that has the same present value, x, as our actual sources of funds. But remember that the present value of consumption also equals the amount x. So suppose that consumption is constant, $c_1 = c_2 = \cdots$ Then the amount of consumption in each period equals the level of permanent income, $\bar{y}$. Hence, permanent income is also the amount of constant consumption that we can sustain forever.

For someone who consumes the same amount in each period, the level of consumption equals the level of permanent income, $\bar{y}$. Hence, when we think in terms of permanent income, the propensity to consume equals one.

Recall that in our previous example the level of real income from the commodity market increased by 1 unit in every period. But then permanent income also increases by 1 unit. We can verify this from the definition in equation (4.10). The change in permanent income, $\Delta\bar{y}$, is

$$\Delta\bar{y} = \frac{R}{(1 + R)} [\Delta y_1 + \Delta y_2/(1 + R) + \Delta y_3/(1 + R)^2 + \cdots] \quad (4.11)$$

In the present case, the changes in real income, $\Delta y_1, \Delta y_2, \ldots$, are all equal to 1. Therefore, since $[1 + 1/(1 + R) + 1/(1 + R)^2 + \cdots] = (1 + R)/R$ (from the formula for a geometric series that we used above), we find that $\Delta\bar{y} = 1$. Finally, since permanent income rises by 1 unit, we conclude that consumption increases by 1 unit. So, the concept of permanent income gives us the same answer as the one we found earlier.

Again, the results are not exact if the initial time path of consumption is either rising or falling over time. Then it is only an approximation that the propensity to consume out of permanent income is one. Generally, this propensity could be slightly above or slightly below one.

Temporary Shifts in the Production Function

In this section we contrast the results for permanent changes in the production function with those for temporary changes. In particular, suppose that the upward shift to the production function applies only for the current period. So instead of discoveries of new technologies or resources, we can think of the effects of weather, temporary cutbacks in the supply of raw materials, strikes, and so on.

If work efforts do not change, then the increase in real income occurs only in the current period. Typically, people want to spread this extra income over consumption in all periods. But they have to raise current saving in order to finance the additional consumption later on. Hence, current consumption, c_1, now rises by much less than the increase in current real income, y_1. In other words, for the case of a temporary improvement in the production function, the propensity to consume is small. Hence, the propensity to save is positive and nearly equal to one.

In terms of permanent income, we see from equation (4.11) that the change is

$$\Delta \bar{y} = \frac{R}{(1 + R)} \Delta y_1 \qquad (4.12)$$

If $R = 10\%$ per year, then an increase in this year's real income by 1 unit means that permanent income rises by only 0.09 units. Hence, we predict that the propensity to consume here is only about 0.09, while the propensity to save is about 0.91.

Empirical Evidence on the Permanent Income Hypothesis

There have been many attempts to test the permanent income hypothesis. Overall, the results of empirical tests indicate strongly that the propensity to consume out of permanent income is much greater than that out of temporary income. However, the propensity to consume out of temporary income seems to be somewhat higher than the permanent income theory would suggest.

Some of the clearest evidence comes from special circumstances where there are windfalls of income, which people surely regard as temporary. One example is the receipt by Israeli citizens of lump-sum, nonrecurring restitution payments from Germany in 1957–58. The payments were large, with an average value that roughly equaled the average family income for a year. In this case, statistical estimates indicate that the typical family's consumption expenditure during the year of the windfall rose by no more than 20% of the amount received.[6] Further, the measure of consumer spending includes purchases of consumer durables. Since these goods last for many years, we should view these purchases as partly saving, rather than consumption. Therefore, the propensity to consume out of the windfall would actually be substantially less than 20%.

Another example is the 1950 payment to United States World War II veterans of an unanticipated, one-time life-insurance dividend of about $175. At the time, this amount represented about 4% of the average family's annual income. In this case, the statistical estimates indicate that consumption rose by 30–40% of the windfall.[7] But since the data again include purchases of consumer durables, the true propensity to consume would be substantially lower than these values.

---

[6]The results are in Mordechai Kreinin, "Windfall Income and Consumption—Additional Evidence," *American Economic Review*, June 1961; and Michael Landsberger, "Restitution Receipts, Household Savings and Consumption Behavior in Israel," Research Department, Bank of Israel, 1970.

[7]See Roger C. Bird and Ronald G. Bodkin, "The National Service Life Insurance Dividend of 1950 and Consumption: A Further Test of the 'Strict' Permanent Income Hypothesis," *Journal of Political Economy*, October 1965.

More generally, statistical studies of consumer spending over time indicate that the propensity to consume out of permanent income is large and not much different from one. By contrast, the propensity to consume out of temporary income is only about 20–30%.[8] Although this response to temporary changes is somewhat greater than that predicted by the permanent-income theory, the important point for our theoretical analysis is that the response of consumer spending to permanent changes in income is much greater than that to temporary changes.

Wealth Effects from Changes in the Interest Rate

So far, we have looked only at intertemporal-substitution effects from changes in the interest rate. Now, let's see whether a change in the interest rate leads to a wealth effect.

We can test for the effect on wealth by using the budget constraint, which is again

$$y_1 + y_2/(1 + R) + \cdots + b_0(1 + R)/P = c_1 + c_2/(1 + R) + \cdots$$

Abstract from the term that involves the initial stock of bonds, $b_0(1 + R)/P$. Remember that this term will, in any case, equal zero when we sum up over all households.

Suppose that we hypothetically hold fixed the time paths of real incomes, y_1, y_2, . . . , and expenditures, c_1, c_2, ... Then consider the separate effects of an increase in the interest rate on the left and right sides of the budget constraint. Clearly, the rise in the interest rate reduces the present values of real income, $y_1 + y_2/(1 + R) + \cdots$, and of real spending, $c_1 + c_2/(1 + R) + \cdots$ But the important question is which sum falls by the greater amount. If the present value of real spending falls by more, then the given path of real income would be sufficient to continue purchasing these goods and still have something left over. Then we could increase consumption for some periods without *necessarily* decreasing it for others.[9] Hence, wealth increases. However, the opposite conclusion obtains if the present value of real spending falls by less than that of real income.

The budget constraint indicates that the terms that decline most with the rise in the interest rate are those that are most distant into the future. That is, the discount factor for period t is $1/(1 + R)^{t-1}$, which is more sensitive to changes

---

[8]Two of the more important studies (which, however, are demanding in terms of the required knowledge of econometric techniques) are Marjorie Flavin, "The Adjustment of Consumption to Changing Expectations about Future Income," *Journal of Political Economy,* October 1981; and Robert Hall and Frederic Mishkin, "The Sensitivity of Consumption to Transitory Income: Estimates from Panel Data on Households," *Econometrica,* March 1982.

[9]The change in the interest rate has intertemporal-substitution effects, which may motivate us to decrease consumption at some dates. But for assessing the wealth effect, the important point is the capacity to raise consumption for some periods without necessarily lowering it for others. This perspective makes it clear that overall utility—and hence, wealth—must increase.

in R the higher the value of t. Therefore, when the interest rate rises, the present value of real spending declines by more than that of real income if the time path of spending is more heavily concentrated in the future than is the time path of income. For the case where the initial bonds, b_0, equal zero, this property applies for someone who has positive saving in most of the earlier years and negative saving in most of the later years. In other words, people who plan usually to be lenders experience an increase in wealth when the interest rate rises. Conversely, those who plan usually to be borrowers have a decline in wealth.

Although either situation may hold for an individual, neither case can apply for the average person. Since the aggregate stock of bonds is always zero in our model, we know that the average household is neither typically a lender nor typically a borrower. Therefore, in the aggregate, the wealth effect from a change in the interest rate is nil.[10] So for the purposes of aggregate analysis, we shall find it satisfactory to neglect wealth effects from changes in the interest rate. This result is very important. It says that for aggregate purposes, the important effects from changes in the interest rate are the intertemporal-substitution effects.

Choosing Work Effort over Many Periods

The Interest Rate and Work Effort over Time

As in our previous analysis for two periods, we can also analyze intertemporal-substitution effects on work effort. Basically, the effects on the time path of leisure are similar to those for consumption. In particular, a permanently higher interest rate motivates people to shift leisure away from the near term and toward the future. Correspondingly, people shift toward work effort for the near term and away from that later on.

We show these results in Figure 4.3. Note especially that the increase in the interest rate raises the ratio, l_t/l_{t+1}, for each date t. Therefore, if the initial plan calls for a constant level of work, then the new one involves a declining path of work.

Wealth Effects on Work Effort

Suppose again that the production function shifts upward permanently. Specifically, consider a parallel shift, which does not change the schedule for labor's marginal product. We know from before that people use part of their higher wealth to raise leisure, as well as consumption in each period. In particular, as with consumption, people tend to increase leisure by roughly the same amount in each period.

Consider again the case where the level of real income, $y_t = f(l_t)$, rises by

---

[10]For further discussion of this result, see Martin Bailey, *National Income and the Price Level*, 2nd ed., McGraw-Hill, New York, 1971, pp. 106–08.

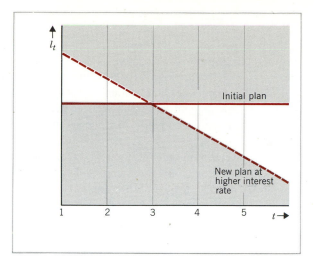

Figure 4.3 **Effect of a Higher Interest Rate on the Time Path of Work**
An increase in the interest rate motivates us to work more now and less later. Therefore, the new time path of work slopes downward, relative to the initial one.

one unit in each period if work effort does not change. Then, in our earlier setting, permanent income also rises by 1 unit. But because people reduce work effort, the actual amount of real income increases by less than 1 unit in each period. For example, it might rise by $\frac{3}{4}$ unit. So from the standpoint of our earlier analysis of consumption, it is just as if permanent income increased by $\frac{3}{4}$ of a unit, rather than 1 unit. Hence, we now predict that consumption will also rise by roughly $\frac{3}{4}$ unit in each period. Notice that real income, $f(l_t)$, and consumption, c_t, still rise by the same amounts in each period. Therefore, there is again no effect on saving when the change in the production function is permanent.

To summarize, a permanent improvement in the production function has the following wealth effects:

- work effort falls in each period by roughly equal amounts
- consumption rises in each period by roughly equal amounts
- the increases in real income, $f(l_t)$, and consumption, c_t, are roughly the same in each period, so that no changes in saving occur

We can also consider the case where the improvement in the production function is temporary. Then, as with consumption, people raise leisure by only a small amount in each period. Therefore, for the current period, we find that the increase in real income, $f(l_1)$, substantially exceeds the rise in consumption, c_1. Hence, as before, there is a strong positive response of current saving when the improvement in the production function is temporary.

Shifts in the Schedule for Labor's Marginal Product

Consider now a rise in the schedule for labor's marginal product. As we know, a higher schedule motivates people to work more. If the change is the same for each period, then we raise work by roughly equal amounts in each period. Therefore, output also increases by nearly the same amount at each date. Permanent income then increases by the same amount as output. Hence, each period's consumption increases by roughly as much as output, which means that no changes in saving occur.

A permanent improvement in labor's productivity, as above, means that consumption becomes cheaper relative to leisure at each date. Therefore, we work and consume more in every period. However, there are no changes in the relative costs of consumption or leisure for different periods. So the responses in work and consumption are nearly the same in each period. Hence, there are no effects on saving.

The results are different if the change in productivity is temporary. As a real-world example, think of a gold rush or other temporary profit opportunity, which makes the reward for today's effort unusually high. In the model we represent this case by shifting the schedule for labor's marginal product only for the current period.

The new element is that today's leisure becomes more expensive relative to leisure or consumption at other dates. Therefore, people have an extra incentive to expand work today in order to increase consumption and leisure later on. Thus, the temporary improvement of productivity stimulates current saving. That is, today's output rises by more than today's consumption.

Note especially that the temporary boost to productivity raises the cost of leisure today relative to leisure later. This change looks just like the intertemporal-substitution effect on work effort that arises from a temporary increase in the interest rate. Thus, we can look at a temporary improvement in productivity as the combination of two positive substitution effects on current work. First, there is the rise in the cost of leisure relative to consumption, which arises also when the improvement is permanent. Then second, there is the intertemporal-substitution effect, which works just like a temporary increase in the interest rate. It is this last element that stimulates the rise in current saving.

Summary

In this chapter, we analyzed the behavior of households over an infinite horizon. We motivated the infinite planning period by thinking about a family in which parents care about their children, who care about their children, and so on.

A permanent increase in the interest rate motivates people to shift away from consumption over the near term and toward that in the future. In particular, the strongest downward effect shows up on today's consumption, while the positive effects become larger the further out we look. The opposite responses apply to work effort. Also, we find that the current levels of consumption and work, and hence, current saving, react more when the change in the interest rate is permanent, rather than temporary.

Improvements in the production function have wealth effects that are positive on consumption and negative on work for each period. If the shift is permanent, then permanent income increases by as much as current income. Hence, the propensity to consume out of current income is near one and the propensity to save is near zero. But if the shift is temporary, then permanent income changes little. Therefore, the propensity to consume is small and the propensity to save is almost one. Finally, we show that a change in the interest rate has no aggregate wealth effect.

A permanent upward shift in the schedule for labor's marginal product raises work and consumption in each period, but has little effect on saving. However, a temporary upward shift in the schedule has a larger effect on current work and a positive effect on current saving. In particular, the temporary improvement in productivity implies an unusual return to today's work. Hence, it has the same intertemporal-substitution effect as that from a temporary increase in the interest rate.

Important Terms and Concepts

planning horizon

life-cycle model

social security

infinite horizon

propensity to consume

propensity to save

permanent income

QUESTIONS AND PROBLEMS

Mainly for Review

4.1 What factors determine the length of a household's planning horizon? If there were no possibilities for lending or borrowing what would the planning horizon be?

4.2 In Chapter 3, the typical household was assumed to have a fixed size of bequest, i.e., b_2 was exogenously given. Based on the reasoning in the present chapter, review this assumption. What factors might cause the household to alter the size of b_2?

4.3 Distinguish clearly between the following:
  a. A temporary change in income.
  b. A permanent change in income.
  c. A change in permanent income.

4.4 What factors determine whether the propensity to consume is less than one or equal to one? Can the propensity to consume be greater than one?

4.5 Suppose that a household has zero initial assets and that its income equals its consumption in every period. Will a change in the interest rate have a wealth effect on this household? Why is the economy as a whole in a position similar to this household?

4.6 Review the effects of the following changes on current consumption and work, distinguishing clearly between wealth effects and substitution effects.
a. A permanent parallel shift in the production function.
b. A change in the interest rate.
c. A temporary change in the marginal product of labor.

Problems for Discussion

4.7 Budget Lines
In Chapter 3, we drew a budget line for consumption today, c_1, versus next period, c_2.
a. Suppose that we consider instead the levels of consumption for periods 4 and 5, c_4 and c_5. What does the budget line look like?
b. Consider now levels of consumption that are separated by two periods—for example, c_1 versus c_3. What is the budget line in this case? What is the slope of the line? How does the result generalize to a comparison of c_1 with c_t for any period t?

4.8 Effects of the Interest Rate on the Time Path of Consumption
Suppose that the interest rate increases permanently. Then, as shown in Figure 4.1, the time path for consumption becomes more steeply sloped than before.
a. Why does the ratio, c_{t+1}/c_t, rise for all periods?
b. Consider the ratio, c_{t+j}/c_t, where j is some number ≥ 1. Why does this ratio rise by more the higher is the value of j?

4.9 Permanent Income With No Receipts From the Commodity Market
Suppose that our initial bond holdings are $b_0 = \$1,000$. All commodity market receipts, Py_t, are zero. The interest rate is $R = 10\%$ per year and the price level is constant over time.
a. What is the level of permanent income? If consumption is constant, what is the volume of saving each year? What is the level of permanent income when we calculate it during period 2?
b. Suppose now that $c_1 = 0$. What is permanent income when we calculate it during the second period? Explain this result.

4.10 Wealth Effects
Consider the household's budget constraint in real terms over an infinite horizon, $y_1 + y_2/(1 + R) + \cdots + b_0(1 + R)/P = c_1 + c_2/(1 + R) + \cdots$ Using this condition, evaluate the wealth effect of the following:

a. An increase in the price level, P, for a household that has a positive value of initial bonds, b_0. (The result has implications for the effects of unexpected price changes on the wealth of nominal creditors and nominal debtors.)

b. An increase in the interest rate, R, for a household that has $b_0 = 0$ and $c_t = y_t$ in each period.

c. An increase in the interest rate, R, for a household that has $b_0 = 0$, $c_t > y_t$ for $t \geq T$, and $c_t < y_t$ for $t < T$, where T is some date in the future.

4.11 Short-Term and Long-Term Interest Rates

Assume that \$1 worth of one-period bonds issued at the end of period 0 pay out $\$(1 + R_1)$ during period 1—that is, the principal of \$1 plus the interest payment of $\$R_1$. Assume that \$1 worth of 1-period bonds issued at the end of period 1 will pay out $\$(1 + R_2)$ during period 2. Suppose that people also market a two-period bond at the end of period 0. \$1 worth of this asset pays out $\$(1 + 2R)$ during period 2. (One payment of $\$R$ could be paid during the first period, but that would complicate the calculations.) Lenders from date 0 to date 2 have the option of holding a two-period bond or a succession of one-period bonds. Borrowers have a similar choice between negotiating a two-period loan or two successive one-period loans.

a. What must be the relation of R to R_1 and R_2? Explain the answer from the standpoint of borrowers and lenders.

b. If $R_2 > R_1$, what is the relation between R (the current "long-term" interest rate) and R_1 (the current short rate)? (The answer is an important result about the "term structure of interest rates.")

c. In March 1980 the yield on Aaa-rated (premium grade, long-term) corporate bonds was 13% per year, while that on three-month maturity prime commercial paper (short-term notes issued by large corporations) was 17% per year. What does this relation suggest for March 1980 about the financial markets' prediction for subsequent commercial paper yields? (You can consult the *Federal Reserve Bulletin* to see what actually happened.)

4.12 The Household's Budget Constraint with a Finite Horizon

Consider the household's budget constraint for n periods from equation (4.4),

$$Py_1 + Py_2/(1 + R) + \cdots + Py_n/(1 + R)^{n-1} + b_0(1 + R)$$

$$= Pc_1 + Pc_2/(1 + R) + \cdots + Pc_n/(1 + R)^{n-1} + b_n/(1 + R)^{n-1}$$

Assume now that $y_t = 0$ for $t > T_1$ and $c_t = 0$ for $t > T_2$. Here, T_2 might represent the expected lifetime and T_1 the anticipated working span for an individual.

a. Assume that we use the planning horizon, $n = T_2$. Why might we want to do this? What value would we select for b_n? What does the n-period budget constraint look like in this case?

b. Discuss the pattern of saving, $b_t - b_{t-1}$, for the "retirement period," where $T_1 < t \leq T_2$. What can be said about saving for the "typical" working year where $0 < t \leq T_1$? (This result concerns the "life-cycle" motivation for household saving.)

c. Suppose that the government forces people to retire earlier than they would otherwise choose. How would this action affect the choices of work effort, consumption, and desired saving for people who are still working, but anticipating an earlier retirement?

d. Given that individuals care about their children (and parents), what difficulties arise in specifying a value for the finite planning horizon, $n = T_2$?

CHAPTER 5
THE DEMAND FOR MONEY

Our model includes two forms of financial assets, money and bonds. But so far, we have not analyzed how much money people hold or how these holdings change over time. Thus, we carried out the analysis in the previous two chapters under the assumption that each household maintained a constant stock of money. Then, whenever people changed the time pattern of consumption or work effort, the resulting changes in saving showed up as lending or borrowing on the credit market. That is, people altered their holdings of bonds, but not their holdings of money.

Now, we provide the remaining building block in the model by explaining people's willingness to place part of their assets into money; that is, we explain the demand for money. Later on, we shall see that this demand is a crucial determinant of the price level.

The Nature of a Monetary Economy

As mentioned before, we assume that money is the sole medium of exchange in the economy. Trades occur between money and commodities and between money and bonds, but not directly between bonds and commodities or between the commodities that different households produce. The direct exchange of goods for goods, which is called **barter,** is inefficient for many types of transactions.[1] In particular, barter requires a **double coincidence of wants,** which is a situation where one person has the goods that someone else desires and vice versa. A general means of payments, such as money, avoids this problem. Buyers use money to purchase goods or bonds. Sellers receive money in exchange for goods or bonds. In this environment people accept money because they can use it later to buy something else. Hence, as long as people hold money they know that they can buy goods or bonds. The problem of double coincidence of wants does not arise.

---

[1]The classic discussion of the difficulties with barter exchange is W. Stanley Jevons, *Money and the Mechanism of Exchange,* D. Appleton, New York, 1896, Chapters 1–3. An interesting model of the evolution of specialized media of exchange appears in Robert Jones, ''The Origin and Development of Media of Exchange,'' *Journal of Political Economy,* August 1976.

Historically, some commodities—especially gold and silver—served as money. These precious metals possess some attractive physical characteristics, which classical economists enumerated as portability, indestructibility, homogeneity, divisibility, and cognizability.[2] But when paper money—such as U.S. dollar bills—replaces commodity money, these physical characteristics no longer enter into the analysis. In our model we think of money as these paper notes, rather than gold, silver, or other commodities.

We assume that the interest-bearing bonds in the model are not money—that is, these paper claims do not function as media of exchange. There are several reasons for this. First, the government may impose legal restrictions that prevent private parties (such as General Motors) from issuing small-size, interest-bearing notes that could serve conveniently as hand-to-hand currency. Further, the government may enact statutes that reinforce the use of its money. As an example, there is the proclamation that the U.S. dollar is "**legal tender** for all debts private and public."[3] Also, U.S. courts are more willing to enforce contracts that are denominated in U.S. dollars, rather than in some other unit. Second, there are costs of establishing one's money as reliable and convenient. These include the prevention of counterfeiting, the replacement of worn-out notes, the willingness to convert notes into different denominations and possibly into other assets, and so on. These costs suggest that money would tend to bear interest at a rate lower than bonds. In fact, because of the inconvenience of paying interest on hand-to-hand currency, the interest rate on money is typically zero.

In our model, we make two basic assumptions about paper money. First, the government has a monopoly in the issue of this stuff. Second, the interest rate on money is zero.

Given that people use money to transact, how much money should they hold? Suppose that everyone synchronizes each sale of goods or bonds with an equal-size purchase of some other good or bond. Then, although people use money for all exchanges, they end up holding virtually zero cash. But in order to hold this low average money balance each person has to spend a lot of effort on financial planning. In particular, they have to synchronize the timing of sales and purchases, and they have to carry out a large number of transactions. Typically, it will be more convenient to allow receipts to accumulate for awhile as cash before spending these funds or converting them into bonds. As Milton Friedman put it, we can usefully employ money as a *temporary abode of purchasing power*. As a general statement, people can reduce their average holdings of cash only by incurring more costs. These costs are often called **transaction costs,** which refer to the expenses of carrying out trades, as well as the costs of making financial decisions.

Given the total of financial assets, a lower average cash balance means a higher average stock of bonds. Hence, by economizing on money, people earn more

[2]See Jevons, op. cit., Chapter 5 and—for an earlier discussion—John Law, *Money and Trade Considered* (1705), Agustus Kelley, New York, 1966, Chapter 1.

[3]However, this provision does not determine the price at which currency exchanges for goods. If the price level were infinite, what would the legal-tender property mean?

interest (or pay less interest if they are borrowing). Thus, the demand for money emerges from a trade-off between transaction costs and interest earnings. Generally, an individual wants to operate at the point where the potential gain in interest earnings just balances the additional transaction costs that arise from economizing on cash. This consideration determines the volume of transaction costs that someone rationally incurs, which then determines the average holding of cash.

A Model of Optimal Cash Management

The following example illustrates the nature of the trade-off between transaction costs and interest earnings. Consider a retired person, who is living off previously accumulated assets. This person keeps financial assets primarily in bonds, but holds some cash in order to facilitate the purchases of consumer goods. For simplicity, assume that consumption expenditure is constant at the amount Pc dollars per year. (We still pretend that the price level, P, does not change over time.) The retiree makes occasional withdrawals of funds from the stock of interest-bearing assets. Suppose that these withdrawals occur at the interval ϕ (ϕ is the Greek letter *phi*). For example, if an exchange occurs every month, then $\phi = \frac{1}{12}$ of a year. Equivalently, the frequency of exchange is 12 per year. Note that this frequency is the reciprocal of the period between withdrawals, $1/\phi$.

Each exchange of interest-bearing assets for cash involves some transaction cost. There may be explicit brokerage charges, but, more likely, the main expense is the time and trouble for carrying out the transfer. If people spend more time transacting, they have less time remaining for work or leisure. Suppose that each exchange costs $\$\gamma$, where γ is the Greek letter *gamma*. (This cost includes the dollar value that people attach to the time needed for the exchange.) We assume a lump-sum transaction cost, which means that the charge is independent of the number of dollars withdrawn. If the retiree transacts at the frequency $1/\phi$ per year, then the total of transaction costs per year is the dollar amount $\gamma \cdot (1/\phi)$. If we divide by the price level, P, we find that the real transaction cost per year is

$$\text{real transaction cost} = (\gamma/P) \cdot (1/\phi) \qquad (5.1)$$

The term, γ/P, is the real cost per transaction.

When the retiree makes a withdrawal, he or she obtains the amount of cash needed to meet expenses until the next withdrawal. In the present case, the money must cover the expenditures over an interval of length ϕ. Since the person spends at the rate $\$Pc$ per year, the amount needed is $Pc \cdot \phi$. Hence, immediately after a withdrawal, the level of cash is $\$Pc \cdot \phi$. (We assume that cash holdings were zero just before—see below.) The retiree spends these funds gradually to buy goods, running out of money when the time ϕ has elapsed. At that point, he or she replenishes cash by making the next withdrawal from the stock of interest-bearing assets.

We show the time pattern of money holdings in Figure 5.1. Notice that a withdrawal of $\$Pc \cdot \phi$ occurs at date 0. The retiree spends gradually out of cash

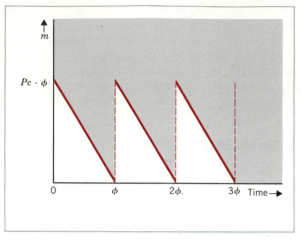

Figure 5.1 The Time Pattern of Money Holdings
Money holdings reach a peak, $Pc \cdot \phi$, just after each withdrawal. Then money declines gradually, reaching zero when it is time to make the next withdrawal. Notice that the withdrawals occur at the interval ϕ.

at the rate $\$Pc$ per year, which just exhausts the stock of money at time ϕ. Therefore, between dates 0 and ϕ, the level of money is shown by the downward-sloping line in the figure. At date ϕ, there is another withdrawal of size $\$Pc \cdot \phi$. Hence, cash jumps upward—along the dashed line in the figure—to the level $Pc \cdot \phi$. Then cash declines steadily again until the time for a new withdrawal at 2ϕ. This saw-tooth pattern for cash holdings keeps repeating with the peaks spaced at interval ϕ.

Given the form of cash management from Figure 5.1, the average cash balance is half the vertical distance to the peak, which is

$$\bar{m} = \tfrac{1}{2}Pc \cdot \phi \tag{5.2}$$

where $\bar{m}$ denotes the average holding of cash. If we divide by the price level, P, we can express the average holdings of cash in real terms as

$$\bar{m}/P = \tfrac{1}{2}c\phi \tag{5.3}$$

Now, suppose that the retiree has a given time path for total financial assets. An increase in the average money balance implies a corresponding reduction in the average holdings of bonds. Hence, if the average holding of money increases, then interest income declines.[4] Specifically, if the interest rate is R (per year), then the dollar magnitude of interest earnings foregone is the quantity $R \cdot \bar{m} = R \cdot (\tfrac{1}{2})Pc\phi$. If all financial assets had been held as bonds, then the interest income per year would have increased by this amount. As usual, we can divide through by the

---

[4]Changes in interest income net of transaction costs show up as a higher or lower level of sustainable consumption. For simplicity, we treat the level of consumption as constant over time.

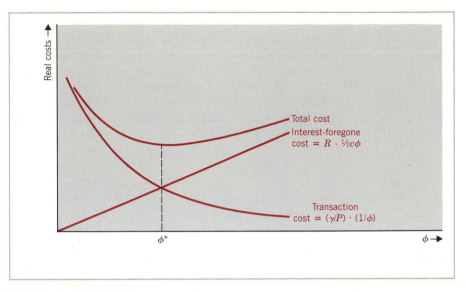

Figure 5.2 The Costs of Cash Management
The interest foregone by holding money, $R \cdot \frac{1}{2}c\phi$, increases with the period between withdrawals, ϕ. Transaction costs, $(\gamma/P) \cdot (1/\phi)$, decline as the period rises. Note that total costs reach a minimum at the point ϕ^*.

price level to express this dollar magnitude in real terms. Therefore, the real amount of interest income foregone per year is given by

$$\text{interest foregone in real terms} = R \cdot \bar{m}/P = R \cdot \tfrac{1}{2}c\phi \qquad (5.4)$$

There are two types of costs in our cash-management problem.[5] First, we can think of the interest foregone in real terms, $R \cdot \frac{1}{2}c\phi$, as a cost of holding money. We graph this cost versus the transaction interval, ϕ, in Figure 5.2. Note that this cost is a straight line from the origin with slope equal to $R \cdot \frac{1}{2}c$. Second, there is the real transaction cost, which is given in equation (5.1) as $(\gamma/P) \cdot (1/\phi)$. This cost appears as the rectangular hyperbola in Figure 5.2. Transaction costs approach zero as the interval between transactions tends toward infinity, and approach infinity as the interval tends toward zero.

---

[5]The model is an example of the ''inventory approach'' to money demand, which was pioneered by William Baumol, ''The Transactions Demand for Cash: An Inventory Theoretic Approach,'' *Quarterly Journal of Economics,* November 1952; and James Tobin, ''The Interest-Elasticity of Transactions Demand for Cash,'' *Review of Economics and Statistics,* August 1956. (The approach is often called the ''Baumol–Tobin'' model.) The two costs for holding money are analogous to those that arise when a firm holds an inventory of its product. The interest-foregone cost for money parallels the costs of foregone interest, storage, and depreciation, which apply to inventories of goods. The transaction cost for financial exchanges corresponds to the costs of restocking—that is, the transaction cost for ordering, shipping, and processing new goods from a supplier. More complicated models of inventories—whether of goods or money—stress the uncertainties in receipts and expenditures.

We show also the total of interest and transaction costs in Figure 5.2. This curve is U-shaped. Costs decline initially as the transaction interval rises above zero, because transaction costs decline by more than interest costs increase. Eventually, we find that transaction costs do not fall as fast as interest costs rise. Therefore, total costs start to increase with increases in the interval, ϕ. There is some amount of time between trips, denoted by ϕ^* in the figure, which minimizes the total costs. Hence, a rational person chooses the interval ϕ^*.[6]

For later purposes, the important point is that the choice of transaction interval, ϕ, determines the average holding of real cash from equation (5.3) as the amount, $\bar{m}/P = (\frac{1}{2})c\phi$. Therefore, a person's choice of transaction interval translates into that person's choice of an average holding of real cash. Our main concern now is how various changes in the economy affect the transaction interval and thereby a person's average holding of real cash.

There are three variables that determine the transaction interval, ϕ^*, in the model. These are the interest rate, R, the real flow of expenditures, c, and the real cost per transaction, γ/P. We can use graphical methods to study the effects of changes in any of these variables.

We consider in Figure 5.3 an increase in the interest rate from R to R'. This change steepens the slope of the line that describes interest-foregone costs. In calculating total costs we find that the interest component has become more important relative to the transaction-cost component. Hence, we reach sooner the position where increasing interest costs dominate over falling transaction costs. It follows that the minimum of total costs occurs at a shorter interval between withdrawals—that is, $(\phi^*)' < \phi^*$ in the figure.

We can interpret the result as follows. An increase in the interest rate makes it more important to economize on cash in order to avoid large amounts of foregone interest income. In our simple model, people can reduce average holdings of money only by transacting more frequently—that is, by shortening the period between financial exchanges, ϕ. Although this process entails a higher transaction cost, people are motivated by the rise in the interest rate to incur these costs. Hence, the rise in the interest rate, R, leads to a decline in the interval between transactions.

Recall from equation (5.3) that the average real money balance equals the amount, $\frac{1}{2}c\phi$. Since the increase in the interest rate lowers the period, ϕ, it follows that average real money holdings decline. In other words, a higher cost of holding money—that is, a rise in the interest rate—reduces the real demand for money. We shall use this important result many times in our subsequent analysis.

We can use a similar method to assess changes in the real flow of spending, c. A rise in the spending flow shifts the interest-foregone cost exactly as shown in Figure 5.3. Hence, someone with a greater annual flow of real expenditure chooses a shorter interval between withdrawals, ϕ. This result obtains because an increase in the real volume of spending, c, makes the interest-foregone cost more important

---

[6]In our example, the period ϕ^* turns out also to equalize the two components of the total costs. That is, in Figure 5.2, the interest-foregone line intersects the curve for transaction costs at the point ϕ^*. This property depends on the details of our example—it does not hold more generally.

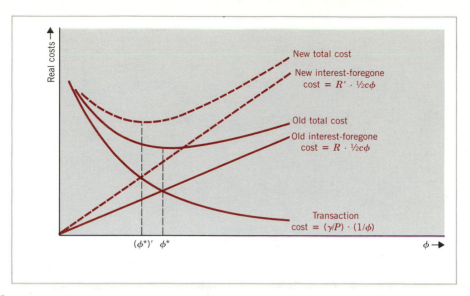

Figure 5.3 **Effect on the Transaction Interval of an Increase in the Interest Rate**
An increase in the interest rate from R to R' steepens the line that describes interest-foregone costs. Therefore, people respond by lowering the period between withdrawals from ϕ^* to $(\phi^*)'$.

relative to the transaction cost. In other words, households with more real spending—typically, households with higher income—find it worthwhile to devote more effort to financial planning in order to economize on their cash.

Average real cash balances equal the quantity, $\frac{1}{2}c\phi$. For a given choice of transaction interval, ϕ, a rise in real spending, c, increases average real cash balances proportionately. But we have just shown that the period, ϕ, declines as the volume of spending increases. This response means that a rise in real spending leads to a less-than-proportionate increase in the average holding of real cash.[7] (We assume here that the interest rate, R, and the real cost of transacting, γ/P, do not change.) Sometimes, people refer to this result as **"economies of scale"** in cash holding. This property means that households with a larger scale of spending hold less cash when expressed as a ratio to their expenditures.

Finally, we can consider an increase in the real cost of transacting, γ/P. We can show graphically that the change leads to a lengthening of the period between exchanges, ϕ. People transact less frequently when the cost of each exchange rises. Because the period, ϕ, lengthens, we know also that average real money balances, $\frac{1}{2}c\phi$, increase.

---

[7]We can show that the decline in the transaction interval, ϕ, is by a smaller proportion than the increase in real spending, c. Therefore, the average real cash balance does rise on net.

Properties of the Demand for Money

The results tell us the effects on average real money balances from changes in the interest rate, R, the real volume of spending, c, and the real cost of transacting, γ/P. We can summarize these findings in the form of a function, h, for average real money demanded,

$$\bar{m}/P = h(R, \quad c, \quad \gamma/P)$$
$$(-) \; (+) \; (+) \tag{5.5}$$

Again, the signs indicate the effect of each independent variable on the dependent variable, $\bar{m}/P$.

Consider what happens when we double the price level, P, but hold fixed the interest rate, R, the level of real spending, c, and the real transaction cost, γ/P. (Hence, nominal spending, Pc, and the dollar cost of transacting, γ, both double along with the doubling of the general price level.) These changes leave unaltered the curves in Figure 5.2, which describe the real cost of transacting and the real value of interest income foregone. Therefore, people do not change their choice of transaction interval, ϕ. It follows that average *real* balances, $\bar{m}/P = \frac{1}{2}c\phi$, do not change. But average *nominal* balances, $\bar{m} = \frac{1}{2}Pc \cdot \phi$, double along with the doubling of the price level.

Equation (5.5) relates the average holdings of money in real terms, $\bar{m}/P$, to a set of real variables. These are the interest rate, R, the real amount of spending, c, and the real cost of transacting, γ/P. Notice that we treat the interest rate as a real variable. In particular, this rate tells us how much real interest income we forego by holding real cash balances.

The Velocity of Money

Economists often think of the relation between the average amount of money that someone holds, $\bar{m}$, and the amount of transactions carried out by that money. In our model, the dollar volume of transactions equals the amount of consumption expenditure, Pc. Then, the ratio of transactions to the average money balance, $Pc/\bar{m}$, is called the **velocity of money.** The velocity indicates the number of times per unit of time, such as a year, that the typical piece of money turns over. The smaller is the average real balance, $\bar{m}/P$, relative to the real flow of spending, c, the greater is the velocity of money.

In our model, a person's average real balance is given from equation (5.3) as the amount, $\bar{m}/P = \frac{1}{2}c\phi$, where ϕ is the period between financial transactions. Therefore, velocity is $c/[\bar{m}/P] = 2 \cdot (1/\phi)$. Notice that the velocity of money depends directly on the frequency of exchange, $1/\phi$, between alternative financial assets (bonds) and cash. Hence, one variable that has an important effect on velocity is the interest rate, R. An increase in the interest rate motivates a higher frequency of financial exchanges, $1/\phi$, so that velocity rises.

The Aggregate Demand for Money

For an individual in our model, the level of real cash follows a sawtooth pattern and varies between zero and the amount, $c \cdot \phi$. Then, equation (5.5) determines the average level of real cash, which is the quantity, $\bar{m}/P = \frac{1}{2}c \cdot \phi$. Now suppose that we sum up over many households, each of which has the same average real balance. Then unless the timing of transactions is synchronized across households, this aggregation smooths out the sawtooth pattern. In particular, aggregate real cash balances at any date look like an individual's average amount, $\bar{m}/P$, multiplied by the number of people.

We can write out a function, H, for aggregate real money demanded as

$$M/P = H(\underset{(-)}{R}, \ \underset{(+)}{C}, \ \underset{(+)}{\gamma/P}) \tag{5.6}$$

Here, the function H looks like the individual's function h, but magnified to incorporate the adding up across many people. Corresponding to the aggregate holding of real balances, we can also define an aggregate concept of velocity, which is the ratio of aggregate real spending to aggregate real cash balances, $C/(M/P)$.[8]

The Velocity of Money in the United States

Figure 5.4 shows the history for the velocity of money in the United States from 1890 to 1980. (The data are plotted at five-year intervals.) Velocity is defined here as the ratio of aggregate personal consumption expenditures for the year, PC, to the annual average of the money stock.[9] For the upper curve in the figure we define money as the public's holding of currency. However, it is more common to use the broader monetary aggregate, $M1$, which includes checkable deposits. In fact, since these checkable deposits are an alternative to currency as a medium of exchange, we can readily apply our theory of the demand for money to the broader concept, $M1$. The lower curve in the figure uses the $M1$ definition of money.

---

[8]More often, economists use gross national product (GNP), rather than consumer spending, to measure aggregate velocity. Although GNP is broader than consumer spending, it still covers only the final goods that an economy produces. The total amount of transactions includes also various intermediate exchanges, such as sales of goods from suppliers to producers, from wholesalers to retailers, and so on. These trades are netted out in measuring GNP. Also, a large and rapidly increasing volume of monetary exchange involves financial trades—such as purchases or sales of stocks and bonds. We do not have data on the total volume of transactions. However, we do know the quantity of expenditures that are made via checks, which are called debits to demand deposits. For 1982, these debits totaled $90.9 trillion, which was 29 times the GNP of $3.1 trillion! The ratio of debits to GNP has increased dramatically in recent years—it was about 16 in 1975, 11 in 1970, 8 in 1965, and between 5 and 7 from 1945 to 1960. The main reason for this change is the explosion of various types of financial transactions. (The data on debits are in issues of the *Federal Reserve Bulletin*.)

[9]The pattern of results is similar if we use the GNP, rather than consumption expenditures, to define velocity.

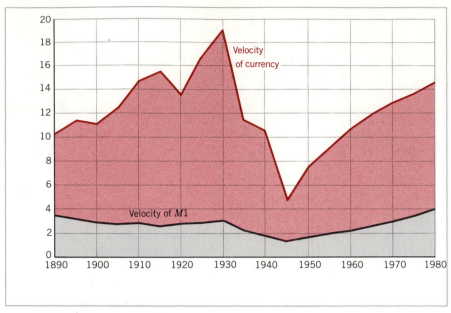

Figure 5.4 The Velocity of Money in the United States, 1890–1980

The upper curve measures the ratio of consumption expenditure for the year to the annual average of currency held by the public. The lower curve uses $M1$, rather than currency. (Prior to 1915, the numbers are based on the broader monetary aggregate, $M2$, which includes all deposits at commercial banks.) Sources: the data on currency and $M1$ are from Milton Friedman and Anna Schwartz, *Monetary Statistics of the United States,* Columbia University Press, New York, 1970, Table 2; and Board of Governors of the Federal Reserve System, *Banking and Monetary Statistics 1941–1970, Annual Statistical Digest 1970–1979,* and the *Federal Reserve Bulletin,* various issues.

One thing to notice from Figure 5.4 is the upward movement in velocity since the end of World War II. This pattern appears whether we define money as currency or as $M1$. Two main factors account for this behavior. First, interest rates have risen substantially since 1945. For example, the interest rate paid on three-month maturity U.S. Treasury Bills rose from 0.4% in 1945 to 2.9% in 1960, 6.5% in 1970, and 14.0% in 1981, but then declined to 10.6% in 1982. The overall rise in interest rates motivated a reduction in real cash balances, relative to the volume of real spending, which meant an increase in velocity. But, the recent decline in interest rates has generated a fall in velocity since late 1981. Second, there have been technological advances in financial management, which enabled people to economize more easily on their cash.[10] In our simple model, these developments

---

[10]However, some of these advances—particularly the ready availability of money-market funds—have themselves been triggered by the rise in interest rates. Therefore, the second factor for explaining the rise in velocity is partly related to the first one.

appear as reductions in the real cost of financial exchanges, γ/P, relative to an individual's real volume of spending, c. Such changes induce people to switch from holdings of money to holdings of alternative financial instruments. Again, the change shows up as a higher velocity of money.

The velocity of currency rises also over most of the period from 1890 to 1930. Changes in interest rates were not a major element here. However, some convenient financial alternatives to currency developed over this period. In particular, checkable deposits became more familiar and accessible. These developments led to decreases in holdings of currency relative to the volume of spending. It is interesting that the peak of currency velocity around 1930 actually exceeds that for 1980. Although there has been much talk recently about the economy's learning to dispense with currency, we see that there was actually less currency outstanding relative to the volume of consumer spending in 1930 than there was in 1980.

The broader monetary aggregate, $M1$, includes demand deposits, which became increasingly popular from 1890 to 1930. Therefore, the velocity of $M1$ behaves very differently from that of currency during this period. In fact, there is a small decline in the velocity of $M1$ from 1890 to 1930.

Major declines in the velocity of currency occurred during World Wars I and II. Here, demand for currency rises, because there are more transactions with strangers, reduced desires to leave records of transactions from checking accounts (because of rationing, higher income taxes, and other legal restrictions on private activities), and increased demand for currency by foreigners.[11] There was also a sharp decrease in the velocity of currency during the Great Depression. In this case, the major financial collapse lessened the attractiveness of alternatives to currency, including demand deposits. Therefore, the velocity of currency fell dramatically from 1930 to 1935.

The influences of the Great Depression and World War II led also to declines in the velocity of $M1$. However, there was no noticeable effect during World War I.[12]

---

[11]For a discussion of these matters, see Phillip Cagan, "The Demand for Currency Relative to the Total Money Supply," *Journal of Political Economy,* August 1958.

[12]For a survey of empirical studies on the demand for money, see David Laidler, *The Demand for Money: Theories and Evidence,* Harper & Row, New York, 2nd ed., 1977, part 2. For a fascinating discussion of longer period developments, see Milton Friedman and Anna J. Schwartz, *A Monetary History of the United States, 1867–1960,* Princeton University Press, Princeton, New Jersey, 1963. The long-term effects of financial developments on the velocity of money in five industrialized countries are studied in Michael Bordo and Lars Jonung, "The Long-Run Behavior of the Income Velocity of Money in Five Advanced Countries, 1870–1975: An Institutional Approach," *Economic Inquiry,* January 1981. For a focus on the implications of recent financial innovations in the United States, see Michael Dotsey, "The Effects of Cash Management Practices on the Demand for Money," unpublished, Federal Reserve Bank of Richmond, September 1982.

Generalizations of the Simple Model

Our simple model captures the basic trade-off that determines the demand for money. Namely, if people put more effort into transacting and financial planning, then they can lower their average holding of cash. A lower cash balance means, in turn, a greater amount of interest earnings. Someone engages in financial planning, and so on, up to the point where the gain in interest income just compensates for the added transaction costs. Consequently, an increase in the interest rate motivates people to incur more costs in order to economize on cash. Similarly, an increase in the volume of expenditures raises the benefits from financial planning. Therefore, although a higher level of spending means more money held, we predict that money balances rise less than proportionately with the scale of spending.[13] Finally, the theory relates the demand for money in real terms to a set of real variables, which include the real flow of spending, the real costs of transacting and financial planning, and the interest rate. A change in the general price level—with all the real variables held fixed—does not change the demand for money in real terms.

In our simple model, the real transaction costs incurred per year, $(\gamma/P) \cdot (1/\phi)$, pertain to transfers from interest-bearing assets to money. More generally, transaction costs apply also to other forms of exchanges. For example, we can think of the costs of depositing funds into bonds or other financial assets, the costs of buying commodities with money, and the costs of making wage payments to workers.[14] We would want also to bring in the costs of finaneial planning and decision making.

---

[13]The empirical evidence on this proposition is mixed. Cross-country studies suggest that real balances per capita rise roughly one-to-one with increases in real income per capita. Thus, there is no evidence here for economies of scale in the holding of money. (See, for example, Nasser Saidi, ''Inflation, Exchange Rates and the Neutrality of Money: International Evidence, 1961–1978,'' Graduate Institute of International Studies, Geneva, 1982.) However, other studies tend to find economies-of-scale in money demand when they include separate variables to measure the level of financial sophistication and the costs of transacting. In our theory, these variables relate to the transaction cost, γ/P. In this context, see Edi Karni, ''The Value of Time and the Demand for Money,'' *Journal of Money, Credit and Banking,* February 1974; David Laidler, op. cit., pp. 148–49; and Michael Bordo and Lars Jonung, op. cit.

[14]Irving Fisher, *The Purchasing Power of Money* (1922), Augustus Kelley, New York, 1971, pp. 83–85, stresses the effect of the payment period for wages on workers' demand for money. The effects of this period are analogous to those we discussed for the case of the period between withdrawals from a financial asset. In particular, a shorter period reduces the average holding of real balances. This effect becomes important during extreme inflations—for example, during the German hyperinflation after World War I. In such situations the cost of holding money becomes very high. Therefore, people incur more transaction costs—such as the costs of making more frequent wage payments—in order to reduce their average holdings of real cash. For 1923, the final year of the German hyperinflation, an observer reported, ''it became the custom to make an advance of wages on Tuesday, the balance being paid on Friday. Later, some firms used to pay wages three times a week or even daily'' (Costantino Bresciani-Turroni, *The Economics of Inflation* (1931), George Allen & Unwin, London, 1937, p. 303). Similarly, during the Austrian hyperinflation after World War I, ''the salaries of the state officials, which used to be issued at the end of the month, were paid to them during 1922 in installments three times per month'' (J. van Walre de Bordes, *The Austrian Crown,* King, London, 1927, p. 163).

Typically, people who do more calculating manage to maintain a smaller average cash balance and thereby achieve a greater amount of interest earnings. Basically, this broader view of transaction costs does not alter our main conclusions with regard to the form of the function for aggregate money demand in equation (5.6).

The costs of transacting change when there are technological innovations in the financial sector. For example, the use of computers by financial institutions makes it easier to shift between money and alternative assets. These improvements tend to lower the demand for money. Similarly, the development of convenient checkable deposits in the late 19th and early 20th centuries in the United States had a negative effect on the demand for currency (and a positive effect on the holdings of demand deposits). The possibilities for economizing on cash holdings are influenced also by the use of credit. It may be easier to synchronize receipts and payments—thereby resulting in a lower average money balance—when we buy with credit rather than cash. In any case, the use of credit favors the use of checks, rather than currency.

In a broader model, we would bring in uncertainties associated with the timing and size of receipts and expenditures. Typically, an increase in the amounts of these uncertainties tends to raise the average holding of money. That is, people hold cash partly because of the possibility that a desirable purchase opportunity will materialize or because of the chance that an income receipt will be late. The uncertainties become more significant if we also introduce delays in liquidating assets to obtain cash. Then people are especially careful to hold money as a precaution against unexpected events.

The introduction of uncertainty does not eliminate the types of influences on aggregate money demand that we summarized in equation (5.6). However, changes in various types of uncertainties may change the aggregate quantity of real cash that people hold. For example, if the degree of uncertainty for receipts and expenses increases, then the aggregate demand for real cash balances tends to rise. This element may have been especially important for holdings of currency during the Great Depression of the 1930s.

Money and Households' Budget Constraints

We want now to incorporate the discussion of money demand into our previous treatment of households' budget constraints. Recall the form of the budget condition for period t,

$$Py_t + (1 + R)b_{t-1} + m_{t-1} = Pc_t + b_t + m_t \qquad (5.7)$$

Before, we simplified the analysis by pretending that each household's cash balance was constant over time—that is, $m_t = m_{t-1}$. Then the cash-balance terms on each side of equation (5.7) cancel. Therefore, terms involving money did not appear in the derivation of the budget constraint over an infinite horizon. Now, we want to reconsider this analysis when households can alter their holdings of cash.

In our model of the demand for money, the cash position moves up and down during a period in accordance with the sawtooth pattern shown in Figure 5.1. But for the purpose of constructing a budget constraint over an infinite horizon, it is satisfactory to neglect these ups and downs of money within a period. That is, we now pretend that a household's money holding is constant during a period, although it can change from one period to the next.

As before, we can use the one-period budget constraint from equation (5.7) to derive a budget condition that applies for any number of periods. When we consider an infinite horizon and express things in real terms, the result turns out to be

$$y_1 + y_2(1 + R) + \cdots + b_0(1 + R)/P + m_0/P =$$

$$c_1 + c_2/(1 + R) + \cdots + R(m_1/P)/(1 + R) \qquad (5.8)$$

$$+ R(m_2/P)/(1 + R)^2 + \cdots$$

Consider the role of the monetary terms in equation (5.8). First, the sources of funds on the left side include the initial real balance, m_0/P. Just like the real value of initial bonds, $b_0(1 + R)/P$, people can use their initial cash to pay for goods. Second, the uses of funds on the right side include a series of terms that reflect the interest foregone by holding money rather than bonds. The first term is $R(m_1/P)/(1 + R)$. The household could have held the real quantity of assets, m_1/P, as bonds rather than money during period 1. Then, the real interest income during period 2 would have increased by the amount, $R(m_1/P)$. Hence the term, $R(m_1/P)/(1 + R)$, is the real present value of this foregone interest. Similarly, the expression, $R(m_2/P)/(1 + R)^2$, is the real present value of the interest foregone during period 3. Overall, the series of monetary terms on the right side of equation (5.8) equals the real present value of interest foregone by holding money.[15]

Let's think about the effect of the monetary terms on the sources of funds, which appear on the left side of equation (5.8), net of that on the uses of funds, which appear on the right side. This net effect equals the difference between the initial real balance and the present-value sum of interest foregone. That is, the net effect is

$$m_0/P - [R/(1 + R)][m_1/P + (m_2/P)/(1 + R) + (m_3/P)/(1 + R)^2 + \cdots] \qquad (5.9)$$

Recall that all of the terms within the brackets relate to planned holdings of real balances, m_1/P, m_2/P, ... In order to understand the nature of expression

---

[15]We can think of this result in another way. It would be correct to omit the monetary terms on the right side of equation (5.8) if people actually carried all assets (positive or negative) after period 0 in the form of bonds. In fact, the usual present-value formula—that is, the discounting of incomes or expenses for period t by the term $1/(1 + R)^{t-1}$—assumes that *all* assets earn interest at the rate R. Since people actually hold some assets as money, the standard method for calculating present values overstates the amount of interest income. Thus, the inclusion of the terms for interest foregone on the right side of equation (5.8) corrects for this error.

(5.9), suppose that these planned real balances were all the same—that is, $m_1/P = m_2/P = \cdots$ Then, we can evaluate the sum within the brackets on the right side of expression (5.9) as

$$(m_1/P)[1 + 1/(1 + R) + 1/(1 + R)^2 + \cdots] = (m_1/P)[(1 + R)/R]^{16}$$

Substituting back into expression (5.9), we find that the net monetary term is $m_0/P - m_1/P$. In other words, the net of sources and uses of funds depends on the difference between the initial real balance, m_0/P, and the real balance that someone plans to hold in future periods, m_1/P. Here, we assumed that all future real balances equaled the amount, m_1/P. But more generally, some average of planned future holdings would appear, rather than just the next period's, m_1/P.

We see now what happens when we include the monetary terms in the household's budget constraint, as we do in equation (5.8). The sources of funds on the left side rise relative to the uses of funds on the right side only if the initial real cash balance, m_0/P, exceeds the amount that someone plans to hold on average in the future. For someone who plans to maintain a constant real balance over time, the net effect is nil. To put this result another way, the initial real balances, m_0/P, provide just enough resources to cover the future holdings of real cash. Thus, there is nothing left over from the initial real cash for people to use to increase consumption or leisure.

The Real-Balance Effect

Let's calculate the wealth effect from a change in the price level, P. Look at the household's budget condition in real terms from equation (5.8). Suppose that we hold fixed the levels of output, $y_1, y_2, \ldots$, and consumption, $c_1, c_2, \ldots$. Also, hold constant the interest rate, R, the planned levels of *real* balances, $m_1/P, m_2/P$, $\ldots$, and the initial *nominal* money holding, m_0. Finally, let's look at the average person, for whom the initial bonds, b_0, equal zero. Consider then the effects on the left and right sides of equation (5.8) from a decline in the price level. Given our assumptions, nothing changes on the right side, which measures the uses of funds in real terms. The only effect on the left side (since $b_0 = 0$) is an increase in the real value of the initial money balances, m_0/P. Thus, wealth increases,[17] because people can use these higher initial real balances either to raise some levels of consumption or to lower some levels of work effort. The increase in wealth

---

[16]We again use the condition for a geometric sum, $1 + z + z^2 + \cdots = 1/(1 - z)$ if $-1 < z < 1$. In our case, $z = 1/(1 + R)$.

[17]We can modify these results to accommodate a nonzero value for the initial level of bonds, b_0. Lenders, for whom $b_0 > 0$, benefit from a decline in the price level. Borrowers lose out by a corresponding amount. In the aggregate, since $B_0 = 0$, the only effect comes from the change in real money balances, M_0/P.

from a decline in the price level is often called the **real-balance effect.**[18] As with other wealth effects, we predict that this one leads to increased consumption and reduced work effort at all dates.

The real-balance effect operates only when there is a change in initial real cash, m_0/P, relative to the average of planned holdings, m_1/P, m_2/P, ... However, in most of our subsequent analyses, we look at situations where the aggregates of actual and planned real balances move by equal amounts. Then, as mentioned before, there are equal changes to the left and right sides of the aggregate form of the budget constraint from equation (5.8). Therefore, in these cases, the change in real balances does not involve an aggregate wealth effect.[19]

Wealth Effects from Transaction Costs

In our simple model of the demand for money, we considered transaction costs and interest-foregone costs. The interest foregone from holding money appears on the right side of the budget constraint in equation (5.8). However, we have not yet incorporated any transaction costs.

Recall from our simple model that each household picks a frequency of transacting, $1/\phi$. Suppose that the chosen frequency during period t is $(1/\phi_t)$. Then, if the real cost of each transaction is (γ/P), the total of transaction costs incurred for period t is $(\gamma/P)(1/\phi_t)$. In terms of the household's budget constraint, the transaction costs are just like the real expenditure on consumption, c_t. (At least this is true if the transaction costs represent payments for financial services, which people buy from the producers of these services.) Therefore, we should augment the right side of equation (5.8) to include the present value of real transaction costs. Assuming that the real cost per transaction, γ/P, is constant over time, this present value equals

$$(\gamma/P)[(1/\phi_1) + (1/\phi_2)/(1 + R) + \cdots]$$

Other things equal, an increase in the present value of real transaction costs

---

[18]The effect has been stressed by many economists. See, for example, Gottfried Haberler, *Prosperity and Depression,* 2nd ed., League of Nations, Geneva, 1939, especially Chapters 8 and 11; A. C. Pigou, "Economic Progress in a Stable Environment," *Economica,* August 1947; Don Patinkin, "Price Flexibility and Full Employment," *American Economic Review,* September 1948, and *Money, Interest and Prices,* 2nd ed., Harper & Row, New York, 1965, especially Chapter 2; and Robert Mundell, "Money, Debt and the Rate of Interest," in *Monetary Theory,* Goodyear, Pacific Palisades, California, 1971.

[19]For some related discussions of real-balance effects, see G. C. Archibald and Richard Lipsey, "Monetary and Value Theory: A Critique of Lange and Patinkin," *Review of Economic Studies,* October 1958; and E. J. Mishan, "A Fallacy in the Interpretation of the Cash Balance Effect," *Econometrica,* May 1958.

reduces wealth.[20] However, most economists believe that in normal times these costs are small relative to a household's total present values of real incomes and expenditures, which appear in equation (5.8). Therefore, it is customary to neglect changes in transaction costs when analyzing the determination of work effort, consumption, and saving. For most purposes, we follow this practice.

Summary

In this chapter, we explained why people hold part of their financial assets as money, rather than interest-bearing bonds. The explanation involves first the role of money (but not bonds) as a medium of exchange, and second the extra transaction costs that arise when people economize more on their holdings of cash. Then we showed that the average amount of real money held involves a trade-off between transaction costs and interest-income foregone. In particular, a higher interest rate motivates people to incur more transaction costs in order to achieve a lower average real cash balance.

We incorporated the holdings of money into households' budget constraints over an infinite horizon. If the average of planned future holdings of real cash equals the initial holding, then there is no impact on the net of sources and uses of funds. Thus, changes in initial real balances involve a wealth effect only when the change is relative to the planned future holdings. In the aggregate, this type of change cannot arise in our model. On the other hand, an increase in the present value of real transaction costs reduces wealth. But in most instances, we assume that this wealth effect is small enough to neglect.

Important Terms and Concepts

barter

double coincidence of wants

legal tender

transaction costs

economies of scale in the demand for money

velocity of money

real-balance effect

demand for money

---

[20]For example, an increase in the interest rate, R, motivates people to transact more frequently in order to economize on cash. There is an increase in the present value of real transaction costs, which implies a decrease in wealth. Similarly, a rise in the real cost of transacting, γ/P, implies a reduction in wealth.

QUESTIONS AND PROBLEMS

Mainly for Review

5.1 What are the costs of transacting between money and financial assets? (You may want to make a list and include such items as the cost of a trip to the bank and the time spent waiting in line.) How would the development of electronic teller services affect this cost?

5.2 Suppose that an individual's consumption expenditure is $6,000 per year and that it is financed by monthly withdrawals of money from a savings account.
  a. Depict on a graph the pattern of the person's money holdings over a period of one year. What is the average money balance?
  b. Graph the pattern of money holdings when withdrawals of money are made only once in two months. Show that the average money balance (and the interest cost) is higher.

5.3 Refer to question 5.2. If consumption expenditure rises to $9,000 per year and withdrawals continue to be made monthly, what is the average money holding? Is it optimal for the frequency of withdrawals to remain the same when consumption increases? Explain.

5.4 What is the definition of the (aggregate) velocity of money? Use the concept of velocity to explain how a given (aggregate) quantity of money balances can be used to pay for a relatively large volume of (aggregate) consumption expenditure over a year.

5.5 Consider the following changes and state whether their effect on the real demand for money is an increase, a decrease, or uncertain.
  a. A decrease in the interest rate.
  b. An increase in transaction costs.
  c. An increase in real consumption.
  d. An increase in the price level.

5.6 Consider again the changes listed in question 5.5, and describe their effect on velocity.

5.7 Suppose for the typical individual that there is an increase in current money holdings and an equal planned increase in money holdings in all periods. Show (a) why there is no increase in wealth through the monetary terms in the budget constraint, and (b) why there is a small increase in wealth through a reduction in the present value of transaction costs. Distinguish this effect from the real-balance effect.

Problems for Discussion

5.8 **Transaction Costs and Households' Budget Constraints**
  Assume that the real cost of transacting between bonds and money, γ/P, rises.
  a. How does this change show up in households' budget constraints? What is the effect on wealth?

b. We neglected transaction costs when considering households' choices of work effort, consumption, and saving. Suppose now that we bring in the wealth effect from part (a). What then is the effect of an increase in the real cost of transacting, γ/P, on households' work effort, consumption, and saving?

c. Have we left out a new substitution effect in part (b)? Think about the choice between consumption and leisure. Consumption involves market exchange, which requires us to use money. But we can "buy" leisure without using money! So what substitution effect arises for consumption versus leisure when the real cost of transacting, γ/P, rises? How does this affect the answer to part (b)?

5.9 Further Aspects of Transaction Costs

In problem 5.8 we considered the effects of transaction costs on households' budget constraints. These costs might show up as purchases of financial services—for example, as brokerage fees or service charges by banks. Alternatively, transaction costs might just represent the time that it takes to go to the bank or to make a decision.

a. How do these two different views of transaction costs affect the way that these costs appear in households' budget constraints?

b. Do these differences affect our other answers to problem 5.8?

c. How should we think about the production of financial services? That is, how can we incorporate this "good" into the model?

5.10 Effects of the Payment Interval and Shopping Trips on the Demand for Money

Think of a worker with an annual income of $12,000. Suppose that he or she receives wage payments once per month. Consumption spending is constant at $12,000 per year. Assume that the worker holds no bonds—that is, he or she holds all financial assets in the form of cash.

a. What is the worker's average cash balance?

b. What would the average cash balance be if the worker gets paid twice per month, instead of once per month?

c. What is the general relation between the average money balance and the interval between wage payments?

Assume again that the worker receives payments once per month. But instead of carrying out consumption expenditures in a uniform flow, he or she now makes periodic shopping trips. At each trip the worker buys enough goods (for example, groceries) to last until the next trip.

d. If the worker shops four times each month, what is the average cash balance? Why is the answer different from that in part (a)?

e. What happens if he or she shops only twice each month?

f. What is the general effect on the average cash balance of the interval between shopping trips? Compare the answer with that for part (c).

g. Suppose that the cost of making shopping trips rises—for example, because of an increase in the relative price of gasoline. How would this affect the frequency of shopping trips? What does this tell us about the effect of an increase in the cost of making shopping trips on the average real holding of money? How does this result compare with the effect of financial transaction costs, γ/P, which we explored in the text?

5.11 Expenditures and the Demand for Money

a. Consider an increase in the aggregate of real spending, C. What is the effect on the aggregate demand for real cash balances, M/P? Notice that aggregate real spending can rise for two reasons. First, there could be an increase in everyone's real spending with no change in the number of people. Second, there could be an increase in the number of people with no change in each person's level of real spending. How does the response of aggregate real cash, M/P, depend on which case applies?

b. What should happen to the velocity of money as an economy develops? (Take a look at Figure 5.4 to see the history of velocity in the United States.) In answering, be sure to specify what happens to the interest rate, R, and the real cost of transacting between money and interest-bearing assets, γ/P.

5.12 The Denominations of Currency

Consider how people divide their holdings of currency between large bills (say, of $100 and over) versus small ones. How would the fraction of the value of currency that someone holds as large bills change with

a. an increase in the price level?

b. an increase in a person's real income?

c. an increase in the interest rate?

d. a greater incentive to avoid records of payments (for example, to evade taxes or to engage in criminal transactions)?

Given the results above, the facts for the United States are hard to understand. Namely, the fraction of currency held as large bills (denominations of $100 and over) stayed nearly constant—between 20 and 22%—from 1944 to 1970. Then the fraction rose to nearly 40% by 1982. What do you think explains these numbers?

CHAPTER 6

THE BASIC MARKET-CLEARING MODEL

Aggregate-Consistency Conditions and the Clearing of Markets

In Chapter 2, we discussed households' choices of work efforts, which determined their production of commodities. In this Robinson Crusoe environment with no possibilities for storing goods, production is equal to consumption for each household. In Chapters 3 and 4, we allowed people to buy and sell goods at the price P, and to borrow and lend at the interest rate R. With these market opportunities, a household can save or dissave, so that consumption and production need not be equal in every period. Here, the accumulation of saving over time determines a household's stock of financial assets, which can be held as money or bonds. Finally, by studying the demand for money in Chapter 5, we saw how people divide their assets between money and bonds.

During our discussion of a market economy in Chapters 3–5, we mentioned three conditions that must hold when we sum up over all households. First, because each dollar lent by someone on the credit market corresponds to a dollar borrowed by someone else, the aggregate stock of bonds, B_t, equals zero in every period. Second, since the stock of money does not change over time, the total that people hold in each period, M_t, equals the given quantity, M_0. Finally, since consumption is the only use for output in the present model, total production, Y_t, equals total consumption, C_t. We shall refer to the three conditions just mentioned as **aggregate-consistency conditions.**

How do we know that the sum totals of individuals' choices satisfy the three aggregate-consistency conditions? For example, on the credit market, each person thinks that he or she can borrow or lend any amount at the going interest rate R. For any particular value of the interest rate, there is no reason to think that the sum total of households' desired holding of bonds, B_t, would be zero. But then we have an inconsistency, because the total that people want to borrow does not equal the total that others want to lend. One way or another the credit market has to operate to balance the overall amounts of actual borrowing and lending. The classical solution is to assume that the interest rate adjusts so that the aggregates

123

of desired borrowing and lending correspond. This viewpoint is called the **market-clearing approach.** We determine the interest rate to be the value necessary to clear the credit market—that is, to balance total desired lending against total desired borrowing.

The market-clearing approach takes a similar view of the commodity market. Here, we have to ensure an equality between the aggregates of production and consumption. Thus, we assume that the price of commodities, P, adjusts to balance the total of desired production against the total of desired consumption.

Note that when the markets for commodities and credit clear—that is, when supply equals demand—no one finds themselves unable to buy or sell goods at the going price, or unable to extend or receive credit at the going interest rate. In other words, when markets clear, everyone can buy and sell as much as they want at the market-clearing prices.

Recall that each participant in the credit market regards the interest rate, R, as a given. Similarly, people take the price level, P, as a given in the commodity market. However, in the market-clearing approach, the aggregates of households' choices in the two markets determine the interest rate and the price level. Namely, these values must be such as to clear the two markets. Hence, the interest rate and the price level cannot be independent of the aggregate of people's desires to lend and borrow funds or to buy and sell commodities. But any individual's transactions are assumed to be a small fraction of the totals in either market. Therefore, as a very good approximation, each person can disregard the effects of his or her behavior on the market-clearing values of the interest rate and the price level. So we can continue to use the analyses of individual choices that we worked out in Chapters 3–5.

In this chapter we study how the interest rate and price level are determined in order to clear the markets for credit and commodities. We suggested above that the interest rate adjusts to clear the credit market, while the price level adjusts to clear the commodity market. However, we shall find it better to say that the interest rate and price level are determined together in order to clear both markets simultaneously. That is because a change in conditions in one place—say, in the commodity market—usually requires changes in both the price level and the interest rate. So, we shall concentrate on conditions for **general market clearing,** which is a position where the markets for credit and commodities both clear.

As mentioned before, we need some device to ensure that the three aggregate-consistency conditions hold. But why do we use the postulate of market clearing in order to ensure these conditions? It turns out in our model that this postulate amounts to assuming that private markets function to allocate resources efficiently. In particular, when the credit and commodity markets clear, it would not be possible to improve on any outcomes by matching potential borrowers and lenders or by bringing together potential buyers and sellers of goods. Cleared markets already accomplish all of these mutually advantageous trades. Thus, the assumption that markets clear is tied closely to the view that the individuals who participate in and organize markets—and who are guided by the pursuit of their own interests—end up generating efficient outcomes.

We could use some other concept, instead of market clearing, to ensure that the aggregate-consistency conditions hold. One alternative is the Keynesian model, where some markets do not clear in the sense of our concept of cleared markets. Rather, some prices are sticky and some rationing of quantities comes into play. (For example, people may be unable to sell all the goods or labor services that they desire at the going price.) It turns out also that outcomes are generally inefficient in the Keynesian model. In particular, some mutually advantageous trades do not take place. We shall explore this viewpoint in detail in Chapter 19. But the subtleties of Keynesian arguments cannot be appreciated without first understanding the workings of a market-clearing model. Therefore, it is best to begin by studying a framework where markets clear.

People often use the term, *equilibrium,* to signify market clearing. But because the concept of an equilibrium has been used in so many different ways in the economics literature, its meaning has become unclear. For example, some people think of the Keynesian model as a *disequilibrium* framework, while others view it as using a different concept of equilibrium. We shall avoid the terms equilibrium and disequilibrium, in our discussion. But let's emphasize two basic ideas that are central to our thinking about markets. First, we have some aggregate-consistency conditions, which must be satisfied by any reasonable model. Second, we assume in most of the analysis that the interest rate, price level, and so on, adjust in order to clear markets. That's how we satisfy the aggregate-consistency conditions in the market clearing model. We shall see later how the Keynesian model modifies the second idea, but not the first one.

Walras' Law of Markets

Consider again an individual who faces a given price level, P, and interest rate, R. Let's label as y_1^s the quantity of goods that the individual decides to produce and *supply* to the commodity market during period 1. Hence, by the term supply, we refer to the quantity that someone offers to sell at a particular price. Similarly, let c_1^d represent the quantity of goods that an individual offers to buy—or *demands*—from the commodity market. Finally, let b_1^d and m_1^d denote the person's planned stocks of financial assets for period 1—that is, b_1^d is the demand for bonds and m_1^d is the demand for money.

Now, suppose that someone carries over from period 0 the stocks of financial assets, b_0 and m_0. Then the budget constraint in real terms for period 1 is

$$y_1^s + b_0(1 + R)/P + m_0/P = c_1^d + b_1^d/P + m_1^d/P \qquad (6.1)$$

If we sum up equation (6.1) over all households, then we get the aggregate form of the budget constraint for period 1,

$$Y_1^s + B_0(1 + R)/P + M_0/P = C_1^d + B_1^d/P + M_1^d/P \qquad (6.2)$$

During period zero, we must have that every dollar lent corresponded to a dollar borrowed, so that $B_0 = 0$. Using this condition, we can simplify equation (6.2) to

$$Y_1^s + M_0/P = C_1^d + B_1^d/P + M_1^d/P \qquad (6.3)$$

Let's use equation (6.3) to see how the market-clearing model deals with the three aggregate-consistency conditions, which we mentioned before. For period 1, these conditions are

- $B_1^d = 0$—any dollar that someone wants to lend corresponds to a dollar that someone else wants to borrow,
- $M_1^d = M_0$—people willingly hold the outstanding stock of money, M_0, and
- $Y_1^s = C_1^d$—the total supply of goods equals the total demand for goods.

But look at equation (6.3). Suppose that the first two aggregate-consistency conditions hold—that is, $B_1^d = 0$ and $M_1^d = M_0$, then equation (6.3) guarantees that the third condition, $Y_1^s = C_1^d$, holds also. In fact, if any two of the three conditions hold, then the third one must hold. Thus, we have only to worry about satisfying two of the three conditions for aggregate consistency. The third one follows automatically from the aggregate form of households' budget constraints in equation (6.3). This result is called **Walras' Law of Markets,** in honor of the 19th-century French economist, Leon Walras, who pioneered the study of models under conditions of general market clearing. (Usually, economists refer to his analysis as *general equilibrium theory*.)

We shall obtain the same results regardless of which pair of aggregate-consistency conditions that we examine. Usually, macroeconomists look at the condition for clearing the commodity market, $Y_1^s = C_1^d$, and at the one for money to be willingly held, $M_1^d = M_0$. We shall find it convenient to follow this practice in our analysis. However, remember that the results do not change if we substitute for one of these conditions the condition that the credit market clear, $B_1^d = 0$.

Clearing of the Commodity Market

We want to ensure that the aggregate quantity of goods supplied, Y_1^s, equals the aggregate quantity of goods demanded, C_1^d. We refer here to the supply and demand for the current period, which is period 1. But it is convenient now to drop the time subscripts.

Our previous analysis pinpoints several variables that influence the aggregate supply and demand for commodities. These include the following:

- The interest rate, R—a higher rate implies intertemporal-substitution effects, which reduce current demand, C^d, and raise current supply, Y^s (by raising current work).
- Wealth effects from changes in the position of the production function—an increase in wealth raises demand, C^d, but lowers work effort. This decline in work offsets the direct effect from an improvement in the production function on the supply of goods, Y^s.
- Substitution effects from changes in the schedule for the marginal product of labor—an upward shift leads to an increase in supply, Y^s (because people work more), and an increase in demand, C^d.

We can write out the condition for clearing the commodity market during the current period as

$$Y^s(R, \ldots) = C^d(R, \ldots)$$
$$(+)(-)$$

$$(6.4)$$

The function Y^s refers to the aggregate supply of commodities, while the function C^d refers to the aggregate demand. We indicate explicitly only the effects of the interest rate in these functions. The omitted variables in the functions, denoted by . . . , include the wealth and substitutions effects that arise from changes in the production function.

Equation (6.4) deals with the summation over a large number of households. We would like to use this analysis even when households are not identical—for example, when they differ by productivity, age, tastes, initial assets, and so on. In some cases, the aggregation over different types of people will not cause major problems. For example, a change in the interest rate implies the same type of intertemporal-substitution effect for everyone. Similarly, we can handle readily shifts in the characteristics of the production functions when these shifts are similar for all households. However, some changes benefit some people and harm others. For instance, we discussed before how movements in the price level or the interest rate have positive or negative effects on wealth, depending on someone's status in the credit market. Thus, these types of changes shift the distribution of resources across households, without changing the aggregate value of these resources. Economists call these kinds of changes **distributional effects.** Typically, we have no presumption about how distributional effects influence the aggregates of commodities supplied or demanded. So, as is customary in macroeconomics, we assume (hope) that we can neglect distributional effects for the purposes of aggregate analysis.

Let's be clear about some variables that do not influence aggregate commodity supply and demand in equation (6.4). We discussed in Chapter 5 how the monetary terms enter into households' budget constraints. Specifically, these terms exert no aggregate wealth effect when the initial real balances, M_0/P, equal the quantity that people plan to hold in all future periods. Because this condition holds in our model, we do not incorporate real-balance terms into the functions in equation (6.4).

The aggregate quantity of bonds, B_0, is zero. Therefore, changes in the price level have no effect on the aggregate real value of these bonds. Hence, on this count, there is no aggregate wealth effect from changes in the price level. Remember that we also have no aggregate wealth effect from the monetary terms. Therefore, the price level does not appear at all in the condition for clearing the commodity market, equation (6.4).

We discussed some types of transaction costs in Chapter 5. Generally, there are some wealth and substitution effects associated with these transaction costs. But as mentioned in Chapter 5, we assume that these effects are small enough to neglect for most purposes. Hence, these effects are also absent from equation (6.4).

Finally, we demonstrated in Chapter 4 that changes in the interest rate, R, have no aggregate wealth effect. (A rise in the interest rate is good for people who

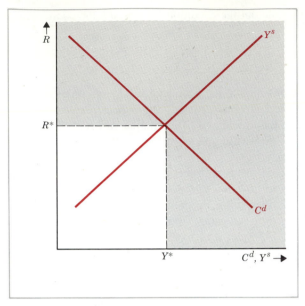

Figure 6.1 **Clearing of the Commodity Market**
Clearing of the commodity market, $C^d = Y^s$, occurs at the interest rate, R^*. At this point the level of aggregate output is $Y^* = C^*$.

are usually lenders, but correspondingly bad for those who are usually borrowers.) Therefore, the effects of the interest rate on aggregate supply and demand, which appear in equation (6.4), refer only to the intertemporal-substitution effects. For this reason, we know that a rise in the interest rate lowers current consumer demand, C^d, and raises current commodity supply, Y^s.

Because the interest rate has important influences on commodities supplied and demanded, we shall find it convenient to depict equation (6.4) graphically with the interest rate on the vertical axis. In Figure 6.1 we show that the interest rate has a positive effect on aggregate supply, Y^s, and a negative effect on aggregate demand, C^d. When the interest rate changes, the responses of supply and demand show up as movements along the curves in the figure. (We show the curves as straight lines only for convenience.)

The positions of the supply and demand curves in Figure 6.1 depend on the omitted elements, denoted by . . . , in equation (6.4). When any of these elements change, the effects on commodity supply and demand show up as shifts of the curves in the figure. Then, for given values of these elements, we can read off from the figure the value of the interest rate, R^*, which corresponds to clearing of the commodity market, $Y^s = C^d$. Generally, we use an asterisk to signal that the value that a variable takes, such as $R = R^*$, derives from a market-clearing condition. Notice from the figure that the market-clearing level of output is the quantity, $Y^* = C^*$.

Remember that each household's quantity of output, y, depends on the level of work, l, through the production function, $y = f(l)$. Here, we assume that we can use an aggregate form of this relation,

$$Y = F(L) \tag{6.5}$$

Notice that the aggregate production function connects the aggregate amount of work, L, to the aggregate quantity of output, Y. Therefore, once we know the market-clearing level of output Y^* from Figure 6.1, we can use equation (6.5) to compute the corresponding level of aggregate work effort, L^*.

The simple market-clearing diagram in Figure 6.1 turns out to be the central graphical tool for our subsequent study of macroeconomic disturbances. Even when we complicate the model, we shall be able to use a version of this diagram to derive the main results. Therefore, let's stress the basic ideas behind this diagram. First, a higher interest rate stimulates the desire to produce and sell goods today, but deters the desire to buy goods. Second, we determine the market-clearing values of the interest rate and the quantity of output by equating aggregate supply to aggregate demand.

The Demand for Money Equals the Quantity of Money

The second aggregate-consistency condition requires the initial stock of money, M_0, to equal the aggregate quantity demanded during period 1, M_1^d. For convenience, we again drop the time subscripts.

In Chapter 5, we derived a function for the aggregate demand for money. When expressed in real terms—that is, as M^d/P—this demand depends negatively on the interest rate, R, and positively on the real amount of spending, C. We also discussed some effects of the real transaction cost, γ/P, although we hold this element fixed for most of our analysis. Therefore, we can write the condition for money to be willingly held as

$$M/P = H(R,\ Y,\ \ldots) \tag{6.6}$$
$$(-)\ (+)$$

Note that the function, H, on the right side of equation (6.6) describes the demand for money in real terms, M^d/P. For convenience, we replace aggregate real expenditure, C, in this function by aggregate output, Y. (When the commodity market clears, we know that real expenditure, C, equals real output, Y.) The omitted terms, denoted by $\ldots$, include any effects on real money demanded other than the interest rate and the level of output. For example, the level of the real transaction cost, γ/P, enters here.

General Market Clearing

We want to determine the values of the interest rate, R^*, and the price level, P^*, that are consistent with the two aggregate-consistency conditions:

- the commodity market clears, as in Figure 6.1, and
- the total money stock is willingly held, as in equation (6.6).

Remember that these two conditions ensure that the credit market clears—that is, $B^d = 0$. We know that from Walras' Law of Markets. So we can refer to R^* and P^* as the general-market-clearing values of the interest rate and the price level.

We can readily see the basic workings of the model. To start with, the market-clearing diagram from Figure 6.1 determines the interest rate, R^*. Then we know also the levels of aggregate output and consumption, $Y^* = C^*$. Hence, we can substitute the values for R^* and Y^* into the money-demand function on the right side of equation (6.6). Then we know what real balances, M/P^*, must be on the left side of this equation. Finally, for a given nominal quantity of money, M, we can find the general-market-clearing value of the price level, P^*.

The procedure for solving the model is this simple because the price level does not appear in the condition for clearing the commodity market, equation (6.4). Or, to put things another way, changes in the price level do not shift the curves in the market-clearing diagram from Figure 6.1. Therefore, we do not have to know the market-clearing value of the price level, P^*, when we determine the interest rate, R^*. Rather, we can just look at the market-clearing diagram to find the interest rate, R^*. Then, conditional on this result, we can use equation (6.6) to solve out for the price level, P^*. But the best way to clarify the workings of the model is to work through some examples, which are of substantial interest for their own sake.

Analyzing Disturbances to the Economy

We begin by studying a variety of changes to the production function. As in some previous discussion, we distinguish temporary changes in production opportunities from permanent changes.

A Temporary Shift of the Production Function

We start with a temporary change to the production function—specifically, let's consider a shift that lasts only for the current period. We can think of bad weather that limits the production of coffee in Brazil, or political problems that reduce the output of agricultural commodities in Poland (if we regard that situation as temporary). Recently, people have called these types of disturbances "**supply shocks.**" For some reason, the term always refers to an adverse shock to the supply of goods. But there can also be temporary improvements to the production function. For example, there may be a bountiful harvest or a run of good luck in labor relations.

Consider first a purely parallel downward shift of the production function, as shown in Figure 6.2. This case is the simplest example of a supply shock. In particular, this type of shift does not alter the schedule for the marginal product of labor. Hence, there are no substitution effects from changes in the relative costs of consumption and leisure.

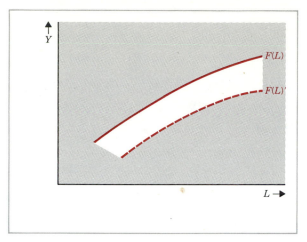

Figure 6.2 **A Parallel Downward Shift of the Production Function**
We examine here a parallel downward shift of the aggregate production function from $F(L)$ to $F(L)'$.

Effects on the Interest Rate and Output. One effect of the supply shock is that output decreases for a given level of work effort. On this count, the supply of goods, Y^s, falls.

Secondly, the disturbance reduces wealth. However, because the change is short-lived, the wealth effects will be small. So we find a small negative response of aggregate consumer demand, C^d, and a small positive response of aggregate work effort. The increase in work implies a rise in goods supplied, Y^s. But, since the wealth effect is weak, this increase offsets only a small part of the initial cutback in supply. Thus, there is a net decrease in aggregate supply, Y^s, which exceeds the small decline in aggregate demand, C^d.

We show the changes to the market-clearing diagram in Figure 6.3. Before the shift, the market clears at the interest rate R^*. Then the disturbance causes the aggregate supply curve to shift leftward from the one labeled Y^s to that labeled $(Y^s)'$. Also, the aggregate demand curve shifts leftward from the one marked C^d to that marked $(C^d)'$. As discussed before, the shift of the supply curve is larger than that of the demand curve. So we find a situation of **excess demand for commodities**—that is, $(C^d)' > (Y^s)'$—at the initial interest rate R^*.

The excess of goods demanded over those supplied means that—at the going interest rate—everybody would like to reduce their saving. That is because the worsening in the production function is temporary. As we know from before, individuals desire to take out most of their temporarily depressed income in the form of less current saving. But we know also that everybody cannot actually reduce their saving—in particular, aggregate saving must end up being zero. So the interest rate has to adjust to make the aggregate of people's desired saving conform to the economy's possibilities—namely, zero total saving. To put this

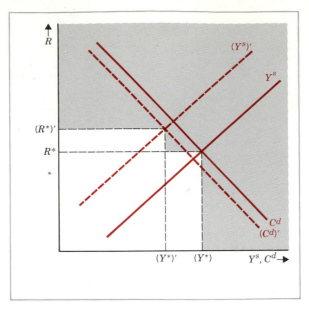

Figure 6.3 **Effect of a Temporary Downward Shift of the Production Function (a "Supply Shock") on the Commodity Market**
The temporary worsening of the production function lowers aggregate supply by more than demand. Therefore, clearing of the commodity market requires the interest rate to rise.

point another way, the interest rate must change in order to ensure the clearing of the commodity market.

We see from the market-clearing diagram in Figure 6.3 that the new interest rate, $(R^*)'$, exceeds the initial one, R^*. Thus, the rise in the interest rate eliminates people's desires to carry out negative aggregate saving. Equivalently, we see that the increase in the interest rate lowers consumer demand along the curve $(C^d)'$ and raises supply along the curve $(Y^s)'$. Note that, at the new interest rate $(R^*)'$, we again have clearing of the commodity market—that is, $(Y^s)' = (C^d)'$.

The new level of output, $(Y^*)'$, can be read off the intersection of the new supply and demand curves in Figure 6.3. Notice that the disturbance—the temporary worsening of the production function—leads to a fall in output. From the perspective of commodity demand, $(C^d)'$, it is clear that output must be lower. First, there is the decrease in wealth, which shifts the demand curve leftward. Then second, there is the increase in the interest rate, which reduces demand along the new curve, $(C^d)'$. So aggregate demand—and hence output, which equals demand—must decline overall.

From the standpoint of commodity supply, $(Y^s)'$, there is the initial leftward shift of the curve. Then the rise in the interest rate raises supply along the curve marked $(Y^s)'$. However, this increase in supply can only partially offset the initial decrease. This result follows since supply and demand are again equal at the new interest rate, $(R^*)'$, and we have just shown that demand is lower.

Effects on Work Effort. The forces that operate on work effort are closely related to those that affect consumer demand. In particular, the decline in wealth leads to more work and less leisure. Then the rise in the interest rate leads to an additional increase in current work, rather than leisure. So aggregate work effort rises, while aggregate leisure falls. This result makes sense because the disturbance does not change the terms on which people can transform leisure into consumption—that is, the schedule for labor's marginal product does not shift. So if the quantities of consumption and leisure change, we would expect them to change in the same direction. In the present example, the aggregates of consumption and leisure both decrease.

Overall, the supply shock leads to less output and consumption, but to more work. Recall from the analysis in Chapter 2 that we reach similar conclusions if we confront Robinson Crusoe with a downward shift in the production function. We might have expected some differences because people can use the credit market to borrow and lend in the present model, whereas Robinson Crusoe cannot borrow and lend. But the interest rate adjusts in the market economy to ensure that the aggregate of desired saving equals zero. Therefore, the typical person ends up saving zero, just like Robinson Crusoe. Accordingly, we also end up with similar predictions about the effects of a worsening in the production function on work effort, production, and consumption.

Effects on the Price Level. In order to determine the price level, we use the condition that all cash be willingly held. Recall that this condition is

$$M/P = H(R, Y, \ldots)$$
$$(-) (+)$$

We know that the disturbance lowers aggregate output and raises the interest rate. Both of these changes reduce the real demand for money, which appears on the right side of the equation. Further, for a given nominal quantity of money, M, real cash balances can decline only if the price level rises. Therefore, the disturbance means that the new price level, $(P*)'$, is higher than the initial one, $P*$.

We can use this analysis to understand the effects on the United States price level from the oil crises of the 1970s. Sharp increases in the price of oil, relative to that of other goods, occurred in 1973 and 1979. For two reasons, this disturbance resembles an adverse shock to production functions. First, oil is an important input to production. Therefore, a cutback in the supply of oil—as reflected in an increase in its relative price—tends to deter the production of other goods. Second, because the United States imports a lot of oil, the increase in oil's relative price means that the United States pays out more of its income to foreigners per unit of oil purchased. Therefore, for a given amount of work effort and production, the United States ends up with less income to spend on consumption.

Overall, the oil crises created adverse shifts of the type shown in Figure 6.3. (At least, these changes apply if people perceive the increase in oil's relative price to be temporary.) Then, we find again that the real demand for money declines. Hence, for a given nominal quantity of money, the price level increases.

We should not conclude that an increase in the relative price of any commodity leads to a rise in the general price level. By the general price level, we mean the number of dollars that it takes to buy a typical market basket of goods. Obviously, this general level of prices can move up or down while some relative prices increase and some decrease.

As an example, consider a poor harvest of grain that affects foreign countries, but not the United States. The price of grain rises, relative to the prices of other goods. But as a large exporter of grain, the United States gains. From the standpoint of the United States, the disturbance amounts to a temporary upward shift of the production function. Hence, we end up with an increase in real money demanded, which leads to a decline in the general level of prices in the United States.

The Dynamics of Changes in the Interest Rate and the Price Level. We have figured out how a particular disturbance, such as a temporary worsening of the production function, changes the general-market-clearing values of the interest rate and the price level. In particular, we know that the aggregate-consistency conditions that we specified before will not be satisfied unless we get to the new position of general market clearing. But we have not really explained how the interest rate and the price level move from one position of market clearing to another. That is, we have not clarified the pressures that lead in our example to increases in the interest rate and the price level.

We mentioned before that a temporary worsening of the production function makes everyone want to save less at the initial interest rate. Consequently, there are less offers to lend funds than there are offers to borrow. Therefore, we anticipate that the interest rate on loans will be bid up. This observation is consistent with the increase in the market-clearing value of the interest rate.

We noted also that the disturbance creates excess demand for commodities. Hence, we can think of suppliers as raising the price, P, at which they are willing to sell. This response accords with the increase in the market-clearing value of the price level.

The above sketch suggests that some plausible dynamic stories of market pressures would lead the economy toward the new position of general market clearing. Actually, some elaborate models of these dynamics have been constructed. But it remains true that economists do not understand these dynamics very well. For one thing, we have trouble explaining how people behave along the way while the aggregate-consistency conditions are not satisfied.[1] But if we look only at positions where these conditions hold, then we limit our attention to situations of general market clearing.

---

[1]Walras thought of an auctioneer who adjusted various prices along the lines of our dynamic sketch. But no trades were actually concluded until a position of general market clearing was achieved. With this view we do not have to worry much about how people behave in situations where the markets do not clear. Of course, the device of an auctioneer who adjusts prices should not be taken literally for most markets. Rather, the idea is that buyers and sellers will manage quickly to establish prices that accord with the aggregate-consistency conditions—that is, which clear markets.

In the subsequent analysis we focus on the characteristics of market-clearing positions. Along the way, we sometimes provide dynamic stories to motivate the changes in the price level and the interest rate. But these stories should be treated with caution, since they do not correspond to fully worked-out models. Our main propositions about the real world come from seeing how particular disturbances influence the conditions for general market clearing. Often, this method provides answers that accord well with real-world observations. So from an empirical standpoint, the lack of a formal dynamic theory of price changes may not be that much of a shortcoming.

Summarizing the Results for the Case of a Harvest Failure. Let's review our findings by seeing how they apply to the case of a harvest failure in the United States. The previous example fits this situation because a harvest failure represents a temporary setback in production. Hence, the conclusions are that a harvest failure leads to cutbacks in output and consumption, but to a rise in work effort. The interest rate and the price level both rise.

Consider why the interest rate rises. Because everyone regards the fall in output as temporary, they would like to borrow funds in order to maintain their levels of consumption. Since not everyone can borrow at once, the interest rate increases in order to restore the balance between desired borrowing and lending. Anyone who lends funds in this depressed situation receives a premium in terms of a high rate of interest.

Consider why the price level rises. The decline in current consumption and output, combined with the rise in the interest rate, reduce the demand for real cash balances. But there is a given amount of nominal cash, M, which people must somehow be induced to hold. Here, the price level rises in order to equate actual to desired real cash balances.

Including a Shift to the Schedule for the Marginal Product of Labor. We have just studied an example where the production function shifted downward in a parallel fashion. But we are usually interested in situations where the cutback in the production function involves also a worsening in the schedule for labor's marginal product. For example, there may be a proportional downward shift in the production function, as shown in Figure 6.4. Here, the marginal product of labor falls at any given level of work effort. But we assume again that the change to the production function applies only for the current period—that is, people perceive the disturbance to be temporary.

We still have the effects on the market-clearing diagram that appear in Figure 6.3. However, we have to add some new effects, which concern the decrease in labor's marginal product. Because of this lower productivity, people want to work less now in order to shift from consumption to leisure. Also, because the worsening in production opportunities is temporary, people want to shift toward current leisure and away from future leisure and consumption. That is, an intertemporal-substitution effect applies. Overall, there is a strong incentive to cut current work, L, and a weaker incentive to reduce current demand for goods, C^d. Note that the decrease in current work means a strong cutback of current goods supplied, Y^s.

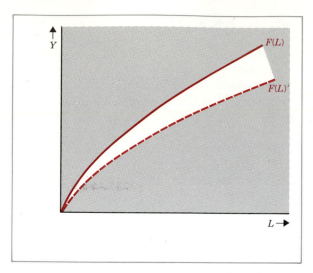

Figure 6.4 A Proportional Downward Shift of the Production Function
We examine here a proportional downward shift of the production function from $F(L)$ to $F(L)'$.

In order to incorporate the new effects, we have to make two modifications to the market-clearing diagram in Figure 6.3. First, we add a large leftward shift to the supply curve, which is labeled $(Y^s)'$. Second, we add a small leftward shift to the demand curve, which is labeled $(C^d)'$. Notice, however, that these changes do not alter the general configuration of the curves shown in Figure 6.3. Hence, we still conclude that output and consumption decrease, while the interest rate rises. But because of the fall in the schedule for labor's marginal product, these effects are all larger than before.

The only qualitative difference in the results concerns the behavior of work effort. We found before that work effort increased. Recall that this response reflected the decrease in wealth and the increase in the interest rate. But now people want to work less because of the fall in the marginal product of labor (MPL). Overall, it is now uncertain whether work effort rises or falls on net.

Think of this last result again in terms of a harvest failure. People want to work a lot today because output is low (the wealth effect) and because the interest rate is high (an intertemporal-substitution effect). But if the harvest failure makes additional labor today relatively unproductive, then people prefer to take leisure instead of work. Overall, it is unclear whether the net of these forces leads people to work more or less.

When we look at the condition that money be willingly held, equation (6.6), we again find that the disturbance raises the price level. However, because output and the interest rate move by more than before, we also conclude that the size of the increase in the price level is greater than previously.

A Permanent Shift in the Production Function

Let's return to the case of a parallel downward shift in the production function, where labor's marginal product does not change. But suppose now that this change is permanent, rather than lasting just for one period.

The difference from the previous case concerns the size of the wealth effects. Now, there is a strong negative effect on consumer demand. Also, there is a strong positive effect on work effort, so that the supply of goods falls by less than before. Recall that the permanent income hypothesis implies that a permanent shift in the production function has little effect on desired saving. That is, if the interest rate does not change, then the decreases in commodities supplied and demanded would now be roughly equal. We use the market-clearing diagram in Figure 6.5 to illustrate this case. Notice that the leftward shifts to the supply and demand curves are the same. Therefore, commodity supply still equals commodity demand at the initial interest rate, R^*. It follows that the new market-clearing interest rate, $(R^*)'$, equals the original one.

We again have declines in output and consumption. Note that, since the interest rate does not change, the reduction in consumer demand now reflects only the decrease in wealth. Similarly, the fall in wealth implies an increase in work effort.

Since output declines and the interest rate does not change, we know that real

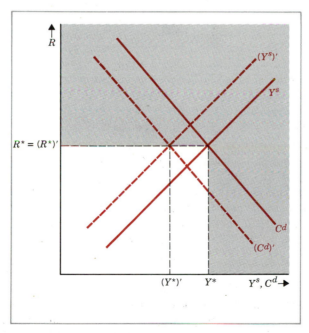

Figure 6.5 Effect of a Permanent Downward Shift of the Production Function on the Commodity Market

The permanent worsening of the production function reduces aggregate supply and demand by comparable amounts. Therefore, the interest rate does not change.

money demanded declines. Therefore, for a given quantity of money, the price level rises. Overall then, the results for output and the price level resemble those that we found before when the change in the production function was temporary.

The major difference in results is the rise in the interest rate when the worsening of the production function is temporary, but no change when the worsening is permanent. The interest rate is a signal that tells people the cost of using resources now rather than later. Specifically, a high interest rate attaches a high cost to current consumption and leisure, relative to future consumption and leisure. When the production function worsens temporarily, there is a scarcity of goods today relative to the future, so a high interest rate makes sense, because it makes people take today's relative scarcity into account when they decide how much to consume and work. On the other hand, a permanent worsening of the production function means that less goods are available at all times. In particular, there is no change in today's position relative to tomorrow's. The interest rate does not change because there is no change in the cost of using resources today rather than tomorrow.

The results tell us something important about movements in interest rates. Mostly, we expect interest rates to change when there are economic disturbances that alter present conditions relative to prospective ones. Harvest failures, natural disasters, and major strikes fall into this category. As we shall stress in a later chapter, war may be empirically the most important example of a disturbance that has a temporary effect on the overall economy. On the other hand, for disturbances that have permanent effects, we do not predict large changes in interest rates. (*Warning:* the analysis has so far left out the important influence of inflation on interest rates. We cover this topic in the next chapter.)

As before, we can modify the analysis to include a downward shift to the schedule for the marginal product of labor. Then we find that this extension does not change most of the results. In particular, we still predict that a permanent worsening of the production function has no effect on the interest rate. However, as in the analysis of a temporary shift, we now find that the response of work effort is ambiguous. Specifically, the reduction in wealth motivates more work, while the fall in labor's marginal product motivates less work. Recall that we discussed the essence of this case in Chapter 2, where we considered the influence of economic development on hours worked. However, that earlier analysis dealt with upward shifts to the production function, rather than downward shifts. Economic development leads to less hours worked over time if the wealth effect dominates over the substitution effect from higher productivity.

Changes in the Stock of Money

In our previous examples, we deduced the change in the price level by examining the condition that money be willingly held. Then we found that changes in output and the interest rate altered the demand for real cash balances. Since the quantity of nominal money, M, is constant, the price level changes in order to equate actual to desired real cash balances. Essentially, we have dealt here with changes in the demand for money, while holding fixed the aggregate supply of nominal money, M.

Many economists have argued that changes in the quantity of money, M, are empirically the major source of variations in the price level. In order to study this linkage, we have to allow for changes in the stock of money. Therefore, we now construct a simple device that enables us to study these changes.

Think of a case where the initial stock of money, M_0, and all subsequent stocks, M_t for $t > 0$, rise by the same amount. So there is a once-and-for-all increase in the quantity of money, which occurs sometime before period 0. Suppose at this earlier date, that the government prints up the extra money and gives it to people. More formally, the government uses the money to finance transfer payments to households. One possibility is that everybody receives the same number of dollars as gifts from the government.

We assume for the present analysis that the government will never repeat this odd business of printing money and giving it to people. So nobody expects to receive any more transfer payments. Therefore, we do not have to modify the analysis of households' budget constraints over an infinite horizon. Remember that this analysis deals with the receipts and expenditures that arise after period 0.

The condition for clearing the commodity market, $Y^s(R, \ldots) = C^d(R, \ldots)$, does not involve the level of the money stock, M_0. Therefore, we know right away that the change in the number of dollar bills outstanding does not change the market-clearing value for the interest rate, R^*. Further, there are no effects on the levels of output and consumption, $Y^* = C^*$.

Consider again the condition that the money stock be willingly held,

$$M_0/P = H(R, Y, \ldots)$$
$$(-)\,(+)$$

The present disturbance is an increase in the aggregate quantity of money, M_0. Since the interest rate and the level of aggregate output do not change, there is no change in the real demand for money, which appears on the right side of the equation. Therefore, in order for real balances, M_0/P, to stay constant, the price level must rise by the same proportion as the stock of money.

As before, we can outline a dynamic story that makes plausible the increase in the price level. At the initial level of prices, people have more real balances, M_0/P, than they wish to hold. So everyone tries to spend their excess cash, partly on goods and leisure and partly on bonds. The positive effect on goods and leisure is the real-balance effect. Remember that this effect operates when—as in the present case—people have more real cash than they plan to hold in the future. Then, because the real-balance effect raises the aggregate demand for goods above the supply, there is upward pressure on the price level.[2] Further, this increase in prices continues until the outstanding amount of real cash, M_0/P, is willingly held.

---

[2]We noted that people also attempt to spend some of their excess cash on bonds. This increase in the demand for bonds tends to drive down the interest rate. A lower interest rate leads, in turn, to excess demand for commodities. Therefore, this channel reinforces the pressure toward higher prices. Note, however, that the interest rate does not change when we get to the new position of general market clearing.

At this point, people no longer have excess cash that they wish to spend and there is no further pressure for the price level to rise.

The Neutrality of Money. Our results exhibit an important property that is called the **neutrality of money.** Once-and-for-all changes in the aggregate quantity of money affect nominal variables, but leave real variables unchanged. For example, if we double the money stock, then we double the price level, P, the nominal values of production and consumption, $PY = PC$, and so on. But we leave unchanged real variables like output and consumption, $Y = C$, real cash balances, M_0/P, and the quantity of work, L. Also, we do not affect the interest rate, R. Note that the interest rate is a real variable, which tells us the cost of buying consumption or leisure today, rather than tomorrow. In later chapters, we explore further aspects of monetary neutrality.

The Quantity Theory of Money and Monetarism. The **quantity theory of money** refers to a body of thinking about the relation between money and prices. This viewpoint goes back hundreds of years, with some of the most interesting statements coming from David Hume, Henry Thornton, and Irving Fisher.[3] There are two common elements in these analyses. First, changes in the quantity of money have a positive effect on the general price level. Second, as an empirical matter, movements in the money stock account for the major longer-run movements in the price level.

Some writers refined the quantity theory to apply to changes in the stock of money relative to changes in the quantity of goods on which people could spend their money. The last element corresponds in our model to the total output of goods, Y. But output is only one variable that affects the demand for real cash balances. So to go further, some quantity theorists stress that the price level increases when the quantity of money rises in relation to the real balances that people want to hold. Empirically then, most movements in prices reflect movements in money if the variations in the nominal quantity of money are much greater than the fluctuations in the demand for real cash balances.[4]

Often, economists identify the quantity theory of money with the statement that monetary changes are neutral. Hence, we have our previous proposition that shifts in the stock of money have proportional effects on the price level, but no effects on real variables. Many quantity theorists regard this hypothesis as accurate in the long run, but not for short-run fluctuations in money. In particular, the

---

[3]David Hume, "Of Money" (1752), in Eugene Rotwein, ed., *David Hume—Writings on Economics,* University of Wisconsin Press, Madison, 1970; Henry Thornton, *An Enquiry into the Nature and Effects of the Paper Credit of Great Britain* (1802), Augustus Kelley, Fairfield, New Jersey, 1978; and Irving Fisher, *The Purchasing Power of Money,* 2nd ed. (1922), Augustus Kelley, New York, 1963, Chapters 2 and 8.

[4]Milton Friedman stresses the stability of the demand for money as the hallmark of a quantity theorist. See his "The Quantity Theory of Money—a Restatement," in M. Friedman, ed., *Studies in the Quantity Theory of Money,* University of Chicago Press, Chicago, 1956, p. 16.

quantity theory allows for the possibility that fluctuations in money have short-run effects on real economic activity. So far, our model does not allow for these short-run real effects of money. But we shall reexamine this possibility in later chapters.

More recently, people use the term, **monetarism,** to describe a school of thought that is similar to the quantity theory of money. As with most terms that are popular in the newspapers, this one has been used in contradictory ways. But it is clear that monetarists regard the quantity of money as the major determinant of the price level, especially over the long run. Thus, monetarists stress control of the money supply as the central requirement for price stability. Also, monetarism allows for important short-term effects of monetary fluctuations on real economic activity. But monetarists typically regard these effects as unpredictable—therefore, they argue that stable money is also the best policy for avoiding erratic movements of the real variables.

Changes in the Demand for Money

As mentioned, we can determine the price level by looking at the condition that money be willingly held,

$$M_0/P = H(R, Y, \ldots).$$
$$(-)\ (+)$$

So, the price level changes if we shift the aggregate nominal quantity of money, M_0, relative to the aggregate real demand for money, $H(R, Y, \ldots)$. We have just studied the effects of changes in the money stock, M_0. Here, shifts in money change the price level in the same direction. Earlier, we examined disturbances to the production function, which ended up changing output, Y, or the interest rate, R. With the money stock held constant, these changes affect the price level by shifting the real demand for money. Notice that the price level moves in the direction opposite to changes in the demand for money.

An economy may experience changes in the demand for money that do not reflect movements in output or the interest rate. For example, in our model of the demand for money from Chapter 5, there may be changes in the cost of transacting between interest-bearing assets and money. These costs have declined significantly in recent years with the development of money-market funds, automated bank tellers, and other financial innovations. We predict that these types of changes reduce the demand for real cash balances, or equivalently, that they raise the velocity of money. That is, people reduce their desired holdings of cash relative to the volume of their expenditures.

Suppose that the real demand function for money, $H(R, Y, \ldots)$, shifts downward. Then, for a given nominal quantity of money, M_0, the price level must rise in order to maintain equality between actual and desired real cash balances. Hence, we predict that the financial innovations of recent years—which reduced the demand for real cash balances—raise the price level for a given behavior of the nominal stock of money. Notice also that these innovations lead to a lower level of real balances, M_0/P.

In our model the change in the real demand for money—and the resulting change in real balances—do not influence the condition for clearing the commodity market, $Y^s(R, \ldots) = C^d(R, \ldots)$. Therefore, there are no changes in the market-clearing values of output or the interest rate. However, this conclusion depends on our earlier approximation, which neglected the role of transaction costs in households' decisions for work effort, consumption, and saving. In particular, we neglected the wealth effects from changes in transaction costs. More generally, if we take account of the resources that people use up in transacting, then financial innovations would affect real variables like output and the interest rate.[5] However, we continue to assume that these effects are small enough to neglect for present purposes.

Summary

Any macroeconomic model must satisfy some conditions for aggregate consistency. In our context these are first, any dollar that someone lends corresponds to a dollar that someone else borrows; second, people hold the outstanding stock of money; and third, total output equals total consumption. Here, we use the idea of market clearing to satisfy these conditions. Specifically, we require that first, the aggregate demand for bonds is zero; second, that the demand for money equal the amount outstanding; and third, the supply of goods equals the demand. But because of the underlying budget constraints of households, these three conditions are not independent. In particular, Walras' Law says that we can work with any two of the three conditions. Here, we focus on the condition for clearing the commodity market—namely, that the supply of goods equals the demand—and on the condition that the stock of money be willingly held.

We construct a market-clearing diagram to show how the condition for clearing the commodity market determines the interest rate and the level of output. Then the condition that money be willingly held determines the price level for a given nominal quantity of money. We use this apparatus to analyze various shifts to the production function. For example, a supply shock—which we model as a temporary downward shift in the production function—lowers output and raises the interest rate and the price level. The effects on work are ambiguous, because the wealth and substitution effects tend to be offsetting. When the adverse shift to the production function is permanent, rather than temporary, the main difference is that the interest rate does not increase. That's because a higher interest rate signals the scarcity of goods today relative to later. When things get permanently worse, there is no reason for the interest rate to change.

Shifts in the nominal quantity of money are neutral in our model. Specifically, the price level changes in the same proportion as money, but no real variables

---

[5]The change in the nominal stock of money, M_0, is different. In this case, people end up holding the same real balances, M_0/P, and incurring the same real flow of transaction costs. Hence, the change in the money stock is neutral even if we take account of the resources used up in transacting.

change. Finally, if we neglect transaction costs, then shifts to the demand for money do not influence any real variables, except for the quantity of real cash balances. But the price level falls when the real demand for money increases.

Important Terms and Concepts

aggregate-consistency conditions	excess demand
market-clearing approach	excess supply
Walras' Law of Markets	neutrality of money
distributional effects	quantity theory of money
supply shock	monetarism

QUESTIONS AND PROBLEMS

Mainly for Review

6.1 How are transactions in different markets, such as consumption and borrowing, linked in individual budget constraints? How does Walras' Law show that this linkage carries over to the markets as a whole?

6.2 How does a change in (a) the interest rate, (b) wealth, and (c) the production function affect the aggregate demand and supply of commodities? Describe the effects graphically, making sure to distinguish between *shifts in,* and *movements along,* the demand and supply curves.

6.3 Why isn't a change in the price level effective in reducing excess demand or supply in the commodity market? Explain how a change in the price level serves to ensure the condition that the outstanding quantity of money is held willingly.

6.4 Consider a parallel shift in the production function that allows the economy as a whole to enjoy more leisure and still get more income, i.e., at the initial interest rate there is an increase (shift) in the aggregate supply of commodities. Use a graph to convince yourself that
  a. If consumption shifts by an equivalent amount, there is no change in the interest rate.
  b. If consumption shifts by a smaller amount, there is a decline in the interest rate.

6.5 Describe your results in question 6.4 in terms of the marginal propensity to consume. Which of the two possibilities is likely to hold when the shift in the production function is temporary?

6.6 What is meant by the neutrality of money? Explain its implications for the popular notion that an increase in the quantity of money will reduce the interest rate.

6.7 Suppose there is a decline in the transaction cost of converting financial assets to money. Describe its effect on (a) the price level, (b) the real quantity of money, and (c) velocity. Do these effects contradict the neutrality of monetary changes?

Problems for Discussion

6.8 Walras' Law of Markets

a. Show how to derive Walras' Law of Markets (equation [6.3]) by using the households' budget constraints.

b. We seem to have three independent conditions for aggregate consistency: zero aggregate demand for bonds, $B_1^d = 0$; the money stock is willingly held, $M_0 = M_1^d$; and equality between commodities supplied and demanded, $Y_1^s = C_1^d$. Walras' Law says that only two of these conditions are independent. Explain this result.

c. How do the number of independent conditions for aggregate consistency compare with the number of market prices that we have to determine in the model? By the term *market prices,* we mean to include both the price level, P, and the interest rate, R. That is, the interest rate is the price of credit.

d. Write out Walras' Law in the form of a sum of aggregate excess demands, $C^d - Y^s$, $M_1^d/P - M_0/P$, and B_1^d/P. What does the law say in this form?

6.9 Aggregate-Consistency Conditions for Robinson Crusoe

We discussed several conditions for aggregate consistency in this chapter. These conditions arise because we have many individuals who come together to trade at marketplaces for commodities and credit. We did not have these markets in Chapter 2, where we discussed the behavior of an isolated individual, such as Robinson Crusoe.

How would you think about aggregate-consistency conditions for Robinson Crusoe? What parallels and differences are there with the conditions that arise in the present chapter?

6.10 Effects of a Change in Population

Assume a one-time decrease in population—that is, the number of households— possibly caused by an onset of plague or a sudden out-migration. The people who left are the same as those who remain in terms of productivity and tastes. The aggregate quantity of money does not change.

What happens to the values of aggregate output, Y, work effort, L, the interest rate, R, and the price level, P?

6.11 Effects of a Change in the Willingness to Work

Suppose (in a magical, unexplained fashion) that all households change their preferences to favor consumption over leisure. That is, people raise their willingness to work. Assume that no change occurs in preferences for expenditures now versus later, so that aggregate desired saving does not change at the initial interest rate.

What happens to the values of aggregate output, Y, work effort, L, the interest rate, R, and the price level, P?

Can you think of some real-world events that might raise everybody's willingness to work?

Note: We will be in trouble if we permit unrestricted fluctuations in preferences. A basic strength of the economic approach—and the basis for forming hypotheses that we can conceivably reject from observed data—is the assumption of stable tastes. Then we can analyze changes to production possibilities and other disturbances in terms of wealth and substitution effects, as we did in the text. In this manner, we end up with predictable influences on observed variables, such as output and the price level. But if tastes are unstable, then we can reconcile any observed behavior by assuming the appropriate shift in unobservable preferences. This capacity for explaining all data means that the model has no predictive value. Also, unaccountable shifts in preferences are more plausible for an individual, rather than for the aggregate of households. Usually, there is no good reason for everyone to become more eager to work precisely at the same time.

6.12 Effects of a Shift in the Rate of Time Preference

Suppose that all households increase their preference for current expenditures over future expenditures. That is, in terms of the language that we used in Chapter 4, there is an increase in the utility rate of time preference, ρ.

What happens to the values of aggregate output, Y, work effort, L, the interest rate, R, and the price level, P?

(The note attached to problem 6.11 applies also to the change in tastes that we assumed in this problem.)

6.13 Temporary Changes in the Interest Rate

Consider the market-clearing diagram in Figure 6.3, which deals with a temporary worsening of the production function. Recall that the interest rate rises from its initial value, R^*, to the higher value, $(R^*)'$. But because the disturbance is temporary, this effect on the interest rate will also be temporary. That is, we would expect the interest rate for later periods to return to the initial value, R^*.

In Chapter 4 we distinguished temporary from permanent changes in the interest rate. Specifically, the intertemporal-substitution effects are weaker when the change in the interest rate is temporary, rather than permanent. How would we use these results for the case shown in Figure 6.3? That is, how do the results change when we recognize that the change in the interest rate is temporary?

6.14 Temporary Changes in the Price Level

Consider again the analysis of a temporary worsening of the production function. We showed that the price level rises from its initial value, P^*, to a higher value, $(P^*)'$. But since the disturbance is temporary, we expect the price level to return in later periods to the initial value, P^*. At least, this should happen if nothing else changes, including the quantity of money.

So far, the analysis assumes that people expect the price level to remain constant over time. But we just showed that the current price level is above its expected future values when there is a temporary worsening of the production function. Think about how to modify the analysis to take account of expected future changes in the price level. (Do not spend too much time on this problem, since we shall study this topic in detail in the next chapter.)

6.15 **Consumption, Saving and the Interest Rate** (optional)

According to the theory, an increase in the interest rate motivates people to reduce current consumption, relative to current income. Correspondingly, people increase current saving. Yet although a temporary downward shift in the production function leads to an increase in the interest rate, it does not lead to any change in the ratio of aggregate consumption to aggregate income (which equals one in this model). Also, there is no change in aggregate saving, which equals zero.

a. Explain these results.

b. Researchers often attempt to estimate the effects of a change in the interest rate on an individual's choices of consumption and saving. Many studies look at the relation between the interest rate and either the ratio of aggregate consumption to aggregate income or the amount of aggregate saving. What does the theory predict for this relation? Why does it not reveal the effect of a change in the interest rate on an individual's choices of consumption and saving?

c. The theory says that an increase in the interest rate motivates people to raise next period's consumption, c_{t+1}, relative to this period's, c_t. Suppose that we look at the relation of the interest rate, R_t, to the ratio of aggregate consumptions, C_{t+1}/C_t. Does this relation reveal something about the behavior of individuals?

d. Suppose that we want to use aggregate data to figure out the effects of the interest rate on an individual's choices of consumption and saving. What do the answers to this question suggest that we should look at?

6.16 **The Dynamics of Changes in the Price Level**

In the text, we examined a case where the real demand for money declined. Then the price level increased, but the interest rate did not change.

a. Outline a dynamic story that describes the pressures for the price level to rise.

b. Does the interest rate stay fixed or move around while the price level adjusts in part (a)?

c. Can you tell a story where the price level jumps immediately to its new market-clearing position, rather than adjusting gradually in accordance with the sketch in part (a)?

6.17 **A Currency Reform**

Suppose that the government replaces the existing monetary unit with a new one. For example, the United States might shift from the old dollar to the Reagan dollar, which equals 10 old dollars. People can exchange their old currency for the new one at a ratio of 10 to 1. Also, any contracts that were written in terms of old dollars are converted at the ratio of 10 to 1 into Reagan dollars.

a. What happens to the price level and the interest rate?

b. What happens to the quantities of output, consumption, and work effort?

c. Do the results exhibit the neutrality of money?

6.18 **Temporary versus Permanent Changes of the Production Function** (optional)

Consider the parallel downward shift to the production function which is shown in Figure 6.2. This type of change does not affect the schedule for labor's marginal product. Suppose first that this change is permanent.

a. We dealt with this type of disturbance for an isolated individual, Robinson

Crusoe, in Chapter 2. We found that Crusoe reduced output and consumption, but raised work effort. How do these results compare with those we obtained in the present chapter, which includes markets for commodities and credit? Think of the typical or representative household: Does that household's responses of output, consumption, and work effort differ from those of Robinson Crusoe?

b. Suppose now that the change to the production function is temporary. Compare again Robinson Crusoe's responses of output, consumption, and work effort with those of the typical household in the model from the present chapter.

c. For Robinson Crusoe, how do the responses of output, consumption, and work effort depend on whether the improvement to the production function is temporary or permanent? (Problem 2.9 in Chapter 2 deals with this matter.)

d. Put together the results from parts (a), (b), and (c). They tell us how to compare temporary and permanent changes to the production function for the model in the present chapter, which includes markets for commodities and credit. How do the responses of output, consumption, and work effort for the typical household depend on whether the change to the production function is permanent or temporary?

PART II

INFLATION

CHAPTER 7
MONEY, INFLATION, AND INTEREST RATES

So far, we have simplified the analysis by holding fixed the general price level, P. But this assumption conflicts with real-world experience, especially in recent years. These days the general level of prices tends to rise over time—that is, there tends to be **inflation.** By inflation, we mean a continuing upward movement in the general price level, P. We begin the study of inflation in this chapter, and continue it in the next chapter.

The theoretical analysis suggests some possible sources of inflation. In order to sort out the possibilities, we shall find it convenient to think about the condition that all money be willingly held

$$M/P = H(R, Y, \ldots) \atop (-)\ (+)$$
(7.1)

One way for the price level to increase is through a downward movement in the real demand for money. For example, there can be a permanent downward shift in the production function, which lowers aggregate output, Y. But notice that a single disturbance of this type creates a single increase in the price level, rather than a continuing series of increases in prices. In order to generate inflation along this line, we would need a succession of downward shifts to the production function. There is no doubt that adverse shocks to the production function—such as oil crises, harvest failures, strikes, and epidemics—can influence the general level of prices over short periods. But there is no evidence that these forces can account for inflation in the sense of persistent rises in prices. In fact, the typical pattern in most countries is one of growing output. Since this growth raises the real demand for money, we predict that prices would fall over time if the nominal stock of money, M, did not change.

There can also be reductions in the real demand for money that reflect increasing financial sophistication. For example, in recent years many countries have developed financial instruments and procedures that make it easier for people to economize on cash. In the United States in the post-World War II period, this factor has led to a downward trend in the real demand for money. However, this

151

element can account only for a small amount of inflation—something like 1–2% per year is a reasonable estimate. Therefore, we cannot use this idea to explain the persistently high rates of inflation that have occurred since the late 1960s.

The remaining suggestion from the previous analysis is a link between inflation and continuing increases in the quantity of paper money, M. At an empirical level it is clear first, that the quantity of money often grows at a high rate over long periods of time, and second, that the **rates of monetary growth** differ substantially across countries and across time periods for a single country. Therefore, monetary growth is a good candidate as a source of inflation.

Cross-Country Data on Inflation and Monetary Growth

In order to assess the role of money as a source of inflation, let's examine some data. Table 7.1 shows the experiences of 83 countries during the post-World War II period. This table reports the average growth rates of an index of consumer prices and of money, which we define as hand-to-hand currency. (The results are similar if we use the broader monetary aggregate, $M1$, which includes checkable deposits. However, because of differences in the nature of financial institutions, the meaning of $M1$ varies more over countries than does that of currency.) The table arranges the countries in descending order with respect to their average rates of inflation. Note the following:

- The average growth rates of prices and money are positive for all countries over the post-World War II period.
- The average growth rates are typically high. For example, the median inflation rate for the 83 countries is 6.2% per year, with 17 of them exceeding 10%. For the average growth rate of currency, the median is 11.4% per year, with 50 of the countries above 10%.
- There is a broad cross-sectional range for the average growth rates of prices and money. The average inflation rates vary from 89% for Chile, 73% for Argentina, and 42% for Uruguay, to about 3% for Venezuela, West Germany, Switzerland, and a few other countries. The rate for the United States is 3.8%. Notice that the growth rates of currency have a comparable range, varying from 97% for Chile, 70% for Argentina, and 42% for Uruguay, to about 5% for the United States, Belgium, and Switzerland.
- The average growth rate of currency exceeds that of prices in almost all cases. That is, growing real cash balances is typical in the post-World War II period. The median growth rate of real currency across the countries is 4.2% per year.[1]
- Most significantly, there is a strong positive association across countries between the average rates of price change and the average rates of monetary growth.

---

[1] For the real stock of $M1$, the comparable figure is 5.0% per year.

Table 7.1 Growth Rates of Prices, Money, and Output for 83 Countries in the Post-World War II Period (Arranged by Decreasing Order of the Inflation Rate)

Country	ΔP	ΔM (Currency)	$\Delta M - \Delta P$	ΔY	Time Span
Chile	89.1	97.1	8.0	2.9	1970–79
Argentina	72.8	70.2	−2.6	3.1	1969–79
Uruguay	42.2	41.5	−0.7	2.1	1960–79
Brazil	29.9	33.2	3.3	8.6	1963–79
Zaire	27.7	18.8	−8.9	4.8	1963–79
Bolivia	22.7	26.8	4.1	3.9	1950–79
Turkey	21.0	24.3	3.3	6.2	1968–78
Peru	16.1	20.7	4.6	4.5	1960–79
Ghana	15.4	15.2	−0.2	2.1	1959–77
Israel	15.1	18.3	3.2	8.0	1950–79
Korea (S.)	15.0	25.4	10.4	7.4	1953–79
Iceland	14.1	15.8	1.7	4.7	1951–79
Nigeria	14.0	26.4	12.4	12.0	1968–77
Yugoslavia	13.7	20.3	6.6	6.3	1960–79
Colombia	11.7	17.1	5.4	5.1	1950–79
Sierra Leone	11.0	15.8	4.8	1.1	1971–78
Paraguay	10.6	15.8	5.2	5.2	1952–79
Saudi Arabia	9.7	24.9	15.2	10.7	1967–69
Central African Republic	9.3	11.6	2.3	1.5	1970–77
Spain	9.1	12.9	3.8	5.2	1954–79
Senegal	7.8	6.7	−1.1	−1.2*	1964–79
Mexico	7.8	14.0	6.2	8.9	1950–78
Pakistan	7.8	10.5	2.7	4.6	1961–79
Ivory Coast	7.6	14.0	6.4	7.1*	1962–79
Jamaica	7.6	13.5	5.9	4.0	1953–79
Portugal	7.5	10.4	2.9	5.1	1953–78
Niger	7.5	13.5	6.0	—	1963–79
Mauritius	7.4	12.9	5.5	3.2	1963–79
Gabon	7.4	11.7	4.3	—	1962–79
Somalia	7.1	16.8	9.7	—	1960–79
Cameroon	6.9	11.3	4.4	6.1*	1962–79
Sudan	6.9	9.7	3.3	3.5*	1951–79
Trinidad & Tobago	6.8	12.1	5.3	4.4	1960–78
Gambia	6.8	10.8	4.0	4.4*	1964–79
Ireland	6.7	9.0	2.3	3.1	1950–79
Finland	6.6	8.7	2.1	4.4	1950–79
India	6.6	8.7	2.1	3.6	1960–78

table continued

Table 7.1 Growth Rates of Prices, Money, and Output for 83 Countries in the Post-World War II Period (Arranged by Decreasing Order of the Inflation Rate) (*Continued*)

Country	ΔP	ΔM (Currency)	$\Delta M - \Delta P$	ΔY	Time Span
Nepal	6.6	11.8	5.2	2.4	1965–79
Greece	6.5	13.8	7.3	6.1	1950–79
Libya	6.2	25.5	19.3	12.2	1964–78
New Zealand	6.2	5.7	−0.5	3.2	1954–79
Thailand	6.2	11.4	5.2	7.8	1965–79
United Kingdom	6.2	7.0	0.8	2.5	1951–79
Egypt	6.1	12.6	6.5	5.0	1965–79
Italy	6.1	10.2	4.1	4.5	1950–79
Togo	6.0	13.9	7.9	5.8	1963–79
France	6.0	7.5	1.5	4.8	1950–79
Congo	6.0	9.5	3.5	—	1960–79
Australia	5.9	7.6	1.7	4.2	1950–79
Denmark	5.9	6.7	0.8	3.5	1950–79
Iran	5.9	16.0	10.1	8.3	1959–77
Philippines	5.9	9.0	3.1	5.7	1950–79
Chad	5.8	7.2	1.4	—	1960–77
Costa Rica	5.7	12.1	6.4	5.9	1960–79
Japan	5.7	12.9	7.2	8.0	1953–79
Ecuador	5.6	11.8	6.2	5.6	1951–79
Netherlands	5.5	7.2	1.7	4.1	1960–79
Norway	5.5	7.0	1.5	4.8	1950–79
Sweden	5.5	7.5	2.0	3.2	1950–79
Iraq	5.4	14.7	9.3	6.0	1965–76
Madagascar	5.3	7.8	2.5	2.4*	1964–78
South Africa	5.2	8.0	2.8	4.6	1950–79
Upper Volta	5.1	10.2	5.1	—	1962–79
Austria	4.8	8.2	3.4	4.7	1950–79
Morocco	4.8	11.6	6.8	5.7	1960–78
Syria	4.8	14.0	9.2	6.0	1957–79
Guyana	4.2	9.7	5.5	2.7	1960–76
Singapore	4.2	12.4	8.2	8.8	1963–79
Haiti	4.1	7.1	3.0	2.0	1953–78
Belgium	4.0	4.9	0.9	3.8	1953–79
Canada	4.0	7.1	3.1	4.7	1950–79
Tunisia	3.9	10.6	6.7	6.6	1960–78
Dominican Republic	3.8	9.1	5.3	5.6	1950–79
El Salvador	3.8	8.0	4.2	4.7	1951–79

Table 7.1 Growth Rates of Prices, Money, and Output for 83 Countries in the Post-World War II Period (Arranged by Decreasing Order of the Inflation Rate) (*Continued*)

Country	ΔP	ΔM (Currency)	$\Delta M - \Delta P$	ΔY	Time Span
United States	3.8	4.9	1.1	3.4	1950–79
Cyprus	3.6	9.7	6.1	4.2	1958–79
Malta	3.6	11.0	7.4	9.1	1960–79
Guatemala	3.4	7.7	4.3	4.9	1950–79
Honduras	3.3	7.7	4.4	4.5	1954–79
Sri Lanka	3.3	8.5	5.2	4.9	1950–79
Switzerland	3.2	5.5	2.3	3.3	1950–79
West Germany	3.1	7.3	4.2	4.6	1953–79
Venezuela	3.1	8.8	5.7	5.8	1950–79
Median	6.2	11.4	4.2	4.7	

Note: All growth rates are annual averages for the sample periods shown in the right-most column. ΔP is the growth rate of consumer prices. ΔM is the growth rate of the stock of currency. ΔY is the growth rate of real gross domestic product. All data are from issues of *International Financial Statistics*.

*Data on real domestic product were unavailable for these countries. ΔY was calculated by subtracting the average growth rate of consumer prices, ΔP, from the average growth rate of nominal gross domestic product.

We bring out the nature of the association between inflation and monetary growth in Figure 7.1. The graph demonstrates the positive correlation between inflation and the growth rate of currency. Further, each increase by 1 percentage point per year in the rate of monetary growth is associated with an increase by roughly 1 percentage point per year in the rate of inflation. However, the relation is closer for the more extreme cases than for the moderate ones. For example, the association is less dramatic if we look only at countries where the average rate of monetary growth is between 5 and 15% per year.

If the growth rate of money exceeds the growth rate of prices, then real cash balances, M/P, increase over time. In fact, the growth rate of real cash balances is the difference between the growth rates of money and prices. But since money is willingly held at each date, the growth rate of real balances must equal the growth rate of real money demanded. Recall that our previous analysis of the demand for money suggests several factors that could lead to increases over time in the quantity of real money demanded. The most important is the growth rate of aggregate output. We show the average growth rate of output for 77 countries (those for which data are available) in Table 7.1. Then Figure 7.2 graphs the average growth rate of real balances versus the growth rate of output. Notice the positive association between the growth rate of output and the growth rate of real balances. Also, observe from the table that the median growth rate of output, which is 4.7% per year, accords with the median growth rate of real cash balances, which

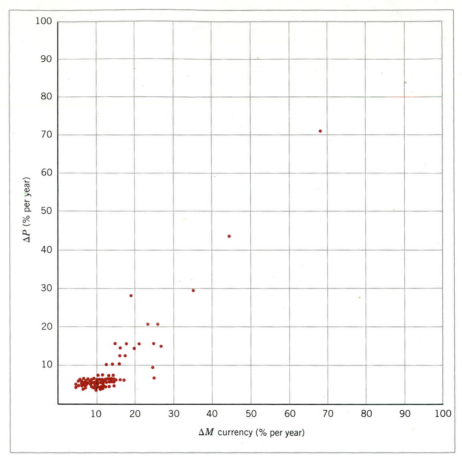

Figure 7.1 Graph of the Inflation Rate Versus the Growth Rate of Currency for 83 Countries
We show here the positive relation between inflation and the growth rate of currency.

is 4.2% per year. Thus we conclude that countries with higher growth rates of output tend to have a lower rate of inflation for a given rate of monetary growth. Therefore, differences in the growth rates of output explain some of the imperfect association between monetary growth and inflation, which shows up in Figure 7.1.

Another variable that influences the demand for money is the interest rate, R, which determines the cost of holding money. Other things equal, we predict that the average growth rate of real cash balances will be lower for countries in which the interest rate has increased, and vice versa. Notice that the change in the interest rate matters here, rather than the average level of the interest rate. Although researchers have verified this proposition for industrialized countries, we cannot

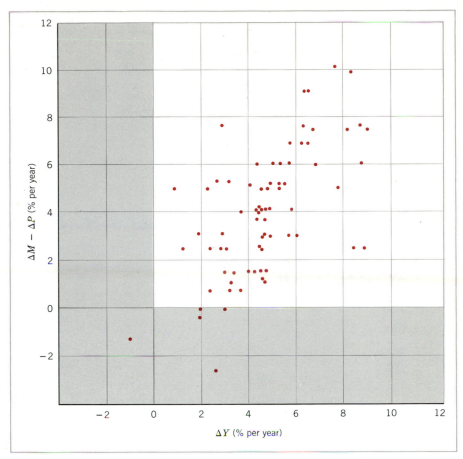

Figure 7.2 **Graph of the Growth Rate of Real Cash Balances Versus the Growth Rate of Output for 73 Countries***

We show here the positive relation between the growth rate of real currency and the growth rate of output.

*In order to provide a clearer picture, we omit four outlying countries. These are Zaire, Nigeria, Saudi Arabia, and Libya. The inclusion of these countries does not change the basic relationship. We had to omit six other countries because of missing data.

demonstrate it for the substantial number of our countries that lack organized securities markets on which interest rates are quoted. However, we shall see in this chapter that interest rates and inflation rates are closely related. In particular, increases in the rate of inflation also mean greater costs of holding money—that is, a higher rate of inflation means that money depreciates in real terms at a faster rate. Therefore, an increase in the rate of inflation tends to reduce the real demand for money. Hence, we predict that the average growth rate of real cash balances will be lower for countries in which the inflation rate has increased. (Notice again that what matters here is the change in the inflation rate, rather than the average level of the rate.) As examples, the sharp rises in inflation rates explain the negative growth rates of real cash balances that show up in Table 7.1 for Argentina, Uruguay, and Zaire.

Overall, the cross-country data suggest a significant, positive association between monetary growth and inflation. Further, this relation is closer than it first appears if we consider additional variables, such as the growth rate of output and changes in interest rates and inflation rates, which affect the real demand for money. We would do better still if we brought in more variables that influence the real demand for currency, such as changing levels of financial sophistication. These changes involve the spread of checking accounts and the increased convenience of other types of financial assets.

U.S. Time Series Data on Inflation and Monetary Growth

Table 7.2 reports data for the United States on average rates of inflation and monetary growth over 20-year periods from 1860 to 1980. Over the entire 120-year span, the average inflation rate is 2.1% per year, while the average growth

Table 7.2 U.S. Time Series Data on Inflation and Monetary Growth: Averages for 20-Year Periods (All figures are average growth rates in % per year)

	ΔP	ΔM (currency)	$\Delta M - \Delta P$	ΔY
1860–1880	1.1	3.4	2.3	4.3
1880–1900	−0.6	3.2	3.8	3.0
1900–20	4.6	6.5	1.9	2.8
1920–40	−1.6	2.4	4.0	2.4
1940–60	4.3	6.8	2.5	3.8
1960–80	4.8	6.9	2.1	3.5
1860–1980	2.1	4.9	2.8	3.3

Note: All growth rates are annual averages for the period shown in the first column. ΔP is the growth rate of the deflator for the gross national product. ΔM is the growth rate of currency. ΔY is the growth rate of real gross national product. All data before 1890 are rough estimates.

Sources: For the price level and real GNP, see Figures 1.1 and 1.4 of Chapter 1. For money, see Milton Friedman and Anna Schwartz, *Monetary Statistics of the United States*, Columbia University Press, New York, 1970, Tables 1 and 13, and *Federal Reserve Bulletin*, various issues.

rate of currency is 4.8% per year. Correspondingly, the average growth rate of real cash balances is 2.7% per year. Notice that this figure accords with the average growth rate of output, which is 3.3% per year. (Again, the results are similar if we look at the broader monetary aggregate, $M1$, rather than currency.)[2]

Although the time series data for the United States do not provide the range of experience that appears in the cross-country sample, there are substantial differences in the various 20-year periods. For example, the average inflation rate is negative over two intervals: -1.6% for 1920–40 (which includes the Great Depression) and -0.6% for 1880–1900. But the rate exceeds 4% in three of the cases: 4.8% for 1960–80, 4.6% for 1900–20, and 4.3% for 1940–60. Note that the two world wars strongly influence the observations for 1900–20 and 1940–60. For currency, the range of growth rates is from 2.4% in 1920–40 to 6.9% for 1960–80.

There is a positive, though imperfect, association between monetary growth and inflation over the different 20-year periods. As in our previous analysis, we can explain some of the divergences between monetary growth and inflation by considering variables that alter the demand for money. These include the growth rate of output, changes in interest rates, and the development of financial institutions.

Inflation as a Monetary Phenomenon

Casual observation of two types of data—across countries and across time for the United States—suggests that we should consider seriously Milton Friedman's famous statement, ''Inflation is always and everywhere a monetary phenomenon.''[3] However, we should remember some important points. First, the analysis will not rule out effects of real disturbances, such as supply shocks, on the price level. However, we expect that these effects will be more important for episodes of price changes, rather than for chronic inflation. Second, we should view the expression, *monetary phenomenon,* as incorporating variables that influence the real demand for money, as well as the nominal supply of money. Third, we would eventually like to know why monetary growth behaves differently in different countries and at different times. However, this question requires us to explore a number of new subjects, including governmental incentives to print more or less money. We sidestep the theory of money supply in this and the next chapter. Here, we look at the consequences for inflation and other variables of a given—unexplained—time path of money. This type of analysis is crucial for an understanding of inflation, although it does not constitute a full study of the topic.

---

[2]For the monetary aggregate, $M1$, the average growth rate is 5.8% per year. Correspondingly, the average growth rate of real $M1$ is 3.7% per year. (In order to calculate these figures, we have to use the broader aggregate, $M2$, before 1915. $M2$ includes all deposits at commercial banks.)

[3]Milton Friedman, ''Inflation: Causes and Consequences,'' in *Dollars and Deficits,* Prentice-Hall, Englewood Cliffs, New Jersey; 1968 p. 29.

Actual and Expected Inflation

Here we begin the process of incorporating inflation into the theoretical model. The inflation rate between periods t and $t + 1$ is

$$\pi_t = (P_{t+1} - P_t)/P_t \tag{7.2}$$

where π is the Greek letter *pi*. Notice that the inflation rate equals the rate of change of the price level between periods t and $t + 1$. By rearranging equation (7.2), we can solve out for the next period's price level as

$$P_{t+1} = (1 + \pi_t)P_t \tag{7.3}$$

Hence, prices rise over one period by the factor, $1 + \pi_t$. Although we focus on situations of rising prices—that is, positive rates of inflation—we can also consider cases where prices decline over time. These cases are called **deflations.**

In making various decisions, such as the choice between consuming now or later, people want to know how prices will change over time. Therefore, people form forecasts or **expectations of inflation rates.** We use the symbol π_t^e to denote an expectation for the inflation rate, π_t. Usually, we think of someone as forming this expectation during period t. Then, since people already know the current price level, P_t, the expectation of inflation, π_t^e, corresponds to a forecast of the next period's price level, P_{t+1}.

In general, forecasts of inflation are not perfectly accurate. That is, the actual rate of inflation is typically higher or lower than the representative person's expectation. Hence, the forecast error—that is, **unexpected inflation**—is usually nonzero. However, people have incentives to form their expectations rationally—making efficient use of the available information on past inflation and other variables—in order to avoid systematic mistakes. Therefore, we should not find that unexpected inflation is either typically positive or typically negative. Further, there ought not to be a systematic pattern of errors over time. For example, if unexpected inflation is positive this period, then it may be either positive or negative in the next period.

Real and Nominal Interest Rates

As before, let R_t be the interest rate on bonds. Specifically, if someone buys \$1 of bonds during period t, then the purchaser gets \$$(1 + R_t)$ as receipts of principal plus interest during period $t + 1$. In other words the dollar value of someone's assets held as bonds rises over one period by the factor $(1 + R_t)$. Accordingly, we can think of the rate R_t as the dollar or **nominal interest rate.**

Now, what happens over time to the real value of assets that people hold as bonds? If the price level is constant, as in previous chapters, then the real value of these assets also grows at the rate R_t. That is, in a world of constant prices, the nominal interest rate, R_t, is also the **real interest rate.**

But what happens if the inflation rate is positive? Then goods next period cost more than those this period. In particular, if the inflation rate is π_t, then equation (7.3) says that the price level rises over one period by the factor, $(1 + \pi_t)$. Hence, if the dollar value of assets rises over one period by the factor, $(1 + R_t)$, then the real value rises by the proportion, $(1 + R_t)/(1 + \pi_t)$. Here, we consider that the dollars available next period—which grow by the factor, $(1 + R_t)$—face a price level that is higher by the factor, $(1 + \pi_t)$.

If people hold assets in the form of bonds, then the real value of these assets rises over one period by the factor, $(1 + R_t)/(1 + \pi_t)$. Now let's define the real interest rate, r_t, to be the rate at which assets held as bonds grow in real terms. Then the real interest rate satisfies the condition

$$(1 + r_t) = (1 + R_t)/(1 + \pi_t) \tag{7.4}$$

We can obtain a more useful expression for the real interest rate, r_t, if we manipulate equation (7.4). In particular, multiply through on both sides by the term, $(1 + \pi_t)$, and then simplify the result to get the condition

$$r_t + \pi_t + r_t\pi_t = R_t \tag{7.5}$$

Now recall that we measure each variable—R_t, π_t and r_t—as a growth rate per "period." For example, suppose that a period is a month. Then think of nominal interest rates and inflation rates that are no larger than, say, 10–20% per year. Then the various rates per month—R_t, π_t and r_t—will be no greater than 1–2%. But in that case, the interaction term, $r_t\pi_t$, will be very small in equation (7.5). In particular, it will be smaller than the amount, $0.02 \cdot 0.02 = 0.0004$. Therefore, we can neglect this term and satisfactorily approximate the real interest rate as

$$r_t \approx R_t - \pi_t \tag{7.6}$$

where the symbol, $\approx$, means approximately equal to.[4]

Recall that the nominal interest rate, R_t, tells people how the dollar value of assets held as bonds grows over time. By contrast, the real interest rate, r_t, determines how fast these assets grow in real terms. Note that equation (7.6) says that the real interest rate, r_t, equals the nominal rate, R_t, less the rate of inflation, π_t. Thus, the real rate is lower than the nominal rate if the inflation rate is positive. Further, the real rate is positive only if the nominal rate exceeds the inflation rate. Otherwise—that is, when the nominal rate is less than the inflation rate—the real interest rate is negative. In this case the rise in dollar value at the rate R_t does not cover the rise in prices at the rate π_t.

Actual and Expected Real Interest Rates

Usually, we think of situations where people can observe directly the nominal interest rate on bonds, R_t. Then, in order to calculate the **expected real interest**

---

[4]The approximation becomes better the shorter is the length of the period. In fact, the length of the period plays no economic role in the model. Rather, we carry out the analysis in terms of periods—which economists call "discrete time"—solely for convenience. Therefore, we can reasonably assume that a period is extremely brief. Then equation (7.6) is a very accurate approximation.

rate between periods t and $t + 1$, people have to subtract from the nominal interest rate their expectation of inflation, π_t^e. Hence, the expected real interest rate, which we denote by r_t^e, is

$$r_t^e \approx R_t - \pi_t^e \tag{7.7}$$

Recall that the actual inflation rate, π_t, can be above or below its expectation, π_t^e. Then, if inflation turns out to be surprisingly high—that is, $\pi_t > \pi_t^e$—we find that the real interest rate r_t is less than its expectation, r_t^e. In other words if we combine equations (7.6) and (7.7), then the unexpected part of the real interest rate, $r_t - r_t^e$, is

$$r_t - r_t^e \approx -(\pi_t - \pi_t^e) \tag{7.8}$$

Thus, errors in forecasts of inflation, $\pi_t - \pi_t^e$, generate errors of the opposite sign in forecasts of the real interest rate.

It is possible to have different institutional arrangements where borrowers and lenders specify in advance the real interest rate, r_t, rather than the nominal rate, R_t. Here, people adjust, ex post, or after the fact, the nominal amount of payments for principal and interest in order to compensate for inflation. Specifically, these adjustments ensure that the actual real interest rate equals the prespecified value. Therefore, people know the real interest rate in advance. However, there is then uncertainty about the nominal interest rate.

The financial arrangements where people contract in advance for real interest rates are called **indexation** or **inflation correction.** These systems tend to exist in countries, such as Brazil and Israel, in which extreme inflation is chronic. Recently, the British government issued a long-term indexed bond of this type. But the U.S. government has so far resisted suggestions to issue this kind of security. Economists do not know why private parties and governments typically prefer to borrow and lend at prespecified nominal interest rates, rather than real rates.[5]

Nominal and Real Interest Rates in the Post-World War II U.S.

Table 7.3 indicates the relation between nominal and real interest rates for the United States over the post-World War II period. The nominal rate, R_t, is the

---

[5]There have been some suggestions: (1) People use and hold money—an asset that is denominated in nominal units—which makes it desirable to borrow and lend in the same units; (2) The government enforces contracts in nominal units more diligently than contracts in other units; (3) The tax treatment of indexed bonds is unclear; and (4) It is hard to agree on a price index to use in making inflation corrections. In his article, "The Ban on Indexed Bonds, 1933–77," *American Economic Review,* December 1980, Huston McCulloch argues that United States courts would not enforce indexing provisions on bonds after 1933. In that year Congress resolved not to honor the "gold clauses" that appeared in some previously issued bonds. These clauses—which were a form of indexing—committed borrowers to repay in a stated amount of gold, rather than U.S. dollars. Then when the Congress voided these gold clauses, the courts interpreted the restriction as applying to all types of indexed bonds. However, Congress rescinded this resolution in 1977, so the ban on indexed bonds no longer applies.

Table 7.3 Inflation Rates, Nominal Interest
Rates, and Real Interest Rates
for Recent U.S. Experience
(% per year)

Year	π_t	R_t	r_t
1948	1.3	1.0	−0.3
9	−1.3	1.1	2.4
1950	8.4	1.2	−7.2
1	1.4	1.6	0.2
2	1.7	1.8	0.1
3	1.4	1.9	0.5
4	1.5	1.0	−0.5
1955	2.6	1.8	−0.8
6	4.0	2.7	−1.3
7	1.8	3.3	1.5
8	2.0	1.8	−0.2
9	2.1	3.4	1.3
1960	0.6	2.9	2.3
1	2.0	2.4	0.4
2	1.6	2.8	1.2
3	1.4	3.2	1.8
4	1.9	3.6	1.7
1965	2.7	4.0	1.3
6	3.2	4.9	1.7
7	3.8	4.3	0.5
8	4.6	5.3	0.7
9	5.5	6.7	1.2
1970	5.0	6.5	1.5
1	4.6	4.4	−0.2
2	4.1	4.1	0.0
3	7.8	7.0	−0.8
4	11.0	7.9	−3.1
1975	5.6	5.8	0.2
6	5.2	5.0	−0.2
7	5.9	5.3	−0.6
8	8.7	7.2	−1.5
9	7.9	10.1	2.2
1980	9.5	11.4	1.9
1	7.0	14.0	7.0
2	4.7	10.6	5.9

Note: The inflation rate, π_t, refers to the
change in the GNP deflator from the first
quarter of each year to the first quarter of the
next year. The nominal interest rate, R_t, is
the average annual yield on secondary markets for U.S. Treasury Bills with three-month
maturity. The real interest rate, r_t, equals R_t
− π_t. For the data on prices, see Figure 1.4
of Chapter 1. Data on interest rates are from
issues of the *Federal Reserve Bulletin* and
U.S. Board of Governors of the Federal Reserve System, *Banking and Monetary Statistics, 1941–1970.*

average yield for each year on 3-month maturity Treasury Bills (short-term U.S. government securities). The inflation rate for each year, π_t, is the rate of change of the general price level, as measured by the deflator for the gross national product. Note that π_t is the actual rate of inflation, which could diverge substantially from people's expectations during the year. Then we calculate the real interest rate for each year from the formula, $r_t = R_t - \pi_t$.

Notice that the nominal interest rate rises dramatically in the post-World War II period. Specifically, this rate increases from 1% per year in 1948 to about 3% in the early 1960s, 5–6% in the late 1960s, 10% in 1979, and 14% in 1981, but then falls to 11% in 1982. Note that the increase is not steady—for example, the interest rate declines from 3.3% in 1957 to 1.8% in 1958, from 6.5% in 1970 to 4.1% in 1972, from 7.9% in 1974 to 5.0% in 1976, and from 14.0% in 1981 to 10.6% in 1982. Further, despite the appearance of a generally upward drift in interest rates, it would not have been easy to forecast this "trend." In any event, someone who foresaw this pattern could have made a fortune by speculating in the bond market.[6]

The behavior of the real interest rate, r_t, differs markedly from that of the nominal rate. Over the full period, 1948–82, the average real interest rate is a very small number, 0.6% per year. Further, roughly similar averages appear for the first and second halves of the period: 0.2% for 1948–1964 and 1.0% for 1965–82.[7] Overall, if we do not give undue weight to the high real rates for 1981–82, the data since 1948 suggest no clear long-term trend in the real interest rate.

The striking observation from Table 7.3 is the tendency for the nominal interest rate and the inflation rate to move together. Notably, the average values for these two rates increase dramatically and roughly in parallel since 1948. Hence, the difference between them—that is, the real interest rate, $r_t = R_t - \pi_t$—shows no clear direction. We display these patterns graphically in Figure 7.3. In our subsequent analysis we shall want to understand why nominal interest rates and inflation rates tend to move together on roughly a one-to-one basis.

Although there is no clear trend in the real interest rate, there are substantial year-to-year variations in this rate. For example, the rates range from lows of -7.2% in 1950 and -3.1% in 1974, to highs of 7.0% in 1981, 5.9% in 1982, 2.4% in 1949 and 2.3% in 1960. In order to understand the main reason for these

---

[6]The greatest returns would have come from going "short" on bonds with long maturities. (The interest rate or "yield to maturity" on long-term bonds changes over time in a way that is roughly similar to that shown for Treasury Bills in the table.) Going short amounts to a bet that prices of bonds will fall over time. Then, as interest rates rose, the prices of these bonds fell dramatically. (Why is that?) But please do not take any of this as advice to speculate on bonds in one direction or the other for the rest of the 1980s!

[7]These real interest rates neglect the taxation of interest income. One important point is that the U.S. income-tax law (and those of most countries) taxes nominal interest returns, which are determined by R_t, rather than the real returns. This element becomes more important for the recent years where the nominal interest rate is relatively high. Consequently, after-tax real interest rates tend to decline over the period since 1948. However, no one is sure exactly what tax rate to use in making these calculations.

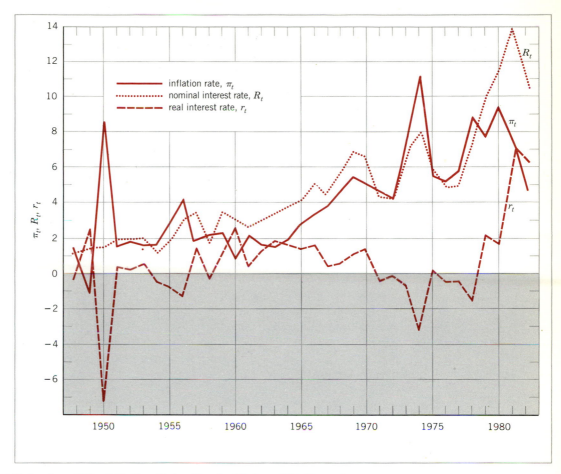

Figure 7.3 **Behavior of the Inflation Rate, Nominal Interest Rate, and
Real Interest Rate in the United States**

The inflation rate and the nominal interest rate rise over the post-World War II period. But except for the high values for 1981–82, there is no clear pattern in the real interest rate.

fluctuations, we have to recall the distinction between actual and expected real interest rates. In particular, unexpectedly high inflation causes the real interest rate to be lower than the expected real rate, and vice versa.

This perspective accounts readily for the two smallest real interest rates. In 1950 the inflation rate of 8.4% is a surprise associated with the start of the Korean War. Therefore, the real interest rate of − 7.2% is well below the anticipated rate. For 1974, the inflation rate of 11.0% is also partly a surprise, which relates to the first oil crisis. Again, the real interest rate of − 3.1% is well below expectations.

In order to use this viewpoint to explain high real interest rates, we have to look for unexpectedly low inflation. The inflation rates for 1949 and 1960, which are − 1.3% and 0.6% respectively, seem to fit this pattern. Also, the inflation rates for 1981 and 1982, which are 7.0% and 4.7% respectively, represent a significant cutback in inflation from prior years. Generally, people did not expect that inflation would be this low. Therefore, at least part of the high real interest rates for 1981–82 derives from the unexpectedly low rates of inflation.

Interest Rates on Money

We have discussed the nominal and real interest rates on bonds. But the same analysis applies to money, once we specify that the nominal interest rate on money is zero, rather than R_t. Recall that the real interest rate on any asset equals the nominal rate less the rate of inflation, π_t. Therefore, for bonds, the real rate is $r_t = R_t - \pi_t$. Similarly, for money, the real interest rate is $-\pi_t$. Positive inflation means that the purchasing power of money erodes over time.

As with bonds, we can distinguish the expected real interest rate on money from the actual rate. Hence, the expected real interest rate on money is just the negative of the expected inflation rate, $-\pi_t^e$. Given the persistent increase in U.S. inflation rates over the post-World War II period, as shown in Table 7.3, it follows that the expected real interest rate on money is much lower than it used to be.

Remember that the money in our model is like currency, which pays a zero nominal interest rate. Recently, some forms of checking deposits have started to pay interest. For these types of ''moneys,'' we calculate the real interest rate just like we do for bonds. That is, the real rate on these deposits equals the nominal interest rate less the rate of inflation.

Incorporation of Inflation and Monetary Growth into the Model

Now, we want to incorporate into the model the various new elements that we have been discussing. These include inflation and the distinction between real and nominal interest rates. Also, as suggested before, we want to analyze the link between monetary growth and inflation. Therefore, we have to extend the model to allow for changes in the stock of money.

In order to simplify matters, we think now of situations where the nominal interest rate, R, and the inflation rate, π, are constant over time. Therefore, the real interest rate, $r = R - \pi$, is also constant.

Monetary Growth and Transfer Payments

Here, we choose the simplest possible way to introduce monetary growth into the model. Namely, we assume that new money shows up as transfers from the government to households. Recall that we used this device before in Chapter 6 in order to study a one-time change in the quantity of money. Now, we allow for persistent growth in money, which means that the transfers are also persistent. Later on, we shall see that this simple device captures the essence of monetary changes. In particular, the main results still hold for other methods of introducing new money into the economy.

Let's denote by v_t the dollar amount of transfer that a household receives during period t. Note that this amount need not be the same for everyone. In any case the government finances the total of transfers, V_t, by printing and distributing new money. Therefore, the change in the aggregate quantity of money, $M_t - M_{t-1}$, equals the aggregate amount of transfers

$$V_t = M_t - M_{t-1} \tag{7.9}$$

Equation (7.9) is a very simple version of a **governmental budget constraint.** Notice that the left side is total government expenditures, all of which take the form of transfers, V_t, at this point. The right side lists government revenues. At present, this revenue derives solely from the printing of new paper money in the amount, $M_t - M_{t-1}$.

We can think of transfer payments as arising via a "helicopter drop" of cash.[8] Thus, our public officials effectively stuff a helicopter full of paper currency and fly around dropping money randomly over the countryside. The transfer payments occur when people pick up the money. However, despite the unrealistic flavor of this story, the only important aspect of it is that each person's transfer is independent of his or her level of income, previous amount of money holdings, and so on. (Let's ignore any dependence on the effort that people exert in searching the countryside for currency.) Economists refer to these as **lump-sum transfers** by which we mean that the amount someone receives is independent of that person's level of work effort, holdings of money, or other choices. In particular, since the transfers are lump-sum, people understand that changes in their holdings of money, M_t and M_{t-1}, have no impact on the size of their individual transfer, v_t.[9]

We have to modify households' budget constraints in order to include the transfer payments. Now, each household's budget constraint for period t is, when expressed in nominal terms

$$P_t y_t + b_{t-1}(1 + R) + m_{t-1} + v_t = P_t c_t + b_t + m_t \tag{7.10}$$

As before, the sources of funds on the left side include the dollar receipts from the commodity market, $P_t y_t$, plus the values of the bonds and money that were held last period, $b_{t-1}(1 + R) + m_{t-1}$. Here, the new element is the dollar amount of transfer, v_t, which is an additional source of funds for a household. The right side of equation (7.10) contains the same uses of funds as before. These are the nominal purchases of commodities, $P_t c_t$, plus this period's holdings of bonds and money,

---

[8]I think that the original source of this popular story is Milton Friedman, "The Optimum Quantity of Money," in his *The Optimum Quantity of Money and Other Essays*, Chicago, Aldine, 1969, pp. 4–5.

[9]The discussion assumes positive transfers, although we could also treat negative ones. Negative transfers are taxes, which may also be lump-sum—that is, independent of individuals' levels of income, amount of money holding, and so on. While we view transfers as financed by a helicopter drop of cash, we can view taxes as collected by a giant vacuum cleaner.

$b_t + m_t$. Notice that we date the price level, P_t, in equation (7.10). That's because the price level will no longer be constant over time. However, as mentioned before, we treat the nominal interest rate, R, as constant.

Inflation and Saving

The national accounts define a household's saving, as we did before, to equal the change in nominal assets—that is, the change in money plus bonds. Using this definition and rearranging the budget constraint from equation (7.10), we get

Nominal Saving (national accounts' version) =

$$(b_t + m_t) - (b_{t-1} + m_{t-1}) = P_t y_t + R b_{t-1} + v_t - P_t c_t \qquad (7.11)$$

The expression on the right side differs from that in earlier chapters only by the inclusion of the transfers, v_t, and by the dating of the price level, P_t.

National income accounting—and standard accounting practices for businesses or governments—do not deal correctly with changing price levels when they measure saving as in equation (7.11). A meaningful concept of someone's dollar saving would—when divided by the price level, P_t—equal the change in the real purchasing power of that person's assets. The standard definition does this when the price level is constant, but does not when the price level changes.

Consider an alternative approach, where we start by defining a household's **real saving** to be the change in the real value of assets—that is,

$$\text{real saving} = (b_t + m_t)/P_t - (b_{t-1} + m_{t-1})/P_{t-1}$$

Now we want to use a version of the budget constraint where everything appears in real terms. So if we divide through equation (7.10) by the price level, P_t, we get the condition in real terms

$$y_t + b_{t-1}(1 + R)/P_t + m_{t-1}/P_t + v_t/P_t = c_t + b_t/P_t + m_t/P_t \qquad (7.12)$$

Then, if we rearrange terms, we determine the real value of assets held for period t

$$(b_t + m_t)/P_t = y_t + b_{t-1}(1 + R)/P_t + m_{t-1}/P_t + v_t/P_t - c_t$$

Therefore, in order to calculate real saving, we have to subtract from both sides of the equation the initial real assets, $(b_{t-1} + m_{t-1})/P_{t-1}$. Then, we get

$$(b_t + m_t)/P_t - (b_{t-1} + m_{t-1})/P_{t-1}$$
$$= y_t + b_{t-1}(1 + R)/P_t + m_{t-1}/P_t + v_t/P_t - c_t - (b_{t-1} + m_{t-1})/P_{t-1}$$

Finally, we can combine terms on the right side, taking account of the relation, $P_t = (1 + \pi)P_{t-1}$. When we carry out the algebra, we end up with the following expression for real saving

$$\text{real saving} = (b_t + m_t)/P_t - (b_{t-1} + m_{t-1})/P_{t-1} \qquad (7.13)$$
$$= y_t + (R - \pi)(b_{t-1}/P_t) - \pi(m_{t-1}/P_t) + v_t/P_t - c_t$$

The important property of our formula for real saving in equation (7.13) is the way that it calculates returns on assets. For bonds, we use the real interest rate, $r = R - \pi$. For money, we use the real interest rate on money, which is $-\pi$. Real saving still equals real income less real expenditures, c_t. But real income must be defined carefully. It equals the real receipts from the commodity market, y_t, plus the real value of transfers, v_t/P_t, plus the real returns on assets, which are $(R - \pi)(b_{t-1}/P_t)$ for bonds and $-\pi(m_{t-1}/P_t)$ for money.

Once we know a person's real saving from equation (7.13), we can calculate the dollar value of this saving from multiplication by the price level, P_t. Then we have

$$\text{nominal saving} = P_t y_t + (R - \pi)b_{t-1} - \pi m_{t-1} + v_t - P_t c_t \quad (7.14)$$

Compare this result with the standard definition of nominal saving from equation (7.11). The differences involve the measures of returns on assets. Specifically, the standard definition uses nominal interest rates, which are R for bonds and zero for money. But our concept of saving uses real interest rates, which are $(R - \pi)$ for bonds and $-\pi$ for money.

Consider some examples in order to clarify the results about saving. Suppose that in each period someone's receipts from the commodity market plus transfers, $P_t y_t + v_t$, just cover consumption expenditure, $P_t c_t$. Assume that the person starts with $1000 in bonds—that is, $b_0 = \$1000$. For simplicity, suppose that he or she holds no money. Then assume that the nominal interest rate, R, and the inflation rate, π, are both 10% per year. Hence, the initial nominal interest income, Rb_0, is $100.

The standard definition, equation (7.11), calculates nominal saving for the first period as $100. This saving shows up as an increase in the dollar value of bonds to $b_1 = \$1100$. Hence, the dollar value of bond holdings goes up by 10% from period zero. But the price level also rises by 10%. So the $1100 of bonds in period 1 buys no more goods than does the $1000 in period 0. Apparently, the person does a lot of "saving," but has added nothing to the purchasing power of his or her assets!

We get a more reasonable answer by using the definition of saving from equation (7.14). Since the real interest rate, $R - \pi$, is zero, we find that nominal saving is zero. (Note that real saving, as calculated from equation [7.13], is also zero.) This answer tells us, correctly, that the purchasing power of assets does not change over time.

Suppose now that we change the example by having all assets—initially $1000—held each period as money, rather than bonds. Then the nominal interest income is zero in each period. Therefore, given the other conditions that we assumed before, the standard definition of saving from equation (7.11) says that saving is zero. Correspondingly, the person's nominal assets—all held as money—remain at $1000 over time. But with 10% inflation, these dollars buy progressively less goods. According to the standard definition, the person does zero saving—yet, the real value of his or her assets deteriorates over time.

Again, we get a more reasonable answer from the definition of saving in equation (7.14). Here, we apply the real interest rate, $-\pi = -10\%$, to the holdings of money. Therefore, the effective interest earnings on money are initially $-\$100$. That is, $\$1000$ of money loses $\$100$ of real value over a year. Thus, nominal saving for the first period is $-\$100$, rather than zero.

So far, the examples assume that someone's holdings of bonds are nonnegative. But the adjustments for inflation just reverse if a person is a debtor. For example, suppose that someone takes out a mortgage on a house for $\$100,000$ at an interest rate, R, of 15%. Then he or she makes annual interest payments of $\$15,000$. (Assume that the mortgage has a long maturity, in which case there is very little repayment of nominal principal.) But the true interest costs are much less than $\$15,000$ per year.[10] Specifically, if the inflation rate is 10%, then the real value of the outstanding principal on the loan declines by 10% in each year. Hence, the true annual interest costs are $\$15,000$ in explicit payments less $\$10,000$ for the decline in the real value of the debt, for a net amount of $\$5,000$.

Aggregate Real Saving

We define an individual's real saving to be the change in his or her holdings of real bonds and money. Therefore, when we sum up over all of the households, we find that aggregate real saving equals the change in the aggregate real stock of bonds, $B_t/P_t - B_{t-1}/P_{t-1}$, plus the change in the aggregate real stock of money, $M_t/P_t - M_{t-1}/P_{t-1}$. But recall that the total stock of bonds, B_t, still equals zero in each period. It follows that the aggregate of real saving equals the change in the aggregate of real cash balances. So if total real money balances change over time, then the aggregate of real saving is now nonzero.

Budget Constraints Over an Infinite Horizon

We have to make some adjustments in order to incorporate inflation into households' budget constraints over an infinite horizon. For the moment, let's put aside the various monetary terms, which include the initial stock of real cash balances, the transfers received from the government, and the interest foregone by holding money. Then, when written in terms of nominal present values, the budget constraint over an infinite horizon looks basically like it did before. Namely, since we assume that the nominal interest rate R is constant, the condition is

$$P_1 y_1 + P_2 y_2/(1 + R) + P_3 y_3/(1 + R)^2 + \cdots + b_0(1 + R) \quad (7.15)$$
$$= P_1 c_1 + P_2 c_2/(1 + R) + P_3 c_3/(1 + R)^2 + \cdots$$

The only new element in equation (7.15) is the dating of the price level.

Now recall that we assume a constant rate of inflation, π. Therefore, the price

---

[10]The discussion here ignores a very important tax benefit, since the interest payments are deductible from taxable income.

levels for any two adjacent periods satisfy the condition, $P_t = (1 + \pi)P_{t-1}$. Hence, we can use this condition repeatedly to express each future level of prices in terms of the current price, P_1, and the constant inflation rate π. Then we get the sequence

$$P_2 = (1 + \pi)P_1,$$

$$P_3 = (1 + \pi)^2 P_1,$$

.

.

.

So if we substitute these results into the budget constraint from equation (7.15), we get the revised condition

$$P_1[y_1 + y_2 \cdot (1 + \pi)/(1 + R) + y_3 \cdot (1 + \pi)^2/(1 + R)^2 + \cdots] + b_0(1 + R) \tag{7.16}$$

$$= P_1[c_1 + c_2 \cdot (1 + \pi)/(1 + R) + c_3 \cdot (1 + \pi)^2/(1 + R)^2 + \cdots]$$

Notice that the next period's real income and spending, y_2 and c_2, enter multiplicatively with the factor, $(1 + \pi)/(1 + R)$. But recall that this expression is just the reciprocal of the term that involves the real interest rate—that is, $(1 + \pi)/(1 + R) = 1/(1 + r)$. Hence, in order to express the next period's real income and spending, y_2 and c_2, as present values we divide by the discount factor, $(1 + r)$. But this makes sense since the real interest rate tells people how they can exchange goods of one period for those of another. In particular, it is the real interest rate, rather than the nominal rate, that matters here.

Now the same idea applies for any future period. For example, the real income and spending for period 3, y_3 and c_3, enter into equation (7.16) as a multiple of the factor, $(1 + \pi)^2/(1 + R)^2$, which equals $1/(1 + r)^2$. So if we make all these substitutions into equation (7.16)—and also divide through by the current price level, P_1—we end up with a simplified form of the budget constraint

$$y_1 + y_2/(1 + r) + y_3/(1 + r)^2 + \cdots + b_0(1 + R)/P_1$$
$$= c_1 + c_2/(1 + r) + c_3/(1 + r)^2 + \cdots \tag{7.17}$$

Equation (7.17) is the budget constraint in real terms over an infinite horizon. As compared with our earlier cases, the new element is the real interest rate, r. Namely, this rate appears, instead of the nominal interest rate, in the various discount factors.

Finally, let's recall our assumption that the real interest rate, $r = R - \pi$, is a known constant. Given this condition, there is no distinction between the expected real interest rate and the actual rate. However, more realistically, when people express prospective real incomes and expenses as present values they must use anticipated real interest rates, rather than the actual values. Therefore, we can think of the real interest rate, r, that appears in equation (7.17) as an expected rate, $r^e = R - \pi^e$.

Intertemporal-Substitution Effects

We discussed before how the interest rate acts as a variable that causes intertemporal substitution of resources by individuals. Namely, an increase in the interest rate motivates people to reduce current consumption and leisure, relative to future consumption and leisure. Then these changes correspond to an increase in currently desired saving.

The intertemporal-substitution effects involve the relative costs of taking consumption or leisure at one date rather than another. In making these comparisons an individual wants to know, for example, how much extra consumption he or she can get next period by reducing consumption this period. But as we worked out before, an individual can save and thus transform each unit of consumption foregone this period into $(1 + r)$ units of added consumption for the next period. Therefore, an increase in the real interest rate, r, motivates people to reduce current consumption and leisure in order to raise future consumption and leisure. In particular, it is the real interest rate, r, not the nominal interest rate, R, that matters here. Thus, all of our previous discussions of intertemporal-substitution effects remain valid, as long as we replace the nominal interest rate by the real rate.[11]

We can also use the budget constraint from equation (7.17) to think about intertemporal-substitution effects. For example, notice on the right side that an increase in the real interest rate, r, effectively cheapens later values of consumption relative to earlier ones. Therefore, an increase in the real interest rate motivates people to shift consumption away from the present and toward the future. Similarly, we can use the budget constraint to show that a higher real interest rate induces people to shift away from current leisure and toward future leisure.

Finally, remember again that we treat the real interest rate, r, as a known quantity. More generally, the expected real interest rate, $r^e = R - \pi^e$, is what matters for intertemporal-substitution effects. In particular, no one shifts their planned time paths of consumption and leisure unless they anticipate that the real interest rate will be either higher or lower. For example, if surprisingly low inflation makes the real interest rate unexpectedly high, then we do not predict a major intertemporal-substitution effect. After all, people could not have expected this unexpectedly low inflation when they decided on their levels of consumption and work. In order for intertemporal-substitution effects to arise, there must be changes in the expected real interest rate, $r^e = R - \pi^e$. That is, there must be changes in the nominal interest rate, R, relative to the expected rate of inflation π^e.

Money and Households' Budget Constraints

Now we can incorporate the various monetary terms into households' budget constraints. Recall that these terms involve initial real cash balances, transfers from the government, and interest foregone on future holdings of money. Before, we

---

[11]It also remains true that a shift in the real interest rate has no aggregate wealth effect. For example, an increase in this rate is good for people who are usually lenders, but correspondingly bad for those who are usually borrowers.

considered these terms when the price level was constant and transfers were zero. Then we found that the monetary terms had no effect in the aggregate on the real present value of households' sources of funds net of the uses of these funds. Hence, aggregate wealth effects arise here only if we bring in the present value of real transaction costs. But then we assumed that these costs were small enough to neglect for most purposes.

Basically, the previous results still hold in our present framework. Specifically, variations in prices and in the quantity of paper money—which show up as transfer payments—cannot, by themselves, create or destroy wealth in the aggregate. Instead, as before, aggregate wealth effects emerge here only when we bring in changes in the present value of real transaction costs. In the appendix to this chapter we go through a fair amount of algebra to prove these results. However, it is possible to skip this material without losing any continuity.

Interest Rates and the Demand for Money

Recall that the demand for money involves a tradeoff between transaction costs and interest-income foregone. Further, the interest foregone depends on the differential between the interest rate on bonds and that on money. For example, if we think of nominal interest rates, then we care about the rate on bonds, R, less that on money, which is zero. Hence, the differential between the nominal interest rates is the amount R, just as in our previous analysis.

Now, we can also make the calculations in terms of real interest rates. Then we take the real interest rate on bonds, r, less that on money, which is $-\pi$. So, the differential is again the amount, $R = r + \pi$.

Since the interest-income foregone still depends on the rate R, we conclude that the form of the demand-for-money function looks the same as before. Namely, the aggregate demand again takes the form

$$(M_t/P_t)^d = H(Y_t, R, \ldots)$$
$$(+)\,(-)$$

(7.18)

Notice an important point. It is the (expected) real interest rate, r, that exerts intertemporal-substitution effects on consumption and work. But it is the nominal interest rate, R, that influences the real demand for money.

Summary

We began by examining some data on monetary growth and inflation across countries and over time for the United States. These data suggest that variations in monetary growth account for a good deal of the variations in inflation rates.

The real interest rate on bonds, r, equals the nominal rate, R, less the inflation rate, π. Hence, if a bond specifies the nominal interest rate in advance, then the expected real interest rate, r^e, depends on the expected inflation rate, π^e. Since World War II the United States data indicate that the nominal interest rate and the rate of inflation have risen dramatically and by roughly equal amounts. Hence, there has been no clear trend in the real interest rate. On the other hand, unexpected inflation leads to substantial year-to-year movements in real interest rates.

We introduced monetary growth into the model by allowing for govermental transfer payments. Here, the government's budget constraint equates aggregate transfers to the change in the stock of money. Then we modified the concept of saving and the formulation of households' budget constraints in order to include inflation. The main result is that saving and budget constraints now involve the real interest rate, rather than the nominal rate. Similarly, the intertemporal-substitution effects on consumption and leisure depend on the real interest rate. Further, when there is uncertainty about future inflation, it is the expected real interest rate that matters for intertemporal-substitution effects.

We discussed how the various monetary terms—initial real cash, the present value of real transfers, and the interest foregone on future money—enter into households' budget constraints. Unless we bring in transaction costs, we find that the aggregate wealth effect from these terms is nil.

Finally, we observe that the nominal interest rate, R, still determines the cost of holding money rather than bonds. Therefore, although the real interest rate matters for choices of consumption and work, it is the nominal rate, R, that appears in the demand-for-money function.

Appendix
The Wealth Effects From the Monetary Terms

Consider the right side of equation (7.17), which shows the real present value of a household's uses of funds over an infinite horizon. Here—if we neglect transaction costs—we have to add the real present value of interest foregone from holding money. Thus, the new terms are

$$R \cdot m_1/[P_2(1 + r)] + R \cdot m_2/[P_3(1 + r)^2] + \cdots \qquad (7.19)$$

In order to understand this series of terms, let's consider the first one. The term, Rm_1, is the dollar interest earnings that someone foregoes during period 2 because he or she holds the quantity of money, m_1, rather than bonds during period 1. Since the foregone interest income applies to period 2, we divide by period 2's price level, P_2, in order to convert to real terms. Then we divide by the discount factor, $(1 + r)$, in order to express the result as a present value. Notice that the subsequent terms in expression (7.19) are similar, except for the discount factor. For example, for the second term, the discount factor is $(1 + r)^2$.

For subsequent purposes, it is convenient to revise expression (7.19). Note that the first part of the expression involves the term, $P_2(1 + r)$. But the price level for period 2, P_2, equals the quantity, $(1 + \pi)P_1$, where π is the constant rate of inflation. Therefore, we have

$$P_2(1 + r) = P_1(1 + \pi)(1 + r) = P_1(1 + R)$$

So we can make this type of substitution for the price level in each term of expression (7.19). Then we obtain a simplified formula for the real present value of the household's new uses of funds, which is

$$[R/(1 + R)] \cdot [m_1/P_1 + (m_2/P_2)/(1 + r) + \cdots] \qquad (7.20)$$

Now consider the left side of equation (7.17), which shows the real present value of a household's sources of funds. To these terms we have to add the real value of the initial cash balances plus the present value of real transfers received from the government. Thus, the additional terms are

$$m_0/P_1 + (v_1/P_1) + (v_2/P_2)/(1 + r) + (v_3/P_3)/(1 + r)^2 + \cdots \qquad (7.21)$$

We can sum up across households in expression (7.21) in order to determine the aggregate real present value of the new sources of funds. Then we get the expression

$$M_0/P_1 + (V_1/P_1) + (V_2/P_2)/(1 + r) + (V_3/P_3)/(1 + r)^2 + \cdots$$

But recall from the government's budget constraint that the aggregate transfer for each period, V_t, equals the change in the stock of money, $M_t - M_{t-1}$. Therefore, if we make this substitution above, we obtain the revised form,

$$(M_0/P_1) + \{(M_1 - M_0)/P_1 + (M_2 - M_1)/[P_2(1 + r)] + (M_3 - M_2)/[P_3(1 + r)^2] + \cdots\}$$

Observe that the first term, M_0/P_1, cancels with one of the terms inside the brackets. Hence, we can rewrite the expression as

$$(M_1/P_1) - M_1/[P_2(1 + r)] + M_2/[P_2(1 + r)] - M_2/[P_3(1 + r)^2]$$

$$+ \text{ terms that involve } M_3, M_4, \ldots$$

Now, recall that we can make the substitution

$$P_2(1 + r) = P_1(1 + \pi)(1 + r) = P_1(1 + R)$$

Therefore, we can combine the terms that involve M_1 in the above expression to get

$$(M_1/P_1)[1 - 1/(1 + R)] = (M_1/P_1) \cdot R/(1 + R)$$

Similarly, the terms that involve M_2 simplify to

$$(M_2/P_2) \cdot [R/(1 + R)]/(1 + r)$$

So if we put this all together, then the expression for the aggregate real present value of the new sources of funds becomes

$$[R/(1 + R)] \cdot [M_1/P_1 + (M_2/P_2)/(1 + r) + \text{ similar terms that involve } M_3, M_4, \ldots] \qquad (7.22)$$

But look at expression (7.20), which shows the real present value of a household's new uses of funds. Clearly, the aggregate of these new uses coincides with the aggregate of the new sources, which appears in expression (7.22). Hence, as we wanted to show, the monetary terms have no impact in the aggregate on the sources net of the uses. Accordingly, we also do not have to consider aggregate wealth effects from the combination of first, real cash balances; second, the present value of real transfers; and third, the interest foregone from future holdings of money.

We can think of the result somewhat differently by asking when the monetary terms will show a net effect for an individual. Basically, there are two things to consider. First, the effect on wealth is positive for someone whose share of total transfers is relatively high. Second, the effect on wealth is positive for someone whose initial share of cash, which is m_0/M_0, exceeds his or her planned share for the typical future period, m_t/M_t. This last result relates to our earlier discussion of the real-balance effect. There, we found a positive effect on wealth when someone's current holdings of real cash were high relative to his or her planned future holdings.[12] Here, we generalize this result by expressing it in terms of the current share of total cash, relative to the planned future share.

Thus, the effect on wealth from the monetary terms may be positive or negative for an individual. But this viewpoint also shows that the wealth effects are zero when we think of the average person. That is, the average person's share of transfers or money cannot be relatively high or low!

Finally, let's stress again that aggregate wealth effects do arise when we consider the present value of real transaction costs. But as before, we assume as an approximation that we can neglect these effects.

Important Terms and Concepts

inflation	expected real interest rate
rate of monetary growth	indexation
deflation	inflation correction
expectation of inflation	governmental budget constraint
unexpected inflation	lump-sum transfer
nominal interest rate	real saving
real interest rate	nominal saving

QUESTIONS AND PROBLEMS

Mainly for Review

7.1 Monetarists hold that changes in the price level are primarily the results of changes in the quantity of money. Can this conclusion be based solely on theoretical reasoning? Explain.

---

[12]In that model aggregate real cash was constant over time. Now, we do not require this condition.

7.2 Consider an individual who lives for two periods, earns a nominal income of $1000 in each period, and has zero initial and terminal assets. The nominal interest rate (R) on dollar loans is 15%, and the expected rate of inflation (π^e) between the two periods is 10%. Assume that the price level in the first period is 1.

a. What is the real value of period 1 income?

b. What is the maximum amount of dollars that could be borrowed in period 1? Find the real value of this amount, and add it to the real value of period 1 income to see the maximum amount of (real) consumption possible in period 1.

c. What is the price level in period 2? What is the real value of period 2 income?

d. What is the maximum amount of dollars that can be obtained in period 2 by saving in period 1? Find the real value (in period 2) of this amount and add it to the real value of period 2 income to see the maximum amount of (real) consumption possible in period 2.

e. As in question 3.4 of Chapter 3, plot a graph showing the consumption possibilities in the two periods.

f. What is the slope of the budget line that you drew in part (e)? Show that it is equal to $-(1 + R)/(1 + \pi^e)$.

7.3 Based on your answer to question 7.2, explain why $(1 + R)/(1 + \pi^e)$, rather than one plus the nominal interest rate, is the correct measure of the tradeoff between real consumption in the two periods. In what situation would it be appropriate to use the nominal interest rate?

7.4 Distinguish between the measures of nominal saving given in equations (7.11) and (7.14). Explain why, when inflation is positive, the first measure is an overestimate of saving for a net lender (an individual for whom $b_{t-1} > 0$). Can we make a similar comparison for a net debtor (an individual for whom $b_{t-1} < 0$)?

7.5 Why is the actual inflation rate typically different from the expected inflation rate? Which is relevant for intertemporal choices of consumption? Which is relevant for the inflation adjustment described in question 7.4?

7.6 Suppose there is a rise in the nominal interest rate that is matched by an equal rise in the expected inflation rate. Explain why consumption demand would be unaffected but the real demand for money would decline.

Problems for Discussion

7.7 Monetary Growth and Inflation

Suppose that the money-demand function takes the form

$$(M/P)^d = H(Y, R, \ldots) = Y \cdot J(R),$$
$$(+) (-)$$

where J is some function. This form says that an increase in real output by, say, 10% raises the real demand for money by 10%.

a. Is it possible that this form of the demand for money accords with our theory of money demand from Chapter 5?

b. Consider the relation across countries between the average growth rates of money and prices. If the functional form shown above for money demand applies, then how does the average growth rate of real output affect the relation between the growth rates of money and prices?

c. What is the relation between the average growth rates of money and prices for a country where the nominal interest rate, R, has increased?

d. If the expected real interest rate is constant, what is the relation between the average growth rates of money and prices for a country where the expected inflation rate, π^e, has increased? How does this result apply to countries for which we do not observe the nominal interest rate, R, on an organized credit market?

7.8 Inflation and the Demand for Money

Suppose that households hold stocks of goods—for example, groceries—as well as money and bonds. Assume that these goods depreciate in a physical sense at the rate δ per year (δ is the Greek letter *delta*).

a. What is the "nominal interest rate" on holdings of these goods? Does this interest rate affect the demands for stocks of goods and money?

b. Assume that the nominal interest rate on bonds, R, does not change, but the expected inflation rate, π^e, rises. What happens to the demand for money?

Note: This problem shows that the demand for money can involve substitution between money and goods, as well as between money and bonds. Therefore, the demand for money may change with a shift in the expected inflation rate, even if the nominal interest rate on bonds does not change.

7.9 Prepayments of Mortgages and Callability of Bonds

Mortgages typically allow the borrower to make early payments of principal, which are called *prepayments*. Sometimes, the mortgage contract specifies a penalty for prepayments, while sometimes there is no penalty. In recent years many state governments have prohibited prepayment penalties on mortgages. (However, there are generally some fees for negotiating a new mortgage.) Similarly, most long-term bonds—although not those of the U.S. government—allow the issuer to prepay the principal after an indicated date and with a specified penalty. When the bond issuer exercises this option to prepay, he or she is said to "call" the bond. Bonds that allow this option are said to be *callable* or to have a *call provision*.

a. When would a borrower want to prepay (or call) his or her mortgage or bond? In particular, would we see more prepayments when nominal interest rates had unexpectedly increased or decreased?

b. Since the late 1970s, banks and savings and loans have been eager for their customers to prepay their mortgages. In fact, the lenders often insist on prepayments when homes are sold by preventing the buyers of the homes from "assuming" the old mortgages. Why did the banks and savings and loans behave this way?

c. Suppose that there is an increase in the year-to-year fluctuations of nominal interest rates, as is true since the early 1970s. From the standpoint of a borrower, how does this change affect the value of having a prepayment option—that is, callability—in his or her mortgage or bond?

7.10 Indexed Bonds

Consider a bond that costs $1000. Suppose that the bond pays a year later the principal of $1000 plus interest of $100.

a. What is the nominal interest rate on the bond? What are the actual and expected real interest rates? Why is the nominal rate known, but the real rate uncertain?

Now, suppose that someone issues an indexed bond, which adjusts the payments to compensate for inflation. For example, suppose that the total amount paid a year later is the quantity $1100 \cdot (1 + \pi)$, where π is the inflation rate over the year.

b. What is the real interest rate on the indexed bond? Why is the real rate known, but the nominal rate uncertain?

c. Can you think of other types of indexed bonds? Are the real and nominal interest rates both uncertain in some cases?

d. Why do you think that indexed bonds are rare in the United States? (*Note:* The famous economist, Irving Fisher, had his company, Cardex Rand, issue an indexed bond in the 1920s. But it was not very popular. Recently, some mining companies have issued bonds that link part of their payout to the price of silver.)

7.11 Wealth and Substitution Effects from Inflation (optional)

Suppose that the expected inflation rate, π^e, and the nominal interest rate, R, each increase by 1 percentage point. Thus, the expected real interest rate on bonds does not change.

a. What happens to the real demand for money?

b. Underlying this demand for money, what happens to the real amount of transaction costs that people incur?

Assume now that we do not neglect the role of transaction costs in households' budget constraints.

c. What is the effect of higher inflation on people's wealth? Therefore, how do consumption and leisure respond?

d. Does higher expected inflation also exert substitution effects on consumption and leisure? (Note that, unlike consumption, leisure does not require people to use money.) Therefore, what is the overall effect of higher expected inflation on consumption and leisure?

CHAPTER 8

MONEY, INFLATION AND INTEREST RATES IN THE MARKET-CLEARING MODEL

In this chapter, we use the market-clearing model to determine inflation and interest rates. Our basic approach will be to specify a given time path of the money stock, M_t. Then we figure out what time path of the price level, P_t—hence, of the inflation rate, π_t—and of the nominal and real interest rates, R_t and r_t, satisfy the conditions for general market clearing. Recall that market clearing is a natural way to satisfy the conditions for aggregate consistency in the model.

Here, we focus on the consequences of different rates of anticipated inflation and monetary growth. In particular, even when the inflation rate, π_t, varies over time, we assume that people forecast these changes accurately. Put another way, people have **perfect foresight** about future price levels, so that there is always equality between the actual and expected inflation rates, $\pi_t = \pi_t^e$. Accordingly, if people know the nominal interest rate, R_t, then there is also equality between actual and expected real interest rates, $r_t = r_t^e$.

On the one hand, the analysis is limited, since it does not address unanticipated inflation and monetary growth. (Later on, we explore these matters.) But, it is useful to study anticipated inflation as a separate topic. In particular, the changes in anticipated inflation explain the principal longer term movements in U.S. nominal interest rates since World War II.

Market-Clearing Conditions

We know from before how to write down the conditions for general market clearing. First, the aggregate supply of goods for period t, Y_t^s, equals the demand, C_t^d. Here, we write this condition as

181

$$Y^s(r_t, \ldots) = C^d(r_t, \ldots)$$
$$(+) \qquad\qquad (-)$$

(8.1)

Equation (8.1) indicates the intertemporal-substitution effect from the real interest rate, r_t. (Recall that the actual rate, r_t, equals the expected rate, r_t^e, in the present analysis.) As usual, this effect is positive on the supply of goods for period t, and negative on the demand.

The omitted terms, denoted by . . . in equation (8.1), include various properties of the production function. For example, shifts in this function can exert wealth and substitution effects. However, we showed in the previous chapter that no aggregate wealth effect arises from the combination of three monetary terms—initial real cash balances, the present value of real transfers, and the present value of interest foregone on future money. Therefore, if we follow our usual practice of ignoring distributional effects, we do not have to consider these terms in the condition for clearing the commodity market. On the other hand, transaction costs generally have some influence on commodities supplied and demanded. As before, we neglect these effects as an approximation.

Second, we have the condition that all money be willingly held. Given our previous discussion of the demand for money, we can write this condition for period t as

$$M_t/P_t = H(Y_t, R_t, \ldots)$$
$$(+) \ (-)$$

(8.2)

On the left, we have the actual quantity of real money balances. On the right, we have the demand for real balances, which depends positively on aggregate output, Y_t, and negatively on the nominal interest rate, R_t. Any other factors that influence money demand, such as the degree of financial sophistication, are denoted by the expression, . . . , in equation (8.2). Here, we assume that these factors do not change over time.

Remember that the two aggregate-consistency conditions—equations (8.1) and (8.2)—guarantee that the aggregate demand for bonds is zero. That is, Walras' Law ensures that the credit market clears.

The Superneutrality of Money

Before we explore the details of the link between monetary behavior and inflation, we can already see an important property from the condition for clearing the commodity market in equation (8.1). Consider the underlying real factors in the model, which include such things as the forms of production functions, population, and the preferences of households. Note that these elements enter into the demand and supply of commodities through the omitted terms, which we denote by . . . in equation (8.1). For given values of these elements, equation (8.1) determines the real interest rate, r_t, and the level of aggregate output, $Y_t = C_t$, at each date.

Further, if the underlying real elements do not change over time, then the market-clearing values of the real interest rate and output are constants.

The important point is that we determine the real interest rate and output independently of the time path of money. Thus, although changes in money end up affecting the time paths of the price level and the nominal interest rate, they do not affect at least some of the real variables in the model. If all real variables were invariant with the behavior of money, we would say that money is **superneutral.** Note that this term suggests an extension of another concept, the neutrality of money, which we discussed before. Neutrality of money means that once-and-for-all changes in the quantity of money affect nominal variables, but not real variables. Superneutrality of money extends this idea from one-time changes in the stock of money to arbitrary variations in the entire time path of money.

Let's consider why money is not superneutral in our model. First, changes in the behavior of money will generally induce people to incur more or less transaction costs. These costs absorb resources directly and may also influence households' choices of work effort, consumption, and saving. Therefore, the superneutrality of money can only be an approximation, which works well when transaction costs are small.

Second, the time path of money matters for inflation, which in turn affects the real demand for money. Hence, the time path of money generally affects the aggregate amount of real cash, which is a real variable. As a related matter, the time path of money affects the nominal interest rate, which tells people the real amount of interest income that they forego by holding money, rather than bonds.

Finally, recall that our analysis assumes perfect foresight about future price levels. Specifically, there is always equality between actual and expected rates of inflation. But we already saw in Chapter 7 that unexpected inflation has important effects on realized real interest rates. Here, when thinking about the real effects of monetary changes, we consider only perfectly anticipated variations in money and prices. Thus, our basic finding above is that the real interest rate and output do not depend on anticipated changes in the quantity of money.

Monetary Growth, Inflation and the Nominal Interest Rate

We want now to examine the details of the linkages among monetary growth, inflation, and the nominal interest rate. We carry out this analysis for given values of the real interest rate, r, and output, Y. By holding these variables fixed, we are making two types of assumptions. First, we use the property that anticipated variations in money and prices do not affect the real interest rate and output. Second, we assume that no other shifts occur over time to the functions for aggregate commodity demand or supply. Generally, these types of changes would lead to movements in the real interest rate and output.

More specifically, the analysis neglects any elements that lead to systematic growth of output. Recall from the discussion in Chapter 7 that the growth of output has some implications for inflation. Namely, countries with higher average growth rates of output tend to have less inflation for a given average growth rate of money. Although it is not hard to incorporate this feature into the analysis, we assume that output is constant in order to deal with the simplest case.

We can illustrate the main results by assuming a constant rate of monetary growth. Therefore, we have

$$M_t = (1 + \mu)M_{t-1} \qquad (8.3)$$

where μ (the Greek letter *mu*) is the monetary growth rate. We assume that equation (8.3) governs the behavior of money at least from the current date, which we label as $t = 1$, and out into the indefinite future.

We want to calculate the price level at each date, given the behavior of money from equation (8.3). Generally, the model determines the time path of prices from the two aggregate-consistency conditions, which we mentioned before. But we already determined the real interest rate and output in order to equate aggregate commodity supply and demand from equation (8.1). Further, if the supply and demand functions do not shift over time, then the real interest rate, r, and output, Y, are constants. Therefore, given these results, the price level, P_t, must satisfy the condition that money be willingly held—that is

$$M_t/P_t = H (Y, R_t, \ldots)$$
$$(+) (-) \qquad (8.4)$$

In Chapter 6 we found that once-and-for-all increases in the quantity of money raise the price level in the same proportion. Therefore, consider the possibility that the price level, P_t, grows at the same rate as the money stock, M_t. In this case the inflation rate, π, is constant and equal to the rate of monetary growth, μ. So let's make this guess and see whether it accords with the condition from equation (8.4) that all money be willingly held.

If money and prices grow at the same rate, then the ratio of these two, which is the level of real cash balances, M_t/P_t, does not change over time. Therefore, the amount of real cash, which appears on the left side of equation (8.4), is constant.

Recall that the nominal interest rate, R_t, equals the quantity, $r_t + \pi_t$. But we already know that the real interest rate is constant. Therefore, if the inflation rate is constant, then the nominal interest rate is also constant. Finally, this result means that the real demand for money, which appears on the right side of equation (8.4), is constant. (Remember that output, Y, does not change over time.)

Since actual and desired real cash balances are constant, we have only to be sure that the two constants are the same. But this condition holds if we determine the current price level, P_1, in order to equate the amount of real cash balances, M_1/P_1, to the real quantity demanded. Then, since actual and desired real cash do not vary over time, we ensure that all money is willingly held at each date. That is, equation (8.4) holds in every period.

To summarize, the solution is as follows:

- Prices grow at the same rate as the money stock—that is, $\pi = \mu$.
- Aggregate real money balances, M_t/P_t, are constant.
- The nominal interest rate, R, is constant and equal to the quantity, $r + \pi$.
- The aggregate demand for real balances, $H(Y, R, \ldots)$, is constant.
- The current price level, P_1, equates the quantity of real cash balances to the amount demanded.

Notice that the results imply that the growth rate of money, μ, shows up one-to-one in the inflation rate, π, and in the nominal interest rate, $R = r + \pi$. But recall that a higher nominal interest rate means a lower level of real money demanded. Therefore, a higher growth rate of money corresponds to a lower level of aggregate real cash balances, M_t/P_t.

A Shift in the Monetary Growth Rate

We can better understand the results about inflation and the nominal interest rate by studying a change in the monetary growth rate. Suppose that the money stock has been growing for a long time at the constant rate, μ. Further, everyone expects this behavior to persist indefinitely. Hence, the inflation rate is the constant, $\pi = \mu$, and the nominal interest rate is given by

$$R = r + \pi = r + \mu$$

We show this initial situation on the left side of Figure 8.1.

Consider how the quantity of money, M_t, behaves over time. We have the sequence

$$M_1 = (1 + \mu)M_0$$

$$M_2 = (1 + \mu)M_1 = (1 + \mu)^2 M_0$$

.

.

.

Therefore, for any period t, the quantity of money is given by

$$M_t = (1 + \mu)^t M_0 \tag{8.5}$$

We shall find it convenient to graph the quantity of money, M_t, on a proportionate scale. On this type of scale (which is also called a logarithmic scale), each unit on the vertical axis corresponds to an equal proportional change in a variable—say, a 1% change in the stock of money. Therefore, since money grows at the constant proportionate rate μ, the graph of money versus time is a straight line on a proportionate scale. Further, the slope of the line equals the growth rate, μ.

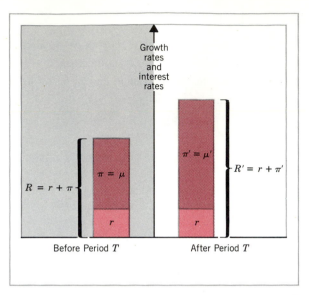

Figure 8.1 Growth Rates of Money and Prices, and Levels of Interest Rates: Effects of an Increase in the Monetary Growth Rate

Before Period T, the growth rate of money is μ. Hence, the left side of the figure shows that the inflation rate is $\pi = \mu$, and the nominal interest rate is $R = r + \pi = r + \mu$. After period T, the growth rate of money is the higher value μ'. Consequently, the new inflation rate is $\pi' = \mu'$, and the new nominal interest rate is $R' = r + \pi' = r + \mu'$.

Accordingly, on the left side of Figure 8.2, we graph the quantity of money, M_t, as a straight line with slope μ.[1]

We found before that the price level grows also at the constant rate, $\pi = \mu$—that is,

$$P_t = (1 + \pi)^t P_0 = (1 + \mu)^t P_0 \qquad (8.6)$$

Therefore, the graph of the price level, P_t, on the left side of Figure 8.2 is a straight line with slope μ. Note that this line parallels the one for the stock of money, M_t.

Assume now that the growth rate of money rises from μ to μ' at some date T. Here, we think of this change as a surprise—that is, before date T no one anticipated the acceleration of money. But once it happens, we assume that everyone expects that the new monetary growth rate, μ', will persist indefinitely. Hence, we study here the consequences of a once-and-for-all increase in the rate of monetary expansion.

After the change in the monetary growth rate, the economy is in the same type of situation as before. The only difference is that the growth rate of money is μ', rather than μ. Therefore, we show on the right side of Figure 8.1 that the new

---

[1]We ignore the discrete length of periods in this graph. In effect, we treat this length as being extremely brief.

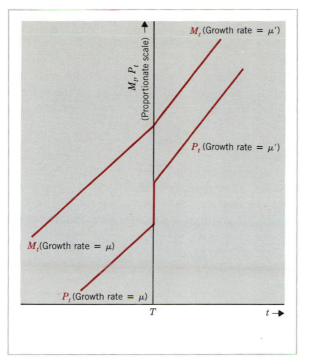

Figure 8.2 **Effect of an Increase in the Monetary Growth Rate on the Path of the Price Level**

We show the behavior of money and prices before and after an increase in the monetary growth rate at date T. Notice that a jump in the price level occurs at date T.

inflation rate is $\pi' = \mu'$. Also, we know that the change in monetary behavior does not affect the real interest rate, which remains at the value r. Therefore, the new nominal interest rate is the value, $R' = r + \pi' = r + \mu'$. In other words, the inflation rate and the nominal interest rate each rise by as much as the increase in the monetary growth rate.

We show the levels of money and prices after date T (on a proportionate scale) on the right side of Figure 8.2. Because the growth rate of money rises after date T, the line for the money stock, M_t, has the slope μ', which exceeds the original slope. Also, since prices grow at the rate $\pi' = \mu'$ after date T, we again show the line for the price level, P_t, as parallel to that for the money stock.

Notice an important complication in the graph of the price level, P_t, in Figure 8.2. Namely, we show a jump in the price level at date T. Let's see why this jump appears.

The acceleration of money at date T raises the nominal interest rate from the value, $R = r + \mu$, to the higher value, $R' = r + \mu'$. But recall that an increase in the nominal interest rate reduces the real demand for money. Hence, the existing amount of cash will be willingly held at date T only if the actual real cash balances, M_T/P_T, fall by as much as the real demand. But there is no sudden change in the nominal quantity of money at date T—only an increase in the rate of growth. Therefore, real balances can fall to equal the smaller amount demanded only if there is an upward jump in the price level at date T.[2]

We can also say something about the size of the jump in the price level at date T. Note that the proportionate rise in the price level equals the proportionate fall in real cash balances, which equals the proportionate decline in the real demand for money. Further, the magnitude of the decline in money demand depends on two things: first, the change in the nominal interest rate, which is $\mu' - \mu$, and second, the sensitivity of real money demanded to changes in the nominal interest rate. Therefore, the jump in the price level is greater the larger is the acceleration of money, $\mu' - \mu$, and the greater is the sensitivity of money demand to changes in the nominal interest rate.

The Increase in the Nominal Interest Rate

Let's think about why the acceleration of money at date T leads to a rise in the nominal interest rate. At date T, people learn that the government will, henceforth, pursue a more expansionary monetary policy. They know also that this policy means a rate of inflation, $\pi' = \mu'$, which exceeds the initial rate, $\pi = \mu$. Consider what the higher expected rate of inflation does at date T in the credit market. Borrowers now regard the old nominal interest rate, R, as a better deal. That's because the real interest rate that they must pay has fallen from the value, $R - \mu$, to the lower value, $R - \mu'$. Hence, if the nominal interest rate did not change, borrowers would raise their demand for loans. On the other side, lenders see that their real rate of return has deteriorated. Therefore, if the nominal interest rate did not change, lenders would decrease their supply of loans. Overall, we can reattain balance between the demand and supply for loans—that is, clear the credit market—only if the nominal interest rate rises.

The new nominal interest rate, R', exceeds the old one, R, by the amount of the increase in the inflation rate, $\mu' - \mu$. Lenders view this rise in the nominal rate as just sufficient to compensate them for the loss of purchasing power over time, because of the higher inflation rate. Similarly, borrowers are willing to pay the higher nominal interest rate because they expect to repay their loans with more heavily deflated dollars. In other words, the increase in the nominal interest rate incorporates fully the change in expected inflation. Thereby, the acceleration of money and prices does not change the real interest rate, r.

---

[2]This type of solution appears in Thomas Sargent and Neil Wallace, ''The Stability of Models of Money and Growth with Perfect Foresight,'' *Econometrica*, November 1973. (This paper is difficult reading.)

The Jump in the Price Level

Let's examine now why the price level jumps upward at date T. The sudden prospect of higher inflation and the consequent rise in the nominal interest rate lead to a sharp fall in the real demand for money at date T. Therefore, if the price level did not adjust, people's actual real cash balances, M_T/P_T, would exceed their desired amount. Consequently, everyone would attempt to spend this excess cash by buying either goods or bonds. (This mechanism is the real-balance effect.) Then the rise in the demand for goods puts upward pressure on the price level. In fact, the economy returns to a position of general market clearing only when the price level rises enough to equate actual and desired real cash. But this condition is the one that we used to determine the size of the jump in the price level in Figure 8.2.

Decreases in Monetary Growth

We can apply the same method of analysis when the rate of monetary growth decreases. Then we reach the following conclusions:

- There are no changes in output and the (expected) real interest rate.
- The inflation rate and the nominal interest rate fall by as much as the decline in the growth rate of money.
- The real demand for money increases.
- The price level jumps downward in order to equate actual real cash balances to the higher quantity demanded.

The Dynamics of Inflation

Return now to the case where monetary growth rises from the initial value, μ, to the higher value, μ'. Let's consider further the transition between the initial rate of inflation, $\pi = \mu$, and the subsequent rate, $\pi' = \mu'$. Because the nominal interest rate increases, the level of real cash balances decreases. Hence, in order for real cash to fall, there must always be a transition period during which prices rise by proportionately more than money. But, in our analysis, this transition occurs in an instant at date T via an upward jump in the price level. In fact, there are a number of real-world considerations that tend to stretch out the transition over several periods. Here, we introduce some of these features in order to study some aspects of the dynamics of inflation.

Anticipated Changes in Monetary Growth

Our analysis can deal with situations where the growth rate of money either rises or falls. But so far, we have looked only at cases where the change in actual monetary growth coincides with the change in perceptions about future monetary growth. That is, two things happen at date T in the previous examples. First, money accelerates or decelerates permanently. Second, people first learn at date T that this acceleration or deceleration will occur.

Sometimes, people receive information in advance that allows them to forecast increases or decreases in the rate of monetary growth. For example, if the end of a war is imminent, then people would project a likely decline in the growth rate of money. Alternatively, during an extreme inflation, there may be promises of a change to a stable monetary regime. For instance, toward the end of the post-World War I **hyperinflation** in Germany, people apparently anticipated that a **monetary reform** was coming.[3] Finally, political developments—such as the outcomes of elections—may indicate that the government will shift to a more or less expansionary monetary policy. For example, William Jennings Bryan campaigned for president in the 1890s on a program of easy money (free coinage of silver). His defeat probably lowered expectations of future monetary growth and inflation—presumably, these expectations would have increased if he had been elected. Similarly, it may be that the election of Ronald Reagan, rather than Jimmy Carter, in 1980 lowered expectations of future monetary growth and inflation.

If people forecast an acceleration or deceleration of money, then the path of inflation differs from those already discussed. Here, in order to avoid a good deal of complicated details, we just sketch the types of effects that arise.

Suppose, as an example, that people learn currently that an acceleration of money is coming at the future date T. Then they know also that inflation rates and nominal interest rates will be higher in the future. But because the cost of holding money rises from date T onward, people tend to reduce their demand for money even before date T. Otherwise, they will get caught holding money at date T when the big increase in prices occurs. Thus, the expectation of future inflation has a negative effect on people's willingness to hold cash today. Then the reduction in today's demand for money means that today's price level rises. In other words, even though the acceleration of money has not yet occurred, the expectation of the future monetary acceleration shows up today as a higher rate of inflation. Finally, since this higher rate of inflation becomes anticipated, the nominal interest rate also rises before the acceleration of money.

The precise time path of inflation depends on when people learn about the acceleration of money. But, as mentioned, one general point is that changes in expectations about future money can generate variations in inflation and the nominal interest rate that precede the changes in monetary growth. Thus, although the analysis stresses monetary factors as the source of inflation, we find that significant divergences can arise in the short run between the growth rates of money and prices. Also, these divergences are likely to be important in an environment—such as the present one in the United States—where a volatile monetary policy induces

---

[3]Peter Garber and Robert Flood quantify these expectations of impending monetary reform in their paper, "An Economic Theory of Monetary Reform," *Journal of Political Economy,* February 1980. See also Laura Lahaye, "Inflation and Currency Reform: a Study of the Effects of Anticipated Policy Switching," unpublished Ph.D. dissertation, University of Chicago, 1980.

frequent revisions in people's forecasts of monetary behavior. Such an environment would also be marked by volatility in inflation rates and nominal interest rates.

Gradual Adjustment in the Demand for Money

Let's return to the case where people first learn at date T that money will be growing at a higher rate. Recall that the size of the jump in the price level at date T depends on the extent of the fall in real money demanded. But suppose that people reduce their demand for money only gradually when the nominal interest rate increases. Then we may find only a small jump—or no jump at all—in the price level at date T. Instead, the extra upward kick to the price level shows up only gradually as people reduce their real demand for money.

Recall that a person's real demand for money reflects some underlying decisions about the frequency of transactions, financial planning, and so on. If the nominal interest rate rises, it is reasonable that people would take some time to alter these aspects of their behavior. Hence, in the aggregate, the real demand for money would decline gradually in response to an increase in the nominal interest rate.

With slow adjustment in the demand for money, we effectively spread out the jump in the price level over a transition interval. Now, when money accelerates at time T, the inflation rate reacts something like the solid line shown in Figure 8.3. Here, the inflation rate, π_t, exceeds the new growth rate of money, μ', over an extended interval. Throughout this period, real cash balances fall gradually as the real demand for money declines. Eventually, the inflation rate approaches its new

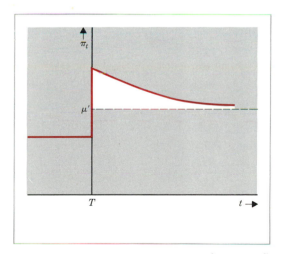

Figure 8.3 **The Effect of Higher Monetary Growth on Inflation, Including Gradual Adjustment in the Demand for Money**

The growth rate of money rises from μ to μ' at date T. The solid line shows that the inflation rate, μ_t, stays above μ' for awhile, but eventually approaches μ'.

long-term value, μ'. Then the level of real cash again remains constant, but at a lower level than initially.

Let's stress a basic feature of these results. Namely, although jumps in the price level need not occur, the acceleration of money must involve a transition during which prices rise by proportionately more than money. This conclusion follows inevitably from the eventual decline in real cash balances.

We can also turn the results around to deal with the case where money decelerates. Then, although a downward jump in the price level need not occur, we find that the transition must involve a period where prices grow by proportionately less than money. This result holds because the lower nominal interest rate raises the real demand for money.

As an example, consider a contractionary monetary policy where the government reduces monetary growth permanently from 10% per year to 5%. Presumably, the objective of this policy is to reduce inflation. Our analysis implies that there is a transition period during which the inflation rate is even less than 5% per year. In fact, there may even be deflation—that is, falling prices—for awhile. Thus, when contemplating a monetary policy to end inflation, we have to think about the potential for very low or negative rates of inflation as a temporary side effect.

Money and Prices During the German Hyperinflation

We can assess some of the theoretical results by examining the data on the post-World War I German hyperinflation. Here, we have something close to a laboratory experiment for studying the consequences of high and variable rates of monetary growth and inflation.[4] In particular, over the period from 1921 to 1923, the rates of inflation ranged from near zero to over 500% per month! Further, the available data suggest that relatively small changes occurred in aggregate real variables, such as total output and employment. (However, the unanticipated part of inflation did cause major redistributions of income, especially in favor of people who began with large nominal debts.) Here, we use the data to focus on the interaction between monetary growth and inflation.

In an environment where inflation rates are volatile, it is impossible to predict accurately the real interest rate on loans that prescribe nominal interest rates. Therefore, as in most extreme inflations, this type of lending tends to disappear. The main exception concerns government loans that bear absurdly low nominal interest rates and which are rationed to favored customers. Also, unlike Israel, Brazil, and some other high-inflation countries at the present day, Germany in the 1920s had no organized credit market in terms of indexed loans. (However, there was an active stock market and much dealing in assets that were denominated in foreign

---

[4]Not surprisingly, the topic has fascinated many economists. Two of the more important studies are C. Bresciani-Turroni, *The Economics of Inflation,* Allen & Unwin, London, 1937; and Phillip Cagan, "The Monetary Dynamics of Hyperinflation," in M. Friedman, ed., *Studies in the Quantity Theory of Money,* University of Chicago Press, Chicago, 1956.

currencies.) So in terms of analyzing the demand for money during the German hyperinflation, we have no useful measures of the nominal interest rate. Hence, the best indicator of the cost of holding money comes directly from the expected rate of inflation, π^e. That is, this rate tells people how much they lose by holding cash, rather than consuming or holding a durable good that maintains its value in real terms.

Table 8.1 summarizes the behavior of the monetary growth rate, μ, the inflation rate, π, and real cash balances, M/P, in Germany from 1920 until 1925. In most cases the table indicates the average growth rates of money and prices over six-month intervals. Then the level of real money balances pertains to the ends of each of these intervals.

At the beginning of 1920 the growth rates of money and prices are already at the very high rate of about 6% per month. (Typically, when talking about hyperinflations, people measure these rates per month, rather than per year!) Then there is a deceleration of money to an average rate of less than 1% per month for the first half of 1921. Notice that, as our theory predicts, the growth rate of prices, π,

Table 8.1 Monetary Growth, Inflation, and Real Cash Balances
During the German Hyperinflation

Period	μ (% per month)	π (% per month)	M/P (end-of-period) (1913 = 1.0)
2/20– 6/20	5.7	6.0	1.01
6/20–12/20	3.0	1.1	1.13
12/20– 6/21	0.8	0.1	1.18
6/21–12/21	5.5	8.4	0.99
12/21– 6/22	6.5	12.8	0.68
6/22–12/22	29.4	46.7	0.24
12/22– 6/23	40.0	40.0	0.24
6/23–10/23	233	286	0.03
- - - - - - - - - - - - - -	**Reform Period**		- - - - - - - - - - - - - - -
12/23– 6/24	5.9	−0.6	0.44
6/24–12/24	5.3	1.4	0.56
12/24– 6/25	2.0	1.6	0.57
6/25–12/25	1.2	0.4	0.60

Note: M is an estimate of the total circulation of currency. Until late 1923 the figures refer to total legal tender, most of which consists of notes issued by the Reichsbank. Later, the data include issues of the Rentenbank, private bank notes, and various ''emergency moneys.'' However, especially in late 1923, many unofficial emergency currencies, as well as circulating foreign currencies, are not counted. We standardize the numbers so that the quantity outstanding in 1913 is 1.0. P is an index of the cost of living, based on 1913 = 1.0.

falls by more than the growth rate of money, μ, when money decelerates. Correspondingly, real cash balances increase by about 20% from early 1920 to early 1921. (The level of real cash in early 1920 is roughly equal to that from before the war in 1913.)

In 1922 money accelerates dramatically to an average growth rate of nearly 30% per month toward the end of the year. Note that during this period, the growth rate of prices, π, exceeds that of money, μ. Hence, by late 1922 real cash balances fall to about one-fourth of the level prevailing in early 1920.

During the first half of 1923 there is some letup in the acceleration of money. Here, money and prices grow together at the extraordinary average rate of 40% per month. Correspondingly, although the rate of inflation is enormous, the level of real cash remains fairly stable. But later in 1923 the hyperinflation builds to its climax with rates of monetary expansion of 300–600% per month for October–November. Again, the acceleration of money leads to rates of inflation that exceed the growth rates of money. Therefore, real cash balances reach their low point in October 1923 at about 3% of the level for early 1920. So, if we neglect variations in aggregate real income from 1920 to 1923—which is satisfactory as a first-order approximation—then the reduction in real cash implies a rise in velocity by over 30-fold. In other words, if in 1920 people held the typical piece of currency for two weeks before spending it, then in October 1923 they held it for about half a day.

A major monetary reform takes place in Germany during November 1923. This reform includes the introduction of a new type of currency, a promise not to print new money beyond a specified limit in order to finance government expenditures or for other purposes, some changes in government spending and taxes, and a commitment to back the new currency by gold.[5] In any event, there is a sharp curtailment in monetary growth and inflation after December 1923. For example, during 1924 monetary growth averages 5–6% per month. But because of the deceleration of money after November 1923, the average inflation rate is even less—below 1% per month for 1924. Most dramatically, the quantity of real cash balances rises from 3% of the early-1920 level in October 1923 to 56% of that level by December 1924. (Much of the increase in real cash arises as an infusion of the new types of currency during the reform months of November–December 1923.)

Finally, in 1925 the growth rate of money falls to 1–2% per month, while the inflation rate remains at roughly 1% per month. Correspondingly, there is a slow rise in real cash, which reaches 60% of the early-1920 level by late 1925. Interestingly, although the inflation rate remains low for the remainder of the 1920s, the level of real cash does not reattain the early-1920 level. Perhaps this discrepancy reflects a long-lasting negative influence of the hyperinflation on people's willingness to hold money.

---

[5]For discussions of the reform, see Thomas Sargent, "The Ends of Four Big Inflations," in Robert Hall, ed., *Inflation: Causes and Effects,* University of Chicago Press for the National Bureau of Economic Research, Chicago, 1982, Section 2.6; and Peter Garber, "Transition from Inflation to Price Stability," *Carnegie-Rochester Conference Series on Public Policy,* Spring 1982.

Some Real Effects of Anticipated Inflation

Real Cash Balances and Transaction Costs

A key theoretical result is the invariance of some real variables, such as aggregate output, from anticipated variations in money. But recall that we do not consider real effects from the unpredictability of inflation. During the German hyperinflation, these effects include massive redistribution of wealth and the disappearance of most organized loan markets. Also, there are some indications that the process of dealing with the severe inflation in late 1923 had some adverse effects on aggregate output. But in any case, one clear real effect from the inflation is the reduction of real cash balances. During the German hyperinflation this response is dramatic, with aggregate real cash falling to about 3% of its initial level.

Corresponding to the increase in expected inflation and the reduction in real cash, people expend more resources on transaction costs. Although we regard these costs as small in normal times, we cannot neglect them during extreme circumstances, such as the German hyperinflation. For example, people spend a significant portion of their time on the process of receiving wage and other payments once or twice per day and in searching rapidly to find outlets for their cash.

The Revenue from Money Creation

A different real effect from inflation concerns the **government's revenue from printing money.** In our theory the government uses this income solely to finance transfers. But more generally, governments use the printing press to pay for a variety of expenditures.

Recall that the real amount of revenue for period t is the quantity, $(M_t - M_{t-1})/P_t$. Using the condition, $M_t = (1 + \mu)M_{t-1}$, we can rewrite this expression as

$$\text{real revenue from printing money} = (M_t - M_{t-1})/P_t = \mu \cdot M_{t-1}/P_t \quad (8.7)$$

Therefore, the real revenue is the product of the growth rate of money, μ, and a term that approximates the level of aggregate real money held, M_{t-1}/P_t. Now, recall that an increase in the monetary growth rate leads to a reduction in real cash balances. Hence, real revenue increases only if the magnitude of the proportionate decline in real cash is smaller than the proportionate increase in the monetary growth rate. Empirically, this condition holds except for the most extreme cases. For example, during the German hyperinflation, the condition was apparently not violated until the growth rate of money approached 100% per month between July and August 1923. Until then, the government successfully extracted more real income by printing money at higher rates.

In normal times for most countries, the government obtains only a small portion of its revenue from printing money. For example, in recent years the Federal Reserve obtains about $10–15 billion from this source. These amounts correspond to between 1 and 3% of total U.S. government revenues, and to less than 1% of the GNP.[6] More broadly, for 14 industrialized countries over the period 1960–78, the revenue from money creation averages about 1% of the GNP.[7]

In a few high-inflation countries, the revenue from money creation is far more important. As an extreme example, for Argentina over 1960–75, money creation accounts for nearly half of government revenues and for about 6% of the GNP. Some other countries where the revenue from printing money is important include Chile (5% of the GNP over 1960–77), Libya (3% of the GNP over 1960–77), and Brazil (3% of the GNP over 1960–78).[8]

During the German hyperinflation and in some other hyperinflations (such as Austria, Hungary, Poland, and Russia after World War I), money creation became the primary source of government revenue. Eventually, the amounts obtained approached 10–15% of the GNP, which appears to be about the maximum obtainable from printing money.[9] Also, there is a close month-to-month connection in Germany between the volume of real government spending and the growth rate of the money supply. That is, the variations in monetary growth—and hence, inflation— were driven in this case by shifts in real government spending.[10] Interestingly, much of the government spending over this period went to reparations payments associated with World War I. Therefore, the reduction in these payments after November 1923 is probably a major factor in the success of the German monetary reform.

Summary

We used the market-clearing model to analyze the interactions among monetary growth, inflation, and nominal and real interest rates. An important result is that the real interest rate and aggregate output are invariant with anticipated variations in the quantity of money. However, money is not superneutral in the model. (By superneutral, we mean that variations in the time path of money have no real effects.) In fact, the behavior of money influences the level of real cash balances, the nominal interest rate, and the volume of transaction costs. Further, the invariance of the real interest rate and aggregate output holds only as an approximation.

An increase in the growth rate of money shows up in the long run as a parallel increase in the inflation rate and the nominal interest rate. However, because the higher nominal interest rate reduces the real demand for money, there must be a

---

[6]See Robert Barro, ''Measuring the Fed's Revenue from Money Creation,'' *Economics Letters,* 1982, Tables 2 and 3.

[7]See Stanley Fischer, ''Seigniorage and the Case for a National Money,'' *Journal of Political Economy,* April 1982, Table A2.

[8]These figures are from Stanley Fischer, op. cit.

[9]These results come from Robert Barro, ''Inflationary Finance and the Welfare Cost of Inflation,'' *Journal of Political Economy,* September/October 1972.

[10]For a detailed analysis of this process, see Zvi Hercowitz, ''Money and the Dispersion of Relative Prices,'' *Journal of Political Economy,* April 1981.

transition interval during which the rate of inflation exceeds the growth rate of money. In a simple case the transition occurs in an instant via an upward jump in the price level. But if we bring in some realistic extensions of the model—such as foreknowledge of the acceleration of money and gradual adjustment of money demand—then we find a richer dynamics of prices during the transition. Here, the inflation rate exceeds the growth rate of money during the transition interval.

Similar results obtain for a decrease in the growth rate of money. Then the process of reducing inflation involves a transition period with unusually low rates of inflation, which may even be negative.

We illustrate some of the results by observing the dynamics of monetary growth and inflation during the post-World War I German hyperinflation. The data show that higher rates of monetary growth lead to lower levels of real cash balances, and vice versa. We also discuss the effects of this inflation on transaction costs and on the real revenue that the government receives from printing money.

Important Terms and Concepts

perfect foresight

superneutrality of money

hyperinflation

monetary reform

government's revenue from printing money

QUESTIONS AND PROBLEMS

Mainly for Review

8.1 Distinguish between a once-for-all change in the quantity of money and growth in the money stock over time.

8.2 Suppose that the commodity market clears at a real interest rate of 4%.
    a. If the inflation rate is zero, what is the nominal interest rate? If the inflation rate is 10%, what is the nominal interest rate?
    b. If the nominal interest rate did not go up by the same amounts as the inflation rate, what would happen to the commodity market, i.e., would there be excess supply or excess demand?

8.3 Suppose that the rate of monetary growth is constant and equal to μ, while the price level grows at a constant rate less than μ. Will the real value of cash balances equal the demand for money?

8.4 Which of the following statements is correct?
    a. A constant rate of increase in the price level will lead to a continuous rise in the nominal interest rate.
    b. A continuous increase in the inflation rate will lead to a continuous rise in the nominal interest rate.

8.5 What would be the effect on the nominal interest rate of each of the following events?

a. The announcement of a one-time increase in the money stock.

b. The announcement of a planned increase in the rate of monetary growth.

Why does the price level jump in both instances? Does the velocity of money increase in both instances?

8.6 Critically review the following statement: "The quantity theory of money predicts that the rate of inflation must equal the rate of monetary growth. In fact, the two are not equal; therefore the theory is wrong." How do factors such as an anticipated increase in inflation or gradual adjustment in the demand for money alter the prediction? What about factors considered in Chapter 7, such as growth in output?

8.7 Can the government always increase its revenue by raising the rate of monetary growth? How does the answer depend on the response of money demand to the nominal interest rate?

Problems for Discussion

8.8 The Superneutrality of Money

a. What is the meaning of the term, *superneutrality of money?*

b. Is money superneutral in our model? In particular, if the behavior of money changes, then which real variables change and which do not change? Explain the factors that underlie these results.

8.9 Stopping Inflation (optional)

Assume that money and prices have been growing for a long time at 10% per year. As the president's chief adviser on monetary affairs, you have been told to design a monetary policy to end inflation. The president says that he wants inflation eradicated within two years. But he also wants a gradual reduction of inflation until then—in particular, deflation is unacceptable. In constructing a policy, assume the following things about the economy:

a. Each decline by 1 percentage point in the nominal interest rate raises the real demand for money in the long run by 2–4 percent. (This range is the right order of magnitude.) However, we have little information about the speed with which people adjust their demand for money to changes in the nominal interest rate.

b. It is unclear whether people will believe any governmental announcements about future policies. (This is surely realistic!)

c. The expected real interest rate and the path of output do not depend on the choice of monetary policy. (This is probably false—but, the problem is hard enough anyway.)

i. What monetary policy would you propose?

In discussing the choice of policy, consider the following:

ii. What is the size of the potential deflation that could occur during the transition to zero inflation? Would it help much if the president were willing to wait four years to eliminate inflation?

8.10 Effects of Supply Shocks on the Price Level

In Chapter 6 we analyzed the effects of permanent and temporary shifts to the production function. A downward shift leads to lower output and a higher price level. If the shift is temporary, as in the case of a harvest failure, then the real interest rate increases. But since the disturbance is temporary, the responses of output, the price level and the real interest rate are also temporary. In particular, if the stock of money does not change over time, then the price level would decline in the future. But so far, the analysis ignores this anticipated deflation.

Use the above discussion to analyze the effects of a temporary downward shift to the production function. Specifically, if the quantity of money is constant over time, then what are the effects on the current values of output, the real interest rate, the nominal interest rate, the price level, and the expected rate of inflation?

PART II

THE LABOR MARKET, INVESTMENT, AND ECONOMIC GROWTH

CHAPTER 9

THE LABOR MARKET AND UNEMPLOYMENT

In order to simplify matters, we pretended that households used only their own labor in order to produce goods. Now we make things more realistic by introducing a market where people can exchange labor services. In particular, some people—whom we can think of as firms or employers—hire others as workers. Then these other people are the employees in the economy.

For now, we assume that everyone's labor services are physically the same. Also, we focus for the moment on whether or not people have jobs, rather than on variations in the hours worked or degree of effort for those that are working. Then we think of aggregate employment, L, as the number of people with jobs. (Here, we include the owners of firms, as well as the employees, in the total of employment.) On the other hand, the **labor force** includes those employed, L, plus those **unemployed,** U. By unemployed, we refer to people who are looking for work, but presently have no job. Thus, those who neither have a job nor are looking for one are classed as being outside of the labor force. Finally, we define the **unemployment rate,** u, to be the ratio of the number unemployed to the labor force—that is

$$u = U/(L + U) \tag{9.1}$$

The Behavior of U.S. Unemployment Rates

Before we theorize about the determinants of unemployment, it is worth taking a quick look at the U.S. data. Table 9.1 shows unemployment rates for all workers and for various categories of workers by age, sex, and race. Note that the data are averages for 1948–82 and for various subperiods.

The average unemployment rate for all civilian workers for 1948–82 is 5.4%. (It is 5.2% if we use the total labor force, which includes military personnel.)[1] But

---

[1]As of January 1983, the official figure on the unemployment rate is based on the total labor force. Since military personnel are employed (!), this change in definition is desirable.

Table 9.1 Behavior of U.S. Unemployment Rates

| | (% of Civilian Labor Force Within Category) | | | | | | % of Total Labor Force All Workers |
	All Civilian Workers	Males 20 yrs. & Older	Females 20 yrs. & Older	Teenagers (16–19)	White	Black & Other Minorities	
1948–54	4.2	3.7	4.2	10.2	3.9	7.0	4.1
1955–61	5.3	4.6	5.1	13.7	4.7	10.1	5.1
1962–68	4.6	3.3	4.6	14.5	4.1	8.7	4.4
1969–75	5.6	4.0	5.4	15.9	5.0	9.6	5.4
1976–82	7.3	5.8	6.8	18.6	6.4	13.4	7.2
1948–82	5.4	4.2	5.2	14.6	4.8	9.8	5.2

Note: The table shows the average unemployment rate over the period indicated for various categories of workers. In the last column the total labor force adds military personnel to the civilian labor force.
Source: Economic Report of the President, 1983.

the average unemployment rates vary substantially by demographic characteristics. For example, among persons 20 years and older, the average rate for females is 5.2%, while that for males is 4.2%. For both sexes, the average unemployment rate declines by age until people reach at least their 50s. But the sharpest distinction applies to teenagers, who have an average unemployment rate of 14.6%, as compared to about 4.5% for those at least 20 years of age. Finally, the average rate for blacks (and other minorities) of 9.8% is roughly double that for whites, which is 4.8%.

Table 9.1 does not indicate much change over time in the relative unemployment rates for the various demographic groups. For example, the unemployment rate for females over 20 is typically close to the overall rate. That for teenagers averages 2.7 times the overall rate, with no clear change in this relation over time. Similarly, the rate for blacks is reasonably stable at around 1.8 times the overall rate.

Aside from the last subperiod, 1976–82, there is no sign of long-term change in the average rate of unemployment for all civilian workers. However, there is some indication that the average rate of unemployment increased by 1–2 percentage points during the 1970s. Also, the increase applies more or less uniformly to the various categories by age, sex, and race.

Job Separations, Job Finding, and the Natural Unemployment Rate

During any period, some fraction of those employed, L, will lose their jobs. We call these **job separations.** Sometimes, economists try to distinguish among *lay-offs, fires,* and *quits,* but these distinctions are hard to apply in practice. Therefore, we consider here only the total number of job losers. Note that, from the standpoint of economic efficiency, there are many good reasons to have job separations. For example, workers may be poorly matched with their existing jobs in terms of skills, preferences for types of work, job location, and so on. Further, changes in the mix of production—such as the reductions for 1980–82 in the U.S. output of automobiles and steel—can generate substantial numbers of job separations.

In Figure 9.1 the box labeled L represents those employed, while the box labeled U represents those unemployed. For now, we pretend that no one either leaves or enters the labor force. Then the arrow pointing from L to U in the figure indicates the number of job separations for the period. (Here, we neglect the possibility that people find a job without ever becoming unemployed.) Finally, for the purpose of an example, we assume that 1% of those employed lose their jobs each period.

The second thing that happens each period is that some fraction of those unemployed find jobs. Note that it would often be inefficient for someone to take a new job immediately upon leaving a previous one. Rather, the process of finding jobs involves a mutual process of search between employers and employees. In Figure 9.1 the arrow pointing from U to L represents the number of unemployed persons who find jobs during a period. Here (in order for the example to generate roughly the right answers later on), we assume that 15% of those unemployed find work each period.

We can work through the process of job separation and **job finding** in order to determine the numbers of people employed and unemployed. In Table 9.2 we assume that the labor force is fixed at 100 million people (the actual size of the total labor force in 1982 was 112 million), and that the economy starts in period 1 with 90 million employed and 10 million unemployed. Thus, the unemployment rate is initially 10%. Then, of the 90 million workers, 1%—or 0.9 million people—lose their jobs in the first period. Simultaneously, 15% of those unemployed—or 1.5 million people—find jobs. Hence, the net change in employment during period 1 is 0.6 million. Correspondingly, unemployment falls by 0.6 million.

As the number of employed increases and the number of unemployed decreases, the quantity of job separations (1% of those employed) rises, while the

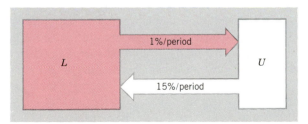

Figure 9.1 Movements Between Employment and Unemployment
In this example, 1% of those employed (L) lose their jobs each period. Simultaneously, 15% of those unemployed (U) find jobs each period. Therefore, the net change in the number employed during the period is $15\% \cdot U - 1\% \cdot L$. Also, the change in the number unemployed is the negative of the change in the number employed.

Table 9.2 The Dynamics of Employment and Unemployment and the Natural Rate of Unemployment

Period	Number Employed (L)	Number Unemployed (U)	Number Who Lose Jobs	Number Who Find Jobs	Net Change in Employment	Net Change in Unemployment
1	90.0	10.0	0.9	1.5	0.6	−0.6
2	90.6	9.4	0.9	1.4	0.5	−0.5
3	91.1	8.9	0.9	1.3	0.4	−0.4
4	91.5	8.5	0.9	1.3	0.4	−0.4
5	91.9	8.1	0.9	1.2	0.3	−0.3
6	92.2	7.8	0.9	1.2	0.3	−0.3
.	.	.	.	.	.	.
.	.	.	.	.	.	.
.	.	.	.	.	.	.
∞	93.8	6.2	0.9	0.9	0	0

Note: We assume that the economy starts with 90 million people employed (L) and 10 million unemployed (U). Then, from Figure 9.1, 1% of those employed lose their job each period, but 15% of those unemployed find jobs. Therefore, the net change in employment is $15\% \cdot U - 1\% \cdot L$. Also, the change in unemployment is the negative of the change in employment. Finally, when the number employed reaches 93.8 million and the number unemployed reaches 6.2 million, the net changes in employment and unemployment are zero. Thus, the natural unemployment rate in this example is 6.2%.

quantity of job findings (15% of those unemployed) falls. Therefore, the increase in employment slows down over time. Eventually, the economy approaches levels of employment and unemployment at which the number of job separations and findings are equal. Then, as long as the rates of job separation and job finding do not change, employment and unemployment are constant.[2] In the example the balance between job separations and job findings occurs when employment equals 93.8 million and unemployment equals 6.2 million—that is, when the unemployment rate is 6.2%. Therefore, in this model, we can say that the **natural unemployment rate** is 6.2%. Namely, the economy tends toward this rate automatically, given the rates at which people lose and find jobs.

Let's observe some important points about the natural unemployment rate. First, although the unemployment rate eventually stays constant at this value, there is still a substantial amount of job turnover going on. Specifically, almost a million people lose and find jobs each period in the example when the unemployment rate is 6.2%. In this model—and in the real world—large flows from employment to unemployment and vice versa are a normal part of the operation of the labor market.

Second, the dynamics of employment and unemployment, as well as the value of the natural unemployment rate, depend on the rates of job separation and job finding. In the example these rates per period are 1 and 15%, respectively. But let's examine things more generally by denoting the rate of job separation by s,

---

[2]If we allowed for a growing labor force, then the numbers employed and unemployed would tend to grow along with the labor force.

and the rate of job finding by η (the Greek letter *eta*). Then the change in the number employed during a period, ΔL, is given by

$$\Delta L = \eta U - sL \tag{9.2}$$

Note that the first term, ηU, is the number of unemployed who find jobs during the period, while the second term, sL, is the number of employed who lose jobs. Accordingly, equation (9.2) says that the change in employment equals job findings less job separations.

Equation (9.2) implies that employment increases if job findings, ηU, exceed job separations, sL. In the reverse case employment decreases. Thus, in order to determine the natural levels of employment and unemployment, we set the change in employment, ΔL, to zero in equation (9.2). Then, using the condition that the labor force, $L + U$, is fixed at 100 million, we find that

$$\eta U = sL = s(100 - U)$$

Solving this equation for the number unemployed, U, determines the natural values for unemployment and employment as

$$U = 100 \cdot s/(s + \eta) \tag{9.3}$$
$$L = 100 \cdot \eta/(s + \eta)$$

Therefore, the natural unemployment rate is[3]

$$u = U/100 = s/(s + \eta) \tag{9.4}$$

Recall that, in our example, $s = 0.01$ per period and $\eta = 0.15$ per period. Thus, $u = 0.01/0.16 = 6.2\%$, as we found before.

Equation (9.4) relates the natural unemployment rate to the rate of job separation, s, and the rate of job finding, η. Specifically, a higher rate of separation, s, raises the natural unemployment rate, but a higher rate of finding, η, lowers it. Thus, when we examine differences in natural unemployment rates—either over groups of people or over time—we should look for differences in the rates of job separation and job finding. People who either lose jobs more frequently or who have more trouble in finding jobs will be unemployed a larger fraction of the time.

Movements in and out of the Labor Force

Before applying the theory to the data on unemployment rates, we can usefully extend the analysis to include movements in and out of the labor force. Conceptually, we classify people as **outside of the labor force** if they neither have a market job nor are currently looking for one. (Hence, the category includes full-

---

[3]For more thorough theoretical analyses of this type of model, see Robert Hall, "A Theory of the Natural Unemployment Rate and the Duration of Unemployment," *Journal of Monetary Economics,* April 1979; and Chitra Ramaswami, "Equilibrium Unemployment and the Efficient Job-Finding Rate," *Journal of Labor Economics,* April, 1983.

time students and homemakers, who might reasonably think of themselves as ''employed.'') In practice, there are sometimes great difficulties in distinguishing those outside the labor force from those unemployed. That's because the distinction comes only from people's answers to a survey question as to whether they are actively ''looking for work'' during a particular time period. To some extent, the number classified as unemployed underestimates the true number, because some of those labeled as outside of the labor force would also like market jobs (at some wage rate!). But on the other hand, many of those who are called unemployed are not actually interested in accepting employment on terms that they could reasonably expect to receive.

For our purposes, the important new effects involve movements from inside the labor force to outside and vice versa. There are many good reasons for these movements—for example, when people retire, when they leave or reenter school, when they have changes in marital status or in the number and ages of children, or when the nature of the available jobs changes.

Figure 9.2 shows the possible transitions among the three categories, employment, unemployment, and outside of the labor force. (Notice that the flows labeled 2 and 3 are those that we studied before.) The list of possibilities is as follows:

1. A change in job, without becoming unemployed or leaving the labor force. (This type of shift is especially popular among sports figures and professors of economics—but, in fact, more than half of all job changes do not involve any unemployment.)[4]

2. A loss of a job with a move to unemployment.

3. The finding of a job from the ranks of the unemployed.

4. A movement from unemployment to outside of the labor force—sometimes described as **discouraged workers.**

5. An entry or reentry to the labor force, but initially unemployed.

6. An entry or reentry to the labor force, with a job obtained at once (as in the case of most graduating majors in business and economics).

7. A loss of a job with a move outside of the labor force (which includes permanent retirements, as well as withdrawals from the labor market in order to raise a family or return to school).

Notice that total job separations are the sum of flows 1, 2, and 7, while total job findings are the sum of flows 1, 3, and 6. Then the difference between separations and findings is the change in employment. On the other hand, the change in unemployment is the sum of flows 2 and 5, less the sum of flows 3 and 4. Thus, because of the movements in and out of the labor force, the change in employment no longer coincides with the negative of the change in unemployment.

As before—but with greater complexity—people's tendencies to experience

---

[4]See Kim Clark and Lawrence Summers, ''Labor Market Dynamics and Unemployment: a Reconsideration,'' *Brookings Papers on Economic Activity,* 1:1979, p. 43.

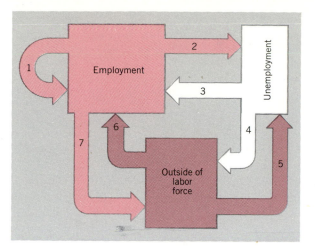

Figure 9.2 The Flows of People Among Three Categories: Employment, Unemployment, and Outside of the Labor Force
The diagram shows the possible moves from one category to another.

the various transitions shown in Figure 9.2 determine the levels of employment and unemployment over time. It is still true that employment tends to be lower the higher is the rate of job separation. Similarly, employment tends to be higher the greater is the rate of job finding. But the movements in and out of the labor force interact with these tendencies to lose and find jobs. For example, people who move frequently in and out of the labor force build up relatively little work experience. Hence, they tend to be the ones who are terminated first and hired last.

For unemployment the new effects concern the possibilities for moving outside of the labor force. For example, the tendency for the unemployed to cease looking for work (flow 4 in Figure 9.2) reduces the number of persons counted as unemployed. But the tendency for people to shift from employment to outside of the labor force (flow 7) tends to raise unemployment. That's because first, these people often become unemployed when they reenter the labor force (flow 5), and second, they are more likely to lose a job later on (flows 2 and 7).

The Behavior of U.S. Unemployment Rates by Demographic Groups

Let's reconsider the data on U.S. unemployment rates, which appear in Table 9.1. Recall that these data show large differences among demographic groups. Now we try to think of these variations as differences in natural unemployment rates, which relate in turn to differences in the rates of job separation and job finding. In order to compare the rates of job separation for the various groups, we look at data on the **duration of jobs.** Basically, people with high rates of job separation end up with short-term jobs, and vice versa. Similarly, in order to get information about job-finding rates, we consider data on the **duration of unemployment.** Those who find jobs quickly end up with brief spells of unemployment, and vice versa.

The Duration of Jobs

The research by Bob Hall[5] on job separations allows us to understand some of the differences in unemployment rates by age, sex, and race. First, most new jobs that people get do not last very long. For example, using data for 1973, Hall estimates that 61% of new jobs last less than one year, while the average duration of a new job is 4 years. But as people get older and try a variety of jobs, most workers eventually find a good job match, which lasts for a long time. In particular (based on data from 1978), by age 50 over 70% of all workers have been on their present job for at least 5 years. Also, by age 40, about 40% of all workers are currently in a very long-term job, which will eventually last at least 20 years. These results mean that job separations (flows 1, 2, and 7 in Figure 9.2) are much more frequent for younger workers, most of whom have not yet found a long-lasting job match. Therefore, this element explains a good deal of the higher unemployment rate for younger persons, especially teenagers.

A lower average duration of jobs can also explain some of the higher average unemployment rate for women than for men. For example, Hall estimates for 1978 that about 50% of women who have jobs will eventually reach a tenure of at least 5 years on their present job, while about 15% will reach at least 20 years. But the comparable figures for men are 64 and 37%, respectively. Basically, women move in and out of the labor force (flows 4, 5, 6 and 7 in Figure 9.2) over their lifetime much more often than men do.

Contrary to popular belief, Hall's figures suggest that blacks have roughly the same chance as whites to stay on a job for a long time. For example, for 1978, his estimate is that 63% of blacks who have jobs will have an eventual tenure of at least 5 years on their current job, while 26% will reach at least 20 years. The figures for whites—which are 57 and 29%, respectively—are basically similar. However, some other data show that blacks are much more likely than whites to experience a job separation in any given month. In particular, Stephen Marston[6] estimates that this element accounts for about one-third of the higher average unemployment rate for blacks. If we put Marston's observations together with Hall's, the suggestion is that blacks have a strong tendency toward very short-term jobs, although no less of a tendency to achieve jobs with a duration of at least five years.

---

[5]"The Importance of Lifetime Jobs in the U.S. Economy," *American Economic Review,* September 1982; and "Employment Fluctuations and Wage Rigidity," *Brookings Papers on Economic Activity,* 1:1980.

[6]Stephen Marston, "Employment Stability and High Unemployment," *Brookings Papers on Economic Activity,* 1:1976, Table 4.

The Duration of Unemployment

The other main element that determines the average unemployment rate is the duration of a typical spell of unemployment. Basically, the longer it takes for an unemployed person to find a job or leave the labor force (flows 3 and 4 in Figure 9.2), the greater will be the measured number of unemployed at any point in time.

The research by Clark and Summers[7] provides some interesting information about the duration of unemployment. One point is that a large fraction of spells end within one month—the percentages are 79% for 1969, 60% for 1974, and 55% for 1975. (Note that 1975 is a year of deep recession, 1974 is an early stage of a recession, and 1969 is a strong boom.) Correspondingly, the average length of a spell is not very long—1.4 months in 1969, 1.9 months in 1974, and 2.2 months in 1975. But Clark and Summers argue that the importance of the long-term unemployed is more significant than these figures suggest. First, in determining the average number of people unemployed at any date, we effectively weight the frequency of each spell by its length. Therefore, although the average length of a spell in 1974 is only 2 months, it also turns out that spells of more than 2 months account for 69% of the number unemployed. (The figures for 1969 and 1975 are 49 and 75%, respectively.) Similarly, spells of 6 months or more still account for 19% of unemployment in 1974. (The values for 1969 and 1975 are 3% and 27%, respectively.)

Secondly, roughly half of all spells of unemployment end in withdrawal from the labor force (flow 4 in Figure 9.2), rather than in employment (flow 3 in the figure). Then many of those who leave the labor force soon reappear as job searchers (flow 5 in the figure), which counts as a new spell of unemployment in the data. Clark and Summers argue that these spells of unemployment and the intervening periods outside of the labor force should be counted as long periods of unemployment. But many of these people (as well as some who never leave the labor force) may not be serious job seekers, who should not be counted as unemployed in the first place. This ambiguity points out the fundamental problems of defining and measuring the concept of unemployment. In general, it is easier to define and measure employment (at market jobs), rather than unemployment.

Teenagers tend to find jobs or leave the labor force more quickly than do older persons. For example, for 1974, the average duration of unemployment for teenagers is 1.6 months, as compared with just over 2 months for those over 20. Therefore, the higher unemployment rate for teenagers reflects mostly the short duration of their jobs, rather than a low rate of job finding.

The main difference by sex is the much higher tendency for unemployed females to leave the labor force (flow 4 in Figure 9.2). For example, in 1974, 58% of unemployed females over 20 eventually leave the labor force, while only 26% of males over 20 do so.

For blacks, particularly those under 25, a greater difficulty in finding jobs

---

[7]Kim Clark and Lawrence Summers, op. cit.

accounts for a large part of their higher unemployment rate. For example, Marston (op. cit., Table 4) estimates that this element accounts for two-thirds of the higher average unemployment rate for blacks from 1967–73.

The Recent Rise in the Natural Rate of Unemployment

The data in Table 9.1 suggest that the average rate of unemployment increased by 1–2 percentage points in the 1970s. The recent research by David Lilien[8] attempts to explain this change as a rise in the natural unemployment rate. Specifically, he argues that the 1970s involve an uncommon amount of change in the composition of United States production, especially away from traditional areas of manufacturing, such as automobiles and steel. These changes may derive, in turn, from dramatic shifts in the relative prices of raw materials—notably oil—and from increases in foreign competition. Then these changes in the composition of production imply increases in the amount of job turnover.

To illustrate the possible effects on unemployment, recall that the natural unemployment rate in our first model is

$$u = s/(s + \eta)$$

where s is the job-separation rate and η is the job-finding rate. (Remember that this model ignores the movements of people in and out of the labor force.) In the example that we considered before, the values $s = 1\%$ per period and $\eta = 15\%$ per period imply a natural unemployment rate of 6.2%. (This value slightly exceeds the average unemployment rate of 5.4% for all civilian workers for 1948–82.) Now, suppose that the shift away from manufacturing means that the rates of job separation and job finding both increase. For example, assume that they rise to $s = 1.5\%$ and $\eta = 15.5\%$. Then the natural unemployment rate increases from 6.2% to 8.8%. Hence, this type of change might account for the higher average unemployment rate in the 1970s.

Lilien quantifies the effects of changes in industrial composition by compiling data on the relative amounts of employment across the various sectors of the economy. Then he demonstrates that the greater shifting around among sectors during the 1970s explains an increase by 1–2 percentage points in the natural unemployment rate. In fact, this increase corresponds roughly to the rise in the average unemployment rate for the 1970s, which shows up in Table 9.1.[9]

---

[8]David M. Lilien, ''Sectoral Shifts and Cyclical Unemployment,'' *Journal of Political Economy*, August 1982.

[9]The increases in the fractions of the labor force that are female and teen-age may also account for a part of the higher natural unemployment rate. See problem 9.10 below.

Factors that Influence the Natural Unemployment Rate

There is a long list of factors—especially government policies—that economists think influence the natural unemployment rate. Here, we consider briefly some of the more important possibilities, which are unemployment insurance, the minimum wage, and labor unions.

Unemployment Insurance

The government's main program of **unemployment insurance** began in 1936. This program provides benefits to eligible persons who have lost their jobs and are currently "looking for work." Hence, those in the category labeled "unemployment" in Figure 9.2 are candidates for these benefits. While the federal government plays some role, the main rules for eligibility and levels of benefits are set by the various state governments. In general, a person's eligibility depends on a long enough work history in a covered job.[10] (In 1981 about 93% of all civilian workers are in covered jobs.) Also, an individual's benefits run out after a period, which typically lasts between 26 and 39 weeks. But in time of recession (such as 1982), the federal government typically extends the period of eligibility.

An employed person can compare his or her current wage with the unemployment benefits that he or she could get by not working. The ratio of the potential benefits to the wage is called the **replacement ratio.** For 1978, this ratio averages about 50% for people who have jobs.[11] Although precise figures are unavailable, there do not seem to have been large changes in this ratio since World War II. For example, a related figure—which is the ratio of the average weekly check from unemployment insurance programs to average weekly earnings for all nonagricultural workers—is 39% in 1947 and 42% in 1981. Over time, the main changes in the unemployment insurance program have been extensions of coverage (especially to small firms and to employees of state and local governments) and increases in the allowable duration of benefits.

Theoretically, the existence of unemployment insurance makes the unemployed who are receiving benefits less eager to accept jobs or leave the labor force (flows 3 and 4 in Figure 9.2). Also, the program makes those employed persons who will be eligible for benefits more willing to accept job separations (flow 2 in Figure

---

[10]In some states, people who quit their jobs or are fired for cause are eligible for benefits, while in others they are ineligible. Of course, it is often hard to tell who quits or is fired for cause, and who loses a job for other reasons. For further discussion of this matter and other issues, see Daniel Hamermesh, *Jobless Pay and the Economy*, Johns Hopkins Press, Baltimore, 1977.

[11]See Kim Clark and Lawrence Summers, "Unemployment Insurance and Labor Market Transitions," National Bureau of Economic Research, working paper no. 920, June 1982, Table 4. Their calculations also consider the taxes that people pay on wages, but not on unemployment benefits.

9.2).[12] On both counts, a more generous program leads to a higher natural rate of unemployment.

Empirically, there is little firm evidence on the sizes of these effects. Most estimates hinge on assessing people's responses to differences across governmental jurisdictions in the levels of benefits and in criteria for eligibility. But we cannot be sure from the data whether a more generous program leads to higher unemployment or, in reverse, whether more unemployment leads a state government to select a more generous program. In any event, some researchers report that the overall program of unemployment insurance raises the natural unemployment rate by roughly 0.5 to 1 percentage point.[13] If these estimates are reasonable, then changes in unemployment insurance cannot account for much of the rise in the average unemployment rate during the 1970s by 1–2 percentage points. That is, the increases that occurred in the coverage of the program and in the allowable duration of benefits would account for an increase in the unemployment rate by much less than 0.5 percentage points.

Another piece of evidence that supports this conclusion is the failure to observe major changes in the ratio of insured unemployment to the total. This ratio averages 49% from 1950 to 1982. But although it tends to rise during a recession, there has been no discernible long-term trend in the ratio. For example, for 1970–82, the average is 48%. If the unemployment insurance program were behind the recent increase in the natural unemployment rate, then it is likely that the ratio of insured unemployment to the total would have risen.

The Minimum Wage

When considering determinants of the natural unemployment rate, economists often mention the **minimum wage.** Since 1938, the federal government has set minimum wage rates in covered industries. In 1946 this regulation covered about 57% of all nonsupervisory employees. But changes in legislation raised the coverage to roughly 85% in 1975; then some further changes led to a decline in coverage, which reached 78% in 1978.

Congress has changed the level of the basic hourly minimum wage numerous times, since the initial choice of 25¢ in 1938. For example, the value was 75¢ in 1950, $1.25 in 1963, $1.60 in 1968, $2.30 in 1977, and $3.35 in 1981. Since

---

[12]This tendency diminishes if the worker's employer must pay for the average benefits given to his or her ex-employees. This process is called **experience rating.** With experience rating, a business that has a lot of job separations pays a larger amount into the fund that finances the unemployment benefits. Then employers have incentives to hold down their rates of job separation. In the United States there is some experience rating, but it is highly imperfect. For a discussion, see Robert Topel and Finis Welch, ''Unemployment Insurance: Survey and Extensions,'' *Economica,* August 1980.

[13]See Hamermesh, op. cit., p. 52; and Clark and Summers, op. cit., Table 10. Hamermesh focuses on the effects on the duration of unemployment. He also distinguishes the effects in a year of high unemployment from those in a year of low unemployment, but the reported differences are small. Clark and Summers' estimates refer to 1978, for which the overall unemployment rate was 5.9%.

1950, the ratio of the minimum to average hourly nonfarm earnings has ranged between 41 and 56%. Although there is no clear trend, the ratio increases each time Congress enacts a minimum, but then declines gradually as average hourly earnings rise.

A higher minimum wage reduces the incentive of employers to hire low-productivity workers in sectors that are covered by the minimum wage. Empirically, researchers find that a higher minimum wage and greater coverage tend especially to reduce the employment of teenagers. Typical estimates suggest that an increase by 10% in the minimum wage lowers the quantity of teenagers employed by somewhat more than 1%.[14] There is also some indication of a negative effect on the employment of young adults (aged 20–24), but no clear effect on older workers. In fact, since the minimum wage makes the labor of low-productivity workers artificially more expensive, it is likely that businesses would shift to more labor from high-productivity workers. Hence, labor unions tend to favor the minimum wage in order to protect their high-paid members from the competition of low-productivity, low-wage workers.

The effects of the minimum wage on teenage unemployment rates depend also on the response of labor-force participation. Because a higher minimum wage reduces the chance of finding a job, it turns out also to reduce the number of teenagers who declare themselves as looking for work. This response lessens the tendency for a higher minimum wage to raise the measured unemployment rate of teenagers.

In any event, the behavior of the minimum wage cannot account for the general rise in unemployment rates during the 1970s. That's because first, the minimum wage has not increased relative to average hourly earnings; second, coverage peaked around 1975 and has since declined; and third, the recent rise in unemployment rates applies as much to older workers as to teenagers and young adults.

Labor Unions

Sometimes, people argue that labor unions cause unemployment. Mostly, unions can raise real wage rates and hold down the levels of employment in covered industries. Correspondingly, there is a higher supply of labor and lower real wage rates in uncovered sectors. Therefore, unions can create inefficiencies, which include the inappropriate distribution of work and production between covered and uncovered areas. Conceivably, more union power may also lead to reductions in aggregate employment and output. But it is less clear that unions have anything to do with the overall unemployment rate. That's because the adverse effects on total work may correspond mostly to reductions in the labor force.

In any event, we should look for effects of unions by observing the changes in unionization over time. In fact, the fraction of the civilian labor force that is

---

[14]For a survey of the evidence, see Charles Brown, Curtis Gilroy, and Andrew Koehn, ''The Effect of the Minimum Wage on Employment and Unemployment: A Survey'', *Journal of Economic Literature,* June 1982.

Table 9.3 Behavior of U.S. Employment Ratios

	Employment Ratio	
	% of Total Population	% of Population 16–64
1948–54	40	64
1955–61	38	65
1962–68	38	66
1969–75	41	66
1976–82	44	68
1948–82	40	66

Note: The table shows the ratio of total employment (including the military) to the total population and to the population aged 16–64.

Source: Economic Report of the President, 1983.

unionized declined from a peak of 27% in the mid-1950s to 21% in 1980. Therefore, we cannot attribute the recent increase in unemployment rates to an increase in unionization. (The principal increases in unionization occurred in the first years of the 20th century, from less than 3 to 6%; in the mid-1930s, from 7 to 15%; and during World War II, from 16 to 26%.)

Changes in Employment Ratios

The increase in unemployment rates for the 1970s contrasts with the behavior of employment when expressed relative to some measure of population. Table 9.3 shows the ratios of total employment (including the military) to total population and to the population aged 16–64. The first ratio varies between 38 and 41% until the mid-1970s, but then increases to 44%. Similarly, the second ratio stays between 64 and 66% until the mid-1970s, but then rises to 68%. Thus, the high unemployment rates for recent years coexist with peak ratios of employment to population.

The high employment ratios for the recent period reflect mainly the increase in the labor-force participation of women. Specifically, the fraction of the civilian labor force that is female rose from 28% in 1948 to 38% in 1969, and 43% in 1982. This development means that there are now many more families with more than one income earner. Accordingly, a given overall rate of unemployment does not have as much significance for the typical family's total earnings as it did previously. (The existence of unemployment insurance and other welfare programs also matters here.)

It is possible that the change in labor-force participation has something to do with the increase in the average rates of unemployment for recent years. Specifically, if someone's spouse is working, then he or she would be less willing to accept work, and more willing to accept a separation from a current job. But if this effect is important, then we should see an increase in the unemployment rates of married persons relative to those of single people. In fact, this has not happened.

Table 9.4 The Dynamics of Employment and Unemployment During a Recession

Period	Job-Separation Rate (s)	Job-Finding Rate (η)	Number Employed (L)	Number Unemployed (U)	Number Who Lose Jobs	Number Who Find Jobs	Net Change In Employment
1	0.015	0.10	93.8	6.2	1.4	0.6	−0.8
2	0.015	0.10	93.0	7.0	1.4	0.7	−0.7
3	0.015	0.10	92.3	7.7	1.4	0.8	−0.6
4	0.015	0.10	91.7	8.3	1.4	0.8	−0.6
5	0.015	0.10	91.1	8.9	1.4	0.9	−0.5
6	0.01	0.15	90.6	9.4	0.9	1.4	0.5
7	0.01	0.15	91.1	8.9	0.9	1.3	0.4
8	0.01	0.15	91.5	8.5	0.9	1.3	0.4
9	0.01	0.15	91.9	8.1	0.9	1.2	0.3
10	0.01	0.15	92.2	7.8	0.9	1.2	0.3
·	·	·	·	·	·	·	·
·	·	·	·	·	·	·	·
·	·	·	·	·	·	·	·
∞	0.01	0.15	93.8	6.2	0.9	0.9	0

Note: During the recession for periods 1 through 5, the job-separation rate rises from 1% per period to 1.5%. Also, the job-finding rate falls from 15% per period to 10%. Consequently, the unemployment rate rises from the natural rate, 6.2%, to 9.4% in period 6. Then, when the job-separation and job-finding rates return to their normal values in period 6, the economy recovers gradually. In particular, the unemployment rate again approaches the natural rate of 6.2%.

Rather, the unemployment rates of married and single people have increased in roughly parallel fashion in recent years.[15]

Employment and Unemployment during Recessions

We can use the theoretical apparatus to see how the unemployment rate rises above the natural rate during a recession, and then falls back toward the natural rate during a recovery. Let's again neglect movements in and out of the labor force. Also, consider the example where the job-separation rate, s, is 1% per period, and the job finding rate, η, is 15%. Hence, the natural unemployment rate is

$$u = s/(s + \eta) = 1/16 = 6.2\%$$

Table 9.4 assumes that the economy begins in period 1 at the natural unemployment rate of 6.2%. But the start of a recession means that the job-separation

---

[15]For 1955–82, the average unemployment rate among single persons is 11.6% for males and 9.2% for females. The corresponding figures for married people with spouse present are 3.2% and 5.3%. For the period 1976–82, the rates for single people are 13.8% for males and 11.7% for females. The corresponding values for married people are 4.0% and 6.2%. (Source: U.S. Bureau of Labor Statistics, *Handbook of Labor Statistics*, 1980; *Employment and Earnings*, January 1983.)

rate rises from 1% to, say, 1.5%, while, the job finding-rate falls from 15% to, say, 10%. That is, a recession is a period where it becomes more common to lose a job, and harder to find a new one.

Although some people still find jobs during a recession, they are outnumbered by those who lose jobs. Hence, Table 9.4 shows that the unemployment rate rises steadily from 6.2% in period 1 to 9.4% in period 6. Correspondingly, the number employed falls from 93.8 million to 90.6 million. Then we suppose that the start of a recovery in period 6 means that the job-separation rate returns to 1% and the job-finding rate to 15%. Now, although some people still lose their jobs, they are outnumbered by those who find jobs. Therefore, the unemployment rate falls gradually toward the natural rate of 6.2%. Correspondingly, employment rises back toward 93.8 million.

We should stress two realistic features of recessions that emerge from this example. First, the buildup of a recession involves a period of gradually rising unemployment and falling employment. Second, even after the recovery begins, it takes a substantial period for the unemployment rate to return to the natural rate.

Unemployment during Recent U.S. Recessions

Table 9.5 brings out the behavior of output, employment, and unemployment during the seven United States recessions since World War II. Consider, for example, the recession of 1957–58. The value of real gross national product (GNP) for 1958 is $680.9 billion. Using the value of real GNP for 1956 as a base, we calculate the real GNP that would have resulted in 1958 if output had grown at an annual rate of 3.0% (which is the average growth rate for 1929–82). This value, labeled $Y^°$ in the table, is $713.1 billion. Hence, we compute for 1958 the shortfall for real GNP of $32.2 billion. This figure is 4.5% of the hypothetical level of output—therefore, the estimated shortfall in output for 1958 is 4.5%.

Table 9.5 shows the results of this calculation for each recession since World War II. Notice that the sharpest contractions are the ones for 1982,[16] where the shortfall in output is by 8.8%, and 1975, where the shortfall is by 7.4%. On average for the seven cases, the shortfall in real GNP is by 4.5%. Overall, this method gives us a reasonable estimate for the magnitude of each recession. But the precise calculations are sensitive to the choices for base years and for the trend growth rate of output.

We make similar computations for employment in the table. When using the total number employed (including the military), the average shortfall for the seven recessions is by 2.4%.[17] These range from less than 1% for 1970 to 4.2% for 1958. By this measure, the 1982 recession is only the second worst, with a shortfall of

---

[16]There is some controversy as to whether to treat 1980 and 1982 as the final years of two distinct recessions, or to consider 1980–82 as one prolonged contraction. Since the intervening recovery in late 1980 and early 1981 is so brief and weak, we treat 1980–82 as a single recession.

[17]We use the trend growth rate of 1.4% per year in order to calculate the hypothetical level of employment, $L^°$.

Table 9.5 The Behavior of Output, Employment, and Unemployment During Recent U.S. Recessions

Year of Recession	1949	1954	1958	1961	1970	1975	1982
Base Year for Comparison	1948	1953	1956	1959	1969	1973	1979
Y	492.2	616.1	680.9	756.6	1085.6	1233.9	1475.5
$Y°$	504.7	642.6	713.1	766.3	1120.7	1332.6	1618.7
$Y°-Y$	12.5	26.5	32.2	9.7	35.1	98.7	143.2
% shortfall	2.5%	4.1%	4.5%	1.3%	3.1%	7.4%	8.8%
(# employed)							
L	59.3	63.5	65.7	68.3	81.9	88.0	101.7
$L°$	60.6	65.6	68.6	69.1	82.6	89.9	105.2
$L°-L$	1.3	2.1	2.9	0.8	0.7	1.9	3.5
% shortfall	2.1%	3.2%	4.2%	1.1%	0.8%	2.1%	3.3%
(total hours)							
L	2.34	2.48	2.53	2.64	3.04	3.18	3.54
$L°$	2.42	2.59	2.68	2.68	3.11	3.31	3.73
$L°-L$	0.08	0.11	0.15	0.04	0.07	0.13	0.19
% shortfall	3.3%	4.2%	5.6%	1.5%	2.3%	3.9%	5.1%
U	5.8%	5.3%	6.5%	6.5%	4.8%	8.3%	9.5%
$U°$	3.7%	2.8%	4.0%	5.3%	3.4%	4.7%	5.7%
$U-U°$	2.1%	2.5%	2.5%	1.2%	1.4%	3.6%	3.8%

Note: Y is real GNP in $ billion (1972 base), L is total employment (millions) or total weekly hours (billions), and U is the unemployment rate for the total labor force. We calculate the hypothetical levels of output, $Y°$, and employment, $L°$, from the base years by the method described in the text. For the unemployment rate, $U°$ is the actual value for the base year.

Source of basic data: *Economic Report of the President,* 1983.

employment by 3.3%. Notice that, for each recession, the percentage shortfall in employment is smaller than that in real GNP. Hence, the ratio of real GNP to the number of workers—which is one measure of "productivity"—tends to fall during a recession.

From the standpoint of aggregate labor input, a measure of total hours is more pertinent than the number of persons employed. In order to get the figures for total hours, we multiply the values for numbers employed by an estimate of average weekly hours of persons employed. It turns out that average weekly hours tend to decline during recessions, because there is less overtime work and more part-time employment. Therefore, there are greater percentage shortfalls in total hours[18] than in numbers employed. In fact, the average shortfall of 3.7% for total hours is only

---

[18]For total hours, we use the trend growth rate of 1.2% per year.

a small amount below that for real GNP, which is 4.5%. Hence, the recessions show little systematic change in productivity when measured as real GNP per worker-hour. The two cases where substantial declines in productivity still show up are those for 1975 and 1982.

Finally, Table 9.5 shows the behavior of the unemployment rate during the seven recessions.[19] On average, the unemployment rate increases by 2.4 percentage points during these recessions. Here, 1982 is again the worst with an increase by 3.8 percentage points. But 1975 is a close second with 3.6 points.

Setup of a Simplified Labor Market

We want to see how the labor market interacts with the markets for commodities and credit. Here, we are interested mainly in determining the aggregate level of employment, L, in conjunction with the aggregate level of output, Y. But given the unemployment rate, determining employment amounts to determining the size of the labor force, which we previously took as a given. For most purposes, we can carry out the analysis by just thinking of the labor market as a place where people supply and demand labor services. Then the clearing of this market—along with those for commodities and credit—determines the aggregate quantities of employment, output, and so on. In particular, we do not detail here the process of job separation and job finding, or the underlying dynamics of the unemployment rate.

Suppose again that everyone's labor services are physically the same. But instead of working on one's own production process, people now sell all of their labor services on the labor market.[20] This market establishes a single **wage rate** for labor services. Denote the wage rate for period t by w_t and measure it in units of dollars per person-hour. In other words, buyers of labor services pay w_t dollars for each hour that someone works for them. Correspondingly, sellers of labor services receive w_t dollars for each hour of work. As in our treatment of the commodity market, we assume that individual buyers and sellers regard the wage rate, w_t, as a given.

Instead of introducing firms as a separate form of economic unit, we continue to think of some of the households as being the employers, who buy the labor services of workers. This device simplifies matters without causing any difficulties. Further, it has the advantage of reminding us that some households own the businesses in the economy.

---

[19]We use the unemployment rate out of the total labor force, which includes the military. But the results change little if we use instead the civilian labor force.

[20]Generally, people do not sell all of their work time, but instead keep some for their own use. But we can think of households as effectively buying back some labor services for various activities at home, such as repair work, cooking, cleaning, child care, and so on. For a discussion of home production versus market production, see Gary Becker, ''A Theory of the Allocation of Time,'' *Economic Journal,* September 1965.

Denote by l_t^s the number of person-hours of labor services that a household supplies to the labor market during period t. Correspondingly, this household receives the dollar quantity, $w_t l_t^s$, of labor income.

Households, in their role as producers, also demand labor services. Let l_t^d denote the number of person-hours of labor services that a household demands during period t. (Notice that labor demand, l_t^d, may include a quantity of the household's own time.) Correspondingly, this household pays the dollar amount, $w_t l_t^d$, as wage payments to workers.

Each household uses the input of labor services, l_t^d, in order to produce commodities. The quantity produced and supplied to the commodity market during period t is

$$y_t^s = f(l_t^d) \tag{9.5}$$

where f is again the production function. Households sell their goods at the price P_t, but must also pay wages to their workers. Hence, the net dollar revenue from production is given by

$$\text{net revenue} = P_t y_t^s - w_t l_t^d = P_t \cdot f(l_t^d) - w_t l_t^d \tag{9.6}$$

If we thought of production as carried out by business firms, then equation (9.6) would describe the profit of a firm. But these profits would go eventually to the individuals who own the firms. Here, we skip the intermediate step where revenues flow first to a firm and then to the households who own the firm. Hence, in our model, the net revenue from production, as shown in equation (9.6), shows up directly as a part of the household's income. Then each household's total income for period t comprises this net revenue from production plus wage income, $w_t l_t^s$, plus interest income.

The Demand for Labor

As before, each household's utility depends on the time paths of consumption, c_t^d, and work, l_t^s. Hence, the demand for labor, l_t^d, matters to the household only through its effect on the net revenue from production, which appears in equation (9.6). Accordingly, households choose their purchases of labor services, l_t^d, in order to maximize this net revenue. (Notice that we reach the same result if we think of business firms, which choose their employment of labor in order to maximize profit.)

An increase in labor input, l_t^d, has two effects on the net revenue from production, which appears in equation (9.6). First, an extra hour of work means that output, $f(l_t^d)$, increases by the marginal product of labor, MPL_t. Hence, gross sales revenue rises by the dollar amount, $P_t \cdot MPL_t$. Second, the wage bill increases by the dollar wage rate, w_t. Therefore, net revenue rises if the value of labor's marginal product, $P_t \cdot MPL_t$, exceeds the wage rate, w_t. In order to maximize net revenue, a producer expands employment, l_t^d, up to the point where the value of the marginal product just equals the wage rate. (Recall that as work increases, the marginal product of labor declines.) If we divide through by the price level, the condition that each producer satisfies is

$$MPL_t = w_t/P_t \tag{9.7}$$

Notice that the right side of equation (9.7) is the **real wage rate,** w_t/P_t. This variable tells a person the quantity of commodities that he or she can buy with the dollar amount w_t. Then a producer chooses the quantity of labor input, l_t^d, so that the marginal product, MPL_t, equals this real wage rate. At that point, the last unit of labor contributes just enough to output, MPL_t, so as to cover the extra cost of this labor in units of commodities, which is the real wage rate.

We illustrate the results in Figure 9.3. The curve shows the negative effect of more labor input on the marginal product, MPL_t. Notice that producers set their demand for labor, l_t^d, at the point where this marginal product equals the real wage rate, w_t/P_t.

Recall that the real wage rate is the same for everyone, since we assume that all labor services are identical. Hence, we know also that labor's marginal product is the same on all production processes. Further, this result holds even if there are differences across households in production functions, in the willingness to work, and so on. Clearly, it is efficient to equalize these marginal products. Otherwise, the economy's total output could rise, without changing total work effort, by shifting workers from one production process to another. In particular, this increase in

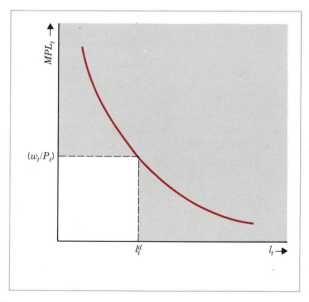

Figure 9.3 **The Demand for Labor**
Labor's marginal product, MPL_t, declines as the quantity of labor input increases. Producers set the demand for labor, l_t^d, at the point where the marginal product equals the real wage rate, w_t/P_t.

output would result if a worker moved from an activity where his or her marginal product was low to one where it was high. But it is only the existence of the labor market that ensures the equality in marginal products. In our earlier model, where people worked only on their own production processes, we might end up with large differences in marginal products. Since one person could not work on another's production activity, there was no mechanism to equalize the marginal products.

It is important to recognize that the existence of the labor market aids economic efficiency. Specifically, this market exhausts all the gains that can obtain from movements of workers from one place to another. Because everyone's marginal product ends up being the same, there are no gains of this type that remain unexploited.

We can use Figure 9.3 to see how various changes affect the demand for labor. It follows at once that a decrease in the real wage rate, w_t/P_t, means a higher quantity of labor demanded. That is, when the real cost of hiring workers decreases, producers expand employment until labor's marginal product falls by as much as the decrease in the real wage.

Second, an upward shift in the schedule for labor's marginal product—that is, an upward shift of the curve in Figure 9.3—leads to a greater quantity of labor demanded for any given value of the real wage rate. Specifically, employment expands until the marginal product again equals the given real wage rate.

We can summarize the results by writing down a function for the aggregate demand for labor. This function takes the form

$$L_t^d = L^d(w_t/P_t, \ldots)$$
$$(-)$$

(9.8)

where the expression, . . . , again refers to the characteristics of the production function.

Recall that each household's choice of labor input determines the supply of goods through the production function, $y_t^s = f(l_t^d)$. Therefore, the function for the aggregate supply of goods takes the form

$$Y_t^s = Y^s(w_t/P_t, \ldots)$$
$$(-)$$

(9.9)

Notice that a decrease in the real wage rate raises the aggregate demand for labor and thereby increases the aggregate supply of goods.

Labor Supply and Consumption Demand

The introduction of the labor market does not greatly alter the analysis of labor supply and consumption demand. The main modification concerns the choice between consumption and leisure at a point in time. In our previous model the schedule for labor's marginal product, MPL_t, tells people the terms on which they can substitute consumption for leisure. That is, when someone works an extra hour on his or her own production process, then he or she can use the additional output (of MPL_t units) to raise consumption. Now people sell their labor services at the real wage rate, w_t/P_t, rather than working on their own production. So the real wage rate tells people the terms on which they can substitute consumption for leisure. If someone works an extra hour, then he or she can use the additional w_t/P_t units of real income to expand consumption.

For an individual, the real wage rate now appears where previously the schedule for labor's marginal product appeared. Specifically, an increase in the real wage rate motivates people to increase labor supply and consumption demand. But recall that the choice of labor demand guarantees that the real wage rate equals the marginal product of labor. Therefore, the present effects from the real wage rate amount, ultimately, to corresponding effects from the schedule for labor's marginal product. The only difference is that the real wage rate and the marginal product of labor must be the same for everyone. In our earlier analysis these marginal products could be unequal, unless all people and production functions happen to be identical.

As before, wealth effects can arise from shifts in production functions. But for given production functions, a change in the real wage rate has a zero aggregate wealth effect. That's because the added benefit to sellers of labor services exactly matches the extra cost to buyers.

The real interest rate, r_t, has the same intertemporal-substitution effects as before. Namely, an increase in this rate motivates households to reduce current consumption demand and raise current labor supply. An additional intertemporal-substitution effect arises if people anticipate variations over time in the real wage rate. Suppose, for example, that workers regard the current real wage rate as high relative to future real wage rates. Then they increase current labor supply and plan to reduce labor supply in the future. Before, we found similar effects if people anticipated changes in the schedule for labor's marginal product.

We can summarize the results in this section by writing down functions for aggregate labor supply and consumption demand. These take the forms

$$L_t^s = L^s(w_t/P_t, r_t, \ldots)$$
$$(+)\ (+)$$

(9.10)

and

$$C_t^d = C^d(w_t/P_t, r_t, \ldots)$$
$$(+)\ (-)$$

(9.11)

The omitted terms, denoted by . . . , include characteristics of the production function. These terms include also any elements that generate departures of future real wage rates or real interest rates from their current values.

Clearing of the Labor Market

The labor market clears when the aggregate supply of labor, L_t^s, equals the aggregate demand, L_t^d. Therefore, using equations (9.10) and (9.11), the condition for clearing the labor market is

$$L^d(w_t/P_t, \ldots) = L^s(w_t/P_t, r_t, \ldots) \qquad (9.12)$$
$$(-) \qquad\qquad (+) \ (+)$$

As before, there are also conditions for clearing the commodity market and for ensuring that all money is willingly held. Thus, these conditions must hold along with equation (9.12) in order to ensure the clearing of all markets. When we take these conditions together we shall be able to determine the nominal wage rate, w_t, as well as the real interest rate, r_t, and the price level, P_t. In other words, we add one new market-clearing condition, equation (9.12), and thereby determine one more ''price''—namely, the price of labor services, w_t.

Figure 9.4 shows the clearing of the labor market. For convenience, we place the real wage rate, w_t/P_t, on the vertical axis, while we put labor demand and supply on the horizontal. Notice that the quantity of labor demanded rises as the real wage rate falls, assuming a given form for households' production functions. For the case of labor supply, we hold fixed the real interest rate, r_t, and the forms of production functions. (Unless we state otherwise, we assume also that prospective values of real wage rates and real interest rates equal their current values.) Then an increase in the current real wage rate means a larger quantity of labor supplied.

Notice from Figure 9.4 that the aggregates of labor demand and supply are equal when the real wage rate is $(w_t/P_t)^*$ and the level of work is L_t^*. In particular, we can use the figure to relate the market-clearing values of the real wage rate and

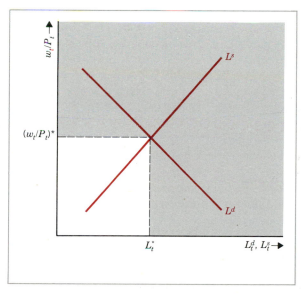

Figure 9.4 Clearing of the Labor Market
For a given value of the real interest rate, r_t, and for given forms of the production functions, the labor market clears when the real wage rate is $(w_t/P_t)^*$ and the quantity of work is L_t^*.

employment to variables that shift either the labor-demand curve or the labor-supply curve. These variables include the real interest rate, r_t, the forms of production functions, and prospective changes in the real wage rate and real interest rate. For example, an increase in the real interest rate, r_t, shifts the labor-supply curve rightward in Figure 9.4. Hence, we find that employment, L_t^*, rises, while the real wage rate, $(w_t/P_t)^*$, declines.

Clearing of the Commodity Market

Using equations (9.9) and (9.11), we can write the condition for clearing the commodity market as

$$C^d(w_t/P_t, r_t, \ldots) = Y^s(w_t/P_t, \ldots) \qquad (9.13)$$
$$(+) \, (-) \qquad\qquad (-)$$

But remember that we can use our analysis of the labor market to relate the market-clearing real wage rate, $(w_t/P_t)^*$, to the real interest rate, r_t, and other variables. Then we can substitute out for the real wage rate in equation (9.13) to obtain a revised condition for clearing the commodity market. This new condition takes the form

$$C^d(r_t, \ldots) = Y^s(r_t, \ldots) \qquad (9.14)$$
$$(-) \qquad\quad (+)$$

Let's examine in detail how the real interest rate, r_t, now enters into the condition for clearing the commodity market. Recall from our study of the labor market that an increase in the real interest rate shifts the labor-supply curve rightward, which leads to a decline in the real wage rate. Then the decline in the real wage leads, as shown in equation (9.9), to an expansion of goods supply, Y^s. Therefore, the positive effect of the real interest rate on the supply of commodities in equation (9.14) picks up this channel of effects.

On the demand side, the change in the real interest rate has two effects. First, from equation (9.11), an increase in the real interest rate lowers consumer demand, C_t^d, for a given value of the real wage rate. Secondly, because an increase in the real interest rate leads to a lower real wage rate, there is a further decline in consumer demand. Therefore, in equation (9.14), the negative effect of the real interest rate on consumer demand picks up both channels of effect.

Similarly, we can work through the consequences of changes in other variables, including the forms of the production functions. Then equation (9.14) combines the direct effects of these changes with those that arise from movements in the real wage rate.

The important point is that equation (9.14) looks just like the condition for clearing the commodity market that we used in previous chapters. The only difference is that the labor market ensures that everybody's marginal product of labor, which equals the real wage rate, is the same. (Recall that we assume that everyone's labor services are physically identical.)[21]

Since the condition for clearing the commodity market looks like it did before, we can still use our previous analysis to determine the real interest rate and the quantities of output and work effort for each period. Further, when we bring in the condition that all money be willingly held, we see that the form of this relation does not change. Therefore, we can continue to use our previous analysis to find the time paths of the price level and the nominal interest rate. However, with the inclusion of the labor market, we can also calculate the time path of wage rates. We can make this calculation as follows. First, once we know the quantity of work, we can figure out the marginal product of labor, MPL_t. Then we know that the real wage rate, w_t/P_t, equals this marginal product. Finally, since we already know the time path of the price level, we can determine the nominal wage rate, w_t, at each date.

An Improvement in the Production Function

Let's bring out the role of the labor market by reexamining a case where everyone's production function improves permanently. We assume a proportional upward shift in the production function so that the level of aggregate output and the marginal product of labor increase for any amount of aggregate work effort.

Figure 9.5 shows the effects on the labor market. Since the disturbance raises wealth, we find that the supply of labor declines for a given value of the real wage rate. (Recall that we hold constant the real interest rate, r_t, when drawing the labor supply curve.) Then, because of the upward shift to the schedule for labor's marginal product, the demand for labor rises for a given value of the real wage. Hence, Figure 9.5 shows that the real wage rate increases. But the change in the quantity of work is uncertain. As in some previous cases, the wealth effect suggests less work, but the improvement in productivity suggests more work.

Figure 9.6 shows the effects on the commodity market. Here, we use the market-clearing condition from equation (9.14), which already takes into account the determination of the real wage rate from the labor market. Notice first the rightward shift in the consumer demand curve. This increase in demand reflects partly the wealth effect from the improvement in the production function, and partly the substitution effect (toward consumption and away from leisure) from the rise in the real wage rate. But since the improvement in the production function and the resulting rise in the real wage rate are permanent in this example, there would be no major change in the aggregate of desired saving at the initial real interest rate. Therefore, Figure 9.6 shows a rightward shift in the goods supply curve that equals the shift in the demand curve at the initial real interest rate, r_t^*. Hence, we

---

[21]More generally, we could expand the analysis to deal with different levels of skills and different characteristics of jobs. Then we find that real wage rates are higher first, for people who are more productive and second, on jobs that are less pleasant. But these considerations do not change the major macroeconomic results.

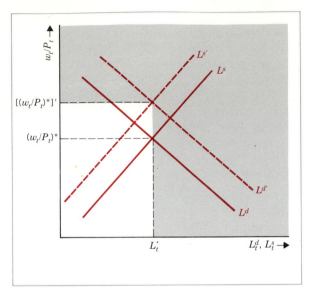

Figure 9.5 Effect of an Improvement in the Production Function on the Labor Market
The permanent upward shift in the production function raises the demand for labor, but lowers the supply. Therefore, the real wage rate increases, but the change in work is uncertain.

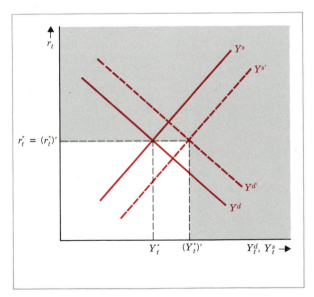

Figure 9.6 Effect of an Improvement in the Production Function on the Commodity Market
The permanent upward shift in the production function raises the demand and supply of commodities by roughly equal amounts. Hence, output increases, but the real interest rate does not change.

conclude that output increases, but the real interest rate does not change. Note also that, since the real interest rate is unchanged, we do not have to modify the analysis of the labor market from Figure 9.5. Recall that this diagram applies for a given value of the real interest rate.

One important observation is that the basic results coincide with those that we reached earlier, when people worked only on their own production processes. Specifically, the permanent improvement in production opportunities raises aggregate output, but has an ambiguous effect on work effort. Further, because the change in the production function is permanent, there is no change in the real interest rate.

Note especially that our earlier simplification, which neglected the labor market entirely, allows us to get reasonable answers about the real interest rate and the aggregate quantities of output and work effort. Therefore, for much of our subsequent analysis, we shall find it satisfactory to return to the earlier framework, which does not deal explicitly with the labor market. Then we can simplify the analysis, but still get the right answers to many important questions.

The introduction of the labor market does deliver an important result about the behavior of the real wage rate. Suppose again that economic development involves a series of permanent improvements to the production function of the sort that we just considered. Then the analysis in Figure 9.5 shows that economic development entails continuing increases in the real wage rate. This proposition accords with data on real wages for a large number of countries. For example, in the United States, the average hourly real wage rate rises at an average rate of 1.4% per year from 1948 to 1982.[22]

Summary

The dynamics of employment and unemployment depend on job turnover, as measured by the rates of job separation and job finding. From the standpoint of economic efficiency, there are many good reasons to have turnover in employment. But if the rates of job separation and job finding are constant, then the economy tends automatically to a natural rate of unemployment. This natural rate rises with an increase in the job-separation rate, but falls with an increase in the job-finding rate. Also, movements in and out of the labor force influence the natural unemployment rate.

We use this framework to analyze differences in average unemployment rates by age, sex and race. Specifically, we can relate these differences to underlying differences in the duration of jobs and of unemployment. Also, we can explain some of the increase in average unemployment rates for the 1970s by an increase in the natural unemployment rate, which stems from greater shifting around of the

---

[22]The wage rate refers to average hourly earnings in the total private, nonagricultural economy. The real wage rate is the ratio of the nominal wage to the GNP deflator. For the data, see *Economic Report of the President,* 1983, Tables B-38 and B-3.

composition of industry. However, some factors that do not seem to contribute much to the rise in unemployment include unemployment insurance, the minimum wage, and labor unions.

During recessions, the high rate of job separation and the low rate of job finding cause the unemployment rate to rise above the natural rate. On average for the seven postwar recessions in the United States, the increase in the overall unemployment rate is by about 2.5 percentage points. Correspondingly, there is a reduction in employment and a proportionately larger reduction in total hours worked. When viewed in conjunction with the shortfall in real GNP, there is some tendency for productivity—that is, output as a ratio to labor input—to fall during recessions. But this tendency is weak if we measure labor input by total hours, rather than by numbers of persons employed.

In order to explore the interaction with the markets for commodities and credit— and to determine the size of the labor force—we set up a simplified labor market that considers the quantities of labor services supplied and demanded at a going wage rate. This market clears when the aggregate demand for labor equals the aggregate supply. One important aspect of a cleared labor market is that it equates each worker's marginal product to the real wage. Thereby, the existence of this market aids economic efficiency—in particular, it exhausts all the gains in output that can result by shifting workers from one production activity to another.

When considering the conditions for general market clearing, we add one new condition—that the labor market clear—and one new "price," which is the wage rate for labor services. But the conditions for determining the aggregate quantities of output and work, as well as the real interest rate and the price level, are similar to those from before. Therefore, for many purposes, we can carry out the analysis without explicitly treating the labor market. However, the inclusion of this market does enable us to determine the wage rate. Specifically, the theory predicts that the real wage will increase as an economy develops. This result accords with the empirical evidence from the United States and other countries.

Important Terms and Concepts

labor force

unemployment

unemployment rate

job separations

job finding

natural unemployment rate

outside of the labor force

discouraged workers

duration of jobs

duration of unemployment

unemployment insurance

replacement ratio (for unemployment insurance)

experience rating (for unemployment insurance)

minimum wage

wage rate

real wage rate

QUESTIONS AND PROBLEMS

Mainly for Review

9.1 What is the definition of the unemployment rate? Since it does not include workers who moved from ''unemployment'' to ''out of the labor force,'' is it an underestimation of the amount of unemployment in the economy? Can you think of any reason that the unemployment rate overestimates unemployment?

9.2 What is the natural rate of unemployment? What factors cause the unemployment rate to rise above the natural rate during a recession? Can the natural rate itself change?

9.3 Consider two individuals, A and B; they have the same production function, but A has a greater willingness to work. If each individual is isolated on an island, who will work more? Who will have the higher marginal product? Show how an increase in output can be obtained by exchanging labor services for goods between the two islands—that is, by opening up a labor market.

9.4 Recall the definitions of superior and inferior goods from Chapter 2. If leisure is a superior good, will a rise in the real wage rate always raise aggregate labor supply? Does your answer depend on whether the rise in the real wage reflects an increase in the marginal product of labor?

9.5 What is the total income for a household that neither buys nor sells labor (except to itself)? Show how a permanent increase in production (with no change in the marginal product of labor) is ''spent'' on both increased leisure and consumption.

Problems for Discussion

9.6 Productivity During Recessions

Suppose that recessions derive from proportional downward shifts in the production function. Then what do we predict for the behavior of ''productivity'' (output per hour of work) during recessions? How does this prediction accord with the data in Table 9.5?

Why does the behavior of productivity during recessions look different when we consider output per worker, rather than output per worker-hour? In particular, why do worker-hours fall by proportionately more than the number of workers during a recession?

9.7 Okun's Law

Okun's Law (named after the economist, Arthur Okun) states that the ratio of the percentage shortfall in output during a recession to the percentage point increase in the unemployment rate is roughly equal to 3.

Calculate these ratios for the seven post-war recessions covered in Table 9.5. How does Okun's Law hold up?

How does Okun's Law relate to the behavior of productivity during a recession?

9.8 Shifts in Industrial Composition

We argued in the text that the higher natural unemployment rate for the 1970s may stem from unusually large changes in the composition of production. Are these effects permanent or temporary? In particular, what does this argument imply for unemployment rates in the 1980s and beyond?

How do shifts in the composition of production affect the levels of aggregate employment and output? Are the effects permanent or temporary?

9.9 The Labor Force during Recessions

The data show little systematic response of the overall civilian labor force to recessions and booms. What response would you predict on theoretical grounds? (Hint: think first about people's incentives to leave the labor force—that is, to stop looking for work—during a recession. But are there also incentives for some people to enter the labor force during bad times?)

On the other hand, the teenage labor force declines during recessions. How can we explain this observation?

9.10 Women and Teenagers in the Labor Force

The unemployment rate for women averages about one percentage point higher than that for men. Further, the fraction of the civilian labor force that is female rises from 28% in 1948 to 43% in 1982. How would this increased role of women in the labor force affect the overall value of the natural unemployment rate?

For teenagers (aged 16–19) the average unemployment rate is about 10 percentage points higher than that for adults. Further, the fraction of the civilian labor force that is teenage rises from about 6.5% in the early 1950s to almost 9.5% in the late 1970s. What does this change mean for the overall value of the natural unemployment rate?

9.11 The Job-Separation Rate, the Job-Finding Rate, and the Natural Rate of Unemployment

Suppose that the labor force has 100 million people, of whom 92 million initially have jobs and 8 million are unemployed. Assume that the job-separation rate is 1% per period and the job-finding rate is 20% per period. Also, suppose that we can neglect movements in and out of the labor force. Trace out the time path of employment and unemployment. What is the natural unemployment rate?

9.12 The Minimum Wage Rate

How does an increase in the minimum wage rate affect the employment of
a. high- and low-productivity workers in covered industries?
b. high- and low-productivity workers in uncovered industries?
What does a higher minimum wage rate mean for the unemployment rate of
a. teenagers?
b. all workers?

CHAPTER 10

INVESTMENT

So far, we simplified matters by pretending that labor services were the only variable input to the production process. Now we want to be more realistic by including capital services as well. We shall think primarily of **physical capital,** such as machines and buildings used by producers. In the national accounts this category is called **producers' durable equipment and structures.** But we can broaden this concept of capital to include the goods held as **inventories** by businesses. We might also add **consumer durables,** such as homes (called residential structures in the national accounts), automobiles, and appliances. In fact, we could usefully go further to include **human capital,** which measures the effects of education and training on the skills of workers. But while our formal analysis applies also to human capital, we shall confine most of our thinking here to physical capital.

The Capital Stock in the United States

Let's start with an overview of the U.S. capital stock. Figure 10.1 shows how a standard concept of physical capital evolves from the end of 1925 until the end of 1981. This concept is called **private fixed capital.** It includes producers' durable equipment and structures, plus residential structures.[1] Thus, it excludes business inventories (which are not part of "fixed" capital), as well as consumer durables other than homes. Also, the measure ignores any capital that is owned by governments. Note that the data are in real terms—that is, they express the quantity of capital in terms of dollar values for the base year, 1972. In addition, the numbers are net of **depreciation,** which we shall discuss later.

Figure 10.1 shows the quantity of capital on a proportionate scale. (Recall that on this scale each unit on the vertical axis corresponds to the same proportionate change in quantity—for example, to a 1% increase in the stock of capital.) Therefore, the slope of the curve indicates the growth rate of the capital stock. Notice

---

[1]The data are from John Musgrave, "Fixed Capital Stock in the United States: Revised Estimates," *U.S. Survey of Current Business,* February 1981. Data for 1980–81 are constructed by adding real net fixed investment to the stock of capital from the end of 1979.

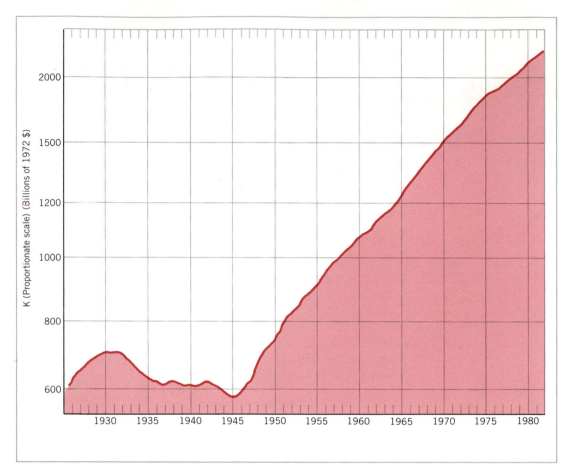

Figure 10.1 The Stock of Private Fixed Capital in the United States
The figure shows the quantity of capital on a proportionate scale. The data run from the end of 1925 until the end of 1981.

that the quantity of capital grows throughout the post-World War II period. In particular, from the end of 1945 until the end of 1981, the average growth rate is 3.8% per year.

The capital stock behaves very differently before 1945. After growing through most of the 1920s (only partially shown in the figure), the stock declines during the depressed years from 1931 through 1938, except for a small increase in 1937. Then, after some growth for 1940–41, the stock declines again during World War II. Overall, the stock of private fixed capital falls at a rate of 0.2% per year from the end of 1925 until the end of 1945.

As mentioned, the data on fixed capital include three major components:

• producers' durable equipment

• producers' structures

• residential structures

During the post-World War II period, the composition among these categories is reasonably stable, with roughly half the total appearing in residential structures and about one quarter in each of the other two categories. For example, at the end of 1979, the breakdown is 26% in producers' equipment, 27% in producers' structures, and 47% in residential structures. By contrast, before World War II, there is a smaller fraction in producers' equipment and a larger fraction in producers' structures. For example, at the end of 1925, the figures are 15% in producers' equipment, 35% in producers' structures, and 50% in residential structures. Throughout the entire period, 1925–81, residential structures account for about half of the total stock of private fixed capital.

Capital in the Production Function

Here, we begin to incorporate capital into the theoretical model. In order to keep things as simple as possible, let's return to the world where each household works only on its own production process. Therefore, we shall not consider explicitly a separate labor market. But the main conclusions do not depend on this simplification.

In order to keep things manageable, we pretend that there is only a single type of capital. Hence, we can measure its quantity in physical units—for example, as a number of standard-type machines. Then we denote by k_{t-1} the quantity of this capital that a producer has at the end of period $t - 1$. Because it takes time to make new capital operational, we assume that the stock from period $t - 1$ is available for use in production during period t. In other words, it takes one period for newly acquired capital to become on-line.

The production function is now

$$y_t = f(\underset{(+)}{k_{t-1}}, \quad \underset{(+)}{l_t})$$

(10.1)

where the variable k_{t-1} measures capital input and the variable l_t measures labor input. In the real world there are variations in the **utilization rate** of capital. For example, a factory, which is a type of capital, may operate for one shift per day or two. But we neglect these possibilities for the production function in equation (10.1). Here, we can think of the quantity of capital, k_{t-1}, as always operating for one standard-length shift per day.

The plus signs under the two inputs in equation (10.1) signify that they are productive at the margin. That is, an increase in either input, with the other held fixed, leads to more output. Remember that the marginal product of labor for period t, MPL_t, measures the effect on output, y_t, from an extra unit of work, l_t. Note that we hold fixed the quantity of capital, k_{t-1}, when we measure the marginal product of labor. Hence, this marginal product indicates the response of output when labor increases by 1 unit, while capital does not change.

We define the **marginal product of capital** in a similar manner. Namely, this marginal product, MPK_{t-1}, measures the response of output, y_t, when capital, k_{t-1}, increases by 1 unit, while the amount of work, l_t, does not change. Notice that the dating on this marginal product shows that it relates to the quantity of capital, k_{t-1}, from the end of period $t - 1$. However, because of the lag in making new capital operational, this marginal product refers to the effect on output for period t.

We discussed before the notion of the diminishing marginal productivity of labor. Specifically, labor's marginal product, MPL_t, falls as the amount of work increases, at least if the quantity of capital does not change. Now we make a parallel assumption about the marginal product of capital. Namely, this marginal product, MPK_{t-1}, declines as the quantity of capital, k_{t-1}, increases, at least if the amount of labor does not change.

Figure 10.2 shows how output responds as a producer uses more capital. Here, we hold fixed the quantity of labor. Notice that the curve goes through the origin, which means that a producer gets no output if the capital stock is zero.

The slope of the curve in Figure 10.2 is the marginal product of capital, MPK_{t-1}. Note that the slope is positive throughout, but declines as the amount of capital increases. In order to stress this relationship, we show it explicitly in Figure 10.3. Here, the marginal product, MPK_{t-1}, declines as the quantity of capital, k_{t-1}, rises. (Recall that the curve assumes a fixed amount of labor, l_t.)

Interactions between Capital and Labor

How does an increase in capital affect the productivity of labor, and vice versa? Usually, these two factors cooperate in the production process. That is, an increase

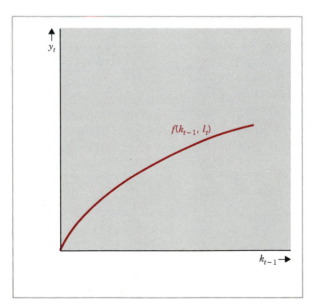

Figure 10.2 The Response of Output to the Quantity of Capital Input
The graph shows the effect on output, y_t, of a change in capital input, k_{t-1}. Here, the quantity of labor, l_t, does not change.

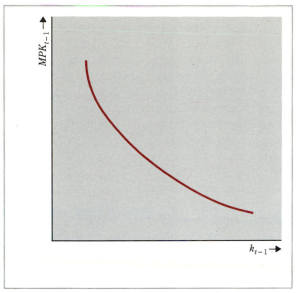

Figure 10.3 **The Relation of the Marginal Product of Capital to the Quantity of Capital**
The graph shows that the marginal product of capital, MPK_{t-1}, declines as the amount of capital, k_{t-1}, increases.

in the quantity of capital, k_{t-1}, raises the marginal product of labor, MPL_t, while an increase in the quantity of labor, l_t, raises the marginal product of capital, MPK_{t-1}.

As an example of this cooperation, think of the effect of better tools on the productivity of a carpenter. An improvement in the tools—that is, more capital, k_{t-1}—raises the marginal product, MPL_t, for each hour of work. Similarly, the more the carpenter works, l_t, the greater is the effect on output, MPK_{t-1}, from having the better tools.

More generally, we can construct examples where an increase in one input, capital or labor, either raises or lowers the marginal product of the other. But for our purposes, we want to model the typical pattern of interaction between capital and labor. Studies of production functions at an economy-wide level indicate that cooperation between the inputs is typical. Therefore, we shall assume in our model that an increase in one factor, capital or labor, raises the marginal product of the other. In particular, if the amount of work, l_t, increases, then the entire schedule for the marginal product of capital, MPK_{t-1}, shifts upward. Thus, in Figure 10.3, an increase in labor input leads to an upward shift of the curve. Similarly, an increase in the quantity of capital, k_{t-1}, shifts upward the schedule for the marginal product of labor, MPL_t.

Returns to Scale

What happens to output if a producer doubles the quantities of both inputs, capital and labor? Does the producer get twice the output, or more or less than twice the output? If output exactly doubles, then we say that the production function exhibits **constant returns to scale.** Alternatively, there are either **increasing or decreasing returns to scale** as output more or less than doubles, respectively. Of course, there may be increasing returns over some range of operations, constant returns over another range, and decreasing returns over a third range.

If a producer actually doubles all of the productive inputs—including not only capital and labor, but also ''land'' (which covers all types of natural resources), managerial talent, and so on—then there would essentially be two identical producing units where there initially was one. Presumably, these 2 units would each produce the same amount of goods—hence, we expect to find constant returns to scale when we think of scale in this broad sense. Also, there would then be no effects from changes in the scale of production on the marginal products of capital and labor.

Usually, when we think about doubling the inputs of capital and labor, we hold fixed some other productive inputs. For example, for a business, we might hold fixed the time of the owner. But if these other inputs had doubled, the producer would have doubled total output. Consequently, when some of these inputs do not change, the producer must end up with less than twice the output. Therefore, the presumption is that a doubling of capital and labor leads to less than twice as much output. That is, there are diminishing returns to scale when we limit the concept of scale to the levels of capital and labor.[2]

When there are diminishing returns to scale, there is also a form of diminishing marginal productivity with respect to changes in scale. Namely, if the quantities of capital and labor double, then the marginal products of both inputs decline. (By contrast, under constant returns, these marginal products would not change if both inputs doubled.)

Investment Goods and Consumer Goods

We define **investment** to be someone's purchases of capital goods—for example, machines or buildings, or goods to be held as inventories—from the commodity market. Generally, capital goods differ physically from consumer goods. But in order to keep things simple, we assume that there is only one physical good that people produce and exchange on the commodity market. One person buys this good for consumption purposes, while another buys it in order to accumulate more capital—that is, for investment purposes.

---

[2]The discussion neglects some setup costs (or ''indivisibilities'') in production, which might make it inefficient to operate at a low scale. For example, the benefits from specialization of labor on an assembly line cannot be attained until the scale of production is large enough.

As an amusing example of our type of multipurpose good, think of a shmoo, which appeared in the Li'l Abner comic strip. According to the comic strip, a shmoo can either be eaten—thereby constituting consumption—or planted in the ground as an investment to yield two shmoos next year. However, a more serious example of our good is livestock, which people use as either a consumer good or an investment good.

The analysis does not actually require consumer goods and capital goods to be physically the same. Instead, we are assuming something about the way people can shift from producing consumables to producing capital goods. For example, suppose that someone can use a combination of the productive inputs to make either X_1 units of consumables or X_2 units of capital. The ratio, X_2/X_1, indicates the terms on which the producer can substitute output of capital goods for output of consumables. Then our basic assumption is that this ratio, X_2/X_1, is constant. Specifically, the terms on which production of capital goods can be substituted for production of consumables do not depend on either the producer's or the economy's levels of production for the two types of goods. Also, we do not allow for any time to elapse while people shift from one type of production to another.[3]

If the substitution ratio for producers, X_2/X_1, is constant, then we may as well pick physical units for consumer goods and capital so that this ratio equals one. That is, we can measure things so that people can shift from producing one unit of consumer goods into producing one unit of capital goods and vice versa. But then this setup amounts to the one that we described before, in which the two types of goods are physically identical. So from now on, we pretend that these two goods are physically the same.

As before, producers sell all of their output, y_t, on the commodity market at the price P_t. Then people buy these goods either for consumption, c_t, or investment, which we denote by i_t. Therefore, a household's total demand for goods, y_t^d, equals the sum of consumption demand, c_t^d, and investment demand, i_t^d. (Note that we can add these two magnitudes, since they are measured in the same physical unit.) Since all goods sell at the same price, suppliers do not care whether their goods are labeled as consumer goods or investment goods. Therefore, we shall focus on a producer's total supply of goods, y_t^s.

---

[3]Our setup is called a *one-sector production technology*. This specification, which appears in most macroanalyses, has only one process that allows people to use inputs in order to produce goods. Some economists use a *two-sector production model*. Then there is one process for producing consumer goods and another for capital goods. (However, there is still only one physical type of capital and only one physical type of consumable.) In this case, there can be changes in the substitution ratio for producers, X_2/X_1. (Recall that X_2 is the quantity of capital goods that someone can make if he or she produces X_1 less units of consumer goods.) For an example of a model with a two-sector production technology, see Duncan Foley and Miguel Sidrauski, *Monetary and Fiscal Policy in a Growing Economy*, Macmillan, New York, 1971, especially Chapter 2.

Depreciation

Capital goods do not last forever, but rather tend to depreciate—or wear out—over time. We model this process in a simple form, where the amount of depreciation during period t is a constant fraction of the stock of capital that someone carries over from period $t - 1$. In other words, if d_t denotes the amount of depreciation in units of commodities, then

$$d_t = \delta k_{t-1} \tag{10.2}$$

where δ (the Greek letter *delta*) is the constant rate of depreciation per period. For example, the depreciation rate δ might be 10% per year. Here, we can think of the quantity of capital goods, d_t, as effectively disappearing or "evaporating" during period t.

Equation (10.2) assumes proportional depreciation—that is, the amount of depreciation is always a given proportion of the existing capital stock. This formulation involves two assumptions that may cause problems empirically. First, it ignores any dependence of depreciation on the composition of the capital stock. For example, if there is a shift from long-lived buildings to short-lived machines, then depreciation rises as a fraction of the capital stock. As noted before, there are some shifts of this type in the United States economy, but the changes occur very slowly. Second, and more importantly, the formulation neglects any effects on depreciation from the intensity with which people use capital.[4] But as mentioned earlier, the model does not consider variations in utilization rates.

We still assume that the capital held over from period $t - 1$, k_{t-1}, is the pertinent input for production during period t. Then, in order to calculate the stock that is available for the next period's production, we have to add investment, i_t, and subtract depreciation, d_t. Therefore, the capital stock at the end of period t is

$$k_t = k_{t-1} + i_t - \delta k_{t-1} \tag{10.3}$$

Recall that a producer purchases the quantity of investment goods, i_t, during period t. But the change in the capital stock $k_t - k_{t-1}$, equals these purchases less the depreciation of existing stocks, δk_{t-1}. Hence, there are two concepts of investment, as follows:

- **Gross investment** is the quantity of capital goods purchased, i_t.
- **Net investment** is the change in the capital stock, $k_t - k_{t-1}$, which equals gross investment, i_t, less the amount of depreciation, δk_{t-1}.

Correspondingly, there are also two concepts of output:

- **Gross product** is the total amount produced, y_t.
- **Net product** equals gross product less depreciation, $y_t - \delta k_{t-1}$. That is, net

---

[4]We also do not consider maintenance, which surely affects the rate of depreciation. However, we can think of maintenance as a form of investment, which we analyze below. Empirically, the main problem here is the lack of data on maintenance expenditures.

product is the quantity of goods that someone produces net of the amount needed to replace the capital goods that wear out during the period.

Gross Investment, Depreciation, and Net Investment in the U.S.

Figure 10.4 shows the behavior of aggregate real gross investment, I_t, depreciation, D_t, and net investment, $I_t - D_t$, in the United States from 1929 to 1982. The numbers refer to private fixed domestic investment, which includes purchases of business plant and equipment, plus residential construction. Thus, the concept of investment corresponds to the measure of the capital stock that we looked at before in Figure 10.1. In particular, this concept does not include changes in the stocks of goods that businesses hold in inventory. In Figure 10.4 we express the amounts of investment as ratios to the stock of capital from the end of the previous year, K_{t-1}.

The numbers for depreciation are rough estimates that assume specified service lives for different types of capital.[5] Therefore, the ratio of measured depreciation to the capital stock changes only when there are shifts in the average service life of the existing capital. For example, the pre-World War II movement away from structures and toward equipment leads to a higher relative amount of depreciation. Quantitatively, the ratio of measured depreciation to the capital stock is very stable, ranging between 5.8 and 6.2% from 1946 to 1975. However, the ratio does rise to 7.1% for 1982. Note also that the ratio is between 4.9 and 5.5% from 1929 to 1945.

By contrast, the ratio of net investment to the capital stock is volatile. From 1946 to 1982, the mean of this ratio is 3.9%. But the numbers range from 1.7% in 1982 to 5.8% in 1948. In fact, low numbers for this ratio identify years of recession—that is, times where output has been growing at a relatively low rate, which may be negative. The list of the lowest ratios for net investment to the capital stock—1.7% for 1982, 2.1% for 1975, 2.4% for 1981, 2.6% for 1976, 2.7% for 1980, 2.8% for 1958, 3.2% for 1961, 3.7% for 1970, and 3.8% for 1954—picks out the recessions of the post-World War II period.[6] Conversely, the ratio tends to be high in years of economic boom, where total output grows rapidly.

We see a stronger version of the same pattern before World War II. Notice that net investment is negative during the years of the Great Depression, 1931–33. In fact, net investment does not become positive again until 1937. Then the recession of 1938 generates another year of negative net investment. Note also that net investment is negative during World War II. However, we shall postpone our

---

[5]Depreciation is calculated on a ''straight-line'' basis. For example, the formula assumes that a building with a 50-year life loses 2% of its initial real value in each year.

[6]Generally, people also view 1949 as a year of minor recession. For that year, the ratio of net investment to the capital stock, 4.2%, does show a significant drop from the previous year.

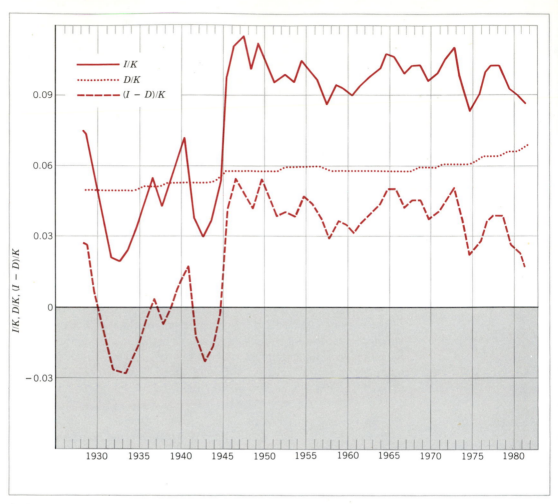

Figure 10.4 The Ratios of Investment and Depreciation to the Capital Stock
The graph shows the ratios to the capital stock, K_{t-1}, of gross investment, I_t, depreciation, D_t, and net investment, $I_t - D_t$. The data on investment and depreciation run from 1929 until 1982.

consideration of this behavior until we study government expenditures in Chapter 13.

Figure 10.5 shows the ratios of gross investment, depreciation, and net investment to real gross national product (GNP). Again, the movements in the net investment ratio indicate the recessions. Here, because net investment fluctuates by proportionately more than total output, we find that net investment's share of output declines during a recession. For example, from 1946–82, the mean of the ratio of net investment to GNP is 5.6%. But the lowest values of this ratio—all

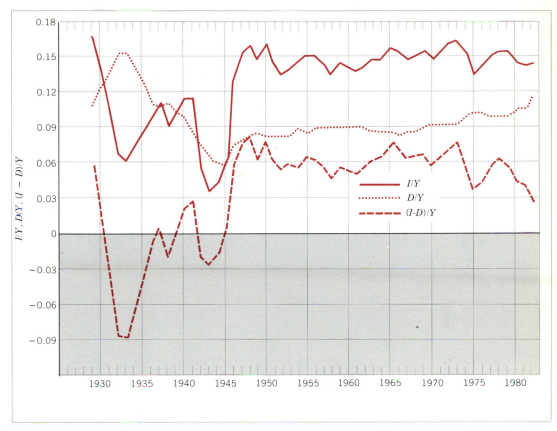

Figure 10.5 The Ratios of Investment and Depreciation to GNP
The graphs show the ratios to real GNP, Y_t, of gross investment, I_t, depreciation, D_t, and net investment, $I_t - D_t$. The data run from 1929 until 1982.

years of recession—are 2.7% for 1982, 3.3% for 1975, 3.6% for 1981, 4.0% for 1976, 4.1% for 1980, 4.3% for 1958, and 4.7% for 1961. Conversely, the ratio of net investment to GNP tends to be high in years where total output grows rapidly.

Consumption and Investment during Recessions

Table 10.1 shows how the shortfalls of real GNP during recessions break down between consumption and investment. Here, we use the method described in Chapter 9 to compute the departure of real GNP and its components from trend values for each recession. For example, for the 1982 recession, the shortfall in real GNP is $143 billion, or almost 9% of the trend value of real GNP. Then we find that 40% of the overall shortfall shows up in personal consumption expenditures, 32%

Table 10.1 Consumption and Investment During Recessions

Final Year of Recession	1933	1949	1954	1958	1961	1970	1975	1982	Mean for 7 Post-War
Base Year for Comparison	1929	1948	1953	1956	1959	1969	1973	1979	Recessions
Shortfall in Real GNP (billions of 1972 dollars)	133.9	12.5	26.5	32.2	9.7	35.1	98.7	143.2	—
Shortfall as % of Trend Real GNP	37.6	2.5	4.1	4.5	1.3	3.1	7.4	8.8	4.5
% of shortfall in real GNP accounted for by:									
Personal consumption expenditures	54	19	17	39	64	16	36	40	33
durables	10	−16	3	20	46	16	16	16	14
non-durables & services	44	34	14	19	19	−1	20	25	19
Gross fixed investment	33	73	4	42	64	30	52	32	42
non-residential	24	53	10	31	8	19	28	14	23
residential	9	21	−6	10	56	11	24	17	19
Change in business inventories	8	81	11	25	45	22	25	12	32
Other*	5	−73	68	−6	−73	32	−13	16	−7
Total investment**	51	138	18	87	155	68	93	60	88

*Government purchases and exports less imports.

**Purchases of consumer durables plus gross fixed investment plus change in business inventories.

Note: The method for calculating the shortfall in each component is discussed in the text.

Source: Economic Report of the President, 1983.

in gross fixed investment, [7] 10% in changes in business inventories, and 16% in other categories.[8] (The last group consists of government purchases and exports less imports.)

For the seven postwar recessions, the mean shares for the shortfall in real GNP are 33% in personal consumption expenditures, 42% in gross fixed investment,

---

[7]Because measured depreciation is very stable, the estimated shortfall for net fixed investment is always close to that for gross fixed investment.

[8]Except for the category labeled as *other,* the calculated shortfall in any component is the difference of a trend value from the actual. The trend value assumes 3% annual growth from the base year. For the category labeled as other, the estimated shortfall is the total shortfall for GNP less the sum of the components calculated separately.

32% in changes in business inventories and -7% in the other components.[9] To put the results another way, although the mean ratio of consumption expenditures to GNP over the post-war period is 62%, the fluctuations in these expenditures account on average for only 33% of the fall in output during recessions. In other words, consumption fluctuates proportionately much less than total output, which in turn fluctuates much less than gross investment.

By using personal consumption expenditures, we substantially overstate the fluctuations in consumption. That's because the figures include purchases of consumer durables (except for residences, which are included with fixed investment).[10] More appropriately, we should think of a person's automobile or home appliance as analogous to a business's machine or factory. In particular, consumer durables last for many years and are used to provide flows of services, such as transportation, food preparation, house cleaning, and so on. Basically, we should view these durables as forms of capital goods that happen to be owned and used in the real world by households, rather than businesses. Hence, we should treat purchases of consumer durables as a form of gross investment.

The last line of Table 10.1 adds together all the investment components—gross fixed investment, changes in business inventories, and purchases of consumer durables. Notice that this total accounts on average for 88% of the total shortfall in real GNP. By contrast, although the mean ratio of consumer expenditures on nondurables and services to GNP is 54%, this component accounts on average for only 19% of the shortfall in output. To put this result another way, the shortfall in the consumption of nondurables and services turns out to average only 1.7% of the trend value of this component.[11] Hence, this measure of consumption is remarkably stable during recessions. As a first approximation, explaining recessions amounts to explaining the sharp contractions in the investment components.

Finally, for comparison, Table 10.1 shows the figures for the Great Depression of 1930–33. Here, the estimated shortfall of real GNP is 37.6% of the trend value. Thus, this experience dwarfs the magnitudes for the postwar recessions. Notice also that the consumption of nondurables and services accounts for 44% of the shortfall in real GNP, while the total of the investment components accounts for 51%. Thus, the cutback in consumption is relatively more important during the Depression than it is for the milder contractions since World War II.

Overall, there are several features of the data that we would like our theory to explain. In particular, we want to know why

---

[9]For the 1954 and 1970 recessions, the large contribution from the other category reflects the sharp cutbacks in military spending after the Korean and Vietnam Wars, respectively. For the 1949 and 1961 recessions, there are substantial increases in government purchases. Therefore, the other category shows large negative contributions to the shortfall of real GNP.

[10]The decision on what is durable and what is not is somewhat arbitrary. For example, clothing is classified as nondurable, although many suits last longer than cars. Also, the service category includes an imputed rental on owner-occupied housing.

[11]However, the largest percentage cutback, which is 4.2%, shows up for the 1982 recession.

- Investment is far more volatile than consumption,
- The ratio of investment to GNP or the stock of capital is low during recessions and high in booms,
- Consumption expenditures—especially on nondurables and services—decline little in proportional terms during mild recessions, but do fall significantly during a severe contraction.

Characteristics of Existing Capital

Let's return now to the theoretical analysis. Remember that producers can call their output either consumables or capital. But once the purchaser has put capital into place—for example, as a factory—it would be grossly unrealistic to assume that these goods can be reclassified as consumables and then eaten up. Hence, we assume that the initial labeling choice as consumables or capital is irreversible. In other words, producers cannot consume their capital at a later date.[12] However, they can allow capital to depreciate and not replace it.

A second issue concerns the possibilities for moving capital goods from one production activity to another. Here, we simplify the analysis by assuming that these movements are possible at negligible cost. This mobility of capital ensures that people place all existing stocks in their most favorable use. Otherwise, someone could do better by shifting capital to another location. Recall also that we treat all units of capital as physically identical. Therefore, each unit must end up with the same physical marginal product.

Sometimes, we shall find it convenient to think of a resale market for used capital. Then, if a piece of capital has a low marginal product for one person, he or she will find it advantageous to sell the capital to someone else.[13] But since old and new capital are identical, the price of a unit of capital during period t on the resale market must equal that for new units, which is P_t. Given this result, we can think of old capital goods as being sold along with new ones on the commodity market. Hence, we do not have to worry about a separate market for resales.

Investment Demand

Consider a producer's incentive to invest during period t. Recall that the stock of capital that will be available for production next period is the quantity

$$k_t = k_{t-1} + i_t - \delta k_{t-1}$$

---

[12]There are examples where capital can be consumed readily, such as livestock. Shmoos are another example! Are there any more? (One of my colleagues predicts that the chefs and wine-growers of France will "consume their capital" if the socialist government becomes too oppressive.)

[13]People might also rent out their capital, rather than sell it. There are organized rental markets for motor vehicles, housing, computers, and copying machines, but not for many other types of capital goods.

Note that, at date t, the previous stock, k_{t-1}, and the amount of depreciation, δk_{t-1}, are givens. Therefore, an increase by 1 unit in gross investment, i_t, means an increase by 1 unit in net investment, $i_t - \delta k_{t-1}$, and also an increase by 1 unit in the stock of capital, k_t. Hence, each producer decides how much to invest during period t by weighing the cost of this investment against the return from having more capital, k_t.

First, in order to raise investment by 1 unit, a producer must purchase an additional unit of goods from the commodity market at the price P_t. Hence, P_t is the dollar cost of an extra unit of investment.

There are two components of the return to investment. First, an additional unit of investment raises capital, k_t, by 1 unit. Hence, if we hold fixed the quantity of work for the next period, l_{t+1}, then next period's output, y_{t+1}, rises by the marginal product of capital, MPK_t. Since producers sell this output at the price, P_{t+1}, the additional dollar sales revenue is the amount, $P_{t+1} \cdot MPK_t$.

Remember that the fraction, δ, of each unit of capital disappears after one period because of depreciation. But the remaining fraction, $1 - \delta$, is still around. Then we can pretend that producers sell all of this old capital on the commodity market at date $t + 1$. (If they like, they can ''buy back'' this capital during period $t + 1$ to use for production at date $t + 2$. But that decision is separate from the choice of investment at date t, which we are now considering.) Since goods sell at price P_{t+1} during period $t + 1$, the dollar revenue from the sale of used capital is the amount, $(1 - \delta)P_{t+1}$. Hence, this term is the second part of the return to investment.

Overall, an additional unit of investment costs P_t during period t and yields the amount, $P_{t+1}(MPK_t + 1 - \delta)$, in period $t + 1$. Therefore, the dollar return on the investment is the difference, $P_{t+1}(MPK_t + 1 - \delta) - P_t$. If we divide by the number of dollars invested, P_t, we determine the nominal rate of return to investment, which is

$$\frac{P_{t+1}(MPK_t + 1 - \delta) - P_t}{P_t} = (1 + \pi_t)(MPK_t + 1 - \delta) - 1$$

Here, we use the condition, $P_{t+1} = (1 + \pi_t)P_t$, where π_t is the inflation rate for period t.

The nominal rate of return from investment looks good or bad depending on its relation to other available returns. Specifically, people can earn the nominal interest rate, R_t, on bonds. Also, they can pay this rate if they decide to borrow funds in order to finance investment. If the nominal rate of return from investment exceeds the nominal interest rate, R_t, producers would like to raise investment— that is, buy more capital goods. (An individual producer can finance this investment either by borrowing or by lowering his or her holdings of bonds.) But as the capital stock rises, diminishing marginal productivity implies that capital's marginal product, MPK_t, falls. Eventually, this decline in the marginal product reduces the nominal rate of return to investment enough to equal the nominal interest rate, R_t. Then producers have no further incentive to expand investment.

Algebraically, investors act to satisfy the condition

$$(1 + \pi_t)(MPK_t + 1 - \delta) - 1 = R_t$$

where the left side is the nominal rate of return from investment. However, recall that the real rate of return on bonds, r_t, satisfies the relation, $(1 + r_t) = (1 + R_t)/(1 + \pi_t)$. Using this condition, we can simplify the above result to the form

$$MPK_t - \delta = r_t \tag{10.6}$$

Equation (10.6) is the basic condition for determining investment demand.

The left side of equation (10.6) is the real rate of return from an additional unit of investment. In the absence of depreciation—that is, $\delta = 0$—this rate of return would be the marginal product of capital, MPK_t. That's because the marginal product tells us the additional goods that we get next year when we invest an extra unit of goods this year. But, when there is depreciation, we also lose δ units of goods per year for each unit of investment. Therefore, we have to subtract the rate of depreciation, δ, from the marginal product, MPK_t, in order to calculate the net **real rate of return from investment.**

Equation (10.6) says that investors act to equate the real rate of return from investment to the real rate of return on bonds, r_t. Any difference between these two rates makes it profitable to select either a higher or lower amount of investment. Therefore, the amount of investment that people choose generates a marginal product, MPK_t, that equates the two real rates of return, as shown in equation (10.6).

We show the results graphically in Figure 10.6. As the quantity of capital k_t rises, the marginal product, MPK_t, declines. Notice that the upper curve in the figure exhibits this property. Recall that the real rate of return from an extra unit of investment is the amount, $MPK_t - \delta$. This magnitude appears on the lower curve in the figure. Finally, a producer chooses the level of capital, denoted by $\bar{k}_t$, where the real rate of return from investment, $MPK_t - \delta$, equals the real interest rate on bonds, r_t.

Given the schedule for capital's marginal product, the **desired stock of capital** $\bar{k}_t$ depends on the real interest rate, r_t, and the depreciation rate. Hence, we can write the desired stock of capital as the function

$$\bar{k}_t = \bar{k}(r_t, \delta, \ldots) \tag{10.7}$$
$$(-)\,(-)$$

Note that an increase in the real interest rate, r_t, or the depreciation rate, δ, means that the marginal product of capital, MPK_t, must be higher in equation (10.6). Therefore, because of diminishing marginal productivity, the desired stock of capital declines.

For given values of the real interest rate and the rate of depreciation, an upward shift in the schedule for capital's marginal product raises the desired stock of capital. (We can show this result graphically by shifting the two curves upward in Figure 10.6). These types of changes show up in the omitted terms, which we denote by . . . , in equation (10.7).

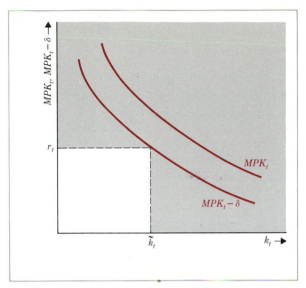

Figure 10.6 The Choice of Capital Stock

Producers aim for the level of capital, $\tilde{k}_t$, where the real rate of return from investment, $MPK_t - \delta$, equals the real interest rate on bonds, r_t.

Once we know the desired stock of capital, $\tilde{k}_t$, we know also the choice of gross investment, i_t. Specifically, in order to attain the stock $\tilde{k}_t$, a producer demands for investment purposes the quantity of goods i_t^d, where

$$i_t^d = \tilde{k}_t - k_{t-1} = \tilde{k}_t - (1 - \delta)k_{t-1}$$

Notice that, for given values of the starting capital stock, k_{t-1}, and depreciation, δk_{t-1}, gross **investment demand** varies one-to-one with changes in the desired stock of capital $\tilde{k}_t$.

Using equation (10.7), we can write out a function for gross investment demand as

$$i_t^d = \tilde{k}(r_t, \ \delta, \ \ldots) - (1 - \delta)k_{t-1} = i^d(r_t, \ \delta, \ k_{t-1}, \ \ldots) \qquad (10.8)$$
$$(-)\,(-) \qquad\qquad\qquad\qquad (-)\,(?)\,(-)$$

The implied amount of net investment demand is

$$i_t^d - \delta k_{t-1} = \tilde{k}(r_t, \ \delta, \ \ldots) - k_{t-1} \qquad (10.9)$$
$$(-)\,(-)$$

Properties of Investment Demand

Here, we summarize the main implications of the analysis for investment demand.

- A reduction in the real interest rate, r_t, raises the desired stock of capital, $\tilde{k}_t$. Therefore, given the initial stock k_{t-1}, investment demand rises.

- Given the real interest rate, an upward shift in the schedule for capital's marginal product, MPK_t, raises the desired stock of capital, $\tilde{k}_t$. Hence, given the initial stock of capital, k_{t-1}, investment demand increases.
- Other things equal, investment demand declines if the previous stock of capital, k_{t-1}, rises. By "other things equal," we mean to include the various elements that determine the desired stock of capital, $\tilde{k}_t$. Recall that net investment demand equals the quantity, $\tilde{k}_t - k_{t-1}$. Therefore, it follows that this demand falls with a rise in the initial stock, k_{t-1}. Then remember that gross investment demand equals the quantity, $\tilde{k}_t - (1 - \delta)k_{t-1}$. Thus, as long as the depreciation rate, δ, is less than 100%, a rise in the initial stock, k_{t-1}, means less gross investment demand, i_t^d.
- An increase in the rate of depreciation, δ, lowers the desired stock of capital, $\tilde{k}_t$. Therefore, net investment demand, $\tilde{k}_t - k_{t-1}$, declines. However, recall again that gross investment demand equals the quantity, $\tilde{k}_t - (1 - \delta)k_{t-1}$. Because the desired capital stock declines, while depreciation rises, the net effect on gross investment demand is ambiguous.
- Gross investment demand is positive as long as the desired stock, $\tilde{k}_t$, exceeds the fraction, $(1 - \delta)$, of the initial stock, k_{t-1}. However, gross investment can be negative for some producers. Remember that we allow resale of old capital goods on the commodity market. So negative gross investment means that someone's sales of old capital goods exceeds his or her purchases of new ones.

We assumed before that capital goods cannot be converted back into consumables. Therefore, one person's negative gross investment (sales of capital goods) must correspond to someone else's positive gross investment. Hence, when we aggregate over all producers, we cannot have negative gross investment, I_t. To put this result another way, the aggregate stock of capital, K_t, cannot fall below the initial stock, K_{t-1}, by more than the amount of depreciation, δK_{t-1}. Correspondingly, aggregate net investment, $K_t - K_{t-1} = I_t - \delta K_{t-1}$, can be negative only up to the magnitude of depreciation, δK_{t-1}.

Recall from Figure 10.4 that the aggregate of private fixed net investment is, in fact, substantially positive for each year since the end of World War II. However, this aggregate is negative during the Great Depression and World War II. Thus, our interpretation is that the aggregate desired stock of capital, $\tilde{K}_t$, fell below the initial stock, K_{t-1}, during these years.

Let's think about the quantitative behavior of net investment demand. Since World War II, aggregate net investment averages about 4% of the initial capital stock, K_{t-1}. Now, consider changes in the real interest rate, r_t, or in the schedule for capital's marginal product, MPK_t. These changes affect the aggregate desired stock of capital, $\tilde{K}_t$. Suppose, as an example, that some change occurs that reduces this desired stock by 1%. Then the aggregate of net investment demand—over a period of, say, a year—declines by about 1% of the capital stock. So if net investment demand were initially equal to 4% of the capital stock, then this change lowers it to 3% of the stock. In other words, a decline by 1% in the desired stock of capital translates into a decline by roughly 25% in one year's net investment demand. Because one year's net investment is a small fraction—on the average about 4%—of the existing capital stock, small percentage changes in the desired stock generate large percentage changes in net investment demand. Therefore, we should not be surprised by two features of the U.S. data, which appear in Figures 10.4 and 10.5. First, because aggregate net investment demand is volatile, the share of net investment in GNP fluctuates substantially from year to year. Second, the desired stock of capital is sometimes low enough—namely, during the Great Depression and World War II—so that aggregate net investment is negative.

Absence of a Resale Market

In determining the choice of investment, we pretended that producers resell the undepreciated portion of their capital, $(1 - \delta)k_{t-1}$, on the commodity market during period t. Then, if they desire, producers can again buy investment goods in period $t + 1$, resell them in period $t + 2$, and so on. By pretending that people resell all of their old capital, we can easily calculate the rate of return to investment over one period. But this device is artificial. Typically, a producer keeps a piece of capital for many years. In fact, the sale of used capital goods is unusual for most types of producers' equipment and structures (although it is common for residences).

In many interesting cases our analysis of investment goes through unchanged even if resales are impossible. In the previous setup, a producer resells the quantity of capital, $(1 - \delta)k_{t-1}$, during period t. But the producer then purchases back the desired stock, k_t. Thus, the difference between purchases and sales of capital goods is the quantity, $k_t - (1 - \delta)k_{t-1}$, which equals gross investment demand, i_t^d. Thus, as long as gross investment demand is positive, the producer does not need to resell old capital. That is, he or she wants only to buy the net positive amount of goods, i_t^d. So, a person who undertakes positive gross investment has no reason to make resales. This person just keeps his or her existing capital, and then buys new goods in the amount, i_t^d.

If we look only at producers who have positive gross investment demand in every period, then the potential for resale is irrelevant. That's because someone with positive gross investment does not choose to resell capital. Therefore, in this case, there are no changes if we eliminate the possibilities for resale. In other words, the previous results go through if gross investment demand is positive in each period for every producer.[15]

Remember that gross investment demand, i_t^d, equals net investment demand, $\tilde{k}_t - k_{t-1}$, plus depreciation, δk_{t-1}. Therefore, in order for the previous results to hold, we do not need net investment demand to be positive for the typical producer.

---

[15]For a discussion of this issue and some related topics on investment, see Robert Hall, "Investment, Interest Rates, and the Effects of Stabilization Policies," *Brookings Papers on Economic Activity*, No. 1, 1977, especially pp. 71–74.

Rather, we need only to rule out net investment demand being so negative that it outweighs the positive amount of depreciation, δk_{t-1}.

For subsequent purposes, we assume that the previous analysis of investment is satisfactory. Recall that this analysis works either if we allow resale of capital or if gross investment demand is always positive for every producer. But, of course, we shall also do okay as an approximation if—as seems plausible—gross investment demand is positive at most times for most producers.

Gradual Adjustment of Investment Demand

In our analysis we assume that producers purchase enough goods in a single period—which might be a year—to attain their desired stock of capital. That is, people invest enough to close the gap between the capital carried over from the previous period, $(1 - \delta)k_{t-1}$, and the desired stock, $\bar{k}_t$.

We have ignored a variety of costs that arise when producers install new capital goods. For example, in order to place new plant and equipment into operation, an investor normally goes through a phase of planning and decision making, then a time of building and delivery, and finally an interval where managers and workers familiarize themselves with the new facilities. Typically, people can speed up parts of this process, but only by incurring extra costs. As examples, quicker decisions mean more mistakes, and faster construction requires larger payments to workers and suppliers.

Because there are substantial costs in adjusting the level of capital, we predict two types of lags in the investment process. First, a gap between the starting stock of capital, $(1 - \delta)k_{t-1}$, and the desired level, $\bar{k}_t$, stimulates higher investment over an extended interval. That is, since it takes time to build and install new plant and equipment, investors stretch out their purchases of new capital goods over an interval of time. Second, the higher capacity for production becomes available only after the investment project is completed. (Note that we capture some of this element by assuming that this period's capital stock affects production for the next period.)

Although adjustment costs for investment are quantitatively important, we continue to ignore these costs in order to simplify matters.[16] That's because the main features of the results do not change when we bring in these complications. Also, we should note that there are other areas where the analysis omits adjustment costs. For example, we assume that producers can shift without delay from producing consumables to producing capital goods, and vice versa. Also, we assume that the existing capital is highly mobile, which ensures that all units have the same

---

[16]For discussions of adjustment costs in investment demand, see Robert Eisner and Robert Strotz, "Determinants of Business Investment," in Commission on Money and Credit, *Impacts of Monetary Policy,* Prentice-Hall, Englewood Cliffs N.J., 1963; and Robert Lucas, "Adjustment Costs and the Theory of Supply," *Journal of Political Economy,* August 1967.

marginal products. Overall, these omissions mean that we should be careful about applying the model in a very short-run context.

Interactions between Capital and Labor

So far, we have ignored the role of labor input in the discussion of investment. Formally, when we drew the schedule for capital's marginal product, MPK_t, in Figure 10.6, we assumed that the associated level of work, l_{t+1}, did not change. Now let's examine how a producer's choice of work effort interacts with his or her choice of capital stock. Here, we still think about people working on their own production processes, rather than hiring workers from outside. However, the results are similar if producers can hire workers.

Consider a decline in the real interest rate, r_t, which raises a producer's desired capital stock, $\bar{k}_t$. Because the two factors of production cooperate in the model, this increase in capital raises the schedule for the marginal product of labor, MPL_{t+1}. Therefore, on this ground, the amount of work effort, l_{t+1}, tends to increase.[17]

We can say something about the size of the increase in labor input. Namely, this increase must be by a smaller proportion than the increase in capital. To see this, consider what would happen if the increases were in the same proportion. Then there would be an expansion in the scale of production—say, an increase by 10% in both capital and labor. But recall that we assume diminishing returns to scale. Therefore, output would rise by less than 10%. Also, the two marginal products, MPK_t and MPL_{t+1}, would decline. But if labor's marginal product falls, people would be unwilling to work more than they used to. Therefore, the increase in labor cannot be in the same proportion as the increase in capital. Rather, the increase in labor must be by a smaller proportion. In other words, the ratio of capital to labor, k_t/l_{t+1}, rises when the real interest rate declines.

The analysis is unfinished because the increase in labor input, l_{t+1}, raises capital's marginal product, MPK_t. Therefore, producers expand capital a bit more, which again motivates an increase in labor, and so on. However, a key element that limits the total of these responses is diminishing returns to scale. Because of this property, the increases in capital and labor lead to progressively smaller marginal products for each input. Therefore, for a given decline in the real interest rate, r_t, we can eventually determine the total amounts by which capital and labor increase.

To summarize, there are two new effects from the interaction between capital and labor. First, the response of work, l_{t+1}, increases the sensitivity of the desired stock of capital, $\bar{k}_t$, to various changes, such as a decline in the real interest rate,

---

[17]The amount of work depends also on intertemporal-substitution effects. Specifically, a higher value for the next period's real interest rate, r_{t+1}, tends to raise next period's work, l_{t+1}, relative to that in later periods. But a higher value for this period's real interest rate, r_t, tends to raise this period's work, l_t, relative to that in period $t + 1$ and in later periods.

r_t. Hence, the effect of the real interest rate on gross investment demand, as shown in equation (10.8), becomes larger in magnitude. Second, there are other reasons for shifts in work effort. For example, there might be a large amount of immigration. Then, because labor and capital cooperate in the production process, these expansions of work effort increase the desired stock of capital for some producers. Therefore, we have to interpret the omitted terms in the investment function, which are denoted by . . . in equation (10.8), as including these types of shifts in work effort.

Summary

We introduce the stock of capital as an input into the production function. An increase in capital raises output and also tends to increase the marginal product of labor. However, as the quantity of capital rises, the marginal product of capital diminishes.

Gross investment demand is the quantity of capital goods that a producer offers to buy from the commodity market. Since we treat capital goods and consumables as physically identical, the total demand for goods is the sum of gross investment demand and consumption demand. The change in a producer's stock of capital—or net investment—equals gross investment less depreciation. In the aggregate, gross investment cannot be negative. However, aggregate net investment can be negative—and was in the United States for most of the 1930s and during World War II.

Empirically, investment fluctuates proportionately by much more than total output, which fluctuates by more than consumption. Further, the ratio of investment to either the stock of capital or GNP is low during recessions and high in booms. For seven postwar recessions, the shortfall in total investment—which includes gross fixed investment, changes in business inventories and purchases of consumer durables—accounts on average for 88% of the shortfall in real GNP. By contrast, the decline in consumer expenditures on nondurables and services accounts on average for only 19% of the shortfall. That is, consumption falls proportionately by only a small amount (on average by 1.7%) during the postwar recessions. However, a large percentage decline in consumption (27%) shows up during the Great Depression.

The real rate of return to investment is the marginal product of capital less the rate of depreciation. Hence, producers determine their desired stocks of capital by equating this rate of return to the real interest rate. It follows that the desired stock of capital rises first, if the real interest rate falls, or second, if the schedule for capital's marginal product shifts upward, or third, if the depreciation rate declines. Given their initial stocks, producers invest enough during a period to achieve the desired stock of capital. Therefore, given the initial stock, investment demand rises if the desired stock of capital increases. Also, given the desired stock of capital, a smaller initial stock means a larger investment demand. Finally, we note that small percentage changes in the desired stock of capital translate into large percentage changes in net investment demand over one year. Therefore, we can see why net investment demand is highly volatile, and can sometimes be negative.

Important Terms and Concepts

physical capital

producers' durable equipment and structures

private fixed capital

inventories

consumer durables

human capital

depreciation

utilization rate

marginal product of capital (MPK)

constant returns to scale

increasing or decreasing returns to scale

gross investment

net investment

gross product

net product

real rate of return from investment

desired stock of capital

investment demand

QUESTIONS AND PROBLEMS

Mainly for Review

10.1 What is meant by private domestic fixed investment? Does it include purchases of consumer durables? What about purchases of bonds?

10.2 Distinguish gross investment and net investment. When is net investment negative? Can gross investment be negative if capital goods cannot be resold?

10.3 Suppose producers expect inflation, i.e., a higher price level in the next period. Will they want to increase their current purchases of capital goods? What if the nominal interest rate rises to reflect the higher expected inflation?

10.4 Given that capital goods last for many periods into the future, why does the condition for determining investment involve only next period's marginal product of capital?

10.5 Use Figure 10.6 to show that a higher real rate of interest reduces the desired capital stock (other things equal). How would you depict the desired amount of net investment on the graph?

10.6 When there are substantial costs in adjusting the level of capital, what is the effect of a decline in the real interest rate on the desired capital stock? On investment demand? Why would you expect investment to be less responsive as compared to a situation where adjustment costs are low?

Problems for Discussion

10.7 The One-Sector Production Function

In our model, output can be labeled as either consumables or capital goods. Economists call this a one-sector production function.

a. Why does the price of a unit of consumables always equal the price of a unit of capital in this model? What would happen if the price of consumables exceeded the price of capital goods, or vice versa?

b. Suppose that everyone wants to undertake negative gross investment—that is, everyone wants to resell old capital on the commodity market. Can the price of capital goods fall below the price of consumables in this case?

c. Consider a "two-sector model," where different production functions apply to consumables and capital goods. Would the price of a unit of consumables always equal the price of a unit of capital goods in this model? (optional)

10.8 Inventory Investment

Businesses hold inventories of goods, partly as finished products and partly as goods-in-process and raw materials. (Over the period, 1958–75, inventories of goods-in-process and materials account on average for 75% of the total in durables-manufacturing industries.)[18] Suppose that we think of inventories as a type of capital, which enters into the production function. Then changes in these stocks represent investment in inventories. (Generally, we assume that the rate of depreciation on inventories is near zero.)

a. How does an increase in the real interest rate affect the quantity of inventories that businesses want to hold? Therefore, what happens to inventory investment?

b. Consider a temporary adverse shock to the production function. What happens to the amount of inventory investment? Therefore, what do we predict for the behavior of inventory investment during recessions? Should we distinguish the response of finished goods from those of goods-in-process and materials?

   (Empirically, inventory investment by businesses during the postwar period averages only 0.7% of GNP. But inventory investment is highly volatile—in fact, during recessions, the change in inventories is often negative. Hence, Table 10.1 indicates that shortfalls in this component account, on average over the seven postwar recessions, for 32% of the shortfall in real GNP.)

10.9 The Investment Tax Credit

For most years since 1962, some types of investments qualify for a credit against income taxes. Assume that this governmental program effectively refunds the fraction, a, of investment expenditures. How does the size of the refund percentage, a, influence producers' desired stocks of capital and, hence, their investment demand? (Assume that someone who resells capital has to return the investment credit on the amount sold.)

---

[18]See Martin Feldstein and Alan Auerbach, "Inventory Behavior in Durable-Goods Manufacturing: the Target-Adjustment Model," *Brookings Papers on Economic Activity*, no. 2, 1976.

10.10 Capacity Utilization (optional)

One way for a producer to generate extra output is to use his or her capital more intensively. That is, a producer can run more shifts per day or allow less "down time" for performing maintenance. Assume that more intensive utilization causes capital to depreciate faster.

a. How does a producer determine the best intensity of use for his or her capital?

b. Show that an increase in the real interest rate, r_t, motivates producers to use their capital more intensively. What does this imply for the effect of the real interest rate on the supply of goods, y_t^s?

c. Aside from faster depreciation, what other costs arise from more intensive use of capital?

10.11 The Ownership of Capital (optional)

In our model, the people who use capital also own the capital. Suppose that these people print up certificates, each of which conveys ownership to one unit of capital. Then these certificates can be sold to others (on a "stock market"). But instead of using the capital themselves, the buyers of these certificates may allow other people ("businesses") to use the capital. Then the users pay a fee to holders of certificates. This fee may be either a fixed rental or a share of the profits.

a. Why might it be a good idea to separate the ownership of capital from the use of that capital? (Remember that people can already finance the purchase of capital by borrowing.) Why might it be a bad idea?

b. What determines the nominal and real value of the ownership certificates when each is a claim to 1 unit of capital?

c. In the real world why is the future real value of a certificate subject to great uncertainty? Specifically, why does the value depend on the fortunes of the company that issued it?

CHAPTER 11

INVESTMENT IN THE MARKET-CLEARING MODEL

In this chapter, we study the implications of investment for the short-run behavior of output, consumption, and the real interest rate. By the term, *short run,* we refer to a situation where changes in the stock of capital are small enough to neglect. Thus, the analysis applies especially to the role of investment during business fluctuations, which typically last for 1–2 years. Here, we focus on an empirical observation from the previous chapter. Namely, investment fluctuates by proportionately much more than consumption during recessions and booms.

We begin by incorporating investment into households' budget constraints and by relating investment to real saving. Then we modify the condition for clearing the commodity market to allow for investment demand. Finally, we use this market-clearing condition to study the interactions among investment, consumption, and total output.

Investment and Households' Budget Constraints

Remember that households carry out the investment expenditures in the model. Therefore, these expenditures are another use of households' funds. When we include investment into a household's budget constraint for period t, we get the condition

$$p_t y_t + b_{t-1}(1 + R) + m_{t-1} + v_t = p_t c_t + p_t i_t + b_t + m_t \qquad (11.1)$$

As before, the left side shows the total sources of funds, while the right side shows the total uses. Note that the new term is the expenditure for investment, $P_t i_t$, on the right side.

Before, we defined someone's real saving as the change in the real value of his or her bonds and money. But aside from these financial assets, people now have another store of value—namely, physical capital goods. Therefore, we now define someone's real saving as the change in the real value of his or her bonds, money, and capital. Accordingly, we have

$$\text{Real Saving} = (b_t + m_t)/P_t - (b_{t-1} + m_{t-1})P_{t-1} + k_t - k_{t-1} \quad (11.2)$$

Notice that the last term in equation (11.2) is the change in the household's stock of capital—that is, net investment. Hence, net investment is one component of the household's real saving.

As in our previous analysis, we can relate someone's real saving to his or her flows of income and consumption by using the budget constraint from equation (11.1). Using this equation and the definition of real saving from equation (11.2), we eventually get the result

$$\text{Real Saving} = y_t - \delta k_{t-1} + (R - \pi)(b_{t-1}/P_t) - \pi(m_{t-1}/P_t) + v_t/P_t - c_t \quad (11.3)$$

We can still interpret real saving as the difference between real income and consumption. But we have to define income carefully. Namely, it equals real *net* product, $y_t - \delta k_{t-1}$, plus the real interest income on bonds, $(R - \pi)(b_{t-1}/P_t)$, and money, $-\pi(m_{t-1}/P_t)$, plus the real value of transfers, v_t/P_t.

Notice that one way for somebody to finance more net investment, $k_t - k_{t-1}$, is to raise his or her real saving, as defined in equation (11.2). Then one way to raise this saving is to reduce consumption, c_t. But we see also from equation (11.2) that people can finance their investments by running down the real value of financial assets, bonds, and money. For example, people can borrow in order to pay for additional capital goods. Hence, an individual's decision to raise investment does not require a corresponding increase in that individual's real saving.

From the standpoint of an individual, there are substantially different forces that influence net investment and real saving. For example, net investment increases with an upward shift in the schedule for capital's marginal product, but falls with a rise in the real interest rate, r_t. On the other hand, desired real saving increases when income is temporarily high or when the real interest rate rises.

If people could not run down financial assets or borrow, then equation (11.2) would say that someone's net investment could be financed only by that person's real saving. Then individuals could exploit productive investment opportunities only if they were willing to abstain from current consumption or leisure. However, the potential for running down financial assets or borrowing means that people can undertake investments even if they are personally unwilling to save very much. In particular, the opportunities to borrow and lend ensure that all investment projects will be undertaken if the real rate of return to investment is at least as great as the real interest rate, r_t. Hence, the separation of individual decisions to invest from individual decisions to save promotes economic efficiency.[1]

How does aggregate real saving behave? Since the aggregate stock of bonds, B_t, is still zero in each period, we find from equation (11.2) that

$$\text{Aggregate Real Saving} = M_t/P_t - M_{t-1}/P_{t-1} + K_t - K_{t-1} \quad (11.4)$$

---

[1]Irving Fisher stresses this feature of a market economy in *The Theory of Interest*, op. cit., especially Chapters 7 and 11.

Let's ignore the part of aggregate real saving that consists of changes in aggregate real cash balances. Typically, that part is small relative to aggregate net investment. Then equation (11.4) says that aggregate real saving equals aggregate net investment, $K_t - K_{t-1}$. Recall that individuals can invest by running down bonds or borrowing. But then, others must be expanding their holdings of bonds—that is, lending. So, for society as a whole, the act of greater net investment does require the same addition to aggregate real saving.

Earlier, we did not allow for possibilities of investment. Then, if we neglected changes in aggregate real cash balances, we found that aggregate real saving must be zero. That's because, without investment, there is no way for the whole economy to save—that is, to change its real assets. But when the capital stock can vary, we find that aggregate real saving can be nonzero. In other words, the economy can now adjust aggregate net investment in order to shift resources from one period to another. These possibilities for shifting resources over time were present before for individuals who can borrow and lend on the credit market at the given real interest rate, r_t. Hence, the total economy now has opportunities for real saving that resemble those that are available to individuals on the credit market. We shall see that these opportunities have some important implications for the analysis of market-clearing conditions.

Clearing of the Commodity Market

There are still two aggregate-consistency conditions to satisfy—first, that the aggregate demand for commodities equal the supply, and second, that all money be willingly held. The existence of investment has major implications for the first condition, but not for the second. So we focus here on the condition for clearing the commodity market.

Clearing of the commodity market requires the aggregate supply of goods to equal the demand—that is

$$Y^s(r_t, \ldots) = C^d(r_t, \ldots) + I^d(r_t, \ldots) \qquad (11.5)$$
$$(+)(-)(-)$$

The left side of the equation shows the positive intertemporal-substitution effect from the real interest rate, r_t, on the aggregate supply of goods, Y_t^s. As before, this response reflects a positive effect on work effort, L_t. The omitted terms in the function, denoted by . . . , include various characteristics of the production function, as well as the quantity of capital from the previous period, K_{t-1}.

The right side of equation (11.5) contains the two components of aggregate demand, consumption and gross investment. As before, the real interest rate, r_t, has a negative intertemporal-substitution effect on consumer demand, C_t^d. As shown in the previous chapter, the real interest rate also has a negative effect on gross investment demand, I_t^d. Again, the omitted terms include the characteristics of the production function, as well as the quantity of capital, K_{t-1}. (Also, we assume a given value for the depreciation rate, δ.)

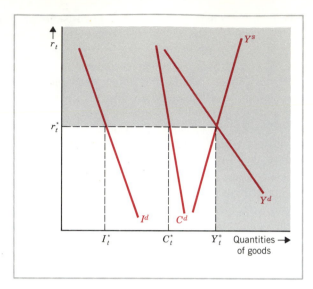

Figure 11.1 **Clearing of the Commodity Market**

The commodity market clears at the real interest rate, r_t^*. Here, the total output, Y_t^*, breaks down into C_t^* of consumption and I_t^* of gross investment.

In the next chapter it will be important to keep track of how the aggregate capital stock changes over time. Then we have to detail the role of the capital stock, K_{t-1}, in the market-clearing condition from equation (11.5). But for now, we carry out the analysis for a given value of this stock. That is, we carry out a short-run analysis in which changes in the stock of capital are small enough to neglect. It turns out that this setting is adequate to study the main role of investment during business fluctuations.

Figure 11.1 graphs the aggregates of commodities supplied and demanded versus the real interest rate, r_t. Notice that the supply curve, Y^s, slopes upward, while the demand curve, Y^d, slopes downward. Also, the figure breaks down aggregate demand into its two components, which are consumption demand, C^d, and gross investment demand, I^d. Each of these curves slopes downward versus the real interest rate.

Figure 11.1 shows that the commodity market clears at the real interest r_t^*. Correspondingly, we label the level of output as Y_t^*. At this point, the uses of output break down between consumption, C_t^*, and gross investment, I_t^*.

A Temporary Shift of the Production Function

Let's bring out some aspects of investment by examining an economic disturbance that we studied before. Consider a temporary downward shift of the production function—that is, a ''supply shock''—such as that caused by a harvest failure. In order to keep things simple, assume to begin with a parallel downward shift of the production function for period t. Then there are no changes in the schedules for the marginal products of labor, MPL_t, or capital, MPK_{t-1}. Also, we assume that there is no change in the schedule for the prospective marginal product of capital, MPK_t.

The decline in the production function lowers the aggregate supply of goods, Y_t^s, on the left side of equation (11.5). Also, there is a negative effect on wealth, which is small since the disturbance is temporary. Therefore, there is a small decline in consumer demand, C_t^d, and a small increase in work effort, L_t. Note that this increase in work offsets part of the initial decline in the supply of goods. Finally, since the schedule for capital's marginal product, MPK_t, does not change, there is no shift to gross investment demand, I_t^d.

Figure 11.2 shows the shifts to aggregate supply and demand. There is a leftward shift in supply and a smaller leftward shift in demand. In the figure the real interest rate labeled r_t^* is the one that clears the market in the absence of the shifts. Therefore, at this real interest rate, there is now an excess of goods demanded over those supplied—that is, $Y_t^d > Y_t^s$. This excess demand arises because people react to the temporary shortfall of production by lowering their desired saving. Thus, we can also say that the disturbance creates an excess of net investment demand over desired real saving.

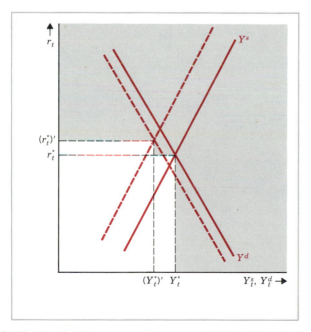

Figure 11.2 Effects of a Temporary Downward Shift of the Production Function
There is a leftward shift to aggregate supply, Y^s, which exceeds the leftward shift to demand, Y^d. Hence, the real interest rate rises, while aggregate output falls.

As in our previous analysis of this situation, the real interest rate must rise in order for the commodity market to clear. Therefore, in Figure 11.2, the new market-clearing real interest rate, $(r_t^*)'$, exceeds the initial value, r_t^*. We can think of this increase in the real interest rate as resulting from the excess of desired borrowing over desired lending. But in our earlier analysis, which did not consider investment, the real interest rate had to rise enough to make aggregate desired saving equal zero.[2] Now, the amount of aggregate real saving equals the quantity of aggregate net investment. Therefore, since the rise in the real interest rate reduces investment demand, we do not require as large an increase in the real interest rate as we did before.

Figure 11.2 shows that the new level of output, $(Y_t^*)'$, is below the initial amount, Y_t^*. Further, this drop in output reflects partly a decline in consumption, $(C_t^*)' < C_t^*$, and partly a decline in gross investment, $(I_t^*)' < I_t^*$. (Since depreciation is fixed at the amount, δK_{t-1}, the fall in net investment equals that in gross investment.) Note that the rise in the real interest rate reduces consumption and investment demand. In addition, the decrease in wealth reinforces the decline in consumer demand. Finally, the higher real interest rate and the reduction in wealth imply that the quantity of work effort, $(L_t^*)'$, exceeds the initial amount, L_t^*.

Consider the quantitative responses of consumption and work effort. Because the wealth effect is weak, these changes are large only if there is a substantial increase in the real interest rate. However, consider what happens if investment demand is highly responsive to movements in the real interest rate. (In the previous chapter we discussed why this is likely.) Then a small increase in the real interest rate is sufficient to equate desired real saving to net investment demand—that is, to clear the commodity market. In this case, most of the drop in output reflects a decline in investment. In particular, there are only small changes in consumption and work effort.[3]

The important conclusion is that fluctuations in investment partially insulate consumption and work from some types of temporary economic disturbances. Let's explain why this happens. When there is a temporary drop in supply—such as a harvest failure—everybody wants to maintain their levels of consumption and work by saving less at the initial real interest rate. But if there are no possibilities for investment, it is infeasible for everyone to save less. So, the real interest rate rises enough to make the total of desired saving equal zero. Then people end up making substantial adjustments in their consumption and work. Now, when we introduce investment, it becomes possible for aggregate saving to change. By lowering aggregate net investment, the economy does what each individual would like to do at a given real interest rate. In fact, if investment demand is strongly responsive to the real interest rate, as we anticipate, then the bulk of the variation in output

---

[2]Here, when referring to aggregate saving, we ignore any changes in aggregate real money balances.

[3]In the present case the rise in the real interest rate is only temporary. Therefore, the intertemporal-substitution effects on consumption and work are relatively weak. Hence, this element reinforces the result that consumption and work move by small amounts.

shows up as movements in investment. By contrast, consumption and work change relatively little.

Notice that the results imply that investment fluctuates by more than consumption, at least in response to some temporary economic disturbances. In particular, adverse shocks—such as a harvest failure—lead to declines in output and to accompanying decreases in investment as a fraction of gross national product (GNP). Conversely, favorable shocks lead to higher output and to increases in the ratio of investment to GNP. Therefore, the theoretical results accord in this respect with the observed behavior of investment. Recall that the discussion in the previous chapter highlighted these features of the United States data.

The Behavior of Employment

One feature of the results that conflicts with the United States data is the behavior of employment. Recessions are invariably accompanied by declines in employment. But the analysis so far suggests that a temporary adverse shock to the production function leads to a small increase in work.

Work effort rises in our example only because we omitted a likely adverse effect on labor's productivity. Specifically, as mentioned in some earlier cases, a downward shift in the schedule for labor's marginal product, MPL_t, usually accompanies a downward shift in the production function. This change motivates people to reduce work effort, L_t. In fact, because the cutback in productivity is temporary, there is an intertemporal-substitution effect, which motivates a strong reduction in work.

The decrease in work effort implies additional leftward shifts to commodity supply and demand of the sort shown in Figure 11.2. Hence, there is a larger decline in output, which reflects the reduction in work effort. Also, there is a larger increase in the real interest rate, which implies a sharper decline in investment. Overall, the main new result is the tendency for a reduction in work to accompany the decline in output. Thus, the results now conform with the behavior of employment during recessions.

A Permanent Shift of the Production Function

Previously, we contrasted permanent shifts of the production function with the type of temporary change that we just examined. Now, consider a permanent downward shift in the presence of investment. But assume again a parallel shift, which leaves unchanged the schedules for the various marginal products. In particular, since there is no change in capital's marginal product, MPK_t, there is again no shift to investment demand, I_t^d.

When the adverse shock is permanent, the wealth effects become important. Therefore, there is a strong negative effect on consumer demand, C_t^d, and a strong positive effect on work effort, L_t. Recall from our discussion of permanent income that this type of permanent change to the production function exerts little net effect

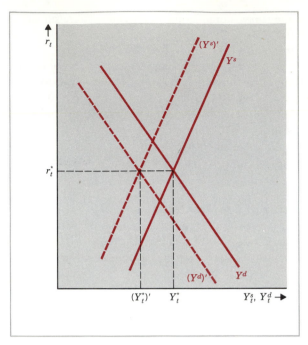

Figure 11.3 Effects of a Permanent Downward Shift of the Production Function (assuming no change in the schedule for capital's marginal product)
With a permanent downward shift of the production function, the leftward shifts of demand and supply are roughly equal. Therefore, output falls, but the real interest rate does not change.

on desired saving. Therefore, in Figure 11.3, we show the leftward shift in demand as equal to that in supply. Also, this result still obtains if we include a permanent downward shift to the schedule for labor's marginal product. But then, the curves in the figure shift leftward by greater amounts.

The main point is that the supply of goods still equals the demand at the initial real interest rate, r_t^*. (Equivalently, net investment demand still equals desired real saving.) Then, since the real interest rate does not change, there is no effect on investment. Hence, in this case, all of the decline in output reflects a fall in consumption.[4]

The main new result concerns the role of investment as a buffer for consumption. When there are temporary shocks to the production function, the sharp fluctuations in investment prevent large changes in consumption. But movements in investment cannot insulate consumption from permanent changes in production

---

[4]The change in work is ambiguous. The fall in wealth tends to increase work, but the decline in the schedule for labor's marginal product tends to reduce work.

possibilities. Hence, permanent shifts in the production function, which have substantial wealth effects, lead to large changes in consumption.

Shifts to the Productivity of Capital

The previous examples dealt with disturbances that left unchanged the schedule for capital's marginal product, MPK_t. Hence, in these cases, there are no shifts to investment demand. However, shifts in this component of demand can also be a source of shocks to the economy. In fact, Keynes stresses this element as a major reason for business fluctuations.[5]

Consider now a change to the production function that involves a downward shift in the schedule for capital's marginal product, MPK_t. Recall that this marginal product refers to the output for period $t + 1$. In order to keep things simple, assume that no changes occur to the production function for period t. Also, we abstract for the moment from any wealth effects (which are likely to be negative here).[6]

Recall that the condition for clearing the commodity market is

$$Y^s(r_t, \ldots) = C^d(r_t, \ldots) + I^d(r_t, \ldots)$$
$$(+) \qquad\qquad (-) \qquad\qquad (-)$$

Given our assumptions, the only initial effect from the disturbance is a decline in gross investment demand, I_t^d, on the right side of the equation. That is, there are no shifts to commodity supply, Y_t^s, or consumer demand, C_t^d. Therefore, Figure 11.4 shows only a leftward shift of the aggregate demand curve, Y^d, which reflects the reduction in investment demand.

Figure 11.4 shows that the real interest rate and output decrease. Note that the fall in output reflects the negative effect of the lower real interest rate on work effort. Also, the lower real interest rate means that consumption rises. Therefore, investment falls by more than the decrease in total output.

Let's go back to the temporary adverse shock that we considered earlier. Usually, this type of disturbance is accompanied by a worsening of investment opportunities—that is, by a decline in capital's marginal product, MPK_t. So, we should combine the effects from Figure 11.4 with those that we found before in Figure 11.2. When we do this, we reinforce the downward effects on output and investment. However, the downward shift in investment demand tends to lower the real interest rate, which offsets the tendency for consumption to decline. In fact, the overall movement in consumption is now ambiguous.

---

[5]John Maynard Keynes, *The General Theory of Employment, Interest and Money*, Harcourt, New York, 1936, Chapters 11 and 12.

[6]The analysis also neglects changes in labor's prospective marginal product, which affect current choices of work and consumption. In addition, we ignore any differences between the current real interest rate, r_t, and future real interest rates.

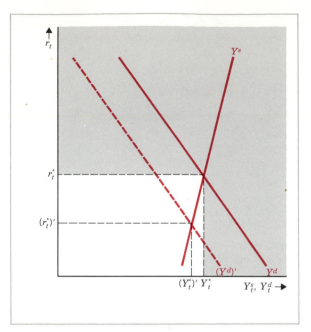

Figure 11.4 Effects of a Decrease in the Marginal Product of Capital
The decrease in the schedule for capital's marginal product reduces investment demand.
Therefore, the real interest rate and the level of output decline.

An important new result concerns the short-run behavior of the real interest
rate, r_t. In Figure 11.2 we found that temporary adverse shocks to the production
function lead to a higher real interest rate. That's because everyone wants to save
less in order to maintain their levels of consumption. But an opposing force arises
if the shock also lowers the marginal product of capital. Then, as shown in Figure
11.4, the downward shift in investment demand tends to reduce the real interest
rate. Thus, the overall effect on the real interest rate is uncertain. The net change
depends on whether the decrease in aggregate desired saving is larger or smaller
than the fall in net investment demand.

Empirically, real interest rates do not have a clear pattern of association with
recessions and booms. Therefore, we should not feel bad that our theory fails to
generate an unambiguous prediction for this pattern.

Summary

We began by incorporating investment as an item of expenditure in households'
budget constraints. Although net investment is one part of an individual's real
saving, the existence of the credit market means that an individual's decision to
invest does not require that individual to save. However, in the aggregate, real

saving equals net investment plus the change in real cash balances. Therefore, ignoring the last term, the existence of investment means that the whole economy can now change its amount of real saving. This possibility has important implications for the characteristics of short-term business fluctuations.

Aggregate gross investment demand enters as a component of aggregate demand in the condition for clearing the commodity market. Because this component tends to be highly sensitive to variations in the real interest rate, we find that investment absorbs the bulk of short-term fluctuations in output. Specifically, a temporary adverse shock to the production function leads to a major proportionate reduction in investment, but to a relatively small decline in consumption. However, the effect on the real interest rate is uncertain—it depends on whether the decline in desired real saving is larger or smaller than the decrease in net investment demand. Finally, changes in investment cannot buffer consumption against permanent shifts to the production function. Here, an adverse shock leads to a strong downward response of consumption.

QUESTIONS AND PROBLEMS

Mainly for Review

11.1 Does higher investment require higher saving on the part of an individual household? For the economy as a whole, how do changes in the interest rate ensure that real saving rises to match an increase in investment?

11.2 How is the demand curve for commodities altered when there is positive gross investment? In particular, why is it flatter than the demand curves in Chapter 6? List the factors that can shift the total demand for consumption and investment.

11.3 Show graphically how the division of total output into consumption and investment is achieved through commodity market equilibrium. How does a temporary shift in the production function alter this division? Does your answer depend on the relative sensitivity of consumption and investment to changes in the interest rate?

11.4 "An increase in the interest rate must be accompanied by a decline in consumption." Is this statement correct when the rise in r is the result of:
  a. A temporary worsening of the production function, with no change in the productivity of capital?
  b. A permanent improvement in the production function, with an increase in the productivity of capital?

11.5 Why does a decline in the productivity of capital reduce the interest rate? Could the interest rate fall so much as to leave the quantity of investment unchanged? Explain.

11.6 When there is a temporary decline in production, could consumption stay the same or increase? If so, what must happen to the interest rate? Could investment stay the same or increase?

Problems for Discussion

11.7 Temporary Shocks to the Production Function and Consumption

Because of the strong response of investment, we found that temporary shocks to the production function have little effect on consumption. Suppose that we look at larger and larger—but still temporary—shocks. How does consumption react as the shocks get bigger? In particular, what happens to the division of the shortfall in output between consumption and investment? How does the answer relate to the Great Depression?

11.8 Investment Opportunities for Robinson Crusoe

In the market economy we find that investment takes the brunt of temporary shocks to the production function. Suppose that we introduce opportunities for investment into the model of Robinson Crusoe, which we constructed in Chapter 2. How would Robinson Crusoe's investment and consumption respond to temporary and permanent shifts to the production function? Are the results basically similar to those for the market economy?

11.9 Saving, Investment, and the Real Interest Rate (optional)

Suppose that shocks to the production function are sometimes favorable and sometimes unfavorable. Also, the shocks are sometimes temporary and sometimes permanent.

a. What pattern of association results between the real interest rate and the aggregate quantities of net investment and real saving?

b. Suppose that we try to deduce the effect of the real interest on an individual's desired real saving by examining the relation between the real interest rate and aggregate real saving. What do we find? What is the source of the problem?

c. Suppose that we try to estimate the effect of the real interest rate on investment demand from the relation between the real interest rate and aggregate net investment. What do we find? What is the source of the problem?

d. Suppose that we look at the relation of the real interest rate, r_t, to the ratio of aggregate consumptions, C_{t+1}/C_t. What will this tell us about an individual's saving behavior?

11.10 Short-Run Movements in the Real Wage Rate

Suppose that we include a separate labor market in the model. Recall that the real wage rate, w_t/P_t, then equals the marginal product of labor, MPL_t.

a. Consider a temporary adverse shock to the production function. Suppose that there is no change in the schedule for labor's marginal product, MPL_t. What happens to the real wage rate? What is the pattern of association between changes in the real wage rate and changes in the quantities of employment and output?

b. Assume, more realistically, that the schedule for labor's marginal product shifts downward. In particular, assume that this shift is large enough so that work effort declines. What happens now to the real wage rate? What is the pattern of association between changes in the real wage rate and changes in the quantities of employment and output?

c. Suppose that business fluctuations result from temporary shifts to the production function. Then what do you predict for the cyclical behavior of real wage rates?

That is, do they move together with or inversely to output and employment? (There is much empirical debate about the cyclical behavior of real wage rates. However, most researchers find a weak procyclical pattern. That is, real wage rates tend to fall somewhat relative to trend during recessions, and vice versa for booms.)

11.11 Effects of Supply Shocks on the Price Level

Consider a temporary downward shift of the production function. Assume that there are also downward shifts in the schedules for the marginal products of labor and capital.

What happens to the general price level, P? In answering, make clear how the results depend on the form of the function for money demand. Specifically, should we use real output, Y_t, as the relevant measure of real transactions, or should we worry about the division of this output between consumption, C_t, and investment, I_t?

11.12 An Energy Crisis (optional)

Assume that each household's production function includes the quantity of energy, z_t, as an input. The new function is

$$y_t = f(k_{t-1}, \quad l_t, \quad z_t)$$
$$(+) \qquad (+) \, (+)$$

Energy has positive and diminishing marginal product. Also, an increase in the quantity of energy input raises the schedules for the marginal products of capital, MPK_{t-1}, and labor, MPL_t. Finally, we assume diminishing returns to scale with respect to changes in the three inputs—capital, labor, and energy.

Suppose that domestic suppliers generate the given aggregate quantity of energy, Z (ignore any imports or exports of energy). The ownership of these supplies of energy is distributed among the households in our model.

a. Assume that P_t^z is the price of a unit of energy at date t. How does the relative price of energy—that is, the ratio, P_t^z/P_t—affect a producer's demand for energy? How does it affect the desired stock of capital, $\tilde{k}_{t-1}$, and the quantity of work, l_t?

b. Suppose that the aggregate quantity of energy declines from Z to Z'. People expect this quantity to return to the earlier level, Z, after a few periods.

  i. What happens to the relative price of energy?

  ii. What happens to the real interest rate, and the aggregates of output, investment, consumption, and employment? (*Note:* did you include a wealth effect?)

  iii. What happens to the general price level? (Assume that the monetary authority does not change the current or prospective quantity of money.)

c. Assume now that all of the energy is owned by one greedy person whom nobody likes (it could just as well be a nasty foreign country). What difference does this make for the analysis? In particular, how does the disturbance change the distribution of income between the greedy person and everyone else?

d. Do you like the assumption that the aggregate supply of energy is a given number, Z or Z'? What would you change here?

CHAPTER 12

THE ACCUMULATION OF CAPITAL AND ECONOMIC GROWTH

So far, we have studied investment in a short-run context, where changes in the stock of capital are small enough to neglect. In this context we focused on the role of investment as a component of the aggregate demand for goods. We now want to allow for the effects of changing capital stocks on productive capacity—that is, on the aggregate supply of goods. Thereby, we bring in one of the central elements of economic growth. Hence, we are able to consider factors that influence a country's development over the long term.

Let's be clear about some important elements that we hold constant initially while we study the process of capital accumulation. One of these is population, which is a major determinant of the aggregate labor force. Another is the accumulation of human capital—that is, education and training—which alters the quality of the labor force. But for most purposes, the economic forces that influence the accumulation of human capital are similar to those that affect physical capital. That is, in our theory, we can take a broad view of capital to include education and training, as well as buildings and machines. (However, although economists have made some estimates, it is difficult to measure human capital empirically.)

Finally, we omit **technological change,** which we might model as shifts in the form of the production function. We can think here of research and experience, which lead over time to better knowledge about methods of production and types of goods. For some purposes, we can think of this knowledge as another form of capital, which producers can accumulate through certain types of expenditures. But there are some important differences: In particular, knowledge about how to produce things does not tend to diminish as producers spread it over a larger scale of operations. Therefore—at least until people start running out of new ideas—there may be increasing returns to scale when we consider technological advance.

Effects of the Capital Stock on Production, Work Effort, and Consumption

Until now, we treated the aggregate stock of capital, K_{t-1}, as a constant. But since this stock will change over time, we have to investigate how these changes affect the quantities of goods supplied and demanded.

Remember that someone's production for period t depends on his or her previous stock of capital, k_{t-1}, through the production function

$$y_t = f(k_{t-1}, l_t)$$

In particular, we assume that people's investment decisions during period t have no impact on productive capacity until the following period. Therefore, from the viewpoint of a producer during period t, a greater amount of capital, k_{t-1}, looks just like an upward shift in the production function. In particular, given the amount of work effort, l_t, an increase in capital, k_{t-1}, means a larger supply of goods, y_t^s.

Second, people are better off at date t if they own a greater amount of capital, k_{t-1}. Of course, in order to acquire this capital, they had to make investments in the past. Then these investments had to be financed, either by borrowing or by running down financial assets or by undertaking more saving. Thus, in deciding how much to invest, people weighed the benefits from having extra capital against the costs of acquiring it.

From the standpoint of society as a whole, the amounts borrowed and lent cancel. Therefore, the total stock of capital, K_{t-1}, must reflect previous acts of saving—that is, abstinence from either consumption or leisure. However, once period t arrives, these costs associated with acquiring the aggregate stock of capital are bygones. Hence, in making decisions, people count the capital as wealth, but make no subtraction in the aggregate for the past hardships that underlie the acquisition of the capital. (An individual subtracts his or her current debts that were incurred to finance investment. But in the aggregate, the stock of debt is always zero.) Hence, from the perspective of period t, if the capital stock K_{t-1} is higher by 1 unit, then aggregate wealth rises just as it would if people received 1 unit of goods as a gift from the sky. Therefore, a larger stock of capital, K_{t-1}, means more aggregate consumer demand, C_t^d.

Finally, there are two effects from more capital, K_{t-1}, on aggregate work effort, L_t. First, the wealth effect motivates less work. But second, the increase in capital raises the schedule for labor's marginal product. Since this change raises work effort, the overall response is ambiguous.

Capital in the Market-Clearing Condition

Putting together the results from above, the condition for clearing the commodity market at date t is now

$$Y^s(r_t, K_{t-1}, \ldots) = C^d(r_t, K_{t-1}, \ldots) + I^d(r_t, K_{t-1}, \ldots) \qquad (12.1)$$
$$(+)\ (+) (-)\ (+) (-)\ (-)$$

Notice the complex role of the capital stock, K_{t-1}, in this equation. First, an increase in this stock raises productive capacity, which underlies the positive effect on goods supplied, Y_t^s. Then, because of the wealth effect, the higher stock of capital raises consumer demand, C_t^d. However, given producers' desired stocks of capital for period t, an increase in the previous stock, K_{t-1}, reduces gross investment demand, I_t^d. Finally, there is also an ambiguous effect of the capital stock on work effort. This effect modifies the overall impact of the capital stock on the supply of goods, Y_t^s, and consumer demand, C_t^d.

The process of capital accumulation works as follows. At any date t there is a given stock of capital, K_{t-1}, from the previous period. Then, as in the analysis from the previous chapter, we determine the real interest rate, r_t, and the quantities of output, Y_t, and investment, I_t, from the market-clearing condition in equation (12.1). Thereby, we determine the stock of capital for the next period from the equation

$$K_t = K_{t-1} + I_t - \delta K_{t-1} \tag{12.2}$$

That is, we add net investment, $I_t - \delta K_{t-1}$, to the previous stock of capital, K_{t-1}, in order to determine the next period's stock, K_t.

Once we know the capital stock, K_t, we can again use the market-clearing condition to determine the next period's real interest rate, r_{t+1}, and the quantities of output, Y_{t+1}, and investment, I_{t+1}. Thus, we determine a sequence of capital stocks, outputs, and so on. That is, we can use the model to chart out a time path of economic development. (But remember that we do not allow yet for changes in population or technology.)

For subsequent purposes, we shall find it convenient to subtract depreciation, δK_{t-1}, from both sides of equation (12.1). Then the market-clearing condition becomes

$$Y^s(r_t,\ K_{t-1},\ \ldots) - \delta K_{t-1} = C^d(r_t,\ K_{t-1},\ \ldots) + I^d(r_t,\ K_{t-1},\ \ldots) - \delta K_{t-1} \tag{12.3}$$
$$\;\;(+)\,(+) \qquad\qquad\qquad (-)\,(+) \qquad\qquad (-)\,(-)$$

Note that the left side is the supply of net product, $Y_t^s - \delta K_{t-1}$, while the right side includes net investment demand, $I_t^d - \delta K_{t-1}$, along with consumption demand, C_t^d.

An Increase in the Capital Stock over One Period

Suppose that at some initial date, $t = 1$, the economy has the aggregate capital stock, K_0. Then, using equation (12.3), the market-clearing condition is

$$Y^s(r_1,\ K_0,\ \ldots) - \delta K_0 = C^d(r_1,\ K_0,\ \ldots) + I^d(r_1,\ K_0,\ \ldots) - \delta K_0 \tag{12.4}$$
$$\;\;(+)\,(+) \qquad\qquad\qquad (-)\,(+) \qquad\qquad (-)\,(-)$$

In Figure 12.1 the upward-sloping solid line shows the supply of net product, $Y_1^s - \delta K_0$, while the downward-sloping solid line shows the demand, $Y_1^d - \delta K_0$. Hence, the market-clearing real interest rate is the value r_1^*, while the corresponding

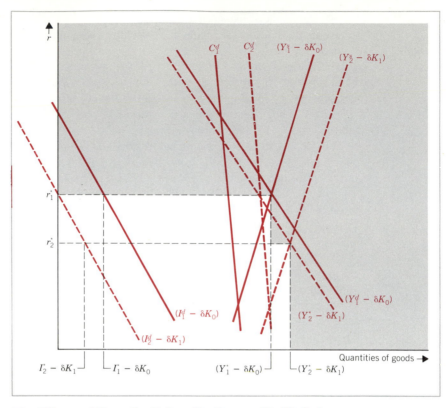

Figure 12.1 **The Effects of More Capital on the Commodity Market**
We show the effects of an increase in capital from K_0 to K_1. The rightward shifts in the supply of net product and in consumer demand are roughly equal. Therefore, since net investment demand declines, the real interest rate falls from r_1^* to r_2^*. The change in net product (shown as positive) is generally ambiguous.

quantity of net product is the amount, $Y_1^* - \delta K_0$. Note that the figure shows also the two components of demand, which are consumption, C_1^d, and net investment, $I_1^d - \delta K_0$. Hence, we can use the figure to determine the quantities of consumption, C_1^*, and net investment, $I_1^* - \delta K_0$.

Assume that aggregate net investment, $I_1^* - \delta K_0$, is positive, as shown in Figure 12.1. Then the next period's stock of capital, K_1, exceeds the initial amount, K_0. Now we have to solve the following problem. How does the increase in the quantity of capital from K_0 to K_1 change the market-clearing condition? In particular, how does the next period's real interest rate, r_2^*, compare with the initial one, r_1^*? Note that in solving this problem we assume that the aggregate capital stock is the only thing that changes between periods 1 and 2.

Using equation (12.3), the market-clearing condition for period 2 is

$$\underset{(+)\,(+)}{Y^s(r_2,\ K_1,\ .\ .\ .)} - \delta K_1 = \underset{(-)\,(+)}{C^d(r_2,\ K_1,\ .\ .\ .)} + \underset{(-)\,(-)}{I^d(r_2,\ K_1,\ .\ .\ .)} - \delta K_1 \qquad (12.5)$$

Consider how the increase in capital from K_0 to K_1 changes the various terms. First, for a given amount of work, an increase in the capital stock makes the supply of net product, $Y_2^s - \delta K_1$, higher than before. In fact, an extra unit of capital raises this net supply by the amount, $MPK_1 - \delta$, which is the real rate of return to investment. (Recall that investors equate this return to the previous period's real interest rate, r_1^*.)

Next, the increase in capital makes consumer demand, C_2^d, higher than before. In order to assess the magnitude of this response, we can use the concept of permanent income. Specifically, if we neglect variations over time in capital's marginal product, then an extra unit of capital provides a constant flow of real income in the amount, $MPK_1 - \delta$. Hence, permanent income increases by this amount. But then if work does not change, consumer demand also rises by approximately the amount, $MPK_1 - \delta$. In other words, the increase in consumption demand roughly equals the increase in the supply of net product. Therefore, the increase in the stock of capital does not lead to a significant change in desired real saving.[1]

So far, we find that the increase in the supply of net product on the left side of equation (12.5) approximately equals the increase in demand on the right side. But the increase in capital from K_0 to K_1 also reduces net investment demand on the right side. Hence, it is uncertain whether the aggregate demand for net product rises or falls. But in any event, we conclude that more capital raises the supply of net product by more than the demand.

The dashed lines in Figure 12.1 show these results for period 2. Note that the rightward shifts to net supply, $Y_2^s - \delta K_1$, and consumer demand, C_2^d, are the same. Then net investment demand, $I_2^d - \delta K_1$, shifts leftward. Notice that this demand is zero at the previous real interest rate, r_1^*. That is, if the real interest rate did not change, producers would have no incentive to alter their capital stocks during period 2. Finally, although the direction of this change is ambiguous, the figure shows a leftward shift in the aggregate demand for net product, $Y_2^d - \delta K_1$.

At the initial real interest rate, r_1^*, the supply of net product during period 2 is greater than the demand. (Equivalently, desired real saving exceeds net investment demand.) Therefore, the real interest rate falls to the value r_2^*. Hence, an increase in the stock of capital leads to a lower real interest rate.

Now, consider what happens to the various quantities. First, consumption must increase, $C_2^* > C_1^*$. That's because the direct effect from more capital and the decline in the real interest rate combine to raise consumer demand. However, the change in work is ambiguous. Here, the decline in the real interest rate and the

---

[1]The change in the amount of work effort is ambiguous. But whatever this change, there will still be little effect on desired real saving.

wealth effect from more capital motivate less work. But the positive effect of the extra capital on labor's marginal product motivates more work.

Unless work effort falls by a great deal, the increase in capital input means that gross and net product expand. In Figure 12.1 we show that the second period's net product, $Y_2^* - \delta K_1$, exceeds the first, $Y_1^* - \delta K_0$.

Figure 12.1 shows graphically that net investment declines—that is, $I_2^* - \delta K_1 < I_1^* - \delta K_0$. We know this must be the case, since otherwise the increase in net product would exceed the rise in consumption. But this outcome is impossible if the rightward shifts to the supply of net product and consumer demand are equal, as assumed in the figure. Thus, an increase in the stock of capital leads to less net investment. Moreover, it follows that net investment declines as a ratio to the previous stock of capital—that is, the growth rate of the capital stock falls. Also, there is a reduction in the ratio of net investment to net or gross product.

Finally, since depreciation rises along with the increase in the amount of capital, we cannot say whether gross investment rises or falls. But recall that gross investment equals net investment plus depreciation. Observe that the first part, net investment, declines relative to the previous stock of capital. Then the second part, depreciation, maintains a constant ratio to this stock. Therefore, gross investment declines overall relative to the previous stock of capital.

Increases in the Capital Stock over Many Periods

As long as net investment is positive, the process described above continues over time. The increase in the capital stock is accompanied by a declining real interest rate, rising consumption, and falling net investment. Also, there are probable increases in net and gross product, but ambiguous changes in work effort.

Recall that the growth rate of capital declines over time. Remember also that the change in the capital stock generates the changes in the other variables. Therefore, the responses of the other quantities—in particular, consumption and total output—tend to become proportionately smaller over time. That is, there are declining growth rates of consumption and of gross and net product.

Let's think about why the real interest rate declines over time. At the start, date 1, the economy has a relatively low capital stock, K_0, and a correspondingly high marginal product of capital, MPK_1. Then the high real interest rate, r_1^*, signals the cost of using up resources during period 1, rather than later. Specifically, this high cost reflects the favorable investment climate. Thus, consuming at date 1, rather than later, is justified only if people are willing to forego returns at the rate r_1^*, which equals the real rate of return to investment, $MPK_1 - \delta$.

Recall our previous analysis of the consumption rate of time preference, which we called λ. People choose their consumptions at dates 1 and 2, c_1 and c_2, so that the consumption rate of time preference, λ_1, between these periods equals the real interest rate, r_1^*. That is, people are just willing to exchange 1 unit of consumption at date 1 for $(1 + \lambda_1) = (1 + r_1^*)$ units at date 2. Since the real interest rate, r_1^*, is high, we know that period 1's consumption, c_1, is low relative to period 2's,

c_2. In other words, consumption grows rapidly at this stage of economic development.

As the economy matures, the capital stock rises and the marginal product of capital declines. Because of these diminishing opportunities for investment, there is a declining real interest rate, r_t^*, which signals a decreasing return from deferring consumption. Therefore, we find also a falling consumption rate of time preference, λ_t, and a declining growth rate of consumption.

The Steady-State Capital Stock and Real Interest Rate

How long does the process of capital accumulation go on? (Recall again that, so far, we ask this question when population and technology are fixed.) As long as capital grows, there must be positive real saving and growth in consumption.[2] But each household chooses a rising time path of consumption—that is, $c_{t+1} > c_t$— only if the real interest rate, r_t^*, exceeds the utility rate of time preference, ρ. (Remember that ρ is the discount rate attached to future utility. Also, the consumption rate of time preference, λ_t, exceeds ρ if consumption grows over time— that is, if $c_{t+1} > c_t$.) Eventually, the real rate of return to investment, $MPK_t - \delta$, and the real interest rate, r_t^*, fall enough to equal the utility rate of time preference. Then households do zero saving and maintain a constant level of consumption. At this point net investment is zero.[3]

Figure 12.2 shows the time path for the market-clearing value of the real interest rate, r_t^*. Remember that producers choose investment in order to equate the return, $MPK_t - \delta$, to the real interest rate in each period. Also, households choose a time path for consumption so that the consumption rate of time preference, λ_t, equals the real interest rate in each period. Therefore, the vertical axis in Figure 12.2 shows the three equal magnitudes, r_t^*, $MPK_t - \delta$, and λ_t.

The real interest rate exceeds the utility rate of time preference, ρ, at date 1. Thereafter, the real interest rate declines and gradually approaches the utility rate of time preference. Along the path, where $r_t^* > \rho$, net investment and real saving are positive. But net investment and real saving decline over time, as the capital stock expands and the real interest rate falls toward the utility rate of time preference.

In the long run the real interest rate approaches the utility rate of time preference, ρ. Since net investment and real saving tend to zero, it follows that the capital stock approaches some constant. Correspondingly, there are constant levels of output, consumption, gross investment (which equals depreciation), and work effort. Economists refer to this situation as a **steady state.** By a steady state, we mean a position where a set of variables stays constant over time. In particular, the growth rates of capital, output, and consumption are all zero in the steady state.

---

[2]Throughout this discussion we neglect any changes in real cash balances as a component of real saving.

[3]This discussion draws on the classic treatment of the dynamics of saving and investment from Frank Ramsey, ''A Mathematical Theory of Saving,'' *Economic Journal,* December 1928.

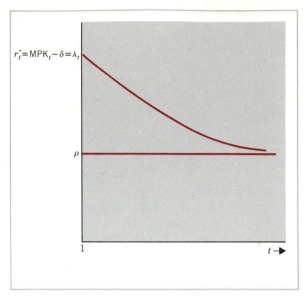

Figure 12.2 The Behavior of the Real Interest Rate Over Time
The market-clearing value of the real interest rate, r_t^*, equals the return to investment, $MPK_t - \delta$, which equals the consumption rate of time preference, λ_t. As the capital stock grows over time, the real interest rate declines and approaches the utility rate of time preference, ρ.

(When we introduce growth of population and technology in the next section, we shall find that the steady-state growth rate is positive.)

What determines the steady-state level of the capital stock? The basic condition is the equality between the real rate of return to investment and the steady-state real interest rate, which equals the utility rate of time preference, ρ. Thus, the steady-state condition is

$$MPK - \delta = \rho \qquad (12.3)$$

We do not date the marginal product, MPK, since it remains constant in a steady state.

The steady-state level of capital is the one that equates the marginal product of capital, MPK, to the quantity, $\rho + \delta$. If we knew the steady-state level of labor input, then we could show the schedule for capital's marginal product as the usual downward-sloping function of the quantity of capital. Then it would be straightforward to pick out the level of capital that satisfies the steady-state condition, $MPK = \rho + \delta$. But there is a minor complication because the level of work generally depends on the quantity of capital. For a full analysis, we have to bring in the response of work to variations in the capital stock. However, our previous analysis shows that the sign of this relation is ambiguous—that is, we do not know whether more capital leads to more or less work.

Let's sketch an example to illustrate the workings of the steady-state results. Suppose that at date 1 the economy is in a steady-state position where capital's marginal product, MPK_1, equals the value, $\rho + \delta$. Then, call this steady-state level of capital K_0. Note that during period 1 the real interest rate is the value, $r_1^* = MPK_1 - \delta = \rho$. Further, the initial quantities of net investment and real saving are zero.

Now assume that there is a permanent improvement in the production technology during period 2. Hence, producers get more output for given inputs. Also, there are permanent upward shifts in the schedules for the marginal products of labor and capital. Recall that we carried out a short-run analysis of this type of disturbance in the previous chapter (although we looked there at a worsening of the production function). Briefly, we get the following effects. Because the change is permanent, there are roughly equal increases in the supply of net product and in consumer demand. That is, desired real saving remains close to zero. However, because of the rise in capital's marginal product, net investment demand becomes positive. Therefore, at the initial real interest rate, $r_1^* = \rho$, there is an excess of commodity demand over supply. Equivalently, net investment demand exceeds desired real saving. Figure 12.3 shows these effects.

During period 2, the real interest rate, r_2^*, rises above its initial value, $r_1^* = \rho$. Now the economy is in the sort of position where we began our previous analysis of capital accumulation. Net investment is positive and the real interest rate exceeds its steady-state value, ρ. Hence, the stock of capital rises over time, while the real-interest rate falls. Eventually, the economy approaches a new steady state, where the stock of capital exceeds the amount, K_0, from the previous steady state. Then the real interest rate returns to the steady-state value, ρ.

To summarize, the permanent improvement in the production function raises net investment and the real interest rate in the short run. But in the long run, the economy ends up with more capital—as well as more output and consumption—and no change in the real interest rate.

Changes in Population

A One-Time Increase in Population

Suppose that at date 1 the economy is again in a steady state with the aggregate quantity of capital K_0. Assume that during period 2 the population increases once and for all by, say, 10%. Let's think of a case where the number of households rises as well by 10%. Then assume that the new households are just like the old ones in terms of average age, tastes, and productivity. Remember that the households are the producing units in the model, so the number of producers also rises by 10%. But the new households might begin life with zero capital. Alternatively, the old households (parents) may provide the new ones (children) with a starting amount of capital. However, the main analysis goes through in either case.

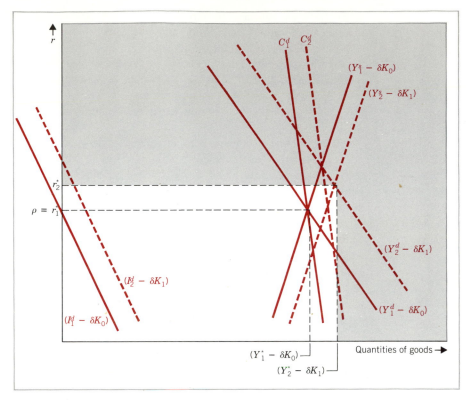

Figure 12.3 Effects of a One-Time Improvement of the Production Function
(beginning from a steady state)
The permanent improvement of the production function during period 2 causes the demand for goods to exceed the supply at the initial real interest rate, $r_1^* = \rho$. Therefore, the real interest rate increases to r_2^*.

If the aggregate stock of capital does not change, then the typical producer has less capital to work with than before. Therefore, the marginal product of capital exceeds its steady-state value, $\rho + \delta$. Hence, in the aggregate, the desired stock of capital increases, which makes aggregate net investment demand positive. There are also increases in the aggregates of work effort, goods supply, and consumer demand. In fact, we can again use Figure 12.3 to show the various responses. In particular, the demand for goods exceeds the supply at the initial real interest rate, r_1^*. Therefore, the real interest rate increases—that is, $r_2^* > r_1^* = \rho$.

The one-time increase in population puts the economy in the familiar position where the real interest rate exceeds its steady-state value, ρ. We can understand this by noting that the rise in population effectively places the typical producer back in an earlier stage of economic development, where he or she has less capital to work with. Then the real interest rate exceeds its steady-state value in this situation.

Following the increase in the real interest rate for period 2, we can trace out the usual time path where the aggregate capital stock increases, while the real interest rate declines toward its steady-state value, ρ. But what can we say about the various quantities in this new steady state? In particular, do the aggregates of capital, output, consumption, and work all rise by 10%—that is, by the same proportion as population?

The aggregate quantities would all be higher by 10% if production exhibited constant returns to scale. Then a 10% increase in the aggregates of capital and labor would produce 10% more goods. Also, the marginal product of capital would be the same as initially—namely, equal to its steady-state value, $\rho + \delta$.

Since the number of people and the number of producing units increase by 10%, why would we expect something other than constant returns? There is some tendency for diminishing returns because there is no change in the aggregate of "land," by which we mean to include various types of natural resources and physical space. Probably, there is a range of production over which constant returns is a reasonable approximation. That is, returns to scale are nearly constant until the fixed quantity of land becomes a major constraint. Then, over the range where nearly constant returns applies, we find that an expansion of population by 10% does lead in the long run to nearly 10% increases in the aggregates of capital, output, consumption, and work effort.

Population Growth

We would like now to study continuing growth in population. However, the details of this subject bring in some complications that would take the discussion far afield. So let's just sketch some results, which are only suggestive.

Continue to assume that returns to scale are roughly constant. But assume now that population grows at a steady rate, rather than jumping all at once. For example, growth rates of population between 0–2% per year are typical for industrialized countries in the post-World War II period. For the United States, the rate was around 3% per year in the early 19th century, but is only 1.0% between 1960 and 1980.[4]

The growth in population has a continuing upward effect on the aggregates of capital, output, consumption and work effort. Specifically, the economy no longer approaches a steady state where these aggregates are constant. Instead, we have a situation that economists call **steady-state growth.** Here, the aggregate quantities of capital, output, consumption, and work effort all grow at the same rate as population. Although the levels of these variables change over time, certain ratios are constant in a position of steady-state growth. These include the per capita

---

[4]Immigration accounts for roughly one-third of the growth in population from the mid-19th century until the 1920s. Then immigration is relatively small from the 1930s through the 1960s. But the numbers rise in recent years. In 1981 the reported figures on immigration account again for nearly 30% of the increase in population. Moreover, if all illegal immigrants were included, this fraction would be much higher.

amounts of capital, output, and consumption. Hence, the per capita growth rates of capital, output, and consumption are all zero in a position of steady-state growth.

Unlike our previous steady states, a position of steady-state growth has positive aggregate net investment and real saving. The net investment provides capital for the new members of society. Thereby, the quantity of capital per person and per worker can remain constant over-time. We can think of parents as carrying out the saving in order to provide for their children—in effect, to establish their children in a business (or to provide them with education). Notice that, with a positive growth rate of population, it is not enough for people just to pass on capital to their descendants. There is more than one child per adult, on average. Therefore, the typical adult must carry out positive real saving over his or her lifetime.

What is the real interest rate in a position of steady-state growth? Since consumption per person is constant, our previous results suggest that the real interest rate still equals the utility rate of time preference, ρ. But remember that the typical parent carries out positive real saving here. The saving goes not to raise consumption per person, but rather to provide for the growing population. In order for this all to make sense, it must be that parents care about their children. That is, they care to the extent of discounting their children's utility by the utility rate of time preference, ρ.

Finally, we should mention that the discussion treats the time path of population as a given. However, we should also be able to apply economic reasoning to determine population. Some classical economists, such as Malthus, Ricardo, and Marx, regarded this topic as a central element of economic analysis (although their theories did not stand up empirically). Recently, some economists are again using economic analysis to study population growth.[5] So far, the empirical results are encouraging, but cannot fully explain the behavior of population growth over time.

Technological Change

Figure 12.3 considers the effect of a permanent improvement in the production function. This change leads in the long run to increases in the per capita quantities of capital, output and consumption. Typically, the process of economic development involves a continuing series of these improvements through a process called technological progress. As in the case of population growth, we shall only sketch some effects from steadily improving technology.

Continuing technological improvements lead to persistent increases in the per capita quantities of capital, output, and consumption. In some cases, the economy approaches a position of **steady-state per capita growth,** where the amounts per

---

[5]See, for example, Gary Becker, ''The Demand for Children,'' in *A Treatise on the Family,* Harvard University Press, Cambridge, Massachusetts, 1981; and Richard Easterlin, *Population, Labor Force, and Long Swings in Economic Growth,* Columbia University Press, New York, 1968.

person of capital, output and consumption all grow at a constant rate. That is, the economy no longer tends toward per capita growth rates of zero.

What about the real interest rate in a position of steady-state per capita growth? Unlike our previous cases, there is now long-run growth in consumption per person. Therefore, people's consumption rates of time preference, λ, exceed their utility rate of time preference, ρ. Accordingly, the real interest rate also exceeds the value ρ in a position of steady-state per capita growth.

Finally, as with population growth, our discussion does not use economic analysis to explain the changes in technology. In particular, we would like to explore producers' incentives to carry out the research and development that leads to new products and better methods of production. One interesting issue here concerns the property rights that people have in their inventions, production techniques, and so on. We should also consider the eventual limitations on new ideas— that is, the likelihood that technology cannot advance forever. Although there is some promising research in this area, the existing economic theory of technological change is not well developed.

Summarizing our Conclusions About Economic Development

Before we look at some evidence, let's summarize the main theoretical conclusions about the path of economic development. Suppose first that we abstract from growth in population and technology. Also, assume that the economy begins with a capital stock below its steady-state value. Then we predict positive, but diminishing growth rates of the capital stock, output, and consumption. These growth rates all approach steady-state values of zero. Correspondingly, the real interest rate falls toward its steady-state value, which is the utility rate of time preference, ρ. We also predict decreases over time in the ratio of net investment to net and gross product, with net investment equaling zero in the steady state. Finally, the levels of capital and the other variables in the steady state depend on the form of the production function and on the utility rate of time preference, ρ. (There are also some ambiguous effects that concern the behavior of work effort.)

When we introduce population growth, we find that the economy approaches a position of steady-state growth. Here, the per capita growth rates of capital, output, and consumption are all zero. But net investment is positive in this situation. (A higher growth rate of population means a larger ratio of net investment to net and gross product.) Otherwise, the results are similar to those summarized above.

Finally, we can allow for continuing improvements in technology. Then the economy may approach a position of steady-state per capita growth, where the growth rates of capital, output, and consumption per person all equal a positive constant. Now, the steady-state real interest rate exceeds the utility rate of time preference, ρ. However, suppose that the economy begins with a relatively low capital stock (in relation to the path for steady-state growth). Then we still predict that the various growth rates and the real interest rate will be high initially, but will then decline toward their values under steady-state growth. Also, the ratio of net investment to net and gross product falls over time toward its steady-state value.

Long-Term Evidence for the United States

Let's see how our theory relates to the long-term performance of the U.S. economy. Table 12.1 contains data from the 19th and 20th centuries on the growth rate of real gross national product (GNP), on a measure of the real interest rate, and on

Table 12.1 Growth Rates, Interest Rates, and Investment Ratios for the U.S. since 1840

	Growth Rates (% per year)			Interest and Inflation Rates (% per year)			Investment Ratios Gross Private Fixed Investment	Investment Ratios Net Private Fixed Investment
	Real GNP	Population	Real GNP per Capita	R†	π	$r = R - \pi$	GNP	GNP
1840–60	4.9	3.1	1.8	8.6	−0.5	9.1	- -	- -
1867–80	5.8*	2.3*	3.5*	6.7	−2.4	9.1	0.17**	0.09**
1880–1900	3.0	2.1	0.9	5.6	−0.7	6.3	0.19***	0.10***
1900–16	3.3	1.8	1.5	5.5	2.4	3.1	0.17	0.07
1920–40	2.4	1.1	1.3	3.3	−1.6	4.9	0.12	0.01
1947–60	3.5	1.7	1.8	2.3	2.5	−0.2	0.14	0.06
1960–80	3.5	1.2	2.3	5.9	4.7	1.2	0.14	0.06

Note: The periods exclude the years around three major wars, 1861–66, 1917–19, and 1941–46.

For the data on real GNP, see Figure 1.1 of Chapter 1.

R is the nominal interest rate on 4–6 month prime Commercial Paper. From 1857–89, the variable refers to 60–90 day rates, as reported in Frederick R. Macaulay, *The Movements of Interest Rates, Bond Yields and Stock Prices in the United States since 1856,* National Bureau of Economic Research, New York, 1938, Table 10. For 1840–56 the rates are Bigelow's estimates for the "New York and Boston money markets," as reported by Macaulay in Table 25. Interest rates since 1890 are in U.S. Commerce Dept., *Historical Statistics for the U.S., Colonial Times to 1970,* p. 1001.

The inflation rate, π, is based on the GNP deflator since 1869. For the data, see Figure 1.4 of Chapter 1. Data on the price level before 1869 refer to the consumer price index, as reported in *Historical Statistics,* p. 211.

The investment ratios equal real fixed, private, domestic investment divided by real GNP. Data on investment for 1869–1928 are from John Kendrick, *Productivity Trends in the United States,* Princeton University Press, Princeton N.J., 1961, Tables A-I and A-III.

Data on all variables for recent years are from U.S. Commerce Dept., *The National Income and Product Accounts of the U.S., 1929–76, U.S. Survey of Current Business,* and the *Federal Reserve Bulletin.*

*1869–80 (data on real GNP for 1867–68 are unavailable).

**1869–78.

***1879–1900.

†Dates for the interest rates are 1840–59, 1867–79, 1880–99, 1900–15, 1920–39, 1947–59, and 1960–79. Thereby, the periods covered correspond roughly to those for the inflation rate.

ratios of gross and net investment to real GNP. Here, we examine averages over 20-year periods, excluding the years around the three major wars (1861–66, 1917–19, 1941–46).

In order to get a long time series, we use the interest rate on prime commercial paper, which covers short-term notes issued by established companies. (U.S. Treasury Bills were first issued in 1929.) However, we do not know how much the riskiness of commercial paper has changed over time. Recall that during the post-World War II period, the real interest rates are small and show no definite trend. However, there is a marked decline in the real interest rate over the long term. Specifically, the average value of the real interest rate is 9.1% for 1840–60 and 1867–80, 6.3% for 1880–1900, 3.1% for 1900–16, 4.9% for 1920–40, −0.2% for 1947–60, and 1.2% for 1960–80. Thus, the numbers conform to our theory, which predicts that capital's marginal product and the real interest rate will decline as the economy develops.

The ratios of gross and net fixed private investment to GNP show some decline over the long term. Specifically, the ratio for net investment decreases from 9–10% for 1869–1900 to 6% for 1947–80. Our theory predicts that this decline will accompany the fall in the real interest rate.

Table 12.1 shows average growth rates of real GNP, of population, and of real GNP per capita since 1840. (The figures on real GNP for the 19th century are rough estimates.) There is a pronounced decline in the growth rate of population— from about 3% per year in the mid-19th century to a little over 1% for 1960–80. There is also some decline in the growth rate of real GNP—from about 5% per year in 1840–60 to 3.5% in 1960–80. But there is no indication of decline since 1880. Finally, there is no clear pattern over time in the growth rates of real GNP per capita. In fact, the value of 2.3% per year for 1960–80 is exceeded only by the value of 3.5% per year for 1869–80.

The strong performance of real GNP per capita during the post-World War II period is a pleasant surprise. Our theory predicts that a fall in per capita growth rates would accompany the decline in capital's marginal product. We can mention some elements that account for some of this behavior.

First, there has been no major economic contraction during the post-World War II period. This outcome distinguishes the recent years from two earlier 20-year periods in the table: 1920–40 and 1880–1900.

Second, there has been an unusually large increase in the rate of labor-force participation. The ratio of the total labor force to the population aged 16–64 increases from 66% in 1950 to 68% in 1965 and 74% in 1980. (This ratio varies between 63% and 65% from 1900 to 1940.) The recent change reflects especially the increasing labor-force participation of women, which relates in part to the reduced birth rate.

Finally, it may be that the rate of technological progress is higher than usual during the post-World War II period. We cannot measure the state of technology directly, but there are some interesting proxies to look at. On the one hand, we do not see an unusually large number of patents issued for inventions, when expressed relative to the size of the population. The figures for the post-World War II years are similar to the averages for 1870 to 1940. But total outlays for research and development and for basic research do grow rapidly since World War II. In real terms the average growth rate of these outlays for 1955–80 is 5.0% per year.

If we look ahead, there seems to be limited scope for further increases in the rates of labor-force participation. There is also no reason to anticipate unusually high rates of technological progress. Therefore, even if the economy avoids major economic contractions, we forecast average growth rates of real GNP per capita that are below those experienced for 1960–80.

Nine Industrialized Countries in the Post-World War II Period

Let's try to apply the theory to the experiences of the major industrialized, primarily free-market economies in the post-World War II period. Here, we want to compare the levels of output across different countries at various points in time. In order to make this comparison, we use the results from a recent research project by Kravis, Heston, and Summers.[6] These researchers measure the prices of a market basket of goods in different countries for some benchmark years. Thereby, they can calculate a time series of real gross product for each country, where all magnitudes are expressed in terms of U.S. dollars for the base year, 1975.

We examine the experiences of nine industrialized or semi-industrialized countries, which Kravis, et al., include in their study.[7] These are the United States, Austria, Denmark, France, West Germany, Italy, Japan, Spain, and the United Kingdom. For most of the countries, we look at the economic performance from 1950 to 1979.

Suppose that these countries are basically similar in terms of production functions, natural resources, and preferences. But at the starting date, which we take to be 1950, there are major differences across countries in the levels of capital stock per person. (Remember that we take a broad view of capital to include human capital and aspects of technology, as well as machines and buildings.) In fact, a large part of the differences in 1950 stem directly from World War II. The losers in that war, which are Japan, Germany, and Italy, lost a larger fraction of their capital stocks than did the winners and neutrals, of which we consider the United States, the United Kingdom, and Spain. Then the occupied countries, as represented by Austria, Denmark, and France are intermediate cases.

The countries that start with more capital per head should have higher initial values for output and consumption per head. But capital's marginal product is greater in the countries with less capital. Hence, these countries would invest a larger fraction of their output and, thereby, experience higher growth rates of

---

[6]Irving Kravis, Alan Heston, and Robert Summers, *World Product and Income, International Comparisons of Real Gross Product*, Johns Hopkins University Press, Baltimore, 1982, Tables 8-3 and 8-4.

[7]They do not include Canada, Sweden, and Switzerland, which we otherwise would have added.

capital, output, and consumption. Eventually, we predict that each country approaches the same path of steady-state growth. Therefore, the countries should come together, not only in terms of growth rates and ratios of investment to output, but also in terms of the levels of output and consumption per person. (The last result would not hold exactly if there are long-term differences across countries in natural resources or some other characteristics.)

The results just mentioned can be offset by major shocks, such as war, depression, or epidemics. In fact, as mentioned above, the effects of wartime account for a significant part of the differences in starting positions among the countries. But the post-World War II period is free from major wars, depressions, and so on. Therefore, this period should isolate the effects that we stress in this chapter.

Table 12.2 shows for each country the growth rates of real gross product, population, and real gross product per capita, along with the ratios to gross product of gross and net fixed investment.[8] The data refer to averages over three decades—the 1950s, 1960s, and 1970s—as well as to the overall period, which is usually 1950–79. The table also indicates the levels of real gross product per person at four dates: 1950, 1960, 1970, and 1979.

As expected, there is a substantial spread for 1950 in the levels of gross output per person. In terms of 1975 U.S. dollars, the numbers are $4,400 for the United States, $2,800 for Denmark, $2,700 for the United Kingdom, $2,300 for France, $2,000 for Germany, $1,700 for Austria, $1,400 for Italy, $1,200 for Spain, and $800 for Japan. We show these amounts on a proportionate scale on the left part of Figure 12.4.

Consider next the ordering of countries by their average growth rates of output per capita from 1950 to 1979. These numbers are 6.7% per year for Japan, 4.3% for Germany and Spain, 4.1% for Austria, 3.9% for Italy, 3.7% for France, 2.9% for Denmark, 2.2% for the United Kingdom, and 2.0% for the United States. This ranking is nearly the reverse of the first one, which is based on starting levels of output per head. That is, as predicted, the countries with the lower starting values of output (and capital) per person are the ones that tend to grow faster. Also, the conclusion is similar if we look at growth rates for the levels of output, rather than output per capita.

Notice that the United States is in last place in terms of the average growth rate of output per capita. (It places eighth, ahead of the United Kingdom, if we consider the average growth rate for the level of output.) Although many people criticize this performance, we may not want to take this criticism seriously. First, the theory predicts relatively low growth for the United States, because the United States starts with the highest level of output per person. Second, remember that the growth rate of output per capita in the United States since World War II looks good when compared to the historical record. In particular, we commented in the previous section that this growth rate is surprisingly high. Basically, the low rank-

---

[8]These figures on investment include investment expenditures by governments, except for military purposes. However, the exclusion of governmental components would not materially change the comparisons across the countries.

Table 12.2 The Behavior of Output and Investment in Nine Industrialized Countries

Country/Period		Real GDP per Capita (1000s of 1975 U.S. dollars at start of period)	Growth Rates (% per year)			Investment Ratios		
			Real GDP	Population	Real GDP per Capita	Period	Gross Fixed Investment/GDP (period average)	Net Fixed Investment/GDP (period average)
U.S.	1950–60	4.45	3.2	1.7	1.5	1950–59	0.18	0.07
	1960–70	5.16	3.8	1.3	2.5	1960–69	0.18	0.08
	1970–79	6.64	3.2	1.0	2.2	1970–79	0.17	0.07
	1950–79	8.06 (1979)	3.4	1.3	2.0	1950–79	0.18	0.07
Austria	1950–60	1.73	5.1	0.2	4.9	1950–59	0.21	0.09
	1960–70	2.81	4.5	0.5	4.0	1960–69	0.26	0.14
	1970–79	4.20	3.4	0.1	3.3	1970–79	0.27	0.15
	1950–79	5.64 (1979)	4.4	0.3	4.1	1950–79	0.25	0.13
Denmark	1950–60	2.81	3.3	0.7	2.6	1950–59	0.19	0.13
	1960–70	3.66	4.5	0.7	3.8	1960–69	0.23	0.16
	1970–79	5.36	2.5	0.4	2.1	1970–79	0.24	0.16
	1950–79	6.45 (1979)	3.5	0.6	2.9	1950–79	0.22	0.15
France	1950–60	2.26	4.4	0.9	3.5	1950–59	0.19	0.08
	1960–70	3.21	5.6	1.1	4.5	1960–69	0.22	0.13
	1970–79	5.04	3.6	0.6	3.0	1970–79	0.23	0.14
	1950–79	6.59 (1979)	4.6	0.9	3.7	1950–79	0.21	0.11
Germany	1950–60	1.99	7.5	1.0	6.5	1950–59	0.22	0.14
(West)	1960–70	3.81	4.5	0.9	3.6	1960–69	0.25	0.16
	1970–79	5.46	2.7	0.1	2.6	1970–79	0.23	0.12
	1950–79	6.92 (1979)	5.0	0.7	4.3	1950–79	0.23	0.14
Italy	1950–60	1.37	5.7	0.6	5.1	1950–59	0.20	0.11
	1960–70	2.28	5.3	0.8	4.5	1960–69	0.21	0.13
	1970–79	3.59	2.5	0.7	1.8	1970–79	0.20	0.11
	1950–79	4.21 (1979)	4.6	0.7	3.9	1950–79	0.20	0.12
Japan	1950–60	0.83	8.1	1.2	6.9	1952–59	0.24	0.14
	1960–70	1.65	10.1	0.9	9.2	1960–69	0.32	0.22
	1970–79	4.12	4.8	1.2	3.6	1970–79	0.33	0.20
	1950–79	5.71 (1979)	7.8	1.1	6.7	1952–79	0.30	0.19
Spain	1950–60	1.18	4.9	0.8	4.1	1954–59	0.18	0.08
	1960–70	1.77	7.1	1.1	6.0	1960–69	0.21	0.11
	1970–79	3.24	3.6	1.1	2.5	1970–79	0.22	0.13
	1950–79	4.05 (1979)	5.3	1.0	4.3	1954–79	0.21	0.11
U.K.	1950–60	2.74	2.6	0.4	2.2	1950–59	0.15	0.07
	1960–70	3.41	2.8	0.6	2.2	1960–69	0.18	0.10
	1970–79	4.24	2.3	0.1	2.2	1970–79	0.19	0.09
	1950–79	5.16 (1979)	2.6	0.4	2.2	1950–79	0.17	0.08

Notes: GDP is gross domestic product, the total value of output produced domestically. The values are expressed as U.S. dollars for the base year, 1975. The figures on investment include purchases of capital goods by governments. However, all defense expenditures are excluded. The fraction of public investment in total investment is about 10–20%, with no major differences across countries. The investment ratios equal nominal investment expenditures divided by nominal GDP.

Sources: The figures on real GDP per capita are from Kravis, et al., op. cit., Tables 8-3 and 8-4. Data on population are from the U.N. *Statistical Yearbook.* Figures on nominal investment and GDP are from OECD, *National Accounts of OECD Countries,* V.I., 1981, 1982. For 1950 (and also 1951 for the U.K.), the data on investment for Austria, Denmark, France, Germany, Italy, and the U.K. are estimated from B. R. Mitchell, *European Historical Statistics,* Columbia University Press, New York, 1975.

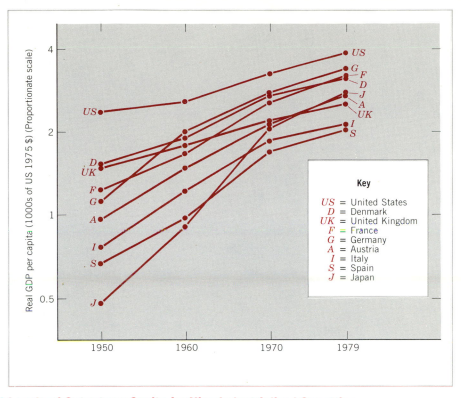

Figure 12.4 Levels of Output per Capita for Nine Industrialized Countries
The figure shows the convergence of output per person across the countries between 1950 and 1979.

ing for the United States growth rate reflects the astonishingly strong performance of the other countries, rather than a low rate of growth in the United States.

The ranking of countries by average growth rates accords reasonably well with a ranking by average ratios of net fixed investment to output. The average values of these ratios from 1950 to 1979 are 0.19 for Japan (for 1952–79), 0.15 for Denmark, 0.14 for Germany, 0.13 for Austria, 0.12 for Italy, 0.11 for Spain (for 1954–79), 0.08 for the United Kingdom, and 0.07 for the U.S. In the main, the countries with the higher investment ratios are the ones with first, the lower starting values of output per capita, and second, the higher average growth rates of output per capita.

Figure 12.4 shows how the differences in growth rates lead over time to convergences in the levels of output per person. The figures on output per capita for 1979, measured again in 1975 U.S. dollars, are $8,100 for the United States, $6,900 for Germany, $6,600 for France, $6,400 for Denmark, $5,700 for Japan, $5,600 for Austria, $5,200 for the United Kingdom, $4,200 for Italy, and $4,000 for Spain. Thus, for example, output per capita for Japan in 1979 is 71% of the

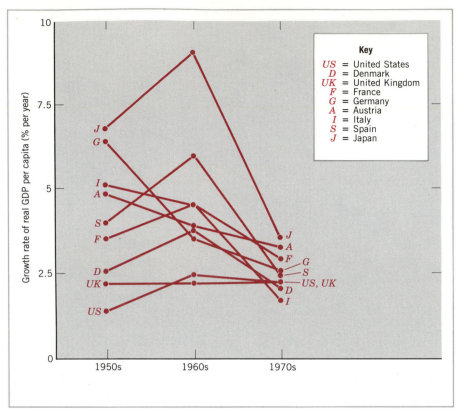

Figure 12.5 Growth Rates of Output per Capita for Nine Industrialized Countries
The figure shows the average growth rates of output per capita for the nine countries during three decades—the 1950s, 1960s, and 1970s.

U.S. level, as compared to 19% in 1950. For Germany, the comparison is between 86% of the U.S. level in 1979, versus 45% in 1950. That for Italy is between 52% of the U.S. level in 1979 and 31% in 1950.

Our theory predicts also that growth rates would decline over time for each country, approaching the rates associated with steady-state per capita growth.[10] Figure 12.5 shows the growth rates of output per capita for each country over three decades—the 1950s, 1960s, and 1970s. Similarly, Figure 12.6 shows the growth rates for the levels of output. Overall, there is a tendency for the growth rates to diminish as we move from the 1950s to the 1970s. For example, the simple averages for the growth rates of output per capita over the nine countries are 4.1%

---

[10]However, these growth rates would not be the same if countries differ by their long-term growth rates of technology or population. As it stands, the theory does not address these questions. With respect to the growth rate of population, the values for the 1970s range from 0.1% per year for Germany and the United Kingdom to 1.2% per year for Japan.

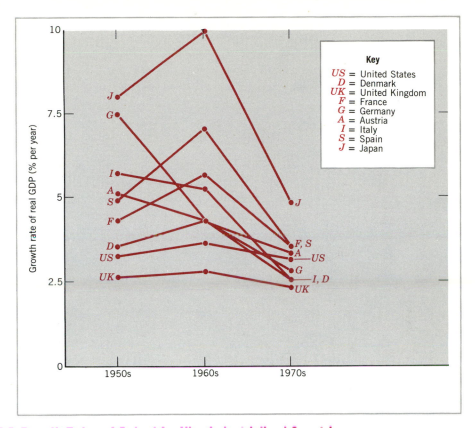

Figure 12.6 Growth Rates of Output for Nine Industrialized Countries
The figure shows the average growth rates of output for the nine countries during three decades—the 1950s, 1960s, and 1970s.

in the 1950s, 4.5% in the 1960s, and 2.6% in the 1970s. For the growth rates of levels of output, the corresponding figures are 5.0%, 5.4%, and 3.2%. Note that the pattern of declining growth rates shows up most clearly for the countries that begin with the highest rates of growth, which are Japan, Germany, and Italy. In particular, the Japanese growth rate of output per capita falls from the extraordinary value of 9.2% per year for the 1960s to 3.6% for the 1970s.

Contrary to the theory, there is no systematic decline over time in the ratios of net investment to output. The simple averages of these ratios for the nine countries (from Table 12.2) are 10% for the 1950s, 14% for the 1960s, and 13% for the 1970s. Notice that for the 1970s, the ratios are 20% for Japan, 16% for Denmark, 15% for Austria, and 14% for France. These values remain strikingly higher than those for the United States and the United Kingdom, which are 7 and 9%, respectively. Since the growth rates of output across the countries have converged substantially, the results on investment ratios are puzzling.

Looking ahead, a key observation is the relatively small spread for the levels of real output per capita in 1979. Therefore, we predict that the rates of growth for the nine countries in the 1980s will be more similar than they were in the previous three decades. Also, the theory predicts more convergence in the ratios of net investment to output. But in order for this to occur, there would have to be declines in the ratios for several countries, especially Japan.

Summary

This chapter studies the process of capital accumulation over the long term. As the quantity of capital increases, the diminishing marginal product of capital implies that the real interest rate falls. Then we trace out a path of economic development where consumption and output rise, but where net investment declines. Work effort may either rise or fall over time. Also, the growth rates of capital, consumption, and output tend to decline. Eventually, the economy approaches a steady state in which output and the quantity of capital do not change. Here, net investment and real saving are zero, and the real interest rate equals the utility rate of time preference.

Steadily growing population leads to persistent growth in output and the quantity of capital. Although the economy no longer approaches a position where net investment and real saving are zero, the per capita growth rates of capital, consumption, and output do tend toward zero. If there is continuing technical progress, then these per capita growth rates can be positive in the long run. But if an economy starts with a relatively small amount of capital per person, then economic development still entails decreases over time in the real interest rate, in the growth rates of the capital stock and output, and in the ratio of net investment to output.

For the United States since 1840, we do find a major decline in the real interest rate and some decrease in the share of net fixed investment in GNP. However, while there is some decline over time in the growth rate of output, there is no systematic decline in the growth rate of output per capita.

We also study the development of nine industrialized countries since 1950. Especially because of World War II, these countries start with major differences in the levels of capital stock and output per person. Then, as the theory predicts, the countries that start with less capital per person experience faster growth rates of output per capita and also invest a larger fraction of their output. Thus, there is substantial convergence over time in the levels of output per capita among the nine countries. Also, there is a tendency for the growth rates of output to fall over time, at least in the countries that start with the higher rates of growth. However, there is a puzzle that concerns the ratios of net investment to output. These tend neither to fall over time nor to converge across the countries.

Important Terms and Concepts

technological change   steady-state growth

steady state   steady-state per capita growth

QUESTIONS AND PROBLEMS

Mainly for Review

12.1 Why does an increase in the capital stock reduce the interest rate? Would the interest rate rise when there is an increase (shift) in aggregate demand for commodities as a result of the higher capital stock?

12.2 Summarize the effect of a higher capital stock on the quantities of:
  a. Consumption
  b. Leisure
  c. Net investment
Distinguish where necessary between wealth and substitution effects.

12.3 What is the immediate effect of a one-time (permanent) improvement in the production function on the interest rate and on net investment? If the rise in the interest rate were equal to the rise in the marginal product of capital, would net investment rise? Explain why this situation is not likely to occur.

12.4 What are the long-run effects of the improvement in the production function considered in question 12.3? In particular, why does net investment remain positive in future periods even though there are no more increases in MPK? Why does the economy eventually reach a steady state, i.e., why does net investment eventually become zero?

12.5 Compare an economy in steady-state growth with one in a steady state. Explain why, in the former, there is positive net investment in every period. Is a rise in the interest rate required to elicit the corresponding amount of real saving?

12.6 Should a decline in the investment/GNP ratio be a cause for public concern? Is it inevitably accompanied by lower growth of GNP per capita?

Problems for Discussion

12.7 The Effects of More Capital on the Commodity Market
Figure 12.1 shows the effects of an increase in the capital stock on the commodity market.
  a. What determines the direction and magnitude of the shift in the aggregate demand for net product, $Y_2^d - \delta K_1$?
  b. Why does the curve for net investment demand, $I_2^d - \delta K_1$, specify zero net investment demand when the real interest rate equals the value r_1^*?
  c. Consider the effect of more capital on the quantity of net investment, $I_2^* - \delta K_1$. Why is this effect negative?
  d. What determines the sign of the effect on net product, $Y_2^* - \delta K_1$?

12.8 Economic Development and the Real Wage Rate
Suppose that we introduce a separate labor market into the model.
  a. Assume that population and technology are fixed, but the economy starts with a capital stock below the steady-state amount. As the economy accumulates capital, what happens to the real wage rate?

b. Suppose that at date 1 the economy is in a steady state. Then there is a once-and-for-all improvement in the production function. Here, the schedules for the marginal products of labor and capital shift upward. (We show this case in Figure 12.3.) What happens to the real wage rate in the short run and the long run?

c. Redo part **b** for the case of a one-time increase in population.

12.9 Population Growth (optional)

Suppose that technology is fixed, but population grows at the constant rate n. Assume that returns to scale in production are nearly constant. How does the value of n affect the following variables *in a position of steady-state growth:*

a. the growth rates of aggregate capital, gross output, consumption, and work effort?

b. the growth rates of capital, gross output, consumption, and work effort per capita?

Assume now that changes in n do not affect the ratio of aggregate capital to either aggregate gross output or aggregate work effort in a position of steady-state growth. Then, how does the value of n affect the following variables under steady-state growth:

c. the ratio of aggregate net investment to the aggregates of capital and gross output?

d. the ratio of aggregate consumption to aggregate gross output?

Explain carefully the answers to parts (c) and (d).

12.10 Growth Rates Across Countries (optional)

We studied nine industrialized countries in the text. We assumed that these countries were similar in terms of production functions and tastes, but differed by their starting values of capital per head. We assumed also that the primary economic organization in these countries involved free markets. Therefore, we predicted that the countries would all approach the same path of steady-state growth. In particular, countries with lower starting values of output per head would grow more rapidly for awhile.

Would you make the same predictions for all countries, including those that are presently at very low levels of economic development? What considerations affect the applicability of the theory to different countries? (No one knows the answer to this!) After you have made your predictions, you can look at data for some cases—for example, for India, Mexico, South Korea, and Brazil. (The data on gross product are in Kravis, et al., as cited in the text.)

PART IV
GOVERNMENT BEHAVIOR

CHAPTER 13
GOVERNMENT PURCHASES AND PUBLIC SERVICES

Up to this point, the government does not play much of a role in the model. In fact, all the government does is print money and give away the proceeds as transfer payments. In the real world the government has important influences on economic activity through its expenditures, taxes, transfer programs, regulations, and debt management. We begin our study of these matters in this chapter by considering government purchases of goods and services and a simple form of tax revenues. But in order to provide some background, let's look first at the history of government spending in the United States.

Government Expenditures in the United States

Figures 13.1 and 13.2 show the evolution of government spending in the United States from 1929 to 1982. Excluding the wartime experiences, total dollar government expenditures when expressed as a ratio to nominal GNP rose from 0.10 in 1929 to 0.18 in 1940, 0.21 in 1950, 0.27 in 1960, 0.32 in 1970, and 0.35 in 1982 (a comparable figure for 1902 is 0.07).

The pattern of steady rise in the relative importance of total government expenditures conceals some different movements in the major underlying components. Figure 13.1 shows how purchases of goods and services have varied over time. Federal purchases rise from 0.01 relative to GNP in 1929 to 0.06 in 1940, but remain at 0.06 in 1950. Following a rise to 0.11 in 1960, the federal purchases' ratio declines to 0.07 in 1979, before rising to 0.08 in 1982. In other words the ratio for 1982 does not differ greatly from that for 1950 or 1940.

Except during the Great Depression from 1933–40, the dominant component of federal purchases is military spending. This spending is 0.02 relative to GNP in 1940 and 0.09 in 1960, but falls from there to a low point of less than 0.05 in 1979; then this ratio rises to 0.06 for 1982. (As a fraction of total government

299

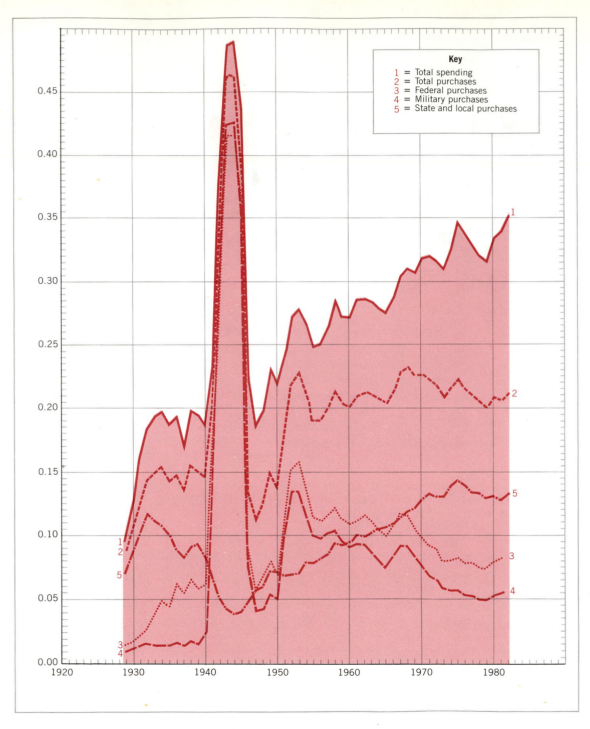

Figure 13.1 Total Government Spending and Government Purchases, Expressed as Ratios to Nominal GNP

The data go from 1929 to 1982.

expenditure, military purchases decline from 33% in 1960 to 16% in 1982.) Notice that Figure 13.1 shows also the peaks in the military purchases' ratio during war-time. These are 0.42 in 1943–44, 0.13 in 1952–53, and 0.09 in 1967–68.

State and local purchases relative to GNP are 0.07 in 1929 and 1950. Then

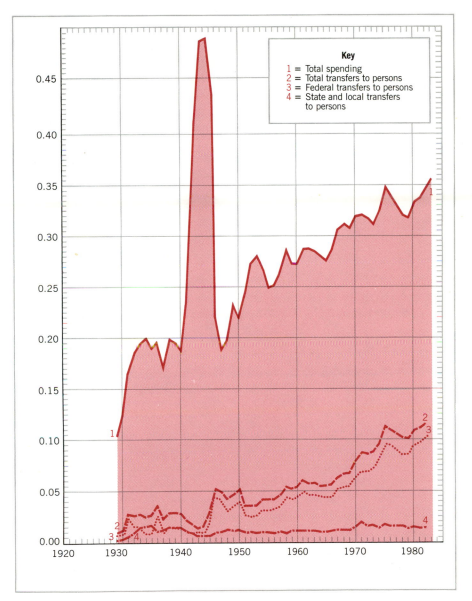

Figure 13.2 Total Government Spending and Transfer Payments, Expressed as Ratios to Nominal GNP
The data go from 1929 to 1982.

this ratio rises to a peak of 0.14 in 1975, but subsequently falls to 0.13 in 1982. About half of the rise in this ratio from 1950 to 1975 represents increases in expenditures for education. (Educational expenditures advance from about one-third of state and local purchases in the years up to 1950 to 42% in 1975.)

Figure 13.2 shows the behavior of transfers. Total transfer payments to persons rise from 0.01 relative to GNP in 1929 to 0.03 in 1940, 0.05 in 1950 and 1960, 0.08 in 1970, and 0.12 in 1982. Note that the state and local part of these transfers (which includes aid to families with dependent children) remains between 0.009 and 0.019 relative to GNP for the peacetime years since the mid-1930s. Hence, the strong upward movement in the transfers' ratio derives from the federal government. The main reason for the increase is the growing benefits paid through social security. For example, the payments for old-age, survivors, and disability, which is the principal social security program, increase from 0.003 relative to GNP in 1950 to 0.050 in 1982. Over the same period, medicare expenditures rise from zero to 0.017 relative to GNP. Although there is much recent discussion about social security, there is no indication as yet that the growth of this spending is slowing down.

We can summarize the movements in government expenditures relative to GNP since the 1950s in terms of three major developments: a sharp drop in spending for the military, a roughly compensating increase in social-security benefits, and a substantial rise in state and local purchases (a major portion of which is for education) until the mid-1970s.

The Government's Budget Constraint

Let G_t denote the government's demand for commodities during period t. In terms of the national accounts, G_t corresponds to real purchases of goods and services by the total of federal, state, and local governments. Total real government expenditure equals these purchases plus the real value of aggregate transfer payments, V_t/P_t. (We do not yet consider governmental interest payments.)

Before, the government's only revenue came from printing money. The real value of this revenue is the amount, $(M_t - M_{t-1})/P_t$. Now we assume that the government also levies taxes on households. (Remember that the households are the producers, as well as the consumers, in our model.) Let T_t be the aggregate dollar amount of taxes for period t. Then the real amount of tax revenues is T_t/P_t.

As before, the government's budget constraint equates total real expenditures to total real revenues. Therefore, we have[1]

---

[1]In the United States economy the revenue from printing money accrues directly to the Federal Reserve, which then turns most of its profits over to the U.S. Treasury. However, for historical reasons, the national accounts treat the Fed as though it were a private corporation, rather than a part of the central government. Therefore, the transfer of funds from the Fed to the Treasury is classified as a tax on corporate profits! (We can almost feel sorry for the Fed, since its "profits" are taxed at nearly a 100% rate!) This quirk in the national accounts can cause trouble for unwary researchers, since the Fed's payments to the Treasury amount to 21% of the reported total for federal taxes on corporate profits in 1981 ($14 billion out of a total of $67 billion) and 31% in 1982 ($15 billion out of $48 billion)!

$$G_t + V_t/P_t = T_t/P_t + (M_t - M_{t-1})/P_t \qquad (13.1)$$

Our earlier formulation fits into equation (13.1) if we set real purchases, G_t, and taxes, T_t/P_t, to zero.

Earlier, we assumed that the transfer payments were lump-sum. This means that the amount of an individual's real transfer, v_t/P_t, does not depend on that person's level of income, effort at soliciting transfers, and so on. Now, we assume also that the taxes are lump-sum. Hence, an individual's real tax liability, t_t/P_t, is independent of that person's level or type of income, effort at avoiding taxes, and so on.

Of course, in the real world, an elaborate tax law specifies the relation of someone's taxes to their amounts of income, business profits, sales, holdings of property, deductions from taxable income, and so on. Generally, there are lots of things people can do—including hiring accountants, working less, underreporting income, and exploiting tax loopholes—in order to lower their obligations. These possibilities imply important substitution effects from the tax system on work effort, investment, relative demands for different goods (even including numbers of children!) and so on. In general, people substitute in favor of activities that lower their taxes.

We shall find it convenient initially to neglect these substitution effects from taxes. That's why we assume **lump-sum taxes,** which do not exert any substitution effects. But we bring in more realistic types of taxes and transfers in the next chapter.

Public Production

The government uses its purchases, G_t, to provide services to households. Further, we assume that the government provides these services free of charge to the users. In most countries public services include national defense, enforcement of laws and private contracts, police and fire protection, elementary education and some parts of higher education, highways, parks, and so on. The range of governmental activities has typically expanded over time, although this range varies significantly from one place to another.

We could model public services as the output from the government's production function. Then the inputs to this function would be the government-owned stock of capital, labor services from public employees, and materials that the government purchases from the private sector. Instead, we simplify matters by neglecting production in the public sector. We do this—as do macromodels generally—by pretending that the government buys only final goods and services on the commodity market. In effect, the government in our model subcontracts all of its production to the private sector. In this setup public investment, publicly owned capital, and government employment are always zero. Ultimately, the introduction of governmental production would affect the main results only if the public sector's technology or management capability differs from that of private producers. Otherwise, it will not matter whether the government buys final goods, as we assume, or buys capital and labor to produce things itself.

Before, we assumed that output could be labeled as either consumables or capital goods. Now we introduce a third function for output; namely, the government can purchase goods in order to provide public services to households. As before, suppliers do not care whether people use the goods for consumption, investment, or to provide public services. That is, the demanders of commodities—which now include the government—determine its use.

Public Services

In our model we consider two types of public services. The first type provides utility directly. As examples we can think of parks, libraries, school lunch programs, subsidized health care and transportation services, and the entertaining parts of the space program. An important feature of these services is that they may substitute closely for private consumer spending. (If the government buys our lunch at school, then we don't buy our own lunch. But we have to be more subtle to find the private substitutes for the space program.)

The second type of service is an input to private production. Examples include the provision and enforcement of laws, aspects of national defense, government sponsored research and development programs, fire and police services, and various regulatory activities. In some cases these services are close substitutes for private inputs of labor and capital. In other cases, such as the provision of a legal system and national defense, the public services are likely to raise the marginal products of private factors.

In many situations a governmental program exhibits features of both types of services that we consider. But the mix varies across the wide range of actual programs. However, in our theory, we proceed as if there were only one type of governmental activity. This activity yields utility directly, and also provides services to producers.

Households' Budget Constraints

Before, we included real transfers, v_t/P_t, as a source of income for a household. Now we also have to subtract real taxes, t_t/P_t, to calculate real income after taxes. That is, people care about the real value of transfers net of taxes, $(v_t - t_t)/P_t$. For example, the budget constraint in real terms for period t is

$$y_t + b_{t-1}(1 + R)/P_t + m_{t-1}/P_t + (v_t - t_t)/P_t = c_t + i_t + (b_t + m_t)/P_t \qquad (13.2)$$

As in previous chapters, we can also calculate someone's real saving for period t. The result is now

$$\text{real saving} = y_t - \delta k_{t-1} + (R - \pi)(b_{t-1}/P_t) - \pi(m_{t-1}/P_t) + (v_t - t_t)/P_t - c_t \qquad (13.3)$$

Before, the household's real income equaled net product, plus the real interest earnings on bonds and money, plus real transfers. Now, we deduct real taxes, t_t/P_t, to compute real income after taxes, which is called **disposable real income.** Then we subtract real consumption expenditures, c_t, to determine real saving.

Earlier, when we calculated a household's budget constraint over an infinite horizon, we included the present value of real transfers, $v_1/P_1 + (v_2/P_2)/(1 + r) + \ldots$ (This expression came up when we added various monetary terms to the budget constraint.) Now, we just replace transfers by transfers net of taxes—that is, the new expression is

$$(v_1 - t_1)/P_1 + [(v_2 - t_2)/P_2]/(1 + r) + \cdots$$

Let's consider the aggregate value of this expression. Each term involves the aggregate of real transfers net of real taxes, $(V_t - T_t)/P_t$. But we know from the government's budget constraint in equation (13.1) that this term equals the real revenue from money creation less real government purchases—that is

$$(V_t - T_t)/P_t = (M_t - M_{t-1})/P_t - G_t \tag{13.4}$$

Suppose for the moment that the money stock were constant, so that the condition, $M_t - M_{t-1} = 0$, holds in each period. Then the aggregate real value of transfers net of taxes, $(V_t - T_t)/P_t$, equals the negative of real government purchases, $-G_t$. Therefore, the aggregate of households' budget constraints over an infinite horizon includes the expression

$$(V_1 - T_1)/P_1 + [(V_2 - T_2)]/(1 + r) + \cdots = -[G_1 + G_2/(1 + r) + \cdots]$$

Note that the present value of real government purchases tells us the amount to subtract from the aggregate real present value of households' funds. So, on this count, an increase in the present value of real government purchases has a negative effect on households' wealth.

What happens when the money stock varies over time? Then, from equation (13.4), the aggregate real present value of households' funds includes the additional terms

$$(M_1 - M_0)/P_1 + [(M_2 - M_1)/P_2]/(1 + r) + \cdots$$

But we looked at this expression before (in Chapter 7). In fact, we found that it cancels along with two other monetary terms—the aggregate of initial real cash balances less the aggregate real present value of interest foregone on holdings of money. Therefore, the results do not change when we allow for revenue from money creation. Namely, the present value of real government purchases still subtracts from the aggregate of households' available funds.

Let's think about this result. From the aggregate of output in each period, Y_t, the government takes the quantity, G_t. Therefore, the expression, $G_1 + G_2/(1 + r) + \cdots$, is the real present value of the goods that the government absorbs. Hence, this expression also tells us the real present value of the goods that are not available for the aggregate of households. But this result does not depend on how much money the government prints in various periods. No matter how much money the government creates, the present value of purchases measures the resources used by the government, which are therefore unavailable for households.

Permanent Government Purchases

Suppose that real government purchases are constant at the amount G. Then the present value of these purchases is

$$G + G/(1 + r) + G/(1 + r)^2 + \cdots = G[1 + 1/(1 + r) + 1/(1 + r)^2 + \cdots]$$

The expression in brackets is a geometric progression, which we have seen before. Recall that it sums to the amount, $(1 + r)/r$.[2] Or, to turn things around, if we multiply the present value by the term, $r/(1 + r)$, we end up with the constant flow of purchases, G.

Now, think of a general time path of purchases, $G_1, G_2, \ldots$ Let's multiply the present value of these purchases by the term, $r/(1 + r)$, and call the result $\tilde{G}$—that is

$$\tilde{G} = \frac{r}{(1 + r)} [G_1 + G_2/(1 + r) + \cdots] \qquad (13.5)$$

If purchases were constant at the amount $\tilde{G}$, then we know from before that the present value would be $\tilde{G}(1 + r)/r$. But equation (13.5) says that the actual present value, $G_1 + G_2/(1 + r) + \cdots$, also equals the amount, $\tilde{G}(1 + r)/r$. Therefore, $\tilde{G}$ is the constant level of purchases that has the same present value as the actual time path of purchases. In effect, $\tilde{G}$ is a type of average for the amounts purchased at different dates. Henceforth, we call $\tilde{G}$ the level of **permanent government purchases,** as evaluated at date 1. Note that we use the term, permanent purchases, because the concept parallels the idea of permanent income. Remember that permanent income is the constant flow of real income that has the same present value as the actual time path of income.

A higher value for permanent purchases means a greater present value of government purchases, which means a lower present value of funds available for households. In fact, if permanent purchases, $\tilde{G}$, rise by 1 unit, then it is just as if the aggregate of households had one less unit of real income available in each period from date 1 onward. On this count, an increase by 1 unit in permanent purchases amounts to a decrease by 1 unit in the aggregate of permanent income.

To illustrate, suppose that the current level of purchases is $G_1 = 100$. But assume that this spending is unusually high because the government is carrying out some foreign military adventure. After period 2, the adventure will end (people think) and purchases will drop forever to 10 units per period. (No more military adventures will ever occur!) We show these numbers for government purchases in Table 13.1. Assume that the real interest rate, r, is 5% per period. Then we can calculate the present value of purchases to be 386. (See the note to Table 13.1.) Using equation (13.5) we find that permanent purchases, $\tilde{G}$, equal 18. Notice that the quantity of purchases during the temporary adventure, $G_1 = G_2 = 100$, is well above the permanent level. Then, after period 2, the quantity of purchases, $G_t = 10$, falls below the permanent level. But from the standpoint of households'

---

[2]We use the formula, $1 + x + x^2 + \cdots = 1/(1 - x)$ if $0 < x < 1$. In our case $x = 1/(1 + r)$.

Table 13.1 A Time Path for Real Government Purchases

Period	G_t
1	100
2	100
3	10
4	10
.	10
.	
.	

Note: Real purchases are temporarily high at the value 100 during periods 1 and 2. Then, at date 3, purchases drop to 10, and stay forever at this level. Assuming that the real interest rate, r, is 5%, the present value of purchases is 386.[3] Therefore, permanent purchases are $\tilde{G} = (0.05/1.05) \cdot 386 = 18$.

budget constraints, it is just as if the government took away 18 units of goods during each period.

Effects of Public Services on Private Choices

We want to explore the effects of government purchases on households' choices of consumption, investment, and work effort. For now, we hold fixed the level of permanent purchases, $\tilde{G}$. As we shall see, the wealth effects from changes in government purchases involve shifts in permanent purchases. Therefore, with this amount held fixed, we do not get any wealth effects.

Consider an increase in the current level of purchases, G_1. (Notice that, if we hold $\tilde{G}$ fixed, then we must reduce some future value(s) of purchases.) The higher current level of purchases means more public services of the two types that we mentioned before.

First, there is a positive effect on utility during the current period. That's because we assume that people like the services that the government provides! Suppose that the public services substitute for some private consumption, but not for leisure.[4] For example, when the government provides free libraries, parks, school lunches, or transportation, then people reduce their private spending in these

$$[3]100 + \frac{100}{1.05} + \frac{10}{(1.05)^2}\left[1 + \frac{1}{(1.05)} + \frac{1}{(1.05)^2} + \cdots\right] = 100 + \frac{100}{1.05} +$$

$$\frac{10}{(1.05)^2}\left(\frac{1}{1 - \dfrac{1}{1.05}}\right) = 100 + 95.2 + 190.5 = 385.7.$$

[4]We follow here the general approach taken in Martin J. Bailey, *National Income and the Price Level,* 2nd ed., McGraw-Hill, New York, 1971, Chapter 9.

areas. Let's use the parameter α (the Greek letter *alpha*) to measure the size of this effect. An increase in current purchases, G_1, by 1 unit motivates households to reduce aggregate private consumption demand, C_1^d, by α units. Thus, if public services are a close substitute for private spending, then the parameter α is high.

It is possible for the parameter α to exceed 1. That is, an extra unit of government purchases may substitute for more than 1 unit of aggregate consumer spending. This outcome is possible because people may benefit jointly from some types of government expenditures, such as the space program. It is this characteristic of joint benefit that economists have in mind when they say that some governmental services are **public goods.** The more the government's services have this characteristic of publicness, the higher the parameter α tends to be.

We assume also that the parameter α declines as the quantity of government purchases rises. That is, as the amount of public services increases, the marginal unit substitutes less closely for private spending. Notice, however, that the value of the parameter α does not necessarily tell us how valuable an extra unit of public services is. People might like these services a lot even if they do not substitute much for private spending—that is, even if α is small.

The second type of public service is an input to private production. Let's use the parameter β (the Greek letter *beta*) to measure the marginal product of public services. In other words, if the inputs of labor and capital do not change, then an increase in current purchases, G_1, by 1 unit raises aggregate output, Y_1, by β units. However, diminishing marginal productivity suggests that the parameter β declines as the quantity of government purchases increases.

Changes in public services may also affect the schedules for the marginal products of labor (MPL) and capital (MPK). In some cases the public services substitute for private inputs. For example, free city police can replace private guards. But more national defense and better enforcement of laws and contracts are likely to raise the marginal products of private factors. So, there is no general presumption about the direction of these effects.

Our main analysis neglects any shifts in the schedules for the marginal products of labor and capital. Therefore, there is no direct effect of current government purchases, G_1, on work effort. Hence, for a given capital stock, an increase by 1 unit in government purchases, G_1, raises the aggregate supply of goods, Y_1^s, by β units.

Recall that net investment demand depends on the schedule for capital's marginal product, on the previous stock of capital, and on the real interest rate. Therefore, since we assume no effect of public services on capital's marginal product, we end up with no direct effect of government purchases on investment demand. Any effects that arise must work through changes in the real interest rate.

Clearing of the Commodity Market

Now, we incorporate government purchases into the market-clearing conditions. The main new effects involve the demand and supply of commodities. Therefore, we focus on the condition for clearing the commodity market. The new condition for period 1 is

$$C^d(r_1, \ G_1, \ \ldots) + I^d(r_1, \ \ldots) + G_1 = Y^s(r_1, \ G_1, \ \ldots) \qquad (13.6)$$
$$(-)\,(-) \qquad\qquad (-) \qquad\qquad\qquad (+)\,(+)$$

(Note that we hold fixed in equation (13.6) the initial stock of capital, K_0, and the level of permanent government purchases, $\bar{G}$.)

The aggregate demand for commodities, Y_1^d, consists of consumption demand, C_1^d, gross investment demand, I_1^d, and government purchases, G_1. Hence, for given values of the two private demands, aggregate demand increases one-to-one with an increase in government purchases. But an increase by 1 unit in purchases, G_1, reduces aggregate consumer demand, C_1^d, by α units. Then, since there is no effect on investment demand, we find that an increase by 1 unit in government purchases raises aggregate demand by $(1 - \alpha)$ units. (We assume below that $\alpha < 1$ applies.) Government purchases also influence the supply of commodities. In particular, since public services are productive, an increase in purchases, G_1, by 1 unit raises the supply of goods, Y_1^s, by β units. (*Warning:* our analysis assumes that taxes are lump sum. When we drop this unrealistic assumption in the next chapter, we introduce some important negative effects from governmental activity on the quantities of goods that people supply and demand.)

Temporary Changes in Government Purchases

Consider a temporary increase in government purchases, where G_1 rises, but permanent purchases, $\bar{G}$, do not change. Empirically, the most important example of this case is military spending during wars. Permanent purchases typically rise also in this situation, but by less than the increase in current purchases. In order to simplify matters, we assume here that permanent purchases do not change.

Recall that the government's budget constraint for period 1 is

$$G_1 + V_1/P_1 = T_1/P_1 + (M_1 - M_0)/P_1 \qquad (13.7)$$

Therefore, an increase in purchases, G_1, must involve some combination of an increase in real taxes, T_1/P_1, a decrease in real transfers, V_1/P_1, or an increase in the real revenue from money creation, $(M_1 - M_0)/P_1$. Because we assume lump-sum taxes and transfers, our analysis of the real variables in the commodity market will be the same, regardless of which combination we specify. Therefore, let's think of the extra purchases as financed by more real taxes, T_1/P_1.

We can use the condition for clearing the commodity market, equation (13.6), to find the responses to a temporary increase in government purchases. As mentioned before, aggregate demand rises by the fraction $(1 - \alpha)$ of the extra purchases, while aggregate supply rises by the fraction β. Notice that, if $\alpha + \beta < 1$, as we assume below, then the increase in aggregate demand $(1 - \alpha)$ exceeds that in supply (β).

Consider the inequality, $\alpha + \beta < 1$. This condition says that if government purchases expand by 1 unit, then people get back less than 1 unit in the combined response from the substitution for consumer spending, α, and the increase in private output, β. One easy way to ensure this condition is to assume that public services are useless—that is, the government essentially buys up goods and then throws them into the ocean. In this case we have the condition, $\alpha = \beta = 0$. Although this viewpoint is popular (and appears implicitly in many macromodels), it may not be the most interesting way to model the functions of government!

More generally, as mentioned before, the two parameters, α and β, tend to decline as the quantity of public services rises. Therefore, our analysis applies in the range where the amount of government purchases is high enough so that the sum, $\alpha + \beta$, is less than one. Notice that, if $\alpha + \beta > 1$ applies, then an increase in public services looks like a good idea. That's because the cost of the additional services—say, 1 unit of goods—is less than the substitution for aggregate consumer spending plus the addition to output. But, the reverse inequality, $\alpha + \beta < 1$, does not necessarily mean that government purchases are too large. Remember that people might like public services a lot even if they substitute little for private spending—that is, even if the parameter α is small.

Figure 13.3 shows the effects on the commodity market when government purchases increase. Without this increase, the market clears at the real interest rate, r_1^*. Then the rise in purchases increases the aggregate quantities of goods demanded and supplied. But notice that the rightward shift of the aggregate demand curve

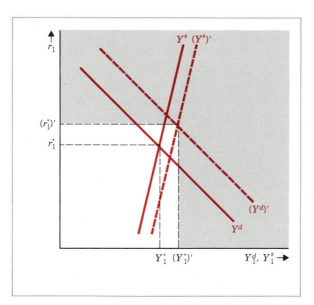

Figure 13.3 **Effect on the Commodity Market of a Temporary Rise in Government Purchases**
The temporary increase in purchases raises aggregate demand by more than supply. Therefore, the real interest rate and output both rise.

exceeds that of the supply curve. Therefore, at the real interest rate, r_1^*, there is now excess demand for commodities. Hence, the real interest rate increases to the value $(r_1^*)'$.

Figure 13.3 shows that output increases. There are two elements behind this increase. First, we assume that public services are productive. Second, the increase in the real interest rate motivates people to work more.

Consider now the composition of output. We know that government purchases rise. But private uses of output—for consumption and investment—decline. Consumption demand falls for two reasons. First, there is the substitution of public services for private spending. However, if we are talking about more military spending, then this effect is likely to be weak—that is, the parameter α is small. Second, the higher real interest rate induces people to postpone their expenditures. This second effect accounts also for the drop in investment demand. Notice that the increase in government purchases **crowds out** private spending. That is, because of the higher real interest rate and the direct substitution of public services for consumer spending, the addition to government purchases induces consumers and investors to spend less.

We suggested before that investment demand is especially sensitive to variations in the real interest rate. Therefore, unless the direct substitution of public services for consumer spending is strong, we predict that the temporary increase in government purchases will mostly crowd out investment (including purchases of consumer durables), rather than consumption.

Since consumption and investment decrease, it follows that total output rises by less than the increase in government purchases. That is, the ratio of the change in output to the change in purchases is positive, but less than one. If the ratio were greater than one, then we would say that a change in government purchases has a multiplicative effect on output. But we do not get this sort of **multiplier** in our model. That's because the economy works to buffer shocks, rather than to magnify them. In particular, the rise in government purchases leads to an increase in work effort, and to decreases in private demands for consumption and investment. Each of these responses serves to alleviate the initial excess demand for goods. (When we study the Keynesian model in Chapter 19 we shall reexamine the potential for a multiplier.)

Let's think about why the temporary increase in government purchases raises the real interest rate. There is a temporarily large governmental demand for goods, which may derive from a war or some other emergency. So, the high real interest rate signals people to work harder, to produce more goods, and to reduce demands for private consumption and investment. Thus, the market uses the real interest rate to achieve the appropriate allocations over time for work effort, production, consumption and investment.[5]

Our discussion refers to wars as cases where government purchases are temporarily high. But there are other aspects of major wars that can substantially affect

---

[5]For some additional discussion, see Robert Hall, ''Labor Supply and Aggregate Fluctuations,'' *Carnegie-Rochester Conference Series on Public Policy,* January 1980.

the analysis. One feature is the widespread use of rationing to hold down private demands for goods. Others are the military draft, confiscation of property, and appeals to patriotism in order to stimulate work and production. Essentially, direct controls can be a rough substitute for a higher real interest rate as a mechanism for crowding out private spending and for stimulating work and production. Then our general conclusions about quantities—output, consumption, investment, and employment—will still hold. But we may no longer see the increase in the real interest rate.

Evidence from Wartime Experiences

The Behavior of Output and Other Quantities

We can assess some effects of temporarily high government purchases by looking at the four most recent wars for the United States—World War I, World War II, Korea, and Vietnam. Table 13.2 describes the behavior of military spending, real gross national product (GNP), and the major components of GNP during these episodes.

The basic method of analysis is similar to one that we used before in order to examine recessions. For example, we contrast the peak year of the Korean War, 1952, with the base year, 1950. Then we find that real military spending is above its trend value by $56 billion, which is 10% of trend real GNP.[6] On the other hand, real GNP is $33 billion or 6% above its own trend.

Next, we calculate the ratio of excess real GNP and its various components to the excess of real military spending. Note that for GNP the ratio in 1952 is 0.59. Hence—assuming that the boost in military spending is the only major change to the economy—this result supports the theory's predictions. Namely, the temporary increase in government purchases has a positive, but less than one-to-one effect on output.

Since GNP rises by less than the increase in military spending, it follows that the nonmilitary components of GNP must decline overall. The figures shown for 1952 in Table 13.2 indicate that total investment (gross fixed investment, purchases of consumer durables and changes in business incentives) declines by the fraction, 0.42, of the increase in military spending. In contrast, consumer expenditures for nondurables and services decline by only the fraction, 0.01. Thus, the temporary excess of military purchases crowds out mostly the investment part of private spending. Recall that the theory predicts this outcome, since military spending would have little direct substitution for consumer spending.

The final rows of the table show the effects on employment. Notice that total employment (numbers of persons working, including military personnel) in 1952 is above trend by 1.5 million or 2.4% of the trend value. This total divides up between 1.9 million extra military personnel and 0.4 million less civilian workers.

---

[6]As before, we use a trend growth rate of 3.0% per year for real GNP and its components.

Table 13.2 The Behavior of Output and Its Components during Wartime

	1918	1944	1952	1968
Peak year of war	1918	1944	1952	1968
Base year for comparison	1916	1947	1950	1965
Excess real military spending (billions of 1972 dollars)	39.7	240.2	56.1	20.0
Excess as % of trend real GNP	18.0	55.9	9.9	2.0
Excess of real GNP (billions of 1972 dollars)	23.2	139.3	32.9	41.3
Excess as % of trend real GNP	10.5	32.4	5.8	4.1
Ratio to excess real military spending for the excess of:				
Real GNP	0.58	0.58	0.59	2.06
Real personal consumption expenditures	0.04	−0.10	−0.14	1.22
durables	—	−0.06	−0.13	0.44
nondurables	—	−0.04	−0.01	0.78
Real gross fixed investment	−0.22	−0.18	−0.17	−0.04
nonresidential	—	−0.11	−0.02	0.14
residential	—	−0.07	−0.15	−0.18
Real change in business inventories	−0.09	−0.01	−0.12	−0.20
Other*	−0.15	−0.13	0.02	0.08
Excess of employment (millions)				
Total employment	2.1	8.4	1.5	2.5
Military personnel	2.7	9.9	1.9	0.7
Civilian employment	−0.6	−1.5	−0.4	1.8
Excess of total employment as % of trend value	5.3	14.8	2.4	3.2

*Nonmilitary government purchases and exports less imports.

Note: The method for calculating the excess or shortfall in each component is discussed in the text.

Sources: For World War II, the Korean War, and the Vietnam War, the data are from *Economic Report of the President,* 1983. For 1916 and 1918, the data on real GNP are from the U.S. Department of Commerce, *The National Income & Product Accounts of the U.S., 1929–76,* p. 72. Estimates for the components of real GNP use the data from John W. Kendrick, *Productivity Trends in the U.S.,* Princeton University Press, Princeton, N.J., 1961, Tables A-I and A-IIa. The shares of real GNP shown in each year from Kendrick's data are applied to the Commerce Department's figures on total real GNP to estimate values for real military spending, real personal consumption expenditures, real gross fixed investment, and real changes in business inventories.

We apply a similar procedure for World War II. However, since the economy had still not fully recovered from the Great Depression in 1940, we use 1947 as the base year. Basically, the findings are similar to those from the Korean War, except that the magnitudes are much larger. For example, the excess of real military spending in 1944 is $240 billion, which is 56% of trend real GNP. Then real GNP is $139 billion or 32% above its own trend. Note that the ratio of excess GNP to excess military spending, 0.58, is virtually the same as that for the Korean War.

For World War II, we find that the excess military spending crowds out total investment (gross fixed investment, purchases of consumer durables, and changes in business inventories) by a fraction of 0.25, and consumer purchases of nondurables and services by a fraction of 0.04. Thus, this breakdown is similar to that for the Korean War. Finally, total employment for 1944 exceeds its trend value by 8.4 million or 15%. This total breaks down into 9.9 million extra military personnel and 1.5 million less civilian workers.

For World War I, we find that the excess of real GNP above trend in 1918 is again 0.58 times the excess of real military spending. (The closeness of the estimated ratios for 1918, 1944, and 1952 must be a coincidence!) Here, we lack the data to break down consumption into durable and nondurable components. But the total of personal consumption expenditures exceeds its trend by 0.04 times the excess of military spending. In contrast, the shortfall in the sum of gross fixed investment and changes in business inventories is 0.31 times the excess of military spending. Thus, we find again that more government purchases mostly crowds out private investment. (We should be cautious about the detailed results for World War I, because the breakdown of GNP into its components is subject to large measurement errors for these years.) Finally, note that total employment in 1918 is above its trend by 2.1 million or 5.3%. In this case there are 2.7 extra military personnel and 0.6 million less civilian workers.

The results for Vietnam differ sharply from those for the other wars. To begin with, using 1965 as the base year, we estimate the excess of real military spending for 1968 as $20 billion, which is only 2% of trend real GNP. Thus, unlike the other cases, it is doubtful that the increase in military spending is the overriding influence on the economy in the middle and late 1960s.

The estimated excess of real GNP for 1968 is $41 billion or 4% of trend real GNP. Thus, the excess real GNP is more than twice as large as the excess real military spending. Correspondingly, we find overall that the nonmilitary components of GNP are above trend in 1968. For example, the ratio to excess military spending is 0.20 for total investment and 0.78 for the consumption of nondurables and services. Hence, the United States really was enjoying ''guns and butter'' at this time.

The most likely explanation for these results is that the economy was experiencing a boom in the 1960s that had little to do with the Vietnam War. This viewpoint is supported by the high growth rate of output in the period before the main increase in military spending. In particular, from 1961 to 1965, the average annual growth rate for real GNP of 5.1% exceeds that from 1965 to 1968, which is 4.3%.

Suppose now that we focus on the results for the Korean War, World War II, and World War I. Then there is an interesting comparison between the behavior of the economy during wartime and during recessions. First, the contrast between wars and recessions concerns the relation between changes in total output and changes in private spending. Total output rises in wars, but falls during recessions. However, private spending declines in both cases. Second, the wartime experiences are similar to recessions in that the major adjustments to private spending occur in the investment components. In particular, as with the seven postwar recessions, we find relatively small reductions in consumer purchases of nondurables and services during the Korean War and World War II. Finally, let's stress the finding that temporarily high government purchases raise total output and employment. But as predicted, the ratio of the excess in real GNP to the excess in purchases is less than one.

The Behavior of Real Interest Rates

The theory predicts that temporarily high government purchases, such as in wartime, raise the real interest rate. However, we have to be careful when matching up this prediction with the wartime behavior of interest rates. Recall that our previous theoretical analysis assumes that government purchases are temporarily high only for the current period. But, during wars, military expenditures tend to build up for awhile and then recede at the end of the war. Also, the length of the buildup and the timing of the war's conclusion (or who wins!) are unknown at the outset.

One implication from the theory is that the average real interest rate should be high over the period from the peak of a war until some time after the war finishes. Thus, Table 13.3 reports averages of interest rates over six-year intervals, beginning with the peak year of each war. Thereby, the figures include between one and five years of peacetime after each war. Notice that the table considers the four wars that we just studied, plus the Civil War. In each case we calculate the average for the nominal interest rate on prime commercial paper over six-year periods. Then we compute real interest rates by subtracting the average rate of change of the GNP deflator. (For the Civil War, we lack data on the GNP deflator and therefore use the consumer price index.)

For the Civil War, the average real interest rate over the period 1863–68 is 2.2%. This rate is substantially less than the averages for 1840–60 and 1867–80, which are each 9.1%. For World War I, the average real interest rate over the

Table 13.3 Interest Rates During Wartime

Period	π_t	R_t	r_t
1863–68	4.8	7.0	2.2
1918–23	2.7	5.8	3.1
1944–49	6.2	1.0	−5.2
1952–57	2.2	2.6	0.4
1968–73	5.2	6.6	1.4

Note: All values are averages, expressed at annual percentage rates, for the periods indicated. π_t is the inflation rate, based on the consumer price index for the period 1863–68, and on the GNP deflator for the other periods. R_t is the interest rate on 4 to 6-month prime commercial paper, $r_t = R_t - \pi_t$.

Sources: See Table 12.1 of Chapter 12.

interval 1918–23 is 3.1%. This value equals the average for 1900–16, but is below the average of 4.9% for 1920–40. Next, for World War II, the average over the period 1944–49 is −5.2%, which is well below the averages of 4.9% for 1920–40 and −0.2% for 1947–60.

For the two most recent wars, Korea and Vietnam, the average real interest rates are 0.4% (for 1952–57) and 1.4% (for 1968–73), respectively. These values do not differ greatly from the average for 1948–82, which is 1.3%.

Overall, the results surely do not confirm a positive effect of wartime spending on real interest rates. In fact, the real interest rates tend to be below average during the wars.

Especially for World War II, we can explain some of the results from the rationing of consumption and private investment, and from the direct pressures to work and produce, which include the military draft. With few goods to buy and little option to take leisure, people may hold financial assets even when they pay negative real interest rates. Also, World War II differs from the Civil War and World War I in that the price level does not decline after the war. Thus, taking the period 1944–49 as a whole, the average inflation rate of 6.2% per year probably exceeded expectations.[7] Correspondingly, the average real interest rate of −5.2% was below expectations.

Some additional evidence on the relation between wartime spending and interest rates comes from a long-period study of the United Kingdom by Dan Benjamin and Levis Kochin.[8] Looking over the period, 1729–1931, they discover a significantly positive effect from temporary increases in real military spending on long-term interest rates. Specifically, for each percentage point that spending exceeds its trend, they find that the interest rate rises by about one-quarter of a percentage point.[9] Thus, these results are more in line with the theory than are those for the United States.

Permanent Changes in Government Purchases

The previous analysis applies to temporary changes in government purchases, such as in wartime. In other cases there are long-lasting shifts in the size of government, with respect to its purchases and public services. For example, the data that we

---

[7]During the war, price controls kept down at least the reported values of the inflation rate. But since these controls were lifted before 1949, this element should not have a major effect on the average inflation rate over the period, 1944–49.

[8]"War, Prices and Interest Rates: Gibson's Paradox Revisited," in Michael D. Bordo and Anna J. Schwartz, eds., *A Retrospective on the Classical Gold Standard, 1821–1931,* University of Chicago Press for the National Bureau of Economic Research, Chicago, in press.

[9]These results refer to the nominal interest rate on British consols, which are bonds that pay a perpetual stream of coupons, but have no maturity date. (The confidence in the durability of the British empire used to be great.) Benjamin and Kochin do not separate the change in the real interest rate from that of the nominal rate. However, over their period of study, the long-term inflation rate in the United Kingdom was close to zero.

looked at before show permanent increases in the ratio of total government purchases to GNP during the 1930s and the 1950s. But we do not see major changes in this ratio for the 1960s and the 1970s.

In order to study the effects of permanent changes in government purchases, we have to allow for a change in permanent purchases, $\tilde{G}$. For convenience, let's now hold fixed the current level of purchases, G_1. (In this case an increase in permanent purchases must reflect a rise in the anticipated values of some future purchases.) Once we work out this case, we can also combine a change in current purchases, G_1, with a change in permanent purchases, $\tilde{G}$.

We found before that an increase by 1 unit in permanent purchases subtracts the equivalent of 1 unit of real income per period from households. However, an increase in permanent purchases also implies an increase in the normal flow of public services. Therefore, in a full sense, an increase by 1 unit in permanent purchases does not subtract the equivalent of 1 unit of real income per period from households. First, if $\tilde{G}$ rises by 1 unit, then in the aggregate households effectively get back α units per period in services that substitute directly for consumer spending. Therefore, people do not have to use their own funds to buy these services. Second, because public services are productive, producers in the aggregate get back β units per period in extra output. Therefore, on net, an increase by 1 unit in permanent purchases, $\tilde{G}$, subtracts the equivalent of $(1 - \alpha - \beta)$ units of real income per period from households. That is, the aggregate of permanent income effectively declines by $(1 - \alpha - \beta)$ units. Recall that we assume the condition, $\alpha + \beta < 1$, which means that permanent income declines when permanent purchases rise.

Let's think about how people respond to an increase by 1 unit in permanent purchases, $\tilde{G}$. We know that the aggregate of permanent income effectively declines by $(1 - \alpha - \beta)$ units. Therefore, if work effort did not change, then households would reduce current aggregate consumption demand, C_1^d, by roughly $(1 - \alpha - \beta)$ units. (Recall that this period's government purchases, G_1, do not change. Therefore, we do not have to worry about the substitution of current public services for current consumer spending.)

More generally, because of the decline in permanent income, households tend also to increase aggregate work effort, L_1, and thereby, to raise the supply of goods, Y_1^s. Then, to the extent that people increase the supply of goods, they can reduce consumption by something less than $(1 - \alpha - \beta)$ units. But we still find that the magnitude of the fall in consumption, when added to the increase in the supply of goods, equals $(1 - \alpha - \beta)$ units.

Now, we can incorporate the level of permanent purchases, $\tilde{G}$, into the condition for clearing the commodity market. The expanded condition is

$$C^d(r_1, \ G_1, \ \tilde{G}, \ \ldots) + I^d(r_1, \ \ldots) + G_1 = Y^s(r_1, \ G_1, \ \tilde{G}, \ \ldots) \quad (13.8)$$
$$(-)\ (-)\ (-) \qquad\qquad (-) \qquad\qquad\qquad (+)\ (+)\ (+)$$

Notice that an increase in permanent purchases, $\tilde{G}$, lowers consumer demand, C_1^d, and raises supply, Y_1^s.

In order to model a permanent increase in government purchases at date 1, we have to allow simultaneously for increases in actual purchases, G_1, and in permanent purchases, $\tilde{G}$. Consider first the effects of this type of change on consumer demand in equation (13.8). Recall that an increase by 1 unit in actual purchases, G_1, lowers consumer demand, C_1^d, by α units. Next, an increase by one unit in permanent purchases, $\tilde{G}$, means that the aggregate of permanent income declines by $(1 - \alpha - \beta)$ units. Thereby, the size of the decline in consumer demand, C_1^d, plus the rise in supply, Y_1^s, is roughly equal to the quantity, $(1 - \alpha - \beta)$. Let the increase in supply be the amount a. Then consumer demand changes by the amount, $-(1 - \alpha - \beta) + a$. [Note that $0 < a < (1 - \alpha - \beta)$ must apply.] Hence, consumer demand changes overall by the amount, $-\alpha$, plus the quantity, $-(1 - \alpha - \beta) + a$, which equals $-(1 - \beta) + a$. We summarize these results in the second column of Table 13.4.

Recall that government purchases have no direct impact on investment demand. Then, since government purchases, G_1, enter one-to-one into aggregate demand, we find that the net increase in aggregate demand, Y_1^d, is the amount $1 - (1 - \beta) + a = \beta + a$. We show this result in column 5 of the table.

Now, let's look at aggregate supply in equation (13.8). An increase by one unit in purchases, G_1, raises supply, Y_1^s, by β units. Also, the increase in permanent purchases raises supply by the amount a. Therefore, column 6 of the table shows that aggregate supply increases by the amount, $\beta + a$.

The important finding is that aggregate demand and supply increase by the same amount, $\beta + a$. Therefore, when actual and permanent purchases increase by equal amounts, we end up with no effect on excess demand. The last column of Table 13.4 shows this result.

Figure 13.4 depicts the effects graphically. Notice that the permanent increase

Table 13.4 Effects of Government Purchases on the Excess Demand for Commodities

(1)	(2)	(3)	(4)	(5)	(6)	(7)
				Impact On		
Increase By 1 Unit In	C_1^d	I_1^d	G_1	Y_1^d	Y_1^s	$Y_1^d - Y_1^s$
G_1	$-\alpha$	0	1	$1 - \alpha$	β	$1 - \alpha - \beta$
$\tilde{G}$	$-(1 - \alpha - \beta) + a$	0	0	$-(1 - \alpha - \beta) + a$	a	$--(1 - \alpha - \beta)$
G_1 and $\tilde{G}$	$-(1 - \beta) + a$	0	1	$\beta + a$	$\beta + a$	0

Note: We show the effects of increases in actual and permanent purchases, G_1 and $\tilde{G}$, on the components of commodity demand—C_1^d, I_1^d and G_1—and on supply, Y_1^s. The effect on aggregate demand, Y_1^d, is the sum of the effects on the three components of demand. Then the effect on excess demand, $Y_1^d - Y_1^s$, is the effect on aggregate demand less that on aggregate supply.

We use the positive parameter a to denote the response of supply, Y_1^s, to an increase in permanent purchases. Note that the impact on consumer demand, C_1^d, is then the amount, $-(1 - \alpha - \beta) + a$. Since the net change in consumer demand is negative, we have the condition, $0 < a < (1 - \alpha - \beta)$.

Notice that a permanent increase in current purchases—where G_1 and $\tilde{G}$ rise together—raises aggregate demand and supply by equal amounts. Hence, excess demand does not change.

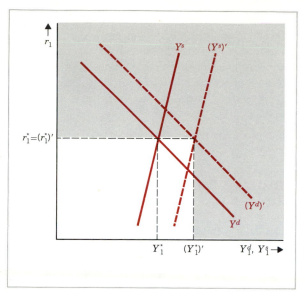

Figure 13.4 **Effects on the Commodity Market of a Permanent Rise in Government Purchases**

The permanent increase in purchases raises aggregate demand and supply by roughly equal amounts. Therefore, output increases, but the real interest rate does not change.

in government purchases shifts the demand and supply curves rightward by equal amounts. Therefore, aggregate demand still equals aggregate supply at the initial real interest rate, r_1^*. In other words, the permanent expansion of government purchases has no effect on the real interest rate.

Figure 13.4 shows that output increases. Note that there are two elements behind this response. First, public services are productive, and second, the decrease in permanent income motivates people to work harder.

Consider next the composition of output. To begin with, government purchases increase. But there are two forces that lower consumer demand. First, public services substitute for private spending, and second, the reduction in permanent income induces people to consume less. However, since the real interest rate does not change, there is no effect on investment. Note that this last result differs sharply from the findings when the change in government purchases is temporary. Then, because of the rise in the real interest rate, more government purchases crowded out both forms of private spending. Now, when the change in purchases is permanent, the extra government purchases crowd out only consumer spending.

Since consumption decreases, while investment does not change, it follows that total output increases by less than the rise in government purchases. That is, the ratio of the change in output to the change in purchases is again positive, but less than one. Thus, we still do not have a multiplier in the model.

Let's think about why the real interest rate increases when the rise in government purchases is temporary, but does not change when the rise in purchases is permanent. A temporary boost in purchases, as in wartime, triggers an incentive to substitute resources intertemporally—in particular, to work and produce more than normal and to consume and invest less than usual during the current period. Then the higher real interest rate guides people toward these responses. But when the increase in government purchases is permanent, people have fewer resources to spend in every period. Therefore, while there is an incentive to reduce consumption and leisure at all dates, there is no reason to do anything unusual in the current period. Hence, the real interest rate does not change.

Permanent and Temporary Changes in Government Purchases— Statistical Estimates of the Effects on Output

I have carried out a statistical study, which divides the observed values of real government purchases into temporary and permanent parts.[10] When considering the ratio of real government purchases to real GNP in the United States, it turns out that most of the changes in this ratio are unpredictable. That is, given the information that people have at any date, it is impossible to forecast the great majority of increases or decreases that occur in this ratio. Therefore, people cannot usually say whether the currently observed ratio of government purchases to GNP is temporarily high or low. Hence, as their best guess, people perceive as permanent most of the observed movements in this ratio. The only systematic exception that I was able to isolate statistically concerns wartime. Not surprisingly, the ratio of defense spending to GNP is unusually high during wars. Therefore, people anticipate declines in this ratio after each war (they also expect each war to end eventually!).

Figure 13.5 plots from 1930 to 1978 the ratio of real defense purchases to real GNP, which is denoted by G^w/Y. Also plotted are my estimates of the permanent part of this ratio, $(\widetilde{G^w/Y})$, and the temporary part, $G^w/Y - (\widetilde{G^w/Y})$. Notice that the estimates of temporary purchases are positive only during and close to the three wars for the period: from 1940–46 for World War II, 1951–54 for the Korean War, and 1967–69 for the Vietnam War.

There are also some important movements in the permanent part of the ratio for defense purchases. The main ones are the net increase during World War II (from 1940 to 1946), the sharp rise at the end of the Korean War (1952–53), and the decrease from the early 1960s through 1978. (This particular study ends in 1978.)

The ratio of real nondefense government purchases to real GNP, denoted by G^p/Y, appears in Figure 13.6. Here, my statistical analysis did not isolate any temporary variations (except for a temporary reduction during wartime). That is, at any date, the current ratio is also the best forecast for future ratios.

---

[10]The results are in Robert Barro, ''Output Effects of Government Purchases,'' *Journal of Political Economy,* December 1981.

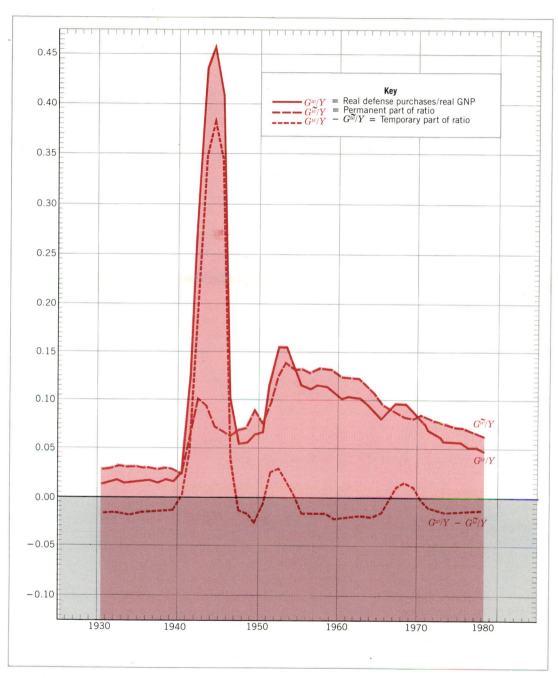

Figure 13.5 The Ratio of Defense Purchases to GNP—A Breakdown into Temporary and Permanent Parts

321

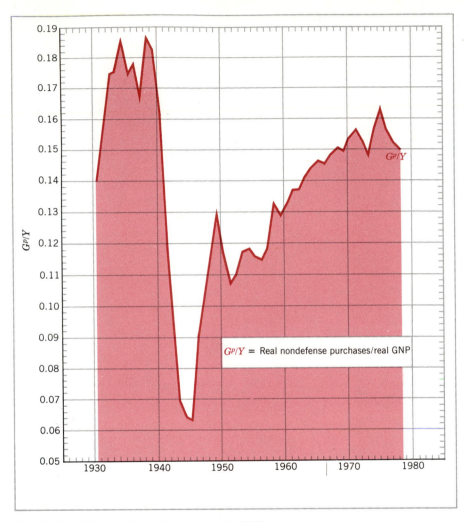

Figure 13.6 The Ratio of Nondefense Purchases to GNP.

I used statistical techniques to estimate the effects on output from temporary and permanent changes in government purchases. The results for the period 1946–78 indicate the following effects on real GNP from a change by one unit in the various categories of purchases:[11]

---

[11]Some problems arise in using the data for World War II. But most of the results are similar if the data for 1942–45 are included. The main change is a lower estimate for the effect of temporary defense purchases on output. Here, the range of effects becomes 0.5 to 0.8.

Change by 1 Unit In	Estimated Number of Units by Which Real GNP Increases
temporary defense purchases	0.5 to 1.2
permanent defense purchases	0.3 to 0.7
permanent nondefense purchases	−0.2 to 1.3

In each case there is a range of estimates for the effects on real GNP. But in a statistical sense, we can be reasonably confident that the true effects lie within these intervals.

For defense purchases, the results show a strong positive impact on output. Also, the estimated responses for temporary changes tend to exceed those for permanent changes. Note that the estimates imply that output rises by between 50% and 120% of a temporary increase in defense purchases. Thus, these findings are broadly consistent with the less formal results that we observed before during wartime. There, we found that the excess of real GNP—during World Wars I and II and the Korean War—was about 60% of the excess of real military spending.

Now, we see that real GNP rises by between 30% and 70% of a permanent increase in defense purchases. Since the response is again less than 100%, we find that a permanent rise in purchases must crowd out some private spending.

For nondefense purchases, there were no temporary changes to analyze. Therefore, the results apply only to permanent changes. Unfortunately, the estimates are imprecise, covering the range of responses for output from −20% to +130% of the change in purchases. Therefore, while a positive effect is likely, we cannot pinpoint the magnitude.

Effects of Government Purchases on the Price Level

People often say that government spending is inflationary. So, let's see what the model says about the effects of government purchases on the price level.

We again look at the condition for all cash to be willingly held. For period 1 we have

$$M_1/P_1 = H(Y_1, \ R_1, \ G_1, \ . \ . \ .),$$
$$(+) \ (-) \ (-)$$

(13.9)

where H is again the function for real money demanded. Here, we assume that total output, Y_1, measures real transactions, which have a positive effect on the real demand for money. As before, the nominal interest rate, R_1, has a negative effect on the real demand for money.

We also enter government purchases, G_1, in the money-demand function with a negative sign. Since public services are provided free of charge to users, there are fewer monetary transactions associated with government purchases than with private consumption or investment. Therefore, for a given level of total output, an increase in government purchases, G_1, means less real money demanded.

Now, let's explore the consequences for the price level of an increase in government purchases, G_1. If the increase is permanent, there is an increase in output, Y_1, but no change in the real interest rate. Thus, unless the direct negative effect of government purchases on real money demanded is substantial, we find that real money demand increases. Therefore, if the behavior of the nominal money stock does not change, then we are likely to get a negative effect of government purchases on the price level, P_1.

If the increase in government purchases is temporary, then there is also an increase in the real interest rate, r_1. Hence, for a given expected rate of inflation, π_1^e, the nominal interest rate, R_1, rises. This element lowers the real demand for money, which makes it more likely that the price level rises.

Overall, for a given behavior of money, there is little basis to predict systematic effects of government purchases on the price level. Moreover, even if there were a positive effect, this channel would not account for chronic rises in prices—that is, for inflation. Rather, each increase in government purchases—relative to the scale of the economy—would generate a one-time rise in the price level. In order to explain inflation on this basis, we would need continuing expansions in the relative importance of government purchases. Yet, as we saw before, government purchases have not changed much in relation to GNP in the 1960s and 1970s, which are the years when United States inflation became significant.

An increase in government purchases may also be inflationary because it stimulates money creation. That is, governments may resort to greater real revenue from printing money in order to finance some part of the higher level of purchases. Of course, this mechanism applies equally well to the government's transfer payments, which are another form of government spending. Notice that this mechanism connects a higher level of real spending to a faster growth rate of money and thereby to a higher rate of inflation. Hence, this route does show how higher real government spending can be inflationary.

Empirically, there is not much evidence that changes in government purchases influence the price level, once we hold fixed the behavior of money. But for some countries, there are important linkages between real government spending and the rate of money creation. In other words, when some governments opt to raise real spending, they use the printing press to pay for part of it. For example, as discussed in Chapter 8, the connection between government spending and monetary growth is very close during the German hyperinflation from 1921–23.

For the United States, there is no evidence that long-term changes in government spending as a ratio to GNP lead to higher rates of monetary growth. However, the sharp expansions of spending that occur during wartime do trigger a lot of money creation. That is, like most countries, the U.S. finances part of its wartime spending with the printing press. Hence, this mechanism accounts for some of the inflation that usually accompanies wars.

Summary

We introduced government purchases of goods and services as another use of output. In order to finance these expenditures and its transfer payments, the government levies lump-sum taxes or prints money. Then the government uses its purchases to provide a flow of public services. An additional unit of these services substitutes for α units of aggregate consumer spending, and also raises production by β units. We assume the condition, $\alpha + \beta < 1$, which means that people get back directly less than the cost of an additional unit of public services.

A temporary increase in government purchases, as in wartime, raises aggregate demand by more than supply. Hence, the real interest rate and output increase. However, the crowding-out of investment and consumption means that total output rises by less than the increase in government purchases. That is, there is no multiplier.

The evidence from World Wars I and II and Korea supports the theory's predictions with respect to quantities. In particular, real GNP rises, but by only about 60% of the increase in real military spending. Thus, there is crowding-out of private spending, especially investment. However, the real interest rate does not tend to rise during wartime—in fact, the rates turn out to be below average at these times. On the other hand, some long-period evidence for the United Kingdom suggests a positive effect of wartime spending on interest rates.

A permanent increase in government purchases amounts to a reduction in permanent income, which lowers consumer demand and raises work effort. The expansions of aggregate demand and supply turn out to be roughly equal. Therefore, output again increases, but there is no change in the real interest rate. In this case, the crowding-out of private spending falls entirely on consumption.

Finally, we examine the connection between government purchases and inflation. For a given behavior of the money stock, the model does not predict any strong linkages. However, more government spending is inflationary if it induces the government to print money at a faster rate.

Important Terms and Concepts

lump-sum taxes

disposable real income

permanent government purchases

public good

crowding out (from government purchases)

multiplier

QUESTIONS AND PROBLEMS

Mainly for Review

13.1 What are the channels by which government spending affects excess demand in the commodity market? How does it affect utility? Can you think of examples of public services that are not close substitutes for consumption ($\alpha = 0$) but nevertheless provide utility?

13.2 Could government services be a substitute for leisure? If so, what additional channel of effect on the commodity market would you expect?

13.3 Explain why it is the present value of government purchases that affects households' budgets. Would this be the case if households did not have access to a credit market? Illustrate your answer by considering the effect on consumption if G_t rises as in Table 13.1, but households are unable to borrow or lend.

13.4 Why does the interest rate rise as a result of a temporary increase in government purchases? Does real saving necessarily decrease?

13.5 Distinguish between (a) a rise in permanent government purchases, and (b) a permanent rise in government purchases. Which of the two has a wealth effect on consumption? Which has an intertemporal substitution effect?

13.6 What is crowding out? Does it involve an intertemporal substitution effect alone? Could there be direct substitution of government purchases for private investment purchases?

Problems for Discussion

13.7 Government Purchases in the National Accounts
The national accounts treat all of government purchases as a part of real GNP. But suppose that these purchases, G_t, are an input to private production—that is, in the aggregate, $Y_t = F(K_{t-1}, L_t, G_t)$. Then public services are an intermediate product—that is, a good that enters as an input into a later stage of production. Hence, we ought not to include these services in real GNP, which tries to measure only final product.

a. Suppose that businesses initially hire private guards. But the government then provides free police protection, which substitutes for the guards. Assume that the private guards and police are equally efficient and receive the same incomes. How does the switch from private to public services affect measured real GNP?

b. How would you change the treatment of public services in the national accounts? Is your proposal practical?
(These issues are discussed in Simon Kuznets, ''Discussion of the New Department of Commerce Income Series,'' *Review of Economics and Statistics*, August 1948, pp. 156–57; and Richard Musgrave, *Theory of Public Finance*, McGraw-Hill, New York, 1959, pp. 186–88.)

13.8 Public Ownership of Capital and the National Accounts

When the government produces goods and services, the national accounts measure the contribution to GNP by the government's purchases from the private sector of labor, materials and new capital goods. But the accounts neglect any contribution to output from the flow of services on government-owned capital. The accounts also do not subtract depreciation of this capital to calculate net product.

a. What happens to measured GNP if the government gives its capital to a private business and then buys the final goods from that business?

b. How would you change the treatment of government-owned capital in the national accounts? Is your proposal practical?

13.9 The Role of Public Services

We assume that an additional unit of public services has two direct effects: first, it substitutes for α units of private consumption, and second, it raises production by β units.

a. Consider various categories of government purchases, such as military spending, police, highways, public transit, research and development expenditures, regulatory agencies, etc. How do you think the parameters, α and β, vary across the categories? Are the parameters always positive?

b. Consider a permanent increase in government purchases. How do the sizes of the responses in output and consumption depend on the values of the parameters, α and β? Explain the results.

c. Repeat part **b** for the case of a temporary increase in government purchases.

13.10 Prospective Changes in Government Purchases

During the current period, date 1, people find out that government purchases will increase permanently in some future period. There is no change in current purchases, or in the time paths of the money stock and real transfers.

a. What happens currently to the real interest rate and the quantities of output, consumption, investment, and employment?

b. What happens to the current price level and nominal interest rate?

c. Can you think of some real-world cases where this question applies?

13.11 Effects of Government Purchases on the Real Wage Rate

Suppose that we include a labor market in the model.

a. What is the effect on the real wage rate from a temporary increase in government purchases?

b. What is the effect from a permanent increase in government purchases?

13.12 Government Employment during Wartime (optional)

In the model we assume that the government buys only final product from the commodity market. In particular, the government neither produces goods nor employs people. This assumption is basically satisfactory if the government's production function is similar to that of private producers. But the assumption is troublesome for wartime. For example, suppose that during World War II the government effectively removes 10 million people temporarily from the civilian labor force. But suppose that the government takes away no privately owned capital. Then, as before, assume that the government also temporarily raises its purchases of goods by a large amount.

a. Analyze the effects on the real interest rate, and on the quantities of output, investment, and consumption. (How did you count the 10 million conscripts in the measure of output?) What happens to total and private employment?

b. If we include a labor market in the model, what happens to the real wage rate?

13.13 The Price Level During the Korean War

With the start of the Korean War, the price level (GNP deflator) rises at an annual rate of 10% from the second quarter of 1950 to the first quarter of 1951. By contrast, the inflation rate is negative for 1949, 1.4% from the first quarter of 1951 to the first quarter of 1952, and 2.0% from the first quarter of 1952 to the first quarter of 1953.

The table below shows over various periods the inflation rate π_t, the growth rates μ_t of currency and $M1$, the growth rate of real government purchases ΔG_t, and the nominal interest rate on three-month Treasury Bills, R_t. Using these data, how can we account for the surge in the price level at the start of the Korean War? (This question does not have a definite answer!)

(*Hint:* Price controls were stringent during World War II. People may have expected a return to these controls under the Korean War in 1950.)

		(Figures in % per Year)			
		($M1$)	(Currency)		
Year and Quarter	π_t	μ_t	μ_t	ΔG_t	R_t
1949.1 to 1950.2	−0.3	1.8	−1.6	2.7	1.1
Start of War					
1950.2 to 1951.1	10.0	4.0	−0.5	24.6	1.3
1951.1 to 1952.1	1.4	5.3	4.7	27.9	1.6
1952.1 to 1953.1	2.0	3.2	4.5	9.2	1.8

13.14 The Optimal Level of Public Services

In our model a permanent increase in government purchases raises output, but lowers consumption and leisure. Recall that we used the condition, $\alpha + \beta < 1$, where α measures the substitution of public services for aggregate consumer spending, and β is the marginal product of public services. We assume also that the parameters, α and β, decline as the quantity of government purchases rises.

Assume first that public services substitute for α units of aggregate consumer spending, but otherwise provide no direct utility. Then

a. What happens to a typical person's utility when the quantity of government purcases rises permanently by 1 unit?

b. If the government wants to maximize a typical person's utility, then where should it set the level of purchases? What condition holds here for the parameters, α and β?

c. Why is it not the right answer in part **b** to choose the level of government purchases that maximizes aggregate output (as measured by real GNP)?

d. Without working through the details, how does the analysis change if public services provide utility in other ways?

CHAPTER 14
TAXES AND TRANSFERS

Thus far, we have taken a highly unrealistic view of the way that governments raise tax revenues. Specifically, we assumed lump-sum taxes, which means that the amount someone pays has nothing to do with their income or other characteristics. In the real world governments levy a variety of taxes, but none of them look like the lump-sum taxes in our theory. Generally, a person's taxes depend on the nature and amount of his or her economic activity. But this dependence motivates changes in behavior. For example, taxes on income deter people from working and investing in order to generate income, while taxes on particular goods deter people from buying them. Overall, the tax system creates a variety of substitution effects on work effort, production, consumption, and investment. In this chapter we extend the theoretical analysis to incorporate some of these effects.

Let's start with an overview of tax collections in the United States. We discuss the different types of levies and indicate how the overall composition has changed over time.

Sources of Government Revenues in the U.S.

Table 14.1 shows the breakdown of revenues by major types for the federal government since 1929. Individual income taxes (including minor amounts of taxes on estates and gifts) are a reasonably stable share of total federal revenues since World War II. For 1982, this share is 49%. The next component, which is corporate income taxes, declines from about 25% of the total after World War II to only 5% in 1982. Then there are levies for social insurance funds, which increase substantially since World War II. In 1982 about 70% of these levies are for social security. The rest are mainly for unemployment insurance and government employees' retirement. Notice that the total of payments into social insurance funds rises from 10% of all federal revenues in 1948 to 35% in 1982. Another part of federal revenues is excise taxes, customs duties, etc., which fall from about 20% of the total after World War II to 8% in 1982. Finally, the Federal Reserve's payments to the Treasury in 1982 amount to 2% of total federal receipts. These proceeds from money creation are near zero before the mid-1950s.

Table 14.1 The Breakdown of Federal Revenues by Types (Figures are Percentages of the Total)

	Individual Income Tax, etc.	Corporate Profits Tax	Excise Tax, Customs Duties, etc.	Social Insurance Levies	Payments from Federal Reserve
1929	33	32	31	3	0
1930	37	24	34	4	0
1	30	21	44	6	0
2	19	19	54	7	0
3	18	17	61	4	0
4	17	18	62	3	0
1935	21	21	55	3	0
6	22	25	45	8	0
7	24	19	34	22	0
8	25	14	34	27	0
9	18	19	35	28	0
1940	16	30	30	23	0
1	13	47	23	16	0
2	21	48	17	14	0
3	42	35	12	11	0
4	43	30	15	12	0
1945	46	24	17	14	0
6	44	22	20	14	0
7	45	25	18	12	0
8	44	27	19	10	0
9	42	24	21	13	1
1950	36	34	18	12	0
1	41	33	15	11	0
2	46	27	15	11	0
3	46	27	16	11	0
4	46	26	15	13	0
1955	43	27	14	12	0
6	45	26	14	14	1
7	46	24	14	15	1
8	47	22	15	16	1
9	44	24	14	17	1

Before World War II, the excise taxes and customs duties are relatively more important. In fact, these items are the major source of federal revenues before World War I. Individual income taxes begin in 1913, except for some levies around the Civil War and in 1895. Corporate taxes start in 1909. Notice also that the levies for social insurance funds are small until the beginning of the unemployment insurance program in 1936 and social security in 1937.

Table 14.2 shows a breakdown for the revenues of state and local governments. Property taxes are traditionally the largest component, but this share falls from about 60% in the early 1930s, to less than 40% after World War II, and to 19%

Table 14.1 (*Continued*)

	Individual Income Tax, etc.	Corporate Profits Tax	Excise Tax, Customs Duties, etc.	Social Insurance Levies	Payments from Federal Reserve
1960	45	21	14	18	1
1	46	21	14	19	1
2	46	20	14	19	1
3	45	21	13	20	1
4	42	21	14	21	1
1965	43	22	13	20	1
6	44	21	11	23	1
7	45	19	11	24	1
8	46	19	10	23	1
9	48	17	10	24	2
1970	48	14	10	26	2
1	45	15	10	27	2
2	48	15	9	28	1
3	44	15	8	31	2
4	46	14	8	31	2
1975	44	13	8	33	2
6	44	15	7	32	2
7	45	15	7	32	2
8	45	15	7	32	2
9	47	13	6	32	2
1980	48	11	8	32	2
1	47	8	10	32	2
2	49	5	8	35	2

Note: In this table the category, corporate profits taxes, does not include the Federal Reserve's payments to the U.S. Treasury, which are shown separately. These items are combined in the national accounts.

Source: U.S. Department of Commerce, *The National Income and Product Accounts of the U.S., 1929–76,* and *U.S. Survey of Current Business,* July 1982, May 1983.

in 1982. In the early period the relative decline in property taxes corresponds to the growth in sales taxes. These increase from 6% of state and local revenues in 1929 to 20% in 1941, but maintain a roughly constant share since World War II. More recently, state and local governments have turned to personal income taxes. This category (which includes minor amounts of levies on gifts and estates) constitutes 4% of state and local receipts in 1929 and 1948, but then increases to 12% in 1982. The other category of state and local revenues that becomes more important since World War II is federal grants-in-aid (transfers of funds from the federal government to state and local governments). These climb from 9% of the total in 1946 to 24% in 1978, but then fall to 19% in 1982. (Federal grants-in-aid are primarily for welfare, medical care, transportation, education, housing, training programs, and general revenue sharing.)

Table 14.2 The Breakdown of State and Local Revenues by Types
(Figures are Percentages of the Total)

	Individual Income Tax, etc.	Corporate Profits Tax	Property Tax	Sales Tax	Social Insurance Levies	Federal Aid	Other
1929	4	2	62	6	2	2	22
1930	4	1	62	7	2	2	22
1	3	1	61	7	2	4	22
2	4	1	62	8	2	2	21
3	2	1	57	9	2	7	22
4	2	1	47	11	2	19	18
1935	3	1	46	13	2	19	16
6	3	2	49	16	2	8	20
7	4	2	47	17	2	8	20
8	4	1	47	17	3	8	20
9	3	2	46	17	3	10	19
1940	3	2	46	18	3	9	19
1	4	3	44	20	3	8	18
2	4	3	43	19	3	8	20
3	4	4	43	18	3	9	19
4	4	4	42	18	3	9	20
1945	5	4	41	20	3	8	19
6	4	4	38	22	5	9	18
7	4	4	36	23	5	11	17
8	4	4	35	23	5	11	18
9	5	3	35	22	5	11	19
1950	4	4	35	23	5	11	18
1	5	4	34	23	6	11	17
2	5	3	34	23	6	10	19
3	5	3	34	23	6	10	19
4	5	3	34	22	7	10	19
1955	5	3	34	22	7	10	19
6	5	3	34	23	7	10	18
7	5	3	34	22	7	11	18
8	5	2	34	24	7	13	15
9	6	3	33	24	7	15	12

Figure 14.1 indicates the federal share of total government revenues. (Federal grants-in-aid are excluded here from total revenues.) Notice that the federal share is 34% in 1929, then falls to a low point of 19% in 1932, but subsequently rises during the New Deal period to reach 49% by 1940. After a peak of 80% during World War II, the share declines to 62% in the early 1970s. For 1982, the number is 64%.

Table 14.2 (*Continued*)

	Individual Income Tax, etc.	Corporate Profits Tax	Property Tax	Sales Tax	Social Insurance Levies	Federal Aid	Other
1960	6	3	34	24	7	13	13
1	6	2	34	24	7	13	14
2	6	3	33	24	7	14	13
3	6	3	33	24	7	14	13
4	7	3	32	24	7	15	12
1965	7	3	32	24	7	15	12
6	7	3	30	24	7	17	12
7	8	3	30	23	7	17	12
8	8	3	29	23	7	17	13
9	9	3	28	24	7	17	12
1970	9	3	28	23	7	18	12
1	9	3	27	23	7	19	12
2	11	3	25	22	6	21	12
3	11	3	24	23	7	21	11
4	10	3	24	23	7	21	12
1975	10	3	23	22	7	23	12
6	11	3	22	22	7	23	12
7	11	4	22	21	7	23	12
8	11	4	20	22	8	24	11
9	12	4	19	22	8	23	12
1980	12	3	18	22	8	23	14
1	12	3	18	22	9	21	15
2	12	2	19	22	9	19	17

Note: Other revenues include hospital and health charges, tuition, fines, motor vehicle licenses, rents and royalties, and some other fees and taxes.

Source: See Table 14.1

Figure 14.2 provides one measure of an overall tax rate. This measure is the ratio of total government revenues (excluding federal grants-in-aid) to GNP. The ratio rises from 11% in 1929 to 18% in 1940 and 25% in 1945. Then, after a fall to 22% in 1949, the ratio increases slowly to 26% in 1956, 28% in 1960, 31% in 1969, and 32% in 1982. Note that the ratio moves from 32% in 1980 to 33% in 1981 and 32% in 1982. Thus, at least the first years of the Reagan tax-cutting program do not produce much change in this overall tax rate.

Figure 14.1 Federal Receipts as a Fraction of Total Government Receipts

Types of Taxes

Notice that some taxes fall on income (individual income taxes, corporate profits taxes and contributions for social security, which are levied on wage earnings), others on expenditures (excise and sales taxes), and some on holdings of property. But one way or another, the amount someone pays depends on their economic activity. That is, none of these look like the lump-sum taxes in our theory.

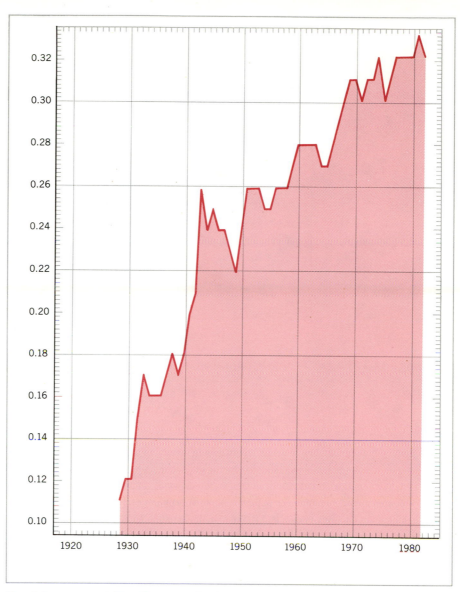

Figure 14.2 Total Government Receipts as a Ratio to GNP

The Federal Individual Income Tax

Let's look briefly at the structure of the federal individual income tax. (In 1982 this category accounts for 48% of federal and 30% of total government receipts.) First, we subtract from someone's reported income the expenses for business purposes, moving, deferred compensation through pension plans, and some other

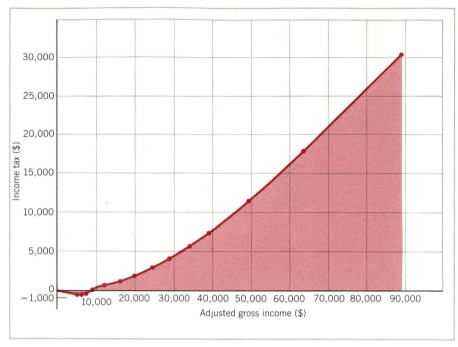

Figure 14.3 The Tax Schedule from the Federal Individual Income Tax in 1982
The graph shows for 1982 the relation of federal income taxes, net of the earned-income credit, to adjusted gross income for a married couple with two children. We assume that all income is "earned" (at least for levels below $10,000) and that deductions are not itemized.

items.[1] That gives us **adjusted gross income.** Then we take out either a standard deduction ($2,300 for a single person, $3,400 for a married couple in 1982) or the itemized deductions for medical care, interest payments, certain taxes, etc. Then we subtract the value of exemptions, which is usually $1,000 per dependent, including oneself. That gives us **taxable income.** Then, aside from any tax credits that apply, the law provides a schedule that relates the amount of tax to taxable income. (Marital status also matters here.) But it is important to note that the tax is not a constant fraction of taxable income—that is, it is not a **flat-rate tax.** Rather, the more income someone receives, the greater is the tax rate on an additional dollar of income. This setup is called a **graduated-rate tax.** (Sometimes, it is called a "progressive tax," which seems to express someone's opinion about its merits. Then a "regressive tax" is one where the rate falls as income rises.)

Figure 14.3 shows the relation of the federal income tax to a family's adjusted gross income. The graph applies in 1982 to a married couple, who have two children and do not itemize deductions. (This assumption is unrealistic at high

---

[1]One of these is the preferential treatment of long-term capital gains. In 1982, when people sell assets that they have held for more than one year, only 40% of the increase in value is subject to tax.

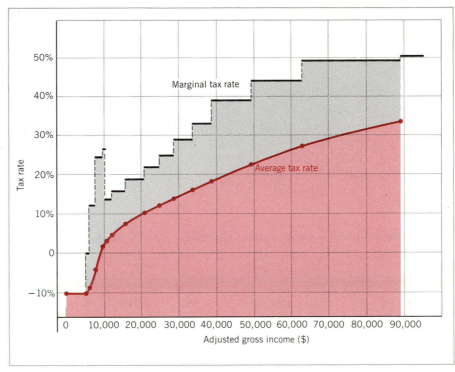

Figure 14.4 Marginal and Average Tax Rates for the Federal Individual Income Tax in 1982
The graph shows for 1982 the relation of marginal and average tax rates to adjusted gross income. We make the same assumptions as in Figure 14.3.

incomes, where most people do itemize their deductions.) So the graph incorporates a standard deduction of $3,400 and an exemption of $4,000. The calculations also include the "earned-income credit," which refunds a portion of taxes to families with adjusted gross incomes below $10,000. The maximum credit of $500 applies to a family that has only earned income (which is basically labor income) and whose income is between $5,000 and $6,000. (The total tax due is negative for incomes below $8,700.)

For levels of income above $10,000—where the earned-income credit is zero—the tax rises with adjusted gross income at a steadily increasing rate. The slope of the curve in Figure 14.3 indicates the tax rate that attaches to an additional dollar of income. Notice that this slope becomes steeper as income rises above $10,000.

Figure 14.4 shows the tax rates that apply to an additional dollar of income for the various ranges of adjusted gross income. These are called **marginal tax rates,** because they prescribe the rate of tax on the marginal dollar of income. Notice that the marginal tax rate rises from 14% at $10,000 to 16% at $11,600, 19% at $15,900, and so on. Eventually, the rate reaches its maximum of 50% when adjusted gross income hits $89,600. (But recall that we do not allow for itemized deductions, which are almost sure to apply at this level of income.) In earlier years the maximum marginal tax rate exceeded 50%.

For incomes below $10,000, we have to consider the earned-income credit, which was introduced in 1975. It is worth looking at some details of this odd feature of the tax law, because it helps us to understand better the notion of a marginal tax rate. Until income reaches $5,000, the credit rises by 10% of each dollar earned. Therefore, the effective marginal tax rate is −10%. That is, someone's tax—which happens to be negative in this range—falls by 10% of each additional dollar of income. Then the credit is constant when income is between $5,000 and $6,000, so the effective marginal tax rate is zero in this range. Next the credit falls by 12.5% of each dollar earned above $6,000. So, the effective marginal tax rate is 12.5% until someone reaches an income of $7,400. Then people start to pay income tax at a marginal rate of 12%, plus they continue to lose the credit at a rate of 12.5%. Hence, the tax system imposes a peculiarly high marginal tax rate of 24.5% for incomes between $7,400 and $9,500. At $9,500, people start to pay income tax at a marginal rate of 14%—hence, the effective marginal tax rate becomes 26.5%. Then the marginal tax rate falls to 14% at an income of $10,000 when the earned-income credit becomes zero.

Figure 14.4 shows also the **average tax rate,** which is the ratio of taxes to adjusted gross income. Notice that the marginal tax rate is above the average rate for incomes above $5,000. Therefore, the average tax rate rises with income when income exceeds $5,000. (Why is that?) Recall, however, that we ignore itemized deductions and various devices that can exclude actual income from adjusted gross income. When we consider these elements, we end up with a weaker tendency for the average tax rate to rise as income increases.

The distinction between average and marginal tax rates is important for our analysis. Average tax rates tell us how much revenue the government collects as a fraction of income—that is, revenue equals the average tax rate multiplied by the amount of income. But the effects of the tax system on people's behavior depend on marginal tax rates. These rates tell people what fraction the government takes from an additional dollar of income. So in deciding how much to work, produce, and invest, people take account of these marginal tax rates.

State and Local Income Taxes

Many states and some cities impose individual income taxes. Overall, in 1982, this category accounts for 12% of state and local and 5% of total government revenues.

Some states have a graduated tax, which resembles the federal setup. For example, in Vermont the tax is 23% of the federal levy, while in California there is a schedule of marginal rates that rise from 0 to 11%. (The highest marginal tax rates seem to be 16% in Minnesota and 18.3% for "unearned" incomes in New York City.) Other states have a flat rate of tax on income, except for a small exemption—for example, the rate for 1982 is 2.5% in Illinois and 2.2% in Pennsylvania. Finally, there are a few states that have no income tax. For people who are looking for a place to move, these are (in 1982) Alaska, Florida, Nevada, South Dakota, Texas, Washington, and Wyoming. (Connecticut, New Hampshire, and Tennessee tax only some forms of property income.)

Social Security Tax

Another important form of tax (which the government amusingly calls a "contribution") is the levy on wage earnings and income from self-employment to finance social security. In 1982 this category accounts for 29% of federal and 18% of total government revenues. At present, almost all workers are covered by social security. The main exceptions are civilian employees of the federal government and of some state and local governments, and workers for some nonprofit institutions. However, the legislation of 1983 moves the system further toward universal coverage.

The social security tax is much simpler than the individual income tax. For example, in 1982 covered employees pay 6.7% of earnings up to a ceiling of $35,700. Employers pay an equal amount. Thus, the combined marginal and average tax rates are 13.4% for labor earnings between 0 and $35,700. Then the marginal tax rate falls to zero, so that the average tax rate declines gradually as earnings increase.[2] Overall, except for the ceiling on earnings, we can describe the social security tax as a flat-rate levy on labor income. However, the tax rates and ceilings have increased substantially over time—for example, in 1960 the rates were 3% for each employee and employer, with a ceiling of $4,800.

The Overall Tax Rate on Personal Income

We can combine the federal individual income tax with state and local income taxes and the social security tax to compute an overall tax on personal income. (The sum over these categories of taxes constitutes 54% of total government revenues in 1982.) We show in Figure 14.5 the ratio of these taxes to personal income from 1929 to 1982. Notice that the ratio stays below 3% before 1940, but then rises to 12% in 1945. After falling to 9% for 1949–50, the ratio varies between 12 and 15% from 1951 to 1966. Then the ratio increases to 18% in 1969, changes little during the 1970s, and reaches 20% in 1982.

The ratios that we just examined and those pertaining to total revenues in Figure 14.2 are aggregate measures of average tax rates. But as mentioned before,

---

[2]In calculating effective marginal tax rates, we should deduct any extra benefits that someone gets *because they pay the tax*. Therefore, some parts of government revenue are not a tax at all—these include charges for school tuition and hospitals, contributions to government employee retirement funds, and some other items. If we include payments for unemployment insurance, then this category accounts for 14% of total government revenues in 1982. Otherwise, it is 12%. For individual income taxes, we treat this extra benefit as nil. That is, even if we like public services, the amounts we get do not depend on the individual taxes that we pay. But for social security, there is some relation of an individual's benefits to that person's lifetime contributions to the program. For an argument that this effect is important for some people, see Roger H. Gordon, "Social Security and Labor Supply Incentives," National Bureau of Economic Research, working paper no. 986, September 1982.

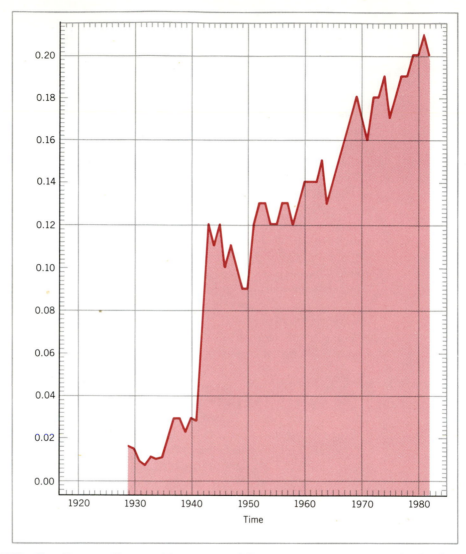

Figure 14.5 The Tax Rate on Personal Income: Individual Income Taxes plus Social Security Taxes as a Ratio to Personal Income

we would like to measure marginal tax rates in order to assess the effects of the tax system on economic activity. Ideally, we would find the marginal tax rate for each family at each point in time. For personal income taxes, we would do this by adding the marginal tax rates for each type of tax—the federal and state and local individual income taxes, and the social security tax. Then we would average these marginal tax rates across families at each date.

Figure 14.6 shows the average marginal tax rate from the federal individual income tax for 1916–80. These values are averages over families' marginal tax rates, when weighted by the adjusted gross income of each family. Note that the

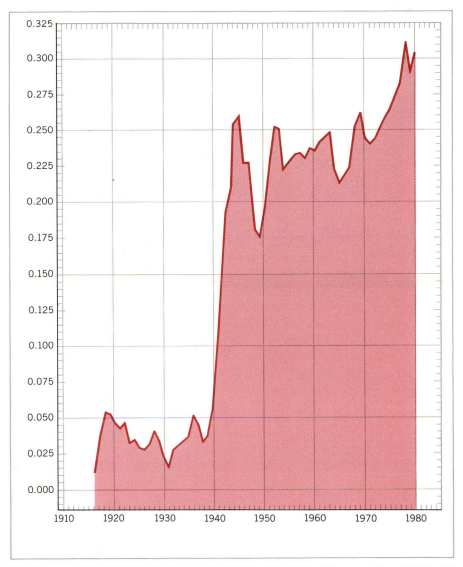

Figure 14.6 **The Average Marginal Tax Rate from the Federal Individual Income Tax, 1916—80**
The graph shows the average of families' marginal tax rates, when weighted by each family's
adjusted gross income. The data are from Robert Barro and Chaipat Sahasakul, "Measuring
the Average Marginal Tax Rate from the Individual Income Tax," *Journal of Business,*
October 1983.

average marginal tax rates go from 5% in 1920 to 2% in 1930, 6% in 1940, 20%
in 1950, 23% in 1960, 24% in 1970, and 30% in 1980. As a rough statement, the
time pattern of average marginal tax rates in Figure 14.6 parallels that for the
average tax rate on personal income in Figure 14.5. (Note that Figure 14.5 also
includes state and local income taxes and the social security tax.) However, the

level of the average marginal tax rate from the federal individual income tax is much higher than the average tax rate from this source. In fact, the ratio of federal individual income tax collections to personal income—that is, the average tax rate for this levy—turns out to be only 30–40% of the average marginal rate, which appears in Figure 14.6. But recall that these values do not include either state and local taxes or the social security tax. At present, we lack data on a broader concept of the average marginal tax rate.

Corporate Profits Taxes

Taxes on corporate profits account for 5% of total government revenues in 1982. For large corporations in 1982, the federal marginal tax rate on taxable earnings is 46%. This rate has been close to 50% since World War II, but a complicated "excess profits tax" applies also during the Korean War and World War II. From 1918 to 1938, the tax rates are between 12 and 15%.

The relation of corporate taxes to corporate profits depends also on various tax credits, and on the rules for computing depreciation allowances and for valuing inventories. Figure 14.7 shows how the ratio of corporate taxes (federal plus state & local) to corporate profits changes over time.[3] For 1946–81, this ratio varies between 39 and 69%, with no regular trend. However, for 1982, the ratio falls to 30%. This decline reflects more favorable depreciation allowances and some other changes in the 1981 tax law.

Recall that corporate profits taxes have declined sharply as a share of government revenues. Specifically, these taxes account for over 20% of total government receipts in the late 1940s, but only 5% in 1982. There are two main elements behind this change. First—at least until 1982—the ratio of corporate profits taxes to corporate profits did not change greatly since World War II. But other taxes rise substantially relative to income. (Of course, the ratio of corporate profits taxes to corporate profits is already very high—near 50%—in the late 1940s.) Second, the ratio of corporate profits to GNP falls significantly in the 1970s. This ratio is about 11% in the late 1940s and is still 10% in 1968. But since then, the ratio falls to 5% in 1982.

We can think of the corporate profits tax as a levy on the capital owned by corporations. But since households ultimately own the corporations, the tax amounts to another levy on individuals' income from capital. In fact, the government taxes the earnings of corporations directly and then taxes them a second time when people receive dividends or capital gains. (Economists call this *double taxation*.) For the purposes of our analysis, we can think of adding the tax on corporate profits to individual income taxes in order to calculate an overall tax on the income from capital.

---

[3]The figures on corporate profits include adjustments for the valuation of inventories and for the calculation of depreciation.

Figure 14.7 Corporate Profits Taxes as a Ratio to Corporate Profits
Corporate profits taxes are amounts paid to federal, state and local governments. The earnings of the Fed are subtracted from corporate profits, and the Fed's transfers to the Treasury are subtracted from corporate taxes. Data are from *Economic Report of the President, 1983.*

Property Taxes

Property taxes provide 9% of total government revenues in 1982. But the various state and local governments use a bewildering array of procedures to determine the taxes on houses, factories, etc. In a general way we can think of the property tax as another form of tax on capital. Therefore, for most purposes, we can combine this tax with the individual income taxes and the corporate profits tax in order to find the overall tax on the income from capital.

Sales and Excise Taxes

Finally, we should mention sales and excise taxes, which constitute 14% of total government revenues in 1982. Many states and localities have general sales taxes, but also have special levies on gasoline, alcohol, tobacco, and some other items. The federal government's excise taxes apply to gasoline, alcohol, tobacco, automobiles, tires, and telephone services. As of 1980, the federal government also levies the ''windfall-profits tax,'' which amounts to an excise tax on petroleum products.

The important feature of these taxes is that they apply to types of expenditures, rather than to income or wealth.[4] In the subsequent theoretical analysis, we focus on income taxes. Thus, in a broad sense, the analysis encompasses the types of taxes discussed in previous categories. But we should remember that sales and excise taxes operate in a different manner.

An Income Tax in the Theoretical Model

We can evaluate the main effects of taxation by examining a simple form of income tax. Here, we assume that a family's real taxes, t_t/P_t, are a fraction, τ, of its real taxable income. (τ is the Greek letter tau.) Hence, for simplicity, we do not introduce a graduate-rate tax structure into the model, but use instead a flat-rate tax. Also, we assume at this stage that the tax rate, τ, does not vary over time.

In the model we assume that a family's real taxable income equals its real net product, $y_t - \delta k_{t-1}$, plus real interest income (which can be negative), less the amount of **tax-exempt real income.** We call the real exempt amount, e_t. Notice that we treat governmental transfers as nontaxable, which is accurate in most cases. Finally, we assume initially that there is no inflation, so that the real and nominal interest rates on bonds are equal—that is, $r_t = R_t$. Therefore, a household's real taxes are given by

$$t_t/P_t = \tau(y_t - \delta k_{t-1} + r_{t-1}b_{t-1}/P_t - e_t) \tag{14.1}$$

If real taxable income is negative, we assume that taxes are negative, rather than zero.[5] Also, we assume that the tax parameters, τ and e_t, are the same for all

---

[4]Many other countries use a *value-added tax,* which amounts to a broad-based sales tax. However, rather than applying to final sales, this levy depends on the value added to goods at various stages of production.

[5]In the real world taxes can be negative because of the earned-income credit and because people can carry over some losses from one period to the next. For example, the Chrysler Corporation has lots of business losses stored up, which it can use to reduce its future taxes (on future profits!).

households. In particular, we neglect any actions that individuals can take to affect either their marginal tax rate, τ, or their quantity of tax-exempt income, e_t. Note that since each household's marginal tax rate is τ, the average marginal tax rate across households is also τ.

A household's average tax rate for period t is

$$\text{average tax rate} = \tau(y_t - \delta k_{t-1} + r_{t-1}b_{t-1}/P_t$$
$$- e_t)/(y_t - \delta k_{t-1} + r_{t-1}b_{t-1}/P_t + v_t/P_t) \quad (14.2)$$

Notice that the average tax rate is below the marginal rate, τ, for two reasons—first, because of the exempt amount, e_t, and second, because of the nontaxable transfers, v_t/P_t. At this point, we continue to treat the transfer payments as lump sum.

Aggregate real income taxes follow from equation (14.1) as

$$T_t/P_t = \tau(Y_t - \delta K_{t-1} - E_t) \quad (14.3)$$

where E_t is the aggregate amount of tax-exempt income. (Remember that aggregate real interest payments, $r_{t-1}B_{t-1}/P_t$, equal zero.) Therefore, the government's budget constraint in real terms is now

$$G_t + V_t/P_t = \tau(Y_t - \delta K_{t-1} - E_t) + (M_t - M_{t-1})/P_t \quad (14.4)$$

Here we measure aggregate real income taxes on the right side by the expression from equation (14.3).

Suppose that we take as givens the amounts of real government purchases, G_t, aggregate real transfers, V_t/P_t, and the real revenue from money creation, $(M_t - M_{t-1})/P_t$. Then for a given amount of aggregate net product, $Y_t - \delta K_{t-1}$, the two tax parameters, τ and E_t, must be set so as to satisfy the government's budget constraint. That is, the government has to generate enough income-tax receipts in each period to meet the expenditures that are not covered by printing money. Often, we shall think about changing the marginal tax rate, τ, and then allowing the exempt amount, E_t, to vary in order for equation (14.4) to hold. But the results end up the same if we change lump-sum transfers, V_t/P_t, instead of the exempt amount, when we shift the marginal tax rate. Note that, at this point, we do not allow the government to borrow and lend on the credit market.

Households' Budget Contraints

Each household's budget constraint in real terms for period t is

$$y_t - \delta k_{t-1} + b_{t-1}(1 + r_{t-1})/P_t + m_{t-1}/P_t + v_t/P_t - t_t/P_t =$$
$$c_t + i_t - \delta k_{t-1} + (b_t + m_t)/P_t \quad (14.5)$$

Notice that we subtract depreciation from both sides, so that net product, $y_t - \delta k_{t-1}$, appears on the left, while net investment, $i_t - \delta k_{t-1}$, appears on the right. Notice also that real taxes, t_t/P_t, subtract from the household's disposable funds on the left side.

Now, substitute for real taxes from equation (14.1) into equation (14.5) and rearrange terms to get

$$(1 - \tau)(y_t - \delta k_{t-1}) + (1 - \tau)r_{t-1}b_{t-1}/P_t + (b_{t-1} + m_{t-1})/P_t$$

$$+ v_t/P_t + \tau e_t = c_t + i_t - \delta k_{t-1} + (b_t + m_t)/P_t \quad (14.6)$$

The first term on the left side equals net product, $y_t - \delta k_{t-1}$, less the tax levy on this product, $\tau(y_t - \delta k_{t-1})$. That is, after-tax net product, $(1 - \tau)(y_t - \delta k_{t-1})$, matters for the household. Similarly, the after-tax quantity of real interest income, $(1 - \tau)r_{t-1}b_{t-1}/P_t$, enters on the left side of equation (14.6).

Notice that the previous financial assets, $(b_{t-1} + m_{t-1})/P_t$, and the transfers, v_t/P_t, appear without the tax rate in equation (14.6). That's because the simple income-tax law from equation (14.1) does not tax either the stock of financial assets or the amounts of transfers. But the term, τe_t, does appear as part of the household's sources of funds. This term represents the saving on taxes because of the tax-exempt income, e_t.

Finally, none of the uses of the household's funds on the right side of equation (14.6) involve the tax rate. This result follows because we assume no tax on the expenditures for consumption or net investment. More generally, any sales or excise taxes would enter here.

The After-Tax Real Interest Rate

People receive real interest at the rate r_t, but they pay the fraction τ of their receipts to the government. Hence, when measured net of tax, people earn interest at the rate $(1 - \tau)r_t$. We refer to this variable as the **after-tax real interest rate.** Notice that this interest rate appears (for period $t - 1$) on the left side of equation (14.6).

In previous chapters we discussed the intertemporal-substitution effects that arise when the real interest rate changes. These effects still apply, but they refer now to the after-tax real interest rate. In particular, an increase in this interest rate, $(1 - \tau)r_t$, reduces the current demands for consumption and investment, but raises current work effort and the supply of goods.

The After-Tax Marginal Product of Labor

When someone works an additional hour, he or she raises output, y_t, by the marginal product of labor, MPL_t. But people keep only the fraction, $1 - \tau$, of their extra product. Hence, the **after-tax marginal product,** $(1 - \tau)MPL_t$, matters for someone's choices of work and consumption.

Suppose that there is a given schedule for labor's marginal product, MPL_t, when graphed versus the amount of work, l_t. Then an increase in the tax rate, τ, lowers the schedule when measured net of tax—that is, as $(1 - \tau)MPL_t$. People respond just as they would to a decrease in the schedule for labor's marginal product. Specifically, they reduce work effort, the supply of goods, and consumption demand.

The After-Tax Rate of Return to Investment

If someone raises their stock of capital, k_t, by 1 unit, then next period's net product, $y_{t+1} - \delta k_t$, rises by the marginal product of capital less the rate of depreciation, $MPK_t - \delta$. Recall that this term is the real rate of return from an extra unit of investment. But people now keep only the fraction, $1 - \tau$, of this return. Therefore, the **after-tax rate of return to investment** becomes $(1 - \tau)(MPK_t - \delta)$. Producers determine the desired stock of capital, $\tilde{k}_t$, by equating this after-tax rate of return to the after-tax real interest rate on bonds, which is $(1 - \tau)r_t$. That is, investors choose the quantity of capital, $\tilde{k}_t$, that satisfies the condition

$$(1 - \tau)(MPK_t - \delta) = (1 - \tau)r_t \qquad (14.7)$$

We shall find it convenient not to cancel out the tax terms, $1 - \tau$, which appear on both sides of equation (14.7). Instead, we think of the desired stock of capital as depending separately on the after-tax real interest rate, $(1 - \tau)r_t$, and the tax rate τ. Then we can write the desired stock of capital, $\tilde{k}_t$, as the function

$$\tilde{k}_t = \tilde{k}[(1 - \tau)r_t, \ \tau, \ \ \delta, \ . \ . \ .] \qquad (14.8)$$
$$\phantom{\tilde{k}_t = \tilde{k}[}(-) \ (-) \ (-)$$

For a given tax rate τ, an increase in the *after-tax* real interest rate on the right side of equation (14.7) raises the required after-tax return from investment. Hence, the desired capital stock falls. Then, for a given after-tax real interest rate, a higher tax rate τ lowers the after-tax return from investment on the left side of equation (14.7). Therefore, the desired capital stock again declines. Finally, as in earlier cases, the desired capital stock rises if the depreciation rate δ falls or if there is an upward shift in the schedule for capital's marginal product, MPK_t.

As before, the desired stock of capital, $\tilde{k}_t$, determines a producer's gross investment demand. Namely, the investment demand function is

$$i_t^d = \tilde{k}[(1 - \tau)r_t, \tau, \ \ \delta, \ . \ . \ .] - (1 - \delta)k_{t-1} = i^d[(1 - \tau)r_t, \tau, \ \ \delta, k_{t-1}, \ . \ . \ .]. \qquad (14.9)$$
$$\phantom{i_t^d = \tilde{k}[}(-) \ (-) \ (-) \phantom{- (1 - \delta)k_{t-1} = i^d[xxxxx}(-) \ (-) \ (?) \ (-)$$

Here, the new features concern the tax rate τ. First, for a given tax rate, it is the after-tax real interest rate, $(1 - \tau)r_t$, that has a negative effect on gross investment demand. Second, for a given value of the after-tax real interest rate, the tax rate τ has a separate negative effect, which comes from the reduction in the after-tax rate of return to investment, $(1 - \tau)(MPK_t - \delta)$.

A Change in the Tax Rate

Suppose that we increase the tax rate, τ. Aggregate real tax revenues are given from the tax law in equation (14.3) as $T_t/P_t = \tau(Y_t - \delta K_{t-1} - E_t)$. If the exempt amount, E_t, did not change, then real tax revenues would increase unless aggregate net product, $Y_t - \delta K_{t-1}$, fell by a great deal. Let's assume for the moment that this is not the case—that is, real tax receipts would increase if the exempt amount did not change.

Now, suppose that we hold constant the levels of government purchases, G_t, and aggregate real transfers, V_t/P_t, as well as the real revenue from money creation, $(M_t - M_{t-1})/P_t$. Then the government's budget constraint from equation (14.4) says that the amount of real taxes collected cannot change. So if we raise the tax rate in this situation, we also have to increase the exempt amount, E_t, in order to keep real tax revenues the same. In effect, we can think of raising the average marginal tax rate, which is what the parameter τ represents in the model, without changing the average tax rate. For example, in the real world, we might increase various exemptions in the income-tax law, but then raise all of the tax rates on taxable income in order to maintain the level of real revenues. Alternatively, we can think of switching from one type of tax, such as the social security tax on wage earnings, to another, such as the individual income tax. Because the social security tax has a low average marginal tax rate, compared to the revenue that it collects, this type of change tends to raise the average marginal tax rate, while leaving unchanged the aggregate of real tax revenues.

The important point is that, conceptually, we want to keep separate the effects of changes in the average marginal tax rate, τ, from those of changes in government purchases, transfers, or money creation. That's why we want to consider first the case where the exempt amount varies along with the tax rate in order to keep fixed the volume of real tax revenues. Then, when we want to, we can also look at cases where tax revenues do change, along with some combination of shifts in government purchases, transfers or money creation.

Finally, does a change in the tax rate, τ, affect wealth? (Recall that by the term, wealth, we refer to the level of utility that the typical person can attain.) Remember that the aggregate of households' budget constraints over many periods involves the present value of aggregate real transfers less aggregate real taxes. Aside from some monetary terms—which we know cancel in the aggregate—this present value depends only on the level of permanent government purchases, which we called $\bar{G}$. Therefore, as long as we hold constant the level of permanent purchases, it seems that a change in the tax rate would not change wealth. In fact, this result turns out to be a satisfactory approximation in many cases. However, we shall see later on that it is not exact. But for now, we neglect any effects on wealth from changes in the tax rate.

Clearing of the Commodity Market

Now, let's incorporate the various effects from the tax rate into the condition for clearing the commodity market. The condition for period 1 is

$$C^d[r_1(1 - \tau), \tau, \ldots] + I^d[r_1(1 - \tau), \tau, \ldots] + G_1 = Y^s[r_1(1 - \tau), \tau, \ldots] \quad (14.10)$$
$$\quad (-) \quad (-) \quad\quad\quad (-) \quad (-) \quad\quad\quad\quad\quad (+) \quad (-)$$

In order to avoid a clutter of terms, we do not write out explicitly some of the variables that influence consumer demand, investment demand, and the supply of goods. These include the initial capital stock, K_0, and the levels of current and permanent government purchases, G_1 and $\tilde{G}$.

One new feature is that the after-tax real interest rate, $(1 - \tau)r_1$, appears where the real interest rate, r_1, used to appear. Then, given the after-tax real interest rate, the tax rate, τ, has some separate effects. First, a higher tax rate reduces the schedule for the after-tax marginal product of labor, $(1 - \tau)MPL_1$, which reduces the incentive to work. Hence, there are reductions in the aggregates of goods supply, Y_1^s, and consumer demand, C_1^d. Further, since the change in the tax rate is permanent, these reductions tend to be roughly equal. That is, there is little change in the aggregate of desired saving.[6] Second, a higher tax rate lowers the after-tax rate of return to investment, $(1 - \tau)(MPK_1 - \delta)$, which means that gross investment demand, I_1^d, decreases (for a given level of the previous capital stock, K_0). Thus, we see generally that a higher tax rate tends to depress market activity—that is, it reduces the demands for consumption and gross investment, as well as the supply of goods. These results follow because an individual's tax liability rises when he or she engages in more market activity. In particular, a higher tax rate motivates people to substitute away from market activities and toward untaxed areas, such as leisure or the "**underground economy**," where the income is not reported.

Figure 14.8 shows the clearing of the commodity market. Here, we find it convenient to place the after-tax real interest rate, $(1 - \tau)r_1$, on the vertical axis. Then the horizontal axis shows the levels of commodity demand and supply. Note that the graph applies for a given position of the production function, and for given values of the starting capital stock, K_0, current and permanent government purchases, G_1 and $\tilde{G}$, and the tax rate, τ.

Effects of a Higher Tax Rate

Assume now that the tax rate rises permanently from τ to τ' at date 1. Figure 14.9 shows the effects on the commodity market. First, there is a leftward shift in the demand curve, which reflects the decreases in consumption demand and gross investment demand. Second, there is a leftward shift in the supply curve. But recall that the cutback in supply is comparable to that in consumer demand. Therefore, the overall fall in demand is greater than that in supply. Hence, the increase in the tax rate creates an excess supply of commodities at the after-tax real interest rate that initially clears the market, $[(1 - \tau)r_1]^*$. In other words, because of the fall in the desired capital stock, there is now an excess of desired real saving over net investment demand.

Figure 14.9 shows that the after-tax real interest rate and the level of output decline. Since the initial capital stock, K_0, is given, the fall in output reflects entirely a decrease in work effort. Here, people work less because the government extracts a larger fraction of a marginal dollar of income.

---

[6]Recall that we hold constant aggregate real taxes. Therefore, the change in the aggregate of desired saving equals the change in goods supply, Y_1^s, less the change in consumer demand, C_1^d.

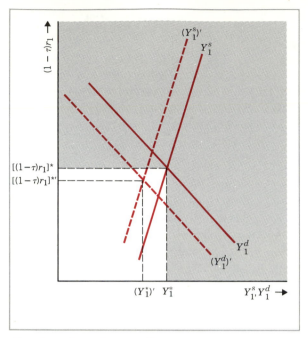

Figure 14.8 Clearing of the Commodity Market
We now graph the demand and supply of commodities versus the after-tax real interest rate, $(1 - \tau)r_1$.

Since government purchases do not change, the total of real private spending for consumption and investment must decline. We know for sure that gross investment decreases. (Since depreciation is a given, net investment also falls.) In fact, the reduced incentive to invest accounts for the drop in the after-tax real interest rate. The lower rate, $[(1 - \tau)r_1]^{*'}$, signals the diminished priority for using resources now—in order, specifically, to accumulate and maintain capital—rather than later. Notice that, from the viewpoint of the private sector, the diminished priority for accumulating capital reflects the adverse effect of a higher tax rate on the after-tax rate of return to investment.

The effect on consumption is uncertain. That's because the decrease in the after-tax real interest rate motivates more consumption, while the higher tax rate motivates less consumption. In other words, although total output falls, the higher tax rate may crowd out enough investment to avoid a decline in consumption in the short run.

The Wealth Effect from a Change in the Tax Rate
We carried out the analysis under the assumption that the change in the tax rate leaves wealth unchanged. This assumption seems reasonable since we varied the amount of tax-exempt income, E_1, in order to hold constant the quantity of real taxes collected, T_1/P_1. But let's consider more carefully whether wealth changes.

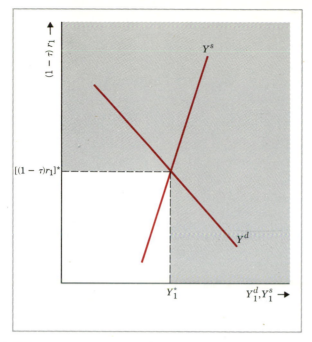

Figure 14.9 Effects on the Commodity Market of a Higher Income-Tax Rate
The increase in the income-tax rate from τ to τ' reduces the demand for commodities by more than the supply. Hence, output and the after-tax real interest rate both fall.

As we discussed back in Chapter 2, the effect of a disturbance on someone's wealth is positive if it enables him or her to achieve a higher level of utility. Similarly, the effect on wealth is negative if the attainable level of utility declines. Now the increase in the tax rate that we have just considered ends up reducing the utility of the typical household. Therefore, the effect on the typical person's wealth is actually negative, rather than zero.

To see why, note first that someone who produces the quantity of output y_1 gets to keep only the portion, $(1 - \tau)y_1$, while the remainder goes as taxes to the government. Therefore, a person's contribution to the economy's product, y_1, exceeds the contribution to that person's after-tax income, which is $(1 - \tau)y_1$. In deciding how much to work and invest, people consider only the fraction, $1 - \tau$, of the marginal products of their labor and capital. Hence, from a social perspective, people have insufficient incentives to work and invest.[7] In particular, the existence of the tax rate distorts private decisions, so that the aggregates of work, consumption, and investment end up below their desirable levels. Further, a higher

---

[7]The fraction τ that goes to taxes reduces the required payments of all other taxpayers (by a very small amount per person). But no individual takes these benefits to others into account when deciding how much to work and invest. Economists call this an "external effect." These effects refer to the benefits that others get from one person's actions, when the person does not take these benefits into account.

tax rate means a greater distortion, which leads to a lower level of utility for the typical household.

We can modify our analysis to include a negative effect on wealth from an increase in the tax rate. However, the general nature of the results does not change. Therefore, for most purposes, we can use the results that we already obtained while neglecting wealth effects.

Long-Run Effects of a Higher Tax Rate

So far, our analysis does not allow for changes in the capital stock. But since a higher tax rate reduces investment in the short run, we anticipate that the stock of capital will be lower in the long run. In order to explore this effect, we have to extend our previous analysis of steady-state situations. But we look here only at cases where population and technology do not change in the steady state. Then we know that the levels of the capital stock, etc., also do not change in the steady state.

The utility rate of time preference, ρ, tells us the real rate of return that savers insist on in the steady state. That is, if the real rate of return exceeds ρ, then people save and increase their quantities of consumption over time. Alternatively, if the real rate of return is less than ρ, then people dissave, so that consumption declines over time. In the steady state, where saving is zero, it must be the case that the real rate of return to saving equals ρ. But, the real rate of return to saving is now the after-tax real interest rate, $(1 - \tau)r$. Therefore, in the presence of taxation, it is the after-tax real interest rate that equals the utility rate of time preference, ρ, in the steady state.

We know also that the after-tax rate of return to investment, $(1 - \tau)(MPK - \delta)$, equals the after-tax real interest rate, $(1 - \tau)r$. Therefore, the full condition for the steady state is now

$$(1 - \tau)(MPK - \delta) = (1 - \tau)r = \rho \qquad (14.11)$$

The condition, $(1 - \tau)r = \rho$, ensures that aggregate saving is zero. Then the other part of the condition, $(1 - \tau)(MPK - \delta) = \rho$, says something about the level of the capital stock in the steady state. Namely, the level of capital corresponds to a marginal product for which the after-tax rate of return to investment, $(1 - \tau)(MPK - \delta)$, equals the utility rate of time preference, ρ. Then producers invest just enough to maintain the levels of their capital stocks—that is, aggregate net investment is zero.

So, what happens in the long run when the tax rate, τ, increases? From equation (14.11), the utility rate of time preference, ρ, pegs the after-tax rate of return to investment, $(1 - \tau)(MPK - \delta)$. Hence, any increase in the tax rate means that the before-tax rate of return to investment, $MPK - \delta$, must rise. But this happens only if the capital stock falls to generate a sufficient rise in the marginal product, MPK. Therefore, in the long run, a higher tax rate means a smaller stock of capital.

Suppose that we compare two steady states; one with the tax rate, τ, and another with the higher tax rate, τ'. We know that the after-tax real interest rate is the same in both steady states, since $(1 - \tau)r$ equals the fixed number ρ. But the one with the higher tax rate has less capital. It is also true that this steady state has lower gross and net product, as well as less consumption. However, the comparison for the levels of work effort is uncertain. First, the higher tax rate deters work. Also, the negative effect from less capital on labor's marginal product reinforces this response. But the negative wealth effect (which we can view as arising in the long run from less capital) works in the opposite direction.

Effects of a Permanent Rise in Government Purchases under Income Taxation

In the previous chapter we studied the effects of a permanent increase in government purchases when financed by lump-sum taxes. Then we found that output increases, partly because the public services are productive, and partly because people work more (in response to a decrease in wealth). Also, consumption decreases, but there are no effects on the real interest rate and investment. The last result suggests that the steady-state stock of capital does not change when government purchases increase permanently.[8] That is, the long- and short-run responses coincide.

In the real world a permanent increase in purchases generally requires a permanent increase in the average marginal tax rate, which we represent by the parameter τ. That is, the tax rate rises along with the increase in total real tax revenues, T_1/P_1. So in assessing the consequences of more government purchases, we want to combine the effects that we found under lump-sum taxes with those that arise when the tax rate increases. (Now we think of a case where the average marginal tax rate τ rises, but the exempt amount E_1 does not change.)

Table 14.3 summarizes the results. Line 1 refers to a permanent increase in government purchases when financed by lump-sum taxes. The responses of the variables are those that we discussed above. Line 2 deals with a permanent increase in the tax rate, τ. Here, we distinguish the short-run results—where the capital stock does not change—from the long-run ones. The findings are those that we worked out earlier in this chapter.

Finally, line 3 combines the permanent rise in government purchases with a permanent increase in the tax rate. The highlights are as follows. The short- and long-run effects on gross and net product are now ambiguous. That's because the negative effects from the higher tax rate offset the positive effects from more government purchases. Similarly, the effects on work effort are uncertain. However, we find again that the after-tax real interest rate, $(1 - \tau)r$, is pegged in the long run to equal the utility rate of time preference, ρ. Therefore, capital's marginal product, *MPK*, must still increase when the tax rate rises, which leads to the long-

---

[8]Here, we neglect an effect from the increase in work on capital's marginal product. This effect tends to raise investment in the short run and to raise the stock of capital in the long run.

Table 14.3 Summary of Economic Effects from Permanent Changes in Government Purchases and the Tax Rate

Nature of Disturbance	Response of								
	K	Y	$Y - \delta K$	L	C	I	$I - \delta K$	$(1 - \tau)r$	r
1. Permanent rise in government purchases, when financed by lump-sum taxes	0	+	+	+	−	0	0	0	0
2. Permanent increase in tax rate, τ									
a. Short run	0	−	−	−	?	−	−	−	?
b. Long run	−	−	−	?	−	−	0	0	+
3. Permanent rise in government purchases, with permanent increase in tax rate									
a. Short run	0	?	?	?	?	−	−	−	?
b. Long run	−	?	?	?	−	−	0	0	+

Note: We show the effects on the variables in each column from the disturbances shown in each row. The possible responses are positive ($+$), negative ($-$), zero (0), or uncertain (?).

run decline in the stock of capital. The counterpart of this result is the short-run decrease in net investment.

Empirically, it is hard to separate the effecs of more government purchases from the effects of a higher tax rate. The reason is that the two changes tend to occur together. We discussed before some estimates for the effect on output of a permanent increase in government purchases. The results suggest a positive effect, although the estimates are imprecise for the case of nondefense purchases. We should interpret these findings as applying to the combined impact of more government purchases and a higher tax rate. Therefore, there is some evidence that this combined effect is positive, although the theory says that the response is ambiguous.

The Relation Between the Tax Rate and Tax Revenues

We combined a permanent increase in government purchases with a rise in the tax rate, τ, in order to generate more real tax revenues for each period, T_t/P_t. But these revenues are given from the tax law as

$$T_t/P_t = \tau(Y_t - \delta K_{t-1} - E_t)$$

Therefore, if we hold the exempt amount E_t constant, then real tax receipts increase with the tax rate only if the fall in output, Y_t, reduces real taxable income, $Y_t - \delta K_{t-1} - E_t$, by proportionally less than the increase in the tax rate.

We can view the long-run movements in aggregate output, Y, in terms of the changes in the two productive inputs, K and L. Then the long-run decline in the capital stock follows from the steady-state condition, which is $(1 - \tau)(MPK - \delta) = \rho$. When the tax rate rises, capital's marginal product must increase sufficiently in the long run to reestablish this equality. So if we need large reductions in the capital stock in order to generate this increase in the marginal product—that is, if diminishing marginal productivity sets in slowly—then the capital stock will fall a great deal in response to an increase in the tax rate.

We know that the long-run response of work effort, L, is ambiguous. However, the main force that motivates a reduction in market work is the higher tax rate on income. This higher tax rate induces people to withdraw from the market in order to spend more time on leisure and other nonmarket (nontaxed) activities. So if these alternative uses of time are close substitutes for the things that people can buy on the market, then the negative effect on market work will be strong.

Overall, we require very substantial depressing effects of income taxation on capital and labor in order for tax revenues to fall when the tax rate rises. However, this outcome does become more likely as the rate of tax, τ, increases. For example, when the tax rate is 10%, a 10% increase means that the new tax rate is 11%. Therefore, the fraction of extra income that people keep, $1 - \tau$, falls from 90 to 89%, or by a percentage of 1.1%. Hence, a 10% increase in the tax rate translates into a decline by only 1.1% in the thing that capital and labor respond to, which is the term, $1 - \tau$. Therefore, we anticipate that the 10% increase in the tax rate would reduce real taxable income by much less than 10%.

Now suppose that we look at higher starting values for the tax rate, but we continue to raise the rate each time by 10%. Then, at a tax rate of 25%, we find that a 10% increase (to a new rate of 27.5%) means that the portion of income that people keep, $1 - \tau$, falls from 75 to 72.5%, or by 3.3%. Similarly, at a starting tax rate of 50%, we see that a 10% increase lowers the term, $1 - \tau$, from 50 to 45%—that is, by 10%. Moreover, at the still higher starting rate of 75%, we find that a 10% increase in the tax rate reduces the part of income that people keep, $1 - \tau$, by 30%. Overall, the higher is the starting value of the tax rate, the greater is the proportional reduction of the term, $1 - \tau$, from a 10% increase in the tax rate. In fact, the proportional effect on the term, $1 - \tau$, approaches minus infinity as the starting tax rate approaches 100%. Table 14.4 summarizes these results.

We have just shown that the term, $1 - \tau$, becomes proportionately more sensitive to a given percentage increase in the tax rate, τ, as the rate of tax increases. But recall that capital and labor—and, therefore, real taxable income—respond to the term, $1 - \tau$. Therefore, we predict that the negative response of real taxable income to the tax rate becomes stronger as the rate of tax increases. At some point—but, surely, for a tax rate below 100%—we shall find that an increase in the tax rate reduces real taxable income by so much that real tax revenues fall.

We show the general form of the relationship between real tax receipts, T/P, and the tax rate, τ, in Figure 14.10. (Think of this relation as applying in the long run, when capital and labor respond fully to a change in the tax rate.) This relationship is often called a **Laffer Curve** (named after the economist, Arthur Laffer). When the tax rate, τ, is zero, the government collects no tax revenues. Then

Table 14.4 Effects of a 10% Increase in the Tax Rate

Old τ	New τ	Old $(1 - \tau)$	New $(1 - \tau)$	% Change in $(1 - \tau)$
1.0	1.1	99.0	98.9	− 0.1
10.0	11.0	90.0	89.0	− 1.1
25.0	27.5	75.0	72.5	− 3.3
50.0	55.0	50.0	45.0	−10.0
75.0	82.5	25.0	17.5	−30.0
90.0	99.0	10.0	1.0	−90.0

Note: We show the effects of a 10% increase in the tax rate, τ, on the fraction of income that people keep, $1 - \tau$. Notice that the percentage decline of the term, $1 - \tau$, becomes larger as the tax rate rises.

revenues increase as the tax rate rises—hence, the curve has a positive slope. However, as the tax rate rises, the negative response of real taxable income to increases in the tax rate becomes stronger. Since this element reduces revenues, we find that the slope of the curve becomes flatter as the tax rate rises. Eventually, the tax rate becomes high enough so that a further increase in the tax rate reduces real taxable income by the same proportion as the increase in the tax rate. Therefore, real tax revenues do not change, and the curve in Figure 14.10 is flat. We label this tax rate as τ^* in the figure. If the government raises the tax rate above τ^*, then real taxable income falls by proportionately more than the increase in the tax rate. Hence, revenues now decline as the tax rate rises. In fact, as the tax rate approaches 100%, tax receipts approach zero. Therefore, if the government wishes to maximize its real tax revenues, it should not choose a tax rate of 100%. Rather, the value τ^* is the tax rate that maximizes receipts.

Some advocates of "**supply-side economics**" have used a picture like the one shown in Figure 14.10 to argue for an across-the-board cut in U.S. income-tax rates. These people contend that the average marginal tax rate on income exceeds the value τ^*, so that a general cut in rates would yield a larger volume of real tax revenues. However, there is no evidence that the United States has reached high enough tax rates for this result to apply.

A recent study for Sweden by Charles Stuart[9] provides some perspective on the U.S. situation. Stuart estimates that the maximum of tax revenues occurs in Sweden when the average marginal tax rate is about 70%. That is, he estimates τ^* to be about 70%. Moreover, the actual value of the average marginal tax rate in Sweden reached 70% in the early 1970s and has since risen to about 80%. (Here, Stuart takes a broad view of taxes to go beyond the income-tax law.) Therefore, Sweden has been operating on the falling portion of the Laffer Curve during the 1970s. In fact, Stuart attributes part of Sweden's low average growth rate of per capita gross product during the 1970s (1.7% per year) to this factor.

[9]Charles E. Stuart, "Swedish Tax Rates, Labor Supply and Tax Revenues," *Journal of Political Economy,* October 1981.

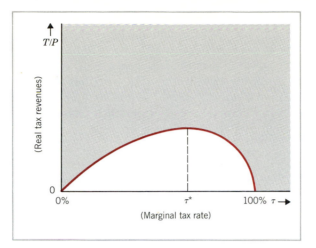

Figure 14.10 **The Relation of Tax Receipts to the Tax Rate (a Laffer Curve)**
Real tax revenues, T/P, initially rise with the tax rate τ. However, revenues reach their maximum when the rate is τ^*. If the tax rate rises above τ^*, then revenues fall. Further, revenues approach zero as the tax rate approaches 100%.

For the United States, the average marginal tax rate in 1980 from the federal individual income tax is about 30% (see Figure 14.6). However, the rate would be substantially higher if we were able to include other taxes. Since we do not have these data, we can draw a rough comparison between the United States and Sweden by considering average tax rates.

For Sweden, the estimated value for τ^* of 70% corresponds to an average tax rate of about 50%. For the United States in 1982, a comparable figure for the average tax rate, when calculated as the ratio of total government receipts to GNP, is 32%. So suppose that Sweden and the United States are roughly the same with respect to first the values of τ^*, and second the relation between marginal and average tax rates. Then we conclude that the United States has a significant way to go before reaching the average marginal tax rate, $\tau^* = 70\%$, at which tax revenues are maximized. However, we should be cautious about this result for two reasons. First, the estimates for Sweden are rough. Second, we cannot be sure that the United States and Sweden have similar Laffer Curves.

Transfer Payments

Suppose now that the government raises the aggregate of real transfers, V/P, and finances these with more tax revenues, T/P. As in the case where government purchases increase, the rise in real taxes typically requires an increase in the average marginal tax rate, τ. Recall that we already discussed the adverse effects on work, production, and investment from an increase in the tax rate. These are summarized in line 2 of Table 14.3. Note especially that an increase in transfers, when financed by an income tax, is no longer neutral in the model.

If transfer payments are lump-sum, as we have been assuming, then our analysis is finished. However, lump-sum transfers actually make little sense. Generally, the point of transfer programs is to provide payments to persons in specified categories—for example, to poor people, to persons who have lost their jobs, to old or sick people, to farmers, to college students, and so on. But none of these transfers are lump sum—that is, the amount depends in some way on a person's status.

Let's think about a welfare program, where the payments depend on a family's current or long-run income. (Similar effects arise for unemployment compensation, food stamps, and a number of other programs.) Typically, individuals face a declining schedule of transfers—possibly subject to some discrete cutoff points—as a function of market income. Then the negative effect of income on benefit payments looks just like a positive marginal tax rate. (Recall our previous example of the earned-income credit in the range where income exceeds \$6,000 but is less than \$10,000.) In particular, since transfers are sometimes cut drastically when a family's income rises, these programs can imply high effective marginal tax rates on the earnings of low-income persons. For example, the Council of Economic Advisers estimates that "typical welfare recipients, namely single mothers with children, face marginal tax rates in excess of 75%."[10] But unfortunately, we do not have estimates for the average marginal tax rate that is implied by the full array of transfer programs.

Suppose again that the government increases taxes in order to finance more welfare payments. We already noted the adverse effects on work, production and investment that derive from the increase in the average marginal tax rate, τ. But it is also likely that the expansion of the welfare program means that low-income people stand to lose more benefits if they earn more market income. That is, there is also an increase in the effective marginal tax rate for potential welfare recipients. Hence, the negative influences of this change on work and production add to the effects from the higher tax rate on market income.

In terms of dollar volume, the most important and rapidly growing transfer program in the United States and in most other countries today is the payments to retirees and survivors under social security.[11] We have already discussed the financing of these programs in the United States. From this standpoint, an expansion of social security leads to a higher marginal tax rate on income, τ, which has the usual negative effects on work and production.[12]

---

[10]*Economic Report of the President,* 1982, p. 129.

[11]One way to measure the size of this program is by the "replacement ratio." This measure equals the ratio of average benefits of retirees to their average earnings for a few years prior to retirement. In 1977 this ratio equaled 45%, as compared to only 30% as recently as 1970. (See Sherwin Rosen, "Some Arithmetic of Social Security," in Colin Campbell, ed., *Controlling the Cost of Social Security,* American Enterprise Institute, in press, Figure 1.)

[12]However, the social security tax depends on labor income, not capital income. Therefore, the effects on investment are different.

If people received their social security benefits without restrictions, except for age,[13] then the distorting influences that arise from welfare programs would not apply. However, the U.S. system involves a test on earned income—specifically, all persons (now below age 70) who earn labor income above a specified amount experience a partial or total cutoff of social security benefits. This income test works like an income standard for welfare—namely, it imposes a high effective marginal tax rate on the potential recipients. Not surprisingly, researchers find that this income test motivates people to retire earlier than they would otherwise.[14]

Summary

In this chapter we add to the model a simple form of income-tax law. The key parameters of this law are the marginal tax rate and the quantity of tax-exempt income. By the term, marginal tax rate, we refer to the extra tax that the government takes from an additional dollar of income. People take this marginal tax rate into account when deciding how much to work, produce and invest. By contrast, the government's tax receipts equal the product of the average tax rate (total taxes divided by total income) and the amount of income.

We show that intertemporal-substitution effects now depend on the after-tax real interest rate. Similarly, the decisions to work and invest consider the after-tax marginal products of labor and capital, respectively. Overall—if we hold fixed total real taxes collected—an increase in the marginal tax rate motivates people to substitute away from market activities, which are taxed, and toward leisure (or the underground economy). Therefore, we find that a higher tax rate leads in the short run to less work, output, and investment. Further, in the long run, there are reductions in the stock of capital, as well as in the levels of output and consumption.

When we combine a permanent increase in government purchases with a rise in the marginal tax rate we change some of the results from the previous chapter. Specifically, because of the adverse effects of higher taxation, the short-run effect on output becomes ambiguous. Further, we now conclude that the stock of capital declines in the long run.

As the marginal tax rate rises, the quantity of real taxable income tends to fall. Further, this sensitivity becomes larger the higher is the tax rate. Therefore, we can draw a Laffer Curve, which shows a diminishing effect of the tax rate on the quantity of real tax revenues. Eventually, the economy reaches a tax rate for which revenues are at a maximum. Then further increases in tax rates mean less real tax receipts. For Sweden, there is an estimate that this marginal tax rate is about 70%,

---

[13]Before 1961 recipients had to be over 65. Since 1961, there is an opportunity to receive reduced benefits at age 62. The 1983 law will eventually raise the basic retirement age from 65 to 67.

[14]See, for example, Michael Boskin, ''Social Security and Retirement Decisions,'' *Economic Inquiry,* January 1977.

which was reached and then surpassed in the early 1970s. But the United States has apparently not yet reached this point.

Finally, we show that transfer payments have allocative effects that resemble those from taxation. In particular, because people tend to lose their welfare payments or social security benefits by earning more income, they effectively face a high marginal tax rate. Thus, an increase in transfers is no longer neutral in the model. Rather, there is a two-dimensional effect, which tends to contract real economic activity. First, tax rates rise to finance the program, and second, the larger transfer payments mean that people stand to lose more benefits by earning income.

Important Terms and Concepts

adjusted gross income

taxable income

flat-rate tax

graduated-rate tax

marginal tax rate

average tax rate

tax-exempt income

after-tax real interest rate

after-tax marginal product of labor

after-tax rate of return to investment

underground economy

Laffer Curve

supply-side economics

QUESTIONS AND PROBLEMS

Mainly for Review

14.1 Distinguish between the average tax rate and the marginal tax rate. Must the two be equal for a flat-rate tax?

14.2 Why must we hold tax revenue constant when studying the effect of a change in the tax rate? What wealth effects would operate if we did not?

14.3 Explain briefly why a rise in the tax rate reduces the after-tax interest rate in the short run but raises the before-tax interest rate in the long run. How does the latter affect the capital stock?

14.4 Ignoring wealth effects from an increase in the tax rate, does the quantity of work decline in the long run? Explain why.

14.5 Could an increase in the tax rate reduce tax revenues? How does your answer depend on the response of labor supply to changes in the (after-tax) marginal product of labor?

14.6 Define supply-side economics. How could the economy benefit from lowering the tax rate? Include in your answer a discussion of the wealth effects of taxes.

Problems for Discussion

14.7 The Flat-Rate Tax

Some economists advocate shifting from the graduated individual income tax to a flat-rate tax. Under the new system, there would be few deductions from taxable income, and the marginal tax rate would be constant. Then, because of the elimination of the deductions (sometimes referred to as "loopholes"), the average marginal tax rate would be lower than that under the current law.

a. What would this change do to the aggregate levels of output, employment, and investment?

b. How does the proposed flat-rate tax compare with the present social security tax?

14.8 Subsidies

Suppose that the average marginal tax rate, τ, is zero. We mentioned that an increase in the tax rate, τ, above zero—with total revenues, T/P, held fixed—reduces the utility of the typical household.

a. Explain this result.

b. Does the result mean that a reduction in the tax rate below zero would be desirable? (A negative value of τ means that the government subsidizes increases in production.)

14.9 Consumption Taxes (optional)

Instead of an income tax, suppose that taxes are levied on the quantity of consumption during each period. An individual's real tax payments for period t are now given by the formula, $t_t/P_t = \tau(c_t - e_t)$. (A comprehensive sales tax on consumables might operate in this manner.)

a. Write down the budget constraints for the government and the representative household.

b. What is the after-tax real interest rate?

c. How does the tax rate, τ, now enter into the functions for consumption demand, C^d, gross investment demand, I^d, and goods supply, Y^s?

d. What is the short-run effect (while the capital stock is held fixed) of an increase in the tax rate, τ? Consider, in particular, the responses of the real interest rate and the quantities of output, work effort, consumption, and investment. Compare the results with those for an income tax.

e. Redo question **d** for the long run, where the stock of capital can change.

14.10 Effects of Inflation on a Graduated Income Tax

In 1982 a married couple in the United States pays income taxes in accordance with the following graduated-rate table:

Range of Taxable Income	Tax Rate on an Extra Dollar of Taxable Income (Marginal Tax Rate) %
$ 3,400– 5,500	12
5,500– 7,600	14
7,600–11,900	16
11,900–16,000	19
16,000–20,200	22
20,200–24,600	25
24,600–29,900	29
29,900–35,200	33
35,200–45,800	39
45,800–60,000	44
60,000–85,600	49
85,600–	50

a. Suppose that each person's real income stays constant over time, so that inflation steadily raises everyone's nominal income. If the tax law shown above remains unchanged, what happens over time to the average marginal tax rate? What happens to total real tax collections?

b. Assume now that the dollar bracket limits that appear in the left column of the table are adjusted proportionately over time for changes in the price level. What then is the effect of inflation on the average marginal tax rate and on total real tax collections? (The indexing rule described in part **b** appears in the tax legislation of 1981. It is scheduled to take effect after 1984. But it will be interesting to see whether this provision—which almost all economists view as sensible—will survive in Congress.)

14.11 Taxes, Inflation and Interest Rates (optional)

Suppose that taxes are levied on nominal interest income. The income-tax rate, τ, does not change over time.

a. What is the after-tax real interest rate on bonds?

Consider a permanent increase in the monetary growth rate from μ to μ', which occurs at date 1. Although the acceleration of money is a surprise, people then anticipate that the higher rate of monetary expansion, μ', will continue forever.

b. Given the presence of the income tax, what is the effect of the increase in monetary growth on the inflation rate, π, the nominal interest rate, R, and the aggregate level of real money balances, M/P? (Assume that the income-tax rate, τ, is unaffected by inflation.)

c. Discuss the relation between changes in the nominal interest rate and the inflation rate, which appears in the answer to part (b).

14.12 Effects of Transfer Programs on Work Effort

Discuss the effects on people's incentives to work of the following governmental programs:

a. The food stamp program, which provides subsidized coupons for purchases of food. The allowable subsidies vary inversely with family income.

b. A negative income tax. This program would provide cash transfers to poor persons. The amount of transfers is reduced as some fraction of increases in family income.

c. Unemployment compensation. People who work for a specified interval and who lose their jobs receive cash payments while unemployed (and "looking for work"). The benefits can last for six months or sometimes for longer periods. What difference does it make if businesses with histories of more layoffs have to raise their contributions to the unemployment-insurance fund? (A program that has this last feature is called "experience rated.")

d. Retirement benefits under social security. What is the consequence of the income test, which reduces benefits to persons (of age less than 70) who earn labor income in excess of a specified amount?

e. The earned-income credit. For families that have no unearned income, the credit is 10% of each dollar earned until income reaches $5,000. Then the credit is constant at $500 until income hits $6,000. Finally, the credit falls by 12.5% of each dollar earned, until it reaches zero when income is $10,000.

CHAPTER 15

THE PUBLIC DEBT

In recent years, one of the hottest economic issues concerns the **government deficit** (which we shall define carefully later on). At least from reading the newspapers, we would think that the economy suffers greatly when—as in 1982—the government runs a large deficit. The most important task in this chapter will be to evaluate this view. As we shall see, the conclusions depart dramatically from those expressed in the newspapers. In particular, deficits turn out to be mainly a symptom of bad times, rather than a cause of difficulties.

In the main, deficits arise when governments choose to finance part of their expenditures by issuing interest-bearing government bonds, rather than levying taxes. The stock of government bonds outstanding is the interest-bearing part of the **public debt.** Hence, a deficit means that the public debt increases over time.

In this chapter we study first the historical behavior of the public debt and government deficits. Along the way, we discuss some measurement problems, which can seriously distort our view about the size of government deficits. With these facts as a background, we extend the theoretical model to allow for public debt. In particular, the government can now run budget deficits, rather than levy taxes. Then we use the model to assess the effects of deficits on interest rates and other economic variables.

The Behavior of the Public Debt in the United States and the United Kingdom

We can gauge the empirical significance of interest-bearing public debt by looking at the long-term history for the United States and the United Kingdom. Table 15.1 shows the behavior over the last two centuries of the central government's nominal, interest-bearing public debt, which we denote by B^g. Note that the data for the United States are net of holdings of public debt by parts of the federal government, which include various agencies and trust funds. Also, we think of the monetary authority—that is, the Federal Reserve—as a part of the central government. There-

Table 15.1 Values for Public Debt in the United States and the United Kingdom

	United States			United Kingdom		
	B^g ($ Billion)	B^g/P	$B^g/(PY)$	B^g (£ Billion)	B^g/P	$B^g/(PY)$
1770	—	—	—	0.13	1.6	1.12
1780	—	—	—	0.17	2.0	1.20
1790	0.08	0.6	0.31	0.24	2.6	1.39
1800*	0.08	0.4	0.18	0.46	2.8	1.43
1810*	0.05	0.3	0.08	0.61	4.0	1.47
1820*	0.09	0.6	0.11	0.84	8.0	2.10
1830	0.05	0.4	0.04	0.80	8.0	1.71
1840	0.00	0.0	0.00	0.84	7.8	1.57
1850	0.06	0.5	0.03	0.83	10.8	1.39
1860	0.06	0.4	0.01	0.82	8.5	1.01
1865	2.2	8.7	0.24	—	—	—
1870	2.0	9.1	0.25	0.79	8.4	0.71
1880	1.7	9.1	0.13	0.77	8.5	0.58
1890	0.7	4.3	0.05	0.69	9.5	0.46
1900	1.0	6.4	0.05	0.63	9.0	0.32
1910	0.9	4.7	0.03	0.71	9.4	0.31
1919	24.2	69.1	0.31	7.4	35.9	1.34
1920	23.3	58.5	0.27	7.8	30.3	1.26
1930	14.8	46.5	0.16	7.5	74.0	1.52
1940	41.5	142.6	0.42	7.9	57.7	1.03
1945	228.2	600.5	1.07	21.4	124.9	2.16
1950	197.6	368.7	0.69	25.8	97.7	1.94
1960	206.6	300.7	0.41	27.7	77.9	1.08
1970	228.0	249.5	0.23	33.1	70.1	0.64
1980	615.1	346.8	0.23	95.3	47.7	0.43
1982	847.8	409.2	0.28	—	—	—

*For the United Kingdom, the dates are 1801, 1811, and 1821.

For the United States:

B^g is the end-of-year value (midyear value before 1916) in billions of dollars of privately held, interest-bearing public debt of the U.S. federal government at nominal par value. The figures are net of holdings by the Federal Reserve and U.S. government agencies and trust funds. (However, they still include holdings by some government-sponsored agencies and by state and local governments.) For the sources, see Robert Barro, "Comment from an Unreconstructed Ricardian," *Journal of Monetary Economics,* August 1978, Table 1.

P is the GNP deflator (1972 = 1.0). For the sources since 1870, see Figure 1.4 of Chapter 1. The earlier data are a wholesale price index, as reported in U.S. Commerce Department, *Historical Statistics of the U.S., Colonial Times to 1970,* p. 201.

Y is real GNP (1972 base). For the sources since 1870, see Figure 1.1 of Chapter 1. Estimates of real GNP from 1834–69 are unpublished data from Robert Gallman. Earlier figures are calculated from the growth rates of real output that are reported in Paul David, "The Growth of Real Product in the United States since 1840," *Journal of Economic History,* June 1967, Table 1; and Alice Jones, *Wealth of a Nation to Be,* Columbia University Press, New York, 1980, Table 3.15.

fore, we also net out the Fed's holdings of U.S. government bonds.[1] The table reports also the real quantity of debt, B^g/P, and the ratio of the public debt to nominal *GNP*, $B^g/(PY)$. We show this last ratio graphically for the United States from 1790 to 1982 in Figure 15.1, and for the United Kingdom from 1770 to 1980 in Figure 15.2.

For both countries the two main positive influences on the ratio of public debt to GNP are wartime and major economic contractions. Superimposed on these infrequent positive shocks is a regular pattern where the ratio declines over time.

Let's focus now on the United States. The major peaks in the ratio of public debt to annual GNP occur at the end of the Revolutionary War (the value for 1784 is 0.33), the end of the Civil War (0.25 in 1865), the end of World War I (0.31 in 1919), and the end of World War II (1.07 in 1945). Smaller effects—which amount to pauses in the usual downward trend in the ratio, rather than to actual increases—show up for the Spanish-American and Korean Wars. However, little impact appears for the Vietnam War. (Recall that this war exhibited only a small excess of real military spending above trend.)

The positive effect of economic contraction on the ratio of public debt to GNP involves partly a negative effect on GNP and partly a positive effect on public debt. A dramatic response to an economic downturn shows up during the Great Depression, where the ratio of public debt to gross national product (GNP) rises from 0.14 in 1929 to 0.38 in 1933. Qualitatively similar behavior arises for less

---

[1]For example, at the end of 1982, the gross amount of interest-bearing debt of the U.S. Treasury is $1,195 billion. But $209 billion of this total is held by various United States government agencies and trust funds, and $140 billion is held by the Federal Reserve. Therefore, the amount in private hands (including about $90 billion with state and local governments) is only $848 billion.

For the United Kingdom:

B^g is the end-of-financial-year value in billions of pounds of the central government's interest-bearing public debt at nominal par value. Since 1855 the dating refers to March 31st of each year. From 1818–54 the date is January 5. Some variation in dating occurs before 1818. Since 1963 the figures refer to the "Net total national debt." From 1836–1962 the data apply to the comparable concept, "aggregate liabilities of the state." Until 1835 the numbers are for the totals of funded and unfunded debt. No corrections were made for "official holdings" of the national debt.

P is a wholesale price index (1975 base).

PY is a nominal GNP.

The sources for B^g are B. R. Mitchell, *Abstract of British Historical Statistics,* Cambridge University Press, 1962, 1971; and Central Statistical Office, *Annual Abstract of Statistics,* London, various issues. The wholesale price index is from B. R. Mitchell, *European Historical Statistics 1750–1970,* Macmillan Press, London, 1975; *International Financial Statistics,* various issues; and *Monthly Digest of Statistics,* various issues. Nominal GNP for 1855–1980 is from B. R. Mitchell, op. cit; *Annual Abstract of Statistics,* various issues; and *Monthly Digest of Statistics,* various issues. For 1830–54 the data are from Phyllis Deane and W. A. Cole, *British Economic Growth 1688–1959,* 2nd ed., Cambridge University Press, 1969. The values for 1770–90 are estimated from figures in Deane and Cole.

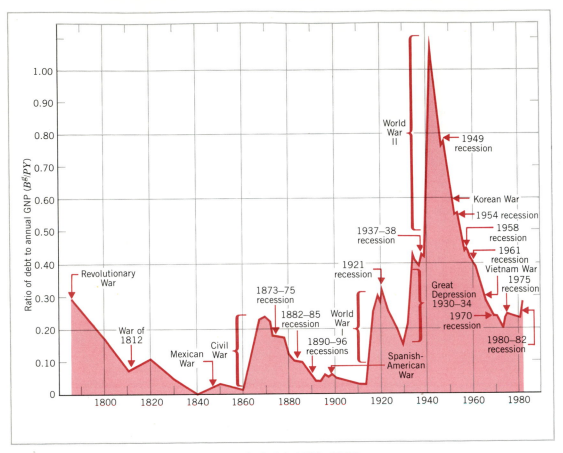

Figure 15.1 Behavior of the U.S. Public Debt, 1790–1982
The figure shows the ratio of the public debt to nominal GNP.

severe contractions: for example, the ratio rises from 0.23 in 1979 to 0.28 in 1982, from 0.20 in 1973 to 0.23 in 1975, and from 0.039 in 1892 to 0.047 in 1894.

During peacetime, nonrecession years, the ratio of public debt to GNP tends to decline. This pattern applies as much to the (mostly peaceful) post-World War II period from 1945 to 1982—where the ratio falls from 1.07 to 0.28—as to earlier times. In fact, the ratio fell to 0.20 in 1973, before the recessions of 1974–75 and 1980–82 raised the value to 0.28. For the earlier peacetime periods aside from the Great Depression, we find that the ratio falls from 0.31 to 0.14 between 1919 and 1929, from 0.24 to 0.02 between 1865 and 1916, from 0.11 to 0.01 between 1820 and 1860, and from 0.33 to 0.08 between 1784 and 1810. Notice also that the ratio for 1982, which is 0.28, is not high by historical standards and is well below the values for the 1950s.

The major element that distinguishes the behavior of the United States public

Figure 15.2 Behavior of the British Public Debt, 1770–1980
The figure shows the ratio of the public debt to nominal GNP.

debt since the late 1960s is the divergent patterns in nominal and real debt. The rapid inflation of recent years means that a declining ratio of the debt to GNP is consistent with a substantial runup in the nominal debt. For example, the nominal debt for 1982 is $848 billion, as compared with $228 billion in 1970. (Recall that these figures refer to the privately held part of the interest-bearing public debt.) By contrast, the nominal debt changed very little between 1945 and 1970. But these changes in the behavior of the nominal debt have not translated into obviously different patterns for the debt when expressed either in real terms or as a ratio to GNP.

The experience for the United Kingdom is broadly similar to that for the United States. The major peaks in the ratio of public debt to annual GNP are again associated with wartime—2.1 after the end of the Napoleonic Wars in 1821, 1.3 at the end of World War I in 1919, and 2.2 at the end of World War II in 1945. It is noteworthy that the high points for the British debt in relation to GNP are more than twice as great as those for the United States. It is also interesting that the ratio of the public debt to GNP for the United Kingdom in 1821 is comparable to that in 1945. Large amounts of public debt are not a new phenomenon.

Economic contractions again have a positive impact on the ratio of the debt to GNP. This response shows up especially for the United Kingdom during the depressed periods from 1920 to 1922 and from 1930 to 1932. The ratio of debt to GNP rises from 1.3 to 1.6 during the first interval, and from 1.5 to 1.7 during the second.

Periods that involve neither war nor economic contraction display a declining pattern in the ratio of public debt to GNP. Again, this behavior applies as much to the post-World War II years as to earlier periods. In particular, the ratio declines from 2.2 in 1945 to 0.4 in 1980. Notice that the ratio for 1980 is not far above the low point over the past two centuries, which is 0.25 in 1913–14.

Characteristics of Government Bonds

In our model the government can now borrow funds from households by selling interest-bearing bonds. We assume that these government bonds pay interest and principal in the same way as private bonds, which are already in the model. In particular, we continue to simplify matters by pretending that all bonds have a maturity of one period.[2] In the main analysis we assume also that bondholders regard public and private debts as equivalent. Specifically, we do not treat the government as more credit-worthy than private borrowers. In this case the government's bonds must pay the same nominal interest rate in each period, R_t, as that on privately issued bonds.

Our assumption about public and private bonds contrasts with our treatment of money. Since currency pays no interest, it seems that private enterprises would find it profitable to produce this stuff. In particular, the higher is the nominal interest rate, R_t, the greater is the gain from entering the business of creating currency. But because of legal restrictions or some technical advantages for the government in providing a medium of exchange, we assume that the private sector does not issue currency.

With respect to bonds, we assume no legal restrictions on private issues and no technical advantages for the government in providing these types of securities. Hence, we do not allow the interest rate on government bonds to differ from that on private bonds. This assumption accords reasonably well with the U.S. data if we interpret private bonds as prime corporate obligations. For example, the market yield on six-month maturity U.S. Treasury Bills averages 6.1% from 1959 to 1982, while that on four- to six-month maturity prime commercial paper averages 6.7%.

---

[2]The average maturity of marketable, interest-bearing public debt in the United States was around 9 years in 1946. Then this figure declined fairly steadily to reach a low point of about 2½ years in 1976. During much of this period, the U.S. Treasury was prohibited from issuing long-term bonds at interest rates that would have made them marketable. With the ending of this restriction, the average maturity rises to about 4 years in 1982. (Source: *Economic Report of the President,* 1975, Table C-73; 1983, Table B-81.)

The rise in Treasury Bill yields from 3.8% in 1959 to 11.1% in 1982 is paralleled closely by the rise in commercial paper rates from 4.0% to 11.9%.[3] Basically similar patterns appear if we look at long-term bonds.

Let's denote by B_t^g the aggregate dollar amount of government bonds outstanding at the end of period t. We still use the symbol b for privately issued bonds. Therefore, an individual's total holdings of bonds for period t are now $b_t + b_t^g$. We still have that the aggregate of privately issued bonds is zero—that is, $B_t = 0$. Hence, the aggregate quantity of bonds held by households now equals the public debt, B_t^g. Usually, we think of cases where the government is a net debtor to the private sector, so that $B_t^g > 0$. However, the government may also become a creditor, where it holds net claims on the private sector.[4] We can represent this case by allowing for $B_t^g < 0$.

The Government's Budget Constraint

The presence of public debt alters the government's budget constraint in two respects. First, the dollar amount of net debt issue for period t, $B_t^g - B_{t-1}^g$, is a source of funds.[5] In this respect the printing of money and the printing of interest-bearing debt play the same role in the financing of the government's expenditures. Second, the government's nominal interest payments, $R_{t-1}B_{t-1}^g$, appear as an expenditure. Recall that this term is zero for the case of money.

The government's budget constraint in dollar terms for period t is now

$$P_t G_t + V_t + R_{t-1}B_{t-1}^g = T_t + (M_t - M_{t-1}) + (B_t^g - B_{t-1}^g) \quad (15.1)$$

The two new terms are the government's interest payments on the left side, $R_{t-1}B_{t-1}^g$, and the net issue of debt on the right side, $(B_t^g - B_{t-1}^g)$. For simplicity, we return to the case where the transfers, V_t, and taxes, T_t, are lump sum.

The Government's Deficit

We can think of the government's saving or dissaving in the same way as for households. Specifically, the national accounts define the government's nominal saving to be the change in the dollar value of the government's holdings of money and bonds. (Recall that the government holds no capital in our model or in the

---

[3]At least some of the positive differential between the yields on commercial paper and Treasury Bills reflects two advantages of the government's notes: first, the interest payments are exempt from state and local income taxes, and second, the Treasury Bills satisfy the requirement that commercial banks hold some amount of government bonds as ''backing'' for the government's deposits in these banks.

[4]The last time this became a serious possibility for the United States was around 1835. A major concern was the outlet for further governmental revenues once the national debt was fully paid off. (We do not have this problem any more.) See the discussion in Davis Dewey, *Financial History of the United States,* 11th edition, Longmans, Green, New York, 1931, p. 221.

[5]Notice that the simple rolling over or reissue of bonds as they come due is not a net source of funds. Rather, what counts is the difference between the stock outstanding at date t, B_t^g, and that outstanding in the previous period, B_{t-1}^g.

national accounts.) Since we think of the government as issuing money and bonds—rather than holding these assets—an increase in money and bonds means that the government is dissaving. Also, people use the term, **surplus,** to refer to positive saving by the government, and the term, **deficit,** to refer to dissaving. (When saving is zero, the government **balances its budget.**)

When we put all this terminology together, we find that the nominal deficit is

nominal deficit (national accounts' version) =

$$\text{government's nominal dissaving} = (M_t + B_t^g) - (M_{t-1} + B_{t-1}^g) \qquad (15.2)$$

When we combine the definition from equation (15.2) with the government's budget constraint from equation (15.1), we can express the nominal deficit as

$$\textbf{nominal deficit (national accounts' version)} = P_t G_t + V_t + R_{t-1} B_{t-1}^g - T_t \qquad (15.3)$$

That is, the nominal deficit equals nominal expenditures—for purchases, transfers, and interest payments—less tax revenues. Finally, in order to calculate the government's real deficit, we divide through by the price level, P_t, to get

$$\textbf{real deficit (national accounts' version)} = G_t + V_t/P_t + R_{t-1} B_{t-1}^g/P_t - T_t/P_t \qquad (15.4)$$

We should note one respect in which our treatment departs from actual practice in the U.S. national accounts. Namely, the accounts treat the Federal Reserve as a private corporation, rather than as a part of the federal government.[6] By contrast, our analysis consolidates the Federal Reserve with the central government. Thereby, we net out the holdings of government bonds by the Fed when we measure the outstanding public debt, B^g. Similarly, we do not count as government expenditures the part of the Treasury's interest payments that are paid on the bonds held at the Fed. But we also do not count as government receipts the earnings that the Fed transfers back to the Treasury. (This last item roughly equals the Fed's interest receipts on U.S. government bonds.) Finally, we count an increase in the quantity of money, M, as part of the government's deficit. But in the United States, this money is formally a liability of the Federal Reserve, rather than the central government.

As with an individual's saving, the standard definitions of the government's deficit in equations (15.2)–(15.4) do not take proper account of inflation.[7] Paralleling our treatment for households, we can define the government's real deficit—that is, its real dissaving—to be the change in the real value of its obligations in the forms of money and bonds. (It is these changes that will matter later on when we think about future taxes or money creation.) Therefore, the natural definition of the **real deficit** is

$$\text{real deficit} = (M_t + B_t^g)/P_t - (M_{t-1} + B_{t-1}^g)/P_{t-1} \qquad (15.5)$$

---

[6]This treatment relates more to the history of the Federal Reserve than to its economic functions. For a discussion of the history, see Paul M. Warburg, *The Federal Reserve System, Its Origin and Growth,* 2 vols., Macmillan, New York, 1930.

[7]For a discussion of these effects from inflation, see Jeremy J. Siegel, "Inflation-Induced Distortions in Government and Private Saving Statistics," *Review of Economics & Statistics,* April 1979.

If we divide through the government's budget constraint from equation (15.1) by the price level, P_t, and use the expression, $P_t/P_{t-1} = 1 + \pi_{t-1}$, then we can show that the real deficit is given by

$$\text{real deficit} = G_t + V_t/P_t + (R_{t-1} - \pi_{t-1})(B^g_{t-1}/P_t) - \pi_{t-1}(M_{t-1}/P_t) - T_t/P_t \quad (15.6)$$

Recall that in measuring households' real saving we had to use the real interest rates on assets—that is, $r_{t-1} = R_{t-1} - \pi_{t-1}$ on bonds and $-\pi_{t-1}$ on money. Thus, the same holds true for the government's real deficit in equation (15.6).

We can calculate an appropriate measure of the **nominal deficit** by multiplying through equation (15.6) by the price level, P_t. The result is

$$\text{nominal deficit} = P_t G_t + V_t + (R_{t-1} - \pi_{t-1})B^g_{t-1} - \pi_{t-1}M_{t-1} - T_t \quad (15.7)$$

Let's compare our concept of the nominal deficit from equation (15.7) with the national accounts' version, which appears in equation (15.3). In both cases the nominal deficit equals total dollar expenditures—for purchases, transfers, and interest payments—less nominal tax revenues. But differences arise in the methods for measuring interest payments. The national accounts' version uses nominal interest rates, which are R_{t-1} for bonds and zero for money. By contrast, the definition in equation (15.7) uses real interest rates, which are $r_{t-1} = (R_{t-1} - \pi_{t-1})$ for bonds and $-\pi_{t-1}$ for money. Recall also where the underlying differences come from. The national accounts' version of the nominal deficit tells us how the government's total dollar obligations change over time. On the other hand, the concept from equation (15.7), when divided by the price level P_t, tells us how the government's total real obligations change over time.[8]

Let's construct a simple example to bring out the differences between the two concepts. Suppose that the government's two nominal obligations, money and bonds, both grow at a steady rate of 10% per year. Assume also that the price level grows at 10% per year, so that the real quantities of money and interest-bearing public debt are constants. Then the national accounts' definition from equation (15.2) says that the nominal deficit is positive and grows at a rate of 10% per year. Hence, when divided by the price level, the national accounts' concept shows a constant, positive real deficit. That is, the national accounts report a positive real deficit in every year, but the government's real obligations never change!

We get the correct answer from our concept of the real deficit in equation (15.5). This definition accurately reports a constant real deficit of zero. Also, when we multiply through by the price level, P_t, we find that the nominal deficit is zero in each year.

Typically, a higher growth rate of money generates a higher rate of inflation and a higher nominal interest rate. In this case, the government effectively imposes a higher tax rate on the holdings of real cash, which usually means that the government gets more real revenue from money creation. But we should think of this

---

[8]Ideally, we would also adjust for changes in the market value of long-term government bonds because of changes in interest rates.

revenue as reflecting a form of tax, which happens to apply to people's holdings of money. Specifically, there is no real deficit because the government's real obligations do not change over time.

The differences between the two concepts of the deficit are large when the inflation rate is high. Therefore, it matters a great deal which definition we use for the years since the late 1960s. Table 15.2 compares the national accounts' concept of the deficit with our measure for the period, 1965–82. The table shows the nominal and real deficits for each year based on the two definitions. (For the years before 1965, where the inflation rate is typically small, the differences are much less significant.)

Table 15.2 Alternative Measures of the U.S. Government's Deficit, 1965–82

	National Accounts' Basis		Correct Measure	
	Nominal	Real	Nominal	Real
1965	1.1	1.5	−5.7	−7.7
6	1.9	2.5	−8.3	−10.8
7	7.5	9.5	−1.1	−1.4
8	11.7	14.2	−2.2	−2.6
9	−2.1	−2.4	−17.4	−19.6
1970	12.2	13.4	−2.8	−3.0
1	23.7	24.7	9.0	9.4
2	18.7	18.7	4.9	4.9
3	7.4	7.0	−18.2	−17.1
4	18.5	16.1	−19.9	−13.1
1975	82.4	65.6	53.1	41.8
6	67.0	50.7	44.4	33.2
7	60.0	42.9	26.9	19.0
8	58.4	38.9	10.2	6.7
9	49.1	30.2	−2.9	−1.8
1980	82.0	46.2	13.8	7.8
1	85.8	43.9	16.8	8.6
2	167.3	80.7	126.6	61.1

Note: For the national accounts' basis, the nominal deficit comes from equation (15.2) as $(M_t + B_t^g) - (M_{t-1} + B_{t-1}^g)$. Then the real deficit is the nominal one divided by the annual average of the GNP deflator. For the correct measure, the real deficit come from equation (15.5) as $(M_t + B_t^g)/P_t - (M_{t-1} + B_{t-1}^g)/P_{t-1}$. Here, P_t is the seasonally adjusted value of the GNP deflator for the fourth quarter of year t. Then the nominal deficit is the real one multiplied by the annual average of the GNP deflator.

Sources (for the table and for Figure 5.3):
The data for government bonds, B^g, are described in Table 15.1. M is the aggregate monetary liabilities of the Federal Reserve (called the "monetary base"), which comprises currency outside the U.S. Treasury plus reserves held at the Federal Reserve. The data, which are values for December of each year, come from the *Federal Reserve Bulletin*, various issues. The data for the GNP deflator are from U.S. Commerce Department, *National Income and Product Accounts of the U.S., 1929–76*, and *U.S. Survey of Current Business*, various issues.

Notice first that the national accounts' concept shows a deficit for 17 of the 18 years since 1965, while the correct measure indicates one for only 9 of the years. That's because, with substantial inflation, the increases in the government's nominal obligations often do not translate into increases in real obligations.

In order to go from the national accounts' measure of the nominal deficit to the correct measure of the real deficit, we make two adjustments. First, we eliminate the inflation part of the nominal interest payments (on bonds and money). Thus, for example, for 1981, this element reduces the deficit from $85.8 billion to only $16.8 billion. To understand this calculation, observe that the total debt (bonds plus money) at the end of 1980 is $773 billion. Hence, the inflation rate of 8.9% from the end of 1980 until the end of 1981 reduces the real value of the debt outstanding by $0.089 \cdot 773 = \$69$ billion. Hence, if the nominal debt had risen by $69 billion, then the real debt would not have changed during 1981. Thus, we subtract $69 billion from the national accounts' version of the deficit in order to correct for the positive rate of inflation.

Second, after we get the correct nominal deficit, which is $16.8 billion in 1981, we divide by the price level to measure the real deficit. This adjustment gives us the final figure for the corrected real deficit, which is $8.6 billion (of 1972 dollars) in 1981. Notice that the first adjustment to the deficit pertains to the *inflation rate* for the year, while the second involves the *price level*.

Since World War II, the two largest real deficits are those associated with the two most recent recessions—$61 billion for 1982 and $42 billion for 1975. Note that the corrections shown in Table 15.2 reduce these figures substantially—from $167 billion to $61 billion for 1982 and from $82 billion to $42 billion in 1975. But even after these adjustments, the real deficits remain large for these two years.

Figure 15.3 graphs the corrected real deficits from 1929 to 1982. The solid line shows the level of the real deficit, while the dotted line expresses it as a ratio to real GNP. There are two important observations from the figure, which correspond to those that we discussed before for the ratio of public debt to GNP. First, there is a positive relation between the real deficit and wars. In particular, this relation stands out for World War II, where the real deficits exceed 20% of real GNP from 1942 to 1944.[9] But there is also some effect during the Korean War for 1952–53 and perhaps during the Vietnam War for 1967–68.

The second important property is the positive relation between the real deficit and economic contraction. This pattern shows up strongly for Great Depression, where the real deficit exceeds 7% of real GNP in 1932. Also, the real deficit tends to be positive during the post-World War II recessions—for example, in 1949, 1958–59, 1961, 1971, 1975–76, and 1980–82. Since World War II, the largest ratios of the real deficit to real GNP are 4.1% in 1982 and 3.4% in 1975.

---

[9]For 1946–47, the large negative real deficits reflect first, decreases in the nominal debt, and second, large increases in the reported price level. Much of these increases in the price level arise from the gradual removal of price controls. Probably, the true price level rises more during World War II and much less for 1946–47. Hence, the true real deficits for 1946–47 are not as negative as those shown in the figure.

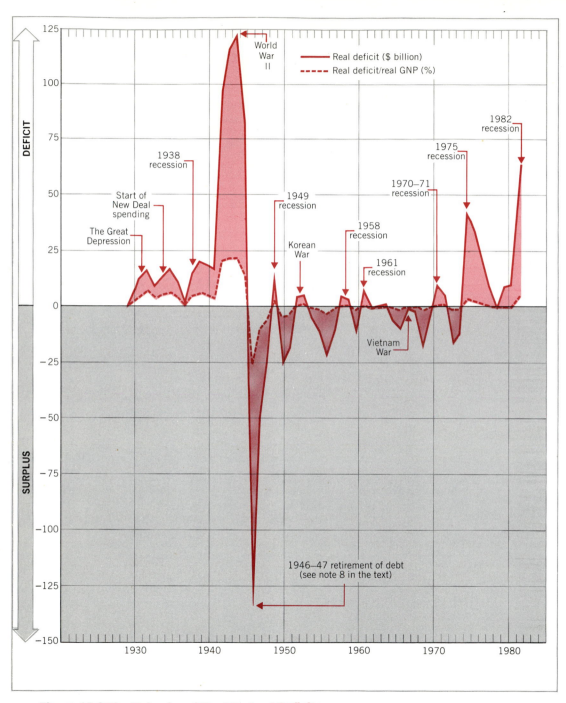

Figure 15.3 The Behavior of Real Federal Deficits
The solid line shows the real deficit, while the dashed line shows the ratio of the real deficit to real GNP.

In recent years there has been an extraordinary amount of attention paid to the size of actual and projected federal deficits. So let's focus on the deficit for 1982 and see why it is so large. First, as already mentioned, the national accounts' figure of $167 billion—which parallels the types of numbers that we read in the newspapers—exaggerates the matter. More appropriately, we can say that the real deficit for 1982 (from Table 15.2) is $61 billion or 4.1% of real GNP.

We can explain the bulk of the real deficit of $61 billion from the recession. A shortfall of real GNP leads to a shortfall in real tax revenues—in fact, the income-tax system has various features that magnify this response. One of these is the graduated-rate structure, which puts people into lower tax-rate brackets when their income falls. Hence, when real GNP declines by 1%, real federal taxes fall by more than 1%. Specifically, I estimate (using data over the period, 1948–76) that a decline by 1% in real GNP causes real federal revenues to decrease by about 1.8%.[10] Now, recall that the shortfall of real GNP in 1982 is by 8.8%. Therefore, real tax revenues tend to fall by 1.8 × 8.8% = 15.8%. Since the trend value of real federal taxes in 1982 is $343 billion, the predicted shortfall in real tax revenues is 15.8% × 343 = $54 billion. Notice that this figure comes close to the real deficit of $61 billion. Hence, most of 1982's real deficit reflects the customary shortfall of real tax revenues during a recession.

Table 15.3 shows similar calculations for some other cases where a recession is the major influence on the real deficit. (Significant movements in real federal expenditures would require separate attention.) Notice that we account for $35

---

[10]This estimate comes from Robert Barro, ''On the Determination of the Public Debt,'' *Journal of Political Economy,* October 1979, Table 2.

Table 15.3 **Recession and Real Federal Deficits**

(1) Year of Recession	(2) Percentage Shortfall in Real GNP	(3) Trend Real Federal Taxes (billions of 1972 dollars)	(4) Predicted Real Deficit = 1.8 × col. (2) × col. (3)	(5) Actual Real Deficit
1982	8.8	343	54	61
1975	7.4	266	35	42
1958	4.5	135	11	4
1933	37.6	14	9	8

Note: For each year of recession, column 4 shows the predicted real federal deficit. This value is the projected shortfall of real federal tax revenues, which is 1.8 times the percentage shortfall in real GNP (col. 2) times the trend value of real federal taxes (col. 3). The trend assumes growth in real taxes at a rate of 4.2% per year (the average over 1948–79) from the base year. Column 5 shows the actual real deficit for each year.

Sources: Column 2 comes from Table 10.1 of Chapter 10. The data on real federal taxes (nominal tax collections divided by the GNP deflator) are from *Economic Report of the President,* 1983. The values for column 5 appear in Figure 15.3.

billion out of the real deficit of $42 billion for 1975. But for 1958, the actual real deficit of $4 billion is well below the projected figure, which is $11 billion. Finally, for 1933, we predict a real deficit of $9 billion, as compared to the actual value of $8 billion.

Overall, at least through 1982, there is no indication that the relation of real federal deficits to the state of the economy has shifted. In particular, there is no evidence yet that the Reagan tax cuts or changes in the behavior of real federal spending have put the economy onto a path where real deficits will be chronically large. Rather, if the economy recovers strongly from the 1982 recession, then we predict that the real deficit would decline sharply. (Further, if inflation were eliminated, then standard measures of the deficit would also become small.)

Public Debt and Households' Budget Constraints

As in Chapter 14, households care about the anticipated present value of aggregate real taxes. (Recall that we treat the taxes as lump sum at this stage.) Therefore, we want to know how the outstanding stock of public debt and the government's current and prospective deficits affect the present value of real taxes.

In order to illustrate the main results, let's start with a number of simplifications. First, assume that the price level and aggregate money stock are constants. Then the government obtains no revenue from the creation of money. Second, we take as given the quantity of government purchases, G_t, in each period. Third, suppose that aggregate transfers, V_t, are zero in each period. Finally, assume that the government starts with no interest-bearing debt—that is, $B_0^g = 0$. Later on, we shall demonstrate that the conclusions do not depend on these unrealistic assumptions.

Given our assumptions, the government's budget constraint in real terms for each period is

$$G_t + RB_{t-1}^g/P = T_t/P + (B_t^g - B_{t-1}^g)/P \tag{15.8}$$

Note that we treat the price level, P, and the nominal interest rate, R, as constants. Also, the real interest rate equals the nominal rate, since there is no inflation.

Recall that the government starts with no interest-bearing debt at date 0. Therefore, if the government balances its budget from date 1 onward—that is, if $B_t^g - B_{t-1}^g = 0$ in every period—then real purchases, G_t, would equal real taxes, T_t/P, at all times, since interest payments would be nil. Now suppose that the government runs a deficit of $1.00 at date 1, so that $B_1^g = 1$. Since we hold fixed the quantity of government purchases, the budget constraint from equation (15.8) says that this period's taxes, T_1, must decline by $1.00. Thus, on this count, the aggregate of current disposable income received by households rises by $1.00.

Now suppose that the government wants to restore the public debt to zero from date 2 onward—that is, $B_2^g = B_3^g = \cdots = 0$. Then, in period 2, the government has to raise taxes enough to pay off the principal and interest on the one dollar of debt that it issued at date 1. Accordingly, the taxes for period 2, T_2, rise by $(1 + R)$ dollars. Since this action pays off the debt, there are no changes in taxes in subsequent periods.

Overall, aggregate taxes fall by \$1.00 during period 1, but rise by $(1 + R)$ dollars for period 2. Thus, the effect on the present value of aggregate real taxes is given by

$$(1/P) \cdot [-1 + (1 + R)/(1 + R)] = 0$$

Note that we discount the increase in next period's taxes of $(1 + R)$ dollars by the discount factor, $(1 + R)$. Hence, the net effect on the present value of aggregate real taxes is nil.

Since there is no change in the present value of aggregate real taxes, the government's deficit during period 1 has no aggregate wealth effect for households. Thus, the shift from current taxes to a deficit has no direct impact on the aggregates of consumer demand and work effort. In this sense, people view as equivalent a current aggregate tax of one dollar and a current deficit of one dollar. This finding is the simplest version of the **Ricardian Equivalence Theorem** on the public debt. (The theorem is named after the famous British economist, David Ricardo, who first enunciated it.)[11]

We can interpret the result as follows. Households receive one dollar of extra disposable income during period 1 because of the cut in taxes. But they also face $(1 + R)$ dollars of additional taxes during period 2. Therefore, if people use the extra dollar of disposable income during period 1 to buy an extra one dollar of bonds, then they will have just enough additional funds—namely, $(1 + R)$ dollars—to pay the extra taxes in period 2. In other words, the tax cut during period 1 provides just enough resources, but no more, for people to pay the higher taxes next period. That is why there is no aggregate wealth effect and no changes in the aggregates of consumer demand and work effort.

In order to generate the results, we assumed that the government paid off the entire public debt during period 2. But this assumption is unnecessary for the results. In order to see this, let's assume instead—and perhaps more realistically— that the government never pays off the principal of one dollar from the debt that it issued at date 1. That is, after the first period, the government always balances its budget, so that $B_t^g - B_{t-1}^g = 0$ holds from period 2 onward. In this case, the stock of debt stays constant over time, so that $B_1^g = B_2^g = \cdots = 1$. But then the government must finance the interest payments of R dollars in each period. (Remember that these payments would have been zero if the government had not run

[11]For discussions, see David Ricardo, "Funding System," in P. Sraffa, ed., *The Works and Correspondence of David Ricardo,* Cambridge University Press, Cambridge, 1951, vol. 4; James Buchanan, *Public Principles of Public Debt,* Irwin, Homewood, Illinois, 1958, pp. 43–46, 114–22; and Robert Barro, "Public Debt and Taxes," in *Money, Expectations and Business Cycles,* Academic Press, New York, 1981. Gerald O'Driscoll, in "The Ricardian Nonequivalence Theorem," *Journal of Political Economy,* February 1977, points out Ricardo's own doubts about the empirical validity of his famous theorem.

a deficit during period 1.) Finally, these extra expenses mean that aggregate taxes, T_t, are higher by $R \cdot B^g = R$ dollars for every period after the first.

Overall, aggregate taxes fall by \$1.00 during period 1, but rise by R dollars for each subsequent period. Therefore, the change in the present value of aggregate real taxes is now given by the expression

$$(1/P) \cdot \{-1 + R[1/(1 + R) + 1/(1 + R)^2 + \cdots]\} =$$

$$(1/P) \cdot \{-1 + [R/(1 + R)] \cdot [(1 + R)/R]\} = 0^{12}$$

That is, the net change in the present value of aggregate real taxes is still zero.

We can think of this result as follows. Households receive \$1.00 of extra disposable income during period 1 because of the cut in taxes. But they also face the stream of additional future taxes, which equal R dollars in each period. If the households use the extra dollar of disposable income during period 1 to buy an extra dollar of bonds, then in period 2 they receive \$1.00 more of principal payments and R dollars more of interest. Then if they use the interest receipts to pay the higher taxes, households can again buy a bond for \$1.00. Continuing in this manner, the households can always use the interest income to meet the extra taxes in each period. In other words, the tax cut during period 1 provides just enough resources, but no more, for the households to pay the stream of higher future taxes. That is why the net change in the present value of aggregate real taxes is again equal to zero. Hence, we still predict no changes in the aggregates of consumer demand and work effort.

The basic conclusion is that shifts between taxes and deficits do not generate aggregate wealth effects. Moreover, this result still obtains if we drop many of our simplifying assumptions. For example, if the initial level of public debt is nonzero, then the conclusion follows by considering the extra future interest payments and taxes that result from today's deficit. Also, the results hold if we superimpose an arbitrary pattern of transfers. Suppose, as an example, that the government reacts to higher future interest payments by reducing transfers, rather than by raising taxes. Then we essentially add a new disturbance—namely, equal decreases in future transfers and taxes—to the one that we already considered. But since this new disturbance has a zero aggregate wealth effect, the basic result remains valid.

We can also allow for money creation and inflation. As one possibility, the government may react to higher future interest payments by printing more money, rather than increasing taxes. In this case economists say that the government **monetizes** part of the deficit or monetizes part of the stock of public debt. But then we essentially add another new disturbance—namely, an increase in future money creation and a decrease in future taxes—to the one that we treated before. We know that changes in money, which finance a cut in taxes, have no aggregate wealth effect. Therefore, there is again no aggregate wealth effect from deficits. However, monetization of the public debt does have important implications for the behavior of prices. These effects work just like the increases in the quantity of

---

[12]Use the condition, $(1 + x + x^2 + \cdots) = 1/(1 - x)$, where $x = 1/(1 + R)$.

money that we studied before. In particular, the monetization of deficits is inflationary.

Finally, we can allow for nonzero deficits—that is, more issues of debt—in future periods. But as with a current deficit, these future ones do not generate any aggregate wealth effects. Therefore, we find that the aggregate wealth effect is nil for any time path of public debt. Thus, we predict that the aggregate of consumer demand does not react either to differences in the initial stock of real government bonds, B_0^g/P, or to variations in current or prospective government deficits.

Fundamentally, there is no aggregate wealth effect from deficits because they do not change the government's use of resources. As before, the quantity of government purchases, G_t, tells us how much goods the government uses during period t. Therefore, aggregate wealth effects do arise when there are changes in the present value of anticipated government purchases—that is, in permanent purchases, $\tilde{G}$. But if we hold constant the value of permanent purchases, then there are no aggregate wealth effects from shifts between taxes and deficits.

The Effects of a Deficit-Financed Tax Cut

Recall that, with lump-sum taxes and transfers, the condition for clearing the commodity market in period 1 is

$$C^d(r_1, \ldots) + I^d(r_1, \ldots) + G_1 = Y^s(r_1, \ldots) \qquad (15.9)$$
$$(-) \qquad\qquad (-) \qquad\qquad\qquad (+)$$

Here, we do not write out explicitly in the demand and supply functions the initial stock of capital, K_0, or the levels of actual and permanent government purchases, G_1 and $\tilde{G}$. Also, recall that our previous analysis implies that the initial amount of real government bonds, B_0^g/P_1, does not matter for aggregate consumer demand, C^d, or goods supply, Y^s.

Suppose that the government cuts current taxes, T_1, and substitutes a corresponding increase in its interest-bearing debt, B_1^g. Generally, economists refer to this type of action as stimulative **fiscal policy.** But assume that the government changes neither the current nor the prospective levels of its purchases. Then the replacement of current taxes by a deficit has no aggregate wealth effect. Hence, there are no effects on consumer demand or work effort. It follows that the tax cut has no impact on the condition for clearing the commodity market, which appears in equation (15.9). Accordingly, there is no effect on the real interest rate, r_1, or on the quantities of output, Y_1, consumption, C_1, investment, I_1, and so on.

The condition that money be willingly held in period 1 is

$$M_1/P_1 = H(Y_1, R_1, \ldots) \qquad (15.10)$$
$$(+) \ (-)$$

Suppose that the government does not change either the current money stock, M_1, or the time path of prospective money stocks. Then the deficit-financed cut in current taxes has no effect on equation (15.10). Hence, the price level, P_1, and the nominal interest rate, R_1, do not change. In this case the quantity of real cash balances, M_1/P_1, still equals the amount demanded. (Notice also that the inflation rate, π_1, and all future price levels are unaffected by the tax cut.)

The government's tax cut means that the real stock of public debt, B_1^g/P_1, increases. But why do households willingly hold this higher real amount of government bonds without any changes in the real or nominal interest rate? They do so because the extra real bonds are just sufficient to cover the additional present value of future real taxes. Therefore, the real and nominal interest rates do not have to change in order to motivate people to hold the bonds.

Open-Market Operations

With public debt in the model, we can analyze **open-market operations.** An open-market purchase of securities occurs when the government—or a monetary authority like the Federal Reserve—buys government bonds with newly created money. In the opposite case there is an open-market sale of bonds for money.

Consider an open-market purchase during period 1, which results in an increase by $1.00 in the stock of money, M_1, and a decrease by $1.00 in the stock of public debt, B_1^g. Let's assume that no subsequent changes in money occur—that is, there is a one-time increase in the quantity of money at date 1. Also, we hold fixed the quantities of real government purchases and transfers in each period.

Table 15.4 shows that an open-market purchase of bonds amounts to the combination of two governmental policies that we have already examined. Suppose first that the government prints an extra dollar of money, M_1, and correspondingly reduces current taxes, T_1, by $1.00. These changes are labeled as policy (1) in the table. Then suppose that the government raises taxes, T_1, back up by $1.00 and uses the proceeds to pay off $1.00 of the public debt, B_1^g. These changes are called policy (2) in the table. The net effect of combining these two policies is to leave taxes unchanged. But the quantity of money rises by $1.00, while the quantity of government bonds falls by $1.00. Thus, we end up with an open-market purchase of bonds, which is policy (3) in the table.

Table 15.4 Open-Market Purchases of Bonds and Other Government Policies

Government Policy	Change in M_1	Change in B_1^g	Change in T_1
1. Print more money and reduce taxes	+$1	0	−$1
2. Raise taxes and retire public debt	0	−$1	+$1
3. Open-market purchase of bonds	+$1	−$1	0

Note: An open-market purchase of bonds—policy (3)—amounts to a combination of policies (1) and (2), which we have already studied.

We know that policy (1) (more money and less taxes) raises the price level in the same proportion as the increase in the quantity of money. But except for a reduction in the real amount of government bonds, there are no changes in real variables. We know that policy (2) (the fiscal policy where taxes rise and public debt declines) has no effects, except for another reduction in the real quantity of government bonds. We can find the effects from an open-market purchase of bonds by combining these two sets of responses. Namely, the price level and other nominal variables (except for the quantity of public debt) rise in the same proportion as the increase in the stock of money. But except for the fall in the real amount of government bonds, there are no changes in real variables. Thus, except for the change in the real quantity of government bonds, our previous results about the neutrality of money apply to open-market purchases (or sales) of bonds.

Why Does the Public Debt Matter?

Our results suggest that the public debt and government deficits do not matter much for the economy. But let's think about the parallel with private debt. The aggregate quantity of private debt is always zero, which also seems uninteresting. But the possibilities for borrowing and lending are important because they eliminate the need for individuals to synchronize their time paths of incomes and expenditures. The public debt plays a similar role. Since the credit market exists, the government need not match its receipts from taxes and money creation to its expenditures in each period.

Using the government's budget constraint, we can write the real amount of revenue from taxation and money creation for period t as

$$T_t/P_t + (M_t - M_{t-1})/P_t = G_t + V_t/P_t + R_{t-1}B_{t-1}^g/P_t - (B_t^g - B_{t-1}^g)/P_t \quad (15.11)$$

Now imagine given time paths for the government's real purchases and transfers. Also, assume for simplicity that the initial stock of interest-bearing debt, B_0^g, is zero. Then, if the government never issues any bonds, its real receipts from taxes and money creation for period t must equal the given total of real expenditures for that period, $G_t + V_t/P_t$. In particular, the receipts have to be high whenever expenditures are high, and vice versa. But the possibilities for issuing interest-bearing debt give the government more flexibility. For example, by borrowing a lot when its expenditures are unusually large, the government can lessen the need for unusually high receipts at that time. In general, the government can manage its issues of public debt in order to alter the quantity of its receipts for a particular period without changing the amount of expenditures for that period. However, remember that the government cannot change the real present value of its receipts from all periods unless it changes the real present value of its spending from all periods.

In order to bring out the main points, let's assume again that the stock of money is constant over time—that is, there is no revenue from money creation. Then the government's choices of public debt dictate the timing of its real tax receipts, T_t/P_t. But if the taxes are lump sum—as we have been assuming—then this timing is unimportant. That's because people care only about the real present value of the taxes, which cannot change unless the real present value of expenditures changes. The important point is that the economy will respond to a different timing of taxes only if the taxes are not lump sum. In order to see the nature of this response, let's reintroduce the type of income tax that we studied before. Then the aggregate real tax collections for period t are given by

$$T_t/P_t = \tau_t(Y_t + R^g_{t-1}B^g_{t-1}/P_t - E_t) \tag{15.12}$$

where τ_t is the marginal tax rate and E_t is the amount of exempt real income for period t. (Note that the interest payments on the public debt—which are taxable—appear in the aggregate of households' real taxable income.)

By managing the public debt over time, the government determines the behavior of real tax revenues, T_t/P_t, which then determines the necessary values of the marginal tax rates, τ_t, from equation (15.12). Suppose, for example, that the government starts with a plan where the marginal tax rate is constant over time. Then reconsider the example where current taxes, T_1, fall by \$1.00, while the public debt rises by \$1.00. Further, assume that the government raises next period's taxes, T_2, by \$(1 + R) in order to pay off the extra debt. Hence, in this example, the taxes collected change only for periods 1 and 2.

Unless the government has gone beyond the point of maximum tax revenues on the Laffer Curve, the changes in taxes collected show up as corresponding changes in marginal tax rates. (Here, we assume no changes in the quantities of tax-exempt real income.) Accordingly, in order to cut today's tax revenues, today's marginal tax rate τ_1 declines, while in order to raise next period's revenues, the next period's tax rate τ_2 rises. But these changes motivate people to shift their income toward the current period and away from the next period. Specifically, people raise today's work, but plan to reduce work in the next period. Notice that this response operates like some intertemporal-substitution effects that we considered before.[13]

Figure 15.4 shows the effect on the commodity market during period 1. Note that the increase in today's work effort shows up as a rightward shift in the supply curve. Since there is no direct stimulus to today's demand,[14] there is an excess supply of goods at the initial value of the after-tax real interest rate, $[(1 - \tau_1)r_1]^*$. Accordingly, Figure 15.4 shows that the after-tax real interest rate declines, while the quantity of output rises. Recall that an increase in work effort underlies the expansion of output. Finally, because of the fall in the after-tax real interest rate, the extra output shows up partly as more consumption and partly as more investment.

The counterpart of this period's lower marginal tax rate is a higher tax rate

---

[13]Since the tax law applies to income, rather than spending, there is no intertemporal-substitution effect on consumer demand.

[14]There may be a direct impact on investment demand, but it depends on the change in the marginal tax rate for the time when the new capital stock is operational. If the changes in marginal tax rates are short-lived, the direct effect on investment demand will be minor. For simplicity, we neglect this effect.

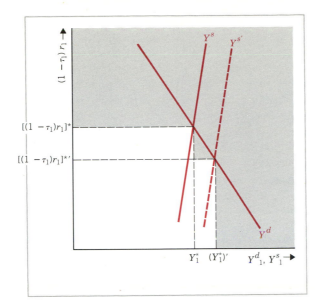

Figure 15.4 The Effect on the Commodity Market of a Deficit-Financed Cut in Today's Marginal Tax Rate
The marginal tax rate falls at date 1. Because of the increase in today's supply of goods, there is an increase in output and a fall in the after-tax real interest rate.

for the next period. Thus, in period 2, the changes to the market-clearing diagram are opposite to those shown in Figure 15.4. Consequently, in comparison with the values that would have arisen with no changes in taxes, there are declines during period 2 in output, work effort, consumption, and investment.

To summarize, when we consider income taxes, there are real effects from fiscal policy. Specifically, a deficit-financed cut in today's marginal tax rate leads to increases in today's real economic activity. But the responses reverse later on when the marginal tax rate is higher than otherwise. In our simple example, the higher future tax rate applies only to period 2. But more generally, the higher tax rate could be spread over many periods. Then the tendency for real economic activity to decline would also be spread out into the future. Overall, fiscal policy turns out to be an instrument that can influence the timing of real economic activity. But if we use this policy to get more output today, then we have to accept less output later on.

The Timing of Taxes

The government can manipulate its deficits in order to change the relative values of marginal tax rates for different periods, and thereby influence the relative levels of output at different times. But it would not be a good idea for the government randomly to make tax rates high in some periods and low in others. These types of fluctuations in tax rates would cause unnecessary distortions, because they would give people the wrong signals in determining how to allocate work and production over time. In practice, the U.S. government has not behaved in this erratic manner—rather, the public debt has typically been managed in order to maintain a pattern of reasonably stable tax rates over time.

An important example of the government's debt management shows up during wartime. Here, real government expenditures are much higher than normal. But as mentioned before, real deficits are also especially high at these times. Thereby, the government avoids abnormally high tax rates during wars. In this way the necessary increases in tax rates are spread roughly evenly over time. Tax rates rise somewhat during wartime, but also rise afterward along with the higher interest payments on the accumulated national debt.

Another interesting example concerns the behavior of income-tax rates during recessions. Typically, real government expenditures do not decline as much as aggregate output during a recession. (In fact, some items like unemployment compensation and welfare payments rise automatically.) Therefore, in order to maintain a balanced budget, the government would have to raise tax rates when the economy contracts. But instead of doing this, the government typically runs a real deficit.[15] In fact, in the United States the federal government tends to run enough of a deficit during a recession so that tax rates are somewhat lower than usual. Therefore, the intertemporal-substitution effect from a relatively low tax rate counteracts the economic contraction.

The Standard view of a Deficit-Financed Tax Cut

Our analysis of fiscal policy differs from that of most macroeconomic models. To see why, let's return to the case of lump-sum taxes, which most macromodels assume. For our analysis, the key point is that the typical household regards as equivalent a current aggregate tax of $1.00 or a government deficit of $1.00. In particular, if the behavior of government purchases does not change, then shifts between taxes and deficits entail no aggregate wealth effects. On the other hand, most macroeconomic models assume that a deficit-financed tax cut raises households' wealth, even if there are no changes in government purchases. Let's look first at the results in this case, and then examine briefly the arguments that some economists have made for a positive effect on aggregate wealth.

---

[15]Economists sometimes modify the measured deficit to take out the usual response to recession or boom. Then people report an estimate of what the deficit would have been if the economy had been operating at a level of ''full capacity'' or ''full employment.'' For discussions of the ''**full-employment deficit,**'' see E. Cary Brown, ''Fiscal Policy in the 'Thirties: a Reappraisal,'' *American Economic Review,* December 1956; and Council of Economic Advisors, *Economic Report,* 1962, pp. 78–82.

Suppose again that the government cuts current taxes by $1.00 and runs a deficit. If the tax cut makes people feel wealthier, aggregate consumer demand rises, but work effort and the supply of goods fall. Hence, the tax cut creates excess demand for goods. Consequently, the real interest rate rises, which means that investment declines. Thus, this analysis predicts that government deficits, which finance a cut in taxes, end up raising real interest rates and thereby **crowding-out** private investment.

What about output and work effort? Because of the increase in wealth, the typical person ends up currently with more leisure to go along with more consumption.[16] But the rise in leisure means less work and hence less output. Recall that the decrease in investment allows the typical person to consume more, even though output is lower.

According to this analysis, the decrease in net investment shows up in the long run as a decrease in the stock of capital. Sometimes, economists refer to this negative effect on the capital stock as a "**burden of the public debt.**" That is, each generation "burdens" the next one by bequeathing them a smaller aggregate stock of capital.[17] Note that these effects arise because deficits make people feel wealthier, which leads to a cutback in desired saving.

From an empirical standpoint, a principal prediction from the standard analysis is that larger real government deficits and larger real stocks of public debt lead to higher real interest rates. In fact, there is little question that most government officials and news reporters, as well as many economists, believe this prediction to be accurate. Nevertheless, this belief does not have evidence to support it.[18] In particular, Charles Plosser[19] carries out a detailed statistical analysis of government deficits and interest rates over the period 1954–78. His major finding is that the size of the deficit and the quantity of public debt outstanding have no significant effect on the interest rates paid on U.S. Treasury Bills or long-term U.S. govern-

---

[16]Notice that the economy's opportunities for shifting between leisure and consumption, which depend on the schedule for today's marginal product of labor, have not changed. Therefore, current consumption and leisure tend to move in the same direction—namely, upward in this case.

[17]For some discussion, see the papers in James Ferguson, ed., *Public Debt and Future Generations,* University of North Carolina Press, Chapel Hill, 1964. Note especially the paper by Franco Modigliani, "Long-Run Implications of Alternative Fiscal Policies and the Burden of the National Debt."

[18]Apparently, a well-known Wall Street "guru" used to forecast nominal interest rates by projecting federal deficits and then assuming a positive relation between deficits and interest rates. Thus, as the deficit grew during 1982, this fellow kept predicting that the prime interest rate (charged by commercial banks on business loans to good customers) would rise from 16–17% to above 20%. But although the deficit continued to expand, interest rates fell after the mid-summer of 1982. (In early 1983 the prime interest rate was 10.5%, but real deficits were still very large.) Eventually, the Wall Street guru changed his forecast to declining interest rates, and stopped talking so much about deficits. (Presumably, he also discarded his forecasting equation.)

[19]"The Effects of Government Financing Decisions on Asset Returns," *Journal of Monetary Economics,* May 1982.

ment bonds.[20] Thus, Plosser's evidence directly contradicts the standard theory in which deficit-financed tax cuts make people feel wealthier.

The Effect of a Tax Cut on Wealth

In order to reach the standard conclusions mentioned above, we have to argue that a tax cut makes people feel wealthier, even if the behavior of government purchases does not change. Here, we consider two of the more important arguments that people have offered, which concern the finiteness of life and the imperfections of private loan markets. It is worth exploring these matters in any case, since they come up in other areas, as well as in the context of public debt.

Finite Lives

Suppose again that the government cuts current taxes by $1.00 and runs a deficit. Then the government has higher interest payments and taxes in the future. Now we know that the present value of the extra future taxes equals $1.00. But assume that some of these taxes will show up after the typical person has already died. Then the present value of the extra future taxes that accrue during the typical person's lifetime falls short of $1.00. Hence, there is a positive effect on wealth when the government replaces current taxes by a deficit.

Why do we get an increase in wealth when people have finite lives? The reason is that the increase in wealth for the aggregate of current taxpayers coincides with a decrease for the members of future generations. Individuals will be born with a liability for a portion of taxes to pay interest on the higher stock of public debt. But these people do not share in the benefits from the earlier tax cut. If these future liabilities on descendants were counted fully by present taxpayers, then there would be no aggregate wealth effect. Essentially, government deficits enable members of current generations to die in a state of insolvency by leaving a debt for their descendants. Current taxpayers experience an increase in wealth if they view this governmental shifting of incomes across generations as desirable. But in fact, most individuals already have private opportunities for intergenerational transfers, which they have chosen to exercise to a desired extent. As examples, parents make contributions to children in the form of educational investments, other expenses in the home, and bequests. In the other direction—and especially before the growth of social security—children provide support for their aged parents. To the extent that private transfers of this sort are operative, the shift from taxes to deficits does not offer the typical person a new opportunity to extract funds from his or her descendants. Rather, the response to higher deficits would be a shift in private transfers by an amount sufficient to restore the balance of income across generations

---

[20]Plosser's results refer to nominal interest rates. Therefore, given his findings, a higher deficit would raise real interest rates only if the expected rate of inflation were to decline.

that was previously deemed optimal. In this case, the shift from taxes to deficits again has no aggregate wealth effect.[21]

As a concrete example, suppose that a couple plans to leave a bequest with a present value of $5,000 for their children. Then the government runs a deficit, which cuts the present value of the couple's taxes by $1,000, but raises the present value of their children's taxes by $1,000. Our prediction is that the parents use the tax cut to raise the present value of their bequest to $6,000. Then the extra $1,000 provides the children with the extra funds to pay their higher taxes. Thereby, parents and children end up with the same amounts of consumption and leisure that they enjoyed before the government ran its deficit.

The important idea is that the typical person is connected via family ties to future generations. In fact, we used this idea before to motivate the use of an infinite planning horizon for households. (Recall that we can then view the utility rate of discount in terms of the lower weight that people attach to the utility of their descendants, rather than their own utility.) That is, people effectively plan with an infinite horizon even though they live for only a finite time. But with an infinite horizon it is clear that a deficit-financed tax cut does not change the typical family's wealth. That is the present value of the extra future taxes exactly balances the cut in current taxes.

Imperfect Loan Markets

The argument that taxes and deficits are equivalent assumes also that private and governmental interest rates are the same. However, the process of lending and borrowing involves transaction costs for loan evaluations, collections, defaults, and so on. In particular, it is relatively easy to borrow if a person has a house, car, or factory to put up as collateral. But it is much harder if someone, such as a student, just promises to repay a loan out of future earnings. Therefore, the interest rates for borrowing are especially high for those with poor collateral, who require large costs of supervision in order to ensure the repayment of loans.

Think of the world as divided into two groups. Group A consists of people who lend or borrow at the same real interest rate, r, as the government. Group B comprises individuals who would like to borrow at this interest rate, but who face higher borrowing rates. Let $\bar{r}$ be the real discount rate that a person from this group uses in calculating the present value of future incomes and expenses. The main point is that the rate $\bar{r}$ exceeds the real interest rate, r, for those from group A.

Now suppose that the government cuts taxes and runs a deficit. The cut in taxes applies partly to people from group A and partly to those from group B. As before, the aggregate of future taxes increases. Let's assume that the division of

---

[21]A rigorous treatment of the interplay between public debt and private intergenerational transfers appears in Robert Barro, ''Are Government Bonds Net Wealth?'' *Journal of Political Economy,* November/December 1974. For a discussion of the role of educational investments as an intergenerational transfer, see Allan Drazen, ''Government Debt, Human Capital, and Bequests in a Life-Cycle Model,'' *Journal of Political Economy,* June 1978.

these future taxes between those from group A and those from group B coincides with the division of the current tax cut. (Otherwise, there is a distributional effect, which we assume has no aggregate effect in our model.) Then, for the people of type A, the present value of the higher future taxes again equals the amount of the tax cut. Therefore, the wealth effect is nil. But the people of type B discount their future taxes at the higher rate, $\bar{r}$. Therefore, for these people, the present value of the extra future taxes is less than the tax cut. Hence, there is an increase in wealth, which leads to more consumption demand and less work effort. Further, as these people raise their current consumption, they tend to reduce the discount rate, $\bar{r}$, that they apply to future incomes and expenses. Therefore, the investment demand from this group tends also to increase. (Think of a small business that faces a high borrowing rate. When the government cuts taxes, the business uses a portion of its extra funds to finance more investment.)

In the aggregate the deficit-financed tax cut leads to an increase in the current demands for consumption and investment, and to a decrease in the current supply of goods. From our usual analysis, we find that the real interest rate, r, rises. But this rate applies to the people from group A. Therefore, these people end up decreasing their current consumption and investment, and raising their work effort. On the other hand, because of the initial stimulus from the tax cut, those from group B increase current consumption and investment, and reduce work. For these people, the discount rate, $\bar{r}$, declines. Note especially the narrowing of the spread between the two discount rates, r and $\bar{r}$.

The overall effects on output, consumption, and investment are uncertain. However, the primary effect is the diversion of current resources away from the consumption and investment of type-A people and toward those of type-B people. Essentially, the tax cut induces the type-A people to hold more than their share of the additional public debt, so as effectively to lend to the type-B people at the real interest rate, r. Thus, the members of group B—whose discount rate $\bar{r}$ exceeds r— are better off. But those of type A are also satisfied, because the yield on their bonds is guaranteed by the government. However, they would have required a real interest rate greater than r in order to lend directly to the people of type B. In other words, the government's issue of public debt somehow avoids the high transaction costs that led in the first place to high borrowing rates for the members of group B.

The analysis assumes implicitly that the government is more efficient than the private market in arranging loans between members of groups A and B. Specifically, we omitted any transaction costs for collecting the additional future taxes from the type-B people. But if these individuals are poor credit risks who require close supervision by private lenders, then they are likely to cause similar problems for the government. On the other hand, some people argue that the ability to levy taxes and to use the police power to collect taxes actually does make the government more efficient in the loan process. Then a deficit-financed tax cut really does raise wealth in the aggregate. Namely, this fiscal policy means that the government carries out more of the loan operations at which, we assume, it is particularly efficient.[22] Of course, if the government is not more efficient, then we no longer get the increase in wealth. That is, when we include the resources that the government uses up to make sure that the people of type B pay their taxes, then the apparent gains disappear.

Even if private loan markets are imperfect—in the sense of being less efficient than the government—the results do not conform to the standard analysis of a deficit-financed tax cut. For instance, although the real interest rate on the well-secured loans increases, that on less well-secured loans tends to fall. That is, we predict a narrowing of the spread between the two rates, r and $\bar{r}$. Also, there need not be crowding-out of private investment. Rather, we find mainly a diversion of all types of spending away from people who have good access to the loan market (the members of group A) and toward those who lack this access (the people of group B).

Social Security and Saving

Some economists argue that, just as in the case of a deficit-financed tax cut, a larger social security program makes people feel wealthier.[23] This effect arises when the social security system is not **fully funded.** In a funded setup workers' payments accumulate in a trust fund, which provides later for retirement benefits. The alternative is a **pay-as-you-go system,** in which benefits to old persons are financed by taxes on the currently young. In this case, the people who are at or near retirement age when the program begins or expands receive benefits without paying a comparable present value of taxes. Correspondingly, the people from later generations pay taxes that exceed their expected benefits in present-value terms (unfortunately, most readers of this book are in this category).

The U.S. system operates mainly on a pay-as-you-go basis. Although the original view of the system in 1935 envisioned an important role for the social security trust fund, the system has evolved steadily since 1939 toward primarily a pay-as-you-go operation.[24] In particular, retirees increasingly received benefits that—in present-value terms—exceeded their prior contributions.

Let's consider the effects of social security in a pay-as-you-go-system. For this purpose, we neglect the substitution effects from the taxes and transfers, since we already discussed these in the previous chapter. Now we look only at the wealth

---

[22]There is no indication that the U.S. government has superior skills in direct loans, as evidenced by its widespread problems in collecting from students. In fact, the tendency is to subcontract the handling of these loans to private financial institutions.

[23]The argument first appears in Martin Feldstein, "Social Security, Induced Retirement, and Aggregate Capital Accumulation," *Journal of Political Economy,* September/October 1974.

[24]For a discussion of the institutional features, see Michael Boskin, ed. *The Crisis in Social Security,* Institute for Contemporary Studies, San Francisco, 1977.

effects from an increase in retirement benefits, when these are financed by higher taxes on workers.

The usual argument goes as follows. Old persons have an increase in the present value of their social security transfers net of taxes. Therefore, they respond to the increase in wealth by consuming more. Young persons face higher taxes, but these are offset partly by the expectation of higher retirement benefits. Hence, the decrease in wealth for the young is smaller in magnitude than the increase for the old. In particular, we predict that aggregate consumer demand rises, so that desired saving falls. Therefore, we also predict an increase in the real interest rate and a decrease in net investment. In the long run, this decrease in net investment shows up as a smaller stock of capital.

The above argument for social security parallels the standard view of a deficit-financed tax cut. In both cases, the increase in aggregate consumer demand arises only if people neglect the adverse effects on descendants. Specifically, an increase in the scale of the social-security program means that the typical person's descendants will be born with a tax liability that exceeds their prospective retirement benefits in present-value terms. If people take full account of these effects on their descendants, the aggregate wealth effect from more social security is nil.

As in the case of a deficit-financed tax cut, more social security enables older persons to extract funds from their descendants. But as before, people value this change only if they give no transfers to their children and receive nothing from their children. Otherwise, people respond to more social security by shifting private intergenerational transfers, rather than by changing consumption. For example, in the United States the growth of social security has strongly diminished the tendency for children to support their aged parents.

On an empirical level, there has been a great debate about the connection of social security to saving and investment. First, Martin Feldstein reported a dramatic negative effect of social security on capital accumulation in the United States.[25] But subsequent investigators disputed these findings.[26] In fact, neither the long-term evidence for the United States nor that from a cross-section of countries in recent years support the proposition that social security substantially depresses saving and investment.

---

[25]See "Social Security, Induced Retirement, and Aggregate Capital Accumulation," *Journal of Political Economy,* September/October 1974.

[26]For a summary of the debate, see Louis Esposito, "Effect of Social Security on Saving: Review of Studies Using U.S. Time Series Data," *Social Security Bulletin,* May 1978; and the papers in the May 1979 issue of the *Social Security Bulletin.* For the popular press (*Business Week,* September 22, 1980), the issue was settled by Dean Leimer and Selig Lesnoy in their paper, "Social Security and Private Saving: A reexamination of the Time Series Evidence Using Alternative Social Security Wealth Variables," Social Security Administration, November 1980. These researchers report that Feldstein's conclusions stem from an error in his computer program!

Summary

The ability to issue and retire interest-bearing public debt allows the government's expenditures to diverge in the short run from the sum of its tax receipts and its revenue from printing money. As an analogue to households' saving, we define the government's real deficit to be the change in the real value of its outstanding liabilities. This concept involves two adjustments to standard measures of the deficit. First, we remove the inflation part of nominal interest payments, and second, we divide by the price level. Then we find that real deficits are large mainly during wars and recessions, and tend to be negative in "normal" times.

Shifts between taxes and deficits affect the timing of tax collections, but not their overall present value. Hence, if we hold fixed the behavior of government purchases, this type of fiscal policy has no aggregate wealth effect, and consequently no impact on aggregate consumer demand. Equivalently, households save the full amount of their extra disposable income in order to provide for the funds to pay the higher future taxes. For the case of lump-sum taxes, it follows that deficits do not alter the real interest rate, or the quantities of investment and output. This result is called the Ricardian Equivalence Theorem, which says that taxes and deficits have the same effect on the economy. A related conclusion concerns open-market operations, which are exchanges between money and public debt. These operations change the price level in the same proportion as the change in the quantity of money, but, aside from the change in the real public debt, there are no effects on real variables.

When we consider an income tax, there are some real effects from a deficit. These concern the timing of taxes, which generate intertemporal-substitution effects on work and production. Generally, it is optimal for the government to manage the public debt in order to avoid large random fluctuations in tax rates from period to period. This motivation accounts for the tendency to run large real deficits during wars and recessions, but to run real surpluses in "good times."

The standard view of deficit-financed tax cuts is that they make people feel wealthier. In this case, deficits would raise the real interest rate and crowd out investment. Sometimes, people-rationalize the wealth effect from a tax cut by appealing to finite lives or imperfect capital markets. But an examination of these ideas suggests that they are unlikely to support the standard conclusions. Also, some statistical evidence reveals no significant relation between deficits and interest rates.

Finally, we note that social security is analogous to the public debt. Thus, if debt-financed tax cuts have little effect on interest rates and capital accumulation, then the same goes for an increase in the scale of the social security program.

Important Terms and Concepts

government deficit (surplus)

public debt

monetize the deficit

fiscal policy

nominal deficit (national accounts' version)

real deficit (national accounts' version)

real deficit

nominal deficit

balanced budget

Ricardian Equivalence Theorem

open-market operations

full-employment deficit

crowding-out (from government deficits)

fully funded system (for social security)

pay-as-you-go system (for social security)

QUESTIONS AND PROBLEMS

Mainly for Review

15.1 What is the real deficit? Why does a rise in the inflation rate reduce the real deficit? Show how the real deficit is altered either by policy changes or by economic events such as recessions.

15.2 Suppose there is a temporary increase in (lump-sum) taxes. Is there any effect on households' wealth? Show how the typical household can use the credit market to offset the reduction in current disposable income.

15.3 Are government budget deficits inflationary? If so, would you expect any effect on the real rate of interest? What about the nominal rate of interest?

15.4 Why are open-market operations neutral?

15.5 Suppose the government announces a reduction in tax rates to take place in some future period. What intertemporal substitution effect will this have on current work? What effect will it have on consumption?

15.6 Compare the effect of (a) government budget deficits and (b) social security on the tax liabilities of younger people. Why do the tax liabilities exceed expected future benefits in the case of social security?

Problems for Discussion

15.7 Inflation and the Government's Budget

Suppose, starting from 1985, that money and prices grow at a steady annual rate of 10%. (Assume that the entire money stock is a liability of the government, as in our theoretical model.) Real cash balances are fixed over time at $200 billion (in terms of 1982 prices). The nominal quantity of interest-bearing public debt also grows at 10% per year. Hence, the real value of this debt is fixed at, say, $1 trillion. Assume that the nominal interest rate on government bonds is constant at 12% per year. Aggregate output is also constant.

a. What is the annual flow of real revenue that the government obtains by printing money? How would this answer change if the rates of growth of money and prices had been assumed to equal 20% per year, rather than 10%?

b. Returning to the original situation, what is the annual flow of real revenue that the government receives by issuing public debt? How does this amount compare with the real value of the government's annual interest payments? Would this comparison change if prices and the stocks of money and public debt had been assumed to be growing at a 20% annual rate, while the nominal interest rate was 22%? What does this result mean for the effect of inflation on the net real revenue from printing bonds?

c. Beginning from the initial setting, suppose that the money stock and price level (but not the nominal public debt) suddenly double. This action is regarded as a one-time surprise. In what ways does this "unexpected inflation" affect the government's revenue position?

d. Returning again to the original situation, how would the national accounts measure the government's deficit over time? How would you measure it?

15.8 The Aggregate Wealth Effect from a Deficit

Assume that taxes are lump sum. Suppose that the government cuts current taxes and runs a deficit. Then assume that the real public debt remains constant from period 2 onward. Also, the time paths of government purchases and real transfers do not change. Discuss the aggregate wealth effect that results from the government's current tax cut. In particular, how does this effect depend on the following considerations:

a. Finite lifetimes?

b. The existence of childless persons?

c. Uncertainty about who will pay the higher future taxes?

d. The possibility that the government will print more money in the future, rather than raising taxes?

e. The imperfection of private loan markets?

15.9 Effects of a Deficit-Financed Tax Cut

Assume that taxes are lump sum. Suppose again that the government cuts current taxes and runs a deficit. Discuss the effects for the current period on first, the real interest rate and the quantities of output and investment, and second, the price level and the nominal interest rate, assuming that

a. The time paths of government purchases, real transfers and money creation do not change.

b. The same as in part **a**, except that people expect the future growth rate of money to rise.

c. The same as in part **a**, except that people expect future real transfers to fall.

d. The same as in part **a**, except that people expect future government purchases to decline.

15.10 The Reagan Tax-Cut Plan for 1981

President Reagan's proposal in 1981 for cutting U.S. federal income-tax rates involved roughly a 23% overall reduction in rates. The full cut was to be phased in over a three-year period ending in 1983. The plan involved also gradual reductions over time in real government expenditures when expressed as a fraction of real GNP.

Consider an alternative plan that yields the same present value of real tax revenues, but which implements the entire cut in tax rates in 1981. Assume that real government expenditures behave the same way as under Reagan's plan. Compare this plan with Reagan's with respect to the effects on work effort, production, and investment over the period 1981–83.

15.11 The Government's Stock of Gold

The U.S. Treasury's gold stock is held at the Federal Reserve. Mostly because of changes in the price of gold, the market value of these holdings rose from $12 billion at the end of 1970 to $117 billion at the end of 1982. In terms of 1972 prices, the increase was from $13 billion at the end of 1970 to $56 billion at the end of 1982.

a. How would you modify the measure of the government's deficit to include these changes in the value of gold holdings?

b. Can you apply your reasoning more generally to the government's holdings of other commodities, capital goods and land?

(Amusingly, the Federal Reserve values its gold holdings at the official price of $42.22 per ounce, rather than at the market price, which was $444 per ounce at the end of 1982.)

15.12 Temporary Consumption Taxes (optional)

Suppose that taxes are levied on consumption, rather than income. An individual's real tax for period t is then $t_t/P_t = \tau_t c_t - e_t$. Suppose that the government runs a deficit during period 1 and cuts the marginal tax rate on consumption, τ_1. For subsequent periods, the marginal tax rates are higher than otherwise.

a. What is the impact of the tax cut on the demand and supply of goods for period 1?

b. What is the effect on the current values of the real interest rate, output, work effort, consumption and investment?

PART V

INTERACTIONS BETWEEN THE MONETARY SECTOR AND THE REAL SECTOR

CHAPTER 16

FINANCIAL INTERMEDIATION

The Role of Financial Intermediaries

In our model the people who hold bonds make direct loans to other people. So a lender may hold a mortgage on someone's house, or a loan collateralized by someone's car, or a loan to a business for investment purposes. But this type of direct lending is often inefficient. First, it requires people to evaluate the credit-worthiness of borrowers, which is costly when strangers are involved (or even when we loan funds to a friend or relative!). Second, unless individuals hold portions of many different types of loans, they may have substantial risks of losing a large part of their assets when a single loan goes bad. But it is hard for an individual to diversify by holding lots of different loans. Finally, the form of claim that someone holds—say, a home mortgage—must match the form of the loan in terms of its maturity. So in the case of a 20-year loan to a homeowner, the lender can cash in this claim only by selling it to someone else or by convincing the borrower to pay it off.

Financial intermediaries can solve the problems that we just mentioned. As examples of these intermediaries, we can think of banks, savings and loan associations, and money-market funds.[1] On the one hand, these institutions are in a good position to evaluate and collect on loans, and to assemble a variety of loans by type and maturity. On the other hand, the financial intermediaries attract funds by providing desirable vehicles for lenders to hold their assets. Often, these take the form of deposits. The main differences in the features of deposits are as follows:

- Whether they can be withdrawn on demand at face value. This privilege applies to **demand deposits** and usually to **savings deposits,** which often have passbooks and legally allow for 30-days notice of withdrawal. In contrast, **time deposits** have a stated maturity date, with some penalties typically attached to premature withdrawals.

---

[1]Others are mutual savings banks, pension funds, investment companies, insurance companies, and the government's mortgage associations.

- Whether people can write checks that instruct the financial intermediary to make payments to a third party. In the United States, all demand deposits are checkable.
- Whether they pay interest and at what rate.
- Whether they are insured by the federal government. At present, this insurance applies to deposits up to $100,000 at most commercial banks, savings and loan associations, and mutual savings banks.

The main point is that the various kinds of deposits are often more attractive for households than the alternative of lending directly to other homeowners, businesses, and so on.

Table 16.1 shows the structure of the balance sheet for a typical depository institution, by which we mean a financial intermediary that provides deposits for its customers. (Insurance companies are examples of financial intermediaries that do not provide deposits.) In order to be concrete, we look at the figures for 1981 on an actual, medium-size commercial bank, which had total assets of about $6 billion at the end of 1981.[2]

Let's look first at the main items on the asset side of the balance sheet. Here we have:

Cash of $.75 billion. This item includes currency (often called **vault cash**), deposits held on the books of the Federal Reserve, and deposits held at other financial institutions. The total of currency and deposits held at the Fed is called **reserves.**

Loans of $4.16 billion. The principal items are commercial loans, mortgages, installment and credit card loans, and foreign loans.[3]

Securities of $.97 billion. This category includes government bonds and short-term ''money-market instruments'' (such as commercial paper and certificates of deposit issued by other financial institutions). Also, we would include here any short-term lending to other financial intermediaries on the **Federal Funds market.** (Financial institutions—primarily commercial banks—borrow funds from each other on a very short-term basis in this market. The interest rate charged on these loans is called the **Federal Funds rate.**)

Buildings and other physical capital of $.15 billion.

Now, let's look at the liability side of the ledger. The principal items are:

Demand deposits of $1.45 billion.
Time deposits of $3.58 billion.

---

[2]The figures are for the Valley National Bank of Arizona. (A principal claim to fame for this bank is that I once owned some stock in it. This investment turned out to be less than brilliant, once it became clear that some of their loans were to Mexico.)

[3]In the United States there are many legal restrictions on the types of earning assets that financial intermediaries can hold. For example, commercial banks cannot hold corporate stock. Also, savings and loan associations and mutual savings banks can hold only very limited amounts of commercial loans.

Table 16.1 **Balance Sheet of Valley National Bank of Arizona
(December 21, 1981) (amounts in billions of dollars)**

Assets		Liabilities	
Cash (includes deposits held at Fed		Demand deposits	1.45
and other financial institutions)	0.75	Time deposits	3.58
Loans (net of loss reserve)	4.16	Borrowing from Federal Funds	
Securities	0.97	Market	0.07
Buildings, etc.	0.15	Borrowing from Fed	0
Other assets	0.11	Repurchase agreements	0.31
		Notes outstanding (acceptances)	0.22
		Other liabilities	0.13
		Shareholders' equity	0.38
Total	6.14	Total	6.14

Source: Moody's Bank & Finance Manual, 1982, pp. 512, ff.

Borrowings from the Federal Funds market of $0.07 billion. Typically, it is the larger banks that borrow in this market, while the smaller banks provide most of the loans.

Borrowings from the Federal Reserve (also called the *Fed*), which are nil in this case. The Federal Reserve lends to financial institutions—principally commercial banks that are members of the Federal Reserve System—at the "discount window." The interest rate charged on these loans is called the Fed's **discount rate.**

Repurchase agreements (or "repos") of $0.31 billion. As an example, a financial intermediary sells a security to a customer—probably a large corporation—but agrees to repurchase this security at a specified price the next day. Thus, the repo provides a known interest rate on overnight loans. In effect, a repo is a short-term deposit, which is typically for a very large amount. But the advantage of the repo is that it escapes the reserve requirement that would apply to a conventional deposit (see below).

Interest-bearing notes issued by the bank (bankers' acceptances) of $0.22 billion.

Shareholders' equity of $0.38 billion.

Reserves—Required and Excess

Intermediaries hold "earning assets"—by which we mean loans and securities—in order to obtain a flow of interest income. They hold physical capital and deposits at other financial institutions in order to carry out their business efficiently. What about cash? Since banks and some other depository institutions stand ready to convert their deposits into currency on demand, they would hold some currency in order to meet the possible withdrawals of depositors. But in the United States in recent years, the key determinant of cash holdings by these institutions is the **reserve requirement** imposed by the Federal Reserve. These requirements specify the quantity of reserves that must be held against various categories of deposits.[4] Legally, the reserves can be held either as currency (vault cash) or as non-interest-bearing deposits on the books of the Federal Reserve.[5] Before 1980, the Fed's requirements applied only to commercial banks that were members of the Federal Reserve System.[6] However, the Monetary Control Act of 1980 extended the reserve requirements to all depository institutions (not including money-market funds), but at lower average percentages than before. By 1984 for member commercial banks and by 1988 for other depository institutions, the requirements will be 12% for all checkable deposits[7] and 3% for all business time deposits of maturity less than five years. But the Fed retains some discretionary authority to vary these requirements.

Figure 16.1 shows how the ratio of required reserves to checkable deposits changes from 1918 to 1982. (For years before the mid-1970s, checkable deposits coincide with demand deposits at commercial banks.) There are two general sources of change in this ratio, the main one being a shift in legal requirements. But some requirements attach also to time and savings deposits, which do not enter into the total of checkable deposits. Also, the requirements depend on the total volume of deposits of the financial institution (or, before 1972, on whether a bank was located in a city or in the "country"). Therefore, some changes in the ratio of required reserves to checkable deposits reflect shifts in the composition of deposits (between checkable and time or savings, and among the categories of financial institutions). We shall discuss later some details and implications of the shifts in the required-reserve ratio.

Instead of keeping non-interest-bearing cash, financial institutions prefer to hold assets that bear interest. Since these institutions can shift rapidly in and out of short-term securities (as well as the Federal Funds Market and repurchase agreements), even a moderate interest rate induces them to hold very little reserves above the required amount. We use the term, **excess reserves,** for the differences between total and required reserves. Figure 16.2 shows that these excess reserves are less than 1% of total reserves throughout the 1970s, when interest rates are high. However, at the lower interest rates that prevailed earlier during the post-

---

[4]Since 1968, reserve requirements depend on deposits held two weeks earlier (which is called *lagged reserve accounting*). However, the vault cash from two weeks before counts as today's reserves. An announcement in 1982 indicates the Fed's plan to return in 1984 to the earlier system where required reserves depend on the contemporaneous amount of deposits. However, vault cash will still count toward meeting reserve requirements with roughly a two-week lag.

[5]Before December 1959 (and since 1917), vault cash did not count at all toward satisfying the reserve requirements. But since November 1960 all vault cash counts.

[6]Membership is optional for state-chartered banks. But nonmembers were subject to a variety of requirements by state and local governments.

[7]The requirement is only 3% of an institution's checkable deposits up to a total of $25 million. For further discussion of the Monetary Control Act, see Robert Auerbach, *Money, Banking and Financial Markets,* Macmillan, New York, 1981, pp. 106, ff.

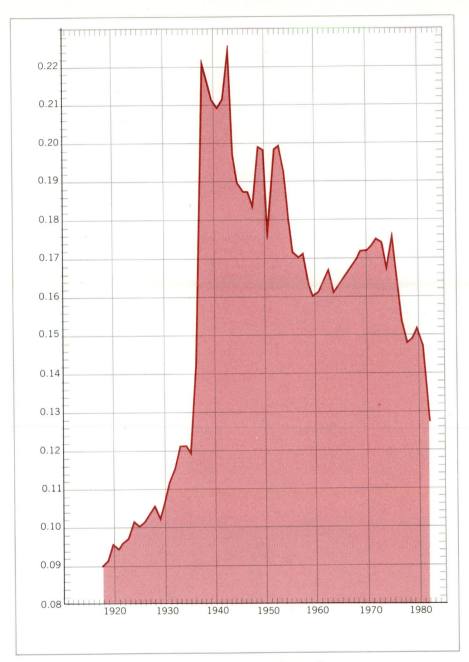

Figure 16.1 **The Ratio of Required Reserves to Checkable Deposits**

Sources (for Figure 16.1 and subsequent figures): Board of Governors of the Federal Reserve System, *Banking and Monetary Statistics; Banking and Monetary Statistics, 1941–1970; Annual Statistical Digest, 1970–79;* and *Federal Reserve Bulletin,* various issues.

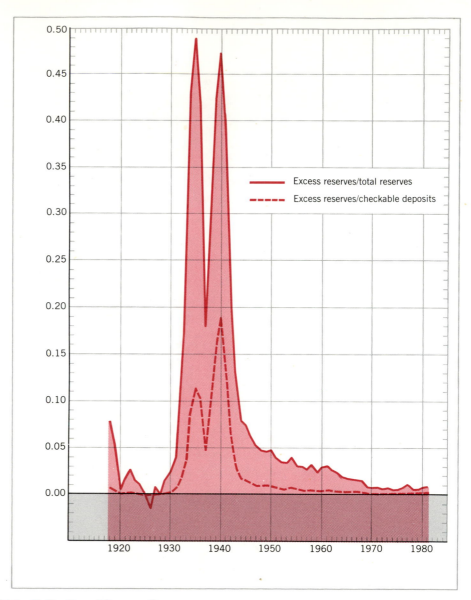

Figure 16.2 The Behavior of Excess Reserves

World War II period, excess reserves are as much as 5% of the total. Notice also the large holdings of excess reserves from 1933 to 1941. Here, the ratio of excess reserves to the total averages 37%. This behavior reflects the financial crises of the Great Depression, as well as the extremely low interest rates on safe assets. We shall discuss this period in detail later on.

We should note that excess reserves provide funds that a financial institution can dip into during emergencies. By contrast, required reserves do not serve this purpose. Specifically, for a given amount of deposits, a depository institution is not permitted to let its reserves fall below the required amount.

Deposits and Earning Assets

Suppose that a depository institution attracts an additional $100 of deposits. It is legally required to hold part of this $100 as non-interest-bearing reserves. (This part is now about $12 for the case of checkable deposits.) The rest of the $100 may be divided as the institution chooses between loans and securities (which bear interest) or excess reserves (which do not bear interest). The change in the institution's net earnings equals the interest on the additional earning assets, less the added costs of evaluating and collecting on loans or dealing in securities, less any extra costs of servicing the deposits (if no separate fees are charged), less the interest paid on the new deposits. In order for the institution to profit from this enterprise, it must be that the interest rate on deposits, call it R^d, is less than that on loans and securities, which we still call R.[8] In particular, the spread, $R - R^d$, must cover at least the following: first, the cost of the funds that the intermediary holds in non-interest-bearing form, second, the transaction costs associated with handling the additional deposits and earning assets, and third, some return on the capital invested in the business of being an intermediary—that is, some amount of "normal profit." Let's call the total of these items the **costs of intermediation.** Then suppose that we neglect for the moment any governmental regulations that limit interest rates on deposits. In this case, competition among intermediaries drives up the interest rate on deposits high enough so that the net earnings from an extra dollar of deposits covers only the normal profit. That is, the spread, $R - R^d$, just balances the costs of intermediation.[9]

As an illustration, suppose that the interest rate on earning assets, R, is 15%, and that the reserve requirement is 12% of deposits. Also, suppose that financial institutions hold no excess reserves. Further, assume that transaction costs are 1% of earning assets and 0.5% of deposits. Finally, suppose that normal profit is 1% of deposits (although this profit would actually relate to the amount of invested capital, rather than directly to the volume of deposits). Then an extra $100 of deposits means:

- $88 of added earning assets, which yield $13.20 per year in interest (15% of $88),
- $12 of added reserves, which yield zero interest,

---

[8]In practice, interest rates differ significantly on different types of loans and securities. The rates depend on the risks of default and on how costly the assets are to evaluate and collect.

[9]For further discussion of this type of result, see Ben Klein, "Competitive Interest Payments on Bank Deposits and the Long-Run Demand for Money," *American Economic Review*, December 1974.

- $0.88 of added transaction costs on earning assets (1% of $88),
- $0.50 of added transaction costs on deposits (0.5% of $100), and
- $1.00 more of normal profit.

Therefore, before paying interest on the deposits, the net return (after an allowance for normal profit) is $10.82 ($13.20—$0.88—$0.50—$1.00). Hence, an interest rate on deposits, R^d, of 10.8% would drive the net earnings on an extra dollar of deposits down to the normal profit.

Overall, competition among intermediaries tells us the following things about the interest rate paid on deposits, R^d. This rate rises with

- An increase in the interest rate on loans and securities, R (but by less than one-to-one).
- A decrease in the required-reserve ratio, which was 12% in the example.
- A decline in the transaction costs associated with handling earning assets and deposits.

Regulation of Interest Rates on Deposits

Since the 1930s, the federal government has regulated the interest rates that banks and other intermediaries can pay on deposits. With the Banking Acts of 1933 and 1935, the government prohibited interest payments on demand deposits. This restriction stayed in force until the middle and late 1970s, when interest-bearing checking accounts began to develop. These mainly take the form of negotiable-order-of-withdrawal (or N.O.W.) accounts. Of course, a negotiable-order-of-withdrawal is just another name for a check. These types of accounts, which bear interest, began in New England in the mid-1970s, but became available nationwide with the Monetary Control Act of 1980.

The Federal Reserve limits interest rates on time and savings deposits through its **Regulation Q.** Figure 16.3 shows how the legal limit for the rate on small-size, short maturity time deposits at commercial banks compares with an open-market interest rate, which we measure as the rate on four- to six-month prime commercial paper. The figure suggests that the ceiling rates on time deposits are high enough not to be binding at least until the 1950s. But the rate on commercial paper rises above this ceiling in the middle and late 1950s, in the late 1960s, and in much of the 1970s. In particular, for 1979–81, the gap exceeds 5 percentage points. So in these periods—and especially in 1979–81—the government's restrictions constrained the interest rates that banks and some other depository intermediaries could offer to their depositors. However, recent regulatory changes effectively remove the restrictions on the interest rates that financial institutions can pay.

What happens when the legal limit on deposits is below the interest rate that would otherwise be paid? One point is that the limits apply only to explicit interest. Thus, institutions often compete for profitable deposits by providing services at below cost. Then the services that people receive by holding deposits amount to

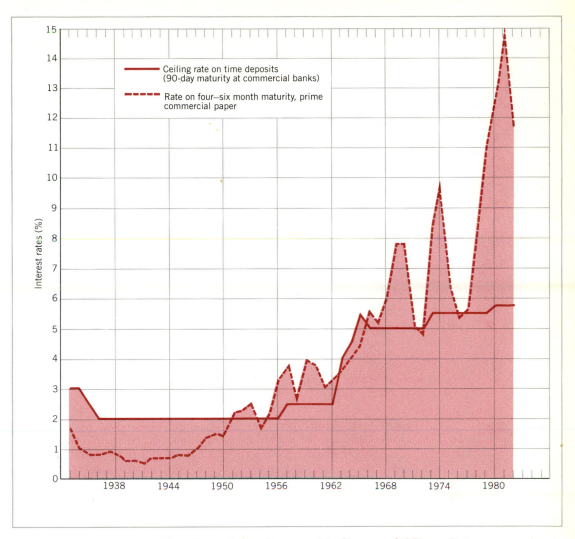

Figure 16.3 **Ceiling Rates on Time Deposits as Compared to Commercial Paper Rates**

implicit interest, which substitutes for the explicit interest that the government prohibits. This mechanism is especially important for demand deposits, where the legal limit on interest, namely, zero, was almost always below the rate the institutions would otherwise pay. In a study of demand deposits, Tony Santomero and I estimated this implicit interest rate by seeing how commercial banks remitted service charges in accordance with the balances that customers held in regular checking accounts. We found that the implicit interest rate on demand deposits rose from about 1.5% in 1950 to about 2.5% in 1968.[10] Presumably, this change reflected the added competition for demand deposits because of the rise in market interest rates. (Commercial paper rates increased from 1.4% in 1950 to 5.9% in 1968.)

Although intermediaries employ numerous methods to evade restrictions on interest rates, we should not conclude that these restrictions are irrelevant. Basically, the implicit methods of paying interest tend to be less efficient than the explicit ones. That's because there are limits to the services that banks can conveniently provide as close substitutes for explicit interest. (However, an offsetting effect is that explicit interest is taxable, whereas free services typically are not.) In any case as market interest rates rise—as they have since the 1950s—the ceiling rates on deposits make it increasingly difficult for the regulated institutions to compete for funds.[11] There have been several predictable responses to this situation:

People move away from deposits and toward direct holding of assets such as bonds and mortgages. This process, which is the reverse of intermediation, is called **disintermediation.**

New types of unregulated financial intermediaries arise, which attract funds away from banks and other institutions. In recent years, the primary example is money-market funds, whose assets grew from near zero in 1977 to over $200 billion by the end of 1982. The money-market funds hold various securities (including large, unregulated certificates-of-deposits that are issued by banks!) and offer deposit-like instruments to their customers. Some of these, like the Merrill Lynch cash-management account (CMA) and its imitators, are checkable without major restrictions.

The government eventually changes its regulations on deposit interest rates, so that banks and other depository intermediaries can again compete effectively for funds. However, according to the regulations established through 1982, there are two remaining distinctions between the money-market funds and the other depository institutions. First, there are no reserve requirements on the money-market funds. But second, unlike the deposits at banks and some other intermediaries, the shares in money-market funds are not insured by the federal government.

Borrowing from the Federal Reserve

From the start of the Federal Reserve System in 1914 until 1980, banks that are members of the Federal Reserve System can borrow short-term funds at the discount

---

[10]See Robert Barro and Anthony Santomero, "Household Money Holdings and the Demand Deposit Rate," *Journal of Money, Credit and Banking,* May 1972.

[11]There is no need to feel sorry for financial intermediaries on this ground. After all, another aspect of the ceiling rates is that they can eliminate some competition among intermediaries, which may result in monopoly profits on deposits. That's why many financial institutions liked Regulation Q until the unregulated money-market funds attracted too many deposits.

rate from a Federal Reserve bank. With the Monetary Control Act of 1980, all depository institutions with checkable deposits can borrow from the Fed.

Borrowing from the Federal Reserve can be advantageous if the Fed's discount rate is below the rates at which banks can otherwise borrow and lend. However, such borrowing may not always be desirable even if the discount rate is relatively low. That's because first, the Fed examines banks more carefully when they borrow frequently at the discount window, and second, the Fed can refuse to lend to banks that ask "too often." In any case the lower the discount rate, relative to market interest rates, the greater the incentive for banks to borrow from the Fed.

Figure 16.4 shows the ratio of borrowings from the Fed to checkable deposits from 1918 to 1982. Notice that these borrowings are important during World War I and through the 1920s. In particular, borrowings peak at 13% of checkable deposits in 1920,[12] and still amount to 4% of these deposits in 1929, 3% in 1932, and 2% in 1933. However, borrowings fall to near zero for 1935–43. During the post-World War II period, some borrowing occurs, but the ratio to checkable deposits never exceeds 1%. For these years, the peak in the ratio occurs in 1974, where the average amount borrowed of $2 billion constitutes about 1% of checkable deposits. Most of these loans are to the Franklin National Bank of Long Island, which was a large bank that engaged in questionable speculations and subsequently failed.

Figure 16.5 shows how the annual average discount rate at the New York Fed compares to the interest rate on four- to six-month maturity prime commercial paper.[13] (The discount rates at the Federal Reserve banks in different cities stay very close to each other.) Although the two interest rates shown in Figure 16.5 tend to move together, the discount rate is typically lower than the commercial paper rate since World War II. Therefore, in these years the loans from the Fed usually involved a subsidy to the borrower. In some years—1966–67, 1969–70, 1973–74, and 1981—the discount rate was more than a full percentage point below the commercial paper rate. Looking at the earlier years, we see that the discount rate exceeded the commercial paper rate from 1932 to 1946. But the discount rate was lower than the commercial paper rate during the 1920s and especially for 1918–20.

The Federal Reserve

Since 1914 the Federal Reserve System has functioned as the central bank in the United States. While there are 12 regional Federal Reserve banks, the main power

---

[12]The borrowings of member banks actually exceeded their total reserves for 1919–21. For example, the average amount borrowed during 1920 was $2.5 billion, while the average amount of reserves was $1.8 billion. Hence, the banks' "unborrowed reserves" (total reserves less borrowings) was negative at this time.

[13]The comparison is similar if we look at the federal funds rate. But these data are available only since 1954.

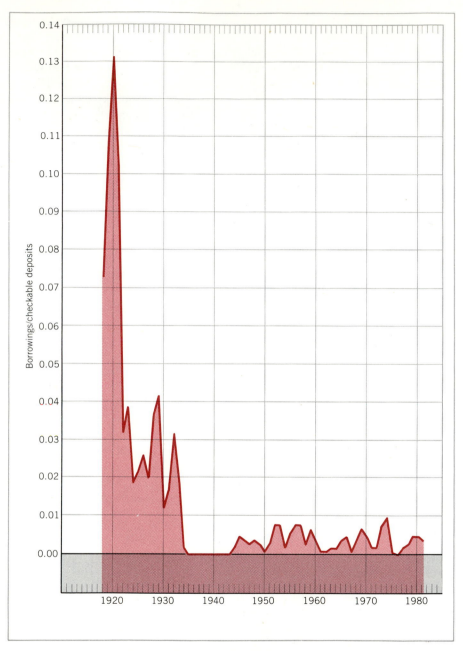

Figure 16.4 Borrowings from the Federal Reserve as a Ratio to Checkable Deposits

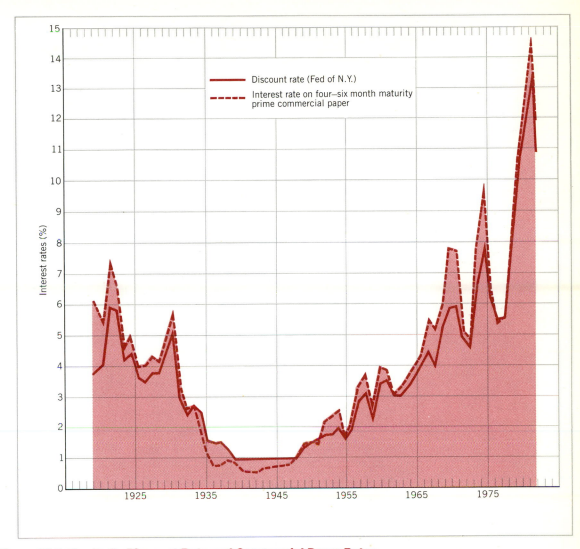

Figure 16.5 The Fed's Discount Rate and Commercial Paper Rates

now resides in the seven-member Board of Governors in Washington. We have already mentioned some of the Fed's activities, which include the setting of reserve requirements, the regulation of interest rates on deposits, and the lending to financial institutions at the discount window.[14] Now we want to focus on the Fed's instruments for controlling the quantity of money. Here, we begin by looking at the balance sheet of the Federal Reserve System.

[14]For discussions of the Federal Reserve System and its policy instruments, see Robert Auerbach, *Money, Banking and Financial Markets,* Macmillan, New York, 1982, Chapters 15 and 16; and Milton Friedman, *A Program for Monetary Stability,* Fordham University Press, New York, 1960, Chapter 2.

Table 16.2 Balance Sheet of all Federal Reserve Banks
(December 31, 1981) (amounts in billions of dollars)

Assets		Liabilities and Capital Account	
Gold account	11.2	Federal Reserve notes (currency)	131.9
Loans to depository institutions	1.6	Deposits of depository institutions	25.2
U.S. government and agency		U.S. Treasury deposits	4.3
securities	140.1	Other deposits and liabilities	4.0
Other assets*	15.1	Paid-in capital and surplus	2.6
Total	168.0	Total	168.0

*Consists of special drawing rights at the International Monetary Fund ($3.3 billion), assets denominated in foreign currency ($5.1 billion), coin ($0.4 billion), accrued interest ($2.2 billion), physical capital ($0.6 billion), and some other items.

Source: U.S. Board of Governors of the Federal Reserve System, *Annual Report,* 1981, pp. 212–13.

Table 16.2 shows the balance sheet at the end of 1981. The main items on the asset side are the following:

- Gold account of $11.2 billion (carried at the official price of $42.22 per ounce). The Fed holds this gold on behalf of the U.S. Treasury. In past years, when the United States was on the gold standard, variations in the quantity of gold resulted mainly from dealings with foreign central banks. Now there are changes if the Treasury auctions off gold or if there are adjustments in the official price of gold. (These changes in price occurred in 1933 and a few times in the 1970s.)

- Loans to Depository Institutions of $1.6 billion. These are the borrowings of depository intermediaries at the discount rate, which we mentioned before.

- U.S. Government and Agency Securities of $140.1 billion. As the balance sheet makes clear, the bulk of the Fed's assets are held in this form.

Finally, the sum of loans to depository institutions, U.S. government and agency securities, and some miscellaneous assets is sometimes called **Federal Reserve Credit.** This amount represents the total of the Fed's claims on the government and the private sector. Note that the great bulk of Federal Reserve credit takes the form of U.S. government securities. That is, in the United States, the central bank engages in little direct lending to the private sector.

On the liability side of the Fed's ledger, we have the following main items:

- Federal Reserve Notes (currency) of $131.9 billion. At present these notes are the only form of currency outstanding. But at earlier dates, currency was issued by the U.S. Treasury and—even earlier—as notes from private banks.

- Deposits of Depository Institutions of $25.2 billion. These are the noninterest-bearing reserves of depository intermediaries, which we mentioned before.

• U.S. Treasury deposits of \$4.3 billion. Essentially, these deposits are the federal government's checking account, which is held at the Federal Reserve.

The total of federal reserve notes and deposits of depository institutions (\$157.1 billion) is called the **monetary base** or **high-powered money.** This sum represents the total of the Fed's monetary liabilities (aside from those held by the U.S. Treasury or as foreign deposits). Note that, in 1981, about 84% of the monetary base takes the form of currency, while only 16% appears as deposits of depository institutions.

Figure 16.6 shows how the monetary base has evolved from 1918 to 1982. For recent years, the definition of the base is the one given above. But at earlier times it included also private holdings of monetary gold (until 1933), as well as paper currency issued by the U.S. Treasury.

Control of the Monetary Base

Open-Market Operations

Under present arrangements, the Federal Reserve has close control over the monetary base. Primarily, the Fed exercises this control through **open-market operations.** For example, in the case of an open-market purchase, the Fed[15] writes a check to buy, say, \$1 million of U.S. government securities. Suppose that the seller of the bonds is a commercial bank, which we call People's Bank. (We would end up with the same results if the seller were a household or, more likely, a large corporation.) Then the Fed credits this bank with \$1 million more of reserves in the form of book-entry deposits at the Fed. Thus, at this point, the balance sheets of the Fed and People's Bank change as shown in Table 16.3. Notice first that the Fed has \$1 million more in assets in the form of government bonds. This amount balances the extra \$1 million of liabilities, which show up as more deposits of depository institutions (in this case of People's Bank). Correspondingly, People's Bank has \$1 million more in assets in the form of deposits held at the Fed, but \$1 million less of government bonds, which are a part of the bank's portfolio of loans and securities.

The balance sheets shown in Table 16.3 are not the end of the story, because People's Bank may not want to hold \$1 million more of non-interest-bearing reserves at the Fed. But let's hold off on this matter for now in order to focus on the behavior of the monetary base. In particular, the open-market purchase of securities shown in Table 16.3 raises the monetary base by \$1 million, which shows up, at least initially, as an extra \$1 million in reserves held by depository institutions at the Fed. Note also that an open-market sale of securities would just reverse the process. That is, if the Fed sells \$1 million of U.S. government bonds, then the monetary base declines by \$1 million.

---

[15]In practice, these decisions are made by the Federal Open-Market Committee (FOMC). The membership of this important committee consists of the seven members of the Federal Reserve's Board of Governors, plus five presidents of the regional Federal Reserve banks.

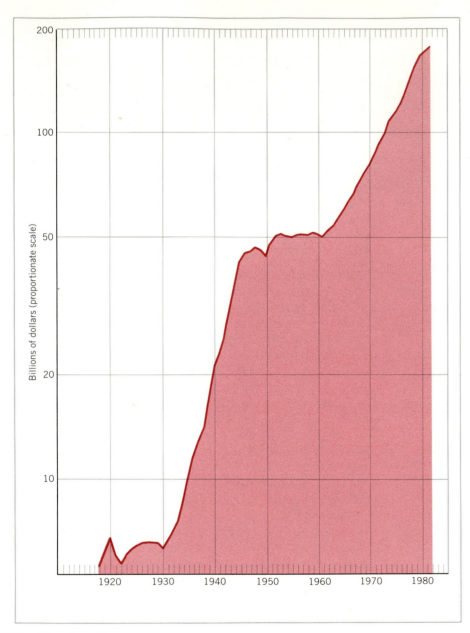

Figure 16.6 The Monetary Base

Source: Milton Friedman and Anna Schwartz, *A Monetary History of the United States, 1867–1960,* Princeton, New Jersey, Princeton University Press, Table B-3; and the sources listed in Figure 16.1.

Table 16.3 Effects on the Balance Sheets of the Fed and Depository Institutions from an Open-market Purchase of Government Bonds

Federal Reserve

Assets	Liabilities
U.S. Government Securities: +$1 million	Deposits of Depository Institutions: +$1 million

People's Bank

Assets	Liabilities
Loans & Securities: −$1 million Deposits at Fed: +$1 million	

In the United States, open-market operations involve government bonds, rather than private bonds, mortgages, shares in General Motors, and so on. That's because the Fed does not hold these types of private obligations.[16] With respect to controlling the monetary base, it would make no difference if the Fed dealt instead in private securities. In fact, it would make little difference all together if the Fed switched from holdings of the public debt to holdings of private bonds.[17] If this switch were made, then the private sector would end up holding more of the public debt, but would owe correspondingly more to the Fed. Then the Fed would have more claims on the private sector, but less on the U.S. Treasury. Overall, there would be no changes in the net positions of the private sector, the Federal Reserve, or the U.S. Treasury.

Loans to Depository Institutions

The Fed can also control the monetary base by varying the quantity of loans to depository institutions. Here, the Fed can change either the discount rate or other aspects of its lending policies in order to induce depository institutions to borrow more of less at the discount window. Suppose, for example, that People's Bank decides to borrow an additional $1 million from the Fed. Then the Fed records a loan of $1 million to People's Bank, and also credits this bank with an extra $1 million of deposits. If People's Bank just holds these deposits at the Fed (perhaps because it would otherwise have fallen short of its reserve requirement), then the balance sheets of the Fed and People's Bank change as shown in Table 16.4.

Notice that the borrowings show up as $1 million more in loans to depository

---

[16]The Fed does hold a small amount of securities issued by banks, which are called bankers' acceptances.

[17]Except that, for political reasons, we may not want the Fed to have ownership rights in private businesses.

Table 16.4 Effects on the Balance Sheets of the Fed and Depository Institutions from Fed Lending at the Discount Window

Federal Reserve

Assets	Liabilities
Loans to Depository Institutions: +$1 million	Deposits of Depository Institutions: +$1 million

People's Bank

Assets	Liabilities
Deposits at Fed: +$1 million	Borrowing from Fed: +$1 million

institutions on the asset side of the Fed's books. Simultaneously, on the liability side, there is an increase by $1 million in the deposits of depository institutions. There are corresponding changes on the books of People's Bank. The main point is that, as before, the monetary base rises by $1 million.

It is important to recognize that an increase in borrowings by depository institutions at the discount window is essentially the same as an open-market purchase of securities by the Fed. In both cases the monetary base increases. The only difference is that in one case (the open-market purchase) the Fed ends up holding more U.S. government bonds, while in the other (lending at the discount window) the Fed ends up with more loans to depository institutions.[18] Correspondingly, People's Bank ends up holding less government bonds in the first case, and more debt to the Fed in the second. Overall, the difference amounts to a shift from the Fed's holdings of U.S. government bonds to holdings of obligations on a private bank. But as mentioned before, these types of changes have no major consequences. In fact, the only significant difference concerns the subsidy that the Fed provides to depository institutions, because the discount rate is typically set below the competitive interest rate.

Economists often say that a shift in the discount rate is significant not for its direct impact on borrowings, but rather as an announcement of the Fed's intentions. Over the longer term, the Fed moves the discount rate to match changes in market interest rates (see Figure 16.5). Hence, most of the movements in the discount rate are reactions to changes in the economy, rather than vice versa. But the timing and sometimes the amount of a shift in the discount rate are at the Fed's discretion. Therefore, it is possible that some of these changes are a useful signal about the future behavior of the monetary base or of other policy instruments, such as the regulation of interest rates on deposits. However, no one has yet shown that changes in the discount rate can actually help to predict the future quantity of the monetary

[18]In fact, the depository institutions often provide some U.S. government securities as collateral for their borrowings at the Fed.

base or other economic variables. So the suggestion that shifts in the discount rate have an "announcement effect" amounts to an interesting idea, which has not been proven.

Finally, many economists suggest that the Fed should stop subsidizing borrowers—that is, it should set the discount rate at a penalty level above market interest rates. Of course, if the discount rate were actually a penalty rate, it would have to be above the rate at which an individual institution could otherwise borrow. For example, for a risky bank like Franklin National in 1974, the penalty rate would be well above the interest rate on commercial paper. But then, no institution would ever borrow from the Fed. So the suggestion for a penalty discount rate amounts to a proposal for closing the discount window.

From the standpoint of controlling the monetary base, it is clear that the discount window is unnecessary. In particular, this lending facility adds nothing to open-market operations. Thus, the argument for the existence of the discount window comes down to the desirability of the Fed's being able to subsidize selected financial institutions—presumably, mainly institutions that are in trouble. So far, no one has come up with good arguments to justify this policy.

The Monetary Base and the Volume of Deposits

Let's return now to the case shown in Table 16.3, where the open-market purchase of government bonds raises the monetary base by $1 million. (For the analysis in this section, we would get the same results if the change in the base reflected more lending at the discount window, as shown in Table 16.4.) Instead of thinking of a single bank, we consider now the effects on financial intermediaries as a whole. Thus, Table 16.5 shows that in step 1 these intermediaries have $1 million more of deposits at the Fed and $1 million less of loans and securities.

Suppose that the extra $1 million of deposits at the Fed are excess reserves, which the financial intermediaries do not wish to hold. (We assume that they also do not wish to pay off borrowings from the Fed.) Rather, these institutions place these funds into earning assets. To be concrete, we assume that they make an additional $1 million of loans to households. However, the results would be the same if the intermediaries bought more securities. In any event, the recipients of the loan have an extra $1 million, which we suppose that they hold initially as deposits at a financial intermediary. Thus the balance sheet of these intermediaries changes as shown in step 2 of Table 16.5. On the asset side there is an additional $1 million of loans and securities which offsets the initial decline by this amount. On the liability side there is an added $1 million of customer deposits.

The recipients of the loan probably do not want to hold an extra $1 million of deposits. But as they spend these funds they are transferred to the accounts of others. Ultimately, people are either induced[19] to hold an extra $1 million of

---

[19]As we shall see in the following section, the motivation derives in the present case from a higher price level.

Table 16.5 Effect of Open-market Purchase of Bonds on the Financial System

| | Financial Intermediaries (F.I.s) | | Households | | The Fed | |
	Assets	Liabilities	Assets	Liabilities	Assets	Liabilities
Step 1:	Loans & Securities: − $1 million Deposits at Fed: + $1 million				U.S. Govt. Bonds: + $1 million	Deposits of F.I.s: + $1 million
Step 2:	Loans & Securities: + $1 million	Customer Deposits: + $1 million	Deposits at F.I.s: + $1 million	Loans from F.I.s: + $1 million		
Step 3:	Loans & Securities + $880,000	Customer Deposits: + $880,000	Deposits at F.I.s: + $880,000	Loans from F.I.s: + $880,000		

deposits at financial intermediaries, or else people are motivated to redeem all or part of this $1 million for currency (which the intermediaries stand ready to provide to depositors). For the moment, suppose that we forget about this (important) possibility of moving into currency. Then we eventually do reach the situation shown as step 2 in Table 16.5.

Now the extra $1 million in customer deposits raises the required reserves of the financial intermediaries. For illustrative purposes, we use a reserve ratio of 12%, which applies currently to most checkable deposits. (But it is important to note that whether these deposits are checkable does not affect the essence of the subsequent analysis.) Thus, required reserves rise by $120,000. But then the financial institutions still have $880,000 ($1 million less the $120,000) of excess reserves. Therefore, they are again motivated to place these funds into earning assets, which we assume take the form of loans. When people are motivated to hold these additional funds as deposits we arrive at step 3 in Table 16.5. Here, the intermediaries' loans and securities and deposits each rise by another $880,000.

If we continue to work through this process, we shall find that the deposits held at financial institutions rise by a large multiple of the expansion in the monetary base. Specifically, the deposits increase eventually by the amount, $1 million · $(1/0.12) = \$8.33$ million. At this point, the intermediaries' required reserves are up by $0.12 · \$8.33$ million $= \$1$ million—that is, the additional base money is all held as required reserves. Notice that this result applies when we use the required-reserve ratio, 0.12, which attaches to checkable deposits. If we take a broader view of deposits to include noncheckable varieties, then a lower reserve ratio applies. Hence, a broader concept of deposits ends up expanding by a larger multiple of the increase in the monetary base.

An important amendment to this **multiple expansion of deposits** concerns the household's increased demand for currency. In particular, the ratio of currency to checkable deposits is currently around 0.4. Thus, if there are no changes in the relative attractiveness of currency and deposits, then for each extra dollar of deposits that people are motivated to hold, they would tend also to be motivated to hold an additional 40 cents of currency.

In Table 16.6 we modify the analysis to take account of the added holdings of currency. Now, with an extra $1 million of funds in step 2a, the public is eventually motivated to hold $700,000 more in deposits and $300,000 more in currency (assuming that the ratio of currency to deposits remains at 0.4). But as the public redeems deposits to obtain this extra currency, the financial intermediaries must get this currency from the Fed by running down the deposits held at the

Table 16.6 **Effect of Open-market Purchase of Bonds on the Financial System, Including the Responses of Currency**

	Financial Intermediaries (F.I.s)		Households		The Fed	
	Assets	Liabilities	Assets	Liabilities	Assets	Liabilities
Step 1a:	Loans & Securities: −$1 million Deposits at Fed: +$1 million				U.S. Govt. Bonds: +$1 million	Deposits of F.I.s: +$1 million
Step 2a:	Loans & Securities: +$1 million Deposits at Fed: −$300,000	Customer Deposits: +$700,000	Deposits at F.I.s: +$700,000 Currency: +$300,000	Loans from F.I.s: +$1 million		Deposits of F.I.s: −$300,000 Currency: +$300,000
Step 3a:	Loans & Securities: +$616,000 Deposits at Fed: −$176,000	Customer Deposits: +$440,000	Deposits at F.I.s: +$440,000 Currency: +$176,000	Loans from F.I.s: +$616,000		Deposits of F.I.s: −$176,000 Currency: +$176,000

Fed. (Equivalently, the intermediaries could reduce their vault cash.) Thus, in step 2a, the liabilities of financial institutions show $700,000 more in customer deposits, while their assets show $300,000 less in deposits at the Fed. Notice that required reserves are now up by $84,000 (0.12 · $700,000 of deposits), rather than the $120,000 in the previous step 2. But actual reserves are up by only $700,000, rather than the previous $1 million. Thus, excess reserves are higher by $616,000 ($700,000 less $84,000), instead of the previous $880,000 ($1 million less $120,000). In other words, the "leakage" of funds into currency means that the financial intermediaries end up with less excess reserves than otherwise.

For the Fed, the additional currency outstanding of $300,000 corresponds to an equivalent reduction in the book-entry deposits of depository institutions. Hence, as shown in step 2a of Table 16.6, there is no change in the monetary base, which consists of currency plus the deposits of the depository institutions at the Fed. Thus, the monetary base remains higher by $1 million.

The remainder of the analysis proceeds as before, except that some funds leak out to currency at each stage. We can find the ultimate position from the following set of equations (which assume that financial intermediaries end up holding no excess reserves). Throughout, the symbol Δ represents the change in the associated variable.

$$\Delta(\text{monetary base}) = \Delta(\text{required reserves}) + \Delta(\text{currency}) = \$1 \text{ million}$$

$$\Delta(\text{required reserves}) = 0.12 \cdot \Delta(\text{deposits})$$

$$\Delta(\text{currency}) = 0.4 \cdot \Delta(\text{deposits})$$

Substituting the second and third conditions into the first leads to

$$0.12 \cdot \Delta(\text{deposits}) + 0.4 \cdot \Delta(\text{deposits}) = \$1 \text{ million}$$

Solving for the change in deposits, we get the results

$$\Delta(\text{deposits}) = \$1 \text{ million}/0.52 = \$1,920,000$$

$$\Delta(\text{currency}) = 0.4 \cdot \Delta(\text{deposits}) = \$770,000$$

$$\Delta(\text{required reserves}) = 0.12 \cdot \Delta(\text{deposits}) = \$230,000$$

Thus, the incorporation of currency has a dramatic effect on the results—instead of rising by $8.33 million, the deposits held at financial intermediaries end up increasing by only $1.92 million. Generally, the ultimate expansion of deposits is larger the smaller is the required-reserve ratio (fixed at 0.12 above) and the smaller is the ratio of currency to deposits (0.4 above).

The Neutrality of Open-Market Operations

In the previous chapter we found that open-market operations were neutral. In particular, a one-time shift in the monetary base led only to proportional responses in the price level and other nominal variables (except for the quantity of public debt).

This result does not change when we introduce financial intermediation. But we have to include as nominal variables the dollar quantities of the various deposits and reserves. Then we find that these nominal magnitudes rise along with the other nominal variables in proportion to the change in the monetary base. Hence, an open-market operation leaves unchanged the real quantities of deposits and reserves, the ratio of deposits to currency, the ratio of reserves to deposits, and so on.

Among the variables that do not change when there is a one-time open-market operation are the nominal interest rate on earning assets, R, and the (explicit or implicit) nominal interest rate, R^d, paid on customer deposits by financial intermediaries. Since these interest rates are unchanged, households would not alter their desired holdings of currency and deposits in real terms. Thus, the results are consistent with the unchanged real quantities of currency and deposits, which we mentioned above.

The financial intermediaries also end up in the same real position as before the open-market operation. Specifically, there are no changes in the intermediaries' real quantities of deposits, reserves, and loans and securities. If these institutions held reserves initially only because of requirements—say, 12% of deposits—then the final holdings of reserves again equal the required amount.

The Amount of Financial Intermediation

Financial intermediation is important because it facilitates the matching of borrowers and lenders,[20] as well as the carrying out of transactions. The reflection of this process is the real quantity of deposits and the real quantity of loans and securities held by financial intermediaries. Thus, we can think of these real quantities as a measure of the amount of financial intermediation in an economy.

Generally, the amount of financial intermediation that occurs depends on the benefits and costs. As mentioned before, the benefits relate to the efficient evaluation of loans, the diversification of assets by risk and maturity, and the convenience of deposits. The costs include the expenses for servicing deposits and loans, the return to capital in the intermediary business, reserve requirements, and the costs of evading restrictions for paying interest on deposits. In particular, if the costs of intermediation rise, then we predict that there would be less intermediation.

As an example, suppose that the Fed increases reserve requirements. Since financial intermediaries must hold more non-interest-bearing reserves for each dollar of deposits, these institutions end up paying a lower interest rate, R^d, on de-

---

[20]Although we focus on financial institutions in this chapter, there are other forms of intermediaries that assist in the efficient channeling of credit. A prime example is the publicly held corporation.

posits. Consequently, households are motivated to switch out of deposits and into either currency or direct holding of earning assets. Ultimately, we find that the real quantity of deposits and the real amount of loans and securities held by financial intermediaries decrease. That is, there is less financial intermediation in the economy. Note that we would reach the same conclusion if, instead of assuming an increase in reserve requirements, we postulated a higher cost for financial intermediaries to service deposits or police loans. Again, we would end up with less financial intermediation.

When there is less financial intermediation it becomes harder for resources to flow toward investors whose projects have the greatest marginal products or toward consumers who have the highest consumption rates of time preference. On both counts, the economy operates less efficiently. Typically, this loss in efficiency shows up as smaller aggregates of the capital stock and output. But the principal conclusion is that less financial intermediation means a poorer match of resources to their ultimate uses.

To some extent, the costs of intermediation reflect the underlying expenses of policing borrowers and servicing deposits. Then we can think of these elements as part of the technology or production function that generates intermediating services. Hence, the amount of intermediation that results tends to be optimal, given this technology. But as already noted, reserve requirements, government regulations of interest rates on deposits, and so on, also affect the cost of intermediation. Specifically, more restrictive policies—such as higher reserve requirements—tend to discourage intermediation, which leads to a less efficient allocation of resources. Often, the reduction in intermediation shows up as smaller levels of the capital stock and output. But in any case, these types of government policies are surely nonneutral.[21]

Financial Intermediation and the Price Level

The degree of financial intermediation also interacts with the determination of the price level. To see how this works, let's use our analysis of price level determination from previous chapters. But we now identify money with the monetary base—that is, as the sum of currency in circulation plus the reserves held by depository institutions at the Fed. Now suppose that the Fed controls the dollar quantity of base money, M, through open-market operations, as discussed above. Then the process of financial intermediation influences the price level because it affects the aggregate demand for real base money, M/P. In particular, for a given dollar quantity of base money, anything that raises the real demand for base money leads to a fall in the price level. Note that this effect works just like the various increases in the real demand for money that we considered in previous chapters.

---

[21]For the argument that the financial industry should be fully deregulated, see Fischer Black, "Banking and Interest Rates in a World without Money," *Journal of Bank Research,* Autumn 1970; and Eugene Fama, "Financial Intermediation and Price Level Control," *Journal of Monetary Economics,* July 1983.

As an example, suppose again that the Fed raises the required-reserve ratio on deposits. Then for a given quantity of deposits there is an increase in the demand for reserves by depository institutions. Hence, on this count, there is an increase in the real demand for the monetary base.

There are some additional effects, because, as noted before, the higher reserve ratio tends to reduce the interest rate paid on deposits, which makes them less attractive to households. To the extent that households shift out of deposits and into currency, there is a further increase in the real demand for the monetary base. (That's because the demand for base money varies one-to-one with the demand for currency, but varies only fractionally with the amount of deposits.) But to the extent that people move away from deposits and into direct holdings of earning assets, the real demand for base money tends to decline. (That's because the reduction in deposits reduces the real demand for reserves by depository institutions.) Thus, the shifting of households' assets among deposits, currency, and earning assets has an ambiguous overall effect on the real demand for the monetary base.[22]

Because of the direct positive effect on the demand for reserves, we can be pretty sure that the overall effect of an increase in the required-reserve ratio is to raise the real demand for base money.[23] Therefore, for a given nominal quantity of base money, the rise in the real demand for base money means that the price level falls.

Historically, the main examples of large short-term variations in the real demand for base money involve banking panics and an experiment with changes in reserve requirements in 1936–37. Therefore, we now consider some details of these episodes.

Banking Panics

Banks and other financial intermediaries promise to convert their demand deposits into currency immediately at face value. Typically, these institutions also extend this instantaneous conversion privilege to savings deposits, for which some notice of withdrawal (usually 30 days) can legally be required. However, intermediaries do not hold nearly enough cash or liquid securities to allow for the simultaneous conversion of all deposits into currency at face value.[24] Therefore, even if the underlying loans and securities are sound, financial institutions can get into trouble

---

[22]For further discussion of these types of effects, see James Tobin, "A General Equilibrium Approach to Monetary Theory," and "Deposit Interest Ceilings as a Monetary Control," in James Tobin, *Essays in Economics,* vol. 1, *Macroeconomics,* Markham, Chicago, 1971.

[23]There is another effect to the extent that the decrease in intermediation leads to lower output. On this count, the real demand for the monetary base tends to fall. But since the effect on output would usually be minor, this effect tends to be less important than those described in the text.

[24]By "liquid," we mean that little cost attaches to the quick sale of an asset. Thus, government bonds are liquid, but real estate is relatively illiquid. Loans that are costly to evaluate—such as those to local businesses and consumers—may also be illiquid.

if too many customers want their cash at the same time. (Of course, the problem is even more serious if other factors—such as movements in interest rates or defaults of borrowers—lead to decreases in the underlying value of an institution's loans and securities.) If people become concerned about a bank's ability to convert its deposits into currency at face value, then each individual has an incentive to get into line first in order to cash in. This incentive is especially great when the deposits are not insured by the government, as was the case in the United States until 1934. When many people attempt to cash in their deposits simultaneously, we have a "run on the bank." Sometimes a bank responds by temporarily "suspending" the privilege of converting demand deposits into currency. When this happens simultaneously at many banks or other financial institutions, we say that a **banking panic** occurs.

The hallmark of a banking panic is a sudden increase in the demand for currency, rather than deposits. Essentially, people perceive deposits to be less desirable because of a greater chance that the conversion privilege will not be honored. As a response, banks and other intermediaries tend to increase their demands for excess reserves and other liquid assets in order to meet their customers' possible demands for cash. Overall, the banking panic leads to increases in the real demand for base money—partly in the form of the public's currency and partly as reserves of financial institutions. Hence, from our previous analysis, a banking panic has two types of effects. First, it makes financial intermediation more difficult, which has adverse consequences for the efficient allocation of resources. Specifically, real output and investment are likely to decline. Then second, unless there is a substantial increase in the nominal quantity of base money, the sharp increase in the real demand for base money puts strong downward pressure on the price level.

Banking panics occurred fairly often before the Federal Reserve began operations in 1914. In particular, there were 12 episodes between 1800 and 1914 that are generally called banking panics. For the period after the Civil War, where better data are available, the most severe crises are those in 1873, 1893, and 1907. Typically, the panics exhibited increases in the ratios of the public's currency and banks' excess reserves to deposits. They also tended to show decreases in prices and in real economic activity. However, it is hard to sort out the independent influence of the banking panics on output and other real variables. That's because, under the monetary system that was in place before the establishment of the Federal Reserve, bad economic conditions tended automatically to generate financial crises.[25] Economists think that these crises also made real economic conditions worse, but it is not easy to prove this through econometric analysis.

---

[25]Phillip Cagan, in *Determinants and Effects of Changes in the Stock of Money, 1875–1960*, Columbia University Press, New York, 1965, pp. 265, ff., argues that the banking panics have major elements that are independent of changes in business conditions. But Gary Gorton, in "Banking Panics and Business Cycles," Federal Reserve Bank of Philadelphia, October 1982, shows a close relationship between business failures and banking panics.

A major reason for the creation of the Federal Reserve was the desire to avoid banking panics. Specifically, the initial idea was that the Fed would serve as the **lender of last resort** through the operation of its discount window. Here, especially when a financial crisis threatened, the Fed would lend liberally to member institutions at the discount rate, which would be set below market interest rates. Thereby, the Fed would provide the extra reserves that bands desired. In fact, this process of direct lending by the Fed was important during World War I and in the 1920s, but has since become less significant.

During the 1920s, the Fed was successful in averting banking panics. In particular, it is likely that the sharp economic contraction of 1921 would have resulted in a banking panic during the pre-World War I monetary regime. However, the worst banking panics in U.S. history occurred from 1931 to 1933 during the Great Depression. Further, Milton Friedman and Anna Schwartz[26] argue convincingly that this financial crisis would have been much less severe if the Fed had not existed. That's because, under the earlier environment, the banks would not have relied on corrective measures from the Fed, which turned out not to materialize.

Between 1930 and 1933 there was an unprecedented number of bank suspensions—roughly 9,000 out of about 25,000 banks that existed at the end of 1929. Then in March 1933, President Roosevelt proclaimed a "banking holiday," which temporarily closed all of the banks. But about one-third of those that had existed in 1929 never reopened.

Because of the banking panics from 1931–33, there were sharp increases in the public's holdings of currency, relative to deposits. We can see this dramatic change in Figure 16.7, which shows the public's holdings of currency relative to the holdings of checkable deposits. Notice that this ratio rose from 0.17 in 1930 to 0.34 in 1933. Similarly, the banking panics sharply increased the ratio of excess reserves to checkable deposits (see Figure 16.2). This ratio increased from near zero in 1930 to 0.04 in 1933 and 0.12 in 1935. As mentioned before, these types of increases in the real demand for base money depress the price level if the nominal quantity of base money does not change.[27] In fact, base money increased from an average of \$6.6 billion in 1930 to \$7.9 billion in 1933 (see Figure 16.6). Yet, the price level, as measured by the GNP-deflator, fell at an annual rate of 7.9% over this period.

The reaction to the banking panics of the Great Depression was a substantial amount of banking legislation. As mentioned before, the various regulations on deposit interest rates began at this time. Also, the Fed obtained the power to change reserve requirements. However, the principal innovation was the federal insurance of deposits at banks and some other financial intermediaries. This insurance came

---

[26]For an excellent discussion of this period, see Milton Friedman and Anna Schwartz, *A Monetary History of the United States, 1867–1960,* Princeton University Press, Princeton, New Jersey, 1963, Chapter 7.

[27]The costs of financial intermediation also rise. Ben Bernanke stresses this feature of banking panics during the Great Depression in his paper, "Non-Monetary Effects of the Financial Collapse in the Propagation of the Great Depression," *American Economic Review,* June 1983.

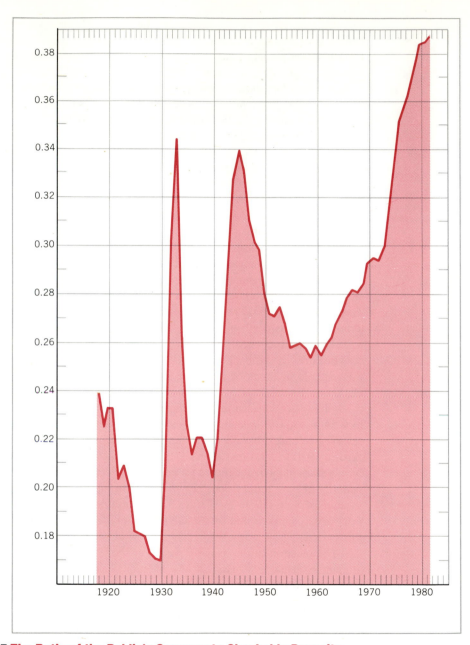

Figure 16.7 The Ratio of the Public's Currency to Checkable Deposits

into effect in 1934.[28] When the government guarantees the redemption of deposits, people lose most of their incentive to withdraw their funds when they are unsure about an institution's financial position. Therefore, it becomes harder for a bank run to start, or for one bank's problems to spread to others. In fact, there have been no banking panics since 1933. Accordingly, we no longer have this major source of instability in the real demand for base money and, hence, in the price level. We can be pretty confident that this dramatic change from the earlier experience derives from the implementation of federal deposit insurance.

Changes in Reserve Requirements in 1936–37

There were no changes in legal reserve requirements from 1917 until 1936. Then, nervous about the large quantity of banks' excess reserves (49% of total reserves and 12% of checkable deposits in 1935), the Fed decided to ''mop them up'' by sharply raising reserve requirements. (The Fed received the authority to make these sorts of changes in reserve requirements only with the Banking Acts of 1933 and 1935.) So the required-reserve ratio for member commercial banks in major cities other than New York and Chicago (the ''central-reserve cities'')[29] went from 10% of net demand deposits in 1935 to 15% in August 1936, 17.5% in March 1937, and 20% in May 1937. (Comparable changes applied to banks in New York City and Chicago, as well as to ''country banks.'') Overall, the ratio of required reserves to checkable deposits rose from an average of 12% in 1935 to 22% in 1937 (see Figure 16.1).

Apparently, the Fed believed that banks would just hold required reserves instead of excess reserves, with no major change occurring in total reserves. But the massive holdings of excess reserves after 1933 (see Figure 16.2) reflected the banks' precautions in order to avoid the kinds of banking panics that occurred from 1931 to 1933. (The interest rate on safe assets was also extremely low at this time—for example, the yield on commercial paper was only 0.75% in 1935.) Therefore, although the ratio of excess reserves to checkable deposits does fall from 12% in 1935 to 5% in 1937, the banks then rebuilt this ratio to 10% in 1938 and 16% in 1939. Accordingly, while the monetary base grew at an annual rate of 13% from 1937 to 1939 (see Figure 16.6), we find that the GNP deflator declined over this period at an annual rate of about 1.5%. We can attribute this behavior of prices to the growing demand for reserves by banks, which followed from the steep rise in required reserves during 1936–37.

---

[28]The Federal Deposit Insurance Corporations—or FDIC—insures the deposits of most banks. The funds for this purpose come from a levy on the deposits of the insured banks. Formally, there is a ceiling for the size of insured deposits, whcih is presently $100,000. But in practice, the government seems to guarantee even the larger deposits.

[29]This designation gives rise to a major trivia question: what city, other than New York and Chicago, was designated as a central-reserve city in 1914? (The answer is St. Louis, which lost the title in 1922.) In 1962 New York and Chicago were also reclassified as reserve cities. Since 1972, reserve requirements depend on an institution's total volume of deposits, rather than its location.

Many economists also attribute the recession of 1936–38 to the Fed's steep increase in reserve requirements. In particular, starting from the trough of the Great Depression in 1933, real GNP grew rapidly at the average rate of 9.6% per year until 1936. But the average growth rate was near zero between 1936 and 1938 (before rising strongly at the average rate of 7.3% per year from 1938 to 1940). At this point, our theory predicts a real effect from the increase in reserve requirements only because of the adverse effect on financial intermediation—that is, on the matching of lenders and borrowers. In particular, we do not predict real effects because of the depressing influence of higher reserve requirements on prices and other nominal variables. However, we shall reexamine the important issue of linkages between nominal and real variables in Chapters 17–19.

Probably because of the economy's poor performance in 1936–38, the Fed has never again engineered a sharp short-run change in reserve requirements. So although the legal requirements shift many times—mostly downward—between 1938 and 1980, Figure 16.1 does not show any short-run movements in the required-reserve ratio that rival those of 1936–37. However, one notable development is the decline in the ratio from 15% in 1979 to 12% in 1982. This change reflected the spread of checkable deposits outside of commercial banks and the reduced reserve requirements under the banking legislation of 1980.

Alternative Monetary Aggregates

Usually, economists, governments, and newspapers define money to be an aggregate that is broader than either currency or the monetary base. The most popular definition, called **M1**, is the sum of the public's currency and checkable deposits.[30] Thus, this concept attempts to include as money the assets that people commonly use as media of exchange. However, economists sometimes use broader definitions of money, which add other assets, such as time deposits at commercial banks, time deposits at savings and loan associations and other financial intermediaries, shares held in money-market funds, and so on. Then, people refer to aggregates like M2, M3, etc. These broader aggregates include liquid assets that do not customarily serve as media of exchange. Of course, once we go beyond the criterion that money be a (common) medium of exchange, there is no clear place to draw the line for the definition.

Often, people say that banks (or other financial intermediaries) create money, in the sense of creating checkable deposits. In our setup, we see that this process is just one example of financial intermediation—namely, a case where the deposits happen to be checkable.[31] Then, as with other forms of intermediation, the amounts that arise depend on the benefits and costs of intermediation. For example, greater

---

[30]In the United States M1 now also includes traveler's checks of nonbank issuers.

[31]For a related viewpoint, see James Tobin, ''Commercial Banks as Creators of 'Money','' in his *Essays in Economics,* op. cit., Chapter 16.

reserve requirements on checkable deposits raise the costs of intermediating through the vehicle of checkable deposits. Therefore, if reserve requirements on checkable deposits increase, then the economy ends up with less checkable deposits in relation to currency and in relation to other forms of deposits.

Let's think about alternative definitions of money from the perspective of the analysis in this chapter. The standard concept, M1, adds a portion of financial intermediation to the quantity of base money. More precisely, the M1 version of money adds deposits of checkable form, but subtracts the part of base money that depository institutions hold as reserves. Then broader concepts of money add in more and more of the quantity of financial intermediation. That is, these definitions include various types of deposits at financial intermediaries, regardless of whether the deposits are checkable or available on demand at face value.

Suppose that our interest in monetary aggregates reflects an underlying concern about the determination of the price level. (We care also about real and nominal income, interest rates, and so on—but we can bring out the main points here by focusing on the price level.) So a guide to a useful definition of money must come from the interplay between money and prices. But we already know that we can analyze the determination of the price level by studying the equality between the quantity of base money and the demand for base money. Further, under present monetary arrangements in the United States, the nominal quantity of base money is controlled accurately by the Federal Reserve through open-market operations. Therefore, the reason for considering other assets—such as checkable deposits—must be that they interact with the real demand for base money. Specifically, these interactions are of two types. First, changes in the attractiveness of deposits affect the public's desire to hold currency. (Recall that these changes may result from banking panics, shifts in reserve requirements, changes in regulations on deposit interest rates, and so on.) Second, financial intermediaries may alter their demand for base money (reserves), either because of shifts in requirements or because of changes in desired holdings of excess reserves.

Consider again the example of a banking panic, where the public increases its real demand for currency and the banks raise their desired ratio of excess reserves to checkable deposits. Recall that these increases in the real demand for base money mean that the price level must fall if the nominal quantity of base money does not change.

What happens to the dollar volume of checkable deposits? Because of the banking panic, a larger fraction of base money is held as either the public's currency or as the banks' excess reserves. Therefore, the fraction held as required reserves must decline. But then, for a given dollar total of base money, we know that the dollar quantity of required reserves falls, which implies a multiple contraction of deposits. It follows that M1—the sum of the public's currency and checkable deposits—tends to decrease during a banking panic.

Suppose now that we can write out a function for the aggregate real demand for M1, which depends only on aggregate output, Y, and the nominal interest rate on earning assets, R. In particular, let's pretend that the banking panic does not change the form of this demand function. Then the decrease in the dollar quantity of M1 means, as we already know, that the price level must fall (at least for given values of output and the nominal interest rate on earning assets). Further, we can use the total stock of M1 as a guide for a monetary policy that stabilizes the price level. Namely, the monetary authority must pump in enough extra base money (for example, through open-market operations) in order to keep the dollar quantity of M1 from falling.

There are a number of problems with the result that we just sketched. First, it is unlikely that the real demand function for M1 would remain fixed during a banking panic or other disturbance that substantially changes the real demand for base money. Hence, constancy of M1 would not generally ensure constancy of the price level, even if output and the nominal interest rate did not change. However, the real demand function for M1 does seem to be more stable historically than the real demand function for the monetary base.[32] At least this is true before World War II, when banking panics and large changes in reserve requirements sometimes occurred. Since World War II, the two demand functions have similar stability.

Second, the policymakers must know by how much to increase the monetary base in order to keep M1 constant. But in order to solve this problem, they have to know by how much the real demand for monetary base rises in the first place. However, if they have this information, then they already know how to stabilize the price level without looking at M1. All the monetary authority has to do is raise the nominal quantity of base money by the same proportion as the increase in the real demand for the base.

Third, the M1 definition of money is not so useful when the private sector develops close substitutes for the checkable deposits that are classified as money. For example, before 1980 M1 included only the checkable deposits at commercial banks. Then, as other financial intermediaries developed checkable accounts, the real demand for the banks' deposits declined. In this circumstance price stabilization does not call for constancy in the quantity of M1, as previously defined. Rather, we would want to hold fixed some broader aggregate, which includes also the checkable deposits at other financial intermediaries. Although the revised definition of M1 includes most of these assets,[33] the basic difficulty remains. Namely, since the financial sector can generate close substitutes for the deposits that appear in M1, we sometimes get substantial shifts in the real demand for M1. Then stabilization of M1 is not such a useful guide for stabilization of the price level.

Finally, the basic idea is to use broader monetary aggregates as an ''indicator'' of how the Fed's underlying policy tool—that is, the monetary base—should be adjusted in order to influence the price level (or other variables). But why is it preferable to look at the monetary aggregates as an ''intermediate target,'' rather than looking directly at the ultimate target, which is the price level? The only

---

[32]That is, if we use variables like output and the nominal interest rate, then we can explain better the movements in real M1 than in the real monetary base. On the other hand, changes in the nominal interest rate seem to have a greater effect on the real demand for M1 than on the real demand for the monetary base.

[33]M1 does not include checkable money-market funds.

possibility is that lags in the economy or in obtaining information mean that we learn things more quickly by looking at monetary aggregates, rather than just at the price level (or the interest rate or other variables). This point may be correct, but it is not important when banking panics or large shifts in reserve requirements produce major changes in the real demand for base money. For example, during the financial crises of 1931–33, the Fed could have looked directly at the sharply falling price level to know that it needed much more monetary base in order to stabilize prices.

Of course, the distinction between the monetary base and M1 matters only when these aggregates behave very differently. In fact, because of the absence of banking panics and sharp changes in reserve requirements, the ratio of M1 to the monetary base does not change greatly from year to year since World War II. Figure 16.8 shows that this ratio varies only between 2.4 and 2.9 between 1946 and 1982. Further, the largest one-year change is the increase by 0.17 in 1950. By contrast, the ratio falls from 3.9 in 1930 to 2.5 in 1933, and from 2.5 in 1936 to 2.0 in 1939.

It also turns out that the ratio of M1 to the monetary base in 1950, 2.6, is nearly the same as that in 1982, 2.7. In other words, the average growth rates of M1 and the monetary base from 1950 to 1982 are very close. However, this correspondence reflects some longer-term changes that happen to cancel. First, as shown before in Figures 16.1 and 16.2, the ratios of required and excess reserve to checkable deposits decline from a total of 0.22 in 1950 to 0.12 in 1982. This element raises the growth rate of M1 relative to that of the monetary base. But as shown in Figure 16.7, the ratio of currency to checkable deposits rises substantially since the mid-1960s (from 0.27 in 1965 to 0.40 in 1982).[34] This factor offsets the changes in the reserve ratios.

Summary

Financial intermediaries perform a number of useful services such as the evaluation and collection of loans, the diversification of assets, and the provision of convenient deposits. Thereby, financial intermediation assists in the matching of borrowers and lenders, as well as in the process of carrying out transactions.

The amount of financial intermediation that goes on depends on the costs, which include the expenses for servicing deposits and loans, the return to capital in the intermediary business, the requirements to hold non-interest-bearing reserves, and the costs for avoiding restrictions on the payments of interest on deposits. An increase in these costs—such as a rise in reserve requirements on deposits—leads

---

[34]The following forces probably underlie this change. First, various financial innovations and increases in interest rates on earning assets apparently reduce the real demand for checkable deposits by more than they reduce the real demand for currency. Second, increases in tax rates and criminal activity motivate people to use more currency in order to conceal their transactions from governments. Third, there may be relatively more U.S. currency held abroad than there used to be.

Figure 16.8 The Ratio of M1 to the Monetary Base

to less financial intermediation. Consequently, there are adverse real effects, which include a greater difficulty of matching borrowers and lenders. These effects tend to show up as reductions in the quantities of investment and output.

The Federal Reserve controls the size of the monetary base (the sum of the public's currency and the reserves of depository institutions) mainly through open-market operations. In the United States these operations typically involve exchanges between base money and U.S. government bonds. However, the Fed's loans to depository institutions also affect the monetary base. Aside from the subsidy to borrowers when the discount rate is below market interest rates, these loans are equivalent to an open-market purchase of bonds.

An increase in the monetary base leads to a multiplicative expansion of deposits. The increase in deposits is greater the smaller is the required-reserve ratio and the smaller is the ratio of currency to deposits.

Open-market operations are still neutral in the model. That is, they affect the price level and other nominal variables, but do not change any real variables (aside from the private sector's holdings of real government bonds). Among the real variables that do not change are the ratios of deposits to currency and of deposits to reserves.

Given the quantity of base money, the price level depends inversely on the real demand for the monetary base. Historically, the major short-term movements in this demand stem from banking panics, which featured sharp increases in the public's demand for currency and in banks' demands for excess reserves. Also, the steep rise in reserve requirements in 1936–37 led to a substantial increase in the real demand for base money. However, the implementation of deposit insurance in 1934 apparently eliminated banking panics. Also, the Fed has not engineered sharp short-run changes in reserve requirements since 1937.

The M1 definition of money adds a portion of financial intermediation—namely, checkable deposits less the reserves of depository institutions—to the monetary base. Then broader aggregates enter more of the quantity of financial intermediation by including additional types of deposits. Under some circumstances, the monitoring of broad monetary aggregates may help the monetary authority to stabilize the price level. But the Fed's main influence on the price level still comes from its control over the quantity of base money.

Important Terms and Concepts

financial intermediaries	costs of intermediation
demand deposits	Regulation Q
savings deposits	disintermediation
time deposits	Federal Reserve credit
vault cash	monetary base
reserves (of depository institutions)	high-powered money
Federal Funds market	open-market operations
Federal Funds rate	multiple expansion of deposits
discount rate (of Fed)	banking panic
reserve requirement	lender of last resort
excess reserves	M1 concept of money

QUESTIONS AND PROBLEMS

Mainly for Review

16.1 What considerations limit the amount of (excess) reserves held by financial institutions? Explain how the volume of reserves can be less than the volume of deposits.

16.2 What factors account for the spread between the interest rate on earning assets and the interest paid on checkable deposits? Is an increase in the spread associated with a lower volume of deposits?

16.3 Show that in order for an increase in the monetary base to be matched by an equivalent increase in reserves and currency held by the public, there must be a multiplicative increase in the volume of deposits. How much would deposits expand if the reserve requirements were 100%?

16.4 Why does the expectation of a bank failure give individuals an incentive to cash in their deposits? Show that this expectation can be a "self-fulfilling prophecy." How does the provision of deposit insurance reduce the likelihood of this event?

16.5 Explain why a shift away from currency holding by the public toward holdings of demand deposits would raise the price level.

16.6 Why would a rise in the interest rate on earning assets reduce public holdings of checkable deposits? What effect would there be on the quantity of M1? Is the quantity of M1 an appropriate target for Fed policy in this circumstance?

Problems for Discussion

16.7 The Fed's Discount Rate and Borrowing at the Fed
How does the volume of borrowing at the Fed depend on the discount rate and the interest rate on earning assets? Do the data shown in Figures 16.4 and 16.5 support the answer?

Suppose that the Fed lowers the discount rate, so that borrowings increase. Are the effects on the economy the same as those from an open-market purchase of bonds?

16.8 Reserve Requirements
Suppose that the Fed increases the required-reserve ratio on checkable deposits.
a. How does this change affect the real demand for base money?
b. How does it affect the price level?
c. How does it affect the nominal quantity of M1?
d. What real effects occur from the increase in reserve requirements?

Let's pretend now that the government imposes reserve requirements on something that has nothing to do with "money." For example, the requirement could be on refrigerators—everyone who owns a refrigerator must hold $10 of non-interest-bearing reserves at the Fed.

How does this new policy affect the real demand for base money and the price level? What other effects arise (for example, on the number of refrigerators)? In what ways do the answers differ from above, where the requirements apply to checkable deposits?

16.9 Vault Cash and Reserve Requirements

From 1917 until December 1959, vault cash did not count toward satisfying the Fed's reserve requirements. Part of it counted until November 1960, after which all of vault cash counted toward the requirements. Just before the change in 1959–60, vault cash at banks that were members of the Federal Reserve System was $2.2 billion, which amounted to about 2% of all checkable deposits.

If the monetary base did not change for 1960–61, then how would the new treatment of vault cash affect the price level? (In fact, base money declined from an average of $50.4 billion in 1959 to $50.0 billion in 1960 and $49.1 billion in 1961.)

16.10 Interest on Reserves Held at the Fed

At present, reserves held at the Federal Reserve bear no interest. Suppose that the Fed pays interest on reserves at a rate that is some fraction of the interest rate on commercial paper. If the quantity of base money stays the same, how would this change affect the following:
a. the interest rate paid on checkable deposits?
b. the dollar amount of checkable deposits?
c. the price level?
d. the amount of intermediation in the economy?
e. the profits of the Federal Reserve (which go to the U.S. Treasury)?

16.11 Gold and the Monetary Base

Suppose the U.S. Treasury receives $1 billion of gold from abroad. Then the Treasury deposits the gold at the Fed, so that the Fed's gold account and the Treasury's deposits at the Fed each rise by $1 billion.
a. What happens to the monetary base if the Treasury holds the extra $1 billion in deposits?
b. What happens if the Treasury spends the extra $1 billion and thereby restores its deposits to their initial level?
c. How can the Fed offset the effect of the gold inflow on the monetary base? (If they take this action, they are said to "sterilize" the inflow of gold.)
d. Suppose that the government raises the official price of gold from $42.22 per ounce to the market price of around $440. Then the capital gains on the Fed's gold holdings (valued at $11.1 billion at the end of 1982, when the price is $42.22) is credited to the Treasury's deposits at the Fed. What might this action do to the monetary base (which is $172 billion at the end of 1982)? What could the Fed do to keep the monetary base from changing?

16.12 Membership in the Federal Reserve System

Until 1980 only commercial banks that were members of the Federal Reserve System were subject to the Fed's reserve requirements. (There were also some services, such as check-clearing and access to the discount window, which were provided free to members.) Membership was optional for banks with state charters, but required for those with federal charters. (In 1980 only 30% of all commercial banks had national charters. But these accounted for 55% of the deposits at commercial banks.)

The fraction of state banks that were members of the Federal Reserve System declined from 21% in 1948 to 10% in 1980. Why do you think this happened?

16.13 Runs on Financial Institutions

In the text we discussed runs on banks. How does the analysis differ if the run applies to other financial intermediaries, which do not offer checkable deposits? (For example, this description would apply until recently to savings and loan associations.)

16.14 Deposit Insurance (optional)

We discussed the role of federal deposit insurance, which has apparently prevented banking panics since 1933. A number of unsolved questions arise here, which you might want to think about.

a. Could private companies satisfactorily provide insurance on deposits? In particular, would the private sector end up providing the "right" amount of insurance? More generally, why is deposit insurance an area where the government should be involved?

b. Is there a reason for the government to be in the insurance business for deposits, but not for other things, such as corporate obligations? (In fact, the federal government has gotten into the business of insuring the debt of doubtful borrowers—such as New York City and the Chrysler Corporation—as well as pension obligations and accounts at stockbrokers. But, so far, the government has not bailed out the Washington (State) Public Power Supply System.)

CHAPTER 17

THE INTERPLAY BETWEEN NOMINAL AND REAL VARIABLES—WHAT IS THE EVIDENCE?

So far, our analysis has not stressed monetary variables as a source of fluctuations in real economic activity. Yet, many economists think that movements in money and prices—that is, nominal disturbances—have a great deal to do with the short-term behavior of real variables, such as aggregate output and employment. In this chapter we concern ourselves mostly with the empirical evidence on this important issue. But before we look at the evidence, let's summarize what our theory says so far about the interaction between nominal and real variables.

First, the theory predicts that changes in the monetary base are neutral. In particular, a one-time shift in the quantity of base money leads to proportional changes in the nominal variables, but to no changes in the real variables. So we get responses in the price level, nominal wage rate, and the dollar values of output, investment, and so on. But there are no changes in the quantities of output and employment, the real interest rate, and so on.

We can also consider complicated monetary disturbances, where the changes do not occur entirely at the present time. Then the anticipations of future monetary changes lead to complicated responses of the price level, as well as to shifts in the nominal interest rate. But the model still predicts no changes in the real variables. At least, the only exception in our theory concerns the transaction costs for moving between money and either goods or interest-bearing assets. Since changes in the nominal interest rate affect the real demand for money, we can get some real effects through this channel. But these influences are probably insufficient to account for sizable fluctuations in aggregate real economic activity.

There are some different results if the monetary fluctuations reflect shifts in the cost of intermediation, rather than just changes in the quantity of base money. For example, there might be a banking panic, which causes people to lose confidence in deposits.[1] Alternatively, there might be changes in reserve requirements. In these cases, as with contractions of the monetary base, there tend to be reductions in the price level and other nominal variables. But because of the higher cost of intermediation, there are also some adverse effects on real variables. Specifically, since it becomes harder to match borrowers and lenders, the levels of investment and output tend to decline. Therefore, these types of disturbances move nominal and real variables in the same direction.

There are also various real disturbances that involve shifts to production functions.[2] For example, an adverse shock reduces output, which lowers the quantity of real money demanded. Hence, for a given amount of base money, the price level rises. Since the price level now moves in the opposite direction of output, we find that the pattern of response differs markedly from the one associated with changes in the cost of intermediation.

Overall, our theory does allow for some relationships between nominal and real variables, although the sign of the interaction depends on the nature of the underlying disturbance. However, let's stress the key theoretical proposition, which concerns monetary neutrality. Namely, purely monetary disturbances—in the sense of changes in the monetary base—have no real effects. To put this point another way, although these monetary disturbances can create substantial variations in prices and other nominal variables, we still predict no responses in the aggregates of output, employment, and so on.[3]

Most economists regard the proposition of monetary neutrality as incorrect, at least in certain contexts. In fact, many researchers attribute a large portion of aggregate business fluctuations to monetary disturbances, which our theory says have no important real effects. More specifically, the common view is that monetary expansion tends to stimulate real economic activity, whereas monetary contraction tends to cause recessions.

The Phillips Curve

Economists often express their ideas about the relation between real and nominal variables in terms of the **Phillips curve** (named after the British economist A. W. Phillips). This curve is intended to summarize the relation between a measure of

---

[1]Of course, banking panics are typically not independent of prior changes in business conditions. However, the potential for panics does depend on some features of the financial structure. In particular, the implementation of federal deposit insurance in 1934 has apparently prevented panics since that time.

[2]For most purposes, we can also include here changes in government purchases and shifts in taxes and transfers. For example, an increase in marginal tax rates is analogous to an adverse shift of the production function.

[3]The variations in prices lead to changes in the distribution of real assets. Specifically, nominal debtors gain from surprise inflation, while nominal creditors lose. But the theory does not allow for effects of these types of distributional shifts on the aggregates of output and employment. One possibility would be to extend the theory, so that these distributional changes do have aggregate consequences.

real economic activity—such as the unemployment rate or the level or growth rate of output—and a nominal variable—such as the rate of change of prices or nominal wages or the stock of money. The basic notion behind the Phillips curve is that more inflation (and more monetary growth underlying this inflation) brings about an economic boom, which shows up as less unemployment and as a higher growth rate of real gross national product (GNP). Initially, this idea was presented (by Phillips) as an empirical, inverse relation between the unemployment rate and the rate of growth of nominal wages. But subsequently, researchers often replace the rate of wage change by the growth rate of either prices or money. Figure 17.1 shows a simple version of the Phillips curve. In this figure a lower inflation rate, π, is associated with a higher unemployment rate, u.

People sometimes argue that more inflation or more monetary growth results in less unemployment and higher growth of output only in the "short run." Eventually, the economy adjusts to any established rate of inflation, so that the real variables no longer depend on the behavior of the nominal variables. Suppose that we think of the expected rate of inflation, π^e, as the rate of inflation to which the economy has adjusted itself. Then, as shown in Figure 17.2, it is only the surprise part of inflation, $\pi - \pi^e$, that would relate systematically (and presumably negatively) to the unemployment rate. This type of relation is called an **expectational Phillips curve,** because the inflation rate enters relative to the amount of expected inflation. One important property of this curve is that a given unemployment rate

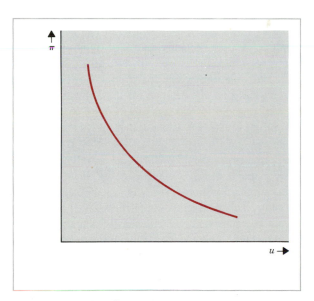

Figure 17.1 A Simple Phillips Curve
The Phillips curve associates a lower value of the inflation rate, π, with a higher unemployment rate, u.

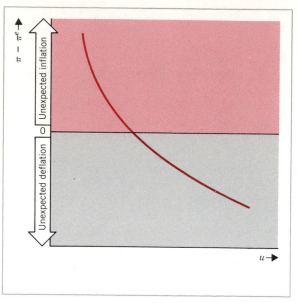

Figure 17.2 An Expectational Phillips Curve
The expectational Phillips curve associates a lower value of unexpected inflation, $\pi - \pi^e$, with a higher unemployment rate, u. Thus, a given unemployment rate (say 6%) can coexist with any rate of inflation.

can coexist with any amount of inflation. That is, an unemployment rate of, say, 6% is consistent with an inflation rate of 0%, 10%, 20%, etc. Equal changes in actual and expected inflation, which leave unchanged the amount of unexpected inflation, $\pi - \pi^e$, have no significance for the unemployment rate. Equivalently, we can say that the simple Phillips curve in Figure 17.1 applies for a fixed value of the expected inflation rate, π^e. When inflationary expectations change, the curve in this figure shifts—specifically, a higher value for expected inflation means that a higher inflation rate is associated with any given value of the unemployment rate.

We can view much of the macrotheorizing since the 1930s as attempts to explain versions of the Phillips curve and, as a related matter, the absence of monetary neutrality. This perspective applies as much to the Keynesian theory as to the more recent monetary theories of business fluctuations. But before we explore these theories, we should understand the nature of the facts that they are trying to explain. In particular, we want to know to what extent the Phillips curve—either the simple one or the expectational variety—and monetary nonneutrality are "facts." So in this chapter we bring out the major pieces of empirical evidence that concern the interplay between nominal and real variables. Throughout this discussion, we look especially for findings that demonstrate the existence of the Phillips curve and the nonneutrality of money.

The Relationship Between Unemployment and the Rates of Change of Wages, Prices, and Money—Long-Term Evidence for the United Kingdom and the United States

The term, Phillips curve, derives from studies of the relationship between unemployment and the growth rate of nominal wages, which were carried out by A. W. Phillips and Richard Lipsey.[4] Lipsey's statistical analysis documents a significant inverse relationship between the unemployment rate and the growth rate of nominal wages in the United Kingdom for the period, 1862–1913. The nature of his findings show up in Figure 17.3, which plots the British data over the period, 1862–1981, excluding the years that are associated with World Wars I and II. The growth rate of the nominal wage, Δw, appears on the vertical axis, while the unemployment rate, u, is on the horizontal. We use dots for the observations from 1862–1913. For these years, we can discern a negative slope, which is also confirmed by a formal statistical analysis.

We see also from Figure 17.3 that the inverse relation between unemployment and the growth rate of nominal wages does not hold up when we look at the behavior after World War I. For the interwar period, 1923–39, the observations appear as asterisks in the figure. Notice that these years exhibit exceptionally high unemployment rates. In particular, the average value of 14.3% contrasts with that of 4.7% for 1862–1913. But there is no significant correlation between the unemployment rate and the rate of change of wages over the period, 1923–39.

A different pattern of association between wage-rate changes and unemployment arises when we look at the post-World War II period (plotted by +'s in Figure 17.3). For the years 1947–81, the relation between the unemployment rate and the rate of change of wages turns out to be significantly positive. In other words, the Phillips curve slopes in the "wrong" direction since World War II! However, the most notable change from the pre-World War I period is the higher average rate of growth of nominal wages—8.1% per year in 1947–81, versus 0.8% for 1862–1913 (and 0.1% for 1923–39). In comparison with the period before World War I, the recent years involve mainly an increase in the average rate of wage change, with no major difference in the unemployment rate. (The average unemployment rate for 1947–81 is 2.9%, but the rate has risen recently to 10.7% in 1981 and 13% toward the end of 1982.)

The results for the United Kingdom look basically similar if we replace the growth rate of nominal wages by the growth rate of either prices or the M1 definition of money. The only indication of an inverse relation between unemployment and the growth rate of the nominal variables—wages, prices, or the money stock—

---

[4]A. W. Phillips, "The Relation between Unemployment and the Rate of Change of Money Wage Rates in the United Kingdom, 1861–1959," *Economica,* November 1958; and Richard Lipsey, "The Relation between Unemployment and the Rate of Change of Money Wage Rates in the United Kingdom, 1862–1957: A Further Analysis," *Economica,* February 1960.

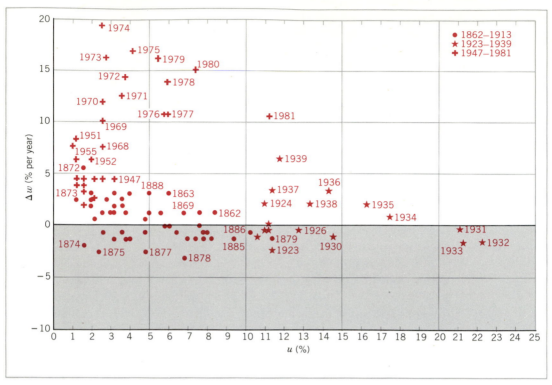

Figure 17.3 **The Relation between the Unemployment Rate and the Rate of Change of Wages in the United Kingdom, 1862–1981**

For the years, 1862–1913 (shown by dots), there is a negative relation between the two variables. But for the interwar period, 1923–39 (shown by asterisks), there is no significant relation. For the recent years, 1947–81 (shown by +'s), the relation is positive.

appears in the years before World War I. Also, for any of the nominal variables, the slope of the Phillips curve has the wrong sign in the recent period.

The pattern of results for the United States resembles that for the United Kingdom.[5] In Figure 17.4 we show the U.S. data for the period, 1890–1982, excluding the years that are associated with World Wars I and II. The growth rate of nominal wages, Δw, appears on the vertical axis, while the unemployment rate, u, is on the horizontal.

A significant negative association between the unemployment rate and the growth rate of wages appears again in the pre-World War I period, 1890–1913

---

[5]Irving Fisher carried out an early statistical study of this type of relationship for the United States. But he used price changes, rather than wage changes. The results appear in Irving Fisher, "A Statistical Relation between Unemployment and Price Changes," *International Labor Review*, June 1926. This paper is reprinted (under the cute title, "I Discovered the Phillips Curve") in the *Journal of Political Economy*, April 1973.

(the observations are indicated by dots in Figure 17.4). As with the United Kingdom, there is no significant correlation between the two variables over the interwar period, 1923–39 (shown by asterisks in the figure). Notice that, unlike the United Kingdom the unemployment rates in the United States are low for 1923–29. But for the 1930s, the unemployment rates are similar in the two countries.

For the post-World War II period in the United States, 1947–82 (shown by +'s in Figure 17.4), we also find no significant correlation between the unem-

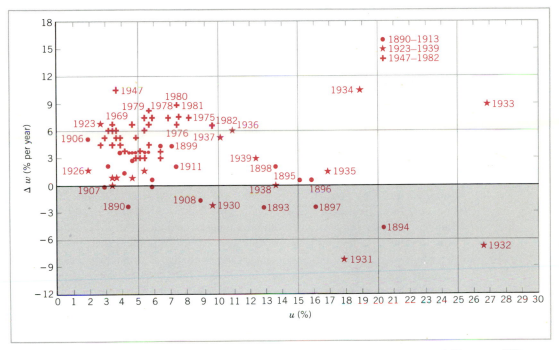

Figure 17.4 **The Relation between the Unemployment Rate and the Rate of Change of Wages in the United States, 1890–1982**

For the period, 1890–1913 (shown by dots), the relation between the two variables is negative. There is no significant relation over the other two periods. *Sources of Data for Figures 17.3 and 17.4. United Kingdom:* The unemployment rate is from B. R. Mitchell, *Abstract of British Historical Statistics,* Cambridge University Press, 1962; B. R. Mitchell, *European Historical Statistics, 1750–1970,* Macmillan, New York, 1975; and *Monthly Digest of Statistics,* various issues. The wage rate index is from B. R. Mitchell, *European Historical Statistics, 1750–1970;* Department of Employment and Productivity, *British Labour Statistics, Historical Abstract 1886–1968,* London, 1971; and *Monthly Digest of Statistics,* various issues. *United States:* The unemployment rate is from Figure 1.3 of Chapter 1. The wage-rate index is from Albert Rees, ''Patterns of Wages, Prices and Productivity,'' in Charles Myers, ed., *Wages, Prices, Profits and Productivity,* Columbia University Press, New York, 1959; and *Economic Report of the President,* various issues. The recent data include an adjustment for overtime pay.

ployment rate and the growth rate of nominal wages. Recall that, for the United Kingdom, we found a positive association between the two variables during these years. Some weak indication of a positive relationship—that is, of a wrongly sloped Phillips curve—shows up for the United States from 1947–82 if we replace the growth rate of wages by that of either prices or a monetary aggregate, such as M1.

What conclusions can we draw from the long-period relationships between the unemployment rate and the growth rates of the nominal variables? First, there is no stable relation between the unemployment rate—or, it turns out, real economic activity more generally—and the growth rates of nominal wages, prices or money.[6] Thus, the sharply higher growth rates of the nominal variables since World War II, as compared to those before World War I, correspond to little change in the average rate of unemployment (or in average growth rates of real GNP). Hence, we can firmly reject the notion of a Phillips curve, such as that shown in Figure 17.1, which is stable over the long term. At least in the long run, it is untrue that more inflation leads to a lower unemployment rate, or that in order to have low inflation a country must accept a high unemployment rate.

What about the negative relation between unemployment and the growth rates of the nominal variables before World War I? One important consideration is that the United Kingdom and the United States (after 1879) were on the gold standard during these years. Under this type of monetary regime, the monetary policy in each country had to conform—at least over the long run—to maintaining a fixed nominal price of gold. (In this period, the U.S. price of gold was $20.67 per ounce.) In particular, it would be infeasible to have high growth rates of money and prices over long periods without having to abandon the gold standard. (We discuss these matters more in Chapter 20.) The main point is that under the gold standard we observe long-term average rates of change of nominal wages and prices that are close to zero. For example, in the case of the United Kingdom, the average rate of change of nominal wages over 1862–1913 is 0.8% per year, while that for prices is −0.4% per year. For the United States from 1890 to 1913, the average growth rate of nominal wages is 1.8% per year, while that for prices is 0.9% per year.[7]

We find that under the gold standard high rates of inflation represent rates that are high relative to the long-term average rate of inflation, which is close to zero. If we think of zero as the expected rate of inflation (at least over long periods), then the results suggest an inverse relation between unexpected inflation,

---

[6]Formal statistical support for this proposition appears in Robert Lucas, ''Two Illustrations of the Quantity Theory of Money.'' *American Economic Review,* December 1980; and John Geweke, ''The Neutrality of Money in the United States, 1870–1972: an Interpretation of the Evidence,'' unpublished, University of Wisconsin, November 1982.

[7]It is possible to get substantial movements in nominal wages or prices from year to year under the gold standard. The range of wage changes for the periods indicated above is from −3.3% (1878) to +6.0% (1872) for the United Kingdom and from −7.7% (1894) to +6.6% (1913) for the United States. For prices, the range for the United Kingdom is from −9.9% (1885) to +6.3% (1866), while that for the United States is from −5.8% (1894) to +5.1% (1900).

$\pi - \pi^e \approx \pi$, and the unemployment rate. That is, we have an expectational Phillips curve of the form shown in Figure 17.2. Note that this form of the Phillips curve can also accommodate the breakdown of the relationship over the longer term. Once countries moved off of the gold standard—as happened in part around World War I and more so in the 1930s and around World War II—we find that the inflation rates no longer average close to zero. Rather, inflation rates tend to be high and unstable. But the general rise in actual and expected rates of inflation, π and π^e—which shows up especially after World War II—does not mean that unexpected inflation, $\pi - \pi^e$, is systematically high or low. Therefore, we no longer see an inverse association between the rate of inflation and the unemployment rate.

What about the positive relation between the unemployment rate and the growth rates of the nominal variables, which shows up for the United Kingdom and weakly for the United States in the post-World War II period? There are two elements that explain at least part of this behavior. First, as noted before, disturbances to production functions ("supply shocks") tend to generate this pattern. For a given quantity of money, an adverse shock lowers output, which reduces the real demand for money, and thereby raises the price level. Second, any tendency of governments to raise monetary growth during recessions reinforces this outcome. That is, lower output triggers more money, which raises the price level. This pattern of active monetary policy arises in the United States and the United Kingdom since World War II, although not during the earlier years under the gold standard.

Overall, the main thing that our theory does not yet explain is the tendency for higher than expected growth rates of the nominal variables to accompany low rates of unemployment. So far, the data indicate the presence of this type of expectational Phillips curve for the period before World War I.

Cross-Country Relations between Nominal and Real Variables

Suppose that we look at average growth rates of real GNP for various countries[8] and compare these with the average growth rates of prices, money, and so on. If we look at averages over one or more decades, then the main variations across countries reflect differences in the long-term average growth rates of real GNP, prices, money, etc. Hence, the relations among these variables should tell us something about how differences in the growth rates of the nominal variables associate in the long run with differences in the real growth rates. That is, the cross-country evidence should resemble the longer-term findings on Phillips curves that we discussed before for the United States and the United Kingdom.

Figure 17.5 uses data from 77 countries to relate the average growth rate of real GNP (over intervals of 1 to 3 decades since World War II) with the average

---

[8]Because of differences in concepts and lack of data, it is hard to compare unemployment rates across countries.

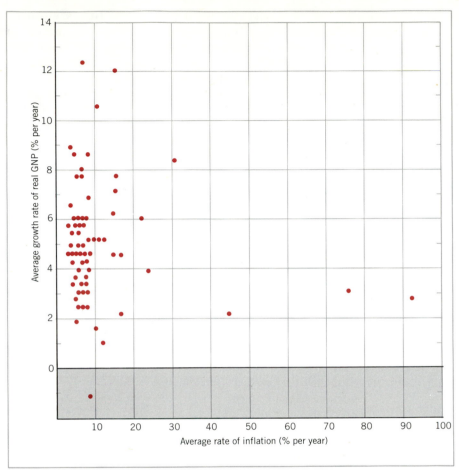

Figure 17.5 The Cross-Country Relation between Inflation and the Growth Rate of Real GNP

Looking at 77 countries, there is no significant relation between the average rate of inflation and the average growth rate of real GNP.

rate of inflation. (Recall that we looked at these data before in Chapter 7.) There is no apparent relation between the two variables in Figure 17.5, as we can verify from a formal statistical analysis.

Figures 17.6 and 17.7 plot the average growth rate of real GNP against the average growth rate of either currency or M1. Again, the average growth rate of real GNP bears no relation to the growth rate of the nominal variables. Thus, as with the long-period evidence for the United States or the United Kingdom, the cross-country data indicate no connection between the growth rates of the nominal variables and the behavior of real variables, such as the growth rate of real GNP. These results are again consistent with the absence of a long-term Phillips curve.

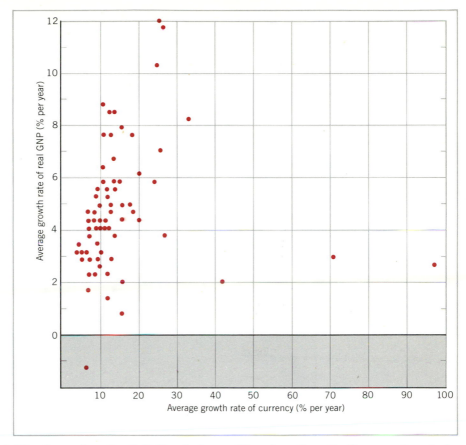

Figure 17.6 The Cross-Country Relation between Monetary Growth (Currency) and the Growth Rate of Real GNP

For the 77 countries, there is no significant relation between the average growth rate of currency and the average growth rate of real GNP.

At least in the long run, more inflation does not associate with better real performance.

The Relation Between Real and Nominal Variables During the Major Recessions Before World War II

The evidence already discussed suggests that the main interplay between nominal and real variables arises when the nominal variables behave in an unusual manner. Hence, we should focus on shocks or surprises in money and prices in order to find interesting interactions with the real variables. Table 17.1 brings out this type

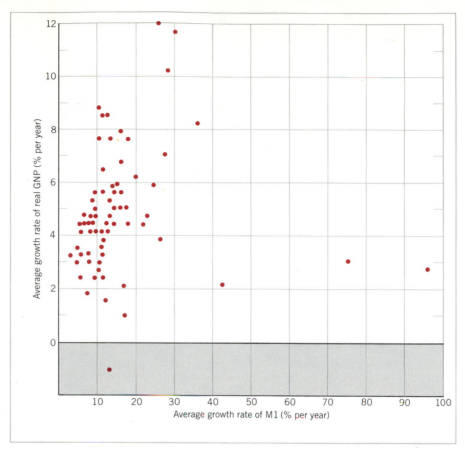

Figure 17.7 The Cross-Country Relation between Monetary Growth (M1) and the Growth Rate of Real GNP
For the 77 countries, there is no significant relation between the average growth rate of $M1$ and the average growth rate of real GNP.

of relationship for the five principal U.S. recessions between 1890 and 1940. Three of these—1892–94, 1906–08, and 1929–33—contain banking panics. Another one, 1937–38, involves the Fed's steep increase in reserve requirements. The fifth episode, 1920–21, occurs along with a dramatic fall in money and prices after World War I.

The first section of Table 17.1 shows the shortfall of real GNP for each recession. These range from 7.2% for 1937–38 to 37.6% for 1929–33. (Our approach for generating these numbers is the one described before in Chapter 9.) These figures imply that the mildest of the five recessions—1937–38—corresponds roughly

Table 17.1 Real and Nominal Variables During Five Major Recessions Before World War II

Final Year of Recession	1894	1908	1921	1933	1938
Base Year for Comparison	1892	1906	1920	1929	1937
Y	89.7	160.8	197.6	222.1	296.7
$Y°$	102.9	183.2	223.0	356.0	319.6
$Y° - Y$	13.2	22.4	25.4	133.9	22.9
% shortfall	12.8	12.2	11.4	37.6	7.2
M	1.57	3.09	6.33	7.92	14.4
$M°$	1.65	2.89	7.15	7.03	14.9
$M° - M$	0.08	−0.20	0.82	−0.89	0.5
% shortfall	4.8	−6.9	11.5	−12.7	3.4
P	0.150	0.183	.340	0.251	0.286
$P°$	0.153	0.185	.404	0.332	0.301
$P° - P$	0.003	0.002	.064	0.081	0.015
% shortfall	2.0	1.1	15.8	24.4	5.0
% change in $M1/M$	−5.4	−12.0	0.3	−32.9	−8.6

Note: Y is real GNP, M is the monetary base, P is the GNP deflator, and $M1$ is the M1 definition of the money stock. (For the two earliest cases, we estimate $M1$ from the available data on $M2$.) The normal or expected values, $Y°$, $M°$, and $P°$, equal the values from the base year, adjusted by the normal growth rates. For real GNP, we use the long-term average growth rate of 3.0% per year. For the monetary base and the price level, we use the average growth rates over the five years prior to the base year. An exception is 1921, where we generate the normal values, $M°$ and $P°$, by using the average growth rates of these variables for 1909–14. We then apply these rates to the values for the base year, 1920.

Sources: See Figures 1.1 and 1.4, Table 7.2, and Figure 16.6.

to the most severe of the post-World War II recessions, which are 1980–82 and 1974–75.[9]

The second section of the table shows the behavior of the monetary base, M;[10] for example, the amount of base money during 1894 is $1.57 billion. We compare this figure with a "normal" or expected amount, which we call $M°$. We compute this amount by asking what the quantity of base money would have been in 1894 if it had grown at a normal or expected rate from the base year, 1892. By a normal rate, we mean the rate that someone would have predicted in 1892 for monetary growth over the next two years (pretending that people were thinking about such

[9]However, the data on real GNP are less accurate for the earlier cases. Conceivably, the magnitudes of these recessions are overstated by the data.

[10]Gold and silver coins and certificates account for roughly half of the monetary base through World War I, and still retain a substantial role until 1933. The reserves held at the Fed appear in the monetary base after the start of the Federal Reserve System in 1914.

matters!). Operationally, we estimate this rate as the average value, 3.4% per year, which applied over the five years prior to 1892. Then we estimate the normal amount of base money, M°, for 1894 as $1.65 billion. Accordingly, the actual stock, M, is 4.8% below this normal value. Although the precise figure depends on the procedure for estimating the normal growth rate of money, we can satisfactorily use a value of about 5% to gauge the rough size of the shortfall in base money for 1892–94.

We apply a similar procedure for three of the other recessions. Thereby, we find that base money actually exceeds the normal amount for two cases—by 6.9% in 1906–08 and 12.7% in 1929–33. But for the 1937–38 recession, the shortfall of base money is 3.4%.

For 1920–21, we have some difficulties in generating the normal growth rate of money. The five years prior to 1920 include the rapid growth of money during World War I. But people would have no reason to expect these high rates of expansion to continue after 1920. So in order to get a rough estimate, we use the growth rate of the monetary base that applies before World War I for 1909–14, which is 2.7% per year. Then we find that the shortfall in the monetary base for 1920–21 is 11.5%. In any event, there is no doubt that the sharp drop in base money during 1921 represents a substantial decline relative to anyone's predictions.

Overall, the five major recessions between 1890 and 1940 do not suggest a close association between contractions of output and shortfalls in the monetary base. In fact, for two of the cases—1929–33 and 1906–08—the movements in base money are expansionary. Only in the case of the post-World War I contraction, 1920–21, do the figures suggest a dominant role for the shortfall in base money. It is also interesting that, for this episode, the fall in the monetary base reflects mostly a sharp decline in borrowing from the Fed. Further, this decline stems at least in part from a dramatic increase in the Fed's discount rate—that is, from a reduction in the subsidy to borrowing by banks.

Conceivably, our focus on the episodes of major economic contraction would mislead us about the overall role of shortfalls in base money. But the notion that this role is minor is confirmed by a more thorough analysis of Mark Rush.[11] His study uses all the data from 1885 to 1913 and also employs more sophisticated techniques for measuring the normal or anticipated growth rate of the monetary base. In addition, he allows for lagged effects of changes in the monetary base on real variables. But his basic finding is that unusual movements in the monetary base play at most a minor role in influencing output and employment over this period.

The third section of Table 17.1 makes calculations for the price level, which parallel those that we made for the monetary base. We find shortfalls in prices relative to the normal or expected level, P^o, by no more than 2% for two cases—1892–94 and 1906–08—by 5% for 1937–38, 16% for 1920–21, and 24% for 1929–33.

---

[11]See Mark Rush, ''Unexpected Monetary Shocks in the United States during the Gold Standard Era,'' unpublished Ph.D. dissertation, University of Rochester, 1982.

Given our earlier results, we know that much of these shortfalls in prices cannot be explained by shortfalls in base money. That is, increases in the real demand for base money must be important during these recessions. But we expect precisely this behavior during banking panics—which occurred in 1893, 1907, and 1931–33—or in response to the sharp increase in reserve requirements in 1936–37.

We can get some idea about the size of the change in the real demand for base money by examining the relation between base money, M, and a broader monetary aggregate, such as $M1$ (the public's currency and checkable deposits). Essentially, the ratio of $M1$ to M tells us something about the amount of financial intermediation in the economy. In particular, our previous analysis implies that this ratio declines when the real demand for base money expands, as in a banking panic.[12] Looking at the fourth section of Table 17.1, we see that the ratio, $M1/M$, declines substantially for four of the five cases.[13] The declines by 5% for 1892–94, 12% for 1906–08, and 33% for 1929–33 reflect the impacts of the banking panics. The reduction by 9% for 1937–38 stems from the increase in reserve requirements. But for 1920–21, the ratio is virtually unchanged.

In any event, the results suggest a positive relation between changes in financial intermediation—as proxied by the ratio of $M1$ to the monetary base—and real economic activity. Further, this indication from the five recessions that we considered is reinforced by the more detailed analysis of Mark Rush, which we mentioned earlier. Over the period, 1885–1913, he finds an important linkage between shifts in the ratio of $M1$ to the monetary base and subsequent changes in output and employment.

An important point is that neither Rush's analysis nor ours tells us for sure whether banking panics cause recessions or, in reverse, that hard economic times make banking panics more likely. But we do know a couple of things about this direction of causation. First, the implementation of deposit insurance in 1934 apparently eliminated the potential for banking panics and thereby lessened the typical size of business fluctuations. Hence, this observation suggests that the potential for banking panics explains part of the magnitude of economic contractions, even if not the timing of these contractions. Second, the increase in reserve requirements in 1936–37 isolates the effect of a financial change on economic activity, rather than the reverse effect.

Overall, the evidence from before World War II indicates important real effects from shifts in financial intermediation, which reflect especially banking panics and changes in reserve requirements. Further, the movements in the ratio of $M1$ to the monetary base serve as a rough proxy for these effects. But there is not much connection between shifts to the monetary base—even when they are surprisingly

---

[12]Before 1914, data on M1 are unavailable because we cannot separate banks' time deposits from their demand deposits. But we can estimate M1 by looking at a broader monetary aggregate, which includes the banks' time deposits. This aggregate used to be called M2, although this term now encompasses some additional assets.

[13]The normal growth rate of the ratio, $M1/M$, would be a small number. Implicitly, we treat it as close to zero.

large—and changes in real economic activity. The one suggestion of this linkage comes from the sharp, but brief, contraction of 1920–21. But even here, the dramatic reduction in the monetary base reflects a major decrease in the Fed's subsidy for borrowing at the discount window.[14] Thus, even this episode does not decisively demonstrate important real effects from a pure reduction in the monetary base (when generated, for example, through open-market sales of bonds).

The Relation Between Real and Nominal Variables Since World War II

For the post-World War II period, there are many detailed studies that attempt to isolate the effects on real variables from unusual movements in the nominal variables. Let's consider first some research that deals with shocks to the price level, and then some work that focuses on monetary disturbances.

Effects From Changes in Prices

Two recent econometric studies analyze the relation between surprise movements in the price level and the amount of real economic activity in the post-World War II United States. The analyses are by Thomas Sargent and Ray Fair.[15]

The two studies focus on the unemployment rate, u_t, as the measure of real economic performance. The statistical procedures seek to estimate the effect on unemployment from surprises in prices, $P_t - P_t^e$, where P_t is the actual price level and P_t^e is the price that the typical person expected for period t. In other words, these studies provide estimates for expectational Phillips curves. Operationally, Sargent and Fair interpret the expected price, P_t^e, as the best forecast for the actual price, P_t, that people could have made with the data available through the previous period, $t - 1$. In practice, the periods are treated as quarters of years. Sargent and Fair use statistical techniques to obtain a best fit between the actual price level, P_t, and the lagged values of a group of explanatory variables. Then they use the fitted values from this relationship as proxies for the expected price, P_t^e—that is, for the best prediction of prices that could have been made from the assumed list of explanatory variables, when observed up to date $t - 1$.

Sargent reports a negative and just statistically significant effect of the price surprise, $P_t - P_t^e$, on the unemployment rate over the period, 1951–73. However, the magnitude of the relationship is weak. Specifically, a 10% rise in prices above expectations—which would be a dramatic shock—lowers that quarter's unemploy-

---

[14]The discount rate averages 1.6 points below the commercial paper rate from 1918 to 1920, but only 0.7 points below for 1921 and 0.3 points below for 1922. Correspondingly, borrowings at the Fed fall by $0.7 billion in 1921 and by $1.2 billion in 1922.

[15]Thomas Sargent, "A Classical Macroeconometric Model for the United States," *Journal of Political Economy,* April 1976; and Ray Fair, "An Analysis of the Accuracy of Four Macroeconometric Models," *Journal of Political Economy,* August 1979.

ment rate by only about two-tenths of a percentage point.[16] In any event, using some improved techniques, Fair finds that the suggested relationship between the unemployment rate and the price surprise is, in fact, statistically insignificant (over the period, 1954–73). Moreover, when he adds data from 1974–77, the estimated effect of price shocks on unemployment reverses sign, becoming positive. That is, the expectational Phillips curve now has the wrong sign.

Recall that our analysis in previous chapters implies that the relation between a real variable, such as the unemployment rate or the level of output, and surprise movements in the price level depends on the nature of the underlying disturbance. Specifically, shifts to production functions can generate a negative relation between movements in output and movements in prices. Hence, this element can account for the positive relation between price shocks and unemployment that Fair reports when he adds the data for 1974–77. Recall that these years include the effects from the first oil crisis of 1973–74, which we can interpret as a major supply shock.[17] For this reason, the expectational Phillips curve, which is the relation between unemployment and price surprises, tends to confound two types of effects. First, there would be the positive relation caused by supply shocks. Second, if monetary disturbances raise prices and lower unemployment, then the expectational Phillips curve would tend to have a negative slope. Thus, even if money is nonneutral, the slope of the Phillips curve could have the wrong (positive) sign. Instead of estimating expectational Phillips curves as Sargent and Fair did, it would be useful to isolate the real effects of monetary disturbances. Then we get a clearer test for the neutrality of monetary shocks.

Monetary Shocks and Real Economic Activity in the Post-World War II U.S.

I have analyzed the real effects of monetary shocks in a number of papers.[18] The starting point is the division of monetary growth into anticipated and unanticipated components. Conceptually, I identified the anticipated part with the prediction that could have been made by exploiting the historical relation between money and a specified set of explanatory variables. Using the $M1$ definition of money over the period since World War II, I found that monetary growth for year t depends positively on three variables: last year's monetary growth, last year's unemployment rate, and this year's level of federal expenditure relative to a measure of normal spending. The positive relation to past unemployment may reflect the Fed's

---

[16]The estimates imply a persisting influence, whereby the unemployment rate falls also in subsequent quarters. The peak response, which is about 50% larger than the initial reaction, occurs with a 2–3 quarter lag.

[17]One study that credits oil shocks with a large influence on aggregate output and employment even before 1973 is James Hamilton, ''Oil and the Macroeconomy since World War II,'' *Journal of Political Economy,* April 1983.

[18]This work is synthesized in Robert Barro, ''Unanticipated Money Growth and Economic Activity in the U.S.,'' in *Money, Expectations and Business Cycles,* Academic Press, New York, 1981.

desire to expand money during a recession, which we call "countercyclical" or "activist" monetary policy. The positive effect of federal spending may involve the incentive for inflationary finance. Some further research indicates a negative reaction of monetary growth to lagged increases in nominal interest rates, which can also be added to the analysis.

I used the estimated relation of monetary growth to the explanatory variables in order to construct a series labeled **anticipated money growth.** Then I took the difference between actual and anticipated monetary change as the empirical counterpart of **unanticipated money.** Essentially, this procedure does for money what Sargent and Fair did for prices in the studies that we discussed above.

I estimated equations for real GNP and the unemployment rate over the post-World War II period in order to ascertain the real effects of anticipated and unanticipated changes in money. Basically, I found that unanticipated money had expansionary real effects that lasted over a 1–2 year period. On the other hand, the anticipated parts of monetary change did not have important real effects. Quantitatively, I estimated that a 1% rise in money above expectations raises next year's output by about 1% and lowers next year's unemployment rate by about six-tenths of a percentage point. Thus, unlike for the price shocks that Sargent and Fair studied, positive monetary surprises seem to have important expansionary effects on real economic activity.

The results just mentioned pertain to the broad monetary aggregate, $M1$. But we can think of disturbances to $M1$ as composed partly of shocks to the monetary base, M, and partly to the ratio of $M1$ to the base. For the post-World War II period, it turns out that these two components contribute roughly equally to the estimated effects on output and unemployment. (But recall that, unlike before World War II, the fluctuations in the ratio of $M1$ to the monetary base have been relatively mild since the war.) In any event, since World War II the unusual movements in the monetary base appear to have significantly positive effects on output and employment.[19]

Overall, the evidence from the post-World War II period suggests that the surprise parts of movements in the monetary base have effects in the same direction on output and employment. Hence, these findings conflict with our theory, which predicts that these types of monetary changes would be neutral. (At least the theory predicts this if we neglect variations in transaction costs and some distributional effects.) Thus, it is worthwhile to try to extend the theory to encompass these findings. We carry out this extension in the next chapter.

---

[19]Empirical analysis of anticipated versus unanticipated money has become popular in recent years. Some of the contributions are C. L. F. Attfield, D. Demery and N. W. Duck, "A Quarterly Model of Unanticipated Monetary Growth, Output and the Price Level in the U.K.," *Journal of Monetary Economics,* November 1981; Roger Kormendi and Philip Meguire, "Cross-Regime Evidence of Macroeconomic Rationality," *Journal of Political Economy,* forthcoming; and Frederic Mishkin, "Does Anticipated Monetary Policy Matter? An Econometric Investigation," *Journal of Political Economy,* February 1982.

Summary

Much of the macrotheorizing since the 1930s can be viewed as attempts to rationalize a strong interplay between nominal and real variables, which shows up in various versions of the Phillips curve. Specifically, we can view the Keynesian theory and more recent monetary theories of business fluctuations in this context. But before considering these theories, we should think about how much evidence there is to explain.

Neither the long-period evidence nor that from across countries suggests important effects on real variables from differences in the average growth rates of money, prices, and wages. That is, in the long run there is no systematic relation between real variables and nominal variables.

Before World War II, the evidence suggests important real effects from banking panics and changes in reserve requirements, which show up as fluctuations in the ratio of M1 to the monetary base. Also, these episodes typically involve some surprise decreases in prices (and nominal wages). But there is not much evidence for real effects from changes in the monetary base.

After World War II, there is an indication that monetary shocks—but not price surprises—have positive effects on real economic activity. The strongest evidence for real effects of money show up when we use a broad aggregate like M1. But there still seem to be some real effects when we look at shocks to the monetary base.

Basically, it is the last observation on monetary nonneutrality that conflicts with our theory. Although this failure deserves some weight in our thinking, it is probable that the weight has usually been too large. That is, the interplay between nominal and real variables is neither as large nor as pervasive as most people believe.

Important Terms and Concepts

Phillips Curve

expectational Phillips curve

anticipated money growth

unanticipated money growth

QUESTIONS

Mainly for Review

17.1 What is the theoretical link between the price level and real variables? The inflation rate and real variables? Why do you think it might be important to distinguish between expected and unexpected inflation?

17.2 Consider the statement, ''Makers of economic policy face a cruel choice between unemployment and inflation.'' Explain why this statement is not supported by either (a) theoretical results or (b) empirical findings on the Phillips curve.

17.3 How does the expectational Phillips Curve explain the negative association between inflation and unemployment rates in the United States prior to World War I? Could the absence of this negative association in subsequent years be ''explained'' by shifts in the Phillips Curve?

17.4 To what extent was the Great Depression (1929–33) accompanied by a change in the nominal quantity of money? In the real quantity of money?

17.5 Explain why it is important to distinguish between shifts in the nominal quantity of money and shifts in money demand. What association would we expect between the price level and real output in periods where both types of shifts occur?

CHAPTER 18

MONEY AND BUSINESS FLUCTUATIONS— THE MARKET-CLEARING MODEL WITH INCOMPLETE INFORMATION

In recent years, some macroeconomists have developed a new line of theory to explain the role of money in business fluctuations. The new approach has been called at least the following: *the equilibrium approach to business cycles, rational expectations macroeconomics,* and the *new classical macroeconomics.* Here, we refer to it, somewhat more descriptively, as the *market-clearing model with incomplete information.*[1]

As with the models that we have discussed so far, this new approach relies on the conditions for general market clearing as its central analytical device. The approach also retains the assumption that people behave rationally, even including the manner in which they form expectations of inflation and other variables. However, we introduce an important source of "friction" by allowing for incomplete

---

[1]For surveys of the research, see Robert Barro, "The Equilibrium Approach to Business Cycles," in Robert Barro, *Money, Expectations and Business Cycles,* Academic Press, New York, 1981; and Ben Mc Callum, "The Current State of the Policy-Ineffectiveness Debate," *American Economic Review,* proceedings, May 1979. The main papers are collected in Robert Lucas, *Studies in Business-Cycle Theory,* M.I.T. Press, Cambridge, Massachusetts, 1981; and in Robert Lucas and Thomas Sargent, eds., *Rational Expectations and Econometric Practice,* 2 vols., University of Minnesota Press, Minneapolis, 1981. Two early papers that stimulated much of the subsequent work are Milton Friedman, "The Role of Monetary Policy," *American Economic Review,* March 1968; and Edmund Phelps, "The New Microeconomics in Employment and Inflation Theory," in Edmund Phelps, ed., *Microeconomic Foundations of Employment and Inflation Theory,* Norton, New York, 1970.

information. Specifically, an important way in which people receive information—and thereby make their allocative decisions—is by observing prices of various goods. But it would be prohibitively expensive for individuals to observe all prices instantly. Therefore, people typically make do with partial knowledge about the prices of different goods, about wage rates in alternative jobs, and so on. In this situation people's decisions often depart from those that they would make with full information.

Variations in money and the general price level make it difficult for people to interpret the limited set of prices that they observe. Hence, when there is an increase in the general price level, people may mistakenly think that the price of their output or their nominal wage rate has increased *relative* to other prices and wages. Consequently, they tend to produce more goods and work more than they would under full information. Because of these responses, we shall find that surprise increases in money and the general price level can lead to expansions in the aggregate level of real economic activity.

The main objective of this line of theory is two-fold. First, we want to account for the positive effect of monetary disturbances on output. (Recall that the previous chapter details the evidence for this effect.) Second, to the extent that we explain the linkage between monetary changes and output, we also account for one of the sources of business fluctuations. (In previous chapters we have discussed supply shocks and variations in government expenditures and taxes as sources of these fluctuations.) Thus, at least after the fact, we might be able to say that a recession or boom during some period stems from past surprises in money.

In this chapter, we work out the details of a representative model from this new line of macroeconomic theory. But it is worthwhile to stress a couple of warnings at the outset. First, in order to bring out the role of incomplete information, we have to set up some new theoretical apparatus and go through some intricate analysis. Second, because this theory is still in its developing stages, there are a number of loose ends that remain. In particular, we cannot yet reach a final verdict on the explanatory power of this theory for business fluctuations. But on the side of rewards, we do end up with some understanding of the real effects from nominal disturbances, as well as with some intriguing results about monetary policy.

The Structure of a Model with Local Markets

Consider again the model where households produce goods and sell them on a commodity market. But in order to study the role of incomplete information, it is necessary to dispense with the notion of homogeneous products that trade in a single marketplace. Rather, we want to imagine goods that differ by physical characteristics, location, and so on. Accordingly, we now index commodities by the symbol z, which takes on the possible values, $1, 2, \ldots, n$, where n is a large number. In order to be concrete and to simplify matters, we usually think of z as a location—that is, as a "local market." But more generally, we could identify this index with various characteristics of goods, occupations, methods of production, and so on. So the value $z = 1$ might signify the automobile industry, $z = 2$ the computer industry, etc.

Since changes in job location or in type of product entail substantial costs, people do not move too often from one place or line of work to another. In order to capture this idea in a workable model, we assume that each household produces and sells goods in only one location during each period. But there is mobility in the sense that people may change locations at some cost from one period to the next.

We now distinguish prices by type or location of product and by date, so that $P_t(z)$ is the price of goods of type z during period t. Thus, $P_t(z)$ might be the price of a car or a pair of shoes, or of a market basket of goods in Detroit or Pittsburgh. Correspondingly, the ratio, $P_t(z)/P_t(z')$, is the price of goods of type (or location) z, relative to that of type (or location) z'. It is important to distinguish this concept of a *relative price* from the general price level, which we have stressed in previous chapters. By the general price level P_t we mean the average of the individual prices at date t.

In order to keep things manageable, we neglect any long-lasting differences among locations or other characteristics of goods. That is, we ignore a variety of things that make goods permanently more or less expensive in different places. So, if the "local price," $P_t(z)$, exceeds the average price, P_t, then market z looks relatively favorable for sellers during period t. But this situation attracts producers (and workers) from elsewhere. Then the expansion of goods supplied to market z tends to drive down the local price toward the general level of prices. Similarly, if the local price is lower than the average price, then producers (and workers) move to other territory. Again, the process tends to bring the local price in line with the general price level. Overall there is a process of entry to and exit from local markets that keep each local price reasonably close to the average price. Hence, if someone makes long-range forecasts, then the expected price in any local market equals that for the average of the markets.

At the beginning of period t, a producer in market z has the stock of capital, $k_{t-1}(z)$. Correspondingly, the amount of goods that he or she produces at location z during period t is given from the production function as

$$y_t(z) = f[k_{t-1}(z), l_t(z)] \tag{18.1}$$

where $l_t(z)$ is the producer's work effort. Note that we again think of each household as working on is own production process, although we could also extend things to include hired workers. Also, we think of last period's capital, $k_{t-1}(z)$, as stuck in market z (Detroit or Pittsburgh), rather than movable across locations.

The dollar revenue from sales equals output, $y_t(z)$, multiplied by the local price, $P_t(z)$. But suppose that people buy goods from many different locations. Then, as an approximation, the typical household pays the average price, P_t, for its purchases of consumables and capital goods. In this case, people calculate the real value of the revenue from local sales—that is, the value in terms of the goods that they buy—by dividing the dollar amount by the general price level, P_t. Hence, the real revenue from production is

$$[P_t(z)/P_t] \cdot y_t(z) = [P_t(z)/P_t] \cdot f[k_{t-1}(z), l_t(z)] \tag{18.2}$$

The term, $P_t(z)/P_t$, is the price of goods sold in market z relative to the average price of goods. Notice that for a given amount of physical product, $y_t(z)$, an increase in the relative price, $P_t(z)/P_t$, means a greater real value of sales.

From the standpoint of a producer, an increase in the relative price, $P_t(z)/P_t$, is equivalent to a proportional upward shift in the production function, f. When deciding how much to work during period t, producers (and workers) looked before at the physical marginal product of labor, $MPL_t(z)$. (Here, the index z means that the marginal product applies to additional work and output in market z.) Now, in order to compute the effect on real sales revenue, producers multiply the change in physical product by the relative price, $P_t(z)/P_t$. Hence, the real value of labor's marginal product is $[P_t(z)/P_t] \cdot MPL_t(z)$. An increase in the relative price looks to the producer just like a proportional upward shift in the schedule for labor's physical marginal product. Therefore, producers respond to changes in the relative price, $P_t(z)/P_t$, just as they did before to changes in the schedule for labor's marginal product.

When deciding how much to invest during period t, producers looked before at the physical marginal product of capital, $MPK_t(z)$. But remember that this marginal product describes the reaction of next period's output, $y_{t+1}(z)$, to increases in this period's stock of capital, $k_t(z)$. That is, it takes one period for investment to raise productive capacity. Accordingly, the real value of capital's marginal product depends on next period's relative price, $P_{t+1}(z)/P_{t+1}$. It follows that investment decisions depend on the real value of capital's marginal product, which is $[P_{t+1}(z)/P_{t+1}] \cdot MPK_t(z)$.[2]

Consider how producers respond to an increase in the relative price, $P_t(z)/P_t$. Suppose first, that this increase applies only for period t—that is, people do not anticipate a higher relative price for subsequent periods. Then the change amounts to an upward shift in the schedule for labor's marginal product during period t, but not for later periods. Therefore, producers increase work effort, $l_t(z)$, and the supply of goods, $y_t^s(z)$. Recall that these responses involve two types of substitution effects. First, there is a shift away from leisure and toward consumption, and second, there is a shift away from today's leisure and toward tomorrow's leisure. The second channel, which is an intertemporal-substitution effect, suggests that the current

---

[2]The returns from investment depend also on the price at which producers can sell their used capital at the end of period $t + 1$. (Remember that we can pretend that producers sell their capital after using it for one period.) But the price of capital in market z at the end of period $t + 1$ depends on the relative price of goods for the subsequent period, $P_{t+2}(z)/P_{t+2}$. Thus, investors generally care about prospective relative prices for periods after $t + 1$. However, in order to simplify matters, we assume that the prospective relative price equals unity for these later periods. In this case, producers think that they can always sell used capital at the general price level, P_{t+1}.

responses of work and production will be particularly strong.[3] As an example, we can think of the strong response of labor supply to the unusually high wages that are offered during overtime periods.

So far, there is no effect on investment because the high relative price does not persist into the next period. That is, there is no change in the real value of capital's marginal product, $[P_{t+1}(z)/P_{t+1}] \cdot MPK_t(z)$. But suppose now that the *prospective relative price*, $P_{t+1}(z)/P_{t+1}$, increases. Then there is a positive response of investment demand in period t. People buy additional capital goods from other markets in order to benefit from the higher relative price for goods sold later in location z.

In order to carry out investment projects—for example, to construct a factory or to install a machine—producers typically have to buy some goods and labor services locally at the high relative price, $P_t(z)/P_t$. (Think of a gold rush, where the prospectors have to pay high local prices for labor and shovels.) For example, the local price likely applies at least to the costs of drawing up plans and making decisions. Further, these parts of an investment project tend to arise first. Consequently, the high prospective relative price, $P_{t+1}(z)/P_{t+1}$, can motivate investors to spend a good deal today in the local market, even though the current relative price, $P_t(z)/P_t$, is high. What's more, in order to obtain favorable returns from investment—that is, to benefit from the high prospective relative price—it is often important for a producer to be ready quickly with the extra capacity. Therefore, we can get a strong positive effect on local investment demand, $i_t^d(z)$, when the prospective relative price rises, even though the current relative price is also high.

A high prospective relative price, $P_{t+1}(z)/P_{t+1}$, means that the high current relative price, $P_t(z)/P_t$, is no longer so much of a temporary opportunity for great rewards. Therefore, the intertemporal-substitution effect on today's work and production becomes weaker. At least, this effect arises if the typical producer plans to remain for awhile in location z. Then we get a smaller response during period t of work effort, $l_t(z)$, and the supply of goods, $y_t^s(z)$.

Our previous discussion indicates that a high relative price cannot persist indefinitely. That's because the entry of producers to favorable markets and their exit from unfavorable ones tends to equalize the prices across the markets. In fact, the incentive to invest, which we just described, is an important part of this entry and exit. Namely, a high prospective relative price motivates investment in the local market, which raises productive capacity in that market in future periods. But then the greater supply of goods later on tends to reduce future relative prices.

These considerations suggest that a high relative price may persist for awhile, but not indefinitely. So the persistence can be long enough to generate important positive effects on investment. But the persistence may also be short enough so

---

[3]The higher relative price, $P_t(z)/P_t$, also increases wealth for sellers in market z. However, for buyers, the effect on wealth is negative. In any case, since the changes in relative prices are temporary, the wealth effects will be small. So in order to focus on the main points, we neglect the wealth effects.

that the intertemporal-substitution effect remains strong. Then we still get substantial positive responses of today's work effort and production.

Buyers in the Local Market

So far, we have examined the behavior of producers in a local market. Now we consider the incentives of buyers, who may come from elsewhere to purchase goods from these producers. For buyers, a high relative price, $P_t(z)/P_t$, deters consumption demand, $c_t^d(z)$, and investment demand, $i_t^d(z)$.[4] (Note that the index z refers to goods bought in market z, although the buyers may use the goods in other locations.)

Clearing of a Local Market

If we put the pieces of the analysis together, then the condition for clearing the local market is

$$Y_t^s(z)[P_t(z)/P_t, P_{t+1}(z)/P_{t+1}, r_t, \ldots] = C_t^d(z)[P_t(z)/P_t, r_t \ldots]$$
$$(+) \qquad (-) \qquad (+) \qquad\qquad (-) \quad (-)$$
$$+ I_t^d(z)[P_t(z)/P_t, P_{t+1}(z)/P_{t+1}, r_t, \ldots]$$
$$(-) \qquad\quad (+) \qquad\quad (-)$$

(18.3)

Here, we use capital letters to denote the total quantity of goods supplied or demanded in market z.

Notice that a higher current relative price, $P_t(z)/P_t$, raises the supply of goods, but lowers consumption and investment demand. Also, a higher prospective relative price, $P_{t+1}(z)/P_{t+1}$, increases investment demand. As mentioned before, this term picks up the expenditures by local investors, who want to act quickly in order to benefit from higher prospective relative prices. In addition, a higher prospective relative price lessens the incentive of suppliers to work and produce during period t. Hence, the prospective relative price has a negative effect on today's supply of goods.

We also include in the supply and demand functions the real interest rate, r_t. As before, this rate equals the nominal interest rate, R_t, less the general rate of inflation, $\pi_t = P_{t+1}/P_t - 1$. We still view the nominal interest rate as an economy-wide variable, which everyone observes on a centralized credit market. (Think, for example, of the organized bond market in New York or of the similar loan rates that are charged by financial intermediaries.) Therefore, the real interest rate, r_t, is also an economy-wide variable.

Given the relative prices, $P_t(z)/P_t$ and $P_{t+1}(z)/P_{t+1}$, the real interest rate has the same effects as before. Specifically, a higher rate means a greater supply of

---

[4] For simplicity, we neglect any effects of prospective relative prices on demand. These effects will be weak unless buyers have a strong attachment to a particular local market.

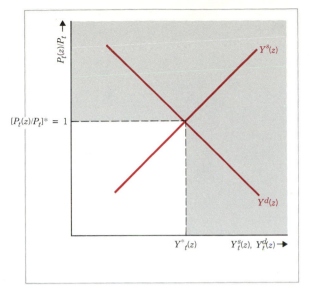

Figure 18.1 **The Clearing of a Local Commodity Market**

We show the dependence of commodity supply and demand on the relative price, $P_t(z)/P_t$. Here, we hold fixed the effects of other variables, including the economy-wide real interest rate, r_t, and the prospective relative price, $P_{t+1}(z)/P_{t+1}$. Note that, for the average market, the market-clearing relative price is one.

goods to each local market, $Y_t^s(z)$, but smaller demands for consumables, $C_t^d(z)$, and investment goods, $I_t^d(z)$.

Figure 18.1 depicts the clearing of a local commodity market. We put the current relative price, $P_t(z)/P_t$, on the vertical axis. The supply and demand curves in the figure assume given values for the prospective relative price, $P_{t+1}(z)/P_{t+1}$, and the real interest rate, r_t. (We also hold fixed the initial stock of capital in the local market, $K_{t-1}(z)$, the forms of production functions, and prospective values of the real interest rate.) Notice that the intersection of the curves determines the market-clearing values of the relative price, $[P_t(z)/P_t]^*$, and local output, $Y_t^*(z)$. Also, for the average market—which, by definition, has not experienced unusual changes in its supply and demand curves—the market-clearing relative price must equal one. That is, in the average market, the local price, $P_t^*(z)$, equals the average price, P_t^*.

Disturbances to Local Markets

We can imagine a variety of changes in tastes and technology that affect the clearing of a local commodity market. For example, there may be shifts in the numbers of producers, or in production functions, or in the numbers of demanders, and so on. Let's think here of an increase in local consumption demand, $C_t^d(z)$. In the model this change could reflect an increase in the number of shoppers in market z. More

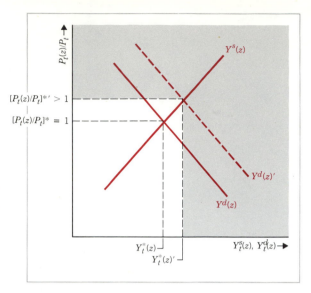

Figure 18.2 **The Responses to an Increase in Local Demand**
The change in consumer demand shows up as a positive shift to the local demand curve. Hence, the relative price and local output increase. Notice that the suppliers respond to the higher relative price by producing more goods (and by working harder). Also, if the market-clearing relative price is initially one (which holds for the average market), then the new value exceeds one.

generally, we can think also of an increase in demand that reflects the popularity of some new or improved product, such as video games or personal computers.

Figure 18.2 shows the effect on a local commodity market from the increase in consumer demand. The solid lines reproduce the supply and demand curves from Figure 18.1. Then the new demand curve is the dashed line, labeled $Y^d(z)'$, which lies to the right of the original curve. Note that we hold constant the real interest rate, r_t, and the prospective relative price, $P_{t+1}(z)/P_{t+1}$. Since the disturbance applies only to the local market, it is reasonable to hold fixed the real interest rate. That is, this economy-wide variable responds to movements in the aggregates of supply and demand, rather than to changes in a single location or for a single type of product. However, we consider in a moment the behavior of the prospective relative price.

Figure 18.2 shows that the current relative price and local output increase. Notice that the rise in the relative price motivates producers to work more and supply more goods. Thus, we can think of the high relative price as the signal that generates the unusually large volume of work and production. However, the higher relative price means that investment falls. Finally, if the market-clearing relative price were initially equal to one—as is true for the average market—then the new relative price must exceed one.

Prospective Relative Prices

The increase in consumer demand tends also to raise the prospective relative price, $P_{t+1}(z)/P_{t+1}$. The main reason is that the high demand typically persists for awhile. (Think again about new products, such as video cassette recorders or six-foot TV screens.) Further, we assume that the entry of new suppliers is insufficient to return the relative price to unity within a single period.

An increase in the prospective relative price raises investment demand, $I_t^d(z)$, but reduces supply, $Y_t^s(z)$. Therefore, we modify the previous analysis as shown in Figure 18.3. The new elements are the leftward shift in the supply curve and the larger rightward shift in the demand curve. There are two important consequences of these modifications. First, the current relative price, $P_t(z)/P_t$, rises by more than the amount shown in Figure 18.2. Second, since the higher prospective relative price boosts investment demand, it is now possible that current investment increases. In particular, this increase is likely if it is crucial for investors to move aggressively in order to capitalize on the opportunities for high prospective relative prices. ●

Note that, so far, we have considered only the response of a local market to a local disturbance. Hence, we have not yet explained movements in aggregate output and investment. But in later sections we show how a monetary disturbance may look, in each market, like a shift to local demand. Then producers in each

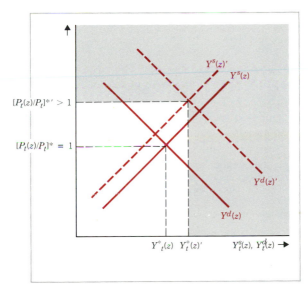

Figure 18.3 **The Responses to an Increase in Local Demand, Including the Higher Prospective Relative Price**

The rise in the prospective relative price raises investment demand, but lowers the current supply of goods. Therefore, the current relative price rises by more than the amount shown in Figure 18.2.

market change output and investment, just as they do in Figure 18.3. When all producers act this way, we end up with movements in the aggregate variables.

Changes in the Stock of Money

Consider a once-and-for-all increase in the quantity of base money, M_t. As in some cases that we explored before, this change might involve an open-market purchase of bonds by the Fed.

Previously, we found that an increase in the quantity of money raises the general price level proportionately, but leaves unchanged real variables like aggregate output and employment. This conclusion still obtains when there are a variety of locations in which people produce and trade goods. As in previous analyses, we can think of people as attempting to spend their excess real cash balances on the goods in various markets. Then the price in each market, $P_t(z)$, ends up rising by the same proportion as the increase in money. Hence, the general or average price level, P_t, moves one-to-one with the quantity of money. Notice that these responses leave unchanged the relative price, $P_t(z)/P_t$, for each market. Also, there is no change in the level of output, $Y_t(z)$, in each market. At this point, we still lack any connection between money and the real variables, which include the quantities of output and the relative prices of the different goods.

Imperfect Information about Money and the General Price Level

Now we make a crucial change in the setup to remove some information that individuals have about money and prices. The basic idea is that people know the prices of things that they recently bought or sold. So they know the wage rate for their labor services (at least on the present job), the price of groceries at the local market, the price of a car that they looked at last week, the rent on their apartment, and so on. Similarly, producers know a good deal about the costs of labor and other inputs, as well as the price of their own product (at least in a local market). However, people have much poorer knowledge about the prices of objects that they shopped for last year or perhaps have never examined.

We can model these general ideas by assuming that sellers and buyers know the local price of goods, $P_t(z)$, but are less sure about the general or average price, P_t. So the local goods correspond to the items that people have dealt with recently, and on which they know the current price. On the other hand, the general price applies to other goods, which are potential alternatives to local product, but for which people have a blurrier notion of the price.

As before, sellers and buyers in market z respond to their perception of the relative price, $P_t(z)/P_t$. But although they know the local price, $P_t(z)$, they no longer are sure about the general price level, P_t. Therefore, we have to analyze how people compute expectations of this average price under incomplete information. Here, we use the idea of **rational expectations.** This approach says that if people do not observe something directly—such as the current price level—then they form the best possible estimate of this variable, given the information that they possess. In other words people make efficient use of their limited data, so as not to commit avoidable errors.[5]

To start with, consider the expectations that people have about prices for period t. For simplicity, we assume now that all markets look the same beforehand. That is, before period t, people cannot predict whether the price in market z, $P_t(z)$, will be higher or lower than the average price P_t.[6] Then we can just think about the expectations that people have before period t for the general price level P_t. We denote this expectation by P_t^e. In order to keep things manageable, we pretend that everyone has the same information beforehand and therefore calculates the same expectation, P_t^e. But recall that people form this expectation before observing any prices or other data for period t. For that reason, we call the variable P_t^e the **prior expectation** (or forecast) of the general price level.

Generally, the prior expectation of prices depends on past information and on knowledge about the workings of the economy. Hence, we can think of this expectation as incorporating information about the quantity of money and about variables that influence the aggregate real demand for money. Often, people will get useful information about these variables from lagged values of money and prices, from interest rates, and possibly from the government's announcements about monetary and fiscal policy. Therefore, the prior expectation, P_t^e, typically depends on all these variables.

During period t, people find that goods sell locally at the price $P_t(z)$. But is this price high or low in relation to prices elsewhere? Sellers and buyers can readily compare the local price with their prior expectation of the general price level, P_t^e. Then if the local price differs from this expectation, there are two possibilities. First, some local condition—such as a shift to demand in this market—may make the relative price of goods in market z either high or low. Second, the forecast of general prices may be inaccurate. That is, the general price level, P_t, may turn out to be either higher or lower than the forecasted value, P_t^e. But by assumption, people cannot check things out directly by immediately sampling lots of prices in other markets or by observing a useful published index of current prices. Because this process of obtaining information is costly, sellers and buyers make do with incomplete knowledge about the prices of alternative goods. Here, we represent this complex matter by assuming that people have only two pieces of useful information. These are the local price, $P_t(z)$, and the prior expectation of the general price level, P_t^e.

---

[5]The basic idea of rational expectations comes from John Muth, "Rational Expectations and the Theory of Price Movement," *Econometrica,* July 1971. For a discussion of applications to macro-economics, see Robert Lucas, "Understanding Business Cycles," *Carnegie-Rochester Conference Series on Public Policy,* 1976.

[6]There is a problem with this assumption, because it eliminates the entry of new producers to markets that have a high expected relative price. But we make the assumption only to ease the analysis.

Once someone has these two pieces of information, $P_t(z)$ and P_t^e, they determine their best estimate (or rational expectation) of today's general price level, P_t. Let's call this estimate $P_{t,z}^e$. The reason it differs from the prior expectation, P_t^e, is that people revise their beliefs about the general price level after they observe the local price. For example, if the local price turns out to be higher than the prior estimate, then it is likely that the current average price, P_t, also exceeds this estimate.

We call the new estimate, $P_{t,z}^e$, the **ex post** (or ''posterior'') **expectation of prices.** Thereby, we distinguish it from the prior expectation, P_t^e. Recall that by the term, prior, we mean an expectation that someone forms *before observing the local price*. In contrast, the ex post expectation, $P_{t,z}^e$, expresses people's beliefs *after they get to examine the local price, $P_t(z)$*. (Note that, since prices differ across markets, the ex post expectation, $P_{t,z}^e$, will depend on someone's location, z.)

Generally, it is best to calculate the ex post expectation by giving some weight to the local price and some to the prior expectation. Hence, we can write a formula for the ex post expectation as

$$P_{t,z}^e = \theta P_t(z) + (1 - \theta)P_t^e \qquad (18.4)$$

Note that the parameter θ (the Greek letter *theta*) determines the weight placed on the local price, $P_t(z)$, relative to that on the prior expectation, P_t^e.

Suppose, as an example, that $P_t^e = 100$ and $\theta = \frac{1}{4}$. Then if we observe the local price, $P_t(z) = 104$, we calculate expectations from equation (18.4) as $P_{t,z}^e = (\frac{1}{4})(104) + (\frac{3}{4})(100) = 101$. In other words, if the local price exceeds the prior expectation by 4%, then we estimate that one percentage point of this excess reflects an increase in the general price level, while the remaining three percentage points come from an increase in the relative price for market z. However, for different values of the parameter θ, we would change this breakdown accordingly.

Now what determines the correct weights, θ and $1 - \theta$? People choose a high value of θ—thereby allowing their ex post expectations to depend heavily on the prices that they see locally—if prices do not differ greatly from market to market. Then any individual price quote mirrors the general level of prices. One element that favors this outcome is a small dispersion of disturbances across markets. Then because all locations face a similar situation, the local price, $P_t(z)$, usually stays close to the average price, P_t.

On the other hand, the prior expectation, P_t^e, is an accurate forecast of the average price when there are few aggregate disturbances that change the general level of prices over time. In particular, the prior forecast is more reliable the smaller are the influctuations over time in money and in variables that influence the aggregate real demand for money. Hence, if the changes in money supply and demand are either small or predictable, then people give more weight, $1 - \theta$, to the prior forecast, P_t^e, when forming ex post expectations in equation (18.4). Conversely, in a volatile monetary environment, people select a high value of θ. Thereby, they rely mostly on their own current observations of prices, $P_t(z)$.

To summarize, the calculation of ex post expectations, $P_{t,z}^e$, assigns the weight

θ to the local price, $P_t(z)$, and the weight $1 - \theta$ to prior expectations, P_t^e. The weight placed on local prices, θ, tends to be large—hence, that placed on prior expectations tends to be small—when there is little dispersion of shocks from one market to another. But the weighting pattern goes the other way when it is relatively easy to predict the changes in the general price level from one period to the next.

Clearing of a Local Commodity Market when Information is Incomplete

A person's ex post expectation of general prices, $P_{t,z}^e$, determines his or her perception of relative prices. In the following we assume that the ratio, $P_t(z)/P_{t,z}^e$, is the perceived relative price that matters for goods supplied and demanded in market z. So, the process now looks as follows. Armed with their prior expectations of prices, P_t^e, sellers and buyers know how to translate observed values of the local price, $P_t(z)$, into ex post expectations, $P_{t,z}^e$. Thus, they form **perceptions of the relative price**, $P_t(z)/P_{t,z}^e$, which in turn determine the quantities of goods that they supply and demand. Finally, the interaction of supply and demand determines local price and output, $P_t(z)$ and $Y_t(z)$, through the usual condition for clearing the local market.

Figure 18.4 shows the supply and demand in a local market when people do not observe the general price level. For the moment, we hold fixed the prospective relative price, $P_{t+1}(z)/P_{t+1}$, and the real interest rate, r_t. Then we plot the ratio of the local price to its prior expectation, $P_t(z)/P_t^e$, on the vertical axis. Recall that the ex post expectation is a weighted average of the local price and the prior expectation—that is, from equation (18.4)

$$P_{t,z}^e = \theta P_t(z) + (1 - \theta)P_t^e$$

Hence, an increase in the price ratio, $P_t(z)/P_t^e$, leads to an increase in the perceived relative price, $P_t(z)/P_{t,z}^e$. However, since the expectation, $P_{t,z}^e$, rises by the fraction θ of the increase in the local price, the perceived relative price rises by less than the price ratio, $P_t(z)/P_t^e$.

To illustrate, suppose again that $P_t^e = 100$ and $\theta = \frac{1}{4}$. Then if the local price is 104, we calculate the ratio $P_t(z)/P_t^e = \frac{104}{100} = 1.04$. As in our previous example, the ex post expectation is $P_{t,z}^e = (\frac{1}{4})(104) + (\frac{3}{4})(100) = 101$. Therefore, the perceived relative price is $P_t(z)/P_{t,z}^e = \frac{104}{101} \approx 1.03$. Hence if $\theta = \frac{1}{4}$, then the perceived relative price responds by roughly 25% less than the price ratio, $P_t(z)/P_t^e$. In general the higher is the value of θ the smaller is the reaction of the perceived relative price to a given change in the price ratio.

Notice that the local market clears in Figure 18.4 when the price ratio, $P_t(z)/P_t^e$, equals one, which occurs along the dashed line labeled A. Correspondingly, the perceived relative price, $P_t(z)/P_{t,z}^e$, also equals one. This result applies to the average market, which, by definition, has not experienced unusual recent changes in local supply and demand. In other words, for the typical market, supply equals demand when the local price, $P_t(z)$, equals the expected price elsewhere,

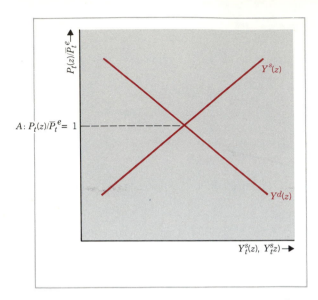

Figure 18.4 Responses of a Local Market to the Ratio of Prices to Prior Expectations
An increase in the price ratio, $P_t(z)/P_t^e$, implies an increase in the perceived relative price, $P_t(z)/P_{t,z}^e$. Hence, the local supply curve slopes upward, while the local demand curve slopes downward. The typical market clears along the dashed line labeled A, where $P_t(z)/P_t^e = 1$.

$P_{t,z}^e$. But this occurs only if the local price, $P_t(z)$, also equals the prior expectation, P_t^e.

Changes in Money When There is Incomplete Information

Now let's reconsider the effects of a once-and-for-all increase in the stock of money, M_t. Here, we deal with a surprise increase in money—that is, one that people did not anticipate when they formed their prior expectation of prices, P_t^e.

Suppose, as before, that the local price, $P_t(z)$, rises in the typical market. (As usual, we can think of people attempting to spend their excess cash balances, which tends to bid up prices.) Then, since the prior expectation P_t^e is given, there must be an increase in the price ratio, $P_t(z)/P_t^e$. Hence, there is also an increase in the perceived relative price, $P_t(z)/P_{t,z}^e$. In other words the typical person now thinks that he or she is located in a market where the relative price is high. Of course, this belief must be incorrect, since the average across markets of the local prices, $P_t(z)$, always equals the general price level, P_t. But the surprise increase in money and prices—together with the lack of direct information about either the average price, P_t, or the quantity of money, M_t—means that the typical person underestimates the rise in the general price level. Thus, this person also overestimates the relative price that he or she faces. Correspondingly, people raise their supplies of goods and lower their demands.

As before, the dashed line labeled A in Figure 18.5 shows the value of the price ratio, $P_t(z)/P_t^e = 1$, which clears the typical local market. However, the surprise increase in money means that the price in a typical market, $P_t(z)$, exceeds the prior expectation, P_t^e. Therefore, the dashed line labeled B in the figure must apply. But then the supply of goods exceeds the demand in the typical market. So something else has to happen in order for this market to clear.

Prospective Relative Prices

So far, we have neglected effects on the prospective relative price, $P_{t+1}(z)/P_{t+1}$. Before, we discussed this variable when people had full information about the current general price level, P_t. There, we explored the tendency for high relative prices to persist. These effects still arise when sellers and buyers do not observe the current general price level. In particular, an increase in the perceived relative price, $P_t(z)/P_{t,z}^e$, raises the relative price that people expect in market z for the next period. Then this expectation raises today's investment demand, $I_t^d(z)$, and lowers today's supply of goods, $Y_t^s(z)$.

We add these new effects to the supply and demand curves in Figure 18.6.

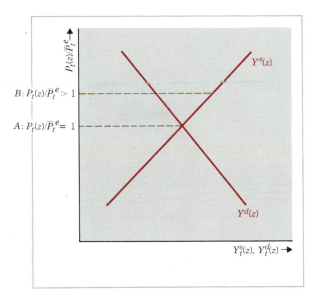

Figure 18.5 The Effect of a Surprise Increase in Money on the Typical Commodity Market
For given values of prospective relative prices and the real interest rate, the typical market clears along line A, where $P_t(z)/P_t^e = 1$. But the surprise increase in money and prices means that the price ratio, $P_t(z)/P_t^e$, exceeds one, as shown along line B. Here, the supply of goods, $Y_t^s(z)$, is greater than the demand, $Y_t^d(z)$.

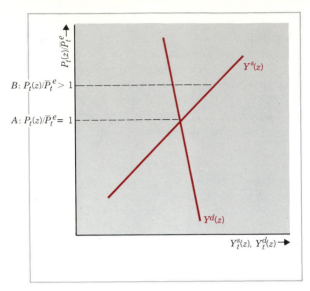

Figure 18.6 **The Effect of a Surprise Increase in Money, Including the Higher Prospective Relative Price**
As the price ratio, $P_t(z)/P_t^e$, rises, the prospective relative price, $P_{t+1}(z)/P_{t+1}$, increases. This increase stimulates investment demand, but deters supply. Hence, as compared with Figure 18.5, the demand curve has less of a negative slope, while the supply curve has less of a positive slope. But we assume that the difference is greater for the case of demand.

As the price ratio, $P_t(z)/P_t^e$, increases, the higher prospective relative price raises investment demand, $I_t^d(z)$, and lowers supply $Y_t^s(z)$. Therefore, the demand curve becomes less negatively sloped than before, while the supply curve becomes less positively sloped. Note that the demand and supply curves now combine two types of effects from changes in the price ratio, $P_t(z)/P_t^e$. First, there are the effects from the current perceived relative price, $P_t(z)/P_{t,z}^e$. Second, there are the effects from the accompanying change in the prospective relative price, $P_{t+1}(z)/P_{t+1}$.

We assume in Figure 18.6 that the more important change from Figure 18.5 comes on the side of demand. That is, the promise of favorable future returns motivates investors to expand aggressively today, even though they perceive the current relative price to be high. Accordingly, we now show the demand curve in Figure 18.6 as being more nearly vertical than the supply curve.

Notice that an excess supply of goods still applies along the dashed line labeled *B* in Figure 18.6, where the price ratio, $P_t(z)/P_t^e$, exceeds one. But the amount of this excess supply is less than that shown in Figure 18.5. That is, the influence of prospective relative prices brings us part of the way toward clearing the commodity markets.

Effects on the Real Interest Rate

The real interest rate, r_t, still equals the nominal rate R_t—which everyone observes on the economy-wide credit market—less the general rate of inflation, $\pi_t = P_{t+1}/P_t - 1$. Hence, the expected value of the real interest rate, which we again call r_t^e, equals the nominal rate R_t less the expected inflation rate, π_t^e.

So far, we have not allowed for any effects of the monetary disturbance on the expected real interest rate. But then Figure 18.6 indicates that the supply of goods exceeds the demand in the typical commodity market. Correspondingly, the aggregate of desired saving exceeds the aggregate of net investment demand. We know from previous analyses that the real interest rate declines in this situation. Specifically, the expected real interest rate falls enough to equate the aggregate of desired saving to the aggregate of net investment demand.[7]

Here we pretend that everyone has the same expectation, r_t^e. In fact, these can differ because of differences in expected inflation rates, π_t^e. However, the basic results do not change if we add this complication.

Let's consider the results from the perspective of the typical commodity market. First, we reproduce the supply and demand curves from Figure 18.6 as the solid lines in Figure 18.7. Then, as the expected real interest rate, r_t^e, declines, the demand curve shifts rightward, while the supply curve shifts leftward. That is, the lower expected real interest rate motivates people to consume and invest more, but to work and produce less. We show the new curves as dashed lines in the figure. Notice that these curves intersect along the line labeled B, where the price ratio, $P_t(z)/P_t^e$, exceeds one. Thus, although people still perceive a high relative price in the typical commodity market, the reduction in the expected real interest rate allows the market to clear.

Monetary Effects on Output, Work, and Investment

Figure 18.7 shows an increase in local output, $Y_t(z)$, although the sign of this change is generally ambiguous. Let's consider the various forces that affect output in the typical market. (By typical, we mean that no unusual shifts in local supply or demand apply to this market.)

First, the high price ratio, $P_t(z)/P_t^e$, stimulates supply but deters consumption and investment demand. Second, the anticipation of a high future relative price, $P_{t+1}(z)/P_{t+1}$, encourages investment but weakens the incentive to supply goods currently. Finally, the decrease in the expected real interest rate, r_t^e, boosts investment and consumption demand but discourages supply.

Our presumption that output increases in the typical market relies on the strong positive effect from the prospective relative price, $P_{t+1}(z)/P_{t+1}$, on local invest-

---

[7]Note that the fall in the expected real interest rate must involve a decrease in the nominal interest rate, R_t, relative to the expected rate of inflation, π_t^e.

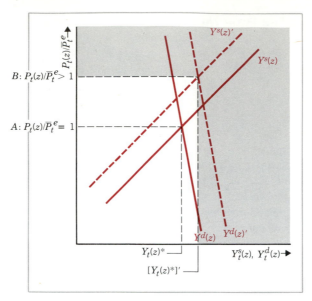

Figure 18.7 **Clearing of the Typical Commodity Market after a Surprise Increase in Money**
The solid lines for supply and demand come from Figure 18.6. Then the decline in the expected real interest rate shifts the demand curve rightward and the supply curve leftward. Hence, the typical commodity market clears where the price ratio, $P_t(z)/P_t^e$, exceeds one.

ment demand. Recall that this assumption motivated the drawing of the demand curve in Figure 18.7 as being more nearly vertical than the supply curve. Given this property, the monetary disturbance tends to raise local investment, output, and work effort. Further, since this result applies to the typical market, it also shows up in the aggregates of investment, output and work.

Let's review the main process by which the surprise increase in money and prices leads to higher work, output, and investment. First, the general rise in prices looks to local suppliers like an increase in their relative price. Therefore, they work more and increase production, just as they would in the case of a true expansion of local demand. In other words the suppliers confuse the change in the general price level with the type of local disturbance that warrants an expansion of their real activity. (Recall that we considered this type of local disturbance before in Figure 18.2.)

Second, the increase in the price ratio, $P_t(z)/P_t^e$, makes people think that the local market will remain favorable to sellers for awhile. That is, people raise their expectations of the future relative price, $P_{t+1}(z)/P_{t+1}$. Then just as in the case of a true increase in local demand, this belief stimulates investment. Further, the investment shows up currently as purchases of goods and services at the local price, which people perceive to be relatively high. Recall that investors make these expensive purchases—at least in the early stages of an investment project—in order to position themselves for the expected high returns later on.

Overall, the expansion of work, output, and investment occurs because the typical person confuses a high general price level for a high relative price in his or her location. Of course, individuals strive to avoid these kinds of mistakes. But given the available information, they cannot distinguish all changes in general prices from those in relative prices. Also, people have to weigh their mistaken reactions to changes in general prices against the potential errors from not responding to true shifts in relative prices. In most instances the local price, $P_t(z)$, accurately signals the reward for local production and investment. Hence, an overly cautious producer who fails to react to these signals—in order to avoid the mistaken responses to change in the general price level—will also fail to exploit a variety of true opportunities for profit.

To summarize, the theory shows how surprise injections of money can be nonneutral. Moreover, unanticipated changes in money can generate the responses in quantities that typify aggregate business fluctuations. For example, the theory explains how a surprise contraction in the monetary base can cause a recession, in which output, employment, and investment decline. Recall that, at least for the post-World War II period, there is some evidence that movements in the monetary base have these sorts of effects.

The Neutrality of Perceived Changes in Money

The analysis in the previous section applies to surprise changes in money and the general price level. But it is important to recognize that the confusion between general and relative prices cannot arise if people fully understand the movements in money and prices. To see this, suppose that everyone accurately anticipates a once-and-for-all increase in the quantity of money between dates $t - 1$ and t. Then the higher value of the money stock, M_t, shows up one-to-one as a higher prior expectation of prices, P_t^e. Hence, the increase of the price level in a typical market, $P_t(z)$, no longer represents a shift relative to prior expectations. Rather, the actual prices and the prior expectations end up increasing in the same proportion. In this case there are no effects on commodity supply and demand in the typical market, which means no effects on the quantities of output and work, or on the real interest rate. Thus, fully understood movements in money and general prices are neutral, just as in our earlier models.

Changes in the long-run averages of monetary growth and inflation would be accompanied by corresponding changes in expectations of monetary growth and inflation. Hence, the theory predicts no effect from these long-term changes on real variables, such as the growth rate of output and the rate of unemployment.[8] Therefore, the theory is consistent with the long-term evidence for the United States and the United Kingdom, and with the data across countries for the post-World War II period. Remember that this evidence indicates that the average rate of monetary growth or inflation bears no relation to the unemployment rate or the growth rate of output.

---

[8]As in most of our analysis, we neglect the effects of inflation on transaction costs. Otherwise, there are some real effects, which economists typically regard as small.

Stagflation

Recently, people use the term, **stagflation,** to describe a situation where inflation is either high or rising during a recession. For example, during the recession of 1973–75, the unemployment rate (for the civilian labor force) reached a peak of 9.0% in May 1975, but the annual rate of change of the GNP deflator increased from about 4% in 1972 to 9% in 1975. Similarly, during 1979–80, the unemployment rate peaked at 7.8% in July 1980, but the inflation rate rose from about 7% in 1978 to 9% in 1980.

The theory in this chapter has no problem accounting for stagflation. First, there is no relation in the theory between the perceived parts of monetary growth or inflation and the real variables. So the increase in the average growth rates of money and prices over the last decade, which are presumably perceived by everyone, give us no reason to predict low unemployment rates. Second, the cutbacks in the supply of oil and some other raw materials during 1973–74 and 1979 constitute supply shocks. As we know from before, these types of disturbances raise the general price level for a given behavior of the money stock. Finally, as also mentioned before, there is some tendency for recessions to lead to an acceleration of money, and thereby of prices.

Persisting Effects of Money on Real Variables

During recessions, variables like output, employment, and investment tend to be depressed for periods of a year or more. Therefore, we want to know whether the theory can account for persisting effects of monetary disturbances on real variables. One possibility is that the misperceptions about the general price level persist for a long time, such as a year or more. Then any real effects from these misperceptions would also persist. But this argument is implausible. Earlier, we argued that people have incomplete information about prices in other markets and about monetary developments, which means that they can be ignorant for awhile about shifts in the general price level. But people presumably receive enough information about prices, so that they would not make the same mistake in estimating the general price level for very long. Thus, it seems unlikely that the persistence in these errors would be as long as the persistence of booms and recessions.

The theory does not require that confusions about prices persist in order to explain why the responses of quantities persist. For example, we showed that the confusions from a monetary disturbance can lead to more investment. Then, perhaps a few months later, investors recognize that they confused an increase in the general price level for an increase in their relative price. But once people start investment projects, it does not always pay to terminate them, even when the past mistakes become clear. Hence, investment demand may remain high even after the confusion about prices disappears. Further, the higher level of investment shows up later as more productive capacity. Then this added capacity tends to raise output and employment long after people learn the truth about past money and prices. Therefore, through this type of mechanism, we find that a monetary disturbance can have a long-lasting influence on investment, output and employment.

Changes in the Monetary Environment

Often, people say that the main cost of inflation stems from its unpredictability, rather than from the magnitude of inflation itself. Here we can use the theory to analyze some aspects of inflation uncertainty.

Suppose that a change in policy makes monetary growth and hence inflation less predictable. Then the prior expectation of prices, P_t^e, becomes less accurate as a forecast of the general price level. Consequently, people rely more on their local observations of prices, $P_t(z)$. That is, people rationally attach a higher weight θ to the local price when they form ex post expectations of prices, $P_{t,z}^e$ (see equation (18.4)). But this means that perceived relative prices, $P_t(z)/P_{t,z}^e$, become less responsive to changes in the price ratio, $P_t(z)/P_t^e$. In other words, since the unpredictable fluctuations in the general price level are large, sellers and buyers have little confidence that movements in the local price reflect a change in relative prices. Instead, people often assume that the change in the local price just reflects a surprise shift in the general level of prices.

Several things happen when people rely more on local prices to infer the behavior of prices in general. First, people become less vulnerable to monetary disturbances. Now when people observe movements in local prices, they appropriately assign a larger fraction of these changes to the underlying shifts in money and general prices. Therefore, they perceive smaller changes in relative prices and, as a consequence, make smaller adjustments in quantities supplied and demanded. Ultimately, this implies that output, employment, and investment respond by less to a given size monetary disturbance.

The last proposition receives empirical support from some recent studies of various countries during the post-World War II period.[9] First, it turns out that monetary disturbances have a positive relation to real GNP for the majority of the countries. But most importantly for the theory, the strength of this relation diminishes substantially as a country's rate of monetary growth becomes less predictable. Specifically, countries such as the U.S. that display relative stability of money turn out to be the ones where monetary shocks have a strong positive relation to real GNP. On the other hand, in places like Argentina and Brazil where monetary growth fluctuates unpredictably, there is essentially no connection between monetary disturbances and real GNP.

Let's return now to the theory to derive some additional results. We already noted that greater fluctuations in money mean that perceived relative prices become less responsive to changes in local prices. On the one hand, this means that people make fewer mistakes when the changes in prices reflect surprises in money and the general price level. But it implies also that people make more mistakes when there actually are shifts in the relative price. Overall, more uncertainty about money

---

[9]See Roger Kormendi and Phillip Meguire, "Cross-Regime Evidence on Macroeconomic Rationality," *Journal of Political Economy*, forthcoming; and C. L. F. Attfield and N. W. Duck, "The Influence of Unanticipated Money Growth on Real Output: Some Cross-Country Estimates," University of Bristol, September 1982.

and the general price level means that observed local prices become less useful as signals of changes in relative prices. Thus, in a general sense, the price system becomes less effective as a mechanism for channeling resources. For example, the economy become less responsive to shifts in the composition of tastes and technology, which require resources to shift from one place to another.[10] Note especially that—in contrast to variations in the average growth rate of money—changes in the predictability of money are nonneutral in this model.

Implications for Monetary Policy

If changes in money have real effects, then it is natural to think about a systematic policy of varying money in order to stabilize the economy. Specifically, economists often advise the Federal Reserve to accelerate money—for example, through open-market purchases of bonds—in order to bring the economy out of a recession. However, the theory developed in this chapter does not support the case for using monetary policy to smooth out business fluctuations.

We can think of monetary policy as a regular procedure for adjusting the quantity of money, M_t, in relation to the state of the economy. For example, the monetary authority may expand money more rapidly than usual in response to a recession, but then hold down the growth rate of money in response to a boom. As noted before, there is some evidence that the Federal Reserve has pursued this sort of countercyclical monetary policy since World War II.

What does the theory predict for the real effects of this type of monetary policy? Given that the policy is in place, our best guess is that people take it into account when they formulate expectations of prices. In particular, if everyone knows that the Fed tends to inflate the economy in response to a recession, then people raise their forecasts of money and prices accordingly. Hence, the prior expectation of prices, P_t^e, incorporates the typical response of the Fed to the observed state of the economy. But this means that the Fed changes money and prices relative to people's perceptions only when it departs from its usual practice. It follows that only the erratic part of the Fed's behavior has real effects. The systematic part of monetary policy—which is the predictable acceleration of money in response to a recession and the contraction in response to a boom—does not create any confusions between general and relative prices. Therefore, these monetary changes are neutral in the model. Sometimes, people call this finding the **irrelevance result for systematic monetary policy**.[11]

---

[10]For some discussions of the adverse consequences from monetary uncertainty, see F. A. Hayek, "The Use of Knowledge in Society," *American Economic Review,* September 1945; and Henry Simons, "Rules versus Authorities in Monetary Policy," in Henry Simons, *Economic Policy for a Free Society,* University of Chicago Press, Chicago, 1948.

[11]For a statement of the result, see Thomas Sargent and Neil Wallace, "Rational Expectations, the Optimal Monetary Instrument, and the Optimal Money Supply Rule," *Journal of Political Economy,* April 1975.

Of course, a great portion of the fluctuations in money are unpredictable, especially in recent years. Therefore, the irrelevance result does not apply to these types of monetary movements. But we also cannot think of this erratic behavior as representing useful policy. Rather, sometimes the changes are expansionary and sometimes contractionary, but not in a way that systematically improves the workings of the economy.

On the other hand, the frequency of the shocks to money is important because it determines the amount of monetary uncertainty. As we saw before, more uncertainty about money is nonneutral—in particular, it makes local prices less useful as allocative signals. Therefore, the theory does have some meaningful advice for policy in this context. Namely, the best monetary policy is the one that contributes least to people's uncertainty about money and prices. Hence, this viewpoint argues for a monetary policy that is predictable, rather than erratic.

Some Problems with the Theory

So far, we have shown how the market-clearing model with incomplete information generates some results that compare favorably with empirical evidence. But before we accept the theory and its intriguing implications for monetary policy, we should investigate more of its properties. Here, we consider some serious criticisms of the theory.

The Behavior of Prices and Real Interest Rates

According to the theory, the real effects of monetary disturbances operate through the channels of price surprises and movements in the real interest rate. But the empirical evidence does not verify these channels of effect. For example, as discussed in Chapter 17, the post-World War II data do not indicate much of a connection between price surprises and fluctuations in real economic activity.[12] Also, some studies for the post-World War II period do not find much connection between monetary disturbances and real interest rates.[13]

Overall, the theory gets mixed reviews for its predictions about monetary disturbances. On the one hand, the analysis neatly accommodates the positive responses of production, employment and investment to monetary shocks. But on the other hand, the available evidence does not support the model's story about the channels of transmission from monetary changes to the real variables.

---

[12]However, as noted in Chapter 17, it is possible that supply shocks obscure the relation. Since these shocks lead to an inverse relation between prices and output, the available studies may not isolate the positive relation that results from monetary shocks.

[13]Some results are in my paper, "Intertemporal Substitution and the Business Cycle," *Carnegie-Rochester Conference Series on Public Policy,* Spring 1981. See also Robert Litterman and Laurence Weiss, "Money, Interest Rates and Output: a Reinterpretation of Post-War U.S. Data," Federal Reserve Bank of Minneapolis, January 1983.

Incomplete Information about Prices and Money

A central element in the theory is that people do not observe immediately the general price level or the stock of money. For instance, if people always know the general level of prices—perhaps because they look regularly at a useful index, such as the deflator for the GNP—then they cannot confuse shifts in the general price level for changes in relative prices. Alternatively, suppose that people observe quickly the quantity of money, but not the general price level. Then—at least if they understand the economics taught in this book!—they can figure out the implications of the monetary movements for the general price level. Therefore, they would not confuse at least the monetary-induced parts of changes in general prices with shifts in relative prices. But then the model predicts that the monetary changes would be neutral.

In fact, it is not difficult for people to observe quickly an index of prices (with a one-month lag for the CPI) or measures of monetary aggregates (with a one-week lag for M1). Lately, the press reports quickly and with great publicity (and often with conflicting interpretations!) the size of each week's monetary aggregate, M1. Also, if people read the *Wall Street Journal,* they can observe the value of each week's monetary base. Of course, most people do not bother to collect and interpret these types of data. But presumably, that's because the information is of minor value to them.[14]

Let's think about the usefulness of the available indices of prices. One reason that they may not be very helpful is that each individual cares about a market basket of goods that differs substantially from the one used in the index. Also, the indices sometimes have conceptual problems, which limit their value. (The CPI's treatment of mortgage interest costs was an example, until the recent change in procedures.) Then in order to keep well informed about prices, people would have to take detailed samples from a variety of markets. But this process is costly. Hence, this viewpoint suggests that people would sometimes make significant errors in their interpretations of observed prices.

A similar argument is that the data on monetary aggregates provide little useful information. Possibly because of seasonal adjustments and the arbitrariness in defining money, the reported measures bear little relation to the concept of money that matters in the theory. However, this argument leads to a puzzle. Namely, it is the reported figures—whether on M1 or the monetary base—that seem to have a positive relation to real economic activity in the post-World War II period. But if the data are meaningless, it is hard to explain this relation. Alternatively, if the reported measures are important, then why would people not bother to observe them?

To put the various points together, it seems reasonable that ignorance about the general price level and the quantity of money can account for small and short-

---

[14]Traders of stocks and bonds pay close attention to monetary developments. So it is likely that all the useful information from observing the quantity of money is already reflected in stock prices and interest rates. Then as long as people look at stock prices and interest rates, they have no reason to look separately at the monetary statistics.

lived confusions about relative prices. That's because people would find it too costly to monitor continuously and interpret the behavior of general prices and the quantity of money. But it is unlikely that large or long-lasting confusions would arise. The costs of being misinformed about relative prices—and therefore making incorrect decisions about production, work, and investment—seem excessive relative to the costs of gathering the necessary information. Hence, this view suggests that monetary-induced confusions of general for relative prices can account only for small fluctuations in the aggregate economy. Specifically, we cannot use this line of theory to explain massive contractions of output and employment.

In terms of the United States history, the theory has promise for explaining a significant role for money in the relatively mild recessions of the post-World War II period. But it is unlikely that the approach can account for a major portion of the more severe contractions from before the war. In particular, the confusion between general and relative prices probably played only a minor part in the Great Depression of 1929–33. On the other hand, we also suggested before that this episode—and some others from before World War I that featured banking panics—involved a cutback in financial intermediation, rather than a contraction of the monetary base. So we probably do not need to rely totally on incomplete information about money and prices in order to understand these experiences.

Summary

There is a new line of macroeconomic theory, which attempts to explain the role of money in business fluctuations. This approach retains the framework of market clearing and rational behavior, but introduces incomplete information about prices in order to explain some real effects from monetary disturbances. In this model surprise increases in money and the general price level make individuals in local markets think that the relative price of their output has risen. Thereby, monetary injections can induce people to expand the quantities of production, work and investment. Hence, the theory accords with some evidence, which suggests that surprise variations in the quantity of base money can be nonneutral.

Perceived changes in money and the general price level do not lead to confusions about relative prices. Therefore, the perceived parts of monetary changes are still neutral. This result conforms with the absence of a long-term relation of real variables to either monetary growth or inflation. Also, the theory is consistent with stagflation, whereby inflation can be high and rising during a recession.

An increase in the amount of monetary uncertainty is nonneutral, because it alters the information that people receive by observing local prices. On the one hand, because people recognize that monetary shocks are often large, the real variables become less sensitive to given-size monetary disturbances. But because the observed prices become less useful as allocative signals, there is also a worsening in the allocation of resources. Specifically, the economy becomes less responsive to variations in the composition of tastes and technology.

The systematic part of monetary policy causes no confusions about relative prices. Therefore, the theory predicts that this part of policy has no significance for real variables. On the other hand, an increase in uncertainty about monetary policy is nonneutral, because it lessens the value of observed prices as allocative signals. Thus, the model's main lesson is that monetary policy should be predictable, rather than erratic.

Although the theory accords with some empirical evidence, it also has some problems. For example, the data do not support either the role of price shocks during recessions or the prediction that monetary disturbances depress the real interest rate. Also, since the costs of obtaining information about money and prices are not very large, the theory cannot fully explain major business contractions, such as the Great Depression. But the theory is especially promising for understanding aspects of mild recessions, such as those experienced since World War II.

Important Terms and Concepts

rational expectations

prior expectation of prices

ex post expectation of prices

perceived relative price

stagflation

irrelevance result for systematic monetary policy

QUESTIONS AND PROBLEMS

Mainly for Review

18.1 Explain why it is reasonable to assume that individuals have imperfect information about the general price level. What are the costs of collecting information about prices?

18.2 Explain what a relative price is. Is the real wage an example of a relative price? Show how a proportional increase in $P_t(z)$ and $P_{t,z}^e$ leaves both buyers and sellers unaffected. Why does a surprise increase in money have a bigger effect on $P_t(z)$ than $P_{t,z}^e$?

18.3 What are the factors that might cause the relative price in a market to remain high for many periods of time? What are the factors that cause changes in the relative price to be offset in later periods? (Include in your answer the effect of changes in the numbers of buyers and sellers and changes in the capital stock.)

18.4 Explain the concept of an average market. How is the average market affected by a fully perceived increase in money? By a surprise increase in money?

18.5 Can there be unexpected changes in the quantity of money when expectations are rational? If so, does a policymaker have the option of counteracting business cycles through ''surprise'' increases in money?

18.6 Why does a decrease in the predictability of monetary growth increase the weight given to $P_t(z)$ when forming estimates of the general price level? Would this result necessarily hold if expectations were irrational?

18.7 When expectations are rational, any errors made in estimating the price level will not persist. How then can we explain persistent deviations of aggregate output from trend?

Problems for Discussion

18.8 Changes in the Predictability of Money

Suppose that the fluctuations of money become less predictable from year to year. What happens to the following:

a. The weight θ that people place on the local price, $P_t(z)$, when calculating ex post price expectations, $P_{t,z}^e$?

b. The relation of the perceived relative price, $P_t(z)/P_{t,z}^e$, to the price ratio, $P_t(z)/P_t^e$?

c. The slopes of the supply and demand curves shown in Figures 18.5 and 18.6?

d. The effect of a given size monetary disturbance on output?

e. The allocation of resources?

18.9 Money and the Dispersion of Relative Prices

The local price, $P_t(z)$, differs across locations because each market experiences its own local shocks to supply and demand. (Think here of changes in the composition of tastes and technology.) Thus, the model generates a dispersion of relative prices across markets at each point in time. Now suppose, as in problem 18.8, that the fluctuations in money become less predictable from year to year. Then what happens to the dispersion of relative prices across markets at a point in time?

(There is evidence that this effect is important during extreme inflations, such as the German hyperinflation, but not for the United States experience. See Zvi Hercowitz, "Money and the Dispersion of Relative Prices," *Journal of Political Economy,* April 1981; and "Money and Price Dispersion in the United States," *Journal of Monetary Economics,* July 1982. For a survey of the related literature on price dispersion, see Alex Cukierman, "Relative Price Variability and Inflation, A Survey and Further Results," *Carnegie-Rochester Conference Series on Public Policy,* forthcoming.)

18.10 Monetary Effects on Consumption (optional)

In the text we noted some shortcomings of the market-clearing model under incomplete information. Here, we explore another problem, which concerns the cyclical behavior of consumption.

We argued that a positive monetary shock could increase output, employment and investment. Suppose, in fact, that work effort increases, so that leisure declines.

a. What must be the effect on consumption? (Hint: does the monetary shock alter the terms on which people can substitute today's leisure for today's consumption?)

b. Would the results change if the monetary disturbance raised perceived wealth?

c. How do the theoretical results about consumption conform with the data on U.S. recessions?

18.11 Revisions of the Monetary Data

a. Suppose that people observe the monetary base as it is reported from week to week. Then what does the theory predict about the effects of changes in base money on real variables?

b. The Federal Reserve often revises its data on money—especially M1—several months after the initial reports. (Mostly, these revisions arise because the Fed has to estimate the monthly figures on checkable deposits for nonmember banks and some other financial institutions.) What does the theory say about the economic effects of these revisions in the monetary figures? (Empirically, the revisions bear no relation to real economic activity—see Robert Barro and Zvi Hercowitz, "Money Stock Revisions and Unanticipated Money Growth," *Journal of Monetary Economics,* April 1980.)

18.12 The Effects of Anticipated Policy

a. What is the irrelevance result for systematic monetary policy?

b. Does the result mean that the unpredictable parts of money do not matter?

c. Does the result mean that the systematic parts of all government policies are irrelevant? Consider, as examples, the following:

  i. The unemployment-insurance program.

  ii. A policy of raising government purchases during a recession.

  iii. A policy of cutting income-tax rates during a recession.

18.13 The Fed's Information and Monetary Policy

Suppose that the Fed has a regular policy of accelerating money during a recession.

a. Why does the theory say that this policy does not matter?

b. If the Fed observes the recession before others do, does the policy still not matter?

c. Suppose that the Fed knows no more about recessions than anyone else does. But the Fed also knows that real activity expands when monetary growth is surprisingly high. Thus, when the economy is in a recession, the Fed attempts to expand money by more than the amount people expect. What problems arise here? (*Hint:* suppose that people understand that the Fed is pursuing this type of policy. What then is the rational expectation of monetary growth and inflation?)

CHAPTER 19

THE KEYNESIAN THEORY OF BUSINESS FLUCTUATIONS

The Keynesian theory was developed in order to understand the tendency of private enterprise economies to experience fluctuations in aggregate business activity. In this respect, the Keynesian theory has the same objective as the market-clearing model with incomplete information, which we explored in the previous chapter. More specifically, Keynes's own analysis[1] sought to explain and suggest policy remedies for the prolonged depressions that occurred in the United States during the 1930s and the United Kingdom during the 1920s and 1930s.

The Keynesian theory focuses on the process by which private markets match up suppliers and demanders. Notably, the theory assumes that prices on some markets do not adjust perfectly to ensure continual balance between the quantities supplied and demanded. Hence, unlike our previous models, some markets do not always clear. (The imbalance between supply and demand is often referred to as "disequilibrium," but we shall avoid that ambiguous term.) Because of the absence of general market clearing, output and employment typically end up below the efficient amounts. That is, although everyone could be made better off by an expansion of economic activity, the private market sometimes fails to generate this higher level of activity.

Typically, Keynesian models assume, at least implicitly, that there are constraints on the flexibility of some prices. For example, the models assume that the nominal wage rate or the dollar price of commodities responds only sluggishly to changes in market conditions. In extreme cases the wage rate or price level is rigid—or at least fully determined from the past. Then current market forces have no influence on these prices. But economists' willingness to accept this type of

---

[1]John Maynard Keynes, *The General Theory of Employment, Interest and Money,* Harcourt Brace, New York, 1935.

assumption as reasonable has diminished with the advent of high and variable inflation in the United States and in other industrialized countries. Thus we shall also consider the possibilities for introducing some flexibility of prices into the Keynesian model.

A Simple Keynesian Model

Keynes's analysis and some subsequent treatments[2] focused on "sticky" nominal wage rages and the resultant lack of balance between labor supply and demand. Prices for commodities were sometimes assumed to be perfectly flexible (leading to the so-called **complete Keynesian model**), but were more often treated also as sticky. In our framework, we can generate the basic Keynesian results without explicitly considering a separate labor market. Here, we treat as sticky the dollar price, P_t, for goods and services that people exchange on the commodity market. (We return now to the case of an economy-wide market for goods.) But as in previous analyses, we allow the nominal interest rate, R_t, to be flexible.

We should stress that the neglect of the labor market is purely a simplification. The same sorts of conclusions emerge if we choose instead to examine this market and postulate a sticky nominal wage rate. In fact, the stickiness of the price level, P_t, may reflect an underlying stickiness in the nominal wage, w_t.

Some early analyses assumed that prices were rigid. This assumption turns out to be unnecessary, because the Keynesian framework can readily accommodate nonzero inflation rates. That is, the crucial feature is not completely fixed prices, but rather the failure of prices to clear all markets instantly. However, it is convenient to begin with a model in which the price level is fixed. Then after we develop this model we can introduce a nonzero inflation rate.

Let's begin by writing down our standard conditions for general market clearing. For the commodity market, the condition for period t is

$$Y^s(R_t, G_t, \tilde{G}, \ldots) = C^d(R_t, G_t, \tilde{G}, \ldots) + I^d(R_t, \ldots) + G_t \quad (19.1)$$
$$(+)\,(+)\,(+) (-)\,(-)\,(-) (-)$$

Notice first that we enter the nominal interest rate, R_t, because the price level is fixed. Hence, the real interest rate, r_t, equals the nominal rate. Second, we include the levels of actual and permanent government purchases, G_t and $\tilde{G}$. Recall that a higher quantity of purchases, G_t, means a larger amount of goods supplied (because public services are productive), but a smaller amount of consumer goods demanded. Also, a higher level of permanent purchases, $\tilde{G}$, means that permanent income declines. Hence, the supply of goods rises, while consumer demand falls. Here,

---

[2]See Don Patinkin, *Money, Interest and Prices*, Harper & Row, New York, 1956, Chapter 13; and Robert Barro and Herschel Grossman, "A General Disequilibrium Model of Income and Employment," *American Economic Review*, March 1971; and *Money, and Employment and Inflation*, Cambridge University Press, Cambridge, England, 1976, Chapter 2.

we assume lump-sum taxes, although an income tax could also be considered. Finally, equation (19.1) takes as given the stock of capital, K_{t-1}, and the characteristics of the production function.

Next we have again the condition that money be willingly held

$$M_t/P_t = H(Y_t, \ R_t, \ . \ . \ .) \tag{19.2}$$
$$(+) \ (-)$$

where M_t is the nominal quantity of money for period t. As usual, the aggregate real demand for money depends positively on output, Y_t, and negatively on the nominal interest rate, R_t.

Equations (19.1) and (19.2) determine the general-market-clearing values for the interest rate and the price level, which we denote by R_t^* and P_t^*. Correspondingly, we denote the general-market-clearing level of output by Y_t^*.

The departure for Keynesian analysis is that the fixed price level, P_t, differs from the general-market-clearing value, P_t^*. Specifically, the standard Keynesian case follows when the price level is excessive—that is, $P_t > P_t^*$—which amounts to assuming downward rigidity of prices. Then it will generally be impossible for the economy to attain full market clearing, as specified in equations (19.1) and (19.2). Consequently, we have to search for some concept other than supply equals demand in order to determine the interest rate and the level of output.

Think of strarting from a position of general market clearing and then arbitrarily raising the price level above its market-clearing value. In this case, equation (19.2) can no longer hold at the general-market-clearing values of output, Y_t^*, and the interest rate, R_t^*. Specifically, the excessive price level means that the quantity of real cash balances, M_t/P_t, would fall short of the aggregate quantity demanded. Then we can think of individuals as attempting to replenish their real balances, partly by selling bonds and partly by reducing consumer demand and leisure. The former response suggests upward pressure on the interest rate, which raises the supply of goods, Y_t^s, and lowers the demand, $C_t^d + I_t^d$. Hence, excess supply of commodities results. Further, any direct reduction in consumer demand or leisure reinforces this outcome. Thus, the excessive price level leads to an excess supply of goods.

The Rationing of Sales

How does the commodity market operate under conditions of excess supply? That is, what happens when—at the going price P_t—the total of offers to sell goods exceeds the overall willingness to buy? Normally, we expect a decline in the price level, but that mechanism is ruled out by assumption. Therefore, we have to study the commodity market when excess supply prevails, but the price level cannot fall.

Some type of quantity-rationing rule must allocate sales when there is an imbalance between the quantities supplied and demanded. The usual mechanism assumes two properties. First, no supplier or demander can be forced to sell or buy more than he or she desires, which follows in a setting of voluntary exchange. Second, trade proceeds as long as some seller and some buyer are both made better off—that is, the market ensures the execution of all mutually advantageous exchanges, given that the fixed price P_t applies to all trades. The first condition means that the total quantity of goods sold, Y_t, cannot exceed the smaller of aggregate supply and demand—otherwise, some involuntary sales or purchases would occur. The second condition guarantees that the amount of sales is at least as great as the minimum of aggregate supply and demand—if not, some mutually advantageous trade at price P_t would be missed. Thus, the combination of the two properties ensures that output is determined by the **short side** of the market—that is, by the condition

$$Y_t = MIN.(Y_t^s, Y_t^d) \tag{19.3}$$

where $MIN.$ denotes the minimum of the variables that appear in the parentheses. Note that we deal here with the rationing of sales on the commodity market. In a more general Keynesian framework, we would include also the rationing of jobs—that is, sales of labor services—on a separate labor market. Then the people who seek jobs but cannot find them are considered to be **involuntarily unemployed.** (The standard Keynesian model does not deal with the sort of natural unemployment that we analyzed in Chapter 9.)

Under conditions of excess supply—that is, $Y_t^s > Y_t^d$—output is determined by aggregate demand, Y_t^d, which defines the short side of the commodity market. Therefore, the typical demander experiences no difficulty in finding goods to purchase from the eager suppliers. However, the representative supplier faces an insufficiency of buyers for the products that he or she offers for sale at the price P_t.[3] Thus we now have to reconsider households' decisions in the presence of this constraint. These modifications play an essential role in Keynesian analysis.

In the standard model of a competitive market, individual sellers and buyers are able to transact any amount desired at the going price. But this condition cannot hold for all suppliers when an excess supply of goods prevails. Here, we want to specify the constraint that confronts an individual supplier of goods. We assume that the total quantity of real sales available, Y_t, is somehow apportioned via some nonprice mechanism among the sellers, who offer the larger quantity, Y_t^s. In other words, there is a rationing process, which assigns each individual producer the quantity of real sales, y_t. Notice that we consider a ration on sales rather than on purchases, which would arise if goods were in excess demand.

We assume that each producer regards his or her real sales limit, y_t, as a given, in the same way that people take as givens the price level, P_t, and the interest rate, R_t. In particular we do not allow an individual to take any actions that would influence the size of his or her ration. That is, we exclude such possibilities as greater search for buyers, black-market activities that could involve price-cutting, overstatement of the true sales offers in order to secure a larger individual ration, political influence to change official rations (in this case, of sales), and so on.

---

[3]In a disaggregated setup, excess supply could appear in some markets and excess demand in others. The standard Keynesian model applies when the great majority of markets experience excess supply.

Basically, the allowance for these features would amount to relaxing the constraint of the fixed price, P_t.

The Choice of Work Effort

The production function implies

$$y_t = f(k_{t-1}, l_t, \quad G_t) \qquad (19.4)$$
$$(+) \quad (+) \, (+)$$

Here, we assume that the ration is an effective constraint on sales—that is, $y_t < y_t^s$ applies for the typical producer.[4] Therefore, the level of output, y_t, is now a given to the producer, rather than a choice variable.

Given the quantity of capital, k_{t-1}, and the level of government purchases, G_t, the quantity of work, l_t, is the minimum amount necessary to produce the assigned level of output, y_t. Therefore, the production function from equation (19.4) determines the amount of labor input for a given quantity of output and for given values of the other inputs, k_{t-1} and G_t. Thus, we can write the quantity of work as the function

$$l_t = l(y_t, \quad k_{t-1}, G_t) \qquad (19.5)$$
$$(+) \, (-) \quad (-)$$

For given values of the other inputs, the amount of work varies directly with the quantity of output, y_t, as shown by the graph of the production function in Figure 19.1. For any value of output on the vertical axis, we can read off the quantity of labor input on the horizontal. Note that more output means more labor input. With the labor market included, more work also means less involuntary unemployment.

Increases in either of the other inputs, k_{t-1} and G_t, mean that less work is needed to produce a given amount of output. Therefore, the quantity of work, l_t, declines in equation (19.5). (In Figure 19.1 we can verify these results by shifting the production function upward.)

In the model without sales constraints, people set the level of work in order to equate the marginal product of labor to the value placed on an extra unit of leisure time. But an effective restraint on sales means that work effort is smaller than otherwise. Because of diminishing marginal productivity, labor's marginal product now exceeds the value placed on an extra unit of leisure. People would like to work and produce more, if only the goods could be sold at the going price. But the constraint on sales prevents the expansion of work and production. Equivalently, this constraint leads to involuntary unemployment on the labor market.

---

[4]Note that we do not allow producers to store up excess output as inventories. This option becomes especially important if people perceive the state of excess supply to be temporary. For extensions of the Keynesian model to include inventories, see Ajit Chaudhury, "Output, Employment and Inventories under General Excess Supply," *Journal of Monetary Economics,* October 1979; and Alan Blinder, "Inventories in the Keynesian Macro Model," *Kyklos,* No. 4, 1980.

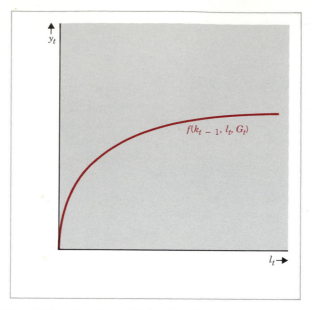

Figure 19.1 **The Determination of Labor Input**
The graph of the production function shows the effect on output of more labor input for given quantities of capital and government purchases. For a given level of output on the vertical axis, the graph determines the quantity of work effort on the horizontal. Note that more output means more labor input.

The Keynesian Consumption Function

The restraint on sales means that people receive less real income than otherwise. In fact, each household's current real receipts from the commodity market equal the real sales ration, y_t. Further, if prospective real sales equal the current value, then variations in the amount y_t have a one-to-one effect on permanent income. Then the effect on consumption demand would also be roughly one-to-one. More generally—when the constraint on sales is temporary—there is a weaker effect on permanent income. Consequently, consumption demand becomes less responsive to variations in current output, y_t.

The main point is that an increase in current output, y_t, has a positive effect on consumption demand. Hence, the consumption function, now denoted by $\hat{c}^d$, takes the form

$$c_t^d = \hat{c}^d(y_t, R_t, \ldots) \tag{19.6}$$
$$(+) \ (-)$$

Notice that the interest rate, R_t, still has a negative intertemporal-substitution effect on current consumer demand.

The expression in equation (19.6) is often called the **Keynesian consumption function.** The distinctive feature of this function is the presence of the quantity of real sales, y_t. In our previous analysis, people chose consumption by considering the real interest rate, the possibilities for substituting between consumption and leisure, the position of the production function, and the nature of their preferences. But now there is a separate effect from the given level of real sales in the commodity market. In particular, anything that raises the quantity of someone's real sales, y_t, spills over to increase consumption demand.

Determination of Output in the Keynesian Model

Putting together the results thus far, we can write the level of aggregate demand, Y_t^d, in the form

$$Y_t^d = \hat{C}^d(Y_t, \ R_t, \ \ldots) + I^d(R_t, \ \ldots) + G_t$$
$$(+)\ (-) \qquad\qquad (-)$$

where $\hat{C}^d$ is an aggregate version of the Keynesian consumption function, and I^d is the investment demand function, which we have studied previously.[5] Recall that the price level exceeds the general-market-clearing value—that is, $P_t > P_t^*$—which means that goods are in excess supply. Consequently, output is demand determined, as follows

$$Y_t = Y_t^d = \hat{C}^d(Y_t, \ R_t, \ \ldots) + I^d(R_t, \ \ldots) + G_t \qquad (19.7)$$
$$(+)\ (-) \qquad\qquad (-)$$

Equation (19.7) is the key relation in the Keynesian model. It says that output, Y_t, equals aggregate demand, Y_t^d. But the tricky aspect is that the consumption part of aggregate demand is itself a function of output. Thus, equation (19.7) says that the level of output, Y_t, determines a level of demand, Y_t^d, which is, in turn, equal to output.

An important element in the determination of output is the responsiveness of aggregate consumer demand to variations in output—that is, the aggregate "**propensity to consume**" out of changes in current real income, Y_t. Typically, this propensity is between zero and one, with the value approximating one when people view a change in output as permanent. We denote the propensity to consume by v (the Greek letter *nu*).

Now assume provisionally that the interest rate, R_t, is a given value. (We shall consider the determination of the interest rate later on.) Then Figure 19.2, which is called the **Keynesian-cross diagram,** shows how equation (19.7) determines the level of output. First, the line labeled Y_t^d indicates the dependence of aggregate demand on the level of output. We show this demand as a straight line only for convenience. Then the slope is the propensity to consume v. Notice that the figure assumes a propensity that is positive, but less than one.

---

[5]In a full analysis of the Keynesian model we would also find a positive effect of output on investment demand. For simplicity, we neglect this effect.

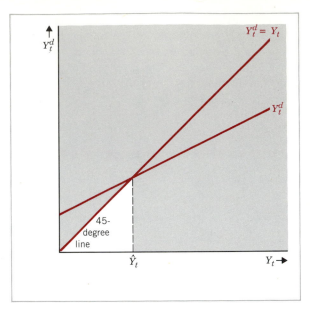

Figure 19.2 **Determination of Output Via the Keynesian-Cross Diagram**

The line denoted Y_t^d shows the response of aggregate demand to changes in output, Y_t. But output equals demand only along the 45-degree line. Therefore, we determine the level of output at the intersection of the curves as the value $\hat{Y}_t$.

Next, the 45-degree line in Figure 19.2 indicates positions where output, Y_t, equals the level of demand, Y_t^d. Therefore, equation (19.7) holds when the aggregate demand curve intersects the 45-degree line. We denote the associated level of output by $\hat{Y}_t$.

The Multiplier

In order to illustrate the determination of output in the Keynesian model, let's consider an increase in aggregate demand, Y_t^d. For example, consumers and investors might decide to spend more for no special reason. Then first, the increase in demand means an increase in output, Y_t. (Recall that, with excess supply of goods, output is demand determined.) But the increase in output means that aggregate demand rises further. Hence, there is another rise in output, which leads to more demand, and so on. But each successive increase in output turns out to be smaller then the one before. Ultimately, this process implies that output rises by a finite multiple of the initial expansion of demand. In order to calculate the exact change, we can use the Keynesian-cross diagram.

In Figure 19.3, the aggregate demand curve is initially the one labeled Y_t^d. Here, the intersection with the 45-degree line determines the level of output, $\hat{Y}_t$. Then an **autonomous** increase in demand of size A shifts the aggregate demand curve upward to the one labeled $Y_t^{d'}$. (By autonomous, we mean that the change comes from out of the blue, rather than being explained within the model.) Accordingly, the level of output, $\hat{Y}'_t$, corresponds to the new intersection with the 45-degree line.

The geometry of the Keynesian-cross diagram in Figure 19.3 reveals the relation between the initial and final levels of output, $\hat{Y}_t$ and $\hat{Y}'_t$. Let $\Delta\hat{Y}$ be the change in output, $\hat{Y}'_t - \hat{Y}_t$. Then observe the smaller right-angle triangle with base $\Delta\hat{Y}$. Note that the slope of the line marked with an arrow is the propensity to consume, ν. Therefore, since the vertical side of the triangle is of length $\Delta\hat{Y} - A$, the slope satisfies the relation

$$\nu = (\Delta\hat{Y} - A)/\Delta\hat{Y}.$$

It follows that the change in output is given by

$$\Delta\hat{Y} = A/(1 - \nu) \tag{19.8}$$

Thus, output changes by a multiple of the autonomous shift in demand, A. Further, the **multiplier** is the term, $1/(1 - \nu)$, which is positive and greater than one. Note that the higher is the propensity to consume, ν, the larger is the multiplier. Also,

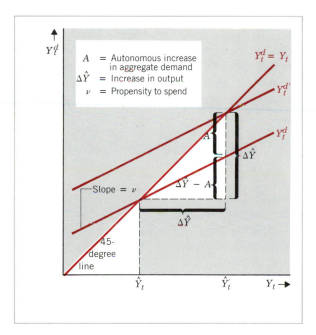

Figure 19.3 The Multiplier
There is an increase in aggregate demand by the amount A. Then the figure shows that the response of output, $\Delta\hat{Y}$, exceeds the initial expansion of demand. Specifically, the geometry implies that $(\Delta\hat{Y} - A)/\Delta\hat{Y} = \nu$, so that $\Delta\hat{Y} = A/(1 - \nu)$. The term, $1/(1 - \nu)$, is the multiplier.

in order for the analysis to make sense, the propensity to consume must be less than one, as we have assumed.

We can better understand the source of the multiplier by deriving equation (19.8) in an alternative manner. The autonomous increase in demand leads initially to an increase in output by the amount A. Then the rise in real income by the amount A leads to an increase in aggregate demand by the quantity, $v \cdot A$. Hence, there is an additional increase in output of size $v \cdot A$, which then causes demand to rise further by the amount, $v \cdot vA$. In other words, there is a continuing sequence where each round's increase in output is the amount v multiplied by the previous round's increase. It follows that the full increase in output comes from summing up all the rounds—namely

$$\Delta \hat{Y} = A + vA + v^2A + \cdots$$
$$= A(1 + v + v^2 + \cdots) \qquad (19.9)$$
$$= A/(1 - v)^6$$

Notice that the result coincides with the one from equation (19.8).

We should stress two points about the derivation of the change in output, $\Delta \hat{Y}$. First, we assume that excess supply of goods prevails throughout, so that producers never hesitate to meet extra demand with more output. Then second, although part of the discussion mentions a sequence of rounds, we do not actually allow any time to elapse while people make adjustments. That is, we do not introduce any lags for the adjustment of either demand or production. Therefore, an autonomous increase in demand leads immediately to the full multiplicative response of output, as shown in equation (19.9). More generally, we could include some dynamics, whereby output adjusts gradually toward the value dictated by the Keynesian-cross diagram in Figure 19.3.

Before going on, let's work out a third way to look at the multiplier. We can rewrite the condition for determining output from equation (19.7) as

$$Y_t - \hat{C}^d(Y_t, R_t, \ldots) = I^d(R_t, \ldots) + G_t \qquad (19.10)$$
$$(+)\,(-) \qquad\qquad (-)$$

The left side is the sum of households' desired saving plus taxes. Hence equation (19.10) says that the level of output is determined so that desired saving plus taxes equals investment demand plus government purchases.

Suppose that an autonomous increase in demand means that the right side of equation (19.10) rises by the amount A. (Equivalently, part of this change could show up as a decrease on the left side of the equation.) Then if taxes do not change, output must rise enough to generate a matching expansion of desired saving on the left side of the equation. Since the propensity to spend is v, the **propensity to save**

---

[6]The formula for a geometric series implies that $1 + v + v^2 \cdots = 1/(1 - v)$ if $-1 < v < 1$.

is the fraction, $1 - v$. Hence, the increment to saving is the amount, $(1 - v)\Delta\hat{Y}$. Since the extra saving must balance the autonomous increase in demand, A, it follows at once that

$$\Delta\hat{Y} = A/(1 - v) \tag{19.11}$$

But this answer for the change in output coincides with those in equations (19.8) and (19.9).

The Determination of Employment

For a given level of output, Y_t, the amount of work, L_t, is just the minimum amount needed to produce this quantity of goods. That is, using an aggregate version of equation (19.5), we have

$$L_t = L(Y_t, \ K_{t-1}, \ G_t) \tag{19.12}$$
$$(+) \, (-) \quad (-)$$

Notice that for given values of the capital stock and government purchases, any disturbance that leads to a change in output leads to a change of the same sign for employment.

Recall that the analysis applies in the range where goods are in excess supply. Here, the marginal product of labor exceeds the value attached to leisure time. Therefore, people eagerly work more whenever it becomes feasible to sell more goods. With a separate labor market where the nominal wage is sticky, we would find that suppliers of labor—who face rationing of jobs—readily accept more work whenever the employers raise their demands. Then the amount of involuntary unemployment would correspond to the gap between the aggregate supply of labor, L_t^s, and the quantity of work. Thus, declines in employment show up as increases in involuntary unemployment.

IS/LM Analysis and the Role of the Interest Rate

Our previous analysis, which includes the multiplier, shows how to determine the level of output for a given interest rate. In particular, as long as there is excess supply of goods, the condition is again

$$Y_t = Y_t^d = \hat{C}^d(Y_t, \ R_t, \ \ldots) + I^d(R_t, \ \ldots) + G_t \tag{19.13}$$
$$(+) \, (-) \qquad\qquad (-)$$

Now, we want to go further by considering the determination of the interest rate, R_t, in the Keynesian model. In order to carry out this analysis, we have to reintroduce the condition that all money be willingly held. This condition is

$$M_t/P_t = H(Y_t, \ R_t, \ \ldots) \tag{19.14}$$
$$(+) \, (-)$$

Given the price level, P_t, equations (19.13) and (19.14) determine simultaneously the interest rate and the level of output. Consider first the condition in equation (19.13). As noted before, this condition determines the level of output, Y_t, for a given value of the interest rate, R_t. But notice that a change in the interest rate affects the level of aggregate demand, Y_t^d, and thereby affects the level of output. What we want to do now is figure out the level of output that corresponds to each value of the interest rate. That is, we want to trace out the combinations of the interest rate and output that are consistent with the equality between output and aggregate demand, as specified in equation (19.13).

An increase in the interest rate lowers aggregate demand on the right side of equation (19.13). Then, as with any decline in aggregate demand, the level of output falls. Therefore, if we map out the combinations of the interest rate and output that satisfy equation (19.13), we determine a downward-sloping relationship. Following standard notation, we label as **IS** the curve in Figure 19.4 that shows this relation. Along the **IS curve,** the interest rate and the level of output are consistent with the condition that output equal aggregate demand.[7]

Consider now the condition that money be willingly held, as specified in equation (19.14). Given the quantity of real cash balances, M_t/P_t, this condition will define another array of combinations for the interest rate and output. What we want to do here is trace out the combinations of the interest rate and output that are consistent with the condition that all money be willingly held. Note that a higher level of output raises the real demand for money on the right side of equation (19.14). Therefore, the interest rate must rise in order to lower the real demand for money back to the given level of real cash, M_t/P_t. Hence, when we map out the combinations of the interest rate and output that satisfy equation (19.14), we determine an upward-sloping relationship. Again following the conventional notation, the curve designated **LM** in Figure 19.4 shows this relation. Along the **LM curve,** the interest rate and the level of output are consistent with the condition that all money be willingly held.[8]

The intersection of the *IS* and *LM* curves in Figure 19.4 picks out the combination of output and the interest rate—labeled as $\hat{Y}_t$ and $\hat{R}_t$—that satisfies two conditions: First, output equals aggregate demand, and second, all money is willingly held. Thus, as long as the price level is fixed, the Keynesian model predicts that the level of output will be the amount $\hat{Y}_t$ and the interest rate will be the value $\hat{R}_t$. Hence, we can use the *IS/LM* apparatus to analyze simultaneously the determination of output and the interest rate in the Keynesian model. In fact, because of the popularity of the Keynesian model, the *IS/LM* diagram has been the favorite analytical tool of most macroeconomists in the last two decades.

---

[7]The terminology, *IS*, refers to an equation of investment demand to desired saving. Recall from equation (19.10) that the condition, $Y_t = Y_t^d$, is equivalent to an equality between desired saving (plus taxes) and investment demand (plus government purchases). The apparatus that we use in Figure 19.4 was introduced by John Hicks in "Mr. Keynes and the 'Classics'," *Econometrica,* April 1937.

[8]People often use the symbol L to denote the function for money demand. Hence, the notation *LM* curve.

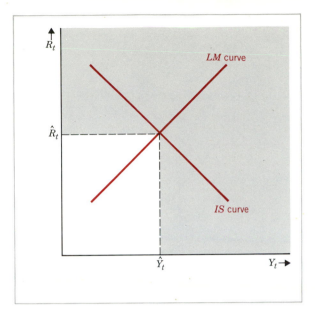

Figure 19.4 **Use of IS/LM Curves to Determine Output and the Interest Rate**

The *IS* curve shows the combinations of Y_t and R_t that satisfy the condition, $Y_t = Y_t^d$. The *LM* curve shows the combinations that induce people to hold all the existing real cash, M_t/P_t. Thus, the levels of output and the interest rate correspond to the intersection of the two curves.

Sources of Variations in Output

In order to bring out the role of the interest rate, let's consider again a case where aggregate demand rises autonomously by the amount A. If the interest rate did not change, then output would rise multiplicatively. However, the expansion of output increases the real demand for money above the given quantity of real cash, M_t/P_t. Consequently, people attempt to move out of bonds and into money. But then the interest rate must increase in order to restore balance on the credit market. This increase in the interest rate reduces the demand for money, but it also decreases aggregate demand. Hence, the overall effect on output turns out to be less than the full multiplicative amount, which we derived before. In fact, it is now possible that the increase in output, $\Delta \hat{Y}$, is less than the autonomous expansion of demand, A. That is, the increase in the interest rate may make the multiplier be less than one.

Figure 19.5 uses the *IS/LM* apparatus to show the results. We reproduce the solid lines from Figure 19.4. Then the boost to aggregate demand appears as a rightward shift in the *IS* curve—that is, output increases for a given value of the interest rate. In fact, the size of this shift is the change in aggregate demand, A, times the multiplier, $1/(1 - v)$. In this example, the *LM* curve does not shift. Therefore, the figure shows that output and the interest rate both rise. But the

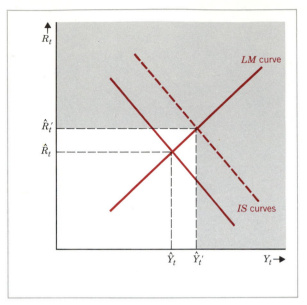

Figure 19.5 Keynesian Analysis of the Effect of an Increase in Aggregate Demand on Output and the Interest Rate

The increase in aggregate demand shifts the *IS* curve rightward. The size of the shift is the autonomous rise in demand, *A*, times the multiplier, $1/(1 - v)$. We find that output and the interest rate both increase. But the rise in output falls short of the full multiplier amount, $A/(1 - v)$.

increase in output is less than the full multiplier amount, which equals the rightward shift in the *IS* curve, $A/(1 - v)$. Finally, underlying the expansion of output is an increase in employment (and a decrease in unemployment).

For a given amount of government purchases, it is clear that total private spending for consumption and investment increases. But because of the rise in the interest rate, it is possible that one of these components would decline. For example, suppose that the autonomous disturbance is an increase in investment demand.[9] Then the rise in output stimulates consumer demand, but the increase in the interest rate depresses this demand. Thus, consumption may fall along with the expansion of output, employment, and investment. Similarly, if the autonomous change applies to consumer demand, then investment may decline. (If investment demand does not depend on output, as we assume in equation [19.13], then investment surely declines in this case.)

---

[9]Keynes attributed a large part of these disturbances to "animal spirits." Here, he referred to spontaneous shifts in optimism or pessimism, which led businesses to alter their aggregate investment plans. In particular, these shifts reflect no changes in the objective environment. The idea of unexplained animal spirits is not very popular among economists. For Keynes's discussion, see Keynes, op. cit., Chapter 12.

Fiscal Policy in the Keynesian Model

The government can influence aggregate demand directly by changing the level of its purchases, G_t. Suppose that the government raises its purchases by 1 unit, and finances this extra spending with lump-sum taxes. Then since consumer demand falls by a fraction of the increase in purchases, aggregate demand expands, but by less than 1 unit.[10] In terms of the *IS/LM* diagram, the disturbance is again the one shown in Figure 19.5.[11] However, the rightward shift in the *IS* curve now equals some fraction of the increase in government purchases, times the multiplier, $1/(1 - v)$. Thus, there is again an increase in output, as well as an increase in the interest rate. Moreover, the increase in output is again less than the full multiplier amount, which equals the rightward shift in the *IS* curve.

Because of the increase in the interest rate, we know that investment declines. That is, government purchases crowd out private investment. (If investment demand depends directly on output, then this result becomes ambiguous.) The effects on consumer spending are uncertain. On the one hand, the expansion of output stimulates consumption demand, but on the other hand, the higher interest rate reduces this demand. In addition, there is the direct negative effect of government purchases on consumer spending.

Another type of fiscal policy that economists consider is a reduction in taxes, which the government finances by issuing more bonds. Often, people argue that this policy is expansionary in the Keynesian model. But in order to get this answer, we have to assume that deficit-financed tax cuts make people feel wealthier. Then the tax cut stimulates consumer demand, which shifts the *IS* curve rightward, as shown in Figure 19.5. Hence, there would again be increases in output and the interest rate.

Because of the higher future taxes, it can still be true (as it was in Chapter 15) that a deficit-financed tax cut has no aggregate wealth effect. In this case there would be no effect on aggregate demand, so that the *IS* curve would not shift. Consequently there would be no effects on output and the interest rate. In other words, the Ricardian Theorem—which states that taxes and deficits are equivalent—can remain valid within the Keynesian model.

If people do treat a tax cut as a signal of more wealth, then the Keynesian model predicts an expansion of output, as shown in Figure 19.5. Since production and employment are constrained initially by lack of demand, the typical person ends up better off in this situation. Thus, people actually do end up being wealthier. But this result has nothing to do with tax cuts *per se*. In the Keynesian model *anything* that makes people feel wealthier generates the increases in output and

---

[10]Remember that public services substitute for α units of private consumer spending, where α is a positive fraction. If permanent purchases increase, then there is effectively a decrease in permanent income. Hence, consumer demand falls further on this count.

[11]This diagram applies if the change in government purchases has no direct effect on the real demand for money. Otherwise, there is also a shift in the *LM* curve.

employment that actually make them wealthier. We shall discuss this unusual property further later on.

The Supply Side in the Keynesian Model

The Keynesian model views aggregate demand as the central determinant of output and employment. Specifically, the analysis pays little attention to aggregate supply. In formal terms the neglect of the supply side arises because the postulated excessive price level, $P_t > P_t^*$, means that excess supply of goods and services prevails. Thereby, the model assumes that productive capacity and the willingness to work do not represent effective constraints on output—only the willingness to spend limits the extent of economic activity in this model. This perspective explains why Keynesian analysis typically pay little attention to some matters that are important in a market-clearing framework. Among these are shifts in the production function, variations in the stock of capital, effects of the tax system on the willingness to work, and so on.[12]

Money in the Keynesian Model

With a fixed price level, an increase in the quantity of money, M_t, means a rise in the amount of real cash balances, M_t/P_t, in equation (19.14). (Here, the increase in money could reflect an open-market purchase of bonds.) For a given level of output, the interest rate must fall in order for people willingly to hold the existing quantity of money. Then the fall in the interest rate stimulates aggregate demand, which leads to the usual expansion of output.

Diagrammatically, we show a rightward shift of the *LM* curve in Figure 19.6. Since the *IS* curve does not shift in this case, the figure indicates that the interest rate falls, while output expands.

Notice from equation (19.14) that a reduction in the demand for money (a rise in velocity) works exactly like an increase in the quantity of money. Therefore, if people decide to hold less real cash, then the effects are again those shown in Figure 19.6. Namely, the *LM* curve shifts rightward, which leads to a fall in the interest rate and a rise in output.

Finally, observe that it is the real quantity of cash, M_t/P_t, that matters in the model. Therefore, a reduction by 1% in the price level, P_t, has the same real effects as an increase by 1% in the quantity of money, M_t. Recall that the Keynesian model assumes that the fixed price level exceeds the general-market-clearing value, P_t^*. Therefore, if the price level adjusts downward toward the market-clearing value, then the effects are again those shown in Figure 19.6. That is, the interest

---

[12]The Keynesian model considers these factors to the extent that they influence investment or consumption demand. Also, the supply of labor services matters when computing the amount of involuntary unemployment.

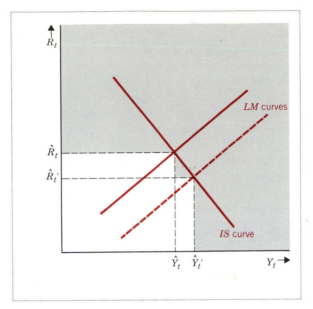

Figure 19.6 **Keynesian Analysis of the Effect of Monetary Expansion on Output and the Interest Rate**

An increase in the quantity of real cash, M/P, shifts the LM curve rightward. Therefore, the interest rate falls and the level of output rises.

rate declines and the level of output rises. In fact, when the price level reaches the general market-clearing value, P_t^*, the level of output reaches the quantity, Y_t^s, that producers are willing to sell. Then any further expansion of aggregate demand would not be met by increases in production and employment.[13]

Keynesian Predictions about Business Fluctuations

Decreases in aggregate demand may reflect autonomous declines in investment and consumption demand, or reductions in government purchases. In the Keynesian

---

[13]We can deal also with cases where the price level is fixed below the general-market-clearing value, so that excess demand for goods prevails. Then it is purchases of goods and services, rather than sales, that have to be rationed. For a theoretical discussion, see Robert Barro and Herschel Grossman, "Suppressed Inflation and the Supply Multiplier," *Review of Economic Studies,* January 1974. For empirical applications to the centrally planned economies of eastern Europe, see David Howard, "The Disequilibrium Model in a Controlled Economy: An Empirical Test of the Barro-Grossman Model," *American Economic Review,* December 1976; and Richard Portes and David Winter, "Disequilibrium Estimates for Consumption Goods Markets in Centrally Planned Economies," *Review of Economic Studies,* January 1980.

model, these changes tend to produce a recession, whereby output, employment, investment, and consumption all decline. Therefore, although the model does not explain the initial disturbance, it does show why the aggregate variables tend to move together during recessions and booms.

The presence of the multiplier suggests that small disturbances can be magnified into significant fluctuations in aggregate activity. But since consumer expenditures on nondurables and services actually change little during mild recessions, this property tends to explain too much. In particular, real-world recessions do not involve small reductions in investment or government purchases that are accompanied by large declines in consumption. Consequently, economists often incorporate some version of the permanent-income hypothesis into the Keynesian model. Then if people view reductions in income as only temporary, the propensity to consume, v, tends to be small. Hence, there would not be much of a multiplier.[14] On the one hand, this modification accommodates the model to some real-world observations: namely, the small fluctuations in consumption and the absence of a multiplicative response of output to increases in government expenditures during wartime. But on the other hand, it also eliminates a distinctive feature of the Keynesian model. Specifically, we can no longer argue that small disturbances are sufficient to set off a recession.

The Keynesian model predicts an expansionary effect from an increase in the quantity of money (relative to the given price level). This effect operates via a reduction in the interest rate. Again, this prediction tends to explain too much. In particular, the empirical evidence indicates no long-term connection between monetary growth and real variables. In order to reconcile the model with this observation, we have to introduce some flexibility of prices (see below). But there is another problem, since the data do not suggest even a short-run relation between monetary fluctuations and changes in real interest rates. Recall that this last finding also causes difficulties for the market-clearing model in the previous chapter.

Notice that shifts to aggregate demand, which affect the *IS* curve, change the real interest rate in the same direction. But movements in the quantity of money (or shifts to velocity), which affect the *LM* curve, cause inverse movements in the real interest rate. Therefore, the Keynesian model does not predict a definite cyclical pattern for the real interest rate. (Remember that the data also reveal no definite pattern.) In the Keynesian model the behavior of the real interest rate depends on whether the dominant disturbance involves aggregate demand or the supply and demand for money.

Inflation in the Keynesian Model

Thus far, we assumed that the price level is fixed. But this assumption is unsatisfactory in modeling present-day economies, where inflation rates are typically

---

[14]The adjustment in the interest rate tends also to eliminate the multiplier.

positive and often highly variable over time. Since the Keynesian model does not rely on market-clearing conditions to determine the price level, we need some other mechanism to replace the assumption that prices are rigid. The usual device is an ad hoc adjustment relationship, whereby the price level adjusts gradually toward the general-market-clearing value, P_t^*. Recall that the condition, $P_t > P_t^*$, corresponds to an excess supply of commodities. Therefore, an adjustment of the price level toward the market-clearing value, P_t^*, means that prices decline when goods are in excess supply, and vice versa for excess demand. This type of price-adjustment relation is sometimes called the **Law of Supply and Demand.**

Formally, the price-adjustment rule says that the inflation rate π_t is given by

$$\pi_t = \sigma(Y_t^d - Y_t^s) \tag{19.15}$$

where σ (the Greek letter *sigma*) is positive. Note that the higher the parameter σ the more rapidly prices adjust to an imbalance between supply and demand. Sometimes, economists regard the reaction of prices to excess demand as different from that to excess supply. Namely, prices are thought to rise quickly in the face of excess demand, but to fall only sluggishly when there is excess supply. Then this asymmetry supports the Keynesian focus on cases where the price level exceeds the market-clearing value. But the reason for this asymmetry in the law of supply and demand has not been explained.

As it stands, the price-adjustment formula in equation (19.15) has some problems. First, inflation is nonzero only if the commodity market does not clear—that is, if $Y_t^d \neq Y_t^s$. But the theory should allow inflation and cleared markets to coexist. Second, as a related matter, inflation is negative in the Keynesian case where goods are in excess supply. Thus, we cannot use equation (19.15) to incorporate positive inflation into the Keynesian analysis.

Recall that equation (19.15) implies that the price level, P_t, moves toward the general-market-clearing price, P_t^*. But monetary growth or some other factors can lead to continuing changes in the general-market-clearing price. Then our intuition suggests that the price level would respond to two things: first, the current discrepancy between the price level and its target, P_t^*, which relates to the current amount of excess demand for goods; and second, the anticipated change in the general-market-clearing price. Let's call this last element π_t^*—that is, π_t^* is the expected rate of change of the general-market-clearing price, P_t^*. Using this concept, we might modify equation (19.15) to the form

$$\pi_t = \sigma(Y_t^d - Y_t^s) + \pi_t^* \tag{19.16}$$

Equation (19.16) says that actual inflation, π_t, exceeds the anticipated rate of change of the market-clearing price, π_t^*, when there is excess demand, and vice versa for excess supply. Thus, the actual price level, P_t, tends to approach the target, P_t^*, even when the target moves over time.

Note that equation (19.16) is consistent with nonzero inflation when the commodity market clears. For example, a high rate of anticipated monetary growth implies a high expected rate of change for the market-clearing price, π_t^*, and thereby, a high rate of inflation, π_t. Moreover, if the expected rate of change of the market-clearing price, π_t^*, is positive, then inflation can be positive even when goods are in excess supply. Hence, positive inflation can appear in the Keynesian model.

We now have the following general description of a recession. First, there is some adverse shock to aggregate demand, perhaps stemming from an autonomous decline in investment demand. Then output, employment, and investment (and probably consumption) fall below their general-market-clearing values. Correspondingly, there is an increase in unemployment.

The shortfalls in quantities persist because prices (and wages) do not adjust downward immediately to reestablish general market clearing. That is, although prices are no longer rigid, they are still sticky. But equation (19.16) says that the inflation rate, π_t, falls below the rate of change of the market-clearing price, π_t^*. Therefore, the price level, P_t, tends to fall relative to the target price, P_t^*. Then there are gradual increases in real cash balances,[15] which lead to decreases in interest rates, and thereby to expansions of aggregate demand. Through this process, the economy tends to return eventually to a position of general market clearing (which economists often call a position of "full employment").

The role for active policy in the Keynesian model appears as a substitute for the economy's automatic, but sluggish, reaction through price adjustment. Specifically, either expansions in the growth rate of money (monetary policy) or increases in government purchases (fiscal policy) can spur aggregate demand. Thereby, the model says that the recovery from a recession can be quickened.

The Role of Sticky Prices in the Keynesian Model

All of the novel features in the Keynesian analysis derive from the assumption that prices (or wages) are sticky. In particular, the key postulate is that prices do not fall quickly (relative to the movements in the market-clearing price) when there is excess supply of goods. Among other things, this assumption delivers the following results:

- Output is determined by aggregate demand—supply-side elements play no important role.
- There may be a multiplier connecting autonomous shifts in aggregate demand to the responses of output.
- Whenever people feel wealthier and raise consumer demand, the expansions of output and employment actually make them wealthier.
- There are real effects from changes in the quantity of money.
- There is a desirable role for active monetary and fiscal policies.

---

[15]We assume here that the growth rate of the market-clearing price, π^*, reflects an equal growth rate for the quantity of money. Therefore, the growth rate of money exceeds that of prices.

Given all the results that follow from sticky prices, we should look further into the meaning of this assumption. Presumably, the stickiness of prices does not to a significant degree reflect the costs of changing prices, *per se*. Instead, economists intend to use sluggish price adjustment as a proxy for other problems that make it difficult for the private sector to operate efficiently. For example, there are costs of obtaining various kinds of information, costs of moving from one job to another, costs of changing methods of production, and so on. Then these considerations mean that the economy does not always react appropriately to changes in the composition of tastes and technology, or to shifts in the levels of aggregate demand and supply.

There is no question that the elements just mentioned are important for explaining variations in the aggregates of output and employment and for understanding unemployment. But it is unclear that we can represent these matters by the Keynesian device of imposing an excessive price level on the trades that the private sector can carry out. For example, incomplete information does not imply that aggregate demand is more important than aggregate supply. Also, the gaps in people's knowledge do not necessarily imply a desirable role for activist monetary and fiscal policies.

When we allow for incomplete information and various adjustment costs, we find that the coordination of economic activity is a hard problem for the private sector to solve. Thus, there are often mistakes, which sometimes show up as unemployment and underproduction. But the key challenge to the Keynesian analysis is to explain why these problems are eased if the government occasionally throws in a lot of money or steps up its purchases of goods. In the type of model that we explored in this chapter, these policy actions look good because the assumption of an excessive price level forces the private economy to commit easily correctable mistakes. Namely, output and employment fall short of the levels at which labor's marginal product equals the value of workers' time. But this type of problem is transparent and easy for the private sector to solve without governmental assistance. What has not been shown is that activist governmental policies can assist when the economy has to deal with incomplete information or other serious problems.

The Role of Long-Term Contracts

It has long been recognized that the weak link in Keynesian analysis is the absence of a theory of sticky prices. Probably the most interesting attempt to explain this behavior involves the role of **long-term contracts.** This approach recognizes that buyers and sellers often form long-term relationships, rather than dealing exclusively on auction markets, such as wholesale markets for agricultural commodities, organized securities markets, and so on. For example, the associations between employers and workers or between firms and their suppliers often extend over many time periods. Frequently, these types of continuing interchanges involve formal—

or more often implicit—contractual obligations between the parties. Some presetting of prices—or, more likely, of wages—may be one feature of these contracts.[16]

Prior agreement on prices or wages may allow one party—for example, a group of workers—to shift some risk from themselves to the other party, such as a large corporation. For example, an automobile company may shield its workers from some—but surely not all—of the fluctuations in the demand for automobiles. This setup is desirable if the company is in a better position than the workers to assume risks—perhaps because the company has better access to insurance and other financial markets.

The presetting of some prices may also prevent one person from demanding excessive payment, *ex post*. For example, a firm might lower the wage rate after the worker incurred significant costs in moving to a job. Similarly, a builder might raise the price for a construction project at a time when delays became prohibitively expensive. In these cases the market—for builders, workers, and employers—may be essentially competitive *ex ante,* but more like a monopoly *ex post.* Then people can avoid some of the problems with *ex post* monopoly by entering *ex ante* into contractual arrangements about prices and other considerations.

Some economists have used the contracting approach to rationalize the stickiness of prices or wages in Keynesian models.[17] For example, suppose that two parties agree on a price, P, over the life of a contract.[18] Then in some cases, the chosen price will be the best estimate of the average market-clearing price during the contract, P^*, given the information available at the outset. But unanticipated events—such as monetary disturbances—create departures of the price from the actual market-clearing value. Eventually, when the contract expires, the parties agree to a new price, which equals the anticipated market-clearing price over the next time interval.

At any point in time, there is an array of existing contracts, which specify prices that likely depart somewhat from market-clearing values. In particular, if there has been a recent monetary contraction, then the typical price will be above its market-clearing value (and vice versa for monetary expansion). But then as

---

[16]Some major papers in this area are Donald Gordon, ''A Neo-Classical Theory of Keynesian Unemployment,'' *Economic Inquiry,* December 1974; Costas Azariadis, ''Implicit Contracts and Underemployment Equilibria,'' *Journal of Political Economy,* December 1975; Martin N. Baily, ''Wages and Employment under Uncertain Demand,'' *Review of Economic Studies,* January 1974; and Herschel Grossman, ''Risk Shifting, Layoffs and Seniority,'' *Journal of Monetary Economics,* November 1979.

[17]See, for example, Jo Anna Gray, ''Wage Indexation: A Macroeconomic Approach,'' *Journal of Monetary Economics,* April 1976; Stan Fischer, ''Long-Term Contracts, Rational Expectations and the Optimal Money Supply Rule,'' *Journal of Political Economy,* February 1977; and John Taylor, ''Aggregate Dynamics and Staggered Contracts,'' *Journal of Political Economy,* February 1980.

[18]Actually, the contracting theory motivates the presetting of a relative price or a real wage rate, rather than dollar prices or wages. Yet, most contracts in the United States are not explicitly ''indexed''—that is, do not contain automatic adjustments of nominal prices or wages for changes in the general cost of living. Apparently, people find it convenient to frame their contracts in terms of the standard unit of account—namely, the dollar—even when inflation is moderately high and variable. But inflation does tend to produce contracts with shorter durations.

more people renegotiate contracts, the average price adjusts gradually toward the average market-clearing value. In other words, we can use this model to rationalize the law of supply and demand for price adjustment, which is again (from equation [19.16])

$$\pi_t = \sigma(Y_t^d - Y_t^s) + \pi_t^*$$

The gradual response of the average price to excess demand corresponds to the process of recontracting, while the inclusion of the anticipated rate of change of the market-clearing price, π_t^*, reflects the known factors that negotiators take into account when setting prices or wages at the start of contracts. Note, however, that the contracting viewpoint suggests that an excessive price—that is, excess supply of goods and services—is no more likely than too low a price. That is, the law of supply and demand would be a symmetric relation, which does not support the Keynesian stress on cases where the average price level is too high.

Although the contracting viewpoint may rationalize the law of supply and demand, there are difficulties in using this approach to explain Keynesian unemployment and underproduction. Specifically, the Keynesian results emerge when prices or wages are above market-clearing values *and* when the quantities of output and employment equal the smaller of supply and demand. Recall that this short-side rule for determining quantities accords with voluntary exchange on an impersonal market. But the rule is not generally sensible in a long-term contract, which is now the theoretical basis for sluggish price adjustment.

In an enduring relationship where long-term contracts arise, we would expect the quantity rule to be efficient. For example, workers can agree in advance that they will work more when the demand for local product (say, automobiles) is high, and less when the demand is low. But unlike an auction market, the contract can allow for these efficient adjustments in work even if dollar wages or prices do not change from day to day. (Payments of overtime wage rates reflect some adjustment in the short run.) Another implication is that work and production would not react to disturbances—such as general inflation—which everyone knows do not affect the efficient levels of work and production. The point is that, over many periods, both parties to a labor contract would benefit from these types of provisions.

As a general matter, the contracting viewpoint implies that stickiness of some prices or wages need not lead to underproduction and unemployment. Within a long-term agreement, it is unnecessary for prices and wages to move all the time in order to induce the appropriate changes in the quantities of output and employment. Then stickiness in prices or wages does not necessarily generate Keynesian results. Rather than supporting the Keynesian model, the perspective of long-term contracting demonstrates that output and employment can be determined efficiently—as if prices and wages always adjusted to clear markets—even if prices and wages are sticky.[19]

---

[19]For an elaboration of this argument, see Robert Barro, ''Long-Term Contracts, Sticky Prices and Monetary Policy,'' *Journal of Monetary Economics,* July 1977; and Robert Hall and David Lilien, ''Efficient Wage Bargains under Uncertain Supply and Demand,'' *American Economic Review,* December 1979.

Summary

In the Keynesian model the price level (or the nominal wage) exceeds the market-clearing value. Then the excess supply of goods and services means that output is determined by aggregate demand. Correspondingly, there is underproduction and unemployment. In the simplest Keynesian model, where the interest rate is given, an increase in aggregate demand leads to a multiplicative expansion of output. Along with this expansion, there tend to be increases in employment, investment, and consumption.

The *IS/LM* analysis shows how to determine the interest rate along with the level of output. In this model, an increase in aggregate demand may no longer have a multiplicative effect on output. That's because the increase in the interest rate crowds out the demands for consumption and investment.

We can incorporate inflation into the Keynesian model by using the law of supply and demand. This relation says that inflation responds positively to excess demand for goods, and negatively to excess supply. Also, when the commodity market clears, the inflation rate equals the anticipated rate of change of the market-clearing price. This mechanism allows the price level to fall, relative to the market-clearing value, during a recession. Then the increases in real cash balances lead to decreases in the interest rate, which stimulate aggregate demand. Thus, the economy adjusts toward the market-clearing levels of output and employment. However, in the Keynesian model, active monetary and fiscal policies can usefully substitute for this slow process of automatic adjustment.

Some novel features of the Keynesian analysis are the following:

- Output is determined by aggregate demand—supply-side elements play no important role.
- There may be a multiplier connecting autonomous shifts in aggregate demand to the responses of output.
- Whenever people feel wealthier and raise consumer demand, the expansions of output and employment actually make them wealthier.
- There are real effects from changes in the quantity of money.
- There is a desirable role for active monetary and fiscal policies.

These features all follow from the postulate of sticky prices. Fundamentally, economists use this postulate to proxy for the private sector's coordination problems in reacting to fluctuations in aggregate supply and demand and in the composition of tastes and technology. But when we model these problems in terms of incomplete information, costs of moving, and so on, the Keynesian features noted above do not tend to emerge.

An interesting rationale for sticky prices concerns long-term contracts. Each (explicit or implicit) contract specifies a wage or price over an interval of time. Then the gradual process of recontracting means that the average wage or price adjusts gradually toward the average market-clearing value. Although this perspective may account for sticky prices, it is less successful in explaining the Keynesian predictions about quantities. That's because sensible agreements would allow for efficient adjustment of work and production even if wages or prices do not change from day to day. Thus, the existence of long-term contracts does not explain the type of unemployment and underproduction that arises in Keynesian models.

Important Terms and Concepts

complete Keynesian model

short-side rule (for determining quantities)

involuntary unemployment

Keynesian consumption function

propensity to consume

Keynesian-cross diagram

multiplier

autonomous change in demand

propensity to save

IS curve

LM curve

Law of Supply and Demand (for adjusting the price level)

long-term contracts

QUESTIONS AND PROBLEMS

Mainly for Review

19.1 Contrast the form of consumption demand in the Keynesian model with that in Chapter 6. Why doesn't a change in current income affect consumption demand in the market-clearing model?

19.2 What is involuntary unemployment? Are the temporary layoffs of workers on long-term contracts an example of involuntary unemployment?

19.3 How does output adjust to ensure the aggregate-consistency condition for the commodity market [equation (19.7)]? Would this result apply if goods were not in excess supply?

19.4 Explain how an increase in the quantity of money reduces the real interest rate in the Keynesian model. Why doesn't this effect arise in the market-clearing model?

19.5 What is the output multiplier for an increase in government purchases? Discuss how the size of the multiplier is affected by
a. Whether government purchases are tax financed or deficit financed.
b. Any increases in the interest rate.
c. Whether government purchases are temporary or permanent.

19.6 If the price level is fixed at a level that is "too high," show that the interest rate and output must adjust to ensure the condition that all money be willingly held. Can the interest rate be too high as a result? How does a downward adjustment of the price level bring down the interest rate and eliminate excess supply of commodities?

Problems for Discussion

19.7 The Paradox of Thrift

Suppose that people become "thriftier" and thereby decide to save more and consume less.

a. For a given interest rate, what happens to the quantities of output and employment? What happens to the amount of saving? (*Hint:* What happens to the quantity of investment?) If the amount of saving falls when people become thriftier, there is said to be a *paradox of thrift*.

b. Redo the analysis when the interest rate is allowed to adjust. What happens now to the amount of saving? Is there a paradox of thrift?

c. Can there be a paradox of thrift in the market-clearing model, where the price level is also allowed to adjust? What accounts for the differences in results?

19.8 The Multiplier

Consider an autonomous increase in investment demand.

a. Why is there a multiplicative effect on output if we hold fixed the interest rate?

b. Is there still a multiplier when the interest rate adjusts? In particular, how does this answer depend on the magnitudes of the following:

  i. The sensitivity of aggregate demand to the interest rate?

  ii. The sensitivity of money demand to output?

  iii. The sensitivity of money demand to the interest rate?

19.9 Perceived Wealth in the Keynesian Model

Suppose that the President makes a speech and announces that we are all wealthier than we previously thought. If we all believe the President, then what does the Keynesian model predict for the changes in output, employment, and "wealth"? Explain these results and contrast them with the predictions from the market-clearing model.

19.10 A Change in Inflationary Expectations

Consider an (unexplained) increase in inflationary expectations, π^e.

a. How does this change affect the *IS* curve? In answering, assume now that we place the expected real interest rate, $r^e = R - \pi^e$, rather than the nominal interest rate, on the vertical axis.

b. How does the increase in expected inflation affect the *LM* curve? Assume again that we place the expected real interest rate on the vertical axis.

c. What happens to the level of output, the real interest rate, and the nominal interest rate? Explain these results and contrast them with those in the market-clearing model. (*Hint:* How does the change in inflationary expectations compare to an autonomous shift in the demand for money?)

19.11 Extreme Cases in the IS/LM Analysis

Consider the following extreme cases (which have sometimes been suggested, but have not been supported empirically).

a. Suppose that money demand is insensitive to the interest rate. What does the *LM* curve look like? In this case what is the effect on output and the interest rate from a disturbance that shifts the *IS* curve?

b. Suppose that money demand is extremely sensitive to the interest rate (which is sometimes called a *liquidity trap*). How does the *LM* curve look in this case? What is the effect now from shifts in the *IS* curve?

c. Suppose that the interest rate has a negligible effect on aggregate demand. How does the *IS* curve look in this situation? What are the effects from shifts in the *LM* curve?

d. Finally, suppose that aggregate demand is extremely sensitive to the interest rate. Draw the *IS* curve and describe the effects from shifts in the *LM* curve.

19.12 Stagflation in the Keynesian Model

Suppose that we define stagflation as an increase in inflation during a recession.

a. Assume that a recession stems from an autonomous decline in aggregate demand. Can we get stagflation from this disturbance in the Keynesian model?

b. Is there some other way to generate stagflation in the Keynesian model?

PART VI
THE INTERNATIONAL ECONOMY

CHAPTER 20

THE INTERNATIONAL ECONOMY

So far, we have dealt with the macroeconomic performance of a single economy. In particular, we have neglected the interactions among countries on international markets. In this chapter we extend the model to allow for trade in goods and credit across national borders.

We shall find that our previous analysis of a single economy now applies to the macroeconomics of the world economy. By contrast, our earlier treatment of individuals carries over to the behavior of a small economy that operates without trade restrictions or transport costs on world markets. We can use this perspective to think about international borrowing and lending, changes in the prices of commodities such as oil, and the factors that determine a country's balance of international payments. Since the U.S. economy is so large, we can view it as an intermediate case between the small economy and the entire world.

Aside from the parallels to our previous discussion, there are some entirely new issues, which concern the determination of exchange rates between different currencies. As part of this analysis, we have to assess the linkages across countries of prices, interest rates, and monetary policies.

The United States in the World Economy

Consider a world economy, within which the United States is one of many countries. For now, we assume that the goods produced in each country are physically identical. We also abstract from transport costs or barriers to trade across national borders.

For the moment, we assume that all countries quote prices of goods in units of U.S. dollars. Then, given all the conditions mentioned above, it follows that goods in all countries must sell at the same dollar price P_t. Otherwise, people would want to buy all goods at the lowest price, and sell all goods at the highest price. This is the simplest version of the **law of one price.** At this point, we also abstract from inflation, so that the dollar price level is the constant P.

Suppose that there is a fixed quantity of a single type of base money in the world. For convenience, we measure this money in dollars. That is, we ignore for now the different currency units (pounds, marks, pesos, etc.) that the various countries employ. Under the **gold-standard regime,** which operated in full force before World War I, we would think of this international base money as gold, and would evaluate it at the fixed price of $20.67 per ounce, which prevailed at that time. Alternatively, we can think of a paper money that is issued by an international agency, such as the **special-drawing rights (SDRs)** that are issued currently by the **International Monetary Fund (IMF).** Also, U.S. currency or the currency of other countries sometimes functions as international base money. In any event, we denote the world quantity of base money by the symbol $\overline{N}$. (Generally, we use an overbar to denote a variable for the entire world.) We also refer to this money as **international reserves.** For present purposes, we assume that international reserves do not bear interest.

We assume that a single credit market exists in the world. Then, if we neglect differences in credit-worthiness among borrowers, the real interest rate, r_t, is the same for all lenders and borrowers in every country. When measured in U.S. dollars—that is, as future dollars paid per current dollar per year—the nominal interest rate is R_t. Since we abstract at this point from inflation, the real interest rate, r_t, equals the nominal rate.

The aggregate dollar quantity of bonds on the world credit market, $\overline{B}_t$, is zero, just as it was for a single country when we neglected foreigners. Part of this debt may be issued or held by governments. Then the holders of government bonds regard them as assets, while the issuers—namely, the governments—treat them as corresponding liabilities. (More basically, as discussed in Chapter 15, the taxpayers of each country regard the public debts as their own liabilities.)

Now consider the situation from the standpoint of the residents of a single country, which might be the United States. We refer to this country as the domestic or home country, while we refer to other countries as foreign. Let Y_t represent the total of goods and services produced domestically, which is called real **gross domestic product.** Correspondingly, the dollar income from this source is the amount, PY_t. We shall see below how this concept differs from the gross national product.

For the residents of a single country, the total of funds lent need no longer equal the total borrowed. Rather, the total amount lent on net by domestic residents (including the government) corresponds to the total borrowed on net from this country by foreigners. Let B_t represent the net holding of bonds by domestic residents at the end of period t.[1] Then, if $B_t > 0$, the home country is a net creditor to the rest of the world, whereas if $B_t < 0$, the country is a net debtor. Corre-

---

[1] Note that we have changed the notation from before, so that B_t is now the total holding of bonds (including government bonds) by the domestic private sector less any net debt outstanding of the home government (which we previously called B_t^g). The last item includes the public debt less any assets held by the government. In other words, we have consolidated the asset position of the government with that of the private sector.

spondingly, the amount R_tB_t is the net interest income for period $t + 1$ to domestic residents from abroad.[2]

We suppose that the central bank of a country holds the quantity of international reserves, N_t. Then we think of the central bank as demanding the real quantity of these reserves, N_t/P, in order to facilitate transactions between domestic residents and foreigners. Basically, the demand for reserves by a central bank is analogous to the demand for real cash balances by individuals.[3] In particular, a greater amount of real transactions with foreigners increases the real demand for international reserves, while a higher nominal interest rate, R_t, reduces this demand.

Recall that, in our theory, the interest rate on international reserves is zero, so that there is no interest income on these holdings. In practice, much of what is called international reserves in the international accounts consists of short-term interest-bearing government securities (often U.S. Treasury Bills) that are held by central banks. We treat these interest-bearing assets as part of the overall earning asset position, B_t, of a country. In contrast, the variable N_t refers to a country's holdings of international base money, which might be gold or U.S. currency or SDRs (although SDRs do bear some interest).

We suppose for convenience that the net interest income from abroad, R_tB_t, is the only source of net income from the rest of the world. In particular, we neglect any net labor income from abroad, which is the labor income of domestic residents working in foreign countries, less that of foreigners working in the home country. This category of income is unimportant for most countries. However, it is a significant negative item for Germany, which imports many foreign workers as *gastarbeiter,* and a significant positive item for countries like Pakistan and Turkey, which export workers to other places. If we included this net labor income, then we would add it to the net interest income to measure the overall **net factor income from abroad.** The term, factor income, means that the income flows either to the factor, labor, or to the factor, "capital," which includes here the net claims on assets abroad, B. Then the total dollar income accruing out of productive activity to domestic residents during period t is the amount, $PY_t + R_{t-1}B_{t-1}$. This total, which is the **gross national product,** equals gross domestic product plus the net factor income from abroad. In our simplified setup the last item includes only the net receipts of interest income from abroad.

Suppose that we neglect any transfer payments that flow from one country to another. (These include gifts, governmental foreign aid, pension payments, etc.)

---

[2]More generally, the variable B_t includes not only interest-bearing securities, but also any other net claims of domestic residents on the rest of the world. Specifically, it includes ownership of capital abroad, which arises from "**direct investment**" in foreign countries. Hence, the term, R_tB_t, encompasses the income from this ownership of capital.

[3]For analyses of the demand for international reserves, see Jacob Frenkel, "International Liquidity and Monetary Control," in International Monetary Fund, *International Money, Credit and the SDR,* Washington D.C., 1983; and Nasser Saidi, "The Square-Root Law, Uncertainty and International Reserves under Alternative Regimes: Canadian Experience, 1950–1976," *Journal of Monetary Economics,* May 1981.

Then the gross national product is the total income of domestic residents. This income can be spent in the following ways:

- Personal consumption expenditures, PC_t, whether on goods and services produced domestically or abroad.
- Private domestic gross investment, PI_t, which is the expenditure on capital goods located at home.
- Government purchases of goods and services, PG_t.
- **Net foreign investment,** which is the name given to the net acquisition of interest-bearing claims from abroad, $B_t - B_{t-1}$, plus any accumulation of international reserves, $N_t - N_{t-1}$.

Putting the results together, we have the budget constraint for the home country during period t

$$PY_t + R_{t-1}B_{t-1} = P(C_t + I_t + G_t) + (B_t - B_{t-1}) + (N_t - N_{t-1}) \quad (20.1)$$

When we consider a single economy in isolation (a **closed economy**), we find that the gross domestic product, PY_t, equals the total expenditure by domestic residents, $P(C_t + I_t + G_t)$. Economists sometimes refer to this sum of expenditures, $P(C_t + I_t + G_t)$, as the value of the **domestic absorption of goods and services.** That is, the absorption equals the total expenditure by domestic residents for consumption, for investment in goods located at home, and for government purchases. When we open the economy to the rest of the world—that is, when we allow for an **open economy**—we introduce some new items, which create a divergence between the gross domestic product and the domestic absorption of goods and services. On the left side of equation (20.1) we include the net factor income from abroad, $R_{t-1}B_{t-1}$. On the right side we include net foreign investment, which equals the net acquisition of interest-bearing claims, $B_t - B_{t-1}$, plus the accumulation of international reserves, $N_t - N_{t-1}$.

The term, $B_t - B_{t-1}$, is called the **balance on capital account** for the home country. If $B_t - B_{t-1}$ is positive, then there is an **outflow of capital.** (If negative, there is an **inflow of capital.**) That is, by acquiring interest-bearing claims on foreigners, the home country provides funds for the purchase of capital goods abroad. (If domestic residents own these goods directly, then the outflow of capital takes the form of **direct investment abroad.**)[4]

Consider the difference between the value of goods and services produced by domestic residents (including the net factor income from abroad), $PY_t + R_{t-1}B_t$, and the expenditure by these residents on goods and services, $P(C_t + I_t + G_t)$. This difference corresponds to the additional assets that domestic residents acquire

---

[4]As mentioned before, the international accounts separate out the short-term interest-bearing claims held by central banks from the remainder of a country's holdings of earning assets. Then the changes in the central bank's holdings are added to the change in international reserves (which are held mainly at central banks) to get the "official-settlements balance." Since we consolidate the interest-bearing assets held by governments with those held by the private sector in the same country, we shall not follow this procedure.

currently from the rest of the world. Hence, it is called the **current-account balance.** Notice from equation (20.1) that

$$\text{Current-account balance} = PY_t + R_{t-1}B_{t-1} - P(C_t + I_t + G_t)$$

$$= \text{net foreign investment} \qquad (20.2)$$

$$= B_t - B_{t-1} + N_t - N_{t-1}$$

This expression is the basic identity for the **balance of international payments.** The equation says that the current-account balance equals net foreign investment, which is the sum of the net capital flow, $B_t - B_{t-1}$, plus the change in international reserves, $N_t - N_{t-1}$. If the current-account balance is positive (negative), then a country is said to have a **surplus (deficit) on current account.**

Now let's take an alternative view of a country's position with respect to the rest of the world. First, the gross national product, $PY_t + R_{t-1}B_{t-1}$, is the total value of the goods and services produced this period by domestic residents. Then the absorption of goods and services, $P(C_t + I_t + G_t)$, is the total current expenditure by domestic residents. Thus, the difference between GNP and absorption equals the value of goods and services produced by domestic residents less the value of goods and services used currently (or absorbed) by these residents. If the difference is positive, then the home country must be selling goods and services on net to the rest of the world. Otherwise, the home country must by buying goods and services on net. We define **exports** to be the goods and services produced by domestic residents that are sold to foreigners, and **imports** to be the goods and services produced by foreigners that are bought by domestic residents. Hence, we have shown that the difference between the gross national product, $P(Y_t + R_{t-1}B_{t-1})$, and absorption, $P(C_t + I_t + G_t)$, equals the value of exports less the value of imports.[5] That is, using equation (20.2)

$$\text{Current-account balance} = PY_t + R_{t-1}B_{t-1} - P(C_t + I_t + G_t) \qquad (20.3)$$

$$= \text{value of exports less value of imports}[6]$$

Finally, we can rearrange equation (20.3) to obtain the customary definition of the gross national product

$$GNP = PY_t + R_{t-1}B_{t-1} = P(C_t + I_t + G_t) + \text{value of exports less} \qquad (20.4)$$
$$\text{value of imports}$$

Usually, people refer to exports less imports as "net exports." Thus, we find that GNP equals consumption plus domestic investment plus government purchases plus net exports.

---

[5] If a tourist buys consumer goods while traveling abroad, then these are treated as imports—in fact they are called "invisible imports." However, direct investment abroad is treated as an acquisition of a financial claim on foreigners, rather than as an import of capital goods.

[6] If the net transfers from foreigners to the home country are nonzero, then these add to exports less imports in the calculation of the current-account balance.

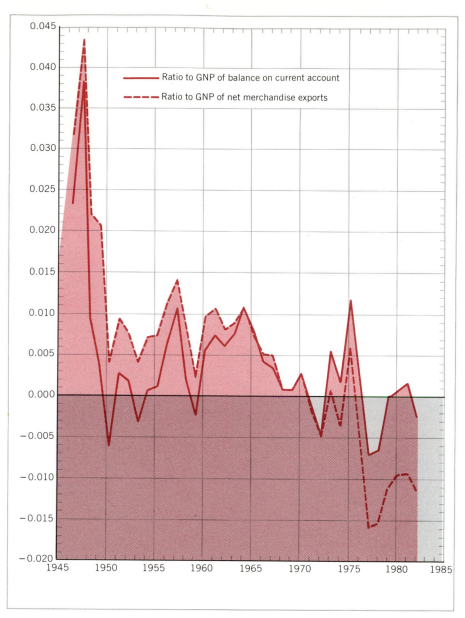

Figure 20.1 The U.S. Current-Account Balance, 1946–82
The figure shows the ratio to GNP of the current-account balance (solid line) and of net merchandise exports (broken line). The data are from *Economic Report of the President,* 1983, p. 276; and *U.S. Survey of Current Business,* March 1983, pp. 33, ff.

Figure 20.1 shows how the U.S. current-account balance behaves from 1946 to 1982. The solid line shows the ratio to GNP of the current-account balance, while the broken line breaks out the portion that corresponds to net merchandise exports (exports of physical commodities less imports of physical commodities). The difference between the solid and broken lines is the ratio to GNP of net income from investments, various service items, net transfers from the rest of the world, and some military transactions.

Notice that in the immediate post-World War II period the balance on current account is strongly in surplus, reaching 4% of GNP in 1947. Then from 1948 to 1976 the current account is typically in surplus, but by an amount that averages only 0.3% of GNP. Subsequently, there are deficits of about 0.7% of GNP in 1977–78, followed by near balance in 1979–81, and a deficit of 0.3% of GNP in 1982.

The short-run fluctuations in the current-account balance reflect mainly those in net merchandise exports. However, the accumulation of current-account surpluses shows up over time in a larger U.S. holding of net assets abroad, B_t. This result follows from the equation for the current-account balance in equation (20.2), given that the change in international reserves, $N_t - N_{t-1}$, is typically a small item. The corresponding increase over time in net investment income shows up in Figure 20.1 as a widening gap between the current-account balance and net merchandise exports. (The gap is initially negative because of the substantial transfers from the United States to the rest of the world.)

Inflation in the International Accounts

As in a closed economy, inflation makes conventional accounting practices less useful as measures of economic changes. For example, in equation (20.2), we would want to measure the flow of interest earnings on the net holding of assets, B_{t-1}, by using the real interest rate, r_{t-1}, rather than the nominal rate, R_{t-1}.[7] Then, when divided by the price level, net foreign investment on the right side of equation (20.2) would measure the change in the real value of a nation's assets. Unfortunately, the available data do not make these adjustments for inflation.[8]

The Role of the International Credit Market

For an individual in a closed economy, the credit market allows for divergences between income and spending. For example, if a disturbance temporarily lowers

---

[7]The real earnings on international reserves would also come into play. Here we would use the real interest rate on these reserves. The appropriate rate depends on whether reserves take the form of a physical commodity, such as gold, or pieces of paper that bear a zero nominal rate of interest.

[8]They also do not adjust for other changes in the real values of assets. For gold, long-term bonds, and direct investments, these changes can be very important. Generally, there turn out to be numerous "errors and omissions" in the international accounts.

someone's income, then he or she can borrow—or spend out of accumulated assets—in order to avoid a temporary decline in consumption or investment. Similarly, an individual can save most of a windfall of income in order to spread it over extra consumption in many periods.

On the other hand, when a closed economy experiences an economy-wide disturbance—such as a temporary decline in everyone's production opportunities—it is impossible for everyone to save less. In this case, the real interest rate adjusts so that the aggregate of desired borrowing equals the aggregate of desired lending. Hence, in a closed economy, the credit market cannot cushion spending against an economy-wide disturbance, even if it is temporary.

Basically, a single country can function in a world credit market much like an individual functions in the credit market of a closed economy. Suppose that there is a temporary supply shock in one country—such as a harvest failure or a natural disaster—which makes everyone in that country desire to decrease saving at the initial real interest rate. Then, especially if the country's economy is small, this decrease in saving can be accommodated on the world credit market without major changes in the world's real interest rate. On the other hand, if the disturbance applied to the entire world, then the universal desire to save less could not be met. In this case, the real interest rate would rise on the international credit market in order to ensure that the world aggregate of desired borrowing equaled the world aggregate of desired lending.

Figure 20.2 illustrates the case of a temporary supply that applies only to the home country. On the vertical axis we plot the real interest rate, r_t, which prevails on the international credit market. Because we think here of a small economy that has little effect on world markets, we hold this real interest rate fixed in the present context. Then the downward-sloping solid curve in the figure shows the domestic residents' aggregate demand for goods or desired real absorption, $Y_t^d = C_t^d + I_t^d + G_t$. As in our previous analysis of a closed economy, a lower real interst rate stimulates this demand.[9]

The upward-sloping solid curve in the figure shows the domestic residents' aggregate supply of goods, $Y_t^s + R_{t-1}B_{t-1}/P$. Note that this concept corresponds to real GNP, which is the total of goods produced by domestic residents, including the real net factor income from abroad. (We abstract here from inflation in calculating the net real interest income from abroad.) As in previous analyses, we assume that a higher real interest rate raises the quantity of goods supplied.

We draw the solid lines in the figure so that, at the given world real interest rate, the domestic residents' aggregate quantity of goods demanded, Y_t^d, is initially equal to the aggregate quantity supplied, $Y_t^s + R_{t-1}B_{t-1}/P$. Hence, the real absorption of goods initially equals real GNP. It follows from equation (20.2) that the current account is in balance. Hence, if the home country's international reserves are constant ($N_t = N_{t-1}$), then the capital account is initially in balance ($B_t = B_{t-1}$).

---

[9]Before we found that the aggregate wealth effect from a change in the real interest rate was nil for a closed economy. In an open economy a nonzero wealth effect can arise. See problem 20.6.

Now suppose that a temporary supply shock reduces the home country's supply of goods, but has a negligible effect on demand. Then the new supply curve is the one shown by the dashed line in Figure 20.2. At the going world real interest rate, r_t, the quantity of goods demanded by domestic residents now exceeds the quantity supplied. In the world economy this imbalance can be accommodated by the home country's borrowing from abroad. Namely, the domestic absorption of goods, $C_t + I_t + G_t$, equals the quantity of goods demanded, Y_t^d; the real GNP equals the quantity of goods supplied, $Y_t^s + R_{t-1}B_{t-1}/P$; and the difference between the two is the real deficit on current account (see equation (20.2)). Further, if there is no change in the home country's international reserves, then equation (20.2) says that the current-account deficit shows up as a capital inflow from abroad—that is, as a negative value for the change in earning assets, $B_t - B_{t-1}$. So the temporary supply shock induces the home country to borrow from abroad in order to avoid a cutback in current spending.

Notice that a world-wide supply shock would be different. In this case, the construction shown in Figure 20.2 applies to each country and, thereby, to the world aggregates of goods demanded and supplied. Consequently, the world real interest rate has to rise in order to clear the international credit market—that is, to equate the quantities of goods demanded and supplied in the world. Then for the typical country, we end up at the point where the new supply curve intersects the

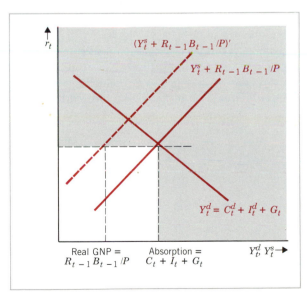

Figure 20.2 **The Effect of a Temporary Supply Shock on a Small Open Economy**
The supply shock lowers the domestic residents' aggregate supply of goods, but has a negligible effect on demand. Thus, at the going world real interest rate, there is a fall in real GNP relative to the absorption of goods. Consequently, the home country runs a current-account deficit, which corresponds to an inflow of capital from abroad.

demand curve in Figure 20.2. At this point, there is a balance on current account—that is, as must always be the case, the typical country has no tendency to borrow from abroad. Notice that this treatment of a world-wide disturbance—including the determination of the world real interest rate—corresponds to the type of analysis that we carried out previously for a closed economy.

We can identify several situations in which a country ends up borrowing heavily on the world credit market. First, consider the example of Poland since 1978, where harvest failures and labor-force problems (both inspired by bad government policies) meant that output fell well below the anticipated average level of future output. In particular, an estimate of real product for Poland shows a decline of about 20% from 1978 to 1981.[10] Thus, the situation resembles that shown in Figure 20.2, where external borrowing prevents a sharp decline in current real spending. In fact, the gross foreign debt of Poland reached $25 billion in 1981, which appears to be on the order of half of annual GNP. Of course, this form of borrowing works out satisfactorily (at least for the lenders) only when the adverse shock is temporary. In the case of a permanent worsening of production opportunities, a country cannot avoid the permanent cutback in spending. If Poland's difficulties turn out to be long lasting, then we can anticipate serious problems with their repayment of international debts.

As a second example, consider a developing country, which has a relatively small amount of capital per worker and thus, a high marginal product of capital. This type of country borrows abroad in order to finance large amounts of investment and, thereby, high growth rates of output. Further, the potential to borrow abroad means that a developing country's level of consumption need not be depressed drastically during the period of high investment.

A recent example of this behavior is Brazil, which sustained an average growth rate of per capita real gross domestic product of about 5% per year from 1971 to 1980. Over this period, Brazil's gross external debt grew from $6 billion or 11% of GDP to $55 billion or 22% of GDP. (In 1982, where a sharp recession also came into play, the Brazilian debt reached $85 billion, which was about 28% of GDP.)[11] For an earlier example of a developing country that borrowed heavily abroad, we can look at the United States in 1890 when the net foreign debt reached $2.9 billion,[12] which amounted to 21% of GNP. Thus, the situation of the United States in the late 19th century is roughly comparable to that for Brazil in recent years.

---

[10]The data on Poland are from the Economist Intelligence Unit, Ltd. (U.K.), *Quarterly Economic Review of Poland,* Annual Supplement 1982, and no. 1, 1983.

[11]The data on gross domestic product for Brazil and Mexico (mentioned below) are from *International Financial Statistics,* 1982 Yearbook, and April 1983. The data on external debt for Brazil and Mexico are from Organization of American States, *Statistical Bulletin of the OAS,* vol. 4, no. 1–2, January–June 1982, Table SA-5, p. 30; and Morgan Guaranty Trust, *World Financial Markets,* February 1983, Table 2, p. 5.

[12]U.S. Commerce Department, *Historical Statistics of the U.S., Colonial Times to 1970,* series U40, p. 869.

For a third situation where a country borrows heavily, we can consider Mexico. In this case, there was a major discovery of a natural resource, namely oil, which promised great amounts of income in future periods. For example, by 1974, Mexico's oil prospects were great, but a significant volume of production had not yet appeared. In this situation, the increase in permanent income motivates external borrowing in order to finance higher consumption (and marvelous government projects) before most of the oil revenue materializes. (In Figure 20.2 we would show this by shifting the demand curve rightward, while keeping the supply curve fixed.) Thus, Mexico's gross external debt rose from $3.5 billion or 9% of GDP in 1971 to $61 billion or 26% of GDP in 1981. With the recent recession and the drop in world oil prices, the debt grew to $80 billion or roughly 32% of GDP in 1982. Of course, this type of foreign borrowing can run into trouble when, as in 1982, the relative price of oil falls unexpectedly, so that Mexico's permanent income turns out to be lower than predicted.

In all of the examples discussed above, a country borrows a great deal abroad when its current real income is low relative to its permanent income. By contrast, the countries that lend internationally are those whose current real income is high relative to permanent income. That is, although prospective real income may exceed current real income, the gap is smaller for these countries than it is for the borrowing countries. Included in the category of international lenders are the mature industrialized countries, such as the United States and Switzerland. For example, the net international investment position of the United States (U.S. assets held abroad including international reserves less foreign assets held in the United States) is estimated to be $59 billion at the end of 1970, and $160 billion at the end of 1981.[13] Another example of an important international creditor is Saudi Arabia, whose flow of oil income (at least through 1981) was high relative to the long-term prospective flow. The estimate for the net international investment position of Saudi Arabia (including international reserves) is $90 billion at the end of 1977 and around $200 billion at the end of 1981.[14]

One important point is that—just as in the case of a credit market in a closed economy—the existence of an international credit market tends to be advantageous for both borrowers and lenders. Obviously, this market enables borrowing countries to spend more than their current income, which is warranted in the cases mentioned above. But the potential to lend abroad also allows countries that have a relatively large amount of desired saving to achieve higher rates of return than would be available domestically. Therefore, although there have been some recent troubles

---

[13]*Economic Report of the President,* 1983, Table B-105. The estimates are very rough because of incomplete coverage and because the assets are carried at book value, rather than market value. For example, gold—which is included in the net international investment position—is valued at the official price, which is about 10% of the market price. Similarly, direct investments are valued at the cost of the initial investment plus the accumulation of retained earnings, which may bear little relation to the market value.

[14]These data are from the Economist Intelligence Unit, Ltd. (U.K.), *Quarterly Economic Review of Saudi Arabia,* Annual Supplement 1982, p. 26.

about foreign loans—such as to Brazil, Poland and Mexico—we should not conclude that the existence of the international credit market is a bad idea overall.

Notice that throughout this analysis we assumed a single world credit market, where the real interest rate was the same for each country. But economists sometimes argue that there are "country risks" associated with loans. As the residents of a country increase their borrowing—with the government of the country often doing the borrowing or guaranteeing the loans—there may be an increasing risk of default. Then the real interest rate paid by that country rises as the amount borrowed increases. (Similar results apply to an individual when borrowing funds on the credit market in a closed economy.) Because of these considerations, a single country, or a single person, has difficulty in using the credit market to smooth out spending when there are major fluctuations in income. In this case, the results turn out to be something like an average of those that we found before for a closed economy with those discussed in this chapter for a single world credit market. Specifically, a temporary disturbance to a country's income shows up partly as a change in that country's real interest rate and level of real expenditure, and partly in the amount of borrowing from abroad. International borrowing then buffers only a portion of the variations in a country's income.

The Terms of Trade

Let's allow now for a divergence between the price of the home country's goods, P, and the average price of goods in the world, which we call $\overline{P}$. (Here, we still measure all prices as dollars per physical unit of goods.) Then there can be changes in the ratios of the prices, $P/\overline{P}$. If the ratio increases, we say that the home country's **terms of trade** improve. That is, for each unit of domestic goods that a country produces and sells abroad (exports), it can now purchase more units of foreign goods (imports).

Recall that, so far, we think of all goods as **tradable** across countries. Often, economists think of some items—especially services—as **nontraded goods.** Because of high transport costs or other considerations, these goods do not move readily from one country to another. Then the terms of trade refer to the relative prices of different tradable goods. However, there are problems in implementing this idea, since considerations such as transport costs mean that tradability is a relative matter. Although some goods enter more easily than others into international commerce, with enough incentive, almost anything—including the services of workers—becomes a tradable good.

Consider a change in the terms of trade, $P/\overline{P}$. Here, we suppose that this change reflects a disturbance that originates in the rest of the world, rather than from a shift in the domestic country. For example, Chile may face a change in the relative price of its main export, copper, or Brazil a shift in the relative price of its main export, coffee. But we assume in this example that Chile's capacity to produce copper or Brazil's to produce coffee does not change.

The shift in the terms of trade, $P/\overline{P}$, looks to the residents of the domestic country—which sells goods at the price P—much like a change in the local relative price, $P(z)/P$, looked to the producers in a local market in the model that we developed in Chapter 18. Specifically, an increase in the terms of trade, $P/\bar{P}$, raises the real values of marginal products in the home country. If the change is temporary, then the main effect is an increase in work effort, production, and the physical volume of exports, with only a small increase in current consumption. The greater real value of exports—reflecting partly the higher relative price and partly the higher physical volume—shows up as a surplus on current account. Thus, there is an outflow of capital, which domestic residents accumulate as greater claims on foreigners. Note that the residents of the domestic country willingly accumulate these extra assets at going interest rates—that is, they raise their desired saving—because the improvement in the terms of trade is temporary. People plan to use the additional assets to finance higher consumption (in the form of imports) in future periods, when they expect the terms of trade to return to the normal value.

If the improvement in the terms of trade is permanent, then there is a strong wealth effect, which motivates an increase in consumption. In fact, there would now be little change in the country's total of desired saving. In this case, we find little change in the assets accumulated from abroad—that is, imports of goods rise (in terms of dollar value) along with exports. Correspondingly, there is no longer a surplus on current account.[15] Thus, the main prediction is that a surplus on current account accompanies a temporary improvement in the terms of trade, but not a permanent improvement.[16]

As an empirical example of these effects from changes in the terms of trade, we can look at the current-account balance for the Organization of Petroleum-Exporting Countries (OPEC). Table 20.1 shows that OPEC's current account is nearly balanced in 1972. Then the sharp increases in oil prices during 1973–74 led to a current-account surplus of $60 billion in 1974. From 1974 to 1978, the relative price of oil fell somewhat. But more importantly, the OPEC countries adjusted their expenditures to their higher permanent income, which corresponded to the growing perception that the relative price of oil would remain high. Thus, by 1978 the current account of OPEC is again nearly balanced—but at much higher dollar levels of exports and imports. Then the surprise increases in oil prices in 1979–80 led once again to a large surplus on current account, which reached $115 billion

---

[15]One additional element concerns investment. If people expect an improvement in the terms of trade to persist, there is a stimulus to domestic investment (for example, for an oil-exporting country, in the oil industry). Here, the increase in the relative price, $P/\bar{P}$, raises the real value of the marginal product of domestic capital (when evaluated by dividing the flow of nominal income by the world price level, $\bar{P}$). This increase in domestic investment demand leads to borrowing from abroad—hence, there tends now to be a deficit on current account (and an inflow of capital from abroad). The point is that a long-lasting improvement in the terms of trade may lead for awhile—during the period of an investment boom—to a current account deficit.

[16]For further analysis of effects from changes in the terms of trade, see Jeffrey Sachs, ''The Current Account and Macroeconomic Adjustment in the 1970s,'' *Brookings Papers on Economic Activity,* no. 1, 1981; and Jeremy Greenwood, ''Expectations, the Exchange Rate and the Current Account,'' *Journal of Monetary Economics,* 1983.

Table 20.1 Current-Account Balance of Oil-exporting Countries (OPEC)

Year	Current-Account Balance ($ billion)
1972	1
1974	60
1976	37
1978	4
1980	115
1982	2

Source: OECD, *Economic Outlook,* July 1983, July 1979.

in 1980. In this case the upward adjustment of expenditures and the fall in oil's relative price in 1982 restored the current account to near balance by 1982.

Restrictions on International Trade

In the context of a closed economy, we mentioned the benefits from the opportunities to exchange goods and services with others on a commodity market. This market allows people to specialize in their production activities, which aids economic efficiency. The existence of international markets widens these opportunities further. In particular, countries can concentrate their production in the areas where they are relatively efficient. What these areas are depends, among other things, on a country's endowments with respect to labor, natural resources, technical expertise, and the initial amounts of capital.

As with taxes in a closed economy, levies on international commerce generate distortions, which prevent efficient outcomes. One common form of these levies is the **tariff,** which is a tax on goods imported into a country. A tariff makes foreign goods artificially more expensive relative to domestic goods. **Quotas**—which are limitations on the quantities of imports—and informal agreements among governments to limit imports are other instruments that raise the relative cost of foreign goods. In addition, there are import licenses, advance deposit requirements, and a variety of other ingenious devices that governments use to keep out foreign goods. Also, governments sometimes subsidize exports, which makes the returns on these sales artificially high.

From the standpoint of economic efficiency, it is preferable to pursue a **free-trade** policy. By free trade, we mean a policy that allows the location of production activities to be determined by open economic competition, without the interference of tariffs, quotas, or similar interventions. However, some groups in an economy tend to benefit from particular restrictions on international trade, which helps to explain the existence of these restrictions. As a recent example in the U.S., the

Reagan administration enacted in 1983 a remarkably high tariff on large Japanese motorcycles, all to benefit the owners and employees of the Harley-Davidson Company in the United States. Of course, the consumers of motorcycles were hurt by this legislation—in fact, because of the overall loss of economic efficiency, we can show that the dollar value of the losses exceeded the dollar value of the gain to the protected industry. Nevertheless, groups sometimes have enough political influence to generate this sort of legislation.

There are also governmental **capital controls,** which interfere with the process of international borrowing and lending. Such restrictions make it difficult for lenders to achieve the highest possible return on their funds, and for borrowers to finance current expenditures on favorable terms. Basically, the argument for free trade in financial transactions parallels the argument for free trade in goods and services.

In calculating the losses from restrictions on international commerce—and from other types of governmental restrictions—we should include the resources that groups expend in attempting to obtain governmental favors. This item is called **rent-seeking activity**—that is, activity directed toward securing excess flows of income or rents. Some estimates suggest that the losses of this type are very large in countries such as India and Turkey where the securing of licenses, quotas, etc., from the government is a national pastime.[17]

International Flows of Money

Recall that the change in a country's holdings of international reserves, $N_t - N_{t-1}$, is one component of the current-account balance in equation (20.2). Any element that increases a country's demand for international reserves—such as a rise in that country's aggregate real income—shows up as a positive flow of reserves, $N_t - N_{t-1}$. Generally, a country can finance this increase in reserves either by running a current-account surplus—that is, exporting more than it imports—or by borrowing from abroad.

Suppose again that the total world supply of international reserves (such as gold or the IMF's special-drawing rights) is a fixed number, $\bar{N}$. (In practice, these amounts would tend to rise over time.) Then somehow, the world's aggregate demand for international reserves must accommodate itself to the given amount that is available. But this problem is analogous to the one that we worked out before for a closed economy, where the nominal quantity of money, M, was a given number. In that case we found that the domestic price level, P, adjusted so that the real quantity of cash, M/P, equaled the real amount demanded. The same idea applies to the world economy. Namely, the world price level, $\bar{P}$, adjusts so that the real value of international reserves, $\bar{N}/\bar{P}$, equals the real quantity de-

---

[17]See Anne Krueger, "The Political Economy of the Rent-Seeking Society," *American Economic Review,* June 1974.

manded. It follows that the world price level depends positively on the world's "money supply," $\overline{N}$, and negatively on the world's real demand for money. This dependence parallels our previous findings for a closed economy.

Different Monies and Exchange Rates

In the real world, each country issues currency in its own unit, whether dollars, pounds, francs, marks, pesos, or whatever. In order to allow for this fact, let M^i be the quantity of domestic money, that is, the monetary base, for country i. We measure this money in domestic currency units, such as Mexican pesos. A typical setup is that the central bank of country i holds the international reserves, N^i, and then issues the domestic monetary base, M^i. Thus, we would have the simplified balance sheet of a central bank as shown in Table 20.2. Note that the central bank's assets consist of international reserves, N^i, foreign interest-bearing assets, and domestic interest-bearing assets, which include bonds issued by the home government. As mentioned in Chapter 16, the holdings of domestic earning assets are called the central bank's domestic credit. Then on the liabilities side, we have currency and deposits of (domestic) financial institutions held at the central bank. The sum of these two items constitutes the home country's monetary base, M^i. (For simplicity, we neglect foreign deposits held at the central bank.)

The domestic price level in country i, P^i, now expresses the number of local currency units, say pesos, that exchange for a unit of goods. To simplify matters, think again of a case where all goods are physically identical. Hence, the same physical object sells for P^i units of one currency (pesos) in country i, and for P^j units of another currency (say, Swiss francs) in country j. Note also that the ratio, M^i/P^i, is the real value of cash held in the form of country i's currency. We assume that this cash is held only by the residents of country i, which is realistic in most cases (although not for the U.S. dollar or, especially in earlier times for the British pound).

We now have to introduce a new market, called an exchange market, on which people can trade the currency of one country for that of another. For example, people might trade Mexican pesos for U.S. dollars or for Swiss francs. The ex-

Table 20.2 Simplified Balance Sheet of a Central Bank

Assets	Liabilities
International Reserves (N^i) Foreign interest-bearing assets Domestic interest-bearing assets (domestic credit)	Monetary Base, M^i (currency and deposits of domestic financial institutions)

change market establishes **exchange rates** among the various currencies. For convenience, we express all exchange rates in terms of the number of units of domestic currency that trade for $1.00 (U.S.). For example, on August 8, 1983, we find that 149 Mexican pesos exchange for $1.00, which means that each peso is worth about 0.7 cents. Similarly, 2.18 Swiss francs exchange for $1.00, so that a Swiss franc is worth about 46 cents.

Notice that the exchange rates for Mexican pesos and Swiss francs in terms of U.S. dollars tell us the exchange rate between pesos and francs. Namely, we can use 149 Mexican pesos to buy $1.00, which we can then convert into 2.18 Swiss francs. Hence, in order to obtain one Swiss franc, we have to sell $149/2.18 = 68$ Mexican pesos. Thus, the exchange rate between pesos and francs is 68 pesos per franc. (In practice, people can make these exchanges directly, rather than going through U.S. dollars.)

Let ϵ^i (the Greek letter *epsilon*) be the exchange rate for country i. In other words, ϵ^i units of country i's currency (say, pesos) exchange for $1.00 (U.S.). Alternatively, we see that the dollar value of 1 unit of country i's currency (1 peso) is $1/\epsilon^i$. Notice that a *higher* value of the exchange rate, ϵ^i, means that country i's currency is *less* valuable in terms of dollars. That's because it takes more of country i's currency to buy $1.00.

For any two countries, i and j, we observe the exchange rates, ϵ^i and ϵ^j. These rates tell us the number of units of each domestic currency that trade for $1.00. Hence, we know that ϵ^i units of currency i (say, 149 Mexican pesos) can buy ϵ^j units of currency j (say, 2.18 Swiss francs). Therefore, the exchange rate between currencies i and j—that is, the number of units of currency i needed to buy one unit of currency j—equals ϵ^i/ϵ^j $(149/2.18)$ $= 68$ pesos per franc). Alternatively, for 1 unit of currency i, we can get ϵ^j/ϵ^i units of currency j.

Purchasing-Power Parity

We are now ready to derive the central theoretical proposition of international finance. This result connects the exchange rate between two currencies to the price levels that prevail in the two countries.

Suppose again that we can think of all goods as physically identical. Then a resident of country i can choose between first, using local currency to buy goods domestically at the price P^i; or second, exchanging money into the currency of country j in order to buy goods at the price P^j. For each unit of currency i, a person can get $1/P^i$ units of goods domestically. In the exchange market, he or she gets ϵ^j/ϵ^i units of currency j for each unit of currency i. Then, buying at the price P^j, the person gets $(\epsilon^j/\epsilon^i) \cdot (1/P^j)$ units of goods. But in order for things to make sense, the two options must result in the same amount of goods. Otherwise, everyone would want to buy goods in the cheap country and sell goods in the expensive country. This idea is a version of the law of one price, which we mentioned before. Thus, we must have that $1/P^i = (\epsilon^j/\epsilon^i) \cdot (1/P^j)$, or, when we rearrange terms

$$\epsilon^j/\epsilon^i = P^j/P^i \tag{20.5}$$

Equation (20.5) says that the ratio of the exchange rates for any two currencies, ϵ^j/ϵ^i, equals the ratio of the prices of goods in the two countries, P^j/P^i. This condition is called **purchasing-power parity (PPP).** It ensures that the purchasing power in terms of goods for each currency is the same regardless of where someone uses the currency to buy goods.

Define the rate of change of country i's exchange rate to be $\Delta\epsilon^i$—that is, $\epsilon^i_{t+1} = (1 + \Delta\epsilon^i)\epsilon^i_t$. Note that a positive value for $\Delta\epsilon^i$ means that country i's currency becomes less valuable over time in terms of dollars. Alternatively, we can say that country i's currency depreciates in value relative to the dollar. Conversely, if $\Delta\epsilon^i$ is negative, then country i's currency appreciates over time relative to the dollar.

The PPP condition in equation (20.5) implies that the rates of change of any two exchange rates, $\Delta\epsilon^j$ and $\Delta\epsilon^i$, are related to the inflation rates in the two countries. Specifically, we can use equation (20.5) to show that

$$\Delta\epsilon^j - \Delta\epsilon^i \simeq \pi^j - \pi^i \qquad (20.6)$$

where π^j and π^i are the respective inflation rates. Equation (20.6) says that the higher a country's inflation rate, π^j, the higher the rate of depreciation of that country's currency, $\Delta\epsilon^j$. Later on we shall look at some empirical evidence on this result.

Equations (20.5) and (20.6) apply when the prices, P^i and P^j, refer to the same physical objects. More realistically, there are differences in the array of goods and services produced in different countries. Think of P^i and P^j as the price of the typical item produced in countries i and j, respectively. (In practice, we might measure these prices by the deflators for the gross domestic product.) Then changes in the relative prices of goods across countries—that is, shifts in the terms of trade—will show up as shifts in the PPP condition. Assume, for example, that the typical good produced in country j (such as coffee in Brazil) becomes more expensive relative to goods produced elsewhere. Then the price ratio, P^j/P^i, must rise for a given ratio of the exchange rates, ϵ^j/ϵ^i.

The general point is that various real disturbances can shift the PPP condition in equation (20.5). Aside from changes in the terms of trade, some other real factors that can affect this condition are shifts in the relative prices of traded and nontraded goods, changes in trade restrictions or transport costs, and some aspects of tax policies.

Interest-Rate Parity

Suppose that there is a market-determined nominal interest rate in each country. The nominal rate in country i, R^i, will be expressed in units of its own currency— for example, as pesos paid per period per peso lent out today. Let's think about this interest rate from the standpoint of U.S. dollars. At date t we can exchange $1.00 for ϵ^i_t units of country i's currency. Then by lending at the interest rate R^i, we receive $\epsilon^i_t(1 + R^i)$ units of country i's currency at date $t + 1$. If we convert back to dollars, using period $t + 1$'s exchange rate ϵ^i_{t+1}, then we obtain the dollar amount

$$\epsilon^i_t(1 + R^i)/\epsilon^i_{t+1} = (1 + R^i)/(1 + \Delta\epsilon^i)$$

where $\Delta\epsilon^i$ is again the rate of change of country i's exchange rate. If the exchange rate rises at a faster rate over time, then the dollar value of next period's holdings falls for a given value of the nominal interest rate R^i.

Instead of holding assets in country i, we could have selected any other country (including the United States). In the case of country j, the dollar value of the next period's holdings would be $(1 + R^j)/(1 + \Delta\epsilon^j)$. But if this amount is not the same for all countries, then everyone would want to lend where the amount is largest and borrow where it is smallest. Thus, as another implication of the law of one price, we find that the amounts must be the same for all countries—that is,

$$(1 + R^j)/(1 + \Delta\epsilon^j) = (1 + R^i)/(1 + \Delta\epsilon^i)$$

We can use this result to derive, as an approximation, a condition that is called **interest-rate parity**—namely,[18]

$$R^j - R^i \simeq \Delta\epsilon^j - \Delta\epsilon^i \tag{20.7}$$

Thus, the higher the rate of change of a country's exchange rate $\Delta\epsilon^j$—that is, the faster the depreciation in value relative to the U.S. dollar—the higher must be that country's nominal interest rate R^j.

In practice, the changes in the exchange rates would not be known in advance. Then we would replace the variables, $\Delta\epsilon^j$ and $\Delta\epsilon^i$, by their expected values. With this modification, equation (20.7) says that a higher expected rate of change of the exchange rate, $(\Delta\epsilon^j)^e$, implies a correspondingly higher nominal interest rate R^j. However, there are a number of real-world considerations that prevent interest-rate parity from holding exactly. These include varying tax treatments of interest income across countries, as well as differences in risks for the various returns.

Finally, if purchasing-power parity holds, then equation (20.6) says that the difference in the growth rates of the exchange rates, $\Delta\epsilon^j - \Delta\epsilon^i$, equals the difference in the inflation rates, $\pi^j - \pi^i$. Then the interest-rate parity condition from equation (20.7) implies that (expected) real interest rates are the same in all countries.

Fixed Exchange Rates

Until the early 1970s and except during major wars, most countries typically maintained **fixed exchange rates** among their currencies. For example, during the post-World War II period, many countries established narrow bands within which they

---

[18]Multiply through by the term, $(1 + \Delta\epsilon^i)(1 + \Delta\epsilon^j)$. Then we get the interest-rate parity condition in equation (20.7) if we neglect the terms, $R^i \cdot \Delta\epsilon^j$ and $R^j \cdot \Delta\epsilon^i$. As the length of the period declines, the approximation becomes more accurate.

would fix the exchange rate, ϵ^i, between their currency and the U.S. dollar. In these cases, the central bank of country i stood ready to buy and sell its currency at the rate of ϵ^i units per U.S. dollar. For example, the German central bank (Bundesbank) provided dollars for marks when people wanted to reduce their holdings of marks, and vice versa when people wished to increase their holdings of marks. In order to manage these exchanges, each central bank maintained a stock of international reserves in the form of U.S. dollars or in other forms that could be readily converted into dollars. Then the United States stood ready to exchange dollars for gold (on the request of foreign official institutions) at a fixed price, which happened to be $35 per ounce.[19] Thus, by maintaining a fixed exchange rate with the U.S. dollar, each country indirectly pegged its currency to gold.

Let P be the dollar price of goods in the United States and note that the United States exchange rate with itself is unity. Then, if the purchasing-power parity condition from equation (20.5) holds, we have that country i's price level is

$$P^i = \epsilon^i \cdot P \qquad (20.8)$$

If the exchange rate ϵ^i is fixed, it follows that the price level in country i, P^i, is determined by the U.S. price level P. For a given U.S. price level and assuming that purchasing-power parity holds, the choice of an exchange rate with the U.S. dollar, ϵ^i, translates into a choice of domestic price level P^i.

We can generalize the result by introducing possibilities for deviations from purchasing-power parity. These include a variety of real disturbances, which we mentioned before. But we would retain the basic result—namely, a country cannot choose independently its exchange rate ϵ^i and its general price level P^i. Given the variety of real factors mentioned above, a fixed exchange rate means that a country's price level is determined by the U.S. price level.

If the U.S. price level, P, changes, then equation (20.8) says that country i's price level, P^i, changes in the same proportion. In other words, any country that maintains a fixed exchange rate with the U.S. dollar experiences roughly the same inflation rate, π^i, as the U.S. rate, π.

The interest-rate parity condition from equation (20.7) implies that country's i's nominal interest rate, R^i, equals the U.S. rate, R. Thus, under fixed exchange rates, there is a single nominal interest rate in the world. (Again, differences in taxes and in riskiness of returns mean that this result does not hold exactly.)

The Quantity of Money under Fixed Exchange Rates

Before, when considering a closed economy, we stressed the relation between a country's quantity of base money, M^i, and the price level, P^i. Yet we have determined a country's price level in equation (20.8) without saying anything about that

---

[19]The arrangement is called the **Bretton-Woods System,** in honor of the meeting in 1944 at Bretton Woods, New Hampshire, where the regime was set up. For a discussion of this system, see James Ingram, *International Economics,* Wiley, New York, 1983, Chapter 9.

country's quantity of money. Let's now investigate the relation betrween money and prices in an open economy.

It is still the case that the residents of country i demand a quantity of real cash, M^i/P^i, which depends on variables like real output, Y^i, and the world nominal interest rate, R. (Recall our assumption that the residents of country i use and hold their own currency, rather than that of the United States or other countries.) The condition that all money in country i be willingly held is

$$M^i/P^i = H(Y^i, R, \ldots) \tag{20.9}$$
$$(+)\ (-)$$

If purchasing-power parity holds, then we can substitute in equation (20.9) for the domestic price level as $P^i = \epsilon^i \cdot P$ from equation (20.8). Then if we multiply through by this term, we get a condition for the domestic quantity of money

$$M^i = \epsilon^i \cdot P \cdot H(Y^i, R, \ldots) \tag{20.10}$$

Given the exchange rate ϵ^i, the U.S. price level P, and the determinants of the real demand for money in country i, $H(\cdot)$, equation (20.10) determines the nominal quantity of money, M^i, that must be in country i. Hence, this quantity of money cannot be regarded as a free element of choice by the monetary authority in country i. Once we prescribe the exchange rate ϵ^i, there is a specific quantity of money, M^i, that is consistent with the maintenance of this exchange rate.

In order to understand these findings, let's assume first that the domestic price level, P^i, accords with purchasing-power parity, as specified in equation (20.8), and that the quantity of money M^i is the amount prescribed by equation (20.10). Then real cash balances equal the amount demanded, as expressed in equation (20.9). Now suppose that the monetary authority of country i increases the quantity of base money M^i—for example, by means of an open-market purchase of government securities. In Table 20.3 we illustrate this case in step 1 by assuming that the monetary base and the central bank's holdings of domestic assets each rise by $1 million.

Table 20.3 Effects of Open-Market Operations on the Central Bank's Balance Sheet

	Assets	Liabilities
Step 1	Domestic interest-bearing assets: +$1 million	Monetary base, M^i: +$1 million
	Assets	**Liabilities**
Step 2	International reserves: −$1 million	Monetary base, M^i: −$1 million

Note: In step 1 the open-market purchase raises the monetary base by $1 million. But in step 2, the loss of international reserves means that the monetary base declines by $1 million.

Our previous analysis of a closed economy suggests that the domestic price level P^i would rise. But then, the price level in country i would exceed the value dictated by purchasing-power parity in equation (20.8). Hence, if the exchange rate did not change, goods bought in country i would become more expensive—per unit of any currency—than goods bought elsewhere. Therefore, people would move away from buying goods in country i and toward buying goods in other countries. This response tends to keep the domestic price level P^i in line with prices that people pay in the rest of the world. But at this price level, domestic residents would be unwilling to hold a larger quantity of domestic money, M^i. We can think of people as returning their excess domestic currency to the central bank in order to obtain U.S. dollars or other forms of international reserves. (Since the central bank fixes the exchange rate, it stands willing to make these exchanges at a fixed conversion ratio.) Thus, in step 2 of Table 20.3, we show that the monetary base and the central bank's holdings of international reserves each decline by $1 million. Then the people who get these reserves use them to buy goods (or bonds) from abroad. In any event, the main point is that the ultimate consequence of the open-market purchase is that the central bank loses international reserves, N^i.

In order to complete the story, we have to assess the central bank's reaction to its loss of international reserves. As one possibility, the bank allows the domestic quantity of money M^i to decline. Then as people return money to the central bank, the domestic quantity of money falls toward the level that is again consistent with purchasing-power parity in equation (20.10). In fact, this automatic response of domestic money to the loss of international reserves is a central element of the gold standard or other systems of fixed exchange rates.

On the other hand, whenever the automatic mechanism tends to reduce the quantity of domestic money, M^i, the central bank can offset this tendency—for example, by further open-market purchases of securities. When the central bank acts this way, we say that it **sterilizes** the flow of international reserves. Thus, by sterilization, we mean that the central bank attempts to insulate the domestic quantity of base money, M^i, from changes in the quantity of international reserves, N^i. Eventually, this type of policy can lead to a sufficient drain on reserves so that the central bank becomes unwilling or unable to maintain the exchange rate. That is, the central bank may no longer provide dollars at the fixed rate of ϵ^i units of domestic currency per dollar. Rather, there may be a **devaluation** of the domestic currency, which means that the exchange rate rises above ϵ^i units per dollar. Thus, the tendency of central banks to sterilize the flows of international reserves threatens the viability of fixed exchange rates.[20] We shall discuss these matters further in a later section.

We should mention another possible reaction of government policy to the loss

---

[20]Our discussion in this and the following sections follows a viewpoint that is often called the **monetary approach to the balance of payments.** This research was pioneered by Robert Mundell—see, for example, his books, *International Economics,* Macmillan, New York, 1968, part II and *Monetary Theory,* Goodyear, Pacific Palisades, California 1971, Part II. Mundell's work has been carried on by some of his bright students—see, for example, Rudi Dornbusch, *Open-Economy Macroeconomics,* Basic Books, New York, 1980, Chapters 7 and 13.

of international reserves. Recall that this drain of reserves is triggered in the present case by excessive monetary creation at home, which tends to make domestic goods more expensive than foreign goods. Thus, the government might step in with trade restrictions, which artificially raise the cost for domestic residents to buy foreign goods. Alternatively, the government might subsidize exports in order to make these goods cheaper for foreigners. The main idea is that the government can interfere with free trade in order to prevent purchasing-power parity from holding. Thus, there are two types of potential ill effects that result from excessive monetary expansion under fixed exchange rates. One is the loss of international reserves, which leads eventually to devaluation. But in order to avoid either this outcome or domestic monetary contraction, governments may pursue a course of extensive interference with international trade. In fact, the frequency of these interferences during the post-World War II period was a major argument used by opponents of fixed exchange rates.[21]

World Prices Under Fixed Exchange Rates

The system of fixed exchange rates, centered on the U.S. dollar, determines each country's price level, P^i, as a ratio to the U.S. price P. In order to complete the picture, we have to determine the U.S. price level. Basically, the analysis is similar to our earlier determination of the world price level. Namely, we have to equate the world's demand for international reserves—including U.S. dollars—to the supply.

Suppose that we add up the total real demand for U.S. money, whether by U.S. residents or by foreigners in the form of international reserves. Then, given the dollar quantity of U.S. money, M, we can determine the U.S. price level, P, in the usual manner. Specifically, a greater amount of money, M, means a higher U.S. price level, P, and a correspondingly higher price level, P^i, in each other country.

Under the international regime that prevailed after World War II, there were a number of factors that constrained the Federal Reserve's choice of the quantity of U.S. money, M. First, if the Federal Reserve pursued a monetary policy that was inconsistent with stabilization of the U.S. price level P—specifically, if there were high and variable U.S. inflation—then U.S. currency would become less attractive as an international reserve currency. Consequently, other countries might no longer find it desirable to fix their exchange rates to the U.S. dollar, or to hold dollars as a form of international reserve. Second, the U.S. had a commitment to exchange U.S. dollars for gold at the rate of $35 per ounce. Therefore, if the U.S. price level rose substantially—as it did during the late 1960s—then it would become attractive for foreign central banks to trade their dollars for gold. As the United States lost more and more gold, it would become unable to maintain the dollar price of gold. Eventually, the system would break down, as it did at the beginning of the 1970s.

---

[21]See Milton Friedman, "Free Exchange Rates," in his *Dollars and Deficits,* Prentice-Hall, Englewood Cliffs, New Jersey, 1968, Chapter 9.

Devaluation

Let's return now to the situation of a typical foreign country in a regime of exchange rates fixed to the U.S. dollar. As suggested before, a country that typically maintains the fixed exchange rate, ϵ^i, occasionally faces pressures to shift this rate. In particular, any force that tends to increase the domestic price level P^i, relative to the U.S. price P, leads to losses of international reserves by the domestic central bank. These pressures could arise, for example, from rapid expansion of the domestic monetary base, M^i, or from a decrease in the demand for country i's real cash balances, M^i/P^i. (The decline in real money demanded might reflect a domestic supply shock, which reduces output in country i.) In response to the outflow of reserves, the central bank has an incentive to raise the exchange rate, ϵ^i, which implies a devaluation of the domestic currency in terms of the U.S. dollar. Conversely, any pressure toward reduction in the domestic price level P^i, relative to the U.S. price P, implies gains in international reserves, which motivate a reduction in the exchange rate ϵ^i. Since the domestic currency then becomes more valuable in terms of the dollar, there is an appreciation of the currency, which is often called a **revaluation.**

Typically, devaluations and revaluations do not involve long periods during which the central bank gradually loses or gains reserves. That's because the expectation of a shift in the exchange rate leads to **speculation,** which tends to hasten the central bank's actions. For example, if people anticipate a devaluation—that is, a rise in the exchange rate ϵ^i—then they have incentives to return their domestic money to the central bank in order to get international reserves, which might be U.S. dollars. People react this way because they expect the domestic money to become less valuable relative to other moneys. But since this decline in the demand for domestic money leads to further losses of international reserves by the central bank, the devaluation tends to occur sooner.

Consider now the effects of a devaluation—that is, an increase in the exchange rate ϵ^i. As noted before, this change may be a symptom of pressure for inflation in the devaluing country, such as excessive expansion of the domestic money stock, M^i. But let's consider here the effects of an autonomous devaluation—that is, a devaluation that comes out of the blue, rather than as a response to changes in domestic money supply or demand.

If the domestic price level P^i (pesos per good) did not change, then an increase in the exchange rate ϵ^i (pesos per dollar) means that goods in country i become cheaper in terms of dollars. Therefore, for a given U.S. price level P, there would be a great increase in the demand for goods sold in country i. Hence, as shown by the purchasing-power parity condition in equation (20.8), a devaluation leads to a higher domestic price level, $P^i = \epsilon^i \cdot P$.

Suppose that we treat the devaluation and the rise in domestic prices as one-time events. Then the higher domestic price means a greater demand for domestic money in nominal terms, M^i. (See equation [20.10].) The rise in the quantity of money, M^i, can come about in two ways. First, the central bank may create more money through open-market operations or other means. Then second, if the central bank does not act, individuals would bring their accumulations of U.S. dollars or other international reserves to the central bank in order to get more domestic currency. As the bank exchanges domestic money for international reserves, the quantity of domestic money, M^i, tends to rise. Thus, a one-time devaluation can lead to an expansion of a country's international reserves, which accompanies the increase in the quantity of domestic money, M^i.

Notice that there is a two-way direction of association between devaluations and the behavior of domestic prices and money. First, expansionary monetary policy creates pressure for devaluation. In this sense we would say that domestic inflation causes devaluation. Then second, an autonomous devaluation tends to raise domestic prices and money. In this sense, a devaluation is, itself, inflationary.

Our analysis treats the changes in the exchange rate ϵ^i and the domestic price level P^i as one-time happenings. But in practice, countries that devalue once tend to devalue again. This outcome makes sense if we think of devaluations as primarily symptoms of pressures for domestic inflation—in particular, as signals that the domestic central bank is pursuing an expansionary monetary policy. Countries that act this way today are likely to continue this behavior later on. Hence, a devaluation can create expectations of future increases in the exchange rate, ϵ^i. Then the interest-rate parity condition from equation (20.7) implies that the domestic nominal interest rate, R^i, must rise above that in the United States. But this change reduces the demand for country i's money, M^i. As a consequence, a devaluation of country i's currency may not generate the increase in international reserves that we discussed above.

Flexible Exchange Rates

The international system of fixed exchange rates, centered on the U.S. dollar, broke down in the early 1970s. One reason for the breakdown was the excessive creation of U.S. dollars after the mid-1960s, which led to increases in the U.S. price level. Thereby, it became difficult for the United States to maintain convertibility of the dollar into gold at the rate of $35 per ounce. Finally, President Nixon acted in 1971 to raise the dollar price of gold. This action signaled the end of the fixed-rate system linked through the U.S. dollar to gold, which had operated since World War II.

Since the early 1970s, countries have allowed their exchange rates to vary or float, more or less freely, in order to clear the markets for foreign exchange. Thus, despite occasional interventions by various central banks (sometimes referred to as ''dirty floating''), we can say that the last decade features **flexible exchange rates,** rather than fixed rates.

If we think of the goods produced in various countries as physically identical, then the condition for purchasing-power parity, $P^i = \epsilon^i P$ from equation (20.8), would still hold under flexible exchange rates. That is, the purchasing power of any currency in terms of goods is still the same regardless of where someone uses the currency to buy goods. Also, deviations from purchasing-power parity can still arise from various real effects, such as shifts in the terms of trade, changes in trade restrictions, and so on.

A new result under flexible exchange rates is that country i's price level, P^i, is no longer tied to the U.S. price P. Rather, the monetary authority of country i can independently determine its money supply, M^i, through open-market operations or other means. Then the domestic price level, P^i, is determined—as in our earlier analysis of a closed economy—to ensure that this cash is willingly held. Finally, the exchange rate adjusts in order to satisfy the condition for purchasing-power parity, $P^i = \epsilon^i \cdot P$ from equation (20.8). This condition implies that the rate of change of country i's exchange rate, $\Delta\epsilon^i$, equals the difference between country i's inflation rate and the U.S. rate, $\pi^i - \pi$ [see equation (20.6)].

The last proposition turns out to work especially well if we examine countries with high average rates of inflation. Not surprisingly, these countries turn out also to be the ones that have maintained flexible exchange rates with the U.S. dollar over most years, even before the 1970s. Table 20.4 reports the relative inflation rates and growth rates of the exchange rate for some high-inflation countries, mainly over the period, 1955–80. (The table covers the high-inflation countries for which data are available.) Notice that the difference between each country's average inflation rate and the U.S. rate, $\pi^i - \pi$, matches up closely with the average percentage change per year in the exchange rate, $\Delta\epsilon^i$.

Table 20.4 **A Comparison of Inflation Rates with Changes in Exchange Rates for Some High-inflation Countries**

	(% per year over 1955–80)	
	$\pi^i - \pi$	$\Delta\epsilon^i$
Argentina	40.8	39.3
Brazil	26.6	26.4
Chile	47.0	44.1
Colombia	9.7	11.7
Iceland	14.2	13.5
Indonesia*	16.4	10.8
Israel	13.2	13.4
Peru**	13.1	11.8
South Korea	11.4	10.0
Uruguay	33.3	31.3
Zaire	12.1	16.1

*1967–80

**1960–80

Note: We show each country's average inflation rate, π^i, less the average U.S. rate, π. These values match up closely with the average percentage change per year in the exchange rate, $\Delta\epsilon^i$.

Sources: The data on price levels (deflators for the gross domestic product) and exchange rates are from IMF, *International Financial Statistics*.

The main point about flexible exchange rates is that they allow each country to pursue an independent monetary policy. Hence, countries can differ in their rates of inflation and monetary growth, as well as in their nominal interest rates. However, the interest-rate parity condition [equation (20.7)] implies that the difference between a country's nominal interest rate and the U.S. rate, $R^i - R$, equals the (expected) rate of change of the exchange rate, $\Delta\epsilon^i$. Also, as noted before, the PPP condition implies that $\Delta\epsilon^i$ equals the difference between the inflation rates, $\pi^i - \pi$. Therefore, the (expected) real interest rate in country i, $R^i - \pi^i$, still equals the U.S. rate, $R - \pi$.

It is important to recognize that flexible exchange rates do not isolate a country economically from the rest of the world. Basically, the nature of the exchange rate system does not have a great deal to do with the role of international trade in commodities (which allows for specialization in production across countries) or of international borrowing and lending. At least, this conclusion holds if we neglect the possible interplay between the exchange rate regime and the extent of restrictions on international commerce. Recall that countries might resort to various restrictions in order to defend a fixed exchange rate without having to undergo domestic monetary contraction. Aside from this possibility, our previous analysis of international trade in goods and earning assets applies as well under flexible exchange rates as with fixed rates.

Purchasing-Power Parity under Flexible and Fixed Exchange Rates

Many economists have noted that purchasing-power parity holds less well under flexible exchange rates since the early 1970s than under the fixed rates that prevailed earlier for most countries. Table 20.5 provides evidence on this idea from the experience of the major industrialized countries—Canada, France, Germany, Italy, Japan, Switzerland, the United Kingdom, and the United States.

Panel 1 of the table shows the exchange rates with the U.S. dollar for selected years from 1950 to 1982. Note that there were few changes between 1950 and 1970, because these countries operated mainly under fixed exchange rates. However, Canada did have a flexible rate over part of this period. Also, there were devaluations by France and the United Kingdom, as well as revaluations by Germany. On the other hand, during the flexible-rate period since the early 1970s, the exchange rates have fluctuated substantially.

Panel 2 of the table shows general price indices, P^i, which we measure as deflators for the gross domestic product. Panel 3 computes what we can call *purchasing-power parity (PPP) ratios*, $(\epsilon^i/P^i) \cdot P$, for each country, where P is the index for the U.S. price level. Since these calculations use price indices, all of which equal 1.0 in 1975, there is an arbitrary unit of measurement in the PPP ratios. We choose to multiply the ratios through by a different number for each country so that all values for a particular year—which we take to be 1970—equal 1.0. Then, if purchasing-power parity holds as a good approximation, we should find that the PPP ratios for other years stay close to 1.0.

Table 20.5 PPP Ratios in Industrialized Countries

Panel 1: Exchange Rates (Domestic Currency per U.S. Dollar)

	Canada (dollar)	France (franc)	Germany (mark)	Italy (lira)	Japan (yen)	Switzerland (franc)	U.K. (pound)	U.S. (dollar)
1950	1.09	3.50	4.20	625	361	4.32	0.36	1
1955	.99	3.50	4.21	625	361	4.29	0.36	1
1960	.97	4.90	4.17	621	360	4.32	0.36	1
1965	1.08	4.90	3.99	625	361	4.33	0.36	1
1970	1.04	5.53	3.65	627	358	4.31	0.42	1
1975	1.02	4.29	2.46	653	297	2.58	0.45	1
1980	1.17	4.23	1.82	856	227	1.68	0.43	1
1982	1.23	6.57	2.43	1352	249	2.03	0.57	1

Panel 2: Price Levels (GDP Deflator, 1975 = 1.0)

	Canada	France	Germany	Italy	Japan	Switzerland	U.K.	U.S.
1950	0.38	0.22	0.38	0.26	0.22	0.36	0.24	0.42
1955	0.45	0.31	0.45	0.33	0.30	0.40	0.31	0.48
1960	0.50	0.43	0.52	0.36	0.36	0.44	0.36	0.54
1965	0.54	0.53	0.61	0.48	0.47	0.56	0.43	0.58
1970	0.67	0.66	0.74	0.57	0.62	0.67	0.54	0.72
1975	1.00	1.00	1.00	1.00	1.00	1.00	1.00	1.00
1980	1.54	1.62	1.21	2.24	1.25	1.12	2.00	1.43
1982	1.88	2.03	1.32	3.11	1.32	1.28	2.40	1.65
Average inflation rate (% per year)								
1950–82	5.0	6.9	3.9	7.8	5.6	4.0	7.2	4.3
1950–70	2.8	5.5	3.3	3.9	5.2	3.1	4.1	2.7
1970–82	8.6	9.4	4.8	14.1	6.3	5.4	12.4	6.9

Panel 3: PPP Ratios, $(\epsilon^i/P^i) \cdot P$, 1970 = 1.0

	Canada	France	Germany	Italy	Japan	Switzerland	U.K.	U.S.
1950	1.07	1.07	1.29	1.25	1.67	1.08	1.12	1
1955	0.92	0.88	1.25	1.13	1.37	1.12	1.01	1
1960	0.93	1.01	1.22	1.15	1.29	1.14	0.97	1
1965	1.02	0.89	1.06	0.96	1.07	0.98	0.88	1
1970	1.00	1.00	1.00	1.00	1.00	1.00	1.00	1
1975	0.89	0.70	0.68	0.81	0.71	0.55	0.80	1
1980	0.95	0.61	0.60	0.68	0.62	0.46	0.55	1
1982	0.96	0.88	0.85	0.89	0.75	0.57	0.69	1

Data are from International Monetary Fund, *International Financial Statistics;* O.E.C.D., *National Accounts, Main Aggregates, V.1, 1952–81,* and *Main Economic Indicators;* and (for Japan for 1950) Irving Kravis, Alan Heston, and Robert Summers, *World Product and Income, International Comparisons of Real Gross Product,* Johns Hopkins University Press, Baltimore, 1982, Table 8-4.

The PPP ratios, $(\epsilon^i/P^i) \cdot P$, tell us the purchasing power of the dollar in country i in comparison to that in the U.S., all expressed as a ratio to the relative purchasing power in 1970. If the PPP ratio falls, it means that goods have become relatively more expensive in country i than in the United States. Or, to put it the other way, U.S. goods have become relatively cheaper.

As an example, for Japan in 1950 the value 1.67 means that in 1950 the dollar bought 67% more goods in Japan relative to the United States in comparison to the relative purchasing power in 1970. Thus, Japanese goods became substantially more expensive relative to U.S. goods from 1950 to 1970. Since the exchange rate was fixed at this time (see panel 1), the fall in the PPP ratio reflected a higher average inflation rate in Japan from 1950 to 1970 (5.2% per year) than in the United States (2.7% per year).

The value 0.62 for Japan in 1980 means that in 1980 the dollar bought only 62% as much in Japan as in the United States, relative to the situation in 1970. But matters reversed from 1980 to 1982. In 1982 the purchasing power of the dollar in Japan relative to that in the United States returned to 75% of the 1970 level. Notice that over the period from 1970 to 1982, the movements in the PPP ratio for Japan reflect mostly the variations in the exchange rate. Namely, the Japanese currency appreciated sharply from 1970 to 1980, but then depreciated from 1980 to 1982. Over the period 1970–82, the average annual inflation rates for Japan and the United States were similar (6.3% and 6.9%, respectively).

The pattern of PPP ratios for Germany is roughly parallel to that for Japan, except that German goods do not start out relatively as cheap in the 1950s. Thus, the PPP ratio in 1950 for Germany is 1.29, as compared to 1.67 for Japan. Notice that, as in the Japanese case, the German currency appreciates sharply relative to the dollar from 1970 to 1980. But also as for Japan, the situation reverses from 1980 to 1982.

Interestingly, the behavior of the PPP ratio in Italy is very close to that for Germany. This result obtains even though the average Italian inflation rate for 1970–82 (14.1% per year) is roughly 3 times the German rate (4.8% per year). Note that the Italian exchange rate rises (the currency depreciates in dollar value) from 1970 to 1980 (panel 1 of the table) at the same time that the PPP ratio declines (panel 3).

Looking at the table for France, Switzerland, and the United Kingdom, we again observe the pattern where the PPP ratio falls from 1970 to 1980, but then rises part of the way back from 1980 to 1982. For Switzerland, these movements reflect mainly changes in the exchange rate, including the sharp appreciation of the Swiss currency from 1970 to 1980. But for the United Kingdom and France, the shifts in the PPP ratios from 1970 to 1980 reflect the excesses of the inflation rates in these countries (13.1% and 9.0%, respectively) over those in the United States (6.9%). On the other hand, from 1980–82, the British and French currencies depreciate relative to the U.S. dollar. In fact, over this period, the dollar becomes more valuable relative to all of the currencies (see panel 1 of the table).

Finally, for Canada, the shifts in the PPP ratio are relatively small. Since the average Canadian inflation rate from 1950 to 1982 (5.0% per year) exceeds that in the United States (4.3%), we do find a moderate depreciation of the Canadian dollar over this period.

Let's try to summarize some of the major facts about PPP ratios in the post-World War II period.[22] Some of these follow readily from observing the data in Table 20.5, while others come from more detailed statistical analysis of these and other data.

1. The PPP ratios do move around more in the flexible-rate period since the early 1970s than in the earlier period where most exchange rates were fixed. But there are some substantial movements in the PPP ratios even under fixed rates (for example, for Japan, Germany and Italy from 1950 to 1970). Thus, fixed exchange rates do not guarantee stability in PPP ratios.

2. The PPP ratios for Canada remain relatively stable even under flexible exchange rates. Thus, flexible rates do not lead necessarily to fluctuations in PPP ratios.

3. It turns out that we cannot use the past experience of movements in the PPP ratios to predict future changes. For example, the fact that all the PPP ratios declined from 1970 to 1975 (panel 3 of the table) would not have allowed us to predict the changes after 1975. Similarly, the rise in the PPP ratios from 1980 to 1982 gives us no basis to forecast changes in the ratios after 1982. People who state confidently that the U.S. dollar is overvalued in 1982–83 should not be taken seriously.

4. There is no clear connection between the behavior of the PPP ratios and a country's experience with inflation (or, it turns out, of monetary growth). As an example, recall our comparison of Germany and Italy. Probably, we can think of the movements in the PPP ratios as reflecting primarily real changes—such as shifts in the terms of trade, in the relative prices of traded and nontraded goods, in trade restrictions and tax policies, and so on. But the details of the links between these real variables and the PPP ratios have not been worked out empirically.

5. The large fluctuations in the PPP ratios under flexible exchange rates probably have more to do with explaining why we have flexible rates, rather than vice versa. That is, since the early 1970s, there have been larger than usual variations in the terms of trade, which have implied larger than usual fluctuations in the PPP ratios. If exchange rates had been fixed, then we would have observed dramatic fluctuations in each country's price level relative to that in the United States. But the flexibility of exchange rates meant that smaller fluctuations in relative price levels were feasible. This finding likely explains the popularity of flexible exchange rates at a time when PPP ratios are unstable. However, we cannot conclude that the existence of flexible rates has contributed to the fluctuations in the PPP ratios.

---

[22]For a related discussion, see Michael Mussa, ''Empirical Regularities in the Behavior of Exchange rates and Theories of the Foreign Exchange Market,'' *Carnegie-Rochester Conference Series on Public Policy,* V. 11, 1979, pp. 10–27.

Summary

We began by introducing international trade in goods and credit. These possibilities allow for the efficient specialization of production across countries, and for an individual country's spending to diverge temporarily from its income. Restrictions on international commerce—such as tariffs and capital controls—interfere with the efficiency of free trade in goods and assets.

A temporary supply shock in one country leads to a deficit on current account, which shows up as more borrowing from abroad. Similarly, temporary movements in the terms of trade have a strong interaction with a country's current-account balance. We show generally that countries borrow abroad when their current real income is substantially below their permanent income. Conversely, the international lenders have relatively high values of current real income.

Purchasing-power parity (PPP) connects a country's exchange rate with the U.S. dollar to the ratio of that country's price level to the U.S. price level. However, a variety of real factors—including changes in the terms of trade, shifts in the relative prices of traded and nontraded goods, and variations in trade restrictions and tax policies—can shift the PPP condition. Interest-rate parity implies that differences in nominal interest rates across countries correspond to differences in (expected) rates of change of exchange rates. However, differences in taxes and in riskiness of returns can lead to violations of interest-rate parity.

When the exchange rate is fixed to the U.S. dollar, a country's price level is determined mainly by the U.S. price level. Then, in order to satisfy the PPP condition, there is a specific quantity of money that is consistent with a country's chosen exchange rate. The flows of international reserves tend to generate this quantity of money automatically. However, countries sometimes sterilize the flows of international reserves in order to maintain a higher quantity of domestic money. These actions tend to lead either to devaluation of the currency or to trade restrictions. Overall, we find a two-way association, where domestic inflation tends to cause devaluation, but where an autonomous devaluation is itself inflationary.

Flexible exchange rates leave intact the main results about international trade in goods and credit. In particular, the conditions for PPP and interest-rate parity apply in the same manner as before. However, under flexible exchange rates, a country can pursue an independent monetary policy, which allows for an independent choice of inflation rate.

Important Terms and Concepts

law of one price

gold standard

special-drawing rights (SDRs)

International Monetary Fund (IMF)

international reserves

gross domestic product (GDP)

terms of trade

tradable and nontraded goods

tariff

quota

free trade

capital controls

direct investment abroad	imports of goods and services
net factor income from abroad	rent-seeking activity
gross national product	exchange rate
net foreign investment	purchasing-power parity (PPP)
closed economy	fixed exchange rate
domestic absorption of goods and services	Bretton-Woods System
	interest-rate parity
open economy	sterilization
balance on capital account	monetary approach to the balance of payments
outflow (inflow) of capital	
current-account balance	devaluation
balance of international payments	revaluation
surplus (deficit) on current account	speculation (on exchange rate)
exports of goods and services	flexible exchange rate

QUESTIONS AND PROBLEMS

Mainly for Review

20.1 Equation (20.2) states that the current account balance is identically equal to net foreign investment. If GNP or domestic absorption changes, why is there a change in foreign investment (or borrowing) rather than a change in the interest rate? What is the accompanying change in net exports?

20.2 Explain why an improvement in the terms of trade need not be associated with an increase in net exports.

20.3 Explain the purchasing-power-parity condition. If the left-hand side of equation (20.5) were greater, would it be better to buy goods in country i or country j?

20.4 Under fixed exchange rates, does the monetary authority have discretion over the money supply? Show how an attempt to exercise an independent monetary policy may result in devaluation or revaluation.

20.5 Under flexible exchange rates, a country that has a persistently high rate of inflation will experience a steady increase in its exchange rate. Why might the monetary authority like this system?

Problems for Discussion

20.6 **Wealth Effects from Changes in the Real Interest Rate**
Consider the wealth effects from a change in the world real interest rate.

a. What is the effect for a single country?

b. What is the aggregate effect for the world?

c. How do these results compare with our earlier findings for a closed economy?

20.7 Shifts in the Demand for Money

Consider an increase in the real demand for money in country i.

a. Under a fixed exchange rate, what happens to country i's price level, P^i, and quantity of money, M^i? What happens to the country's quantity of international reserves, N^i?

b. Under a flexible exchange rate—with a fixed quantity of money, M^i—what happens to the country's price level, P^i, and exchange rate, ϵ^i?

20.8 Nixon's Departure from Gold in 1971

Under the Bretton-Woods System, which prevailed from the end of World War II until 1971, the United States pegged the price of gold at $35 per ounce.

a. Why did trouble about the gold price arise in 1971?

b. Was President Nixon right in eliminating the U.S. commitment to buy and sell gold (from and to foreign official institutions) at a fixed price? What other alternatives were there—in particular,

   i. What was the classical prescription of the gold standard?

   ii. The French suggested a doubling in the price of gold—would that have helped?

20.9 Flexible Exchange Rates and Inflation Rates

a. Show, by using the PPP condition, that the percentage change in the exchange rate, $\Delta\epsilon^i$, equals the difference between country i's inflation rate, π^i, and the U.S. inflation rate, π.

b. Using the IMF's *International Financial Statistics* (yearbook issue), calculate the values of $\Delta\epsilon^i$ and $\pi^i - \pi$ for some countries in the post-World War II period. (Pick some other than those appearing in Table 20.4.) What conclusions emerge?

20.10 Nontraded Goods and PPP Ratios (optional)

Suppose that each country produces some goods and services (such as haircuts and rents on buildings) that are not traded internationally. Assume that the price of nontraded goods in country i rises relative to the price of traded goods. But no change occurs in the relative price of nontraded and traded goods in the United States. What happens to country i's PPP ratio, $(\epsilon^i/P^i) \cdot P$? In answering, note the following: First, the general price levels, P^i and P, include the prices of both traded and nontraded goods. Second, the law of one price says that the purchasing power of any currency should be the same for traded goods, regardless of where they are produced, but the same may not hold for nontraded goods.

    Can you use the result to suggest an explanation for the movement in Japan's PPP ratio from 1.67 in 1950 to 1.0 in 1970 (see Table 20.5)?

GLOSSARY

adjusted gross income   Gross income less adjustments for tax purposes, such as business and moving expenses and deferred compensation through pension plans.

after-tax marginal product of labor   The **marginal product of labor** less the increase in the tax levied on the product.

after-tax rate of return to investment   The **real rate of return from investment** less the tax levied on the resulting increase in **net product.**

after-tax real interest rate   The **real interest rate** less the tax paid on the interest earnings.

aggregate-consistency conditions   Conditions on quantities that must hold when we add up the actions of all participants in a market—for example, the total of goods sold equals the total bought and the total of funds lent equals the total borrowed; in the basic model we use **market-clearing conditions** to ensure that the aggregate-consistency conditions are satisfied.

anticipated money growth   The public's forecast of the **rate of monetary growth,** based on the historical relationship between the quantity of money and economic variables.

average tax rate   The ratio of taxes to a measure of income. See **marginal tax rate.**

balance on capital account   The net acquisition of interest-bearing assets from abroad.

balance of international payments   The summary statement of a country's international trade in commodities, bonds, and reserves.

balanced budget   A situation in which there is no change in the real amount of money and bonds issued by government; zero real saving by government.

banking panic   Simultaneous runs on many banks and financial institutions, where depositors attempt to convert their deposits to cash.

barter   Direct exchange of one good for another, without the use of money. See **medium of exchange.**

bond   A contract that gives the holder (lender) a claim to a specified stream of payments from the issuer (borrower).

boom   A period of time in which aggregate economic activity or real GNP is high and rising.

Bretton-Woods System   A system of international payments established after World War II in which each country pegged the exchange rate between its currency and the U.S. dollar; the United States exchanged dollars for gold at a fixed price ($35 per ounce), thus pegging the value of each country's currency to gold.

budget constraint   The equation relating a household's sources of funds in a period, such as income from the commodity market and initial assets, to the uses of funds in that period, such as consumption and end-of-period assets.

budget line   A graph of the combinations of consumptions over two periods that satisfy the two-period **budget constraint.**

capital controls   Governmental restrictions on international borrowing and lending.

closed economy   An economy that is isolated from the rest of the world.

complete Keynesian model   A version of the Keynesian theory that assumes sticky nominal **wage rates** but a perfectly flexible **general price level.**

constant returns to scale   The property of some production functions that a proportionate increase in all inputs results in an equi-proportionate increase in output.

consumer durables   Commodities purchased by households for the purpose of consumption, which last for more than one period of time, such as homes, automobiles, and appliances.

consumer nondurables and services   Commodities and services purchased by households for consumption, which last for only one period of time.

consumer price index (CPI)   A weighted average of prices of consumer goods relative to a base year.

consumption rate of time preference   A measure of the relative value that people attach to consumption in different periods. The higher the consumption rate of time preference, the higher the amount of future consumption that is required to compensate for a one-unit loss in current consumption.

costs of intermediation   The total cost of operating as a financial intermediary, including a return (normal profit) on the capital invested.

crowding-out (from government deficits)   The decline in private investment that results from a tax cut that is financed by a **government deficit;** investment declines due to the accompanying rise in **real interest rates.**

crowding-out (from government purchases)   The decrease in private consumption and investment that accompanies an increase in government purchases; private spending declines because of higher **real interest rates** and the direct substitution of government services.

current-account balance   The value of goods produced by domestic residents (including the net factor income from abroad) plus net transfers from abroad, less the expenditure by domestic residents on goods; if the current-account balance is positive (negative), then there is a **surplus (deficit) on current account.**

currency   Noninterest-bearing paper money issued by the government.

deflation   A sustained decrease in the **general price level** over time. See **inflation.**

deflator for GNP   The price index that converts GNP in **nominal terms** to GNP in **real terms.**

demand deposits   Deposits held at a financial institution that can be withdrawn at face value without restrictions.

demand for money   The amount of money that someone desires to hold, expressed as a function of the volume of spending, the interest rate, **transaction costs,** and other variables.

depreciation   The wearing out of **capital goods** over time; often expressed as a fraction of the stock of capital.

desired stock of capital   The stock of capital that is chosen by a producer, depending on factors such as the **marginal product of capital,** the **real interest rate,** and the **depreciation** rate.

devaluation   An action by the central bank of a country that raises the number of units of its currency that exchange for 1 U.S. dollar; a rise in the **exchange rate.**

diminishing marginal productivity   A characteristic of the **production function** by which successive increments of an input yield progressively smaller increments in output.

direct investment abroad   Purchase of capital goods that are located in foreign countries.

discount factor   The relative value of a dollar in different periods of time; for example, between one period and the next the nominal discount factor is one plus the nominal interest rate.

discount rate of Fed   The interest rate charged on loans from the Federal Reserve to financial institutions.

discouraged workers   Workers who leave the labor force following a period of unemployment.

disintermediation   The decline in the use of the services of financial intermediaries that results when the public moves away from holding deposits toward direct holding of bonds and mortgages.

disposable income   **Personal income** less taxes.

distributional effects   Shifts in the distribution of resources across households, with no change in the aggregate of resources; changes such that some sectors in the economy gain at the expense of others.

domestic absorption of goods and services   The total expenditure on goods and services by the residents and the government of a country.

double coincidence of wants   The situation required for **barter** to take place, in which the type and quantity of goods offered by one trader match those desired by the other trader.

duration of jobs   The average length of time that a job is expected to last; the duration of jobs is inversely related to the rate of **job separations.**

duration of unemployment   The length of time that a period of unemployment is expected to last; the duration of unemployment is inversely related to the rate of **job finding.**

economies of scale in the demand for money   The property of the demand for money that the desired average cash holding increases less than proportionately with a rise in income.

excess demand   A situation in a market where, at the prevailing market price, the quantity demanded exceeds the quantity supplied.

excess reserves   The difference between the total **reserves** held by financial institutions and the amount required to be held under the **reserve requirement** of the Federal Reserve.

excess supply   A situation in a market where, at the prevailing market price, the quantity supplied exceeds the quantity demanded.

exchange rate   The number of units of the currency of a country that trade for 1 U.S. dollar.

expectation of inflation   The public's forecast of the inflation rate. See **inflation.**

expectational Phillips curve   The relation between **unexpected inflation** and the **unemployment rate;** according to this curve, an unexpected increase in the **inflation rate** has a negative effect on the unemployment rate.

expected real interest rate   The **real interest rate** that is expected to be earned (or paid) after adjusting the **nominal interest rate** by the **expectation of inflation.**

experience rating (for unemployment insurance)   The feature of the U.S. program of **unemployment insurance** that taxes employers more heavily if they have a history of a larger amount of **job separations.**

exports   Goods that are produced by the residents of a country but are sold to foreigners.

ex post expectation of prices   The forecast of the **general price level** that is based on the individual's observation of the current price in a local market, as well as on the **prior expectation of prices;** posterior expectation of prices.

Federal Funds Market   The market for very short-term borrowing and lending between financial institutions, primarily commercial banks.

Federal Funds Rate   The interest rate on loans made in the **Federal Funds Market.**

Federal Reserve credit   The sum of the Fed's holdings of loans to depository institutions, U.S. government securities, and miscellaneous assets. The total of the Fed's claims on the government and the private sector.

financial intermediaries   Institutions that obtain funds from deposits made by individuals and make loans to households and businesses. Examples are banks, savings and loan associations, and money-market funds.

fiscal policy   The choice of levels of government spending, taxation, and borrowing in order to influence the level of aggregate economic activity.

fixed exchange rate   The system of international payments, prevalent until the early 1970s, in which countries control the rate at which their **currency** exchanges against the U.S. dollar; by buying or selling its currency the central bank would limit variations in the **exchange rate** to a narrow range.

flat-rate tax   A kind of income tax in which the amount of the tax is a constant fraction of **taxable income.** See **graduated-rate tax.**

flexible exchange rate   The system of international payments, prevalent since the early 1970s, in which countries allow the **exchange rates** for their currencies to fluctuate so as to clear the exchange market.

free trade   International trade of goods and assets, without restrictions in the form of **tariffs, quotas, capital controls,** and so on.

full-employment deficit   The **government deficit** after adjusting for the automatic response of government spending and taxes to a recession or boom; an estimate of what the deficit would be if the economy were operating at a full employment level.

fully funded system (for social security)   A system in which each individual's payments accumulate in a trust fund and retirement benefits are paid out of the accumulated funds. See **social security; pay-as-you-go system.**

general market clearing   Simultaneous clearing of all markets. See **market-clearing approach; Walras' Law of Markets.**

general price level   The dollar price per unit of a (physically uniform) aggregate of commodities.

gold standard   A system of international payments under which countries agree to buy or sell gold for a fixed amount of their currencies; the high point of this system was from 1879 to 1914.

government deficit (or surplus)   In **real terms,** the increase (or decrease) in the real value of the government's obligations to the private sector in the forms of money and bonds.

government purchases of goods and services   Expenditures by government on commodities and services produced by the private sector.

governmental budget constraint   The equation showing the balance between total expenditures and total revenues of the government.

government's revenue from printing money   The real income that government obtains by increasing the quantity of **high-powered money.**

graduated-rate tax   A kind of income tax in which the **marginal tax rate** rises with **taxable income.** See **flat-rate tax.**

Great Depression   The decline in aggregate economic activity in the United States that occurred from 1929–1933.

gross domestic product (GDP)   The market value of an economy's domestically produced goods and services over a specified period of time.

gross investment   The purchases of **capital goods.**

gross national product (GNP)   The total market value of the goods and services produced by the residents of a country over a specified period of time; GNP equals **gross domestic product** plus the **net factor income from abroad.**

high-powered money   The total amount of Federal Reserve Notes (**currency**) and noninterest-bearing deposits (**reserves**) held at the Fed by depository institutions; the **monetary base.**

human capital   Skills and training that are embodied in workers and add to productivity.

hyperinflation   A period with an extraordinarily high **inflation rate,** such as that in Germany after World War I.

implicit GNP price deflator   The **price index** that relates the **gross national product,** measured in **nominal terms,** to **real GNP.**

imports   Goods that are produced in foreign countries and purchased by the domestic residents of a country.

increasing (or decreasing) returns to scale   A characteristic of the **production function** such that a proportionate increase in all inputs results in a more than (or less than) proportionate increase in output.

indexation   A system of contracts in which payments are revised upward or downward according to increases or decreases in the **general price level,** so as to keep the real value of payments independent of **inflation;** inflation correction.

indifference curve   A graph showing the combinations of two items, such as consumption and labor (work effort), that yield the same level of **utility.**

inferior goods   Goods for which the **wealth effect** is negative.

infinite horizon   The household's planning horizon when plans extend into the indefinite future; used in models that stress the role of intergenerational transfers.

inflation   A sustained increase in the **general price level** over time.

inflation correction   See **indexation.**

inflation rate   The percentage change in a **price index** between two periods of time.

interest rate   The ratio of the interest payment to the amount borrowed; the return to lending or the cost of borrowing.

interest-rate parity   The equalization of **interest rates** across countries, taking account of an adjustment for prospective changes in **exchange rates.**

intermediate goods   Commodities that are purchased for resale or for use in the production and sale of other commodities.

International Monetary Fund (IMF)   An international agency that provides assistance to member countries in making international payments; the agency that issues **special-drawing rights.**

international reserves   The total quantity of base money—gold, **special-drawing rights,** U.S. dollars, and some types of foreign exchange—used in international payments.

intertemporal-substitution effect   The effect on current consumption (leisure) when the cost of future consumption (leisure) changes relative to that of current consumption (leisure).

inventories   Stores of commodities held by businesses either for sale or for use in production.

investment demand   The quantity of **investment** that is desired by firms and households, expressed as a function of the **real interest rate,** the **depreciation rate,** and the existing stock of capital.

involuntary unemployment   The inability of workers to obtain employment at the prevailing market wage; a feature of Keynesian theory.

irrelevance result for systematic monetary policy   The theoretical finding that a policy of changing the quantity of money in response to the state of economy is predictable and therefore powerless to affect the economy.

IS curve   A graph used in Keynesian theory showing the combinations of aggregate output and the interest rate which satisfy the condition that aggregate output equals the aggregate demand for commodities.

IS/LM model   The analytical tool used in Keynesian theory to study the simultaneous determination of aggregate output and the **interest rate.**

job finding   The movement of workers from a state of being unemployed or out of the labor force to an employed state.

job separations   The movement of workers from an employed state to a state of being unemployed or out of the labor force.

Keynesian consumption function   The relationship between aggregate consumption demand on the one hand and aggregate output and the interest rate on the other; a central element of Keynesian theory.

Keynesian cross diagram   The graph depicting the determination of the level of aggregate output when the level of aggregate demand and the **interest rate** are given.

Keynesian model   The theory developed by John Maynard Keynes and published in 1935 that sought to explain aggregate business fluctuations.

labor force   The total number of employed workers plus the number of **unemployed.**

Laffer curve   A graph showing that tax revenues initially rise as the **marginal tax rate** rises but eventually reach a maximum and decline with further increases in the marginal tax rate.

law of one price   The condition that identical goods in different countries must sell at the same dollar price.

Law of Supply and Demand (for adjusting the price level) The assumption that the price level declines when goods are in **excess supply** and rises when goods are in **excess demand.**

legal tender A characteristic of money, whereby its use as a medium of exchange is reinforced by government statute.

lender of last resort A function of the Federal Reserve, which provides for liberal lending to member banks, particularly during a financial crisis.

life-cycle model The theory of the choices of consumption and leisure that are made when the **planning horizon** is equal to the individual's expected remaining lifetime; it predicts that the individual will build up savings during working years and exhaust them during retirement years. See **infinite horizon.**

LM curve A graph used in Keynesian theory, showing all the combinations of aggregate output and the **interest rate** which satisfy the condition that the **real demand for money** equals the given real quantity of money.

long-term contracts Agreements between buyers and sellers or between firms and workers that specify the terms of exchange over a number of periods of time.

lump-sum taxes Taxes paid to the government so that the amount paid does not depend on any characteristic of the individual, such as income or wealth.

lump-sum transfer A **transfer payment** from government to an individual in which the amount paid does not depend on any characteristic of the recipient, such as income or wealth.

M1 concept of money The sum of **currency** plus checkable deposits plus travelers' checks; a measure of the volume of assets that serve regularly as media of exchange.

marginal product of capital (MPK) The increment of output obtained per unit increment in the input of **physical capital,** while holding fixed any other inputs.

marginal product of labor (MPL) The increment of output obtained per unit increment in labor input while holding fixed any other inputs; the slope of the graph of the **production function** relating output to labor input.

marginal tax rate The fraction of an additional dollar of income that must be paid as tax. This rate varies according to the level of **adjusted gross income.** See **average tax rate.**

market-clearing approach The viewpoint that prices, such as the **interest rate** and the **general price level,** are determined in order to clear all markets, such as those for credit and commodities; that is, supply equals demand in each market.

medium of exchange The commodity or other item that people use as a means of paying for purchases; money.

microeconomic foundations The theoretical analysis of individual behavior that underlies the macroeconomic model of the economy.

minimum wage   The wage level below which the wage paid by a firm cannot legally fall.

monetarism   A school of thought, based on the **quantity theory of money,** that changes in the nominal quantity of money primarily account for movements in the price level in the long run and for fluctuations in **real GNP** in the short run.

monetary approach to the balance of payments   Analyses of the **balance of international payments** and **exchange rates** that stress the quantity of money and the real demand for money in each country.

monetary base   See **high-powered money.**

monetary reform   A fundamental change in the monetary system or in the formulation of monetary policy.

monetize the deficit   Raise revenue to meet interest payments on government debt by increasing the quantity of money.

multiple expansion of deposits   The effect of an increase in the **monetary base** on the volume of deposits held at financial institutions.

multiplier   The change in aggregate output per dollar autonomous increase in aggregate demand; assumed in simple **Keynesian models** to be positive and greater than one.

national income   The income earned from aggregate production; GNP adjusted for **depreciation** and sales and excise taxes.

national-income accounts   The summary statement of GNP and the components of GNP during a year.

natural unemployment rate   The average **unemployment rate** that prevails in the economy, depending on the average rates of **job separation** and **job finding.**

net exports   The difference between the value of **exports** and the value of **imports.**

net factor income from abroad   Income earned by the residents of a country from labor supplied to foreign countries or from net claims on foreign assets.

net foreign investment   The change in a country's net holdings of interest-bearing assets from abroad plus the change in its **international reserves.**

net investment   The change in the capital stock; **gross investment** minus the amount of **depreciation.**

net national product (NNP)   **Gross national product** minus the **depreciation** of capital.

neutrality of money   The theoretical finding that once-and-for-all changes in the nominal quantity of money affect nominal variables such as the **general price level** but leave real variables such as **real GNP** unaffected.

nominal deficit   The current dollar value of the **real deficit** of the government. See **nominal deficit (national accounts' version).**

nominal deficit (national accounts' version)   The change in the nominal value of government-issued money and bonds. See **nominal deficit.**

nominal interest rate   The amount paid as **interest** per dollar borrowed for one period of time; the rate at which the nominal value of assets that are held as **bonds** grows over time.

nominal saving   The current dollar value of **real saving,** calculated by multiplying real saving by a **price index.**

nominal terms   Measured in current dollar magnitudes; valued at current dollar prices; unadjusted for changes in the **general price level.**

open economy   An economy that conducts trade with the rest of the world.

open-market operations   The purchase or sale of government securities by the Federal Reserve in exchange for newly created **high-powered money.**

outflow (inflow) of capital   The positive (negative) **balance on capital account** for a country.

outside of the labor force   The classification of a person who is neither employed nor currently looking for a job.

pay-as-you-go system (for social security)   A system in which benefits to old persons are financed by taxes on the current young generation.

perceived relative price   The ratio of the observed price in a local market to the **ex post expectation** of prices; a measure of the level of the local price relative to the perceived **general price level.**

perfect competition   The assumption that individuals participating in a market each view themselves as sufficiently small that they can each buy or sell any amount without affecting the established price.

perfect foresight   An assumption that **expectations of inflation** or of other variables are accurate, so that there are no forecast errors.

permanent government purchases   The hypothetical level of government purchases that, if maintained permanently, would have the same total present value as the actual pattern of government purchases; the per-period equivalent of the present value of government purchases.

permanent income   The hypothetical amount of real income that, when received constantly throughout the individual's planning horizon, has the same total present value as the actual pattern of the individual's income; the per-period equivalent of the total present value of income. A temporary change in income entails a less than equivalent change in permanent income.

personal consumer expenditures   Purchases of goods and services by households for use in consumption.

personal income   Income received directly by persons; **national income** adjusted for undistributed corporate profits, social security contributions, and transfer payments to households from government and business.

Phillips curve   The relationship between nominal variables such as the **inflation rate** and real variables such as the **unemployment rate** or growth rate of aggregate output.

physical capital   Capital inputs into production, such as machinery and buildings.

planning horizon   The number of future periods that enter the household's **budget constraint;** the length of time for which the household plans consumption and leisure choices.

present value   The value of future dollar amounts, after dividing by the discount factor.

price index   A weighted average of individual prices in a particular year, relative to prices in some given base year; a measure of how much the average price has changed since the base year.

principal of bond   The amount borrowed, to be repaid at maturity.

prior expectation of prices   The forecast of the current **general price level,** based on information that people have before observing any current variables.

private fixed capital   The sum of **producers' durable equipment and structures** and residential structures; a measure of the capital stock that excludes business **inventories** and **consumer durables** other than homes.

producer price index (PPI)   A weighted average of prices of raw materials and semi-finished goods, relative to base-year prices.

producers' durable equipment and structures   The measure of **physical capital** that includes machinery and buildings used in production.

production function   The relationship between the quantity of output obtained and the quantities of inputs into production, such as labor and capital.

propensity to consume   The change in current consumption per dollar change in current income; the fraction of an increase (decrease) in income that is spent on consumption expenditure.

propensity to save   The change in current saving per dollar change in current income; the fraction of an increase (decrease) in income that is saved.

public debt   The volume of interest-bearing government obligations to the public; the stock of government bonds outstanding.

purchasing-power parity (P.P.P.)   The condition that the ratio of the **exchange rates** for the currencies of any two countries must equal the ratio of the prices of goods in each country.

quantity theory of money   The theory that changes in the nominal quantity of money account for the majority of long-run movements in the **general price level.**

quota   A limitation on the quantity of **imports.**

rate of monetary growth   The percentage increase in the nominal quantity of money between two periods of time.

rational expectations   The viewpoint that individuals make forecasts or estimates of unknown variables, such as the current **general price level,** in the best possible manner, utilizing all information currently available.

real-balance effect   The effect of a change in wealth resulting from a change in the **general price level;** the **wealth effect** of a rise in the real value of money balances.

real deficit   The change in the real value of the government's obligations to the public in the form of money and bonds. See **real deficit (national accounts' version).**

real deficit (national accounts' version)   The change in the nominal value of the government's obligations to the public in the form of money and bonds, deflated by the current price level. See **real deficit.**

real gross national product   The **gross national product** divided by a **price index** in order to adjust for changes in the average level of market prices; GNP in constant dollars.

real interest rate   The rate at which the real value of dollar assets that are held as **bonds** grows over time; the interest rate on an asset after adjusting for **inflation.**

real rate of return from investment   The net real proceeds from investment over one period expressed relative to the real cost of the investment.

real saving   The change in the real value of assets of a household or of the economy as a whole.

real terms   Measured in units of commodities; valued at base-year prices; dollar magnitudes that are adjusted for inflation by deflating by a price index.

real wage rate   The value in **real terms** of the dollar amount paid for an hour of labor services.

recession   A period of decline in the level of aggregate economic activity or real GNP.

Regulation Q   The legal limit imposed by the Federal Reserve on the **interest rate** payable on time deposits and savings deposits held at banks.

relative price   The price of a commodity or service relative to the price of other goods or services; the ratio of the dollar price of a commodity to the **general price level.**

rent-seeking activity   The expenditure of time and other resources in attempting to benefit from government regulation. An example is the attempt to obtain a larger share of imports that are limited by a **quota.**

replacement ratio (for unemployment insurance)   The ratio of unemployment benefits to the wage earnings of a worker.

reserve requirement   The requirement imposed by the Federal Reserve that depository institutions must hold a certain quantity of **reserves.** For each category of deposits, the requirement is specified as a fraction of the amount of deposits.

reserves (of depository institutions)   The total amount of currency and noninterest-bearing deposits at the Fed held by banks and other depository institutions.

revaluation   An increase in the value of a country's currency in terms of the U.S. dollar.

Ricardian Equivalence Theorem   The theoretical finding that, given the amounts of government purchases, an increase in current taxes has the same effect on the economy as an equal increase in the **government deficit.**

saving   The change in an individual's assets during a period of time.

savings deposits   Deposits held at banks that usually allow funds to be withdrawn without penalty with a 30-days notice of withdrawal.

short-side rule (for determining quantities)   The condition that the quantity of output or sales in a situation of **excess demand** or **excess supply** is determined by the lesser of the quantity demanded and the quantity supplied.

social security   **Transfer payments** made by government to households through social insurance programs such as old age and survivors insurance and disability insurance.

special-drawing rights (SDRs)   A type of paper asset, issued by the **International Monetary Fund,** and used to make international payments.

speculation (on exchange rates)   Sale (or purchase) of a currency in exchange for U.S. dollars whenever a **devaluation** (or **revaluation**) is expected.

stagflation   A situation where a **recession** is accompanied by high and rising **inflation.**

steady state   A situation where the rate of growth of the economy is zero and output, consumption, gross investment and work effort are all constant.

steady-state growth   A situation in a growing economy where output, the stock of physical capital, consumption, and work effort all grow at the same rate as population, so that the amounts of output, etc., per person are constant.

steady state per capita growth   A situation in a growing economy where the amounts of output, capital stock, and consumption per person all grow at some constant rate.

sterilization   An action by the central bank of a country that prevents increases (decreases) in the amount of **international reserves** from increasing (decreasing) the **quantity of money** in the country.

substitution effects   The response of households to changes in the relative cost of obtaining any two goods, such as consumption and leisure.

superior goods (or normal goods)   Goods for which the **wealth effect** is positive.

superneutrality of money   The theoretical finding that a change in the pattern over time of monetary growth does not affect real variables such as aggregate output and the **real interest rate.** See **neutrality of money.**

supply shock   Changes that alter the **production function,** that is, raise or lower the output obtainable from given inputs or alter the **marginal products** of the inputs. Examples are harvest failures and technological changes.

supply-side economics   The study of the causes and effects of changes in the supply of work effort and the productivity of labor. This approach emphasizes the negative effect of income taxes on the incentive to work.

surplus (deficit) on current account   A positive (negative) **current-account balance.**

tariff   A tax on goods imported into a country.

taxable income   **Adjusted gross income** minus the value of tax exemptions.

tax-exempt income   Income from production, interest earnings, or government transfers that is not liable for income taxes.

technological progress   Improved knowledge about methods of production that shifts the **production function** upward.

terms of trade   The price of a country's tradable goods expressed relative to the price of a market basket of the world's tradable goods; often approximated by the ratio of a country's export prices to its import prices.

time deposits   Deposits at banks and other depository institutions that have a stated maturity date and carry penalties for early withdrawal.

tradable goods   Goods that are actually exchanged or could potentially be exchanged with foreign countries.

transaction costs   Costs incurred in the process of making sales or purchases, such as brokerage fees or the cost of the time involved.

transfer payments   Transfers of funds from government to individuals, such as welfare payments, which do not constitute payments for goods or services.

unanticipated money growth   The difference between the actual amount of monetary growth and **anticipated money growth.**

underground economy   The collection of economic activities from which the income earned is not reported and therefore not taxed.

unemployment   The situation of a worker who has no job and is looking for work.

unemployment insurance   The government program of providing temporary benefits to workers who have lost their jobs and are eligible by virtue of their work history.

unemployment rate   The ratio of the number of unemployed workers to the total number of employed and unemployed workers; the fraction of the labor force that is unemployed.

unexpected inflation   The difference between the actual rate of inflation and the **expectation of inflation;** the forecast error made in predicting inflation.

utility   The level of happiness of a household, measured in units called utils. Utility increases with increases in either consumption or leisure. See **utility function.**

utility function   The relationship between the amount of utility obtained and the amounts of consumption and labor chosen by the household.

utility rate of time preference   The parameter that determines the relative weights applied to utility in different periods of time. The higher the utility rate of time preference, the higher the discount applied to future utility.

utilization rate   The percentage of time that capital is used in production. For example, an increase in the number of shifts per day in a factory increases the utilization rate of machinery.

vault cash   **Currency** that is held by a depository institution.

velocity of money   The ratio of the dollar volume of transactions per period to the average money holding; the number of times per period that the average dollar turns over in making transactions.

wage rate   The dollar amount that is paid to a worker in exchange for an hour of labor services.

Walras' Law of Markets   The finding that if all but one of the conditions for **general market clearing** hold, then the final one must hold as well; this result follows because, in the aggregate, households' **budget constraints** must be satisfied.

wealth effects   The response of consumption and leisure (or labor) to changes in the household's opportunities for increasing **utility.** An increase (decrease) in wealth occurs when the household can raise (must reduce) consumption while leisure remains unchanged.

AUTHOR INDEX

SUBJECT INDEX